Lecture Notes in Computer Science   10599

Commenced Publication in 1973
Founding and Former Series Editors:
Gerhard Goos, Juris Hartmanis, and Jan van Leeuwen

More information about this series at http://www.springer.com/series/7410

Phong Q. Nguyen · Jianying Zhou (Eds.)

Information Security

20th International Conference, ISC 2017
Ho Chi Minh City, Vietnam, November 22–24, 2017
Proceedings

 Springer

Editors
Phong Q. Nguyen
Inria
Paris
France

and

Inria
Tokyo
Japan

Jianying Zhou
Singapore University of Technology and
Design
Singapore
Singapore

ISSN 0302-9743   ISSN 1611-3349   (electronic)
Lecture Notes in Computer Science
ISBN 978-3-319-69658-4   ISBN 978-3-319-69659-1   (eBook)
https://doi.org/10.1007/978-3-319-69659-1

Library of Congress Control Number: 2017956937

LNCS Sublibrary: SL4 – Security and Cryptology

Printed on acid-free paper

This Springer imprint is published by Springer Nature
The registered company is Springer International Publishing AG
The registered company address is: Gewerbestrasse 11, 6330 Cham, Switzerland

Preface

This volume contains the papers presented at ISC 2017: the 20th Information Security Conference held during November 22–24, 2017, in Ho Chi Minh City, Vietnam.

The Information Security Conference is an annual international conference covering research in theory and applications of information security. ISC aims to attract high-quality papers in all technical aspects of information security. ISC 2017 was hosted by the Vietnamese German University (VGU).

There were 97 submissions to ISC 2017. Each submission was reviewed by three Program Committee members on average, and the reviewing process was double-blind. After careful reviews and intensive discussions, 25 papers were selected for presentation at the conference. In addition to the contributed talks, there were two invited talks given by Thai Duong (Google, USA) and Adi Shamir (Weizmann Institute, Israel), whom we heartily thank for accepting our invitation despite a very busy schedule. Adi Shamir talked about "Towards Quantitative Analysis of Cyber Security", and Thai Duong talked about "Security at Scale: Shipping Secure Software at Google."

We would like to thank the Program Committee members and the external reviewers for all the hard work they put in evaluating the papers. We thank Easy Chair for providing a good platform on paper submission and review. We also thank Springer for supporting the conference and publishing the conference proceedings in the LNCS series. We are very grateful to all the people whose work ensured a smooth organization process: the ISC Steering Committee, and Masahiro Mambo in particular, for their advice; the local organizing team led by General Chairs Martin Kappes and Dinh-Thuc Nguyen, and Local Chairs Thuc-Vien Ha and Van-Song Pham. Last but not least, our thanks go to all the authors who submitted papers and all the attendees.

September 2017

Phong Q. Nguyen
Jianying Zhou

ISC 2017

20th International Conference on Information Security
Ho Chi Minh City, Vietnam
November 22–24, 2017

Program Chairs

Phong Q. Nguyen   Inria, France and CNRS/JFLI/University of Tokyo, Japan
Jianying Zhou   Singapore University of Technology and Design, Singapore

General Chairs

Martin Kappes   Vietnamese German University, Vietnam and Frankfurt am Main University, Germany
Dinh-Thuc Nguyen   University of Science, VNU-HCM, Vietnam

Steering Committee

Ed Dawson   Queensland University of Technology, Australia
Javier Lopez   University of Malaga, Spain
Masahiro Mambo   Kanazawa University, Japan
Dinh-Thuc Nguyen   University of Science, VNU-HCM, Vietnam
Eiji Okamoto   University of Tsukuba, Japan
Susanne Wetzel   Stevens Institute of Technology, USA
Rui Zhang   University of Delaware, USA
Yuliang Zheng   University of Alabama at Birmingham, USA

Program Committee

Shweta Agrawal   Indian Institute of Technology Madras, India
Gail-Joon Ahn   Arizona State University, USA
Yoshinori Aono   National Institute of Information and Communications Technology, Japan
Jean-Philippe Aumasson   Kudelski Security, Switzerland
Gildas Avoine   INSA Rennes, France
Sherman S.M. Chow   Chinese University of Hong Kong, SAR China
Carlos Cid   Royal Holloway, University of London, UK
Yuval Elovici   Ben-Gurion University, Israel
Debin Gao   Singapore Management University, Singapore
Juan A. Garay   Texas A&M University, USA
Stefanos Gritzalis   University of the Aegean, Greece

Tibor Jager	Paderborn University, Germany
Sokratis Katsikas	Norwegian University of Science and Technology, Norway
Stefan Katzenbeisser	TU Darmstadt, Germany
Noboru Kunihiro	University of Tokyo, Japan
Qi Li	Tsinghua University, China
Zhiqiang Lin	University of Texas at Dallas, USA
Javier Lopez	University of Malaga, Spain
Mark Manulis	University of Surrey, UK
Weizhi Meng	Technical University of Denmark, Denmark
Chris Mitchell	Royal Holloway, University of London, UK
David Naccache	Ecole Normale Supérieure, France
Khoa Nguyen	Nanyang Technological University, Singapore
Martín Ochoa	Singapore University of Technology and Design, Singapore
Tatsuaki Okamoto	NTT, Japan
Yanbin Pan	Chinese Academy of Sciences, China
Duong-Hieu Phan	University of Limoges, France
Indrakshi Ray	Colorado State University, USA
Matt Robshaw	Impinj, USA
Pierangela Samarati	Università degli Studi di Milano, Italy
Gang Tan	Penn State University, USA
Lei Wang	Shanghai Jiao Tong University, China

Local Organizing Chairs

Thuc-Vien Ha	Vietnamese German University, Vietnam
Van-Song Pham	Vietnamese German University, Vietnam

Local Organizing Committee

Quoc-Binh Nguyen	Vietnamese German University, Vietnam
Thanh-Duy Nguyen	Vietnamese German University, Vietnam
Quoc-Hung Nguyen	Vietnamese German University, Vietnam
Thuy-Trang Nguyen	Vietnamese German University, Vietnam
Hai-Dinh Pham	Vietnamese German University, Vietnam
Thuan-Anh Tran	Vietnamese German University, Vietnam
Thu-Huong Tran	Vietnamese German University, Vietnam
Hong-Ngoc Tran	Vietnamese German University, Vietnam

Additional Reviewers

Albrecht, Martin
Alcaraz, Cristina
Alderman, James
Anagnostopoulos, Marios
Bai, Shi
Bauman, Erick
Belyaev, Kirill
Bezawada, Bruhadeshwar
Bhattacherjee, Sanjay
Bi, Jingguo
Bost, Raphael
Bourse, Florian
Brotzman-Smith, Robert
Castellanos, John Henry
Chakraborty, Suvradip
Chandra, Swarup
Chang, Jinyong
Chen, Zhigang
Chotard, Jeremy
Chuadhry, Mujeeb
Datta, Pratish
Davidson, Alex
Du, Minxin
Fernandez, Carmen
Gellert, Kai
Gong, Junqing
Gougeon, Thomas
Guarnizo, Juan David
Haefner, Kyle
Harilal, Athul
Hou, Xiaolu

Janson, Christian
Jin, Xin
Kakvi, Saqib A.
Kalloniatis, Christos
Karande, Vishal
Katsumata, Shuichi
Kolokotronis, Nicholas
Konstantinou, Elisavet
Kundu, Ashish
Kurek, Rafael
Lacovazzi, Alfonso
Lai, Russell W.F.
Le Trieu, Phong
Lee, Hyung Tae
Li, Baiyu
Li, Jianwei
Li, Qinyi
Liu, Shen
Ma, Jack P.K.
Maitra, Monosij
Mukherjee, Subhojeet
Niehues, David
Nieto, Ana
Nuñez, David
Papamartzivanos,
    Dimitrios
Patsakis, Constantinos
Pelosi, Gerardo
Quinonez Tirado, Raul
Ramanna, Somindu C.
Rios, Ruben

Rizomiliotis, Panagiotis
Rothstein, Eric
Scotti, Fabio
Shiehian, Sina
Striecks, Christoph
Su, Chunhua
Sun, Bing
Tai, Raymond K.H.
Tan,
    Benjamin Hong Meng
Tang, Bo
Tardif, Florent
Toffalini, Flavio
Trinh, Viet Cuong
V., Santhoshini
Wang, Huibo
Wang, Jiafan
Wang, Xiuhua
Wang, Yuntao
Wong, Harry W.H.
Wudel, Wojciech
Xagawa, Keita
Xu, Yanhong
Zeng, Dongrui
Zhang, Juanyang
Zhang, Kai
Zhang, Tao
Zhao, Qingchuan
Zhao, Yongjun
Zuo, Chaoshun

Contents

Software Security

Network and System Security

Symmetric Cryptography

Rate-One AE with Security Under RUP

Shoichi Hirose[1](✉), Yu Sasaki[2](✉), and Kan Yasuda[2](✉)

[1] University of Fukui, Fukui, Japan
hrs_shch@u-fukui.ac.jp
[2] NTT Secure Platform Laboratories, Tokyo, Japan
{sasaki.yu,yasuda.kan}@lab.ntt.co.jp

Abstract. This paper investigates what sort of security can be retained by the most efficient (namely, rate-one) AE schemes like OCB under the release of unverified plaintext (RUP). At CT-RSA 2016, Chakraborti et al. have presented an impossibility result, which says that any rate-one AE scheme cannot ensure INT-RUP, a strong integrity requirement under RUP. In this paper we show that any rate-one AE scheme cannot satisfy PA2 (plaintext awareness 2) either, a strong privacy requirement under RUP introduced by Andreeva et al. at Asiacrypt 2014. Given these impossibility results, we relax the security requirements and identify new notions of tag-PA and tag-INT. The new notions are strictly weaker than PA2 and INT-RUP yet have considerable significance in the practical sense. In particular, tag-PA is strictly stronger than PA1 defined by Andreeva et al. at Asiacrypt 2014. Unfortunately, OCB is neither tag-PA nor tag-INT. We present a new rate-one AE scheme which is both tag-PA and tag-INT. The new scheme is essentially as efficient as OCB, consuming just one extra call to a block cipher.

Keywords: AE · Decryption misuse · RUP · Rate-one · Tag feedback · OCB

1 Introduction

Authenticated encryption (AE) provides authenticity and privacy in one scheme. Several AE schemes are internationally standardized and used in daily life, e.g. GCM [9] in IPsec and CCM [16] in TLS. In addition, the CAESAR competition [4] is currently conducted to determine the portfolio of the AE schemes having several advantages over AES-GCM. In general, efficiency and security are two important aspects of the AE design.

With respect to efficiency, OCB [8,11,13] shows outstanding performance. OCB has several attractive features e.g. fully parallelizable, rate-one (only requires 1 block cipher call per message block without universal hash function), fast tag computation. OCB is a nonce-based AE. The assumption that protocols never repeat the same nonce enables such an efficient construction.

With respect to security, AE schemes are designed to be secure when they are properly used. Meanwhile, cryptographers should not rule out the potential

© Springer International Publishing AG 2017
P.Q. Nguyen and J. Zhou (Eds.): ISC 2017, LNCS 10599, pp. 3–20, 2017.
https://doi.org/10.1007/978-3-319-69659-1_1

misuses of the cryptographic schemes especially because those schemes are often implemented by non-expert of cryptography.

Among several misuses, our focus is *decryption misuse*. In many AE schemes, the decrypted results can be released only if verification succeeds, while the users may release them from implementation reasons, e.g. insufficient buffer, which is formalized as *releasing unverified plaintext (RUP)* [3]. Then, the plaintext information will be leaked.

It is a big challenge to design an AE scheme that ensures a certain robustness against misuses but simultaneously satisfies good implementation properties such as *rate-one* and *parallelizability* as OCB does. The difficulty is that misuse resistant AE schemes are often heavy or lose functionalities.

- The scheme may require two block cipher calls per message block (rate-2), e.g. SIV mode [14], robust AE [7], RIV mode [1], etc.
- The scheme may require to send additional information, e.g. additional nonce in nonce-decoy [3], which consumes communication bandwidth.
- The scheme may require to introduce dependency between ciphertext C and values to be misused, thus generation of C may become expensive or complicated. For example, SIV makes C dependent on the tag T, thus requires to process message M twice. APE [2] makes M dependent on T during the decryption, thus requires unusual backward decryption.

Related Work. *Nonce decoy* [3] offers some robustness against decryption misuse, in which the users generate dummy nonce IV' by encrypting original nonce IV, and then run the encryption/decryption with IV'. When the attacker modifies IV' to something unknown during decryption, the computational result becomes random, thus receives no damage even if it is released (IV'-robust decryption). However, such RUP security is limited to the case that the attacker modifies IV'. No RUP security is provided when A, C, or T are modified. Moreover, nonce decoy needs to send both of IV and IV' to the receiver, which consumes bandwidth. A permutation based AE, APE [2], has a unique decryption algorithm, namely "decrypting" tag and then proceeds to decrypting ciphertext. Because of this feature, APE has the property, which we call "T-robust decryption." APE is single pass, but cannot be parallelizable.

Our Contributions. This paper presents an efficient AE scheme which provides a certain level of robustness against decryption misuse. Considering the efficiency of OCB, our goal is designing AE with rate-one and full parallelizability.

As mentioned above, aiming the perfect security for decryption misuse is costly. Thus we take an opposite approach. Namely, by starting an efficient construction (OCB), we slightly modify it, possibly with a few more primitive calls, to enhance its security as much as possible. Regarding efficiency, we avoid communicating additional information to avoid consuming bandwidth.

The main contribution of this paper is the conversion method named *tag feedback*, which turns conventional nonce-based AE to satisfy the above goals.

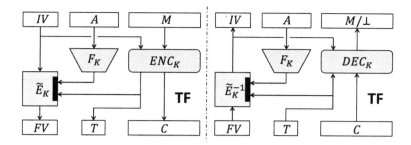

Fig. 1. Tag feedback (TF). Left and right diagrams show encryption and decryption/verification algorithms, respectively. ENC_K is a nonce-based encryption, DEC_K is a corresponding decryption, F_K is a (keyed) hash function and $\tilde{E}_K$ is a TBC.

In short, our scheme takes as input nonce IV, associated data A and message M, and then computes ciphertext C and tag T. Our core idea is then converting IV to finalization vector FV by applying tweakable block cipher (TBC) that takes T and hash of A as tweak. The sender does not need to transmit IV, because the receiver can recover it from FV, T and A. The construction is shown in Fig. 1.

Our construction provides a certain level of robustness against decryption misuse which we call (FV, T, A)-*robust decryption* defined as follows.

Definition 1 ((FV, T, A)-Robust Decryption). *An AEAD scheme should not leak any information about plaintext to an adversary that has access to the decrypt-anyway oracle $DEC_K(\cdot, \cdot, \cdot, \cdot)$, except if the adversary makes a query (FV, T, A, C) to its DEC_K-oracle where (FV, T, A) is a legitimate triplet generated by the encryption algorithm ENC_K.*

From the viewpoint of mode of operation, the two-pass, offline construction seems essential for realizing ciphertext-robustness. Thus (FV, T, A)-robust decryption achieves maximal level of robustness with rate-one and parallelizable AE. Because no additional data is communicated, our construction achieves higher security with lower communication cost than nonce-decoy.

We then propose a concrete construction called ΘCBt by applying tag feedback to ΘCB mode, which is a tweakable block cipher level of OCB. We also prove privacy and authenticity of ΘCBt against (FV, T, A)-respective adversary and privacy against (FV, T, A)-repeat adversary.

Table 1 summarizes our results. We first show that achieving PA2 [3], a strongest form of privacy under RUP, is impossible with rate-one AE schemes. Together with the previous result [6] for INT-RUP [3], a strongest form of authenticity under RUP, our result implies that any rate-one AE scheme cannot ensure privacy or authenticity in their strongest forms under RUP. This motivates us to define new security notions under RUP that are slightly weaker than PA2 and INT-RUP. We call these tag-PA and tag-INT. We propose a new scheme ΘCBt, which satisfies both tag-PA and tag-INT. ΘCBt maintains the efficiency of the original ΘCB, which is neither tag-PA nor tag-INT.

Table 1. Summary of our results; the impossibility result for INT-RUP is due to Chakraborti et al. [6]

Scheme	Privacy			Authenticity		
	PA2	tag-PA	PA1	INT-RUP	tag-INT	For new tags
Any rate-one	✗			✗		
Our OCB-based scheme	✗	✓	✓	✗	✓	✓
OCB	✗	✗	✗	✗	✗	✓

Finally, our schemes can protect the confidentiality of IV, because IV is transformed to FV using TBC. This feature fits the use of secret message number (SMN) discussed in CAESAR [4], which is useful for protocols in practice.

2   An Impossibility Result for PA2

In this section, we show that any rate-one AE scheme does not satisfy PA2. We first define rate-one AE schemes by generalizing OCB2 mode of operation.

2.1   Rate-One AE Schemes

Put $\mathbb{B} := \{0,1\}^n$. We have a message $M = (M_1, M_2, \ldots, M_\ell) \in \mathbb{B}^\ell$. We can regard $\mathbb{B}$ as $\mathrm{GF}(2^n)$, the field of 2^n elements, by mapping $\mathbb{B}$ to $\mathrm{GF}(2)[x]/f(x)$ with some irreducible polynomial $f(x)$, where $\mathrm{GF}(2)[x]$ denotes the polynomial ring in variable x with coefficients in the binary field $\mathrm{GF}(2) = \{0,1\}$.

Description of OCB2. We can summarize OCB2 mode of operation as follows. Given a nonce $N \in \mathbb{B}$ and an ℓ-block message $M = (M_1, \ldots, M_\ell) \in \mathbb{B}^\ell$, the OCB2 algorithm outputs ciphertext $C := (C_1, \ldots, C_\ell) \in \mathbb{B}$ and a tag $T \in \mathbb{B}$. The secret mask L is computed from the nonce N as $L := E_K(N)$. Then intermediate inputs are computed as $X_i := M_i \oplus 2^i L$ and intermediate outputs as $Y_i := E_K(X_i)$. The ciphertext C is defined as $C_i := Y_i \oplus 2^i L$. Similarly for computing the tag T, we have $\overline{X} := M_1 \oplus \cdots \oplus M_\ell$ and $\overline{Y} := E_K(\overline{X} \oplus 3 \cdot 2^\ell L)$. The tag is simply set as $T := \overline{Y}$. Hence, there exists a $(2\ell + 2)$-by-$(2\ell + 2)$ binary matrix $\boldsymbol{E}$ such that

$$\boldsymbol{E} \cdot \begin{pmatrix} L \\ M \\ Y \\ \overline{Y} \end{pmatrix} = \begin{pmatrix} \boldsymbol{E}_{11} & \boldsymbol{E}_{12} & \boldsymbol{E}_{13} & \boldsymbol{E}_{14} \\ \boldsymbol{E}_{21} & \boldsymbol{E}_{22} & \boldsymbol{E}_{23} & \boldsymbol{E}_{24} \\ \boldsymbol{E}_{31} & \boldsymbol{E}_{32} & \boldsymbol{E}_{33} & \boldsymbol{E}_{34} \\ \boldsymbol{E}_{41} & \boldsymbol{E}_{42} & \boldsymbol{E}_{43} & \boldsymbol{E}_{44} \end{pmatrix} \cdot \begin{pmatrix} L \\ M \\ Y \\ \overline{Y} \end{pmatrix} = \begin{pmatrix} X \\ \overline{X} \\ C \\ T \end{pmatrix} \tag{1}$$

where $X := (X_1, \ldots, X_\ell)$ and $Y := (Y_1, \ldots, Y_\ell)$. We note that $\boldsymbol{E}_{13}$ and $\boldsymbol{E}_{24}$ are strictly lower triangular and we must have $\boldsymbol{E}_{14} = \boldsymbol{E}_{34} = 0$.

Similarly for decryption, OCB2 mode of operation computes intermediate inputs as $U_i := C_i \oplus 2^i L$ and intermediate outputs as $V_i := E_K^{-1}(U_i)$.

The plaintext M is recovered as $M_i := V_i \oplus 2^i L$. Therefore, there exists a 2ℓ-by-$(2\ell + 1)$ binary matrix D such that

$$
D \cdot \begin{pmatrix} L \\ C \\ V \end{pmatrix} = \begin{pmatrix} D_{11} & D_{12} & D_{13} \\ D_{21} & D_{22} & D_{23} \end{pmatrix} \cdot \begin{pmatrix} L \\ C \\ V \end{pmatrix} = \begin{pmatrix} U \\ M \end{pmatrix} \tag{2}
$$

where $U := (U_1, \ldots, U_\ell)$ and $V := (V_1, \ldots, V_\ell)$ are re-ordering of Y and X, respectively.

Rate-One AE Schemes. We can define rate-one AE scheme via generalizing the OCB mode of operation. Namely, we say that an AE scheme is rate-one if its encryption and decryption can be written with binary matrices E and D in the form (1) and (2), respectively.

2.2   Any Rate-One AE Scheme Is Not PA2

Now given the above definition of rate-one AE schemes, we show that a rate-one AE scheme cannot be PA2. PA2 means that the output of the decrypt-anyway oracle (i.e. plaintext candidates) for invalid ciphertext cannot be distinguished from uniform random strings. We make use of the following result:

Lemma 1 (Chakraborti et al. [6]). *For the rate-one AE scheme to preserve privacy, the submatrix D_{23} must be invertible.*

Now recall that $X = E_{11}L + E_{12}M + E_{13}Y$ where E_{13} is strictly lower triangular. Hence for two different queries (N, C, T) and (N, C', T) we must have $\Delta X = E_{12}\Delta M + E_{13}\Delta Y$, where the symbol Δ means for example $\Delta X := X \oplus X'$. Also recall that we have $M = D_{21}L + D_{22}C + D_{23}V$. We have $\Delta M = D_{22}\Delta C + D_{23}\Delta V$, where the submatrix D_{23} is invertible. Since ΔV is a re-ordering of ΔX, one can easily distinguish the outputs of decrypt-anyway oracle from random strings by for example setting $V_1 = V_1'$ (hence $\Delta V_1 = 0$) and checking these conditions.

3   Basic Idea and Formulation

3.1   Tag Feedback TF in a Nutshell

In this section we explain how one could use our tag feedback TF for the purpose of secure and efficient authenticated encryption. We refer back to Fig. 1.

Encryption. The encryption algorithm of TF takes as its input an initialization vector IV that is a nonce, a message M, associated data A and outputs ciphertext C, a tag T and a *finalization vector* FV whose length is equal to that of IV. Then the quadruplet (FV, T, A, C) gets sent in a channel or put in storage, depending on the application in use. Here it is important that the value of IV does not need to be communicated between the parties or saved along with the encrypted data.

Decryption. Now the decryption algorithm of TF, upon receiving (FV, T, A, C), first recovers the initialization vector IV from the finalization vector FV using the associated data A and the tag T. Then, using this IV, the decryption algorithm of TF proceeds to verification and decryption of T and C. At the end, it outputs either the decrypted message M or a reject symbol $\perp$. In case of decryption misuse, the decrypted "message" M gets always released instead of $\perp$.

3.2   Generalized AEAD Formulation by Shrimpton and Terashima

In order to formally capture the idea of tag feedback, we need slightly generalized formulation of AEAD, which has been given by Shrimpton and Terashima [15]. In this section we review this formulation and recast it to our syntax of tag feedback.

The formulation by Shrimpton and Terashima is a natural generalization of the classical nonce-based AEAD. Let IV denote the initialization vector, which is a nonce. In the classical AEAD framework [12], the same, synchronized IV must be used both by the sender for encryption and by the receiver for decryption. On the other hand, in the generalized AEAD, only the sender, who encrypts, uses IV. Shrimpton and Terashima introduces the idea of *reconstruction information* [15] whose specific form corresponds to the finalization vector FV in the current work. The value of FV is calculated in the encryption process and sent along with the encrypted data. The receiver, who decrypts, uses FV instead of IV. Obviously, in the special case where $FV = IV$, this formulation simply reduces to the classical AEAD framework.

Syntax. We split encryption and authentication (tag generation) functionalities. Syntactically a combined approach would also work, but there are a few reasons why we adopt the disjointed syntax. First, in the setting of online ciphers, ciphertext and tag play fundamentally different roles, and indeed many existing online AE algorithms (e.g. CCM [16], GCM [9] and OCB [13]) have two clearly-separated algorithmic parts to produce ciphertext and tag. Second, in the setting of release of unverified plaintext (RUP) [3], we have independent notions of privacy and integrity, and as a result we need disjointed oracles in order to define the security notions.

An AEAD scheme $\Pi = (\mathcal{E}_K, \mathcal{G}_K, \mathcal{V}_K, \mathcal{D}_K)$ is a set of four algorithms, where K is a key in some space $\mathbb{K}$. The first two, encryption $\mathcal{E}_K$ and generation $\mathcal{G}_K$, are used by the sender. The last two, verification $\mathcal{V}_K$ and decryption $\mathcal{D}_K$, are used by the receiver. We set $\mathbb{N} := \{0,1\}^n$ where n denotes a block length (e.g. $n = 64, 128$). Let $\mathbb{A}, \mathbb{M}, \mathbb{C} \subset \{0,1\}^*$ denote the associated data space, message space and ciphertext space, respectively. Let $\mathcal{L}$ be the set of valid tag lengths. For example, $\mathcal{L} = \{32, 64, 96, 128\}$. The parameter $\tau \in \mathcal{L}$ denotes the tag length. We set $\mathbb{T} := \bigcup_{\tau \in \mathcal{L}} \{0,1\}^\tau$, which is nothing but the tag space.

1. **Message encryption.** The encryption algorithm $\mathcal{E}_K$ takes as its input an initialization vector $IV \in \mathbb{N}$, associated data $A \in \mathbb{A}$, a message $M \in \mathbb{M}$, and

outputs ciphertext $C \in \mathbb{C}$ as $\mathcal{E}_K(IV, A, M) \to C$. For simplicity we assume that the equality $|C| = |M|$ always holds.

2. **Tag generation.** The generation algorithm $\mathcal{G}_K$ takes as its input a tag length $\tau \in \mathcal{L}$, an initialization vector $IV \in \mathbb{N}$, associated data $A \in \mathbb{A}$, a message $M \in \mathbb{M}$, and outputs a finalization vector $FV \in \mathbb{N}$ and an authentication tag $T \in \{0, 1\}^{\tau}$, as $\mathcal{G}_K(\tau; IV, A, M) \to (FV, T)$.

So one receives a quadruple (FV, T, A, C). Note the major difference from the classical nonce-based AEAD framework that the plain IV does not get communicated, and hence the receiver in general does not know the value of IV upon decryption.

3. **Tag verification.** The verification algorithm $\mathcal{V}_K$ takes as its input a finalization vector $FV \in \mathbb{N}$, a tag $T \in \mathbb{T}$, associated data $A \in \mathbb{A}$, ciphertext $C \in \mathbb{C}$, and outputs a symbol, either $\top$ or $\bot$. Succinctly, we have $\mathcal{V}_K(FV, T, A, C) = \top$ or $\bot$. Here note that the tag length τ is not explicitly input to $\mathcal{V}_K$, but rather it should become clear from the input value T.

4. **Ciphertext decryption.** This is so called "decrypt-anyway" algorithm [3]. The decryption algorithm $\mathcal{D}_K$ takes as its input a finalization vector $FV \in \mathbb{N}$, a tag $T \in \mathbb{T}$, associated data $A \in \mathbb{A}$, ciphertext $C \in \mathbb{C}$, and outputs a message $M \in \mathbb{M}$. Succinctly written, $\mathcal{D}_K(FV, T, A, C) \to M$. Note that this algorithm invariably outputs "something" in $\mathbb{M}$ regardless of the authenticity of input. For simplicity we assume that the equality $|M| = |C|$ always holds.

***IV* Recovery (Optional).** Sometimes a receiver may want to recover the value of original IV. Such a demand occurs when IV contains some useful information (e.g. managed counter, secret message number [4,5], and plaintext via nonce stealing [10]).

Such a functionality is not required by the generalized AEAD formulation, and it will not appear in our security analysis, either. This is optional and not mandatory. However, our tag feedback TF provides this useful functionality, so for the sake of completeness we describe the algorithmic syntax here.

5. ***IV* Recovery.** The recovery algorithm $\mathcal{R}_K$ takes as its input a finalization vector $FV \in \mathbb{N}$, a tag $T \in \mathbb{T}$, associated data $A \in \mathbb{A}$, ciphertext $C \in \mathbb{C}$, and outputs an initialization vector $IV \in \mathbb{N}$, as $\mathcal{R}_K(FV, T, A, C) \to IV$. Note that the recovery algorithm $\mathcal{R}_K$ outputs a value in $\mathbb{N}$ regardless of the authenticity of input, just like the decryption algorithm $\mathcal{D}_K$.

***FV* Synchronization.** In the classical nonce-based AEAD framework, it is outside its scope how to synchronize IV between parties [12]. The most common way is to directly communicate the current value of IV. Another way is possible when the parties are both stateful and decide to use predictable IV, like a counter. In such a case, theoretically, they may be able to agree on the same IV without directly communicating its value. However, in practice, the communication channel is often unreliable, and hence the synchronization of IV is not so easy. Indeed, most protocols such as IPSec and SSL/TLS adopt the solution of sending (part of) IV along with ciphertext, tag and associated data.

In the generalized AEAD formulation, the synchronization (or "coupling") of IV and FV is a priori explicitly specified, because the value of FV is computed in the encryption process and sent to the receiver together with ciphertext, tag and associated data. It should be noted that the generalized formulation excludes the above (though rather hypothetical) case of synchronizing IV without direct communication.

4   ΘCBt Construction

In this section, we present an OCB-based AEAD scheme that we call ΘCBt, following the conversion TF. We describe our scheme using an ideal tweakable block cipher, so we should rather say that our scheme is based on ΘCB, the OCB mode having an ideal tweakable block cipher as its underlying primitive (hence our name ΘCBt). Of course one could use an ordinary block cipher via XEX and XE (and realizes "OCBt"). The construction is given by Algorithm 1. It is also depicted in Fig. 2. Among the different versions of OCB, our scheme is most similar to OCB2 [11].

In Algorithm 1, $\pi : \mathcal{T} \times \{0,1\}^n \to \{0,1\}^n$ is the encryption function of the ideal tweakable block cipher, where $\mathcal{T}$ is the tweak space. The encryption function with tweak $Tw \in \mathcal{T}$ is denoted by $\pi^{Tw}(\cdot)$. It is assumed that $\mathcal{T} = \{0,1,2\} \times (\mathbb{N} \cup \mathbb{N} \times \mathbb{T}) \times \{1, \ldots, \eta\} \times \{0,1,2\}$, where $\eta = \max_{X \in \mathsf{M} \cup \mathsf{A}} \lceil |X|/n \rceil$.

The function partition takes $X \in \{0,1\}^*$ as input and divides it into blocks $X_1, X_2, \ldots, X_x$ such that $x = \max\{\lceil |X|/n \rceil, 1\}$ and $X = X_1 \| X_2 \| \cdots \| X_x$, where $|X_i| = n$ for $1 \le i \le x - 1$, and $0 \le |X_x| \le n$. For $Y \in \{0,1\}^*$ such that $|Y| < n$, $Y \| 0^*$ means that the minimum number of 0's are appended so that $|Y \| 0^*| = n$. $Y \| 10^*$ means that the minimum number of 0's are appended so that $|Y \| 10^*| = n$. The function $_\ell(Z)$ returns the ℓ-bit prefix of Z, where $Z \in \{0,1\}^n$ and $0 \le \ell \le n$. The function $\mathsf{len}(Y)$ returns the n-bit binary representation of $|Y|$.

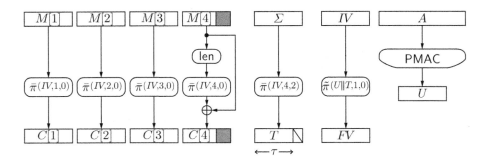

Fig. 2. The ΘCBt construction. $\pi^{(0,\cdot,\cdot,\cdot)}$ and $\pi^{(2,\cdot,\cdot,\cdot)}$ in Algorithm 1 are denoted by $\bar{\pi}^{(\cdot,\cdot,\cdot)}$ and $\tilde{\pi}^{(\cdot,\cdot,\cdot)}$, respectively.

Algorithm 1. OCB-based construction ΘCBt

100: **function** Θt.$\mathcal{E}(IV, A, M)$
101:    $T, C \leftarrow \Theta.\mathcal{E}(IV, M)$
102:    **return** C
103: **end function**

200: **function** Θt.$\mathcal{G}(\tau; IV, A, M)$
201:    $T, C \leftarrow \Theta.\mathcal{E}(IV, M)$
202:    $U \leftarrow \mathsf{PMAC}(A)$
203:    $FV \leftarrow \pi^{(2, U \| T, 1, 0)}(IV)$
204:    **return** FV, T
205: **end function**

300: **function** $\Theta.\mathcal{E}(IV, M)$
301:    $M[1], \ldots, M[m] \leftarrow \mathsf{partition}(M)$
302:    $\Sigma \leftarrow 0^n$
303:    **for** $i = 1$ to $m - 1$ **do**
304:       $C[i] \leftarrow \pi^{(0, IV, i, 0)}(M[i])$
305:       $\Sigma \leftarrow \Sigma \oplus M[i]$
306:    **end for**
307:    $pad \leftarrow \pi^{(0, IV, m, 1)}(\mathsf{len}(M[m]))$
308:    $C[m] \leftarrow M[m] \oplus_{|M[m]|} (pad)$
309:    $\Sigma \leftarrow \Sigma \oplus (C[m] \| 0^*) \oplus pad$
310:    $T \leftarrow_\tau (\pi^{(0, IV, m, 2)}(\Sigma))$
311:    $C \leftarrow C[1] \| C[2] \| \cdots \| C[m]$
312:    **return** T, C
313: **end function**

400: **function** $\mathsf{PMAC}(A)$
401:    $A[1], A[2], \ldots, A[a] \leftarrow \mathsf{partition}(A)$
402:    $\varsigma \leftarrow 0^n$
403:    **for** $i = 1$ to $a - 1$ **do**
404:       $\varsigma \leftarrow \varsigma \oplus \pi^{(1, 0^n, i, 0)}(A[i])$
405:    **end for**
406:    **if** $|A[a]| = n$ **then**
407:       $U \leftarrow \pi^{(1, 0^n, a, 1)}(\varsigma \oplus A[a])$
408:    **else**
409:       $A'[a] \leftarrow A[a] \| 10^*$
410:       $U \leftarrow \pi^{(1, 0^n, a, 2)}(\varsigma \oplus A'[a])$
411:    **end if**
412:    **return** U
413: **end function**

500: **function** Θt.$\mathcal{D}(FV, T, A, C)$
501:    $M, d \leftarrow \Theta$t.$\mathcal{VD}(FV, T, A, C)$
502:    **return** M
503: **end function**

600: **function** Θt.$\mathcal{V}(FV, T, A, C)$
601:    $M, d \leftarrow \Theta$t.$\mathcal{VD}(FV, T, A, C)$
602:    **return** d
603: **end function**

700: **function** Θt.$\mathcal{VD}(FV, T, A, C)$
701:    $U \leftarrow \mathsf{PMAC}(A)$
702:    $IV \leftarrow (\pi^{(2, U \| T, 1, 0)})^{-1}(FV)$
703:    $C[1], \ldots, C[m] \leftarrow \mathsf{partition}(C)$
704:    $\Sigma \leftarrow 0^n$
705:    **for** $i = 1$ to $m - 1$ **do**
706:       $M[i] \leftarrow (\pi^{(0, IV, i, 0)})^{-1}(C[i])$
707:       $\Sigma \leftarrow \Sigma \oplus M[i]$
708:    **end for**
709:    $pad \leftarrow \pi^{(0, IV, m, 1)}(\mathsf{len}(C[m]))$
710:    $M[m] \leftarrow C[m] \oplus_{|C[m]|} (pad)$
711:    $\Sigma \leftarrow \Sigma \oplus (C[m] \| 0^*) \oplus pad$
712:    $T' \leftarrow_\tau (\pi^{(0, IV, m, 2)}(\Sigma))$
713:    $M \leftarrow M[1] \| M[2] \| \cdots \| M[m]$
714:    $d \leftarrow \perp$
715:    **if** $T = T'$ **then**
716:       $d \leftarrow \top$
717:    **end if**
718:    **return** M, d
719: **end function**

5   Security Definitions

We define security notions for an AEAD scheme $\Pi = (\mathcal{E}_K, \mathcal{G}_K, \mathcal{V}_K, \mathcal{D}_K)$ in this section. Our security goals are privacy and authenticity under decryption misuse (i.e. release of unverified plaintext). We start with describing the adversarial model.

5.1   Adversarial Model

An adversary A is an oracle machine. The adversary A is given access to oracles $\mathcal{E}_K(\cdots)$, $\mathcal{G}_K(\cdots)$, $\mathcal{V}_K(\cdots)$ and $\mathcal{D}_K(\cdots)$. We write $A^{\mathcal{O}}$ to denote an experiment of running A interacting with its oracle $\mathcal{O}$.

Sometimes adversary A outputs a value at the end of its execution. With abuse of notation we also write $A^{\mathcal{O}}$ to indicate this value. Therefore, the notation $\Pr\left[A^{\mathcal{O}} = 1\right]$ stands for the probability that A returns 1 after interacting with its oracle $\mathcal{O}$. All probabilities are taken over random coins used in the experiment, i.e. keys and other random variables chosen by the oracles and random tapes used by the adversary, if any.

For simplicity we only consider computationally unbounded adversaries, and in our analysis only the query complexity is bounded. This is possible because we assume that the underlying block cipher is ideal. It is straightforward to translate our results into the standard model, where the underlying primitive is replaced with an actual block cipher like AES, with an additional term in the security bound arising to the security of the block cipher itself.

Nonce-IV-Respecting. We require that the adversary A never makes queries of different messages $M \neq M'$ having the same IV, to $\mathcal{E}$-oracle or $\mathcal{G}$-oracle. Each IV corresponds to at most one message M.

Note that the adversary is allowed to repeat the same pair (IV, M) with different values of A and τ. In some AEAD schemes (e.g. ciphertext translation [10]), most part of ciphertext would not be affected by A, and hence the two outputs $\mathcal{E}_K(IV, A, M)$ and $\mathcal{E}_K(IV, A', M)$ may be almost identical. Also, in many AEAD schemes, the generated tags $\mathcal{G}_K(\tau; IV, A, M)$ and $\mathcal{G}_K(\tau'; IV, A, M)$ for different tag lengths $\tau \neq \tau'$ may look much related (e.g. tag truncation).

We treat these distinguishability not as violating the confidentiality of M (or authenticity by T) but rather as providing us with engineering benefits, because our definitions still require security in a strong sense. This leads to a privacy notion similar to deterministic AE [14]; that is, the adversary is able to tell that the exact same message M must have been encrypted for these multiple instances (either with changing A or with changing τ), but that is all what the adversary is able to tell about the message M.

Nonce-(FV, T, A)-Respecting. We require that adversary A never makes queries with an "old" triplet (FV, T, A) to its $\mathcal{D}$-oracle. Here we say that a triplet (FV, T, A) is *old* if there has been already a query to $\mathcal{G}$-oracle such that $\mathcal{G}_K(\tau; IV, A, M) \rightarrow (FV, T)$.

We also require that adversary A never repeats the same triplet (FV, T, A) to its $\mathcal{D}$-oracle. On the other hand, our scheme ΘCBt still ensures some confidentiality (a form of plaintext awareness [3]) even against such (FV, T, A)-repeating adversaries. We refer to Sect. 7 for details.

Algorithm 2. Ideal objects to define privacy

---

function INITIALIZATION
  $K \xleftarrow{\$} \mathbb{K}$
  $\mathsf{S} \leftarrow \varnothing$
end function

function $\mathcal{E}_K^{\$}(IV, A, M)$
  if $\mathsf{S}[IV, M]$ undefined **then**
    $\mathsf{S}[IV, M] \xleftarrow{\$} \{0,1\}^{|M|}$
  end if
  $S \leftarrow \mathsf{S}[IV, M]$
  $C \leftarrow \mathcal{E}_K(IV, A, S)$
  return C
end function

function $\mathcal{G}_K^{\$}(\tau; IV, A, M)$
  if $\mathsf{S}[IV, M]$ undefined **then**
    $\mathsf{S}[IV, M] \xleftarrow{\$} \{0,1\}^{|M|}$
  end if
  $S \leftarrow \mathsf{S}[IV, M]$
  $(FV, T) \leftarrow \mathcal{G}_K(\tau; IV, A, S)$
  return (FV, T)
end function

function $\mathcal{D}_K^{\$}(FV, T, A, C)$
  $S \xleftarrow{\$} \{0,1\}^{|C|}$
  return S
end function

5.2   Security Notions

Privacy: tag-PA. The privacy notion is defined in a form of indistinguishability. The adversary A is given access to $\mathcal{E}$-, $\mathcal{G}$- and $\mathcal{D}$-oracles. The corresponding ideal objects $\mathcal{E}_K^{\$}, \mathcal{G}_K^{\$}, \mathcal{D}_K^{\$}$ are defined in Algorithm 2. The first two, $\mathcal{E}_K^{\$}$ and $\mathcal{G}_K^{\$}$, are essentially the same as the real objects, except that they use a random message $S \in \{0,1\}^{|M|}$ instead of M. This is due to the fact that the tags do not need to "look random" for different tag lengths. Indeed, it can be just truncation. The last object $\mathcal{D}_K^{\$}$ simply returns a random string $S \xleftarrow{\$} \{0,1\}^{|C|}$.

Now we define the privacy as

$$\mathrm{Adv}_{\Pi}^{\mathrm{priv}}(A) := \Pr\big[A^{\mathcal{E}_K, \mathcal{G}_K, \mathcal{D}_K} = 1\big] - \Pr\big[A^{\mathcal{E}_K^{\$}, \mathcal{G}_K^{\$}, \mathcal{D}_K^{\$}} = 1\big],$$

where the probabilities are taken over all random coins used in each experiment. Note the presence of the decryption algorithm. This notion guarantees robustness against decryption misuse under nonce-IV, nonce-(FV, T, A)-respecting.

Authenticity: tag-INT. The authenticity notion is defined in a form of unforgeability. The adversary A is given access to all four oracles $\mathcal{E}_K, \mathcal{G}_K, \mathcal{V}_K$ and $\mathcal{D}_K$. We define

$$\mathrm{Adv}_{\Pi}^{\mathrm{auth}, \tau}(A) := \Pr\big[A^{\mathcal{E}_K, \mathcal{G}_K, \mathcal{V}_K, \mathcal{D}_K} \text{ forges a } \tau\text{-bit tag}\big],$$

where "forges a τ-bit tag" means that adversary A makes a non-trivial $\mathcal{V}$-query (FV, T, A, C) with $|T| = \tau$ so that $\mathcal{V}$-oracle returns $\top$. A $\mathcal{V}$-query is *trivial* if both the queries $\mathcal{E}_K(IV, A, M) \to C$ and $\mathcal{G}_K(\tau; IV, A, M) \to (FV, T)$ have been already made. Previous $\mathcal{G}$-queries with $\tau' \neq \tau$ do not count.

Note that the parameter τ is explicit in this definition. This is because we want to ensure τ-bit security for τ-bit tags, which we demand even under tag truncation. We want to avoid such a situation as 2^{96} trials would be sufficient to guess a 128-bit tag after seeing its truncated 32-bit part.

6   Security of ΘCBt

The security of OCB-based construction ΘCBt is discussed on the assumption that the underlying tweakable block cipher is ideal. To simplify the proof, PMAC is replaced with a function $\rho : \mathbb{A} \to \{0,1\}^n$ chosen uniformly at random. It is justified since the tweaks of π used in PMAC and those of π used in $\Theta.\mathcal{E}$ are disjoint [11, Theorem 15].

Without loss of generality it is assumed that, for any $\mathcal{E}$-query (IV, A, M), adversary A makes a $\mathcal{G}$-query $(\tau; IV, A, M)$ right after the $\mathcal{E}$-query. Values for the i-th query made by A are represented with subscript i. For example, if the i-th query is a $\mathcal{G}$-query, then it is denoted by $(\tau_i; IV_i, A_i, M_i)$ and the corresponding reply is denoted by (FV_i, T_i). For a query made by A, a value or a tuple of values in the query or the corresponding reply are said to be fresh if they do not appear before the query.

Let Col_ρ be an event that there exist some distinct i and j such that $A_i \neq A_j$ and $\rho(A_i) = \rho(A_j)$.

Let $\mathsf{Col}_{\mathrm{IV},1}$ be an event that there exists some $\mathcal{D}$-query (FV_i, T_i, A_i, C_i) such that $IV_i = IV_j$ for some j such that $1 \leq j < i$ and $(FV_i, T_i, A_i) \neq (FV_j, T_j, A_j)$. Let $\mathsf{Col}_{\mathrm{IV},2}$ be an event that there exists some $\mathcal{E}$-query (IV_i, A_i, M_i) with fresh IV_i such that $IV_i = IV_j$ for some $\mathcal{D}$-query (FV_j, T_j, A_j, C_j) such that $1 \leq j < i$ and $(FV_i, T_i, A_i) \neq (FV_j, T_j, A_j)$.

Theorem 1 (Privacy). *Let A be any adversary against privacy of ΘCBt. Suppose that A makes at most q_{e}, q_{g} and q_{d} queries to Θt.$\mathcal{E}$, Θt.$\mathcal{G}$ and Θt.$\mathcal{D}$, respectively. Let $q = q_{\mathrm{e}} + q_{\mathrm{g}} + q_{\mathrm{d}}$. Then,*

$$\mathrm{Adv}^{\mathrm{priv}}_{\Theta\mathrm{CBt}}(A) \leq \frac{q^2}{2^n} + \frac{2\,q\,q_{\mathrm{d}}}{2^n - q} \ .$$

Proof. Notice that A does not repeat the same (FV, T, A) to the $\mathcal{D}$-oracle. In addition, A does not ask *old* (FV, T, A) to the $\mathcal{D}$-oracle. Thus, as long as $\mathsf{Col}_{\mathrm{IV},1} \cup \mathsf{Col}_{\mathrm{IV},2}$ does not occur, $(\Theta.\mathcal{E}, \Theta.\mathcal{G}, \Theta.\mathcal{D})$ and $(\Theta.\mathcal{E}^{\$}, \Theta.\mathcal{G}^{\$}, \Theta.\mathcal{D}^{\$})$ look identical to each other. Both $(\Theta.\mathcal{E}, \Theta.\mathcal{G})$ and $(\Theta.\mathcal{E}^{\$}, \Theta.\mathcal{G}^{\$})$ evaluate π on a single point for each tweak to produce C's and T's. Thus,

$$\Pr\left[A^{\Theta\mathrm{t}.\mathcal{E}, \Theta\mathrm{t}.\mathcal{G}, \Theta\mathrm{t}.\mathcal{D}} = 1\right] - \Pr\left[A^{\Theta\mathrm{t}.\mathcal{E}^{\$}, \Theta\mathrm{t}.\mathcal{G}^{\$}, \Theta\mathrm{t}.\mathcal{D}^{\$}} = 1\right] \leq \Pr[\mathsf{Col}_{\mathrm{IV},1} \cup \mathsf{Col}_{\mathrm{IV},2}] \ ,$$

where $\Pr[\mathsf{Col}_{\mathrm{IV},1} \cup \mathsf{Col}_{\mathrm{IV},2}] \leq \Pr[\mathsf{Col}_\rho] + \Pr[\mathsf{Col}_{\mathrm{IV},1} \,|\, \overline{\mathsf{Col}_\rho}] + \Pr[\mathsf{Col}_{\mathrm{IV},2} \,|\, \overline{\mathsf{Col}_\rho}]$.

Since ρ is a uniform random function, $\Pr[\mathsf{Col}_\rho] \leq q^2/2^n$.

Suppose that Col_ρ does not occur. For $\mathcal{D}$-query (FV_i, T_i, A_i, C_i), if (T_i, A_i) is fresh, then IV_i is chosen uniformly at random from 2^n elements, and the probability that IV_i is not fresh is at most $(i - 1)/2^n$. On the other hand, if (T_i, A_i) is not fresh, then $FV_i \neq FV_j$ for every (FV_j, T_j, A_j) such that $(T_i, A_i) = (T_j, A_j)$ and $1 \leq j < i$. Thus, IV_i is chosen uniformly at random from at least $2^n - (q_{\mathrm{g}} + q_{\mathrm{d}})$ elements, and the probability that IV_i is not fresh is at most $(i - 1)/(2^n - (q_{\mathrm{g}} + q_{\mathrm{d}}))$. Thus, $\Pr[\mathsf{Col}_{\mathrm{IV},1} \,|\, \overline{\mathsf{Col}_\rho}] \leq q\,q_{\mathrm{d}}/(2^n - q)$.

For $\mathcal{D}$-query (FV_i, T_i, A_i, C_i), the corresponding IV_i is not disclosed and chosen uniformly at random from at least $2^n - (q_g + q_d)$ elements. It implies that $\Pr[\mathsf{Col}_{\mathrm{IV},2} \,|\, \overline{\mathsf{Col}_\rho}] \leq q_e q_d / (2^n - q)$. $\qquad\qquad\qquad\square$

Theorem 2 (Authenticity). *Let A be any adversary against authenticity of ΘCBt. Suppose that A makes at most q_e, q_g, q_v and q_d queries to $\Theta t.\mathcal{E}$, $\Theta t.\mathcal{G}$, $\Theta t.\mathcal{V}$ and $\Theta t.\mathcal{D}$, respectively. Let $q = q_e + q_g + q_v + q_d$. Then,*

$$\mathrm{Adv}_{\Theta\mathrm{CBt}}^{\mathrm{auth},\tau}(A) \leq \frac{q^2}{2^n} + \frac{2\,q\,q_d}{2^n - q} + \frac{q_v}{2^\tau (1 - (q_v + 1)2^{-n})} \ .$$

Proof. Let $\mathsf{Col}_{\mathrm{IV}} = \mathsf{Col}_{\mathrm{IV},1} \cup \mathsf{Col}_{\mathrm{IV},2}$. Let Suc be the event that A is successful in forgery of a τ-bit tag. Then, $\Pr[\mathsf{Suc}] \leq \Pr[\mathsf{Col}_{\mathrm{IV}} \cup \mathsf{Suc}] \leq \Pr[\mathsf{Col}_{\mathrm{IV}}] + \Pr[\mathsf{Suc}\,|\,\overline{\mathsf{Col}_{\mathrm{IV}}}]$.

Similarly to the proof of Theorem 1, $\Pr[\mathsf{Col}_{\mathrm{IV}}] \leq q^2/2^n + 2\,q\,q_d/(2^n - q)$.

Notice that A does not make queries with old (FV, T, A) to its $\mathcal{D}$-oracle. Thus, as long as $\mathsf{Col}_{\mathrm{IV}}$ does not occur, $\mathcal{D}$-queries gives A no information on encryption with tweaks using IV's in $\mathcal{E}$- or $\mathcal{G}$-queries.

A can ask (FV, T, A) obtained by a $\mathcal{G}$-query in the $\mathcal{V}$-queries. A can also repeat the same (FV, T, A) in the $\mathcal{V}$-queries. Then, similar to the proof of Theorem 4 in [11], the probability that a $\mathcal{V}$-query is successful is at most $2^{n-\tau}/(2^n - q_v - 1)$. Thus, $\Pr[\mathsf{Suc}\,|\,\overline{\mathsf{Col}_{\mathrm{IV}}}] \leq q_v/(2^\tau(1 - (q_v + 1)2^{-n}))$. $\qquad\square$

7   Privacy Against (FV, T, A)-Repeating Adversaries

In this section, we show that some sort of privacy still remains even against (FV, T, A)-repeating adversaries. What we prove here is a type of plaintext awareness [3] against (FV, T, A)-repeating adversaries under RUP. It is quite general and immediately implies the privacy theorem proven in Sect. 6 against (FV, T, A)-*respecting* adversaries under RUP.

The pa1-advantage of adversary A is defined as

$$\mathrm{Adv}_{\Pi}^{\mathrm{pa1}}(A) = \Pr\big[A^{\mathcal{E}_K, \mathcal{G}_K, \mathcal{D}_K} = 1\big] - \Pr\big[A^{\mathcal{E}_K, \mathcal{G}_K, D} = 1\big] \ ,$$

where D is an extractor. The extractor D is a probabilistic but stateless algorithm that takes as its input a query (FV, T, A, C) and its associated history string $\alpha[FV, T, A]$ and tries to mimic the output of the "real" oracle. The history string $\alpha[FV, T, A]$ contains the record of previous adversarial activities (i.e. queries to and replies from the oracles) associated with the triplet (FV, T, A).

Theorem 3. *Let A be any adversary against plaintext awareness of ΘCBt. Suppose that A makes at most q_e, q_g and q_d queries to $\Theta t.\mathcal{E}$, $\Theta t.\mathcal{G}$ and $\Theta t.\mathcal{D}$, respectively. Let $q = q_e + q_g + q_d$. Then,*

$$\mathrm{Adv}_{\Theta\mathrm{CBt}}^{\mathrm{pa1}}(A) \leq \frac{q^2}{2^n} + \frac{2qq_d}{2^n - q} \ .$$

Proof. A is allowed to make a $\mathcal{D}$-query (FV, T, A, C) such that (FV, T) is produced as a reply to some previous $\mathcal{G}$-query $(\tau; IV, A, M)$, where (IV, A, M) is an $\mathcal{E}$-query prior to the $\mathcal{G}$-query. For $\mathcal{D}$-query (FV, T, A, C), the extractor $\Theta\mathsf{t}.\mathcal{D}$ works as follows:

1. Suppose that (FV, T, A) is fresh. Namely, it does not appear prior to the $\mathcal{D}$-query. Then, return M chosen uniformly at random from $\{0, 1\}^{|C|}$.
2. Suppose that (FV, T, A) is not fresh. Then, return M computed as follows. Let $\boldsymbol{C}$ be the set of C' such that (FV, T, A, C') is produced by some previous $\mathcal{E}$-query and $\mathcal{G}$-query, or it is a previous $\mathcal{D}$-query. Let $\mathsf{partition}(C) = (C[1], C[2], \ldots, C[m])$.
   (a) For $1 \leq i \leq m - 1$, if there exists some $C' \in \boldsymbol{C}$ such that $C[i] = C'[i]$ and $C'[i]$ is not the last block of C', then $M[i] \leftarrow M'[i]$, where M' is a message of C'. Otherwise, $M[i]$ is chosen uniformly at random from $\{0, 1\}^n \setminus \{M'[i] \mid C' \in \boldsymbol{C} \text{ and } C'[i] \text{ is not the last block of } C'\}$.
   (b) For the last block, if there exists some $C' \in \boldsymbol{C}$ such that $|C'| = |C|$, then $M[m] \leftarrow M'[m] \oplus C'[m] \oplus C[m]$. Otherwise, $M[m]$ is chosen uniformly at random from $\{0, 1\}^{|C[m]|}$.

$(\Theta\mathsf{t}.\mathcal{E}, \Theta\mathsf{t}.\mathcal{G}, \Theta\mathsf{t}.\mathcal{D})$ and $(\Theta\mathsf{t}.\mathcal{E}, \Theta\mathsf{t}.\mathcal{G}, \Theta\mathsf{t}.D)$ look identical to each other as long as $\mathsf{Col}_{IV,1} \cup \mathsf{Col}_{IV,2}$ does not occur. Thus,

$$\Pr[\boldsymbol{A}^{\Theta\mathsf{t}.\mathcal{E}, \Theta\mathsf{t}.\mathcal{G}, \Theta\mathsf{t}.\mathcal{D}} = 1] - \Pr[\boldsymbol{A}^{\Theta\mathsf{t}.\mathcal{E}, \Theta\mathsf{t}.\mathcal{G}, \Theta\mathsf{t}.D} = 1] \leq \Pr[\mathsf{Col}_{IV,1} \cup \mathsf{Col}_{IV,2}] .$$

Similarly to Theorem 1, we can prove $\Pr[\mathsf{Col}_{IV,1} \cup \mathsf{Col}_{IV,2}] \leq q^2/2^n + 2qq_\mathsf{d}/(2^n - q)$.
$\square$

8 Discussion

8.1 Implementation Choices

In general, computation resources of encrypting and decrypting devices are unbalanced. In some network, end-devices with restricted resource collect sensitive data which is then encrypted and sent to the server. While in other network, the server generates sensitive orders and transfers to the end devices. In the former case, encryption must be as light as possible while decryption will be done in a resource-rich environment. The situation is opposite in the latter case. ΘCBt can be implemented in several ways depending on which of encryption and decryption implementors want to optimize as summarized in Table 2.

Implementation 1: Optimizing Encryption. The natural implementation of ΘCBt is optimized for encryption. The plaintext is encrypted block by block from the beginning, and the ciphertext is sent to the decryption player online.

On the other hand, tag generation requires the checksum of all message blocks. Decryption only can start after FV is sent, thus decryption may not be able to start immediately after receiving the first ciphertext blocks. However, considering that taking checksum of all message blocks is much faster than computing E_K for all blocks, delay of receiving FV is small.

Implementation 2: Optimizing Decryption. We can choose to minimize the cost of decryption by allowing the encryption to be two-passes. The idea is first generating and sending FV to the decryption player. After FV is sent, encryption starts from the first block. Because FV has already been sent, decryption can immediately start after receiving each ciphertext block.

Encryption can be implemented in two ways. To optimize latency, both encryption and FV generation are simultaneously computed by storing the ciphertext in a large buffer. After FV is sent, the ciphertext in the buffer is released. To optimize throughput without using buffer, the encryption player first computes FV. After FV is sent, the encryption starts.

Table 2. Implementation choices

		Rate	Pass	On-the-fly
Implementation 1	Enc	1	1	✓
	Dec	1	2	–
Implementation 2	Enc	1	2	–
	Dec	1	2	✓

8.2   Supporting Secret Message Number (SMN)

SMN defined in CAESAR [4] is a type of IV having two features; confidentiality of SMN is ensured, and SMN is recovered during decryption.

IV Confidentiality. Bernstein [5] listed importance of IV confidentiality.

- Suppose that IV is set to some unique data from earlier in the protocol, e.g. the number of message packets processed so far. Such sensitive information should not be exposed.
- Suppose that IV is set to user's CPU dependent data, e.g. a high-resolution monotonic clock. Actual CPU clocks are not exactly real time. If it is leaked, the difference may reveal some sensitive CPU information, e.g. CPU's load.

In our scheme, only FV is communicated, which efficiently supports SMN.

Security Against Replay Attacks. SMN is useful to prevent replay attacks, in which the attacker first eavesdrops correct (FV, T, A, C), and later sends the same quadruplet to the verifier. Because the quadruplet is correct, authentication can succeed. To prevent replay attacks, protocols need to be stateful. A popular countermeasure is embedding the counter of the number of messages processed before in the message, which raises several concerns [5]:

- Real world users can wrongly implement countermeasures.

- Replays should be detected immediately. Spending long to detect replays consumes bandwidth and decreases performance. It also increases the risk of denial of service.

A simple implementation of the countermeasure which detects replays efficiently possibly without embedding the counter in the message, is important. Our scheme allows implementors to simply set the counter in IV. Decryption first recovers IV, thus replays can be detected at the very beginning of the decryption.

Appendix

A   Rational of Associated Data Computation in ΘCBt

In Sect. 4, we presented ΘCBt as an instantiation of the tag-feedback, where A is processed with PMAC and the result is used as a part of tweak. We stress that identifying the best construction for incorporating A is non-trivial. Here, we explain the rational behind ΘCBt especially about the incorporation of A.

A.1   Synthetic Approach

We incorporate associated data A into the tag feedback. One can immediately notice that associated data A cannot be just input to the underlying ΘCB, even if it accepts associated data. This is because we need to make FV dependent *directly* on A, not via tag T, to achieve (FV, T, A)-robust decryption.

So we use a keyed function F_K to "hash" associated data $A \in \mathbb{A}$. By following the design of OCB2, we use PMAC as F_K. Write $U \leftarrow \mathsf{PMAC}_K(A)$. Write W the tag output of the underlying ΘCB. Then we make the tweak input, tw, and the final tag, T, by using or combining U and W. There are four possibilities: U, W, $U \oplus W$ and $U \| W$, and thus 16 combinations as shown in Fig. 3.

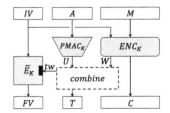

Fig. 3. Synthetic approach for tw and T

tweak (tw)	tag (T)			
	U	W	$U \oplus W$	$U \| W$
U	$-^{2,3}$	$-^3$	$-^3$	$-^{1,3}$
W	$-^2$	$-^4$	TF1	$-^1$
$U \oplus W$	$-^2$	TF2	$-^5$	$-^1$
$U \| W$	$-^2$	TF	TF3	$-^1$

Fig. 4. Sixteen choices for tw and T

The analysis for those sixteen cases is summarized in Table 2.

In Fig. 4, '$-$' represents that the construction is not suitable with respect to efficiency or security, and superscript numbers indicate the reasons as follows.

$-^1$: The new tag size $|T|$ increases from the original $|W|$.

$-^2$: By using U as new tag T, only A is authorized. Integrity can be violated.

$-^3$: Recovering IV from FV during decryption is not dependent on T, thus correct M for invalid T is leaked by querying invalid T (violating confidentiality). This clearly illustrates the fact that the tag feedback is essential for (FV, T, A)-robust decryption.

$-^4$: U is not used anywhere, which is obviously insecure.

$-^5$: T is directly used as tweak, thus recovering IV from FV during decryption is not dependent on U, which is insufficient for (FV, T, A)-robust decryption.

In the end, we have four secure constructions. Among them TF is more advantageous on the simplicity of the security proof. To simply describe the concept of our construction, we chose TF to build ΘCBt.

B   Authenticity against Adversaries Asking Old Triplets

In this section, we show that some sort of authenticity still remains even against adversaries asking *old* triplets (FV, T, A). For an old triplet (FV, T, A), if adversary $\boldsymbol{A}$ makes a $\mathcal{D}$-query (FV, T, A, C), then we call the triplet corrupted. We want that all uncorrupted triplets (FV, A, T) remain secure. This motivates us to define the auth-advantage of $\boldsymbol{A}$ as

$$\mathrm{Adv}_{\Pi}^{\mathrm{auth},\tau}(\boldsymbol{A}) := \Pr\left[\boldsymbol{A}^{\mathcal{E}_K, \mathcal{G}_K, \mathcal{V}_K, \mathcal{D}_K} \text{ forges a } \tau\text{-bit tag with uncorrupted}\right],$$

where by "forges with uncorrupted" we mean $\boldsymbol{A}$ being able to make the $\mathcal{V}$-oracle return $\top$ for a query (FV, T, A, C) such that (FV, T, A) is uncorrupted.

Theorem 4. *Let $\boldsymbol{A}$ be any adversary against authenticity of ΘCBt. Suppose that $\boldsymbol{A}$ makes at most q_{e}, q_{g}, q_{v} and q_{d} queries to Θt.$\mathcal{E}$, Θt.$\mathcal{G}$, Θt.$\mathcal{V}$ and Θt.$\mathcal{D}$, respectively. Let $q = q_{\mathrm{e}} + q_{\mathrm{g}} + q_{\mathrm{v}} + q_{\mathrm{d}}$. Then,*

$$\mathrm{Adv}_{\Theta\mathrm{CBt}}^{\mathrm{auth},\tau}(\boldsymbol{A}) \leq \frac{q^2}{2^n} + \frac{2qq_{\mathrm{d}}}{2^n - q} + \frac{q_{\mathrm{v}}}{2^\tau(1 - (q_{\mathrm{v}} + 1)2^{-n})} \ .$$

The proof is omitted due to the page limit.

References

1. Abed, F., Forler, C., List, E., Lucks, S., Wenzel, J.: RIV for robust authenticated encryption. In: Peyrin, T. (ed.) FSE 2016. LNCS, vol. 9783, pp. 23–42. Springer, Heidelberg (2016). doi:10.1007/978-3-662-52993-5_2

2. Andreeva, E., Bilgin, B., Bogdanov, A., Luykx, A., Mennink, B., Mouha, N., Yasuda, K.: APE: authenticated permutation-based encryption for lightweight cryptography. In: Cid, C., Rechberger, C. (eds.) FSE 2014. LNCS, vol. 8540, pp. 168–186. Springer, Heidelberg (2015). doi:10.1007/978-3-662-46706-0_9

3. Andreeva, E., Bogdanov, A., Luykx, A., Mennink, B., Mouha, N., Yasuda, K.: How to securely release unverified plaintext in authenticated encryption. In: Sarkar, P., Iwata, T. (eds.) ASIACRYPT 2014. LNCS, vol. 8873, pp. 105–125. Springer, Heidelberg (2014). doi:10.1007/978-3-662-45611-8_6
4. Bernstein, D.: CAESAR Competition (2013). http://competitions.cr.yp.to/caesar.html
5. Bernstein, D.: Re: secret message numbers. Posted to CAESAR Mailing List (2013). https://groups.google.com/forum/#!topic/crypto-competitions/n5ECGwYr6Vk
6. Chakraborti, A., Datta, N., Nandi, M.: INT-RUP analysis of block-cipher based authenticated encryption schemes. In: Sako, K. (ed.) CT-RSA 2016. LNCS, vol. 9610, pp. 39–54. Springer, Cham (2016). doi:10.1007/978-3-319-29485-8_3
7. Hoang, V.T., Krovetz, T., Rogaway, P.: Robust authenticated-encryption AEZ and the problem that it solves. In: Oswald, E., Fischlin, M. (eds.) EUROCRYPT 2015. LNCS, vol. 9056, pp. 15–44. Springer, Heidelberg (2015). doi:10.1007/978-3-662-46800-5_2
8. Krovetz, T., Rogaway, P.: The software performance of authenticated-encryption modes. In: Joux, A. (ed.) FSE 2011. LNCS, vol. 6733, pp. 306–327. Springer, Heidelberg (2011). doi:10.1007/978-3-642-21702-9_18
9. McGrew, D.A., Viega, J.: The security and performance of the Galois/counter mode (GCM) of operation. In: Canteaut, A., Viswanathan, K. (eds.) INDOCRYPT 2004. LNCS, vol. 3348, pp. 343–355. Springer, Heidelberg (2004). doi:10.1007/978-3-540-30556-9_27
10. Rogaway, P.: Authenticated-encryption with associated-data. In: Atluri, V. (ed.) ACM CCS 2002, pp. 98–107. ACM (2002)
11. Rogaway, P.: Efficient instantiations of tweakable blockciphers and refinements to modes OCB and PMAC. In: Lee, P.J. (ed.) ASIACRYPT 2004. LNCS, vol. 3329, pp. 16–31. Springer, Heidelberg (2004). doi:10.1007/978-3-540-30539-2_2
12. Rogaway, P.: Nonce-based symmetric encryption. In: Roy, B., Meier, W. (eds.) FSE 2004. LNCS, vol. 3017, pp. 348–358. Springer, Heidelberg (2004). doi:10.1007/978-3-540-25937-4_22
13. Rogaway, P., Bellare, M., Black, J., Krovetz, T.: OCB: a block-cipher mode of operation for efficient authenticated encryption. In: Reiter, M.K., Samarati, P. (eds.) ACM CCS 2001, pp. 196–205. ACM (2001)
14. Rogaway, P., Shrimpton, T.: A provable-security treatment of the key-wrap problem. In: Vaudenay, S. (ed.) EUROCRYPT 2006. LNCS, vol. 4004, pp. 373–390. Springer, Heidelberg (2006). doi:10.1007/11761679_23
15. Shrimpton, T., Terashima, R.S.: A modular framework for building variable-input-length tweakable ciphers. In: Sako, K., Sarkar, P. (eds.) ASIACRYPT 2013. LNCS, vol. 8269, pp. 405–423. Springer, Heidelberg (2013). doi:10.1007/978-3-642-42033-7_21
16. Whiting, D., Housley, R., Ferguson, N.: Counter with CBC-MAC (CCM). Internet Engineering Task Force (IETF), RFC 3610 (2003)

An Improved SAT-Based Guess-and-Determine Attack on the Alternating Step Generator

Oleg Zaikin[(✉)] and Stepan Kochemazov

Matrosov Institute for System Dynamics and Control Theory SB RAS,
Irkutsk, Russia
zaikin.icc@gmail.com, veinamond@gmail.com

Abstract. In this paper, we propose an algorithm for constructing guess-and-determine attacks on keystream generators and apply it to the cryptanalysis of the alternating step generator (ASG) and two its modifications (MASG and MASG0). In a guess-and-determine attack, we first "guess" some part of an initial state and then apply some procedure to determine, if the guess was correct and we can use the guessed information to solve the problem, thus performing an exhaustive search over all possible assignments of bits forming a chosen part of an initial state. We propose to use in the "determine" part the algorithms for solving Boolean satisfiability problem (SAT). It allows us to consider sets of bits with nontrivial structure. For each such set it is possible to estimate the runtime of a corresponding guess-and-determine attack via the Monte-Carlo method, so we can search for a set of bits yielding the best attack via a black-box optimization algorithm augmented with several SAT-specific features. We constructed and implemented such attacks on ASG, MASG, and MASG0 to prove that the constructed runtime estimations are reliable. We show, that the constructed attacks are better than the trivial ones, which imply exhaustive search over all possible states of the control register, and present the results of experiments on cryptanalysis of ASG and MASG/MASG0 with total registers length of 72 and 96, which have not been previously published in the literature.

Keywords: Keystream generator · Alternating step generator · Cryptanalysis · Guess-and-determine attack · SAT · Monte Carlo

1 Introduction

The alternating step generator (ASG) was proposed in [16]. It consists of two stop/go clocked binary Linear Feedback Shift Registers (LFSRs), $LFSR_X$ and $LFSR_Y$, and a regularly clocked binary LFSR, $LFSR_C$. The clock-control bit defines which of the two stop/go LFSRs is clocked, and the keystream bit is obtained as the bitwise sum of stop/go LFSRs' output bits. There exist many attacks on ASG. The majority of them (e.g., [14, 15, 19, 20]) follow the divide-and-conquer approach, where a correlation attack is performed on stop/go LFSRs.

© Springer International Publishing AG 2017
P.Q. Nguyen and J. Zhou (Eds.): ISC 2017, LNCS 10599, pp. 21–38, 2017.
https://doi.org/10.1007/978-3-319-69659-1_2

There is a number of ASG modifications. In [32] two of its modifications (MASG and MASG0) were proposed. They are based on replacing stop/go LFSRs by Nonlinear Feedback Shift Registers (NLFSRs). Because of the non-linearity of the controlled registers, it is unlikely that most attacks on ASG can be easily extended to them.

In the present paper we develop the guess-and-determine approach to ASG, MASG and MASG0 cryptanalysis. The most simple variant of a guess-and-determine attack on ASG looks as follows. First, we "guess" the initial state of the control register (e.g., see [16, 34]). By guessing we mean assigning values to corresponding bits. After this we write a system of equations over bits corresponding to states of controlled LFSRs and "determine" using appropriate methods if the system is consistent and has a solution. It is clear that to find a correct "guess" we need to perform an exhaustive search over all possible states of the control register. An interesting question is whether there exist less trivial sets of bits than that comprising the control register, and if they do, how can one solve the systems of (in a general case) nonlinear equations produced by assigning values to the corresponding bits? In the present paper we positively answer the former question thanks to applying algorithms for solving Boolean satisfiability problem (SAT) [4] to the latter.

SAT is formulated as follows: for a given propositional formula to either find its satisfying assignment (the assignment of all its variables that makes formula True), or to prove that it is unsatisfiable. Because SAT is an NP-hard problem, it means that even if our simplified system of equations contains nonlinear entries, we can still reduce it to SAT and solve it in such form. It is important to notice, that while state-of-the-art SAT solving algorithms (usually referred to as SAT solvers) show remarkable performance on a huge variety of test samples, it is impossible to know in advance how long will it take to solve each particular SAT instance. Nevertheless, following a number of papers [10, 30] we show that it is possible to construct a runtime estimation of cryptanalysis of a keystream generator for each chosen set of bits to guess, SAT solver and keystream fragment size. This runtime estimation is constructed computationally via the Monte Carlo method [12] and can not be expressed by formula.

Thus, we can construct a guess-and-determine attack for an arbitrary subset of a set of bits, corresponding to an initial state of a keystream generator and estimate its runtime. It means, that using black-box optimization algorithms we can in fact organize an automatic procedure for finding good subsets of bits that yield better attacks. It was done before in application to several generators [10, 28–30], but the previous papers did not take into account a number of important SAT-related issues, thus the approach presented in our paper simply works better in one or the other aspect.

Let us present a brief outline of the paper. In Sect. 2 we briefly describe ASG and its modifications studied in the paper, and focus on particular configurations of ASG, MASG and MASG0 (as well as their SAT encodings). In Sect. 3 we suggest a new Monte-Carlo based algorithm, which for a given generator allows to construct a SAT-based guess-and-determine attack with a good runtime estimation and discuss why the runtime estimations constructed can be believed to be reliable. In Sect. 4 we construct such attacks on ASG (with 72-bit, 96-bit, and 192-bit initial states), MASG and MASG0 (both of them with 72-bit initial states). For each considered generator configuration (except the 192-bit ASG version) we prove that our runtime estimations are correct by solving 20 cryptanalysis instances. We also show that the constructed SAT-based guess-and-determine attacks are better than the trivial SAT-based guess-and-determine attacks in all cases. In the rest of the paper we observe the related work and draw conclusions.

2   Considered Cryptanalysis Problems

As it was outlined above, unlike most cryptanalytic attacks our approach does not make it possible to construct a general formula that would express its complexity. Rather, we can construct runtime estimation for each particular cryptanalysis problem. As such, hereinafter we consider cryptanalysis problems for three configurations of ASG – with total length of registers equal to 72, 96 and 192 (further we will refer to them as ASG-72, ASG-96 and ASG-192). Below we show the primitive polynomials used in each version.

ASG-72:

- LFSR$_C$ (23 bits): $X^{23} \oplus X^{22} \oplus X^{20} \oplus X^{18} \oplus 1$;
- LFSR$_X$ (24 bits): $X^{24} \oplus X^{23} \oplus X^{22} \oplus X^{17} \oplus 1$;
- LFSR$_Y$ (25 bits): $X^{25} \oplus X^{24} \oplus X^{23} \oplus X^{22} \oplus 1$.

ASG-96:

- LFSR$_C$ (31 bits): $X^{31} \oplus X^7 \oplus 1$;
- LFSR$_X$ (32 bits): $X^{32} \oplus X^7 \oplus X^5 \oplus X^3 \oplus X^2 \oplus X \oplus 1$;
- LFSR$_Y$ (33 bits): $X^{33} \oplus X^{16} \oplus X^4 \oplus X \oplus 1$.

ASG-192:

- LFSR$_C$ (61 bits): $X^{61} \oplus X^{60} \oplus X^{46} \oplus X^{45} \oplus 1$;
- LFSR$_X$ (64 bits): $X^{64} \oplus X^{63} \oplus X^{61} \oplus X^{60} \oplus 1$;
- LFSR$_Y$ (67 bits): $X^{67} \oplus X^{66} \oplus X^{58} \oplus X^{57} \oplus 1$.

We also consider cryptanalysis problems for MASG and MASG0, which were proposed in [32]. In these modifications LFSR$_X$ and LFSR$_Y$ are replaced by NLF-SRs, to which we refer below as NLFSR$_X$ and NLFSR$_Y$. In MASG a keystream bit is produced similarly to the original ASG: as a bitwise sum of output bits of NLFSR$_X$ and NLFSR$_Y$. In MASG0 a keystream bit is produced as a bitwise sum of outputs of all three registers (LFSR$_C$, NLFSR$_X$ and NLFSR$_Y$). For both MASG and MASG0 the following feedback polynomials were used:

- LFSR$_C$ (23 bits): $X^{23} \oplus X^{22} \oplus X^{20} \oplus X^{18} \oplus 1$;
- NLFSR$_X$ (24 bits): $X^{19} \cdot X^8 \oplus X^{16} \oplus X^{10} \oplus X^9 \oplus X^2 \oplus X$;
- NLFSR$_Y$ (25 bits): $X^{24} \cdot X^{22} \cdot X^2 \oplus X^{17} \oplus X^5 \oplus X$.

It should be noted, that here we used the same LFSR$_C$, as in ASG-72. The polynomials for NLFSRs were taken from [7,25]. So, we consider MASG and MASG0 configurations with total length of registers equal to 72 (further we will refer to them as MASG-72 and MASG0-72).

The transition from an original problem to SAT is usually quite nontrivial (see survey [27]). There exist several openly available automatic tools that make it possible to reduce cryptanalysis problems to SAT [11,18,26,31]. These tools produce relatively similar encodings, thus we applied the Transalg tool [26] to construct the SAT encodings for considered configurations of generators. In particular, for each considered configuration we obtained a Conjunctive Normal Form (CNF). In Table 1 we present the size, number of clauses, number of variables and keystream fragment size for the constructed CNFs. In Sect. 4 we will describe, why exactly these keystream fragment sizes were used.

Table 1. Characteristics of CNFs encoding the considered keystream generators.

Generator	Size, Mb	Variables	Clauses	Keystream fragment size
ASG-72	0.3	3 426	15 382	76
MASG-72	0.5	3 426	20 454	76
MASG0-72	0.5	3 426	20 758	76
ASG-96	0.7	6 658	32 166	112
ASG-192	1.9	22 705	95 326	200

3   Algorithm for Constructing SAT-based Guess-and-Determine Attacks

Let C be a CNF encoding a cryptanalysis problem for some keystream generator. Assume that X^{in} is a set of Boolean variables corresponding to an initial state of generator registers. In the case of ASG-96 (see Sect. 2), $|X^{in}| = 96$ (while there are 6658 Boolean variables in the corresponding CNF in total). We can choose some subset $X^* \subset X^{in}$ and consider all possible assignments of variables from X^*. Below let us refer to X^* as to set of *partitioning variables* and to a family of subproblems, formed by adding information about a particular assignment of variables from X^* to an original CNF for a considered problem, as to a *partitioning* [17].

It is easy to see, that on the one hand any subproblem from a partitioning should most likely be much easier to solve compared to an original problem (since we "know" a sizable chunk of information we need), and on the other hand by processing all such subproblems we will be able to obtain a solution of a considered hard problem. Of course, there exists some trade-off between the size and contents of X^* and the difficulty rate of constructed subproblems. It is not always possible to evaluate this trade-off analytically, so in a number of papers [5, 10, 29, 30] there were studied several ways how it can be achieved automatically or at least semi-automatically. Basically it all boils down to the problem of how to choose the best X^*.

It is clear, that any X^* corresponds to some guess-and-determine attack on a considered keystream generator. The nontrivial fact consists in the fact that for a given X^* it is possible to estimate a runtime of a corresponding attack. Essentially, the estimation can be done by means of the Monte Carlo method [12]: we choose relatively small random sample of subproblems from our partitioning, solve them, compute the average time required to solve one subproblem and scale it to the number of subproblems. However, in reality, there are many important nuances.

Let us describe the basic Monte-Carlo-based procedure, which is usually used to obtain the runtime estimation for a set of partitioning variables. The procedure takes as an input a CNF C, a known keystream fragment F, a set of partitioning variables X^*, and the number N, representing the size of a random sample. The procedure works as follows.

1. Construct a random sample S by choosing N binary words from $\{0, 1\}^{|X^*|}$ according to the uniform distribution.
2. Launch Conflict-Driven Clause Learning (CDCL, [21]) solver on N SAT instances formed by appending information from F and $s_i \in S$ to C and record the runtime of the solver on this instance to t_i.
3. Compute the runtime estimation by averaging t_i over S and multiplying the constructed value by the size of a partitioning: $R = 2^{|X^*|} \times \frac{\sum_{i=1}^{N} s_i}{N}$.

The described procedure defines an objective function – using some optimization algorithm one can try to find a set of partitioning variables with minimal value of this function. For this purpose it is natural to first construct a search space of all possible sets of partitioning variables (i.e. all possible subsets of a set of Boolean variables corresponding to an initial state of a considered keystream generator). Each point in this search space corresponds to some guess-and-determine attack. For every point we can calculate a runtime estimation using the objective function defined above. By traversing a search space via some optimization algorithm we can find a set of partitioning variables with a good runtime estimation. In our experiments in the role of such algorithm we use a simple tabu-based local search algorithm. As its starting point we always choose a set X^{in}. The optimization algorithm stops after reaching a given time limit. The output of this algorithm is a best found attack (compared to that, processed by the algorithm during its work).

We implemented the procedure described above and applied it to construct guess-and-determine attacks on several ASG configurations. However, it turned out that it could only find sets of partitioning variables for which the runtime estimations were very inaccurate: sometimes the solving time was several times larger (and sometimes lower) than runtime estimation. Also, in most experiments the found guess-and-determine attacks were worse than the trivial attack that implies guessing the bits corresponding to the initial state of the control register.

When we studied, why the described procedure gives very inaccurate estimations for the considered problems, we found out that it often gives overly optimistic or overly pessimistic estimations for a given set of partitioning variables because of the way the random sample is constructed. For cryptographic instances it is a common situation when for some set of partitioning variables the percentage of very simple subproblems in a partitioning is very large. By simple problems we mean here the ones that can be solved effectively – by means of Unit Propagation algorithm [6]. Meanwhile, the rest of the subproblems (not solved by Unit Propagation) can be exceptionally hard, such that one hard subproblem is solved many times longer than a whole random sample of simple subproblems. In other words, if we generate a random sample in the most simple way possible without additional consideration, it is often the case that a constructed sample does not adequately represent a partitioning, and even increasing its size has little to no effect.

Thus, the problem with the outlined scheme lies mainly in the first step of the procedure — how a random sample is constructed. So we decided to modify the procedure in such a way that it works well on the considered problems. Basically, on the one hand, we want the new procedure to construct random samples which contain subproblems that are not all solved by Unit Propagation. For this purpose we need to introduce some filtering procedure that determines if a problem can be solved by unit propagation or not. This procedure can be constructed by stripping a SAT solver down. On the other hand, we do not want to just neglect unit propagation stage at all – it can provide a sizable chunk of runtime.

New procedure takes as an input several parameters: X^* – the set of partitioning variables, D – a number of diapasons to be processed, s – a diapason size, K – a number of problems that have to be constructed within the diapason and not be solved by unit propagation. It works as follows.

1. Construct D binary words chosen randomly according to the uniform distribution from $\{0, 1\}^{|X^*|}$. These D points serve as diapason starting values.
2. Process each constructed diapason beginning from a starting value. Attempt to construct K problems that are not solved by unit propagation, by sequentially applying the filtering procedure to each next word taken from a diapason in a lexicographic order.
3. If K such words were constructed, while not exceeding the diapason size, then the corresponding K words are returned as a result, along with the number of words P that did not pass filtering.
4. Solve K corresponding subproblems by a CDCL solver (without any limitations) in the incremental mode [9] (this mode prevents runtime estimation from being too pessimistic).
5. Calculate an average runtime for each diapason, taking into account both runtime on subproblems solved by unit propagation and that on the subproblems solved by a CDCL solver in the incremental-based loop.
6. Compute the runtime estimation for X^* by averaging t_i over D and multiplying the constructed value by the size of a partitioning.

The suggested procedure, augmented by the aforementioned black-box optimization algorithm, was implemented in the form of a parallel program, which is based on Message Passing Interface (MPI) [13]. To solve subproblems we employ the ROKK CDCL-solver, which is a slightly modified version of MiniSat 2.2 [8]. According to our experience [26], it shows good results in cryptanalysis of keystream generators.

One thread of our program is a control thread, while the others are computing threads. Each computing thread receives tasks from the control thread, performs the corresponding calculations and sends obtained results. This program works in two modes – the estimating mode and the solving mode. In the estimating mode, in order to calculate a runtime estimation for a particular X^*, the control thread first randomly generates D binary words of size $|X^*|$ and forms D computing tasks containing X^* and one of D words. Then every computing thread works with one task per process at a time. After performing the processing of a corresponding diapason according to the procedure outlined above, a computed average runtime for a diapason is sent to the control thread, which then takes all D such values and based on them computes a runtime estimation for X^*.

In the solving mode, our program takes as an input a set of partitioning variables. This set can be found in the estimating mode, or it can be constructed manually. For example, one can use the set of variables, which encode the initial state of a clock control register of a generator. Given a set of partitioning variables, the program solves all subproblems from a corresponding partitioning.

4   Computational Experiments

Using the algorithm, described in Sect. 3, we constructed guess-and-determine attacks on ASG-72, ASG-96, ASG-192, MASG-72 and MASG0-72. For each of them (excluding ASG-192) 20 cryptanalysis instances were constructed by randomly generating 20 initial states values. For each configuration the size of the corresponding keystream fragment is discussed below.

Hereinafter by *total solving time* we mean the time required to solve all subproblems from a partitioning. Of course, for the majority of satisfiable SAT instances we find a satisfying assignment faster. In particular, each considered SAT instance has exactly 1 satisfying assignment, so on average it usually takes twice less time. However, we compare our estimations with total solving time for all subproblems, because in fact it is this runtime that we estimate.

It should be noted, that we applied our program to construct a set of partitioning variables only for 1 instance out of 20 in every case (in particular, for the first one from a series). After this the constructed guess-and-determine attack was performed on all 20 instances from a series (including the one, which was used to find a set of partitioning variables). Our empirical evaluations and the results of computational experiments show that the SAT-based guess-and-determine attack for a particular cryptanalysis instance with fixed keystream fragment can be extended to cryptanalysis instances that have different keystream fragments. This fact allows us to say, that by finding a set of partitioning variables for a considered generator configuration, we construct a guess-and-determine attack not only on this particular instance, but on the generator itself.

All calculations were performed on the HPC-cluster "Academician V.M. Matrosov" [23]. Each computing node of this cluster is equipped with two 18-core CPUs Intel Xeon E5-2695 (36 CPU cores in total) and 128 gigabytes of RAM. In order to automatically construct guess-and-determine attacks, we used the following values of parameters for the procedure described in Sect. 3: $D = 1000, s = 1000000, K = 1000$.

For each generator configuration we compared the automatically constructed guess-and-determine attack with the trivial one, based on guessing the bits of the control register. We also compared it with two multithreaded CDCL solvers: `plingeling` and `treengeling` [3]. In the SAT competition 2016 they won the first two prizes in the parallel category [1]. We chose these standard solvers in order to check, if the high-ranked CDCL-based parallel SAT solvers can efficiently solve the considered problems directly, without constructing a guess-and-determine attack. It should be noted, that in the solving mode we employed exactly 1 computing node of the cluster in all cases, because the mentioned multithreaded solvers can work only within 1 workstation (i.e. they can not be launched on a HPC cluster using MPI). In the following subsection we will present the results of computational experiments for the considered generators configurations.

4.1 Additional Optimization: Choosing the Right Keystream Fragment Size

In the case of ASG-72, we first considered cryptanalysis problem for the keystream fragment length of 100 bits (this value is four times greater, than the length of the largest employed LFSR). We constructed 1 CNF encoding randomly formed cryptanalysis problem, and on this CNF we launched our parallel program (see Sect. 3) in the estimating mode for 2 h to find a set of partitioning variables (as a subset of a set of 72 variables corresponding to the initial state). In this case (as well as in all other launches in estimating mode) our program used 10 computing nodes (360 CPU cores in total). As a result, for ASG-72 we found the set, consisting of 21 variables with runtime estimation equal to 32 s (if running on the same workstation). This set contains the following variables: 5 6 7 8 9 10 11 12 13 14 15 16 17 18 19 20 21 (LFSR$_X$); 45 (LFSR$_X$); 69 70 71 (LFSR$_Y$). Here we use end-to-end numbering – variables of the control register LFSR$_C$ have numbers from 1 to 23, for the controlled register LFSR$_X$ – from 24 to 47, for the controlled register LFSR$_Y$ – from 48 to 72. In Table 2 the set is depicted – here "+" denotes that the corresponding variable belongs to the set.

In [20] it was stated, that the average number of ASG preimages for any keystream fragment with length m is about $2^{3L-m}, m \leq 3L$, where L is the length of the controlled stop/go register. In [20] an ASG with the controlled registers of equal lengths was considered. In our case (with controlled registers of different lengths) as L we used a length of the largest controlled register.

Table 2. The set of partitioning variables, found for ASG-72.

LFSR$_C$	$- - - - + + + + + + + + + + + + + + + + + + + - -$
LFSR$_X$	$- + - -$
LFSR$_Y$	$- + + + -$

So, for ASG-72 $L = 25$, and about 75 bits of a given keystream fragment should be enough to get only 1 preimage. We decided to find the length of a keystream fragment, which yields the best runtime estimation for the considered crypt-analysis problem when the set of partitioning variables is fixed. We randomly constructed 7 more cryptanalysis instances for ASG-72 – with keystream fragment lengths from 72 to 96 with the step of 4. We then solved each of them using the constructed guess-and-determine attack. In order to compare the total solving time (in seconds), all subproblems from each partitioning were solved. It turned out, that on 72-bit fragment two preimages were found, on the other variants there was only 1 preimage. The obtained results are presented in Table 3. Along with the total solving time, for each variant we show the runtime estimation (calculated for the set of 21 variables, found on the 100-bit variant). We can conclude, that the total solving time agrees well with the estimation – the difference is about 18%. As it was mentioned before, in the estimating mode our program uses 10 computing nodes, while in the solving mode it uses 1 node. So, further all runtime estimations are given for 1 computing node.

Table 3. The comparison of ASG-72 total solving time (in seconds) with different sizes of keystream fragment

Keystream length	72	76	80	84	88	92	96	100
Estimation	31	31	32	31	32	32	32	32
Total solving time	35	35	35	36	37	37	41	38
Preimage number	2	1	1	1	1	1	1	1

According to the table, the fragments of sizes 72, 76, 80 and 84 bits provide the best efficiency. We chose the least value, for which only 1 preimage was found. So we used a fragment of size 76 in all our further experiments for ASG-72 (as well, as for MASG-72 and MASG0-72).

We did the similar calculations for ASG-96. We first considered the crypt-analysis problem for the keystream fragment length of size 132 (this value is four times greater than the length of the largest employed LFSR). We constructed 1 CNF encoding randomly formed cryptanalysis problem, and on this CNF we launched our parallel program (see Sect. 3) in the estimating mode for 12 h to find a set of partitioning variables (as a subset of a set of 96 variables corresponding to the initial state). As a result, we found the set, consisting of 30 variables with runtime estimation equal to 29 497 s (8 h and 12 min). The found set consists of the following 30 variables: 2 3 4 5 6 12 13 14 15 17 19 20 22 23

Table 4. The set of partitioning variables, found for ASG-96.

LFSR$_C$	$- + + + + + - - - - - + + + + - + - + + - + + - + + + - + + -$
LFSR$_X$	$- + + + + + - + -$
LFSR$_Y$	$- + - + + + + + - -$

25 26 27 29 30 (LFSR$_C$); 56 57 58 59 60 62 (LFSR$_X$); 89 91 92 93 94 (LFSR$_Y$). This set is depicted in Table 4.

We then randomly constructed 8 more cryptanalysis instances for ASG-96 – with keystream fragment lengths from 100 to 128 with the step of 4. We solved each of 9 SAT instances using the constructed guess-and-determine attack. As in the case of ASG-72, all subproblems of each partitioning were solved. As a result for a 100-bit fragment 2 preimages were found, on the other variants there was only 1 preimage. The obtained results are presented in Table 5. We can conclude, that the total solving time agrees well with the estimation – the difference is about 7%.

Table 5. The comparison of ASG-96 total solving time with different keystream fragment lengths

Keystream length	100	104	108	112	116	120	124	128	132
Total solving time	30 905	32 195	30 608	30 292	31 132	32 627	31 311	31 558	31 566
Estimation		31 671	33 137	31 571	30 946	31 931	33 763	32 427	31 971	29 497
Preimage number	2	1	1	1	1	1	1	1	1

According to the table, the fragment length of 112 bits provides the best efficiency. So we used the fragment of size 112 bits in our further experiments for ASG-96.

4.2 ASG-72

We used the found set of 21 variables (Table 2) to solve 20 cryptanalysis instances for ASG-72 (in each instance 76 bits of a keystream were known). The average time required to solve them turned out to be 16 s (we stopped processing of each partitioning when a correct initial state value was found). We can conclude, that this average solving time agrees well with the constructed estimation (remind that it is equal to 31 s). We also tried to solve all these instances by `plingeling`, `treengeling`, and by our program using the trivial set – formed by 23 variables corresponding to the initial state of the control register. The results of the comparison are depicted in Fig. 1. Here GDA is an abbreviation for "guess-and-determine attack". The runtime was limited by 5000 s for every launch. On the figure we used the so-called cactus plots. On such plot the values are sorted in the ascending order. From these figures it follows, that `plingeling`

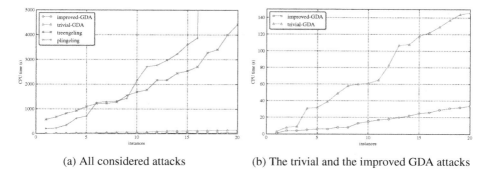

(a) All considered attacks   (b) The trivial and the improved GDA attacks

Fig. 1. Comparison of the considered SAT-based attacks on ASG-72

and `treengeling` work much worse, than other two variants. It also follows, that the constructed guess-and-determine attack is better, than the trivial one.

In Table 6 for each program the number of solved instances and the average time (in seconds) on solved instances are shown. Our improved guess-and-determine attack turned out to be about 4.7 times better, than the trivial one. We would like to emphasize, that in these experiments an estimation is considered as accurate, if it is about 2 times greater, than the average solving time. As it was said above, on average one needs to process half of a partitioning to find a solution.

Table 6. The comparison of different SAT-based attacks on ASG-72.

Attack	Solved	Avg. time on solved	Estimation
`plingeling`	16	1 795	-
`treengeling`	20	1 997	-
Trivial GDA	20	75	121
Improved GDA	20	16	31

4.3   ASG-96

We used the found set of 30 variables (it was described above) to solve 20 randomly constructed cryptanalysis instances for ASG-96 (in each instance 112 bits of keystream were known). The results of the comparison are depicted in Fig. 2. The runtime was limited by 12 h (43 200 s) for every launch. As a result, `plingeling` and `treengeling` could not solve any instance in time, while both guess-and-determine attacks solved all of them. Here in the trivial attack the set of 31 variables, corresponding to the control register, was used. From the figure it follows, that the constructed guess-and-determine attack is better, than the trivial one.

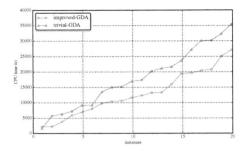

Fig. 2. Comparison of the trivial and the improved guess-and-determine attacks on ASG-96

In Table 7 for each SAT-based attack the number of solved instances and the average time (in seconds) on solved instances are shown. Our improved guess-and-determine attack turned out to be about 38% better, than the trivial one.

Table 7. The comparison of different SAT-based attacks on ASG-96.

Attack	Solved	Avg. time on solved	Estimation
plingeling	0	-	-
treengeling	0	-	-
Trivial GDA	20	18 211	40 357
Improved GDA	20	13 181	30 946

4.4 MASG-72 and MASG0-72

In the cases of MASG-72 and MASG0-72 the keystream length of 76 was used (similar to ASG-72). For both generators our program was launched in the estimating mode for 2 h on the cluster.

As a result for MASG-72 we found the set of partitioning variables consisting of 22 variables with runtime estimation equal to 71 s. The set consists of the following variables: 7 8 9 10 11 12 13 14 15 16 17 18 19 20 21 (LFSR$_C$); 40 41 42 45 (LFSR$_X$); 64 67 68 (LFSR$_Y$). This set is also presented in Table 8.

Table 8. The set of partitioning variables, found for MASG-72.

LFSR$_C$	$------ ++++++++++++++++ --$
LFSR$_X$	$----------------- +++--+--$
LFSR$_Y$	$----------------+--++ +----$

We used this set to solve 20 randomly generated cryptanalysis instances for MASG-72. We also launched plingeling, treengeling and trivial guess-and-determine attack on them. In Table 9 for each SAT-based attack the number of solved instances and the average time (in seconds) on solved instances are shown. Our improved guess-and-determine attack turned out to be about 29% better, than the trivial one. The results of experiments are also presented in Fig. 3.

Table 9. The comparison of different SAT-based attacks on MASG-72.

Attack	Solved	Avg. time on solved	Estimation
`plingeling`	10	1 935	-
`treengeling`	14	2 418	-
Trivial GDA	20	58	89
Improved GDA	20	45	71

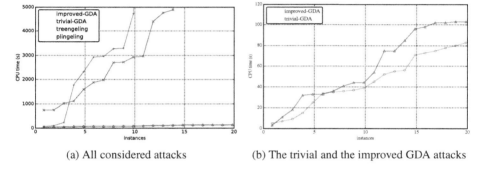

(a) All considered attacks   (b) The trivial and the improved GDA attacks

Fig. 3. Comparison of the considered SAT-based attacks on MASG-72

For MASG0-72 in the same conditions we found the set of 22 variables with runtime estimation of 74 s. The set consists of the following variables: 3 7 8 9 10 11 12 13 14 15 16 17 18 20 21 22 (LFSR$_C$); 41 42 46 (LFSR$_X$); 65 67 68 (LFSR$_Y$). This set is also presented in Table 10.

Table 10. The set of partitioning variables, found for MASG0-72.

LFSR$_C$	$-\ -\ +\ -\ -\ -\ +\ +\ +\ +\ +\ +\ +\ +\ +\ +\ +\ -\ +\ +\ +$
LFSR$_X$	$-\ -\ -\ -\ -\ -\ -\ -\ -\ -\ -\ -\ -\ -\ -\ -\ -\ +\ +\ -\ -\ -\ +\ -$
LFSR$_Y$	$-\ -\ -\ -\ -\ -\ -\ -\ -\ -\ -\ -\ -\ -\ -\ -\ +\ -\ +\ +\ -\ -\ -\ -$

In Table 11 for each SAT-based attack the number of solved instances and the average time (in seconds) on solved instances are shown. Our improved guess-and-determine attack turned out to be about 20% better, than the trivial one. The results of experiments are also presented in Fig. 4.

Table 11. The comparison of different SAT-based attacks on MASG0-72.

Attack	Solved	Avg. time on solved	Estimation
`plingeling`	9	1 746	-
`treengeling`	13	1 667	-
Trivial GDA	20	55	92
Improved GDA	20	46	74

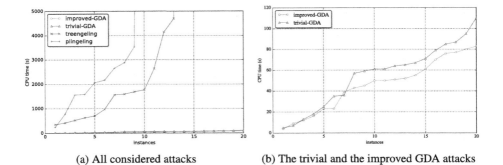

(a) All considered attacks   (b) The trivial and the improved GDA attacks

Fig. 4. Comparison of the considered SAT-based attacks on MASG0-72

4.5 ASG-192

We launched our program for 24 h in order to construct a guess-and-determine attack on ASG-192. As a result we found the set of 63 variables with the runtime estimation of 7.55e+13 s. This set is presented in Table 12. The set consists of the following variables: 6 7 8 9 11 13 14 15 16 17 18 19 20 21 22 25 29 30 31 33 34 37 38 39 40 42 43 44 45 46 47 48 50 51 52 55 57 60 ($LFSR_C$); 94 97 100 101 105 106 113 114 115 116 117 118 119 121 124 ($LFSR_X$); 160 161 162 166 167 168 172 174 175 186 ($LFSR_Y$).

We also used our program to estimate the trivial set (61 variables, corresponding to the control register). The corresponding estimation turned out to be 3.60e+14 s, i.e. our attack is about 4.77 times better (by estimation). According to the obtained estimations, we decided not to perform the constructed improved attack in practice. This example shows, that using our approach for a given guess-and-determine attack, one can determine, if this attack can be performed in reasonable time in practice.

5   Related Work

The cryptographic resistance of the alternating step generator was analyzed in a number of papers [14–16,20,34]. The majority of these attacks implement different variants of correlation attacks on one or both controlled LFSRs [14,15, 20]. A good overview of these attacks can be found in [20]. Hereinafter, assume

Table 12. The set of partitioning variables, found for ASG-192.

LFSR$_C$	$- - - - - + + + + - + - + + + + + + + + + + + - - + - - - - + + + - + +$
	$- - + + + + - + + + + + + + + - + + + - - + - + - - + -$
LFSR$_X$	$- + -$
	$- + - - + + - - - - + + - - - - - - - - + + + + + + + + - + - - + -$
LFSR$_Y$	$- -$
	$+ + + - - - + + + - - - + - + + - - - - - - - - - - - + - - - - - -$

that l is the length of the control LFSR, and m and n are the lengths of two controlled stop/go LFSRs. The attack with lowest time complexity was proposed in [19]: $O(m^2 \times 2^{2m/3})$, but it requires a lot of keystream $(O(2^{2m/3}))$ and has a number of specific requirements regarding the keystream fragment. The same can be said about the attack from [20].

Since our attack does not have such requirements and uses a fragment of keystream of relatively small size, we compare it with the best attacks with similar properties. From this point of view the best attack among previously published results is the divide-and-conquer attack from [16], because in all configurations considered in our paper the control register is the smallest.

The attack from [16] has the time complexity of $O(min(m, n) \times 2^l)$, however, since we can not express the complexity of our attack analytically, it is necessary to get into details. In the attack from [16] we perform an exhaustive search over all possible variants of the initial value of control register (it corresponds to 2^l component in $O(\cdot)$). Intuitively, after guessing the value we derive a system of linear equations over bits corresponding to initial values of controlled registers and apply to it the so-called Linear Consistency Test (LCT) [33]. Essentially, LCT consists in solving the constructed system by means of Gaussian elimination or more state-of-the-art algorithm [2] and simultaneously checking if it is consistent. If the system yields a solution then with overwhelming probability it is the solution of our cryptanalysis problem. Now, for ASG-72 (for which $l = 23$, $m = 24$ and $n = 25$) the average runtime of our attack is 16 s on 36 cores, so about 576 s on one core of Intel Xeon E5 2695v4. It means, that in order for attack from [16] to be equally fast as our attack, it would need to be able to process about $2^{23}/576 = 14563.5$ states of control register per second on the same processor core. For ASG-96 the corresponding number of states per second is $2^{31}/(13181 \times 36) = 4525$. It is very hard to say what will be the performance of this attack if implemented properly without actually implementing it. We could not find ready implementations and implementing attack ourselves is out of the scope of the present research. Our guess is that if programmed properly it would be in the general vicinity of our approach. The important consideration here is that we present the results of a practical attack – it involves a lot of auxiliary work, such as actual decomposition of the problem into partitioning, sending commands to computing processes, processing the results, etc. Meanwhile the attack in [16] has only general outline.

We are not aware of any SAT-based and/or guess-and-determine attacks on ASG. Meanwhile, the corresponding approach works quite well in other areas of cryptanalysis. The overview of possible applications of SAT in algebraic cryptanalysis can be found in [2]. In [22] a SAT-based attack on a reduced variant of DES was proposed. In [24] there were studied several applications of SAT solvers to finding collisions of cryptographic hash functions.

In [10,29,30] using a relatively similar way to our approach, the Monte Carlo algorithms were applied to construct SAT-based guess-and-determine attacks on several keystream generators. However, we suggest a Monte Carlo-based algorithm with the new significantly improved functionality that takes into account several previously ignored issues, that greatly improve its accuracy.

Another relatively similar approach to cryptanalysis of ASG and other generators was proposed in [34]. In that paper it was suggested to use a straightforward backtracking algorithm to determine if a system of equations, specifying the cryptanalysis instance, can be solved. In a way, our work can be considered as a development in this direction, however we replace simple backtracking algorithm by the accumulated experience and methods from the area of SAT solving in the form of state-of-the-art CDCL algorithms.

As for MASG/MASG0, we have not found any papers considering the cryptanalysis of these generator modifications. Since we replace controlled LFSRs by NLFSRs, it means that the vast majority of correlation attacks or their variants, that work well for ASG, can not be applied to MASG/MASG0. The same can be said about the attack from [16]. Theoretically, the attack employing backtracking scheme proposed in [34], can be extended to considered modifications, but evaluating its complexity is a nontrivial task.

Overall, from our point of view, the method for constructing guess-and-determine attacks presented in our paper is interesting because despite relying on black-box optimization algorithms and algorithms for solving Boolean satisfiability problem (which is NP-hard) it shows competitive results on cryptanalysis of ASG/MASG/MASG0, and makes it possible to extend the paradigm of guess-and-determine attacks by considering non-trivial sets of bits to guess.

6 Conclusions

In the present paper, we proposed a new algorithm for constructing a SAT-based guess-and-determine attack on ASG and two its modifications (MASG and MASG0). Using this algorithm we obtained new guess-and-determine attacks that are better than the trivial ones (where we guess an initial state of the control clock register). The constructed attacks were used to perform in practice the cryptanalysis of the considered generators (with the initial states of size up to 96 bits).

Acknowledgments. Authors thank all anonymous reviewers for valuable comments.

The research was funded by Russian Science Foundation (project No. 16-11-10046) and by Council for Grants of the President of the Russian Federation (stipends no. SP-1184.2015.5 and SP-1829.2016.5).

References

1. Balyo, T., Heule, M.J.H., Järvisalo, M.: SAT competition 2016: recent developments. In: Singh, S.P., Markovitch, S. (eds.) Proceedings of the Thirty-First AAAI Conference on Artificial Intelligence, San Francisco, California, USA, pp. 5061–5063. AAAI Press, 4–9 February 2017
2. Bard, G.V.: Algebraic Cryptanalysis, 1st edn. Springer, US (2009)
3. Biere, A.: Splatz, Lingeling, Plingeling, Treengeling, YalSAT entering the SAT competition 2016. In: Balyo, T., Heule, M., Järvisalo, M. (eds.) Proceedings of SAT Competition 2016 – Solver and Benchmark Descriptions. Department of Computer Science Series of Publications B, vol. B-2016-1, pp. 44–45. University of Helsinki (2016)
4. Biere, A., Heule, M., van Maaren, H., Walsh, T. (eds.): Handbook of Satisfiability. Frontiers in Artificial Intelligence and Applications, vol. 185. IOS Press (2009)
5. Courtois, N.: Low-complexity key recovery attacks on GOST block cipher. Cryptologia $37(1)$, 1–10 (2013)
6. Davis, M., Logemann, G., Loveland, D.W.: A machine program for theorem-proving. Commun. ACM $5(7)$, 394–397 (1962)
7. Dubrova, E.: A list of maximum period NLFSRs. IACR Cryptology ePrint Archive 2012, 166 (2012). Informal publication
8. Eén, N., Sörensson, N.: An extensible SAT-solver. In: Giunchiglia, E., Tacchella, A. (eds.) SAT 2003. LNCS, vol. 2919, pp. 502–518. Springer, Heidelberg (2004). doi:10.1007/978-3-540-24605-3_37
9. Eén, N., Sörensson, N.: Temporal induction by incremental SAT solving. Electr. Notes Theor. Comput. Sci. $89(4)$, 543–560 (2003)
10. Eibach, T., Pilz, E., Völkel, G.: Attacking bivium using SAT solvers. In: Kleine Büning, H., Zhao, X. (eds.) SAT 2008. LNCS, vol. 4996, pp. 63–76. Springer, Heidelberg (2008). doi:10.1007/978-3-540-79719-7_7
11. Erkök, L., Matthews, J.: High assurance programming in Cryptol. In: Sheldon, F.T., Peterson, G., Krings, A.W., Abercrombie, R.K., Mili, A. (eds.) Fifth Cyber Security and Information Intelligence Research Workshop, CSIIRW 2009, Knoxville, TN, USA, p. 60. ACM, 13–15 April 2009
12. Fishman, G.S.: Monte Carlo: Concepts, Algorithms, and Applications. Springer Series in Operations Research. Springer, New York (1996)
13. Foster, I.: Designing and Building Parallel Programs: Concepts and Tools for Parallel Software Engineering. Addison-Wesley Longman Publishing Co., Inc., Boston (1995)
14. Golić, J.D., Menicocci, R.: Edit distance correlation attack on the alternating step generator. In: Kaliski Jr., B.S. (ed.) CRYPTO 1997. LNCS, vol. 1294, pp. 499–512. Springer, Heidelberg (1997). doi:10.1007/BFb0052258
15. Golic, J.D., Menicocci, R.: Correlation analysis of the alternating step generator. Des. Codes Crypt. $31(1)$, 51–74 (2004)
16. Günther, C.G.: Alternating step generators controlled by De Bruijn sequences. In: Chaum, D., Price, W.L. (eds.) EUROCRYPT 1987. LNCS, vol. 304, pp. 5–14. Springer, Heidelberg (1988). doi:10.1007/3-540-39118-5_2
17. Hyvärinen, A.E.J.: Grid Based Propositional Satisfiability Solving. Ph.D. thesis, Aalto University (2011)
18. Janicic, P.: URSA: a system for uniform reduction to SAT. Logical Methods Comput. Sci. $8(3)$, 1–39 (2012)

19. Johansson, T.: Reduced complexity correlation attacks on two clock-controlled generators. In: Ohta, K., Pei, D. (eds.) ASIACRYPT 1998. LNCS, vol. 1514, pp. 342–356. Springer, Heidelberg (1998). doi:10.1007/3-540-49649-1_27

20. Khazaei, S., Fischer, S., Meier, W.: Reduced complexity attacks on the alternating step generator. In: Adams, C., Miri, A., Wiener, M. (eds.) SAC 2007. LNCS, vol. 4876, pp. 1–16. Springer, Heidelberg (2007). doi:10.1007/978-3-540-77360-3_1

21. Marques-Silva, J.P., Lynce, I., Malik, S.: Conflict-driven clause learning SAT solvers. In: Biere et al. [4], pp. 131–153

22. Massacci, F., Marraro, L.: Logical cryptanalysis as a SAT problem. J. Autom. Reasoning **24**(1/2), 165–203 (2000)

23. Irkutsk Supercomputer Center of SB RAS. http://hpc.icc.ru

24. Mironov, I., Zhang, L.: Applications of SAT solvers to cryptanalysis of hash functions. In: Biere, A., Gomes, C.P. (eds.) SAT 2006. LNCS, vol. 4121, pp. 102–115. Springer, Heidelberg (2006). doi:10.1007/11814948_13

25. Maximum period NLFSRs. https://people.kth.se/~dubrova/nlfsr.html

26. Otpuschennikov, I., Semenov, A., Gribanova, I., Zaikin, O., Kochemazov, S.: Encoding cryptographic functions to SAT using TRANSALG system. In: ECAI 2016 - 22nd European Conference on Artificial Intelligence, 29 August-2 September 2016, The Hague, The Netherlands. Frontiers in Artificial Intelligence and Applications, vol. 285, pp. 1594–1595. IOS Press (2016)

27. Prestwich, S.D.: CNF encodings. In: Biere et al. [4], pp. 75–97

28. Semenov, A.A., Zaikin, O.S.: Using Monte Carlo method for searching partitionings of hard variants of Boolean satisfiability problem. In: Malyshkin, V. (ed.) Proceedings of the 13th International Conference on Parallel Computing Technologies, 31 August - 4 September, Petrozavodsk, Russia, pp. 222–230 (2015)

29. Semenov, A., Zaikin, O.: Algorithm for finding partitionings of hard variants of Boolean satisfiability problem with application to inversion of some cryptographic functions. SpringerPlus **5**(1), 1–16 (2016)

30. Soos, M., Nohl, K., Castelluccia, C.: Extending SAT solvers to cryptographic problems. In: Kullmann, O. (ed.) SAT 2009. LNCS, vol. 5584, pp. 244–257. Springer, Heidelberg (2009). doi:10.1007/978-3-642-02777-2_24

31. Soos, M.: Grain of salt - an automated way to test stream ciphers through SAT solvers. In: Tools 2010: Proceedings of the Workshop on Tools for Cryptanalysis, pp. 131–144 (2010)

32. Wicik, R., Rachwalik, T.: Modified alternating step generators. IACR Cryptology ePrint Archive 2013, 728 (2013)

33. Zeng, K., Yang, C.H., Rao, T.R.N.: On the linear consistency test (LCT) in cryptanalysis with applications. In: Brassard, G. (ed.) CRYPTO 1989. LNCS, vol. 435, pp. 164–174. Springer, New York (1990). doi:10.1007/0-387-34805-0_16

34. Zenner, E.: On the efficiency of the clock control guessing attack. In: Lee, P.J., Lim, C.H. (eds.) ICISC 2002. LNCS, vol. 2587, pp. 200–212. Springer, Heidelberg (2003). doi:10.1007/3-540-36552-4_14

Efficient Masking of ARX-Based Block Ciphers Using Carry-Save Addition on Boolean Shares

Daniel Dinu$^{(\boxtimes)}$, Johann Großschädl, and Yann Le Corre

Laboratory of Algorithmics, Cryptology and Security (LACS),
SnT and University of Luxembourg, 6, Avenue de la Fonte,
4364 Esch-sur-Alzette, Luxembourg
{dumitru-daniel.dinu,johann.groszschaedl,yann.lecorre}@uni.lu

Abstract. Masking is a widely-used technique to protect block ciphers and other symmetric cryptosystems against Differential Power Analysis (DPA) attacks. Applying masking to a cipher that involves both arithmetic and Boolean operations requires a conversion between arithmetic and Boolean masks. An alternative approach is to perform the required arithmetic operations (e.g. modular addition or subtraction) directly on Boolean shares. At FSE 2015, Coron *et al.* proposed a logarithmic-time algorithm for modular addition on Boolean shares based on the Kogge-Stone carry-lookahead adder. We revisit their addition algorithm in this paper and present a fast implementation for ARM processors. Then, we introduce a new technique for direct modular addition/subtraction on Boolean shares using a simple Carry-Save Adder (CSA) in an iterative fashion. We show that the average complexity of CSA-based addition on Boolean shares grows logarithmically with the operand size, similar to the Kogge-Stone carry-lookahead addition, but consists of only a single AND, an XOR, and a left-shift per iteration. A 32-bit CSA addition on Boolean shares has an average execution time of 162 clock cycles on an ARM Cortex-M3 processor, which is approximately 43% faster than the Kogge-Stone adder. The performance gain increases to over 55% when comparing the average subtraction times. We integrated both addition techniques into a masked implementation of the block cipher Speck and found that the CSA-based variant clearly outperforms its Kogge-Stone counterpart by a factor of 1.70 for encryption and 2.30 for decryption.

1 Introduction

The concrete security of a cryptographic system depends not only on the cryptanalytic complexity of the underlying algorithm, but also on the quality of its implementation. This became apparent some 20 years ago with the emergence of Side-Channel Analysis (SCA) [13], a special form of cryptanalysis that aims to exploit measurable physical phenomena (e.g. variations in the response time or power consumption) of a device executing a cryptographic algorithm so as to reveal information about the secret key. The most advanced variant of SCA is

Supported by FNR Luxembourg (CORE project ACRYPT, ID C12-15-4009992).

© Springer International Publishing AG 2017
P.Q. Nguyen and J. Zhou (Eds.): ISC 2017, LNCS 10599, pp. 39–57, 2017.
https://doi.org/10.1007/978-3-319-69659-1_3

Differential Power Analysis (DPA) [14], which involves two phases, namely an acquisition phase and an analysis phase. In the former phase, the attacker captures power consumption traces from the target device for different plaintexts or ciphertexts under the same secret key. Thereafter, in the analysis phase, she adopts sophisticated statistical techniques to determine the correlation between the power consumption and certain intermediate values that depend solely on the plaintext/ciphertext and (parts of) the secret key. Numerous case studies reported in the literature confirm that DPA attacks pose a real-world threat to the security of unprotected (or insufficiently protected) cryptosystems and can be mounted in relatively short time with relatively cheap equipment.

From a high-level point of view, countermeasures to thwart DPA attacks on symmetric cryptosystems can be broadly divided into two main categories; one is *hiding* (i.e. eliminating the data-dependency of the power consumption) and the second is *masking* (i.e. randomizing the intermediate values that are computed) [16]. Common approaches for hiding countermeasures aim to make the device's power consumption profile either constant for all possible values of the secret key or fully random (i.e. statistically independent from the key). Hiding can be implemented in hardware (e.g. by using a so-called DPA-resistant logic style) and software (e.g. by randomly shuffling the order in which the sensitive operations are executed or through the insertion of dummy operations) [16]. In both cases, the intention is to break (or, at least, to obscure) the link between the sensitive intermediate values that are computed during the execution of an algorithm and the power consumption traces. Masking, on the other hand, aims to conceal every key-dependent variable with a random value, called "mask," in order to break the link between the intermediate values that are computed on the device and the (unmasked) intermediate values of the algorithm. The basic principle is related to the idea of secret sharing since every sensitive variable is split into $n \geq 2$ "shares," so that any combination of up to $d = n - 1$ shares is statistically independent of any secret value. These n shares must be processed separately during the execution of the algorithm and then re-combined in the end to yield the correct result. When implemented properly, masking forces an attacker to combine n leakages originating from the n shares in order to obtain the secret information.

Depending on the actual operation to be protected against DPA, a masking scheme can be Boolean (using logical XOR), arithmetic (using modular addition or modular subtraction) or multiplicative (using modular multiplication). When a cryptographic algorithm involves arithmetic and Boolean operations, which is generally the case for all ARX-based block ciphers, then the masks have to be converted from one form to the other without introducing any kind of leakage [21]. Goubin was the first to describe secure algorithms for conversion between arithmetic and Boolean masks in [9]. While his method is very efficient for the Boolean-to-arithmetic conversion, it introduces a high overhead for conversions in the other direction. Coron and Tchulkine [5], as well as Debraize [6], came up with improved variants of Goubin's algorithm for switching from arithmetic to Boolean masking. At FSE 2015, Coron *et al.* [4] introduced a novel conversion technique with logarithmic complexity based on a special "parallel-prefix" form of a carry-lookahead adder, known as *Kogge-Stone Adder (KSA)* [15]. Besides mask conversion, there exists a second principal approach for efficient masking of ARX-based ciphers, namely to perform the necessary arithmetic operations (e.g. modular addition/subtraction) directly on Boolean shares. This idea was originally proposed for hardware implementation [1], but can also be applied to protect software implementations of ARX-based block ciphers against DPA as demonstrated in [12]. The latency of the implementations in [1] and [12] grows linearly with the bit-length of the two operands. However, Coron *et al.* showed in [4] that the KSA allows not only logarithmic-time mask conversion, but also logarithmic-time modular addition on Boolean shares.

The KSA for modular addition on Boolean shares introduced in [4] comes with a formal security proof embedded into the framework of Isai, Sahai, and Wagner [11]. Furthermore, the authors of [4] present a software implementation of their addition technique written in ANSI C and analyzed its execution time on a 32-bit processor. They also report the execution time of first-order secure implementations of HMAC-SHA1 and the SPECK cipher [2]. Unfortunately, an implementation written in C is not suitable for performance evaluations since optimizations introduced by the compiler may break the security of a masking scheme, even if the source code looks perfectly sound. On the other hand, when preventing a compiler from performing sophisticated optimizations, the results are not meaningful. Therefore, it is still unclear how fast a modular addition on Boolean shares can be in the real world and how its execution time impacts the performance of an ARX-based cipher. Another important question arising from [4] is whether there exists an alternative addition technique that could lead to better execution times than the KSA. Based on the work described in the present paper, we can answer this question positively. We propose a new technique for performing modular additions and subtractions directly on Boolean shares that uses a basic *Carry-Save Adder (CSA)* [17] in an iterative fashion, which is not only faster but also smaller (in terms of code size) than the KSA.

A masking scheme that uses the proposed CSA-based addition on Boolean shares is a lightweight countermeasure with relatively low impact on execution time and binary code size. The design of DPA countermeasures always involves a trade-off between security (i.e. the achieved "degree" of DPA resistance) and performance/resource requirements (RAM footprint, code size). Such trade-offs yield a wide spectrum of countermeasures along an axis between security and efficiency, whereby most existing proposals (including the KSA-based masking from [4]) are at the far end towards security. These countermeasures were typically developed for smart card applications where the secret key is fixed and an attacker can measure an arbitrary number of traces. Such applications require advanced DPA countermeasures, which usually introduce massive overheads in execution time [16]. However, applications outside the smart card domain can have different threat models, different assumptions about the number of traces the attacker can measure, and different security requirements. For example, in

Table 1. The cost (in number of elementary operations) of different secure operations.

Secure operation	Cost
SecNot	1
SecXor	2
SecShift	4
SecShiftFill	5
SecAnd	8
SecOr	11

the Internet of Things (IoT), the secret key used to encrypt the communication between two devices is often provisioned dynamically (e.g. through ephemeral ECDH key exchange) and the amount of transmitted data is, in general, small (e.g. up to a few kB), which means that at most a few hundred data blocks are encrypted with one and the same key. In this case, an attacker can just capture a few hundred power or EM traces. The proposed masking using CSA addition on Boolean shares is a (relatively) inexpensive DPA countermeasure that can meet certain relaxed security requirements at significantly lower cost than the sophisticated countermeasures used for smart cards.

2   Preliminaries

A first step towards masked implementations of ARX-based ciphers is to define "secure" (i.e. masked) variants of the used arithmetic/logical operations: modular addition and subtraction, rotations, and bitwise exclusive OR. All bitwise logical operations and shifts (including rotations) are relatively easy to perform directly on Boolean shares, whereas the non-linear addition/subtraction require more complex algorithms. Coron *et al.* [4] presented a provably-secure method to perform a modular addition on Boolean shares using only secure algorithms for AND, XOR and bit shifts.

We specify in Table 1 all secure operations required to mask an ARX design and their cost expressed in the number of "elementary" operations, which can normally be executed via a single instruction. SecAnd, SecShift, and SecXor are described in detail in [4, Sect. 4]. Besides these, we need provably-secure algorithms for two further operations: SecOr and SecShiftFill. The former computes an OR on Boolean shares, while SecShiftFill shifts a sensitive value represented by Boolean shares n bit-positions to the left and fills the n least significant bits with 1 (see [7] for a more detailed treatment). We divide the secure operations on Boolean shares into three classes according to their computational cost. The first class includes all secure operations with a cost of at most six instructions (e.g. SecXor, SecShift). Then, the second class contains operations that can be masked using up to a dozen instructions (e.g. SecAnd, SecOr). Finally, the third class is represented by operations that need more than 12 instructions. Secure algorithms for modular addition/subtraction on Boolean shares belong to this latter class since they rely on secure operations from the first two classes.

Algorithm 1. Kogge-Stone Addition

Input: Operands $a, b \in \{0, 1\}^k$
Output: Result $r = a + b \mod 2^k$
1: $p \leftarrow a \oplus b$
2: $g \leftarrow a \wedge b$
3: **for** i from 1 to $\max\left(\lceil \log_2(k-1) \rceil, 1\right)$ **do**
4:     $g \leftarrow \left(p \wedge (g \ll 2^{i-1})\right) \oplus g$
5:     $p \leftarrow p \wedge (p \ll 2^{i-1})$
6: **end for**
7: $g \leftarrow \left(p \wedge (g \ll 2^{n-1})\right) \oplus g$
8: $r \leftarrow a \oplus b \oplus (g \ll 1)$
9: **return** r

The Kogge-Stone Adder (KSA) [15] belongs to the family of parallel-prefix carry-lookahead adders, which parallelize the computation of the carry signal in order to reduce the carry propagation delay. The structure of a parallel-prefix adder can be represented through prefix graphs that generate at each stage two signals: a propagate signal p and a generate signal g. The KSA is very fast due to its minimal depth (which grows logarithmically with respect to the size of the operands) and minimal fan-out, but has a high node count and, thus, it suffers from wiring congestion when implemented in hardware.

The structure of the KSA can be easily parallelized in software as specified in Algorithm 1. If the adder does not get an input carry signal along with the two operands a and b, then the bitwise ORs can be replaced by bitwise XORs as in Algorithm 1. The addition on Boolean shares benefits tremendously from this optimization because the secure SecXor operation is much faster than the secure SecOr operation. Unfortunately, this optimization can not be applied to the subtraction (i.e. two's complement addition) because the input carry signal has to be set to 1 and distributed to all stages of the adder. Hence, a software implementation of KSA subtraction needs to fill the least significant bits of the generate word g with the value of the input carry after each left-shift. This leads to less efficient software implementations of subtraction versus addition.

3   Carry-Save Addition

The design of algorithms and respective hardware architectures for the addition of integers is one of the central research topics in computer arithmetic and has a history stretching back more than 50 years [18]. The efficiency of the various techniques proposed in the literature depends to a large extent on how the two operands to be added are represented. In the most basic case, i.e. the standard binary system, one uses a number representation radix of $r = 2$ and the digit set $D = \{0, 1\}$, which means a k-bit integer a is given as

$$a = \sum_{i=0}^{k-1} a_i \, 2^i \quad \text{with} \quad a_i \in \{0, 1\} \tag{1}$$

Throughout this paper, we shall use indexed lowercase letters to denote the individual bits of an integer (a_0 is the least significant bit of a and a_{k-1} is its most significant bit). The most basic way of adding up two k-bit integers is to apply a so-called *Ripple-Carry Adder (RCA)* consisting of k Full Adders (FAs) [18]. Each FA gets besides the two operand bits a_i and b_i also a carry bit c_{in} as input and produces a sum bit s_i and an outgoing carry bit c_{out} as follows.

$$s_i = a_i \oplus b_i \oplus c_{in}, \quad c_{out} = (a_i \wedge b_i) \vee (a_i \wedge c_{in}) \vee (b_i \wedge c_{in}) \tag{2}$$

The carry output c_{out} of each FA is connected to the carry input c_{in} of the next-higher FA. When analyzing the latency of an RCA, one needs to take into account the maximum possible length of a carry chain. As defined in [18], the length of a carry chain is the number of bit positions from where the carry is generated up to (and including) where it is finally absorbed or annihilated. The longest possible carry chain of a k-bit RCA covers all k FAs since, in the worst case, a carry generated at the least significant position ripples all the way up to the most significant position. As a consequence, the latency of an RCA grows linearly with the operand size. However, a single carry chain of length k occurs only for very few combinations of operands as we will discuss further below. In the case of random inputs, one can normally (i.e. on average) expect to have several, but much shorter, carry chains. It was already shown in 1946 that, on average, the carry chains in a k-bit addition are $\log_2(k)$ bits long [3].

Although RCAs are easy to implement in hardware, they are rarely used in high-speed arithmetic circuits. The maximum frequency with which an RCA is capable to process operands is determined by the worst-case signal propagation path, which, in turn, is determined by the maximum length of the carry chains (i.e. k) and not their average length (i.e. $\log_2(k)$) [18]. This has motivated the development of advanced adder circuits having a worst-case latency that grows logarithmically with the operand length. A good example for such an advanced adder is the KSA described in the preceding section. A logarithmic worst-case behavior is the optimum that one can achieve with the binary number system [18]. However, when using a redundant number system (i.e. a number system with a digit set D containing more than r elements), it is even possible to add two integers in constant time, independent of their length.

A very important redundant number system is the *Carry-Save (CS)* system [17], which uses a radix-2 representation with the digit set $D = \{0, 1, 2\}$. Since any digit a_i can take three possible values (namely 0, 1, and 2), it needs to be encoded using two bits, a sum bit a_i^s and a carry bit a_i^c, as shown below.

$$0 \leftrightarrow (0, 0) \qquad 1 \leftrightarrow (0, 1) \text{ or } (1, 0) \qquad 2 \leftrightarrow (1, 1) \tag{3}$$

The actual value of a k-digit number a given in CS form is

$$a = \sum_{i=0}^{k-1} a_i \cdot 2^i = \sum_{i=0}^{k-1} (a_i^s + a_i^c) \cdot 2^i \text{ with } a_i^s, a_i^c \in \{0, 1\} \tag{4}$$

A k-digit CS integer a is always composed of a sum-word a^s and a carry-word a^c, each of which consists of k bits. Thus, we can write $a^s = (a^s_{k-1}, \ldots, a^s_1, a^s_0)$ and $a^c = (a^c_{k-1}, \ldots, a^c_1, a^c_0)$. The redundancy in the digit set D, which enables two encodings for the digit 1, means that the CS representation of an integer is not unique [18]. An integer a given in CS representation can be converted into conventional binary form by simply adding up its sum-word a^s and carry-word a^c using e.g. an RCA or KSA, i.e. the redundant-to-binary conversion involves always a propagation of carries. In some way, the sum-word a^s and carry-word a^c can be interpreted as two *arithmetic shares* of the integer a since their sum $a^s + a^c$ is exactly a. In practice, the CS representation is typically used for the implementation of complex arithmetic operations that require a multi-operand addition; a typical example is the addition of partial products performed in an integer multiplication [18]. The CS representation is attractive for this purpose because it allows partial products to be added up in constant time, irrespective of k, yielding a result in CS form. Only at the end of a multiplication, a single carry-propagating addition is needed for the redundant-to-binary conversion.

Let a be a k-digit integer in CS form and b a binary integer of k bits. The result $r = a + b$ of a CS addition can be computed in parallel for all digits and consists of a sum-word r^s and a carry-word r^c, obtained as follows.

$$r^s_i = a^s_i \oplus a^c_i \oplus b_i \quad \text{for } 0 \leq i \leq k - 1 \tag{5}$$
$$r^c_i = (a^s_{i-1} \wedge a^c_{i-1}) \vee (a^s_{i-1} \wedge b_{i-1}) \vee (a^c_{i-1} \wedge b_{i-1}) \quad \text{for } 1 \leq i \leq k \tag{6}$$

A *Carry-Save Adder (CSA)* can be easily implemented in hardware through an array of k FAs, similar to the RCA [18]. However, the carry-propagation in the CSA is limited to a single position, which becomes immediately evident from Eq. (6) because r^c_i depends solely on bits with index $i - 1$. A carry generated by an FA just goes to the next-higher FA, but can not ripple up further. The overall latency of a k-digit CSA is, therefore, determined by the latency of an FA and does not depend on k anymore. The least significant bit of the result's carry-word, i.e. r^c_0, must be set to 0 when performing an addition, and to 1 in the case of a subtraction, as we will explain further below.

3.1   Using a CSA for Single-Operand Addition

Traditionally, CSAs are employed for multi-operand addition, i.e. in situations where many operands (e.g. partial products of an integer multiplication) are to be summed up. However, in the present paper we use a CSA to perform single-operand additions to add two k-bit integers, a and b, in standard binary form with the goal of obtaining a binary result. Computing the sum $r = a + b$ in CS form is easy and requires just a logical AND and a logical XOR operation:

$$r^s_i = a_i \oplus b_i \quad \text{for } 0 \leq i \leq k - 1 \tag{7}$$
$$r^c_i = a_{i-1} \wedge b_{i-1} \quad \text{for } 1 \leq i \leq k \tag{8}$$

An arithmetic circuit computing r^s_i and r^c_i according to the equations above is commonly referred to as a Half-Adder (HA). Similar as before, i.e. Eqs. (5)

Algorithm 2. Carry-Save Addition

Input: Operands $a, b \in \{0, 1\}^k$
Output: Result $r = a + b \bmod 2^k$
  1: $t \leftarrow a \wedge b$
  2: $r^s \leftarrow a \oplus b$
  3: $r^c \leftarrow t \ll 1$
  4: **while** $r^c \neq 0$ **do**
  5:     $t \leftarrow r^s \wedge r^c$
  6:     $r^s \leftarrow r^s \oplus r^c$
  7:     $r^c \leftarrow t \ll 1$
  8: **end while**
  9: **return** r^s

---

and (6), the sum bits r_i^s are kept "in place," whereas all the carry bits r_i^c move one position to the left. Since, in this paper, additions and subtractions are always done modulo 2^k, we can simply discard the most significant carry bit r_k^c. When implemented in software, a HA consists of an AND instruction, an XOR, and a 1-bit left shift, which is a lot more efficient than the sequence of instructions carried out by the KSA (Algorithm 1). Another advantage of the CSA over the KSA is that a subtraction is only slightly more complex than an addition. The most common way to perform a subtraction $r = a - b$ is to add the two's complement of b to a. To generate the two's complement of b, we have to first form the one's complement (through an inversion of all bits of b) and then add 1 to it [18]. Fortunately, this addition of 1 can be simply realized by just setting the least significant carry bit r_0^c to 1. Adding 1 in this way is always possible when using a CSA[1], but not with a KSA. Hence, a CS subtraction is essentially the same as a CS addition with inverted addend bits.

While the benefit of the CSA for multi-operand addition (multiplication) is clear, it may seem counterintuitive to use a CSA for a single addition since the result is obtained in CS form and still needs to be converted into the standard binary representation, which requires a propagation of carries. This raises the question of why one does not simply use a KSA or some similar kind of carry-propagating adder in the first place. The answer lies in the rather little-known fact that a CSA can not only be employed to perform a CS addition, but also for the redundant-to-binary conversion of the result. Namely, when we feed the sum-word r^s and carry-word r^c obtained through Eqs. (7) and (8) as input into a CSA, we get again a result in CS representation, but with fewer 1 bits in the carry-word r^c (i.e. lower Hamming weight) or no 1 bits at all. When repeating this procedure, all bits of the carry-word r^c will eventually become 0, and the latest sum-word r^s represents the result in binary form. In each iteration, the Hamming weight of r^c is reduced by (at least) 1 since the lowest carry bit r_0^c is set to 0. Algorithm 2 specifies this addition technique in a formal fashion. The first three lines do the actual CS addition of the operands a and b according to

---

[1] As mentioned before, r_0^c is normally set to 0 when performing an addition.

Eqs. (7) and (8), yielding a sum in CS form consisting of r^s and r^c. Then, the sum is converted into standard binary representation using the while-loop.

The overall execution time of Algorithm 2 depends on the number of loop-iterations needed for the redundant-to-binary conversion of the result r, i.e. the number of iterations that have to be executed until the carry-word r^c becomes 0. Intuitively, one expects the number of iterations to be closely related to the average length of the carry chains that occur when a is added to b, which, as explained earlier in this section, is approximately $\log_2(k)$ for k-bit operands. In [10], Hendrickson experimentally assessed the accuracy of the $\log_2(k)$ approximation and concluded that $\log_2(5k/4)$ makes a better estimate for the average length of the carry chains. This suggests an average of around 4.3 bit positions for the carry-chain length when 16-bit operands are added, and about 5.3 bits in the case of $k = 32$. However, these results are not immediately applicable to the estimation of the number of loop iterations of Algorithm 2 since the carries are generated outside the loop (namely in the actual CS addition of a and b in line 1–3). Therefore, the number of iterations is one less than the length of the carry chains, i.e. based on Hendrickson's formula we can estimate the average number of iterations to be about $\log_2(5k/4) - 1$. In this way, we finally obtain $\log_2(20) - 1 \approx 3.3$ iterations if $k = 16$ and $\log_2(40) - 1 \approx 4.3$ iterations for the redundant-to-binary conversion when $k = 32$. Thus, the average execution time of the CSA addition specified in Algorithm 2 increases *logarithmically* with the operand length k, similar to the execution time of the KSA.

3.2   Security Aspects

Even though both the CSA and KSA have logarithmic time complexity, there exists a significant difference, namely that the execution time of the former is not constant for a given operand length. Based on above analysis, the average number of iterations of the while-loop for redundant-to-binary conversion can be approximated as $\log_2(5k/4) - 1$. In the best case, however, the while-loop is not iterated at all, which happens when $(a \wedge b) \ll 1$ is 0. On the other hand, in the worst case, a total of $k - 1$ iterations need to be performed until all k bits of the carry-word r^c become 0. The $k - 1$ iterations are the absolute maximum since, in each iteration, the least significant carry bit r_0^c is set to 0. When the operands are short, e.g. when $k = 16$, it is feasible to (exhaustively) determine the *exact* number of iterations for all 2^{2k} combinations of input words. Figure 1 shows the probabilities of all possible iteration counts for $k = 16$, which ranges from 0 to 15. Out of the total of 2^{32} possible operand combinations, only some 1.34% (or 57,395,628 combinations to be precise) directly yield a final result in binary form (i.e. $r^c = 0$) such that the loop is not iterated at all. An iteration count of three has the highest probability; it occurs for roughly 27.72% of the input combinations, closely followed by two iterations with a probability in the area of 27.01%. The maximum possible 15 iterations happen only with 65,536 input combinations, i.e. the probability of the worst case for $k = 16$ amounts to only 2^{-16}, or roughly 0.0015%. The average over all 2^{32} possible combinations of pairs of 16-bit input words is approximately 3.25 iterations, which confirms

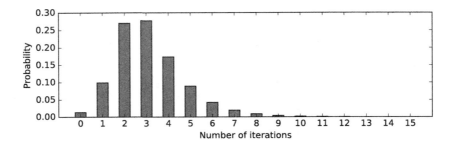

Fig. 1. Probability of each possible number of iterations of the loop for redundant-to-binary conversion when $k = 16$.

that the estimated iteration-count of $\log_2(5k/4) - 1 \approx 3.3$ was pretty accurate and the same also holds for $k = 8$ as we experimentally verified.

An attacker may be able to count the number of iterations executed in the redundant-to-binary conversion, which raises the question of what information the iterations reveal about the operands or the result. Let us first consider the scenario that the loop is not iterated at all, which can only happen if after the left-shift operation (line 3 of Algorithm 2), the carry-word r^c is 0. This means an attacker learns that $a \wedge b$ is either 0 or 2^{k-1} because only in these two cases r^c can become 0. Answering the question of what information the attacker can learn about the obtained result r (i.e. the sum-word r^s) in this scenario is less obvious and boils down to the question of whether r can take all 2^k possible values between 0 and $2^k - 1$ or not. Due to our experiments with $k = 16$ from above, we know already that there are 57,395,628 different input combinations for which the loop is not executed at all. A further analysis reveals that these combinations cover all 2^{16} possible values for the resulting sum, i.e. r can have any value between 0 and $2^{16} - 1$. However, this does not hold any longer when the redundant-to-binary conversion consists of exactly one loop iteration since now only $2^{16} - 2 = 65{,}534$ different values for the sum can be obtained. In the most extreme case, i.e. when the maximum number of $k - 1 = 15$ iterations is performed, the resulting sum can only be either 0 or 2^{15}, which means that an attacker has a 50% chance to simply guess the value of the sum. However, the probability of 15 iterations is extremely small, namely $2^{-16} \approx 0.0015\%$.

The above analysis of the iteration counts is based on an exhaustive testing of all possible pairs of input words, which is feasible for $k = 16$, but not when $k = 32$ anymore since the number of combinations of 32-bit words amounts to 2^{64}. However, one can expect that for $k = 32$, the distribution of probabilities for iteration counts will be similar to Fig. 1, meaning the highest probabilities are centered around four iterations and the probability of $k - 1 = 31$ iterations is extremely small, namely 2^{-32}. Concretely, an attacker would have to observe on average some $4.29 \cdot 10^9$ CS additions to reduce the guessing entropy for the result to 1. However, the attacker can "trade" the number of guesses she has to make for the number of traces she has to acquire to mount a DPA attack.

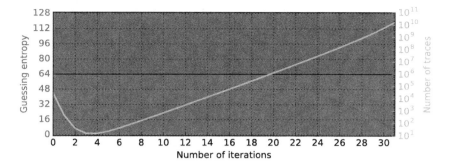

Fig. 2. The number of traces necessary to reduce the guessing entropy of a 128-bit key for different number of iterations of four 32-bit CS additions protected against DPA. (Color figure online)

The relation between the guessing entropy and the number of iterations, as well as the probability of each of the 32 iteration counts, is graphically represented in Fig. 2. We generated the information shown in this figure through experiments with 2^{46} pairs of 32-bit words since exhaustively testing all 2^{64} combinations is not feasible. Concretely, in these experiments, we added a 128-bit secret key to a 128-bit state consisting of four 32-bit words.

Due to our experiments, we can confirm that an iteration count of four has the highest probability among the 32 possible counts and occurs in about 25% of the 32-bit CS additions. In a real DPA attack on a 128-bit key addition, one can therefore expect approximately one out of 16 power consumption traces to contain four additions with four iterations each. As indicated by the yellow line in Fig. 2, an exponentially increasing number of power traces must be captured as the number of iterations gets larger. For example, an attacker would need to measure (at least) 10^6 power traces before she can expect to encounter a trace with more than 20 iterations. The blue line in Fig. 2 shows that the larger the number of iterations gets, the more information about the sum is "leaked." As analyzed before for $k = 16$, the number of distinct values that the result of an addition can take decreases with the number of loop iterations executed in the redundant-to-binary conversion. In the most extreme case of $k - 1$ iterations (which happens with a very small probability of 2^{-32} for $k = 32$), the result can only take two distinct values, namely 0 and 2^{k-1}. Fortunately, the restriction of the value space for the result is much lower for the iteration counts with the highest probabilities, which are centered around four iterations. Nonetheless, it is possible to exploit the number of iterations in our experiments to reduce the guessing entropy for the 128-bit key. For example, our results show that if an attacker is able to observe some 600,000 additions, the guessing entropy would be reduced from 128 to 64 bits. Similarly, the ability to measure power traces of roughly 62,000 additions would reduce the guessing entropy to 80 bits. However, the assumption that an attacker is capable to measure power traces from several 10,000 or even 100,000 encryptions with one and the same key may

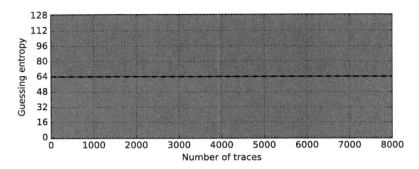

Fig. 3. The evolution of the guessing entropy for a Correlation Power Analysis (CPA) attack against four unprotected 32-bit modular additions.

be reasonable for smart cards, but is extremely unrealistic in many other contexts (we discussed in Sect. 1 secure communication in the IoT as an example where secret keys are ephemeral and only used to encrypt small amounts of data).

The best attack against a protected (i.e. masked) version of the CSA takes the number of loop-iterations performed in the redundant-to-binary conversion into account to reduce the guessing entropy of the key. This raises the question of how much harder a protected CSA implementation is to attack in relation to an unprotected 32-bit modular addition. To answer this question, we mounted a Correlation Power Analysis (CPA) attack against an unprotected implementation of modular addition executed on an ARM Cortex-M3 processor clocked at 33 MHz. The result, depicted in Fig. 3, shows that four 32-bit additions can be attacked with some 6,800 power traces on average. On the other hand, when using a similar amount of traces (namely 7,467), to attack a protected implementation of the CSA, the guessing entropy of a single 32-bit addition can be reduced by only 5.18 bits. Therefore, the protected CSA considerably increases the attacker's effort compared to an unprotected modular addition.

The leakage caused by the operand-dependent number of loop-iterations in the redundant-to-binary conversion reduces the guessing entropy of the secret key and, hence, the effective security level, depending on the number of traces an attacker is able to capture. However, for an effective security level of e.g. 96 bits, a masked implementation of 128-bit SPECK (i.e. SPECK-64/128) based on the protected CSA is still much faster (namely about 17.5% for encryption and roughly 42.4% for decryption) than a masked implementation of 96-bit SPECK (i.e. SPECK-64/96) using the protected KSA, as we will see in Subsect. 4.2.

Although the protected CSA could be applied to operands of any size, the trade-off between the number of traces and the guessing entropy must be taken into account. This trade-off must be particularly carefully analyzed for operand lengths below 32 bits. As a general guideline, we only recommend the protected CSA for operands with a bitlength of $k \geq 32$ as otherwise the security margin might become too tight. Yet, even with this restriction, the protected CSA can be used to efficiently mask numerous cryptographic primitives that are used in practice, including a diverse range of ARX-based lightweight symmetric ciphers (like Chaskey, SPECK, RECTANGLE, LEA, etc.) and the keyed-hash message authentication code based on SHA-256 (HMAC-SHA-256).

4   Implementation Details and Evaluation

We implemented secure addition/subtraction on Boolean shares using both the KSA and CSA algorithm in Assembly language for a 32-bit ARM Cortex-M3 processor. Then, we applied the mentioned addition techniques to protect two variants of the block cipher SPECK [2] against first-order DPA attacks.

4.1   Secure Addition on Boolean Shares

The implementation results for secure addition/subtraction on Boolean shares are shown in Table 2. Before discussing the results in detail, we briefly describe the implementations. Like other 32-bit ARM processors, the Cortex-M3 has 13 general-purpose registers, which we allocate as follows: Four registers hold the shares of the two masked inputs. Either two or three registers (depending on the algorithm) store the randomly generated 32-bit values needed for the execution of the secure Boolean functions like SecureAnd and SecureShift. Each algorithm also occupies a certain number of registers for intermediate results: three in the case of the CSA and four for the KSA. A special property of ARM processors is their ability to execute a shift operation together with most arithmetic/logical instructions within a single clock cycle. We exploited this feature to reduce the execution time of both the CSA-based and KSA-based addition technique.

The secure KSA performs additions in constant time and can be implemented with either "rolled" or unrolled loops. The entirely unrolled version of the KSA is between 28% (addition) and 21% (subtraction) faster than a standard implementation with rolled loops, but this gain in speed comes at the expense of almost doubling the binary code size. In both cases, the KSA subtraction is significantly slower than the addition because the SecureXor operation has to be replaced by the less efficient SecurOr and the left-shifts by n bits performed on the shares of the generate word require the insertion of n bits set to 1 (i.e. the

Table 2. Execution time and code size of secure addition on Boolean shares using the secure Kogge-Stone Adder (KSA) and the secure Carry-Save Adder (CSA). Since the execution time of the CSA is not constant, we specify the average number of cycles over 100,000 executions with random inputs.

Adder	Time (cycles)		Code size (bytes)	
	Addition	Subtraction	Addition	Subtraction
KSA rolled	282	369	292	408
KSA unrolled	202	291	544	808
CSA (average)	161.75	165	136	148

SecShift must be replaced by SecShiftFill). However, in the unrolled version, the execution time of SecShiftFill can be sightly reduced by using immediate values instead of registers (see [7] for further implementation details).

The secure CSA is very efficient thanks to its simple structure that involves only SecXor, SecAnd, and SecShift operations. Unlike the "rolled" version of the KSA, it does not need a separate register to hold a loop counter. However, the main advantage of the CSA over the KSA is that a subtraction is only slightly slower than an addition since it requires just two extra operations, namely an inversion and the insertion of a 1 at the LSB-position of the carry-word.

A direct comparison of the results of the rolled version of the KSA and the CSA allows us to conclude that the carry-save approach is not only faster, but also notably smaller than the Kogge-Stone technique. While the CSA addition is, on average, about 43% faster than the KSA addition (162 vs. 282 cycles as per Table 2), the difference increases to some 55% for subtraction (165 vs. 369 cycles). The benefit of the CSA over the KSA is even more significant in terms of code size since the difference amounts to a factor of about 2.14 for addition and 2.75 for subtraction. However, as we mentioned before, the execution time of the KSA can be improved by full loop unrolling, but the resultant code-size penalty may be undesirable for certain highly constrained environments where every single byte matters. In summary, using the proposed carry-save technique to directly perform a modular addition or subtraction on Boolean shares shows clear speed and size advantages over the KSA.

4.2   Masked Implementation of Speck

SPECK is a family of lightweight block ciphers designed by cryptographers from the U.S. National Security Agency [2]. SPECK-64/128 uses a two-branch Feistel network to encrypt 64-bit plaintexts with a 128-bit master key. Its round function is iterated 26 times and consists of simple operations on 32-bit words: two rotations, a modular addition, and two XORs. In the case of a straightforward (i.e. unprotected) implementation, the cipher's state fits into two registers, and a third register is needed for the round key. The remaining eleven registers are available for other purposes, e.g. the implementation of a masking technique to protect the cipher against DPA attacks.

The implementation results presented in Table 3 show that the unprotected version of SPECK-64/128 is quite efficient compared to the secure addition on Boolean shares (Table 2). Concretely, the encryption time is just a little worse than the execution time of the slowest addition on Boolean shares (i.e. rolled KSA), while the code size is at least six times smaller than the code size of the KSA. The code size of the unprotected implementation of SPECK is also more than three times smaller than the size of the CSA, which is the adder with the smallest footprint. This high-level comparison clearly illustrates the enormous cost of masking just a single nonlinear operation, the modular addition. It can therefore be expected that the integration of masking will entail a massive performance degradation and also inflate the code size. Hence, any effort spent on optimizing masking is well spent. Even a modest improvement by a few cycles

Table 3. Execution time, code size and performance penalty factor of different implementations of SPECK-64/96 and SPECK-64/128. Since the execution time of the CSA is not constant, we specify the average number of cycles over 100,000 executions with random inputs.

Implementation	Time (cycles)		Code size (B)		Penalty factor	
	Enc	Dec	Enc	Dec	Enc	Dec
Unprotected SPECK-64/96	306	510	44	52	1	1
SPECK-64/96 (KSA rolled)	6639	9525	340	480	21.69	18.67
SPECK-64/96 (KSA unrolled)	4921	7447	592	876	16.08	14.60
SPECK-64/96 (CSA average)	3902.9	4071.8	180	204	12.75	7.98
Unprotected SPECK-64/128	318	530	44	52	1	1
SPECK-64/128 (KSA rolled)	6892	9889	340	480	21.67	18.65
SPECK-64/128 (KSA unrolled)	5108	7731	592	876	16.06	14.58
SPECK-64/128 (CSA, average)	4061.3	4290.8	180	204	12.77	8.09

when performing a masked addition has the potential to yield a non-negligible overall performance gain.

A masked implementation of SPECK occupies four registers to store the two shares of the 64-bit state. Depending on the implementation methodology, one or two registers have to be used to manipulate the shares of the round key. An ARM Cortex-M3 processor does not provide enough general-purpose registers to hold all operands needed during the execution of a masked implementation of SPECK-64/128 using the secure KSA algorithm. Thus, at the beginning of an addition (or subtraction), two registers have to be spilled to RAM so that the necessary number of registers becomes available for the KSA. The original content of these registers is recovered at the end of the operation. However, for the fully unrolled implementation, it suffices to save only a single register onto the stack. These stack instructions (i.e. push and pop) add quite some overhead to each execution of the secure KSA-based modular addition/subtraction. On the other hand, the protected implementations of SPECK-64/128 using the secure CSA are able to execute all operations directly on registers (i.e. no push/pop is required) since the underlying algorithm operates on fewer variables.

We compare in Table 3 the execution time and code size of an unprotected implementation of SPECK-64/96 and SPECK-64/128 with three DPA-protected versions[2]. All implementations have received a similar amount of optimization and perform a single iteration of the round function in a loop, i.e. we refrained from full loop unrolling to keep the code size small. The penalty factor on the execution time of SPECK-64/128 introduced by the different masking schemes varies between 8.09 and 21.67. As expected, the efficiency of the three variants reflects the performance of the underlying method for addition or subtraction on Boolean shares. When comparing the masked implementation based on the

---

[2] The results exclude the generation of (pseudo-)random numbers for masking.

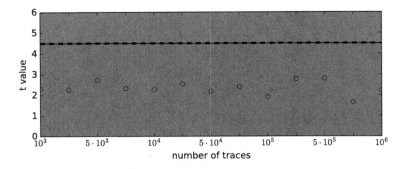

Fig. 4. T-statistic (absolute values) of the CSA under a HW leakage model.

CSA with the two KSA versions, it turns out that the encryption time of the former is more than 20% better than that of the unrolled KSA and 3.28 times smaller in size. The performance gain even doubles to 41% (which corresponds to a considerable speed-up factor of 1.70) when we compare the CSA with the rolled-loop KSA version. Furthermore, the CSA-based SPECK implementation clearly outperforms its two KSA-based SPECK counterparts in decryption; it is 1.80 times faster than the unrolled KSA variant (4291 vs. 7731 cycles) and 2.30 times faster than the KSA with a "rolled" loop (9889 cycles).

4.3   Leakage Assessment

We evaluated the DPA-protected implementation of CSA addition on Boolean shares as well as the masked implementation of SPECK based on the CSA using Welch's t-test [8] on simulated power traces. Doing the test on simulated traces facilitates experiments with a large number (e.g. millions) of traces and reduces time and memory complexity in relation to real measurements. Our evaluation framework is inspired by the tool described in [19], but applies a "fixed versus random" leakage detection methodology. We eliminated the leakage related to the number of loop iterations performed in the redundant-to-binary conversion by simply executing the maximum number of iterations (i.e. 31) for all possible combinations of 32-bit input words. Then, we judiciously applied the t-test to avoid any wrong outcome [20]. Yet, we did not observe any significant leakage above the ±4.5 threshold (which corresponds to a high statistical significance level of $\alpha = 0.001$) in our evaluation.

The maximum absolute value of the t-statistic of the secure implementation of the CSA addition is graphically represented in Fig. 4 for different numbers of simulated traces under a Hamming Weight (HW) leakage model. The t value is always well below the threshold of 4.5 in all our experiments and only shows small variations when increasing the number of traces from 10^3 to 10^6. To give a concrete example, the result of the t-test applied to 10^6 power traces of the secure CSA addition is depicted in Fig. 5. Again, we can observe that the value of the t-statistic is inside the ±4.5 interval for each point in time, which

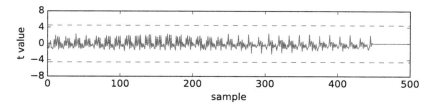

Fig. 5. The result of the t-test applied to the CSA under a HW leakage model.

implies that the null hypothesis holds. In other words, the masking scheme is effective against first-order DPA attacks because it passes the t-test evaluation. All these results strongly indicate that the implementation will also not leak when more than 10^6 traces are used for the t-test. Therefore, the described implementation of CSA addition can be deemed secure against first-order DPA attacks.

We obtained similar results when we applied the t-test to the secure implementation of KSA addition on Boolean shares and the masked implementation of the SPECK cipher based on the KSA. This suggests that our implementation of the KSA can be considered secure against first-order DPA attacks.

5   Conclusions

The implementation of lightweight symmetric cryptosystems requires a careful balance between efficiency and security, including a certain degree of resistance against DPA attacks. In this context, we introduced a new masking technique for block ciphers that involve both arithmetic and Boolean operations, which is the case for SPECK and many other ARX designs. Our main contribution is an algorithm for performing CSA-based modular addition/subtraction directly on Boolean shares, which makes expensive mask conversions obsolete. The CSA is much simpler and, hence, faster than the KSA presented at FSE 2015, but has operand-dependent execution time. Concretely, a CSA-based 32-bit addition on Boolean shares requires 162 clock cycles when executed on an ARM Cortex-M3 processor, which is between 20% and 41% faster than the KSA, depending on whether the loops are unrolled or not. We integrated both addition techniques into a masked implementation of SPECK and found the CSA to outperform the "looped" KSA by a factor of 1.70 for encryption and 2.30 for decryption. The main drawback of the CSA is its operand-dependent execution time, which can be exploited to reduce the guessing entropy of the secret key. Nonetheless, the CSA is a practical and useful alternative to the KSA, especially for applications that encrypt only small amounts of data with one and the same key.

References

1. Baek, Y.-J., Noh, M.-J.: Differential power attack and masking method. Trends Math. **8**(1), 53–67 (2005)
2. Beaulieu, R., Shors, D., Smith, J., Treatman-Clark, S., Weeks, B., Wingers, L.: The SIMON and SPECK families of lightweight block ciphers. Cryptology ePrint Archive, Report 2013/404 (2013)
3. Burks, A.W., Goldstine, H.H., von Neumann, J.: Preliminary discussion of the logical design of an electronic computing instrument. Report to U.S, Army Ordnance Department (1946)
4. Coron, J.-S., Großschädl, J., Tibouchi, M., Vadnala, P.K.: Conversion from arithmetic to Boolean masking with logarithmic complexity. In: Leander, G. (ed.) FSE 2015. LNCS, vol. 9054, pp. 130–149. Springer, Heidelberg (2015). doi:10.1007/978-3-662-48116-5_7
5. Coron, J.-S., Tchulkine, A.: A new algorithm for switching from arithmetic to Boolean masking. In: Walter, C.D., Koç, Ç.K., Paar, C. (eds.) CHES 2003. LNCS, vol. 2779, pp. 89–97. Springer, Heidelberg (2003). doi:10.1007/978-3-540-45238-6_8
6. Debraize, B.: Efficient and provably secure methods for switching from arithmetic to Boolean masking. In: Prouff, E., Schaumont, P. (eds.) CHES 2012. LNCS, vol. 7428, pp. 107–121. Springer, Heidelberg (2012). doi:10.1007/978-3-642-33027-8_7
7. Dinu, D.: Efficient and secure implementations of lightweight symmetric cryptographic primitives. Ph.D. thesis, University of Luxembourg (2017)
8. Goodwill, G., Jun, B., Jaffe, J., Rohatgi, P.: A testing methodology for side-channel resistance validation. In: Proceedings of the NIST Non-invasive Attack Testing Workshop (NIAT 2011), pp. 158–172, September 2011
9. Goubin, L.: A sound method for switching between Boolean and arithmetic masking. In: Koç, Ç.K., Naccache, D., Paar, C. (eds.) CHES 2001. LNCS, vol. 2162, pp. 3–15. Springer, Heidelberg (2001). doi:10.1007/3-540-44709-1_2
10. Hendrickson, H.C.: Fast high-accuracy binary parallel addition. IRE Trans. Electron. Comput. **9**(4), 465–469 (1960)
11. Ishai, Y., Sahai, A., Wagner, D.: Private circuits: securing hardware against probing attacks. In: Boneh, D. (ed.) CRYPTO 2003. LNCS, vol. 2729, pp. 463–481. Springer, Heidelberg (2003). doi:10.1007/978-3-540-45146-4_27
12. Karroumi, M., Richard, B., Joye, M.: Addition with blinded operands. In: Prouff, E. (ed.) COSADE 2014. LNCS, vol. 8622, pp. 41–55. Springer, Cham (2014). doi:10.1007/978-3-319-10175-0_4
13. Kocher, P.C.: Timing attacks on implementations of Diffie-Hellman, RSA, DSS, and other systems. In: Koblitz, N. (ed.) CRYPTO 1996. LNCS, vol. 1109, pp. 104–113. Springer, Heidelberg (1996). doi:10.1007/3-540-68697-5_9
14. Kocher, P., Jaffe, J., Jun, B.: Differential power analysis. In: Wiener, M. (ed.) CRYPTO 1999. LNCS, vol. 1666, pp. 388–397. Springer, Heidelberg (1999). doi:10.1007/3-540-48405-1_25
15. Kogge, P.M., Stone, H.S.: A parallel algorithm for the efficient solution of a general class of recurrence equations. IEEE Trans. Comput. **22**(8), 786–793 (1973)
16. Mangard, S., Oswald, E., Popp, T.: Power Analysis Attacks: Revealing the Secrets of Smart Cards. Springer, Heidelberg (2007)
17. Metze, G., Robertson, J.E.: Elimination of carry propagation in digital computers. In: Proceedings of the International Conference on Information Processing, Paris, France, June 15–20, 1959, pp. 389–395. UNESCO (1960)

18. Parhami, B.: Computer Arithmetic: Algorithms and Hardware Designs. Oxford University Press, Oxford (2000)
19. Reparaz, O.: Detecting flawed masking schemes with leakage detection tests. In: Peyrin, T. (ed.) FSE 2016. LNCS, vol. 9783, pp. 204–222. Springer, Heidelberg (2016). doi:10.1007/978-3-662-52993-5_11
20. Standaert, F.-X.: How (not) to use Welch's t-test in side-channel security evaluations. Cryptology ePrint Archive, Report 2017/138 (2017)
21. Vadnala, P.K., Großschädl, J.: Faster mask conversion with lookup tables. In: Mangard, S., Poschmann, A.Y. (eds.) COSADE 2014. LNCS, vol. 9064, pp. 207–221. Springer, Cham (2015). doi:10.1007/978-3-319-21476-4_14

Improved Automatic Search Tool for Related-Key Differential Characteristics on Byte-Oriented Block Ciphers

Li Lin[1,2(✉)], Wenling Wu[1,2], and Yafei Zheng[1,2]

[1] TCA Laboratory, SKLCS, Institute of Software,
Chinese Academy of Sciences, Beijing, China
{linli,wwl,zhengyafei}@tca.iscas.ac.cn
[2] University of Chinese Academy of Science, Beijing, China

Abstract. The security of modern block ciphers against related-key attacks, especially the automatic search algorithm for the related-key differential characteristics, attaches a lot of academic attention in recent years. Many search algorithms have been proposed, including depth-first algorithm, breadth-first algorithm and mixed-integer linear programming algorithm. However, the algorithm with reasonable time and memory is still very ad hoc. In this paper, we propose a heuristic algorithm for automatic search for related-key truncated differential characteristics. The goal of our tool is to output a good characteristic within reasonable time and memory, so that it can be used to evaluate the resistance against related-key differential attacks. Our tool combines the precomputation phase of breadth-first algorithm and the depth-first algorithm. To demonstrate the usefulness of our approach, we apply our tool to AES, Deoxys, Joltik and Midori. For AES, we for the first time get a searching result of the best related-key differential characteristic on 10-round AES-128 using the truncated differential form directly. For Deoxys and Joltik, we get more results than the designers under the related-key related-tweak setting. For Midori, we get a two-round related-key cyclic characteristic with weight two, which means that Midori is weak under the related-key setting. We also give a way to calculate the complexity of depth-first algorithm, breadth-first algorithm and our heuristic algorithm, and this is meaningful for us to choose the proper parameters of the algorithm to make the search feasible.

Keywords: Automatic search tool · Related-key differential characteristics · Heuristic algorithm · AES · Deoxys · Joltik · Midori

1 Introduction

Differential cryptanalysis [3] is one of the most well-known attacks on block ciphers, based on which many cryptanalytic techniques have been developed, such as truncated differential attack [15], impossible differential attack [4] and boomerang attack [21]. Evaluation of the security against differential attack

© Springer International Publishing AG 2017
P.Q. Nguyen and J. Zhou (Eds.): ISC 2017, LNCS 10599, pp. 58–76, 2017.
https://doi.org/10.1007/978-3-319-69659-1_4

becomes a basic requirement for the design of block ciphers. Methodologies for constructing block ciphers provably resistant to differential attacks are readily available under the single-key setting. However, things get worse under the related-key setting [2]. In this kind of attacks, the attacker knows or chooses the relation between several keys and is given access to encryption/decryption functions with all these keys. The goal of the attacker is to find the actual keys. The relation between the secret keys is a function chosen by the attacker with some extra care taken to avoid trivial attacks, and quite often it is just an xor with a chosen constant. While less relevant in practice than the classical single-key model, related-key attacks are also very important when the block cipher is used as inner primitive of a hash function, and in that setting one can even consider the known-key [16] or chosen-key models [6] to exhibit some non-ideal properties of the primitive. AES [8] is the most significant standard for block ciphers. The result on full-round AES is still an open problem. A breakthrough in analysis of full-round AES has been presented under the related-key setting. In [6], a related-key attack on 14 rounds of AES-256 was presented. In [5], related-key boomerang attacks on full-round AES-192 and AES-256 were shown.

Automatic search for best differential characteristics under the single-key setting was first performed by Matsui [20] for DES. The automatic search tool for related-key truncated differential characteristic was first proposed by Biryukov et al. at EUROCRYPT 2010 [7]. Their strategy to find the best n-round truncated characteristic first starts by computing the best ones on 1 to $n-1$ rounds. This algorithm works by recursive and can be seen as a tree traversal in a depth-first manner. The advantages of this algorithm are that it can be implemented in parallel and it can output the best characteristics at the end of the algorithm. The disadvantages are that the time complexity increases exponentially with the number of rounds and there are few limits in the middle rounds. At CRYPTO 2013, Fouque et al. proposed a breadth-first algorithm to search the best related-key truncated differential characteristic [11]. This algorithm is made up of two phase, i.e., precomputation phase and online phase. In the precomputation phase, a graph G that contains all the possible one-round transitions is built. In the online phase, all the best r-round related-key truncated differential characteristics corresponding to all the shortest paths in the $(r+1)$-equipartite directed acyclic graph G_r are built by concatenating r copies of G. The advantage of this algorithm is that its time complexity of online phase is linear in the number of rounds. The disadvantages are that the precomputation phase needs to store a graph containing all the possible one-round transitions which may be too large to store, and the online phase isn't feasible to be implemented in parallel.

Our contributions. In this paper, we describe a heuristic tool for searching related-key truncated differential characteristics. The goal of our tool is to output a good characteristic within a reasonable time and a reasonable memory, so that it can be used to evaluate the resistance against related-key differential attacks. This algorithm is also made up of a precomputation phase and an online phase. In the precomputation phase, we also need to build a graph G that contains some one-round transitions as in the precomputation phase of the breadth-first algorithm. The difference is that we introduce a number $\overline{W}_{2round}$ which is the upper-bound for two-round characteristics. In the online phase, we use the depth-first algorithm under the restrain of $\overline{W}_{2round}$. For the AES-like block ciphers, we can get an improved algorithm which can use the early-abort technique between columns, and the time and memory complexities of precomputation phase can be ignored.

To demonstrate the usefulness of our approach, we apply our tool to AES, Deoxys, Joltik and Midori. For AES, we get the searching result of the best related-key differential characteristic on 10-round AES-128 under the truncated differential form. Although the authors of [11] also get a 10-round best characteristic, they use the semi-compression form to compress the entropy and get the characteristic under semi-compression form. Then they convert the semi-compression form to truncated differential form, and get the best truncated differential characteristic. To the best of our knowledge, this is the first time one can get the 10-round best characteristic using the truncated differential form directly and the running time is short. For Deoxys [12] and Joltik [13], since they use the tweakey framework [14], the authors use the number of active S-boxes to evaluate the ciphers against related-key related-tweak attacks. However, they can only get the best 6-round related-key related-tweak differential characteristics using the depth-first algorithm. For seven and more rounds, they can only give a lower bound using the extended split approach. With the help of our tool, we get the characteristics up to 9 rounds for Deoxys-128-128/Joltik-64-64 and characteristics up to 11 rounds for Deoxys-256-128/Joltik-128-64, which are enough to reach the security goal. For Midori, we find more than one 2-round related-key cyclic characteristics with weight two, suggesting that Midori is weak under the related-key setting.

Finally, we give the ways to calculate the time and memory complexities of depth-first, breadth-first and our heuristic algorithms. Although Fouque et al. gave the way to calculate the memory complexity of the precomputation phase of the breadth-first algorithm in [11], we find that their results are too ideal and the real memory complexity is much greater. Meanwhile, they ignored the time complexity of the precomputation phase, which is much greater than the memory complexity. Since our calculation is quite general, it is meaningful for us to choose the proper parameters (e.g., $\overline{W}_{2round}$) of the algorithm to make the search feasible.

The source code of our tool is available at http://alturl.com/pocz7.

Organization of this paper. The rest of this paper is organized as follows. Section 2 gives some notations, definitions and a brief recall of the depth-first and breadth-first algorithms. Section 3 gives our automatic search tool. Sections 4, 5 and 6 give our results on AES, Deoxys/Joltik and Midori, respectively. Section 7 gives our calculation processes for depth-first, breadth-first and our heuristic algorithms. Finally, Sect. 8 concludes this paper.

2 Preliminaries

In this section, we first give some notations and definitions, then recall the depth-first algorithm and breadth-first algorithm proposed respectively in [7] and [11].

2.1 Notations and Definitions

In this paper, $W(x)$ or W_x means the number of active S-boxes of one state x, and sometimes we call it the weight of x. Since our tool works for word-oriented block ciphers, one state of these ciphers can be represented by one $N_r \times N_c$ matrix, where N_r is the number of rows and N_c is the number of columns. Let (s, k) or (S, K) denote one state/key pair, and let $S[i]$ and $K[i]$ denote the ith column of S and K, respectively. The branch number of MixColumn operation is denoted as N_{br}.

In this paper, we consider truncated differential attacks [15]. That is, for a state of differences, we only consider the presence of differences in every word, regardless of their actual values. We call the former truncated differences and the latter actual differences, and a trail of truncated differences is called truncated differential characteristic.

Definition 1 (Truncated differences). *Let $S_0 = [S_0^{i,j}]$ and $S_1 = [S_1^{i,j}]$ be two states. We denote their truncated differences by $\Delta = [\Delta^{i,j}]$ with $\Delta^{i,j} = 1$ if and only if $S_0^{i,j} \neq S_1^{i,j}$ (active), and $\Delta^{i,j} = 0$ otherwise (inactive).*

2.2 Depth-First Algorithm for Related-Key Characteristics

At EUROCRYPT 2010, Biryukov et al. gave a depth-first algorithm for finding truncated differential characteristics both in the state and in the key [7]. They introduced three variants of the algorithm for different scenarios, and we recall the first variant here. This algorithm is based on the automatic search algorithm for best differential characteristics and linear approximations under the single-key setting which is proposed by Matsui for DES [20]. This algorithm works by induction: to find the best n-round characteristic, first it finds the best $1, 2, \cdots, (n-1)$-round characteristics. Let $W_1, W_2, \cdots, W_{n-1}$ be the weights of the $1, 2, \cdots, (n-1)$-round characteristics found previously with the algorithm and let $\overline{W}_n$ be the weight of some (not necessarily optimal) n-round characteristics. Firstly, the algorithm builds all possible one round characteristics with a weight at most $\overline{W}_n - W_{n-1}$. This is for the reason that if the weight of the first round is more than $\overline{W}_n - W_{n-1}$, then it can not be extended to an n-round characteristic because the weight of $n-1$ rounds is at least W_{n-1}, so in total it will have a weight more than $\overline{W}_n$. The upper-bound for the search of the ith round is $\overline{W}_n - W_{n-(i-1)} - \sum_{j=1}^{i-1} \omega_j$, where ω_j is the weight of state/key pair of the jth round. Then n-round characteristic can be formed. Let $\Delta X \rightarrow \Delta Y$ be one round differential transition, where ΔX is the input difference in both the state and the subkey, and ΔY is the output difference. The pseudo-code is described in Algorithm 1.

Algorithm 1. Pseudo-Code for Depth-First Algorithm

1: **for all** $\{\Delta X \mid W(\Delta X) + W_{n-1} \leq \overline{W}_n\}$ **do**
2:     Call NextRound(ΔX, $W(\Delta X)$,2)
3: **end for**
4:
5: **function** NextRound(ΔX, W, r)
6:     **for all** $\{\Delta Y \mid \Delta X \rightarrow \Delta Y$ and $W(\Delta Y) + W + W_{n-r} \leq \overline{W}_n\}$ **do**
7:         **if** $r = n$ **then**
8:             Update the best characteristic
9:             $\overline{W}_n \leftarrow W + W(\Delta Y)$
10:        **else**
11:            Call NextRound(ΔY, $W + W(\Delta Y)$, $r + 1$)
12:        **end if**
13:    **end for**
14: **end function**

The advantages of this algorithm are that it can be implemented in parallel and it can output the characteristics of the best weight at the end of the algorithm. The disadvantages are that the time complexity increases exponentially with the number of rounds and there are few limits of weights in the middle rounds. We propose an algorithm to calculate the time complexity of the depth-first algorithm in Sect. 7.2.

2.3 Breadth-First Algorithm for Related-Key Characteristics

At CRYPTO 2013, Fouque et al. presented a breadth-first algorithm for the best related-key truncated differential characteristics [11]. This algorithm is made up of two phases, i.e., precomputation phase and online phase. In the precomputation phase, a graph G which contains all the possible one-round transitions need to be built. G can actually be described as a special product of two smaller graphs G_{BC} and G_{KS}, such that an edge $(s_i, k_j) \rightarrow (s_{i'}, k_{j'})$ exists in G if and only if $k_j \rightarrow k_{j'}$ exists in G_{KS} and $(s_i, k_{j'}) \rightarrow s_{i'}$ exists in G_{BC}. In the online phase, all the best r-round related-key truncated differential characteristics corresponding to all the shortest paths in the $(r + 1)$-equipartite directed acyclic graph G_r are built by concatenating r copies of G. To achieve the goal for an i-round cipher, the function to be minimized for each state/key pair ΔX is:

$$W(\Delta X) + \min_{\Delta Y \in \{x \mid x \rightarrow \Delta X\}} C(\Delta Y),$$

where $C(\Delta Y)$ represents the minimum weight to get ΔY through $i - 1$ rounds. This can be done by creating a list containing all the ΔY sorted increasingly according to the cost of their shortest path $C(\Delta Y)$. Then, starting from the cheapest ΔY and ending to the most expensive one, we set the minimum weight of all the successors ΔX of ΔY to $W(\Delta X) + C(\Delta Y)$ if and only if ΔX is not reached yet. The pseudo-code of round-i is shown in Algorithm 2.

The advantage of this algorithm is that its time complexity of online phase is linear in the number of rounds. The disadvantages are that: First of all, it needs

---

Algorithm 2. Pseudo-Code for Breadth-First Algorithm

1: **function** SEARCH$_i$(all ΔY with $C(\Delta Y)$)
2:     Sort ΔY by $C(\Delta Y)$
3:     **for all** ΔY, by increasing $C(\Delta Y)$ **do**
4:         **for all** $\Delta X \in \{x \mid \Delta Y \to x\}$ **do**
5:             $\alpha \leftarrow C(\Delta Y) + W(\Delta X)$
6:             **if** ΔX was not reached yet **then**
7:                 $C(\Delta X) \leftarrow \alpha$
8:                 Record this transition
9:             **else if** $C(\Delta X) = \alpha$ **then**
10:                 Record this transition
11:             **end if**
12:         **end for**
13:     **end for**
14: **end function**

---

to store a graph containing all the possible one-round transitions which may be too large to store; Secondly, the online phase isn't feasible to be implemented in parallel; After that, although the time complexity is linear in the number of rounds, we still need to run through all the possible edges of one-round transitions, which makes the time complexity to be still very large; Finally, we need to store a table in the online phase to retrieve the best characteristics which sometimes is even larger than the precomputation table.

Although the authors give the best related-key truncated differential characteristics on 10-round AES-128. They use the semi-compressed form instead of the truncated form to compressed the entropy and make the search available. Then they convert the semi-compression form to truncated differential form, and get the best truncated differential characteristic. However, for many other block ciphers, they don't have such a good structure as AES to compress the entropy. Therefore, we give the first searching result of AES using truncated differential form directly in Sect. 4.2.

In [11], the authors gave a way to calculate the memory complexity of G_{BC}. However, their results are too ideal and they ignore the time complexity of the precomputation phase which is even larger. We give a general way to calculate the time and memory complexities of both online phase and precomputation phase in Sect. 7.1.

3   Improved Tool for Search of Related-Key Differential Characteristics

The designers of word-oriented block ciphers often use the number of active S-boxes to evaluate the resistance against related-key differential attacks. However, the fast diffusion of encryptions and key schedules, large block and key size and small S-boxes (e.g. use 4-bit S-boxes in the 128-bit block cipher) make the search of the best characteristics almost impossible.

In this section, we describe a heuristic tool for searching related-key truncated differential characteristics. The goal of our tool is to output a good characteristic within a reasonable time and a reasonable memory, so that it can be used to evaluate the resistance against related-key differential attacks. To fulfill this goal, the algorithm must be implemented in parallel to make full use of the computational resources and we can get the characteristics to test the correctness. If we choose the depth-first algorithm as Sect. 2.2, the time complexity increases exponentially with the number of rounds and there are few limits of weights in the middle rounds. If we choose the breadth-first algorithm as Sect. 2.3, since the online phase cannot be implemented in parallel and a large maybe unreasonable memory space is needed both in the precomputation phase and online phase. To overcome the disadvantages of each algorithm, we propose a heuristic algorithm in the following section.

3.1   Tool for Related-Key Differential Characteristics

The idea of this tool comes from the observation of the propagation of related-key differential characteristics. For one cipher with good diffusion layer, the differential characteristic may include some rounds which have a lot of active S-boxes under the single-key setting (e.g., the best differential characteristic of 5-round AES which satisfies $1 \to 4 \to 16 \to 4 \to 1$). However, under the related-key setting, an AddRoundKey layer follows the diffusion layer, and the number of active words for a "bad" state after an AddRoundKey layer may decrease. Let t denote the number of active S-boxes of a two-round characteristic in an n-round "good" related-key differential characteristic and T denote the total number of active S-boxes in these two rounds, t is always small compared to T (e.g., for the 10-round best related-key differential characteristic of AES-128 in [11], the maximum number of t is 10 and $T = 40$).

Therefore, we combine the precomputation phase of breadth-first algorithm and the depth-first algorithm together to form a heuristic algorithm for the related-key differential characteristics, i.e., this algorithm is also made up of a precomputation phase and an online phase.

In the precomputation phase, we also need to build a graph $\overline{G}$ which contains some one-round transitions. The difference is that we introduce a number $\overline{W}_{2round}$, which is the upper-bound for two-round characteristics, i.e., $(s_i, k_j) \in \overline{G}$ if and only if $W(s_i, k_j) + W(s_{i'}, k_{j'}) \le \overline{W}_{2round}$. $\overline{G}$ can still be described as a special product of two smaller graphs $\overline{G}_{BC}$ and G_{KS}. Since an edge $(s_i, k_j) \to (s_{i'}, k_{j'})$ exists in $\overline{G}$ if and only if $k_j \to k_{j'}$ exists in G_{KS} and $(s_i, k_{j'}) \to s_{i'}$ exists in $\overline{G}_{BC}$, an edges $(s_i, k_{j'}) \to s_{i'}$ is in $\overline{G}_{BC}$ if $W(s_i, k_{j'}) + W(s_{i'}) + \min\{W(x) \,|\, x \to k_{j'}\} \le \overline{W}_{2round}$.

In the online phase, we use the depth-first algorithm as Sect. 2.2. However, instead of running through all $\{\Delta Y \,|\, \Delta X \to \Delta Y$ and $W(\Delta Y) + W + W_{n-r} \le \overline{W}_n\}$, we only run through the members in $\overline{G}_{BC} \times G_{KS}$ with $W(\Delta X) + W(\Delta Y) \le \overline{W}_{2round}$. The pseudo-code for this breadth-depth heuristic algorithm is shown in Algorithm 3.

For the reasonable value of $\overline{W}_{2round}$, since our goal is to construct an algorithm within reasonable time and memory, we give a relation function between $\overline{W}_{2round}$ and the time/memory complexity in Sect. 7. We can choose a proper value of $\overline{W}_{2round}$ to make the search feasible.

For the state of block cipher which can be divided into some small parts (e.g., AES-like ciphers which can be divided into columns), instead of storing G_{BC} for the whole state, we only need to store a small table for column. So we can get an improved algorithm whose memory complexity can be ignored and we can also get an improved algorithm which can use the early-abort technique between columns. The detailed description of this algorithm is given in Sect. 4.2.

Algorithm 3. Pseudo-Code for Breadth-Depth Algorithm

1: **for all** $\{(s_0, k_0) \mid W(s_0, k_0) + W_{n-1} \leq \overline{W}_n\}$ **do**
2:     Call NEXTROUND$((s_1, k_1), W(s_1, k_1), 2)$
3: **end for**
4:
5: **function** NEXTROUND$((s_{r-1}, k_{r-1}), W, r)$
6:     **for all** $\{k_r \mid (k_{r-1} \rightarrow k_r) \in G_{KS}, W(k_r) + W + W_{n-r} \leq \overline{W}_n$ and $W(s_{r-1}, k_{r-1}) + W(k_r) \leq \overline{W}_{2round}\}$ **do**
7:         **for all** $\{s_r \mid ((s_{r-1}, k_r) \rightarrow s_r) \in \overline{G}_{BC}, W(s_r, k_r) + W + W_{n-r} \leq \overline{W}_n$ and $W(s_{r-1}, k_{r-1}) + W(s_r, k_r) \leq \overline{W}_{2round}\}$ **do**
8:             **if** $r = n$ **then**
9:                 Update the best characteristic
10:                 $\overline{W}_n \leftarrow W + W(s_n, k_n)$
11:             **else**
12:                 Call NEXTROUND$((s_r, k_r), W + W(s_r, k_r), r + 1)$
13:             **end if**
14:         **end for**
15:     **end for**
16: **end function**

Next, we will give some tips for the search:

1. We sort the sets of successors in both $\overline{G}_{BC}$ and G_{KS}, so that we can perform an early-abort manner. This means that if the ith successor of one state is pruned, we don't need to go on since the following successors must be pruned.
2. For the loop of (s_0, k_0) in Algorithm 3, we should loop it from weight low to high.
3. Both the online phase and precomputation phase of this algorithm can be implemented in parallel. Suppose we have N_p processors and the number of pairs (s_1, k_1) with weight ω is $N_W(\omega)$, we should divide $N_W(\omega)$ into N_p parts and run the algorithm. After that, we can deal with weight $\omega + 1$.
4. For the value of $\overline{W}_n$, we can let the best $(n-1)$-round characteristic go forward/backward one more round, and let $\overline{W}_n$ be the best weight so far.

4   Applications to AES

4.1   Former Results of AES

In [7], Biryukov et al. gave the best related-key truncated differential characteristics on 11-round AES-192 and 14-round AES-256, but they cannot find
best related-key truncated differential characteristics on 9-round and 10-round
AES-128 since the complexity is too high. We calculate the complexity of the
depth-first algorithm in Sect. 7.2. In [11], Fouque et al. gave the best related-key
truncated differential characteristics on 10-round AES-128. They use the semi-
compressed state, i.e., store the weight of one column except for the columns
with weight one, instead of truncated state to compress the entropy of states
and make the search feasible. If they use the truncated differential characteristics directly, the complexity will make the search infeasible. In [11], the authors
also calculated the memory complexity of the precomputation phase for truncated differences. However, their calculation is too ideal, the precomputation
table is much larger than their result, and the time complexity ignored by the
authors is even larger. We show the counting process of the time complexity
and memory complexity of both the online phase and precomputation phase in
Sect. 7.1.

4.2   Improved Applications to AES-like Ciphers

In [20], Matsui described level of recursion over the 8 S-boxes of DES (i.e.,
$Round - 2 - j$), with which the probability of a partial trail is computed up to
round $r - 1$ and up to S-box j at round r, where $1 \leq j \leq 8$. Thanks to his
original proposal, we can give an improved search tool for AES-like ciphers [11].

For AES-like ciphers, the states can be divided into some small parts, called
columns. The linear layer of these ciphers consists of an operation inside one
column, called MixColumn (MC), and a simple permutation between columns.
After that, the round-key is xored into the state. We can give recursion over
columns just as Matsui.

For one column of state $S[i]$ and one column of key $K[i]$, let $RS(S[i], K[i])$
be the set of outputs of $MC(S[i]) \oplus K[i]$, and the members in this set are sorted
by their weights. Suppose $\overline{W}_{limit}$ is the upper-bound of weight of this round, we
have the following situations:

- For column-0, if it takes the j_0^{th} member of $RS(S[0], K[0])$, the search can go
  on if and only if $W(RS(S[0], K[0])[j_0]) + \sum_{t=1}^{N_c-1} W(RS(S[t], K[t])[0])$ is at
  least as good as $\overline{W}_{limit}$. Otherwise, we stop the search and go back to the
  previous round. This is for the reason that $RS(S[i], K[i])$ is sorted by the
  weight.
- For column-k, if the ith column takes the j_i^{th} member of $RS(S[i], K[i])$ for $i =
  0, \cdots, k$, the algorithm can go on if and only if $\sum_{i=0}^{k} W(RS(S[i], K[i])[j_i]) +
  \sum_{i=k+1}^{N_c-1} W(RS(S[t], K[t])[0])$ is at least as good as $\overline{W}_{limit}$. Otherwise, we stop
  the search and go back to the previous column.

– For column-$(N_c - 1)$, the algorithm can go on if and only if $\sum_{i=0}^{N_c-1} W(RS$ $(S[i], K[i])[j_i])$ is at least as good as $\overline{W}_{limit}$. Otherwise, we stop the search and go back to the previous column.

Therefore, for AES-like ciphers, instead of sorting all the possible one round transitions with weight less than $\overline{W}_{limit}$, we only need to store a small table for columns, and the time and memory complexity of precomputation phase of our tool can be ignored.

Let $\overline{W}_{2round} = 11$, the searching results of AES-128 are shown in Table 1. The numbers in this table are in hexadecimal, each hexadecimal number represents one column.

Table 1. Results of the related-key characteristics on AES-128.

Round	$\overline{W}_n$	Best weight	Time	Trail
8	23	21	12 min	$(a000, 033f) \rightarrow (0c00, fcf0) \rightarrow (0000, ff00) \rightarrow$ $(f000, f000) \rightarrow (0005, ffff) \rightarrow (0060, f0f0) \rightarrow$ $(0400, ff00) \rightarrow (0000, f000)$
9	25	23	1 min	$(1000, 0ff0) \rightarrow (0b00, 0f00) \rightarrow (0005, 0fff) \rightarrow (0060, f0f0)$ $\rightarrow (0000, ff00) \rightarrow (ff00, ff00) \rightarrow (0006, ffff) \rightarrow$ $(0040, 0ff0) \rightarrow (0000, 0f00)$
10	27	25	1 min	$(0800, 0ff0) \rightarrow (0b00, 0f00) \rightarrow (0005, 0fff) \rightarrow$ $(0060, f0f0) \rightarrow (0000, ff00) \rightarrow (f000, f000) \rightarrow$ $(0005, ffff) \rightarrow (0060, f0f0) \rightarrow (0400, ff00) \rightarrow (0000, f000)$

★: $\overline{W}_{2round} = 11$. (a, b) means that the state is a and the key is b.

5   Applications to Deoxys and Joltik

5.1   Descriptions of Deoxys and Joltik

Deoxys [12] and Joltik [13] are two families of authenticated encryption algorithms with state sizes of 128-bit and 64-bit designed by Jean et al. and are two of the 29 submissions which are chosen as the second-round candidates of CAESAR competition. The design of Deoxys and Joltik follows the TWEAKEY framework proposed by the same authors at ASIACRYPT 2014 [14]. The tweakable block cipher used in these two submissions can be represented as $E_K(T, P) = C$, where P is the plaintext, K is the key and T is the tweak. The AES-based tweakable schedule $(p = 2)$ that Deoxys-128-128 and Joltik-64-64 based on is shown in Fig. 1. For the description of Deoxys-256-128 and Joltik-128-64 $(p = 3)$, we refer to their papers. One round of Deoxys/Joltik, similar to one round of AES, has four transformations: AddRoundTweakey, SubWords, ShiftRows and MixColumn. The biggest difference between them is the AddRoundTweakey operation, which xor the round key and tweak which are produced by the tweakey schedule to the state.

The tweakey schedule can be seen in Fig. 1, where h is a permutation between words, ② means a multiplication with 2 and RC_i are the round constants.

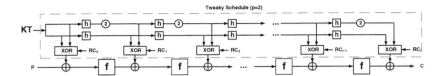

Fig. 1. Instantiation of the TWEAKEY framework for Deoxys and Joltik ($p = 2$).

5.2   Applications to Deoxys-128-128 and Joltik-64-64

In [12,13], the authors use the number of active S-boxes to evaluate the resistance against related-key related-tweak attacks. However, they can only get the best 6-round related-key related-tweak differential characteristics using the depth-first algorithm. For seven and more rounds, they can only give a lower bound using the extended split approach [10]. Also, they don't give the strategy to search this kind of characteristics since this attack scenario is quite new and the searching strategy is quite complicated.

For Deoxys-128-128 or Joltik-64-64, since the state, key and tweak are all made up of 16 words, it's impossible to run through all possible triples and get the best trail. Meanwhile, the tweakey-schedule includes a multiplication with 2, which means that for one word w_K of key and one word w_T of tweak, $w_K \oplus w_T = 0$ can only appear once during the tweakey-schedule. Suppose there are i positions where the key and tweak are both active[1], the total number of possibilities of the tweakey-schedule is $1 + \binom{i}{1}R + \cdots + \binom{i}{i}R^i = (1 + R)^i$ for an $(R+1)$-round cipher. This number is quite large for $i = 0, \cdots, 15$, and we should also limit the value since large values of i unlikely give a good characteristic.

We let $\overline{W}_{2round} = 8$, the searching results are shown in Table 2, and the characteristic of 8-round Deoxys-128-128/Joltik-64-64 is shown in Fig. 2. The characteristic in the tweakey structure is the xor of the key and tweak.

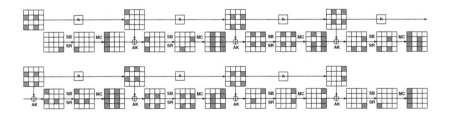

Fig. 2. Truncated differential characteristic of 8-round Deoxys-128-128/Joltik-64-64.

---

[1] For the case that the key (or the tweak) is active, it is included in the case that the key and tweak are both active.

Table 2. Results of the related-key related-tweak characteristics on Deoxys-128-128/Joltik-64-64.

Round	Weight	Time	Trail
7	16	20 min	$(0180, 0a55) \rightarrow (4228, 4298) \rightarrow (0000, f005) \rightarrow$ $(8228, 8228)$ $\rightarrow (2004, 500a) \rightarrow (1882, 1862) \rightarrow (0, 05f0)$
8	20	53 min	$(0001, 5050) \rightarrow (5000, a000) \rightarrow (0a0a, 0505) \rightarrow$ $(0105, 0a0a) \rightarrow (a020, 5050) \rightarrow (5050, a0a0) \rightarrow$ $(0208, 0505) \rightarrow (0001, 000a)$
9	23	10 min	$(0004, 5050) \rightarrow (0050, 00a0) \rightarrow (0a0a, 0505) \rightarrow$ $(0105, 0a0a) \rightarrow (a0a0, 5050) \rightarrow (1010, a0a0) \rightarrow$ $(0a0a, 0505) \rightarrow (0104, 0a0a) \rightarrow (4020, 4050)$

★: $\overline{W}_{2round} = 8$. The second number in one pair is the xor of key and tweak.

5.3 Applications to Deoxys-256-128 and Joltik-128-64

For Deoxys-256-128 and Joltik-128-64, there are three branches in the tweakey-schedule with one multiplying 2 and one multiplying 4, which means that for one word w_j of the three branch, $w_0 \oplus w_1 \oplus w_2 = 0$ can appear twice during the tweakey-schedule. The total number of possibilities is $(1 + R + \binom{R}{2}))^i$.[2]

We also let $\overline{W}_{2round} = 8$, the searching results are shown in Table 3. The characteristic in the tweakey structure is the xor of the key and tweak. The number of active S-boxes for 11-round Deoxys-256-128/Joltik-128-64 is greater than 23, which is enough to reach the security goal.

6 Applications to Midori

Midori is a lightweight block cipher designed by Banik et al. at ASIACRYPT 2015 [1] and is based on the Substitution-Permutation Network (SPN). One version of Midori uses a 64-bit state, another uses a 128-bit state and we denote these versions Midori-64 and Midori-128. Each of these versions uses a 128-bit key. In this paper, we focus on the related-key truncated differential characteristic of Midori-128 (the related-key truncated differential characteristic of Midori-128 is obviously the related-key truncated differential characteristic of Midori-64). One round of Midori-128 consists of a SubByte, a ShuffleByte, a MixColumn and an AddRoundKey operations. We refer to [1] the detailed description of Midori.

For Midori-128, we find more than one 2-round related-key cyclic characteristics with weight 2, and we show one example in Fig. 3. Therefore, Midori is weak under the related-key setting.

---

[2] (1) All active: 1; (2) One inactive word: R; (3) Two inactive words: $\binom{R}{2}$.

Table 3. Results of the related-key related-tweak characteristics on Deoxys-256-128/Joltik-128-64.

Round	Weight	Time	Trail
7	12	2 h	$(2000, 1c43) \rightarrow (0000, 00f0) \rightarrow (4411, 4411) \rightarrow (1002, a005)$ $\rightarrow (4418, 4318) \rightarrow (0000, f00a) \rightarrow (1000, 1000)$
8	15	8 h	$(8000, 70d8) \rightarrow (5000, b000) \rightarrow (0822, 072d) \rightarrow (a000, 5e00) \rightarrow (2880, d870) \rightarrow (0a00, 00b0) \rightarrow (0208, 0d07) \rightarrow (0000, 000e)$
9	18	10 h	$(8080, 5e0a) \rightarrow (2880, d870) \rightarrow (0a00, 05b0) \rightarrow (2208, 2d07) \rightarrow (00a0, 005e) \rightarrow (8020, 70d0) \rightarrow (5000, b000) \rightarrow (0802, 070d) \rightarrow (0000, 0e00)$
10	21	12 h	$(0100, 1c43) \rightarrow (0000, 00f0) \rightarrow (4411, 4411) \rightarrow (1002, a005) \rightarrow (4418, 4318)$ $\rightarrow (0000, f00a) \rightarrow (1144, 1144) \rightarrow (0840, 05a0) \rightarrow (1142, 1c42) \rightarrow (0000, 0af0)$

★: $\overline{W}_{2round} = 8$. The second number in one pair is the xor of key and tweak.

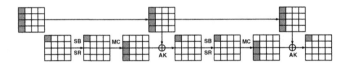

Fig. 3. Two-round related-key cyclic characteristic of Midori-128.

7   Evaluating the Complexity

In [11], Fouque et al. gave a way to evaluate the average branch number of nodes/edges of G_{BC} and G_{KS}. In this section, we generalize their model and evaluate the time complexity of breadth-first, depth-first and our breadth-depth algorithms. We use the number of edges the algorithm goes through to evaluate the time complexity. We take the SPN block cipher, i.e., the cipher consists with an S-box substitute layer, a permutation layer and an AddRoundKey layer, of size $N_r \times N_c$ as an example. The permutation layer is made up of a permutation between words and N_c MixColumn operations on each column using a finite-field multiplication as $S[i] \leftarrow M \cdot S[i]$, where M means a $N_r \times N_c$ matrix. Since the permutation (e.g., ShiftRow of AES) doesn't change the number of active S-boxes, we start with a state after this operation. The branch number of M is N_{br}. The size of the intermediate state and the size of the key are the same. The source code of this section is also available at http://alturl.com/pocz7.

7.1   Evaluating the Complexity for Breadth-First Algorithm

We evaluate the time complexity[3] and memory complexity of this algorithm here. Since we consider all keys and intermediate states, we can ignore the permutation operation.

Theorem 1. *For one column difference c_i with $W_{c_i} = W(c_i)$, the time complexity for all key differences xor c_i is $f_{xor}(W_{c_i}) = 2^{N_r - W_{c_i}} \times 3^{W_{c_i}}$.*

Proof. Let $p_0, \cdots, p_{W_{c_i}}$ denote the bit positions of c_i which are active. Let $2^{N_r - W_{c_i}}$ keys which are equal in positions $p_0, \cdots, p_{W_{c_i}}$ and take all different values in the other positions be a cluster. The number of clusters which have i active bits among $p_0, \cdots, p_{W_{c_i}}$ is $\binom{W_{c_i}}{i}$, where $i \leq W_{c_i}$. Let k be one key in a cluster which has i active bits among $p_0, \cdots, p_{W_{c_i}}$, number of output states after $k \oplus c_i$ is 2^i.

Therefore, the time complexity for all keys xor c_i is $2^{N_r - W_{c_i}} \times \sum_{i=0}^{W_{c_i}} \binom{W_{c_i}}{i} \cdot 2^i = 2^{N_r - W_{c_i}} \cdot (1+2)^{W_{c_i}} = 2^{N_r - W_{c_i}} \cdot 3^{W_{c_i}}$. $\qquad\square$

Theorem 2. *The time complexity of the precomputation phase of breadth-first algorithm is $\sum_{i_1=0}^{N_r} \cdots \sum_{i_{N_c}=0}^{N_r} \prod_{j=1}^{N_c} \binom{N_r}{i_j} f_{mc/xor}(i_j)$ and the memory complexity of G_{BC} is $\sum_{i_1=0}^{N_r} \sum_{i_2=0}^{N_r} \cdots \sum_{i_{2*N_c}=0}^{N_r} \prod_{j=1}^{N_c} \binom{N_r}{i_{2*j}} \binom{N_r}{i_{2*j-1}} M_{off}(i_{2*j}, i_{2*j-1})$, where*

$$f_{mc/xor}(W_{c_i}) = \begin{cases} \sum_{i=N_{br}-W_{c_i}}^{N_r} \binom{N_r}{i} f_{xor}(i), & if \ W_{c_i} < N_{br} - 1 \\ \sum_{i=1}^{N_r} \binom{N_r}{i} f_{xor}(i), & if \ W_{c_i} \geq N_{br} - 1 \end{cases}$$

and

$$M_{off}(W_{c_s}, W_{c_k}) = \begin{cases} 1, & if \ W_{c_s} = 0 \\ N_{br} - W_{c_s}, & if \ W_{c_k} = 0 \\ 2^{W_{c_k}} + \sum_{i=1}^{N_r - (N_{br} - W_{c_s})} \binom{N_r - W_{c_k}}{i} & if \ W_{c_s} \neq 0 \end{cases}$$

Proof. For the time complexity, if the weight of one column c_i is W_{c_i} and the branch number of MixColumn operation is N_{br}, the number of states after Mix-Column and AddRoundKey layer is:

$$f_{mc/xor}(W_{c_i}) = \begin{cases} \sum_{i=N_{br}-W_{c_i}}^{N_r} \binom{N_r}{i} f_{xor}(i), & if \ W_{c_i} < N_{br} - 1 \\ \sum_{i=1}^{N_r} \binom{N_r}{i} f_{xor}(i), & if \ W_{c_i} \geq N_{br} - 1 \end{cases}$$

Therefore, the time complexity of the precomputation phase of breadth-first algorithm is $\sum_{i=0}^{2^{N_r N_c} - 1} \prod_{j=0}^{N_c - 1} f_{mc/xor}(W((i \gg (j \times N_r)) \& (2^{N_r} - 1)))$, i.e., $\sum_{i_1=0}^{N_r} \cdots \sum_{i_{N_c}=0}^{N_r} \prod_{j=1}^{N_c} \binom{N_r}{i_j} f_{mc/xor}(i_j)$.

For the memory complexity, since for one column of state/key pair (c_s, c_k), we have the following three situations:

---

[3] In [11], the authors did not give the time complexity of this phase. Since we cannot know whether the output state already exists in G_{BC} in advance, we cannot ignore it.

1. If $W_{c_s} = 0$, the number of states after MixColumn and AddRoundKey layers is 1.
2. If $W_{c_k} = 0$, the number of states after MixColumn and AddRoundKey layers is $N_{br} - W_{c_s}$.
3. Otherwise, since $W_{c_s} \neq 0$, the outputs of MixColumn must include one column like $11 \cdots 1$, and the number of $11 \cdots 1 \oplus c_k$ is $2^{W_{c_k}}$. For other MixColumn outputs, states after MixColumn and AddRoundKey layers that are not in $11 \cdots 1 \oplus c_k$ are states with 0 in the positions which are 1 in c_k, so the extra number is $\sum_{i=1}^{N_r - (N_{br} - W_{c_s})} \binom{N_r - W_{c_k}}{i}$.

We use $M_{off}(W_{c_s}, W_{c_k})$ to denote the above situations, i.e.,

$$
M_{off}(W_{c_s}, W_{c_k}) = \begin{cases} 1, & if\ W_{c_s} = 0 \\ N_{br} - W_{c_s}, & if\ W_{c_k} = 0 \\ 2^{W_{c_k}} + \sum_{i=1}^{N_r - (N_{br} - W_{c_s})} \binom{N_r - W_{c_k}}{i} & if\ W_{c_s} \neq 0 \end{cases}
$$

Therefore, the memory complexity of the precomputation phase of breadth-first algorithm is $\sum_{i=0}^{2^{N_r N_c}} \sum_{j=0}^{2^{N_r N_c}} \prod_{k=0}^{N_c-1} M_{off}(W((i \gg (k \times N_r))\&(2^{N_r} - 1)), W((j \gg (k \times N_r))\&(2^{N_r} - 1)))$, i.e.,

$$
\sum_{i_1=0}^{N_r} \sum_{i_2=0}^{N_r} \cdots \sum_{i_{2*N_c}=0}^{N_r} \prod_{j=1}^{N_c} \binom{N_r}{i_{2*j}} \binom{N_r}{i_{2*j-1}} M_{off}(i_{2*j}, i_{2*j-1}). \tag{1}
$$

□

For AES-128, the time complexity of the precomputation phase is $2^{48.9}$, the memory complexity is $2^{42.8}$, which is much larger than [11].

Theorem 3. *The time complexity of the online phase of breadth-first algorithm is* $O(\sum_{s=0}^{2^{N_r N_c}} \sum_{k=0}^{2^{N_r N_c}} T_{on}(s, k))$, *where* $T_{on}(s, k) = \sum_{\tilde{k} \in \mathbb{KS}_k} \prod_{i=0}^{N_c-1} \prod_{j=0}^{N_c-1} M_{off}(W((s \gg (i \times N_r))\&(2^{N_r} - 1)), W((\tilde{k} \gg (j \times N_r))\&(2^{N_r} - 1)))$ *and* $\mathbb{KS}_k$ *denotes the set that one key* k *can get after one key-schedule.*

Proof. For one state/key pair (s, k), the number of edges that it needs to go through is $T_{on}(s, k) = \sum_{\tilde{k} \in \mathbb{KS}_k} \prod_{i=0}^{N_c-1} M_{off}(W((s \gg (i \times N_r))\&(2^{N_r} - 1)), W((\tilde{k} \gg (i \times N_r))\&(2^{N_r} - 1)))$. Therefore, the time complexity of the online phase is $\sum_{s=0}^{2^{N_r N_c}-1} \sum_{k=0}^{2^{N_r N_c}-1} T_{on}(s, k)$.

For an R-round block cipher, the time complexity is $O(\sum_{s=0}^{2^{N_r N_c}} \sum_{k=0}^{2^{N_r N_c}} T_{on}(s, k))$. □

For AES-128, the time complexity of online-phase is $O(2^{48.6})$. Both the time complexity and memory complexity of AES-128 are quite large, and it's almost impossible to implement it in reality.

7.2 Evaluating the Complexity for Depth-First Algorithm

Suppose we want to find n-round best related-key differential characteristic, since $W_1, \cdots, W_{n-1}$ are the weights of the best $1, \cdots, (n-1)$-round characteristics and $\overline{W}_n$ is the upper-bound of W_n, the upper-bound for the search of the ith round is $\overline{W}_n - W_{n-(i-1)} - \sum_{j=1}^{i-1} \omega_j$, where ω_j is the weight of state/key pair of the jth round .

For one state/key pair with weight W_I, we need to calculate the average number of states it can propagate to with weight W_O. For one column of state/key pair (c_s, c_k), let $T_{coldepth}(c_s, c_k, t)$ denote the number of columns $MC(c_s) \oplus c_k$ with weight t. For one state/key pair (s, k) with weight W_I, we can get the number of state/key pairs (s, k) can propagate to with weight W_O with the help of $T_{coldepth}(c_s, c_k, t)$ and $\mathbb{KS}_k$. Therefore, we can run through all the state/key pairs (s, k) with weight W_I, and get the number of state/key pairs they can propagate to with weight W_O. We use $T_{depth}(W_I, W_O)$ to denote the number of state/key pairs from weight W_I to weight W_O. For AES-128, we list parts of the results of $T_{depth}(W_I, W_O)$ in Table 4. Let $N_W(t)$ denote the number of state/key pairs with weight t, then the average number of output pairs with weight W_O for one input pair with weight W_I is $Aver(W_I, W_O) = \frac{T_{depth}(W_I, W_O)}{N_W(W_I)}$.

After getting $T_{depth}(W_I, W_O)$, we have the following situations:

1. For the first round, the nodes which can reach the second round must satisfy that their weights cannot be greater than $\overline{W}_n - W_{n-1}$.
2. For the second round, the nodes which can reach the third round must satisfy that their weights cannot be greater than $\overline{W}_n - W_{n-2} - \omega_1$. For one ω_1, the number of output pairs of this round with weight ω_2 is $T_{depth}(\omega_1, \omega_2)$.
3. For round-i with $2 < i < n$, the nodes which can reach round-$(i+1)$ must satisfy that their weights cannot be greater than $\overline{W}_n - W_{n-i} - \sum_{j=1}^{i-1} \omega_j$. Suppose the number of pairs with weight ω_{i-1} for this round is $N_W(\omega_{i-1})$, the number of output pairs of this round with weight ω_i is $Aver(\omega_{i-1}, \omega_i) \times N_W(\omega_{i-1})$ in average.
4. For round-n, suppose the input weight of this round is ω_{n-1} and the number is $N_W(\omega_{n-1})$, the time complexity of this round is the average number of nodes these nodes can propagate to, i.e., $N_W(\omega_{n-1}) \times \sum_{i=0}^{W_{total}} Aver(\omega_{n-1}, i)$, where W_{total} is the maximum weight of one pair.

For an R-round block cipher with $R \geq 4$, the time complexity of the depth-first algorithm is

$$\sum_{\omega_1=0}^{\overline{W}_n - W_{n-1}} \cdots \sum_{\omega_i=0}^{\overline{W}_n - W_{n-i} - \sum_{j=1}^{i-1} \omega_j} \cdots \sum_{\omega_n=0}^{W_{total}} T_{depth}(\omega_1, \omega_2) \cdots Aver(\omega_{i-1}, \omega_i) \tag{2}$$
$$\cdots Aver(\omega_{n-1}, \omega_n).$$

For 10-round AES-128 with $\overline{W}_{10} = 25$, the time complexity of this algorithm is more than 2^{39}. Since we only calculate the average number in the middle rounds, this is a lower bound. It's impossible for us to get the best weight for 10-round AES-128 using the original tool of [7] in reality.

Table 4. Table of $T_{depth}(W_i, W_o)$ with $W_i \leq 10$ and $W_o \leq 10$.

W_O	W_I										
	0	1	2	3	4	5	6	7	8	9	10
0	0.0	3.0	5.0	6.4	7.4	8.3	9.2	9.9	10.4	10.8	11.2
1	3.0	7.0	9.8	11.8	13.1	14.1	15.0	15.9	16.6	17.2	17.8
2	8.3	12.0	14.5	16.3	17.7	18.8	19.8	20.7	21.6	22.5	23.4
3	11.2	15.1	17.8	19.7	21.2	22.5	23.7	24.9	26.2	27.4	28.5
4	13.0	17.1	20.0	22.2	24.0	25.6	27.2	28.9	30.5	31.9	33.1
5	13.7	18.1	21.5	24.2	26.5	28.7	30.8	32.7	34.5	35.9	37.1
6	13.7	19.9	23.9	27.0	29.6	31.9	34.1	36.1	37.9	39.3	40.5
7	19.6	23.9	27.3	30.0	32.5	34.8	37.0	39.0	40.8	42.2	43.3
8	22.4	26.6	29.8	32.4	34.8	37.2	39.4	41.5	43.2	44.6	45.7
9	24.1	28.3	31.4	34.1	36.6	39.1	41.5	43.5	45.2	46.6	47.7
10	24.8	29.0	32.3	35.2	38.1	40.7	43.1	45.1	46.8	48.2	49.2

★: The numbers in this table are after log base 2.

7.3   Time Complexity of Breadth-Depth Algorithm

The method to calculate the time complexity of our breadth-depth Algorithm is almost the same as the depth-first algorithm in Eq. 2, the only difference is that for round-i, the upper-bound of the maximum weight is $min(\overline{W}_n - W_{n-i} - \sum_{j=1}^{i-1} \omega_j, \overline{W}_{2round} - \omega_{i-1})$. We can use this formula to choose the reasonable value of $\overline{W}_{2round}$. The memory complexity of our tool is almost the same as the memory complexity of Theorem 2. The only difference is that we should restrain the values of $i_1, \cdots, i_{2*N_c}$ and M_{off} to make sure the weight is lower than the two-round limit.

Since we can use the column-pruning method described in Sect. 4.2, the time complexity is much less than the equation for AES-128. Choose $\overline{W}_n = 27$ and $\overline{W}_{2round} = 11$, we can get the best trail within one minute using our tool.

8   Conclusions

In this paper, we gave a heuristic tool to search for the related-key truncated differential characteristics based on the precomputation phase of the breadth-first algorithm and the depth-first algorithm. The goal of our tool is to output a good characteristic within a reasonable time complexity and a reasonable memory complexity. Then, we applied our tool to AES, Deoxys, Joltik and Midori, and found some results that cannot be got using the original tools. Finally, we gave a way to calculate the time and memory complexities of the depth-first, breadth-first and our algorithms, which is meaningful for us to choose the proper parameters of the algorithm to make the search feasible.

Acknowledgments. We would like to thank anonymous referees for their helpful comments and suggestions. The research presented in this paper is supported by the National Natural Science Foundation of China (No. 61672509 and 61232009), National Cryptography Development Foundation of China (No. MMJJ20170101) and National Basic Research Program of China (No. 2013CB338002).

References

1. Banik, S., Bogdanov, A., Isobe, T., Shibutani, K., Hiwatari, H., Akishita, T., Regazzoni, F.: Midori: A Block Cipher for Low Energy (Extended Version). Cryptology ePrint Archive, Report 2015/1142 (2015), http://eprint.iacr.org/
2. Biham, E.: New types of cryptanalytic attacks using related keys. J. Crypto. **7**(4), 229–246 (1994)
3. Biham, E., Shamir, A.: Differential cryptanalysis of DES-like cryptosystems. J. Crypto. **4**(1), 3–72 (1991)
4. Biryukov, A.: Impossible differential attack. In: Encyclopedia of Cryptography and Security, p. 597. Springer, US (2011)
5. Biryukov, A., Khovratovich, D.: Related-key cryptanalysis of the full AES-192 and AES-256. In: Matsui, M. (ed.) ASIACRYPT 2009. LNCS, vol. 5912, pp. 1–18. Springer, Heidelberg (2009). doi:10.1007/978-3-642-10366-7_1
6. Biryukov, A., Khovratovich, D., Nikolić, I.: Distinguisher and related-key attack on the full AES-256. In: Halevi, S. (ed.) CRYPTO 2009. LNCS, vol. 5677, pp. 231–249. Springer, Heidelberg (2009). doi:10.1007/978-3-642-03356-8_14
7. Biryukov, A., Nikolić, I.: Automatic search for related-key differential characteristics in byte-oriented block ciphers: application to AES, Camellia, Khazad and Others. In: Gilbert, H. (ed.) EUROCRYPT 2010. LNCS, vol. 6110, pp. 322–344. Springer, Heidelberg (2010). doi:10.1007/978-3-642-13190-5_17
8. Daemen, J., Rijmen, V.: The Design of Rijndael: AES-the Advanced Encryption Standard. Springer, Heidelberg (2002)
9. Derbez, P., Fouque, P.-A., Jean, J.: Improved key recovery attacks on reduced-round AES in the single-key setting. In: Johansson, T., Nguyen, P.Q. (eds.) EUROCRYPT 2013. LNCS, vol. 7881, pp. 371–387. Springer, Heidelberg (2013). doi:10.1007/978-3-642-38348-9_23
10. Emami, S., Ling, S., Nikolić, I., Pieprzyk, J., Wang, H.: The resistance of PRESENT-80 against related-key differential attacks. Crypt. Commun. **6**(3), 171–187 (2014)
11. Fouque, P.-A., Jean, J., Peyrin, T.: Structural evaluation of AES and chosen-key distinguisher of 9-round AES-128. In: Canetti, R., Garay, J.A. (eds.) CRYPTO 2013. LNCS, vol. 8042, pp. 183–203. Springer, Heidelberg (2013). doi:10.1007/978-3-642-40041-4_11
12. Jean, J., Nikolić, I., Peyrin, T.: Deoxys v1. Submitted to the CAESAR Competition (2014)
13. Jean, J., Nikolić, I., Peyrin, T.: Joltik v1. Submitted to the CAESAR Competition (2014)
14. Jean, J., Nikolić, I., Peyrin, T.: Tweaks and keys for block ciphers: the TWEAKEY framework. In: Sarkar, P., Iwata, T. (eds.) ASIACRYPT 2014. LNCS, vol. 8874, pp. 274–288. Springer, Heidelberg (2014). doi:10.1007/978-3-662-45608-8_15
15. Knudsen, L.R.: Truncated and higher order differentials. In: Preneel, B. (ed.) FSE 1994. LNCS, vol. 1008, pp. 196–211. Springer, Heidelberg (1995). doi:10.1007/3-540-60590-8_16

16. Knudsen, L.R., Rijmen, V.: Known-key distinguishers for some block ciphers. In: Kurosawa, K. (ed.) ASIACRYPT 2007. LNCS, vol. 4833, pp. 315–324. Springer, Heidelberg (2007). doi:10.1007/978-3-540-76900-2_19
17. Ko, Y., Hong, S., Lee, W., Lee, S., Kang, J.-S.: Related key differential attacks on 27 rounds of XTEA and full-round GOST. In: Roy, B., Meier, W. (eds.) FSE 2004. LNCS, vol. 3017, pp. 299–316. Springer, Heidelberg (2004). doi:10.1007/978-3-540-25937-4_19
18. Li, L., Jia, K., Wang, X.: Improved single-key attacks on 9-Round AES-192/256. In: Cid, C., Rechberger, C. (eds.) FSE 2014. LNCS, vol. 8540, pp. 127–146. Springer, Heidelberg (2015). doi:10.1007/978-3-662-46706-0_7
19. Li, R., Jin, C.: Meet-in-the-middle attacks on 10-round AES-256. Des. Codes Cryptogr., 1–13 (2015)
20. Matsui, M.: On correlation between the order of S-boxes and the strength of DES. In: De Santis, A. (ed.) EUROCRYPT 1994. LNCS, vol. 950, pp. 366–375. Springer, Heidelberg (1995). doi:10.1007/BFb0053451
21. Wagner, D.: The boomerang attack. In: Knudsen, L. (ed.) FSE 1999. LNCS, vol. 1636, pp. 156–170. Springer, Heidelberg (1999). doi:10.1007/3-540-48519-8_12

Post-quantum Cryptography

Choosing Parameters for the Subfield Lattice Attack Against Overstretched NTRU

Dung Hoang Duong[1,2]($\boxtimes$), Masaya Yasuda[1,2], and Tsuyoshi Takagi[1,2]

[1] Institute of Mathematics for Industry, Kyushu University,
744 Motooka Nishi-ku, Fukuoka 819-0395, Japan
{duong,yasuda,takagi}@imi.kyushu-u.ac.jp
[2] JST, CREST, 4-1-8 Honcho, Kawaguchi, Saitama 332-0012, Japan

Abstract. Albrecht et al. [1] at Crypto 2016 and Cheon et al. [4] at ANTS 2016 independently presented a subfield attack on overstretched NTRU problem. Their idea is to map the public key down to the subfield (by norm and trace map respectively) and hence obtain a lattice of smaller dimension for which a lattice reduction algorithm is efficiently applicable. At Eurocrypt 2017, Kirchner and Fouque proposed another variant attack which exploits the presence of orthogonal bases within the cyclotomic number rings and instead of using the matrix of the public key in the subfield, they use the multiplication matrix by the public key in the full field and apply a lattice reduction algorithm to a suitable projected lattice of smaller dimension. They also showed a tight estimation of the parameters broken by lattice reduction and implementation results that their attack is better than the subfield attack.

In this paper, we exploit technical results from Kirchner and Fouque [12] for the relative norm of field elements in the subfield and we use Hermite factor for estimating the output of a lattice basis reduction algorithm in order to analyze general choice of parameters for the subfield attack by Albrecht et al. [1]. As a result, we obtain the estimation for better choices of the subfields for which the attack works with smaller modulus. Our experiment results show that we can attack overstretched NTRU with modulus smaller than that of Albrecht et al. and of Kirchner and Fouque.

1 Introduction

The NTRU encryption scheme is one of the first cryptosystems based on lattices proposed in 1998 by Hoffstein, Pipher and Silverman [11]. Up to present, NTRUEncrypt remains secure and is considered as one of the fastest post-quantum public key encryption schemes. The NTRU assumption is that, given the quotient ring $R = \mathbb{Z}[x]/(\phi(x))$ where $\phi(x)$ is a polynomial of degree n and q a positive integer, finding a "short" element in

$$\Lambda_h^q = \{(x,y) \in R^2 \mid hx = y \bmod q\}$$

is hard. Here h is the public polynomial in $R_q = \mathbb{Z}_q[x]/(\phi(x))$ which is of the form $h = gf^{-1} \bmod q$, where f and g are sampled from R such that they have

© Springer International Publishing AG 2017
P.Q. Nguyen and J. Zhou (Eds.): ISC 2017, LNCS 10599, pp. 79–91, 2017.
https://doi.org/10.1007/978-3-319-69659-1_5

small coefficient norms and f is invertible modulo q. In the original proposal [11], the authors used R to be the convolution ring $\mathbb{Z}[x]/(x^n - 1)$ and the coefficients of f and g are normally taken from the set $\{-1, 0, 1\}$. Even though there is no efficient attack against NTRUEncrypt, there is no security reduction to a hard mathematical problem; see [10] for current updates on the security of classical NTRUEncrypt. It is later recommended by Lyubashevsky and Micciancio [14] to replace the polynomial $x^n - 1$ by the cyclotomic polynomial $x^n + 1$ with n a power of 2, based on which they constructed a hash function proven collision-resistant under the assumed hardness of worse-case lattice problem over ideal lattices. Stehlé and Steinfeld used the polynomial $x^n + 1$ and defined a variant of NTRUEncrypt. They showed that if f and g are sampled from a Gaussian distribution with wide enough standard deviation, then NTRUEncrypt is proven to be secure under the hardness of lattice problems in ideal lattices; see [15] for more details. In this paper, we consider only the cyclotomic number ring $R = \mathbb{Z}[x]/(x^n + 1)$ where n is a power of 2.

Coppersmith and Shamir [6] showed that in order to break an NTRU cryptosystem, it suffices to find a short multiple of the secret key (f, g). The goal of the attack against NTRU problem then is to find a short enough vector in Λ_h^q, which is corresponding to an integral lattice of dimension $2n$; such a short vector will be a short multiple of the secret key (f, g) (see Theorem 8).

Albrecht et al. [1] and Cheon et al. [4] independently at Crypto 2016 and ANTS 2016 proposed a subfield attack on NTRU. Their idea, attributed to Gentry, Szydlo, Jonsson, Nguyen and Stern [9], is to exploit the presence of a subfield $\mathbb{L}$ in the cyclotomic number field $\mathbb{K} = \mathbb{Q}[x]/(x^n + 1)$. They then map the public key h down to the subfield $\mathbb{L}$ using the relative norm and trace map respectively. The obtained element h' in the subfield $\mathbb{L}$ gives rise to the NTRU problem with the associated lattice $\Lambda_{h'}^q$ of dimension much smaller than Λ_h^q. A solution for this NTRU problem in $\mathbb{L}$ will later be lift to a solution for the NTRU problem in the full field $\mathbb{K}$, and hence solves NTRU problem with large (overstretched) modulus q. At Eurocrypt 2017, Kirchner and Fouque [12] proposed a variant of the attack and claim that their attack is more efficient than that of Albrecht et al.'s and Cheon et al.'s. Their idea is to exploit the presence of orthogonal basis within the cyclotomic number ring and hence instead of mapping the public key down to the subfield, they use the projected lattices to the subring corresponding to the subfield. Their implementation results show that their attack is applicable with smaller modulus q compared to the subfield attack by Albrecht et al. The aforementioned attacks [1,4,12] against overstretched NTRU problem then can break several instances of NTRU-based cryptosystems, such as multilinear maps GGH13 [8], and fully homomorphic encryption LTV [13] and YASHE [3].

Our contribution. In this paper, we use tighter bound for norms of elements in the corresponding subfield from Kirchner and Fouque [12] and use the Hermite factor for approximating the output of a lattice reduction algorithm (e.g., LLL) to analyze the subfield attack by Albrecht et al. [1]. As a result, we derive better choice for the subfield for which the attack is applicable with smaller modulus q.

Our implementation results support our theoretical estimation for the choice of the subfield (see Table 1):

- For the same $n = 2^{11}$, with the choice of subfield $\mathbb{L}$ such that $|\mathbb{K} : \mathbb{L}| = 4$ while Albrecht et al. (cf. Table 5 in [1]) chose $\mathbb{L}$ such that $|\mathbb{K} : \mathbb{L}| = 8$, we can break the NTRU problem with $\log(q) = 72$ while Albrecht et al. succeeded with $\log(q) = 95$; it is a tradeoff that we have to work on a higher dimension lattice. Our succeeded modulus $\log(q) = 72$ for $n = 2^{11}$ is close to $\log(q) = 70$ of Kirchner and Fouque which is the smallest succeeded modulus and both have the same choice for the subfield to attack.
- For $n = 2^{12}$, with the choice of subfield $\mathbb{L}$ such that $|\mathbb{K} : \mathbb{L}| = 8$ while Albrecht et al. (cf. Table 6 in [1]) chose $\mathbb{L}$ such that $|\mathbb{K} : \mathbb{L}| = 16$ (same as Kirchner and Fouque), we can break the NTRU problem with $\log(q) = 135$ while Albrecht et al. succeeded with $\log(q) = 190$. Our succeeded modulus $\log(q) = 120$ for $n = 2^{12}$ is better than $\log(q) = 144$ of Kirchner and Fouque.

What we notice from experimental results of Kirchner and Fouque is that, although their method succeeded with small modulus q, it does not guarantee the success of larger modulus, whereas the subfield attack yields the exact limit of success, like in our and Albrecht et al.'s experiments.

2 Preliminaries

Let n be a 2-power number and $m = 2n$. Let $\mathbb{K} = \mathbb{Q}[x]/(x^n+1)$ be the cyclotomic number field. Let $\mathbb{L}$ be the subfield of $\mathbb{K}$ of degree n' with $n = rn'$. Let G be the Galois group of $\mathbb{K}$ over $\mathbb{Q}$ and H the subgroup of G fixing $\mathbb{L}$. Let $R = \mathcal{O}_{\mathbb{K}} = \mathbb{Z}[x]/(x^n+1)$ be the ring of integers of $\mathbb{K}$. Define the relative norm $N_{\mathbb{K}/\mathbb{L}} : \mathbb{K} \to \mathbb{L}$ by

$$N_{\mathbb{K}/\mathbb{L}}(a) = \prod_{\psi \in H} \psi(a).$$

and denote $L : \mathbb{L} \hookrightarrow \mathbb{K}$ be the canonical inclusion.

The number field $\mathbb{K}$ (or $\mathbb{L}$) is viewed as a Euclidean $\mathbb{Q}$-vector space by endowing with the inner product

$$\langle a, b \rangle = \sum_e e(a)\bar{e}(b),$$

where e ranges over all the n (or n') embeddings $e : \mathbb{K} \to \mathbb{C}$ and $\bar{e}$ its complex conjugate. This defines a Euclidean norm denoted by $\|.\|$. Define the operator norm $|.|$ as

$$|a| = \sup_{x \in \mathbb{K}^*} \frac{\|ax\|}{\|x\|}.$$

It is easy to check that $|a|$ is equal to $\max_e |e(a)|$, the maximal absolute complex embedding of a, and that $\|L(a)\|^2 = r\|a\|^2$, $|L(a)| = |a|$. Moreover for any $a \in \mathbb{K}$, one has

$$|a| \leq \|a\| \leq \sqrt{n} \cdot |a|,$$

and using the inequality of arithmetic and geometric means yields

$$|N_{K/\mathbb{Q}}(a)| \le \left(\frac{\|a\|}{\sqrt{n}}\right)^n. \tag{1}$$

The discriminant of the number field $\mathbb{K}$ is denoted by $\Delta_{\mathbb{K}}$. One has that $\sqrt{|\Delta_{\mathbb{K}}|} = \mathrm{Vol}(\mathcal{O}_{\mathbb{K}})$ and

$$\mathrm{Vol}(a\mathcal{O}_{\mathbb{K}}) = |N_{K/\mathbb{Q}}(a)| \cdot \sqrt{|\Delta_{\mathbb{K}}|}.$$

Lemma 1 ([12, Lemma 1]). *Let $M \subseteq \mathbb{K}^d$ be a discrete $\mathcal{O}_{\mathbb{K}}$-module of rank 1. Then for any $0 \ne v \in M$, one has*

$$\mathrm{Vol}(M) \le \left(\frac{\|v\|}{\sqrt{n}}\right)^n \cdot \sqrt{|\Delta_{\mathbb{K}}|}.$$

Proof. Since the rank of M is 1, one can build a $\mathbb{K}$-linear isometry from $\mathbb{R} \otimes M$ to $\mathbb{K} \otimes \mathbb{R}$. Hence we can assume that $d = 1$. Let v be a non-zero vector in M, then $v\mathcal{O}_{\mathbb{K}} \subseteq M$, which implies

$$\mathrm{Vol}(M) \le \mathrm{Vol}(v\mathcal{O}_{\mathbb{K}}) = N_{K/\mathbb{Q}}(v) \cdot \sqrt{|\Delta_{\mathbb{K}}|} \le \left(\frac{\|v\|}{\sqrt{n}}\right)^n \cdot \sqrt{|\Delta_{\mathbb{K}}|},$$

where the last inequality follows from (1). □

Definition 2 (Gaussian Distribution). *Given $s > 0$, the discrete Gaussian distribution over the lattice $\mathcal{L}$ with zero mean is defined as $\mathcal{D}_{\mathcal{L},s}(x) = \rho_s(x)/\rho_s(\mathcal{L})$ for any $x \in L$, where $\rho_s(x) = \exp(-\pi\|x\|^2/s^2), \rho_s(\mathcal{L}) = \sum_{x \in \mathcal{L}} \rho_s(x)$.*

Lemma 3. *For any lattice $\mathcal{L}$, any $t \ge 1$, then*

$$\mathrm{Pr}_{x \leftarrow \mathcal{D}_{\mathcal{L},s}}\left[\|\mathbf{x}\| > st\sqrt{\frac{n}{2\pi}}\right] < \exp(-n(t-1)^2/2).$$

It follows from Lemma 3 (by taking $t = \sqrt{2\pi}$) that $\|x\| \le s\sqrt{n}$ with high probability.

Definition 4 (NTRU Problem). *Given a ring $R = \mathbb{Z}[x]/(x^n + 1)$ as above, a modulus q, a distribution $\mathcal{D}$ on R, and a target norm B. The NTRU problem is defined as the following: given $h = [gf^{-1}]_q$ where f, g are sampled from $\mathcal{D}$ (with the condition that f is invertible modulo q), find a vector $(x, y) \in R^2$ such that $(x, y) \ne (0, 0) \mod q$ and of Euclidean norm less than B in the lattice*

$$\Lambda_h^q = \{(x, y) \in R^2 : hx - y = 0 \mod q\}.$$

One can express a basis $\mathbf{B}$ for Λ_h^q as follows

$$\mathbf{B} = \begin{pmatrix} q\mathbf{I}_n & \mathbf{h} \\ 0 & \mathbf{I}_n \end{pmatrix} \tag{2}$$

where $\mathbf{I}_n$ is the identity matrix of degree n and $\mathbf{h}$ stands for an $n \times n$ matrix whose i-th column is the coefficient vector of the polynomial $x^{i-1} \cdot \mathbf{h} \mod x^n + 1$.

Remark 5. *Coppersmith and Shamir [6] showed that recovering short enough vectors may be sufficient; the NTRU Problem is essentially to recover the secret key (f, g). Hence, in order to attack the NTRU problem, we need to find a short non-zero vector (x, y) of Λ_h^q. We follow Albrecht et al. [1] to require that the solution (x, y) to have norm at most $q^{3/4}$.*

Heuristic 6 (Lattice reduction algorithms). *There is an algorithm which, given as input a basis of a d-dimensional integer lattice L, outputs a non-zero vector v of L such that*

$$\|v\| \leq \delta_L \cdot \mathrm{Vol}(L)^{1/d}.$$

Here $\delta_L = c^d$ is the Hermite factor of a lattice reduction used for the lattice L. One has ([7]):

(i) $c \cong 1.0219$ for LLL algorithm on average for $d \geq 100$.
(ii) $c \cong 1.0128$ for BKZ algorithm with block size 20 on average.

Remark 7. *Heuristic 6 holds for random lattices (cf. [7]). For NTRU lattices (2), if the modulus q is large, then the NTRU lattices (2) contain vectors shorter than $(0, \ldots, 0, q, 0, \ldots, 0)$, and hence a lattice reduction algorithm (e.g. LLL) can recover a multiple of the secret key. Experiments in Tables 2 and 3 show that the root Hermite factor c for which our attack succeeds is much smaller than the approximation in Heuristic 6.*

3   Overview of the Subfield Lattice Attack

Let $\mathbb{K} = \mathbb{Q}[x]/(x^n + 1)$ with n a 2-power. Denote by $\mathbb{L} = \mathbb{Q}[x^r]/(x^n + 1)$ a subfield of $\mathbb{K}$ with $n = rn'$. Let $\mathcal{D}_{\mathcal{O}_{\mathbb{K}}, s}$ be the discrete Gaussian distribution over $\mathcal{O}_{\mathbb{K}}$ with standard deviation s, and let q be an integer. We consider the NTRU problem with f, g withdrawn from $\mathcal{D}_{\mathcal{O}_{\mathbb{K}}, s}$ such that f is invertible modulo q. Set $h = gf^{-1} \bmod q$ and consider the NTRU lattice

$$\Lambda_h^q = \{(x, y) \in \mathcal{O}_{\mathbb{K}}^2 \mid hx = y \bmod q\}.$$

The subfield attack by Albrecht et al. [1] works in three steps as the following.

- Step 1: Norming down the public vector h to an element h' in the subfield $\mathbb{L}$
- Step 2: Using a lattice reduction algorithm of the lattice $\Lambda_{h'}^q$ in the subfield $\mathbb{L}$ which has dimension smaller than the original lattice.
- Step 3: Lifting up the results from Step 2 to the full field $\mathbb{K}$ and prove that they are short vectors in the lattice Λ_h^q, which are short multiples of secret key (f, g).

3.1 Norming down to the Subfield

Let $h' = \mathrm{N}_{\mathbb{K}/\mathbb{L}}(h), g' = \mathrm{N}_{\mathbb{K}/\mathbb{L}}(g)$ and $f' = \mathrm{N}_{\mathbb{K}/\mathbb{L}}(f)$. Then $f', g' \in \mathcal{O}_{\mathbb{L}}$ and (f', g') is a vector of the following lattice

$$\Lambda_{h'}^q = \left\{ (x', y') \in \mathcal{O}_{\mathbb{L}}^2 \mid h'x' = y' \bmod q \right\}$$

and depending on the parameters, it may be an unusually short one. We now have reduced our NTRU problem in the full field $\mathbb{K}$ (for the lattice Λ_h^q) to the NTRU problem in the subfield $\mathbb{L}$ (for the lattice $\Lambda_{h'}^q$). The lattice $\Lambda_{h'}^q$ has dimension $2n'$ and volume $q^{2n'}$.

3.2 Lattice Reduction in the Subfield

We now apply a lattice reduction algorithm (cf. Theorem 6) to the lattice $\Lambda_{h'}^q$ we obtain a non-zero vector $(x', y') \in \Lambda_{h'}^q$ of norm

$$\|(x', y')\| \leq \delta_{\mathbb{L}} \cdot \mathrm{Vol}(\Lambda_{h'}^q)^{1/2n'}.$$

where $\delta_{\mathbb{L}} = c^{2n'}$ is the Hermite factor of the lattice $\Lambda_{h'}^q$, and c is a constant depending on the corresponding lattice algorithm (cf. Theorem 6).

The following shows that if the vector (x', y') is short enough then it must be an $\mathcal{O}_{\mathbb{L}}$-multiple of (f', g').

Theorem 8 ([12, Theorem 8]). *Let $f', g' \in \mathcal{O}_{\mathbb{L}}$ be such that $\langle f' \rangle$ and $\langle g' \rangle$ are coprime ideals and that $h'f' = g' \bmod q\mathcal{O}_{\mathbb{L}}$ for some $h' \in \mathcal{O}_{\mathbb{L}}$. If $(x', y') \in \Lambda_{h'}^q$ has length satisfying*

$$\|(x', y')\| < \frac{n'q}{\|(f', g')\|}$$

then $(x', y') = v(f', g')$ for some $v \in \mathcal{O}_{\mathbb{L}}$.

Proof. We first prove that $B = \{(f', g'), (F', G')\}$ is a basis of the $\mathcal{O}_{\mathbb{L}}$-module $\Lambda_{h'}^q$ for some $(F', G') \in \mathcal{O}_{\mathbb{L}}^2$. By coprimity, there exist (F', G') such that $f'G' - g'F' = q \in \mathcal{O}_{\mathbb{L}}$. We note that

$$f'(F', G') - F'(f', g') = (0, q);$$
$$g'(F', G') - G'(f', g') = (-q, 0);$$
$$[f'^{-1}]_q(f', g') = (1, h') \bmod q.$$

Hence the module M generated by B contains $q\mathcal{O}_{\mathbb{L}}^2$ and $(1, h')$, i.e., $\Lambda_{h'}^q \subseteq M$. Moreover, $\det_{\mathbb{L}}(B) = f'G' - g'F' = q = \det_{\mathbb{L}}\{(1, h'), (0, q)\}$, we have $\mathrm{Vol}(M) = |\Delta_{\mathbb{L}}|q^{n'} = \mathrm{Vol}(\Lambda_{h'}^q)$ and therefore $M = \Lambda_{h'}^q$.

Denote by $\Lambda = (f', g')\mathcal{O}_{\mathbb{L}}$ and by Λ^* the projection of $(F', G')\mathcal{O}_{\mathbb{L}}$ orthogonally to Λ. We have $\mathrm{Vol}(\Lambda)\mathrm{Vol}(\Lambda^*) = q^{n'}\Delta_{\mathbb{L}}$. Let $0 \neq u \in \Lambda^*$ be a shortest vector in Λ^*. By Lemma 1, one has

$$\mathrm{Vol}(\Lambda) \leq \left(\frac{\|(f', g')\|}{\sqrt{n'}}\right)^{n'} |\Delta_{\mathbb{L}}|^{1/2}, \text{ and } \mathrm{Vol}(\Lambda^*) \leq \left(\frac{\|u\|}{\sqrt{n'}}\right)^{n'} |\Delta_{\mathbb{L}}|^{1/2}.$$

We deduce that $\lambda_1(\Lambda^*) = \|u\| \geq n'q/\|(f', g')\|$. The hypothesis implies that $\|(x', y')\| < \lambda_1(\Lambda^*)$. Hence $(x', y') \in \Lambda$ as desired.   □

Remark 9. *It is proven in [1, Section 2.2] that with high probability (approximately 75%), f' and g' are coprime. However, the experiments succeeded even when they are not coprime.*

3.3   Lifting up the Short Vector

Assume that we have found a short non-zero vector $(x', y') \in \mathcal{O}_{\mathbb{L}}^2$ in the lattice $\Lambda_{h'}^q$ subject to the condition of Theorem 8, i.e., (x', y') is a short multiple of (f', g'). We now lift up (x', y') to $(x, y) \in \mathcal{O}_{\mathbb{K}}^2$ by computing

$$x = L(x') \text{ and } y = L(y') \cdot h/L(h') \bmod q \tag{3}$$

where $L : \mathbb{L} \hookrightarrow \mathbb{K}$ is the canonical inclusion map of $\mathbb{L} \subset \mathbb{K}$.

   Obviously $(x, y) \in \Lambda_h^q$. It follows from Theorem 8 that $x' = vf', y' = vg'$ for some $v \in \mathcal{O}_{\mathbb{L}}$. Let $\bar{f} = L(f')/f$, $\bar{g} = L(g')/g$ and $\bar{h} = L(h')/h$. Note also that $\bar{f}, \bar{g}$ and $\bar{h}$ are integers over $\mathbb{K}$. We write

$$x = L(x') = L(v) \cdot \bar{f} \cdot f \bmod q$$
$$y = L(y') \cdot h/L(h') = L(v) \cdot \bar{f} \cdot g \bmod q$$

and hence $(x, y) = u \cdot (f, g)$ is a multiple of (f, g), for $u = L(v) \cdot \bar{f} \in \mathcal{O}_{\mathbb{K}}$.

4   Revisiting Albrecht et al.'s Attack [1]

In this section, we analyse the subfield attack proposed by Albrecht et al. [1]. First, we analyse in Sect. 4.1 theoretically the modulus q and yield better choice of r for which the subfield attack is feasible with smaller modulus q. In Sect. 4.2, we compare the theoretical estimation and implementation results.

4.1   Theoretical Analysis

Set $D = s\sqrt{n}$ to be the upper bound for the norm of a secret polynomial sampling from the discrete Gaussian distribution $\mathcal{D}_{\mathcal{O}_{\mathbb{K}}, s}$ over $\mathcal{O}_{\mathbb{K}}$ (see Lemma 3). Hence for $f, g \leftarrow \mathcal{D}_{\mathcal{O}_{\mathbb{K}}, s}$, one has $\|f\|, \|g\| \leq D$. Let $\mathbb{L}$ be the subfield of $\mathbb{K}$ of degree n', i.e., $n = rn'$, and let

$$f' = \mathrm{N}_{\mathbb{K}/\mathbb{L}}(f), \ g' = \mathrm{N}_{\mathbb{K}/\mathbb{L}}(g), \ h' = \mathrm{N}_{\mathbb{K}/\mathbb{L}}(h).$$

Then

$$\|f'\| \leq \sqrt{n'}D^r, \ \|g'\| \leq \sqrt{n'}D^r,$$

and hence

$$\|(f', g')\| \leq \sqrt{2n'}D^r.$$

Applying a lattice reduction algorithm to the lattice $\Lambda_{h'}^q$, we obtain a non-zero vector (x', y') of norm

$$\|(x', y')\| \leq c^{2n'}\sqrt{q},$$

and therefore

$$\|(x', y')\| \cdot \|(f', g')\| \leq c^{2n'}\sqrt{2n'}D^r\sqrt{q}.$$

It follows from Lemma 1 that if

$$c^{2n'}\sqrt{2n'}D^r\sqrt{q} < n'q \tag{4}$$

then (x', y') will be a multiple of (f', g'). Inequality (4) is equivalent to

$$4n'\log(c) + 2r\log(s) + r\log(n) + 1 - \log(n') < \log(q). \tag{5}$$

Notice that

$$4n'\log(c) + 2r\log(s) + r\log(n) = \frac{4n\log(c)}{r} + r(2\log(s) + \log(n))$$
$$\geq 2\sqrt{4n\log(c)(2\log(s) + \log(n))}$$

with equality if and only if

$$r = \sqrt{\frac{4n\log(c)}{2\log(s) + \log(n)}} \ . \tag{6}$$

Hence the choice of r in (6) optimizes the left-hand side of (5), and hence yields the estimation of the modulus q that makes NTRU problem vulnerable to the subfield attack.

Table 1. Comparison of succeeded modulus $\log(q)$ for the subfield attacks. We use LLL algorithm as in Albrecht et al. and Kirchner-Fouque.

$\log(n)$	$t = \log(r)$	Succeeded $\log(q)$	Method	Estimated $\log(q)$
9	2	40	Ours	44
10	2	52	Ours	63
11	3	95	Albrecht et al. [1]	109
11	2	70	Kirchner and Fouque [12]	
11	**2**	**72**	**Ours**	98
12	4	190	Albrecht et al. [1]	208
12	4	144	Kirchner and Fouque [12]	
12	**3**	**120**	**Ours**	148

4.2   Implementation Results

In Table 1, we show our choice of r, which is the index of the subfield $\mathbb{L}$ in $\mathbb{K}$, to which we apply the subfield attack, and compare the actual succeeded values of $\log(q)$ by our, Albrecht et al.'s [1] and Kirchner-Fouque's experiments. As in previous works of Albrecht et al. and Kirchner-Fouque, we use LLL algorithm in our experiments. We take $s = \sqrt{2/3}$, and use constant $c = 1.0219$ (see Heuristic 6) for estimating the choice of r. Experimental results for the cases $n = 2^{11}$ and $n = 2^{12}$ can be seen from Tables 2 and 3 respectively. The requirement for success

Table 2. Implementation results for $n = 2^{11}$ and $\log(r) = 2$. Here we work with lattices of dimension $2n' = 1024$. The third column rhf stands for root Hermite factor obtained from our experiments (cf. the constant c in Heuristic 6)

$\log(q)$	$\log(\|(f',g')\|)$	rhf	$\log(\|(x',y')\|)$	$\log(\|(x,y)\|)$	Is $\|(x,y)\| \leq q^{3/4}$?
95	21.40	0.9925	36.37	36.75	Yes
94	21.19	0.9934	37.30	37.66	Yes
93	21.37	0.9933	36.61	36.90	Yes
92	21.20	0.9936	36.63	36.81	Yes
91	21.28	0.9938	36.44	36.66	Yes
90	21.34	0.9942	36.42	36.60	Yes
89	21.30	0.9944	36.33	36.47	Yes
88	21.27	0.9949	36.49	36.55	Yes
87	21.35	0.9952	36.45	36.57	Yes
86	21.12	0.9959	37.05	37.24	Yes
85	21.17	0.9958	36.35	36.61	Yes
84	21.24	0.9962	36.42	36.78	Yes
83	21.15	0.9966	36.54	36.63	Yes
82	21.27	0.9973	37.11	37.28	Yes
81	21.26	0.9971	36.29	36.53	Yes
80	21.26	0.9979	37.00	37.13	Yes
79	21.18	0.9978	36.31	36.45	Yes
78	21.53	0.9983	36.56	36.75	Yes
77	21.22	0.9989	36.92	37.18	Yes
76	21.30	0.9992	36.87	37.17	Yes
75	21.28	0.9992	36.46	36.66	Yes
74	21.12	0.9996	36.42	36.49	Yes
73	21.45	1.0003	36.97	37.03	Yes
72	21.33	1.0005	36.80	36.92	Yes
71	21.27	1.0223	68.17	74.70	No
70	21.33	1.0225	67.89	73.70	No

Table 3. Implementation results for $n = 2^{12}$ and $\log(r) = 3$. Here we work with lattices of dimension $2n' = 1024$

$\log(q)$	$\log(\|(f',g')\|)$	rhf	$\log(\|(x',y')\|)$	$\log(\|(x,y)\|)$	Is $\|(x,y)\| \le q^{3/4}$?
150	46.31	0.9898	59.88	60.35	Yes
149	45.71	0.9903	60.12	60.62	Yes
148	46.11	0.9951	59.75	60.25	Yes
147	46.22	0.9910	60.23	60.82	Yes
146	46.91	0.9913	60.13	60.56	Yes
145	45.47	0.9914	59.81	60.48	Yes
144	46.11	0.9918	59.97	60.28	Yes
143	45.79	0.9921	59.84	60.22	Yes
142	45.87	0.9924	59.84	60.22	Yes
141	45.55	0.9929	60.05	60.51	Yes
140	46.20	0.9934	60.31	60.58	Yes
135	46.45	0.9948	59.88	60.28	Yes
130	46.26	0.9965	59.82	60.36	Yes
125	45.90	0.9984	60.14	60.42	Yes
120	45.77	0.9998	59.83	60.17	Yes
115	46.34	1.0225	90.41	119.21	No
100	45.87	1.0224	82.81	104.21	No

of the attack is that the obtained solution (x, y) is a multiple of (f, g) and has norm at most $q^{3/4}$ (following Albrecht et al. [1]).

- For $n = 2^{11}$, we choose $r = 2^2$ which is the same as Kirchner-Fouque and different from Albrecht et al. (vs. $r = 2^3$). We succeeded with $\log(q) = 72$, which is much smaller than $\log(q) = 90$ by Albrecht et al. and close to $\log(q) = 70$ by Kirchner-Fouque.
- For $n = 2^{12}$, we choose $r = 2^3$ whereas Albrecht et al. and Kirchner-Fouque's chose $r = 2^4$. We succeeded with $\log(q) = 120$ which is smaller than $\log(q) = 190$ by Albrecht et al. and $\log(q) = 144$ by Kirchner-Fouque.

The last column of Table 1 gives our estimated values of breakable $\log(q)$ in the subfield attack which are larger than the results from experiments. One reason is that our estimation for the upper bound of the norms of $N_{\mathbb{K}/\mathbb{L}}(f)$ and $N_{\mathbb{K}/\mathbb{L}}(g)$ is not tight; for example, for $n = 2^{12}$, our estimated for $\log(\|(f',g')\|)$ is around 57.75 while it is approximately 46 by experiments.

Table 2 shows our implement results for the subfield attack against NTRU problem for $n = 2^{11}$ in which we choose the subfield $\mathbb{L} \le \mathbb{K}$ with $|\mathbb{K} : \mathbb{L}| = r$ and $\log(r) = 2$ according to (6). Note that for the case $\log(q) = 70, 71$, the attack is successful, i.e. the obtained results are multiple of the secret key (f, g), but they are not short enough as required. Table 3 shows our implement results for the subfield attack against NTRU problem for $n = 2^{12}$ in which we choose the subfield $\mathbb{L} \leq \mathbb{K}$ with $|\mathbb{K} : \mathbb{L}| = r$ and $\log(r) = 3$ according to (6). Experimental results for $n = 2^9$ and $n = 2^{10}$ are shown in the Appendix.

5 Conclusion

In this work, we exploit technical results from Kirchner and Fouque [12] to re-analyze the subfield attack by Albrecht et al. [1] against the overstretched NTRU problem. We derives better choices of the subfields for which the attack is successful with smaller modulus. Our experiments show that our succeeded modulus is much smaller than that of Albrecht et al. [1]. However, with our choices of subfields, we have to work with lattices of higher dimensions (as twice as those of Albrecht et al.) and hence the attack takes longer. Our implementation results for the case $n = 2^{11}$ (with same choice of subfield) are close to that of Kirchner and Fouque [12] ($\log(q) = 72$ vs. $\log(q) = 70$), while for the case $n = 2^{12}$ (with different choice of subfield), we can break the NTRU problem with smaller modulus ($\log(q) = 120$ vs. $\log(q) = 144$). Whereas Kirchner and Fouque's method can break NTRU problem with smaller modulus q in some cases (e.g., $n = 2^{11}$), it does not guarantee to succeed with bigger q, in contrast to the subfield attack which gives the exact limit of success. Recently, Cheon et al. [5] proposed an attack against overstretched NTRU problem which exploits the existence of the sublattice in the NTRU lattice similar to that of Kirchner and Fouque. Their attack can apply for NTRU problem with general modulus polynomial $\phi(x)$ and they also give an improved subfield attack. One of our future work is to give a complete comparison between those attacks against overstretched NTRU problem.

Acknowledgments. We are grateful for the anonymous reviewers for their useful comments and suggestions. The first author would like to thank Martin Albrecht, Shi Bai and Paul Kirchner, for their kindness and helpful discussions. This work was supported by JST CREST Grant Number JPMJCR14D6, Japan. The first author thanks the Japanese Society for the Promotion of Science (JSPS) for financial support under grant KAKENHI 16K17644.

Appendix

Tables 4 and 5 show implementation results for the case $n = 2^9$ and $n = 2^{10}$ respectively, with the same choice of subfield $\mathbb{L}$ such that $|\mathbb{K} : \mathbb{L}| = 4$.

Table 4. Implementation results for $n = 2^9$ and $\log(r) = 2$

$\log(q)$	$\log(\|(f',g')\|)$	rhf	$\log(\|(x',y')\|)$	$\log(\|(x,y)\|)$	Is $\|(x,y)\| \leq q^{3/4}$?
44	17.07	0.9950	20.16	20.39	Yes
43	17.11	0.9960	20.03	20.40	Yes
42	17.19	0.9978	20.22	20.34	Yes
41	17.15	0.9997	20.40	20.63	Yes
40	17.18	0.9996	19.85	20.14	Yes
39	17.12	1.0228	27.83	41.71	No
38	17.21	1.0215	26.87	40.67	No

Table 5. Implementation results for $n = 2^{10}$ and $\log(r) = 2$

$\log(q)$	$\log(\|(f',g')\|)$	rhf	$\log(\|(x',y')\|)$	$\log(\|(x,y)\|)$	Is $\|(x,y)\| \leq q^{3/4}$?
63	19.31	0.9926	26.07	26.23	Yes
62	19.24	0.9931	25.95	26.09	Yes
61	19.15	0.9942	26.27	26.43	Yes
60	19.14	0.9943	25.85	26.09	Yes
59	19.31	0.9955	26.23	26.58	Yes
58	19.46	0.9964	26.38	26.61	Yes
57	19.21	0.9965	25.95	26.37	Yes
56	19.14	0.9976	26.24	26.50	Yes
55	19.40	0.9982	26.22	26.48	Yes
54	19.19	0.9988	26.16	26.24	Yes
53	19.09	0.9996	26.21	26.49	Yes
52	19.08	1.0000	26.05	26.22	Yes
51	19.22	1.0223	41.83	54.24	No
50	19.43	1.0221	41.15	53.19	No

References

1. Albrecht, M., Bai, S., Ducas, L.: A subfield lattice attack on overstretched NTRU assumptions. In: Robshaw, M., Katz, J. (eds.) CRYPTO 2016. LNCS, vol. 9814, pp. 153–178. Springer, Heidelberg (2016). doi:10.1007/978-3-662-53018-4_6
2. Banaszczyk, W.: New bounds in some transference theorems in the geometry of numbers. Math. Ann. **296**(1), 625–635 (1993)
3. Bos, J.W., Lauter, K., Loftus, J., Naehrig, M.: Improved security for a ring-based fully homomorphic encryption scheme. In: Stam, M. (ed.) IMACC 2013. LNCS, vol. 8308, pp. 45–64. Springer, Heidelberg (2013). doi:10.1007/978-3-642-45239-0_4
4. Cheon, J.H., Jeong, J., Lee, C.: An algorithm for NTRU problems and cryptanalysis of the GGH multilinear map without an encoding of zero. LMS J. Comput. Math. **19**, 255–266 (2016). ANTS XII 2016

5. Cheon, J.H., Hhan, M., Lee, C.: Cryptanalysis of the overstretched NTRU problem for general modulus polynomial. ePrint 2017/484. https://eprint.iacr.org/2017/484
6. Coppersmith, D., Shamir, A.: Lattice attacks on NTRU. In: Fumy, W. (ed.) EUROCRYPT 1997. LNCS, vol. 1233, pp. 52–61. Springer, Heidelberg (1997). doi:10.1007/3-540-69053-0_5
7. Gama, N., Nguyen, P.Q.: Predicting lattice reduction. In: Smart, N. (ed.) EUROCRYPT 2008. LNCS, vol. 4965, pp. 31–51. Springer, Heidelberg (2008). doi:10.1007/978-3-540-78967-3_3
8. Garg, S., Gentry, C., Halevi, S.: Candidate multilinear maps from ideal lattices. In: Johansson, T., Nguyen, P.Q. (eds.) EUROCRYPT 2013. LNCS, vol. 7881, pp. 1–17. Springer, Heidelberg (2013). doi:10.1007/978-3-642-38348-9_1
9. Gentry, C., Szydlo, M.: Cryptanalysis of the revised NTRU signature scheme. In: Knudsen, L.R. (ed.) EUROCRYPT 2002. LNCS, vol. 2332, pp. 299–320. Springer, Heidelberg (2002). doi:10.1007/3-540-46035-7_20
10. Hoffstein, J., Pipher, J., Schanck, J.M., Silverman, J.H., Whyte, W., Zhang, Z.: Choosing parameters for NTRUEncrypt. In: Handschuh, H. (ed.) CT-RSA 2017. LNCS, vol. 10159, pp. 3–18. Springer, Cham (2017). doi:10.1007/978-3-319-52153-4_1
11. Hoffstein, J., Pipher, J., Silverman, J.H.: NTRU: a ring-based public key cryptosystem. In: Buhler, J.P. (ed.) ANTS 1998. LNCS, vol. 1423, pp. 267–288. Springer, Heidelberg (1998). doi:10.1007/BFb0054868
12. Kirchner, P., Fouque, P.-A.: Revisiting lattice attacks on overstretched NTRU parameters. In: Coron, J.-S., Nielsen, J.B. (eds.) EUROCRYPT 2017. LNCS, vol. 10210, pp. 3–26. Springer, Cham (2017). doi:10.1007/978-3-319-56620-7_1
13. López-Alt, A., Tromer, E., Vaikuntanathan, V.: On-the-fly multiparty computation on the cloud via multikey fully homomorphic encryption. In: Proceedings of the Forty-Fourth Annual ACM Symposium on Theory of Computing, STOC 2012, pp. 1219–1234. ACM (2012)
14. Lyubashevsky, V., Micciancio, D.: Generalized compact knapsacks are collision resistant. In: Bugliesi, M., Preneel, B., Sassone, V., Wegener, I. (eds.) ICALP 2006. LNCS, vol. 4052, pp. 144–155. Springer, Heidelberg (2006). doi:10.1007/11787006_13
15. Stehlé, D., Steinfeld, R.: Making NTRU as secure as worst-case problems over ideal lattices. In: Paterson, K.G. (ed.) EUROCRYPT 2011. LNCS, vol. 6632, pp. 27–47. Springer, Heidelberg (2011). doi:10.1007/978-3-642-20465-4_4

Zero-Knowledge Password Policy Check from Lattices

Khoa Nguyen, Benjamin Hong Meng Tan$^{(\boxtimes)}$, and Huaxiong Wang

Division of Mathematical Sciences, School of Physical and Mathematical Sciences,
Nanyang Technological University, Singapore, Singapore
{khoantt,tanh0199,hxwang}@ntu.edu.sg

Abstract. Passwords are ubiquitous and most commonly used to authenticate users when logging into online services. Using high entropy passwords is critical to prevent unauthorized access and password policies emerged to enforce this requirement on passwords. However, with current methods of password storage, poor practices and server breaches have leaked many passwords to the public. To protect one's sensitive information in case of such events, passwords should be hidden from servers. Verifier-based password authenticated key exchange, proposed by Bellovin and Merrit (IEEE S&P, 1992), allows authenticated secure channels to be established with a hash of a password (verifier). Unfortunately, this restricts password policies as passwords cannot be checked from their verifier. To address this issue, Kiefer and Manulis (ESORICS 2014) proposed zero-knowledge password policy check (ZKPPC). A ZKPPC protocol allows users to prove in zero knowledge that a hash of the user's password satisfies the password policy required by the server. Unfortunately, their proposal is not quantum resistant with the use of discrete logarithm-based cryptographic tools and there are currently no other viable alternatives. In this work, we construct the first post-quantum ZKPPC using lattice-based tools. To this end, we introduce a new randomised password hashing scheme for ASCII-based passwords and design an accompanying zero-knowledge protocol for policy compliance. Interestingly, our proposal does not follow the framework established by Kiefer and Manulis and offers an alternate construction without homomorphic commitments. Although our protocol is not ready to be used in practice, we think it is an important first step towards a quantum-resistant privacy-preserving password-based authentication and key exchange system.

1 Introduction

One of the most common methods of user authentication is passwords when logging in to online services. So, it is very important that passwords in use are hard to guess for security. Password policies was introduced to guide users into choosing suitable passwords with high entropy. Ur et al. [51] discovered that users are more likely to choose easily guessable passwords in the absence of a password policy. Examining the password policies of over 70 web-sites, Florêncio

© Springer International Publishing AG 2017
P.Q. Nguyen and J. Zhou (Eds.): ISC 2017, LNCS 10599, pp. 92–113, 2017.
https://doi.org/10.1007/978-3-319-69659-1_6

and Herley [17] found that most require passwords with characters from at least one of four sets, digits, symbols, lowercase and uppercase letters and a minimum password length. Hence, it is reasonable to focus on password policies with a minimum password length, sets of valid characters and maybe constraints on the diversity of characters used.

Even with strong passwords and good policies, leaks will occur if servers do not properly store passwords. Improperly stored passwords can cause serious problems, as seen by hacks on LinkedIn [19] and Yahoo [47] and the web-site "Have I Been Pwned?" [25]. Sadly, such poor practices are not uncommon: many popular web-sites were discovered by Baumann et al. [4] to store password information in plaintext.

If servers cannot be trusted, then no password information should be stored there at all. Thus, protocols that avoid storing secret user information at external servers become necessary. However, even with secret passwords, password policies are important to enforce a base level of security against dictionary attacks, leaving a dilemma: how do users prove compliance of their password without revealing anything?

Kiefer and Manulis [30] showed how to address this problem with zero knowledge password policy check (ZKPPC). It enables blind registration: users register a password with a server and prove password policy conformance without revealing anything about their passwords, thereby solving the dilemma. With ZKPPC, some randomised password verification information is stored at the server and it does not leak information about the password, protecting against server compromises. Furthermore, ZKPPC allows a user to prove, without revealing any information, that the password conforms to the server's policy. Blind registration can be coupled with a verifier-based password-based authenticated key exchange (VPAKE) protocol to achieve a complete system for privacy-preserving password-based registration, authentication and key exchange. Password-based authenticated key exchange (PAKE) [5,6,8,14,20,27] is a protocol that allows users to simultaneously authenticate themselves using passwords and perform key exchange. However, these protocols store passwords on the server and thus, users have to trust the security of the server's password storage and may be vulnerable to password leakages in the event of server compromise. Verifier-based PAKE [5,7,11,21] extends PAKE to limit the damage caused by information leakage by storing a verifier instead. Verifiers are a means to check that users supplied the correct passwords and are usually hash values of passwords with a salt, which makes it hard to extract the passwords from verifiers.

A ZKPPC protocol allows users to prove that their password, committed in the verifier, satisfies some password policy. VPAKE can then be used to securely authenticate and establish keys whenever communication is required. Together, the password is never revealed, greatly increasing the user security over current standards. Passwords are harder to guess and no longer easily compromised by server breaches.

Kiefer and Manulis [30] proposed a generic construction of ZKPPC using homomorphic commitments and set membership proofs. In the same work, a concrete ZKPPC protocol was constructed using Pedersen commitments [45], whose security is based on the hardness of the discrete logarithm problem. As such, it is vulnerable to attacks from quantum adversaries due to Shor's algorithm [49] which solves the discrete logarithm problem in quantum polynomial time. With NIST issuing a call for proposals to standardize quantum resistant cryptography [44], it is clear that we need to prepare cryptographic schemes and protocols that are quantum resistant, in case a sufficiently powerful quantum computer is realized. As there is currently no proposal of ZKPPC protocol that has the potential to be quantum resistant, it is an interesting open problem to construct one.

OUR CONTRIBUTIONS AND TECHNIQUES. In this work, attracted to the emergence of lattice-based cryptography as a strong quantum resistant candidate, we aim to construct a ZKPPC protocol from lattices. Our contribution is two-fold. A randomised password hashing scheme based on the hardness of the Short Integer Solution (SIS) problem is designed. Then, a SIS-based statistical zero-knowledge argument of knowledge, allowing the client to convince the server that his secret password, committed in a given hash value, satisfies the server's policy is constructed. This yields the first ZKPPC protocol that resists quantum adversaries.

Our first technical challenge is to derive a password encoding mechanism that operates securely and interacts smoothly with available lattice-based cryptographic tools. In the discrete log setting considered in [30], passwords are mapped to large integers and then encoded as elements in a group of large order. Unfortunately, this does not translate well to the lattice setting as working with large-norm objects usually makes the construction less secure and less efficient. Therefore, an alternative that encodes passwords as small-norm objects, is desirable. To this end, we encode passwords consisting of t characters by mapping them to a binary vector of length $8t$. The vector contains t blocks, where each is the ASCII value of the corresponding password character in binary. Further increasing its entropy, we shuffle the arrangement of these blocks with a random permutation χ, then commit to the permuted vector and a binary encoding of χ via the SIS-based commitment scheme proposed by Kawachi, Tanaka and Xagawa [28]. This commitment value is viewed as the randomised hash value of the password.

The next technical challenge is to prove in zero-knowledge that the committed password satisfies a policy of the form $f = \big((k_D, k_U, k_L, k_S), n_{\min}, n_{\max}\big)$, which demands that the password have length $n_{\min}$ between $n_{\max}$ inclusive, and contain at least k_D digits, k_S symbols, k_L lower-case and k_U upper-case letters. To this end, we will have to prove, for instance, that a committed length-8 block-vector belongs to the set of vectors encoding all 10 digits. We thus need a lattice-based sub-protocol for proving set membership. In the lattice-based world, a set membership argument system with logarithmic complexity in the cardinality of the set was proposed in [35], exploiting Stern-like protocols [50] and Merkle hash trees. However, the asymptotic efficiency does not come to the front when the underlying set has small, constant size. Here, we employ a different approach, which has linear complexity but is technically simpler and practically more efficient, based on the extend-then-permute technique for Stern's protocol, suggested by Ling et al. [37]. Finally, we use a general framework for Stern-like protocols, put forward by Libert et al. [33], to combine all of our sub-protocols for set membership and obtain a ZKPPC protocol.

From a practical point of view, our lattice-based ZKPPC protocol is not yet ready to be used: for a typical setting of parameters, an execution with soundness error 2^{-30} has communication cost around 900 KB. We, however, believe that there are much room for improvement and view this work as the first step in designing post-quantum privacy-preserving password-based authentication and key exchange systems.

RELATED WORK. The only construction of ZKPPC was proposed by Kiefer and Manulis [30] using Pedersen commitments [45] and a randomised password hashing scheme introduced in the same work. It commits each character individually and uses set membership proofs to prove compliance of the entire password to a password policy. The password hash is the sum of the committed characters and thus is linked to the set membership proofs through the homomorphic property of the commitments used. As mentioned previously, their protocol is vulnerable to quantum adversaries and greater diversity is desirable.

Improving the efficiency of secure password registration for VPAKE [31] and two server PAKE [32], Kiefer and Manulis proposed blind password registration (BPR), a new class of cryptographic protocols that prevent password leakage from the server. Building on techniques introduced in [30], Kiefer and Manulis used an efficient shuffling proof from [18] to achieve $\mathcal{O}(1)$ number of set membership proofs instead of $\mathcal{O}(n_{max})$ in ZKPPC. However, the security model considered for BPR is aimed at honest but curious participants. Security in ZKPPC is defined to prevent malicious users from registering bad passwords that violate the given password policy. Malicious servers also do not gain any information on passwords from running the ZKPPC protocol. Overall, the security model of BPR is weaker than the capabilities of ZKPPC and available instantiations are not resistant to quantum adversaries.

An alternate approach using symmetric key primitives, secure set-based policy checking (SPC), was proposed in [16]. Policies are represented by monotone access structures and mapped to linear secret sharing schemes (LSSS). Then, policy compliance corresponds to the membership of some set in the access structure, i.e. the set of shares derived from the password can reconstruct the secret in the LSSS. To obtain a privacy-preserving protocol for SPC, oblivious bloom intersection (OBI) from [15] is used. The server constructs an LSSS that only users who fulfil the policy can obtain the right shares from the OBI and recover the secret. Knowledge of the secret is proved with a hash of the secret with the transcript of the protocol execution and identities of the two parties, tying the protocol to the proof of knowledge. In the proposed SPC protocol, the one-more-RSA assumption is used to guarantee that the password registration protocol is sound when used by a malicious client. Thus, in the presence of a quantum adversary, the SPC protocol cannot be considered sound anymore.

Since the focus is on quantum resistant blind registration of passwords with malicious participants, the SPC protocol is insufficient.

ZERO-KNOWLEDGE PROOFS IN LATTICE-BASED CRYPTOGRAPHY. Early work on interactive and non-interactive proof systems [23,43,46] for lattices exploited the geometric structure of worst-case lattice problems, and are not generally applicable in lattice-based cryptography. More recent methods of proving relations appearing in lattice-based cryptosystems belong to the following two main families.

The first family, introduced by Lyubashevsky [40,41], uses "rejection sampling" techniques, and lead to relatively efficient proofs of knowledge of small secret vectors [2,9,12,13], and proofs of linear and multiplicative relations among committed values [3,10] in the ideal lattice setting. However, due to the nature of "rejection sampling", there is a tiny probability that even an honest prover may fail to convince the verifier: i.e., protocols in this family do not have perfect completeness. Furthermore, when proving knowledge of vectors with norm bound β, the knowledge extractor of these protocols is only guaranteed to produce witnesses of norm bound $g \cdot \beta$, for some factor $g > 1$. This factor, called "soundness slack" in [2,12], may be undesirable: if an extracted witness has to be used in the security proof to solve a challenge SIS instance, we need the $\mathsf{SIS}_{g \cdot \beta}$ assumption, which is stronger than the SIS_{β} assumption required by the protocol itself. Moreover, in some sophisticated cryptographic constructions such as the zero-knowledge password policy check protocol considered in this work, the coordinates of extracted vectors are expected to be in $\{0,1\}$ and/or satisfy a specific pattern. Such issues seem hard to tackle using this family of protocols.

The second family, initiated by Ling et al. [37], use "decomposition-extension" techniques in lattice-based analogues [28] of Stern's protocol [50]. These are less efficient than those of the first family because each protocol execution admits a constant soundness error, and require repeating protocols $\omega(\log n)$ times, for a security parameter n, to achieve negligible soundness error. On the upside, Stern-like protocols have perfect completeness and can handle a wide range of lattice-based relations [33–36,38,39], especially when witnesses have to not only be small or binary, but also certain prescribed arrangement of coordinates. Furthermore, unlike protocols of the first family, the extractor of Stern-like protocols can output witness vectors with the same properties expected of valid witnesses. This feature is often crucial in the design of advanced protocols involving ZK proofs. In addition, the "soundness slack" issue is completely avoided, so the hardness assumptions are kept "in place".

ORGANIZATION. In the next section, we define notations used in the paper and briefly describe the building blocks for our ZKPPC protocol. Following that, in Sect. 3, we instantiate the building blocks and ZKPPC protocol with lattices-based primitives. Finally, we summarize and conclude in Sect. 4.

2   Preliminaries

NOTATION. We assume all vectors are column vectors. A vector $\mathbf{x}$ with coordinates $x_1, \ldots, x_m$ is written as $\mathbf{x} = (x_1, \ldots, x_m)$. For simplicity, concatenation of $\mathbf{x} \in \mathbb{R}^k$ and $\mathbf{y} \in \mathbb{R}^m$ is denoted with $(\mathbf{x}\|\mathbf{y}) \in \mathbb{R}^{k+m}$. Column-wise concatenation of matrices $\mathbf{A} \in \mathbb{R}^{n \times k}$ and $\mathbf{B} \in \mathbb{R}^{n \times m}$ is denoted by $[\mathbf{A}\,|\,\mathbf{B}] \in \mathbb{R}^{n \times (k+m)}$. If S is a finite set, then $x \xleftarrow{\$} S$ means that x is chosen uniformly at random over S. For a positive integer n, $[n]$ denotes the set $\{1, \ldots, n\}$ and $\mathsf{negl}(n)$ denotes a negligible function in n. The set of all permutations of n elements is denoted by $\mathcal{S}_n$. All logarithms are of base 2.

2.1   Some Lattice-Based Cryptographic Ingredients

We first recall the average-case problem SIS and its link to worst-case lattice problems.

Definition 1 ($\mathsf{SIS}^\infty_{n,m,q,\beta}$ [1,22]). *Given a uniformly random matrix* $\mathbf{A} \in \mathbb{Z}_q^{n \times m}$, *find a non-zero vector* $\mathbf{x} \in \mathbb{Z}^m$ *such that* $\|\mathbf{x}\|_\infty \leq \beta$ *and* $\mathbf{A} \cdot \mathbf{x} = \mathbf{0} \bmod q$.

The hardness of the SIS is guaranteed by the worst-case to average-case reduction from lattice problems. If $m, \beta = \mathsf{poly}(n)$, and $q > \beta \cdot \widetilde{\mathcal{O}}(\sqrt{n})$, then the $\mathsf{SIS}^\infty_{n,m,q,\beta}$ problem is at least as hard as the worst-case lattice problem SIVP_γ for some $\gamma = \beta \cdot \widetilde{\mathcal{O}}(\sqrt{nm})$ (see, e.g., [22,42]).

The KTX commitment scheme. In this work, we employ the SIS-based commitment scheme proposed by Kawachi, Tanaka and Xagawa [28] (KTX). The scheme, with two flavours, works with lattice parameter n, prime modulus $q = \widetilde{\mathcal{O}}(n)$, and dimension $m = 2n\lceil \log q \rceil$.

In the variant that commits t bits, for some fixed $t = \mathsf{poly}(n)$, the commitment key is $(\mathbf{A}, \mathbf{B}) \xleftarrow{\$} \mathbb{Z}_q^{n \times t} \times \mathbb{Z}_q^{n \times m}$. To commit $\mathbf{x} \in \{0,1\}^t$, one samples randomness $\mathbf{r} \xleftarrow{\$} \{0,1\}^m$, and outputs the commitment $\mathbf{c} = \mathbf{A} \cdot \mathbf{x} + \mathbf{B} \cdot \mathbf{r} \bmod q$. Then, to open $\mathbf{c}$, one reveals $\mathbf{x} \in \{0,1\}^t$ and $\mathbf{r} \in \{0,1\}^m$.

If there exists two valid openings $(\mathbf{x}_1, \mathbf{r}_1)$ and $(\mathbf{x}_2, \mathbf{r}_2)$ for the same commitment $\mathbf{c}$ and $\mathbf{x}_1 \neq \mathbf{x}_2$, then one can compute a solution to the $\mathsf{SIS}^\infty_{n,m+t,q,1}$ problem associated with the uniformly random matrix $[\mathbf{A}\,|\,\mathbf{B}] \in \mathbb{Z}_q^{n \times (m+t)}$. On the other hand, by the left-over hash lemma [48], the distribution of a valid commitment $\mathbf{c}$ is statistically close to uniform over $\mathbb{Z}_q^n$ which implies that it is statistically hiding.

Kawachi et al. [28] extended the above t-bit commitment scheme to a string commitment scheme $\mathsf{COM} : \{0,1\}^* \times \{0,1\}^m \to \mathbb{Z}_q^n$. The extended scheme shares the same characteristics, statistically hiding from the parameters set and computationally binding under the SIS assumption.

In this work, we use the former variant to commit to passwords, and use COM as a building block for Stern-like zero-knowledge protocols.

2.2 Zero-Knowledge Argument Systems and Stern-Like Protocols

We work with statistical zero-knowledge argument systems, interactive protocols where the zero-knowledge property holds against *any* cheating verifier and
the soundness property holds against *computationally bounded* cheating provers.
More formally, let the set of statements-witnesses $R = \{(y, w)\} \in \{0, 1\}^* \times \{0, 1\}^*$
be an NP relation. A two-party game $\langle \mathcal{P}, \mathcal{V} \rangle$ is called an interactive argument
system for the relation R with soundness error e if two conditions hold:

- Completeness. If $(y, w) \in R$ then $\Pr[\langle \mathcal{P}(y, w), \mathcal{V}(y) \rangle = 1] = 1$.
- Soundness. If $(y, w) \notin R$, then $\forall$ PPT $\widehat{\mathcal{P}}$: $\Pr[\langle \widehat{\mathcal{P}}(y, w), \mathcal{V}(y) \rangle = 1] \leq e$.

Here and henceforth, PPT denotes probabilistic polynomial time. An argument
system is statistical zero-knowledge if for any $\widehat{\mathcal{V}}(y)$, there exists a PPT simulator
$\mathcal{S}(y)$ which produces a simulated transcript that is statistically close to that of
the real interaction between $\mathcal{P}(y, w)$ and $\widehat{\mathcal{V}}(y)$. A related notion is argument
of knowledge, which requires the witness-extended emulation property. For 3
move protocols (*i.e.*, commitment-challenge-response), witness-extended emulation is implied by *special soundness* [24], which assumes the existence of a PPT
extractor, taking as input a set of valid transcripts with respect to all possible
values of the "challenge" to the same "commitment", and returning w' such that
$(y, w') \in R$.

Stern-like protocols. The statistical zero-knowledge arguments of knowledge
presented in this work are Stern-like [50] protocols. In particular, they are Σ-
protocols as defined in [9, 26], where 3 valid transcripts are needed for extraction
instead of just 2. Stern's protocol was originally proposed for code-based cryptography, and adapted to lattices by Kawachi et al. [28]. It was subsequently empow-
ered by Ling et al. [37] to handle the matrix-vector relations associated with the
SIS and inhomogeneous SIS problems and extended to design several lattice-
based schemes: group signatures [33, 35, 36, 38, 39], and group encryption [34].

The basic protocol has 3 moves. With COM, the KTX string commitment
scheme [28], we get a statistical zero-knowledge argument of knowledge (ZKAoK)
with perfect completeness, constant soundness error $2/3$, and communication
cost $\mathcal{O}(|w| \cdot \log q)$, where $|w|$ is the total bit-size of the secret vectors.

An abstraction of Stern's protocol. We recall an abstraction of Stern's
protocol, proposed in [33]. Let n, ℓ, q be positive integers, where $\ell \geq n$, $q \geq 2$,
and VALID be a subset of $\{0, 1\}^\ell$. Suppose $\mathcal{S}$ is a finite set and every $\phi \in$
$\mathcal{S}$ is associated with a permutation Γ_ϕ of ℓ elements, satisfying the following
conditions:

$$\begin{cases} \mathbf{w} \in \mathsf{VALID} \iff \Gamma_\phi(\mathbf{w}) \in \mathsf{VALID}, \\ \text{If } \mathbf{w} \in \mathsf{VALID} \text{ and } \phi \text{ is uniform in } \mathcal{S}, \text{ then } \Gamma_\phi(\mathbf{w}) \text{ is uniform in } \mathsf{VALID}. \end{cases} \quad (1)$$

We aim to construct a statistical ZKAoK for the following abstract relation:

$$R_{\text{abstract}} = \left\{ (\mathbf{M}, \mathbf{v}), \mathbf{w} \in \mathbb{Z}_q^{n \times \ell} \times \mathbb{Z}_q^n \times \mathsf{VALID} : \mathbf{M} \cdot \mathbf{w} = \mathbf{v} \bmod q. \right\}$$

Stern's original protocol has $\mathsf{VALID} = \{\mathbf{w} \in \{0,1\}^\ell : \mathsf{wt}(\mathbf{w}) = k\}$, where $\mathsf{wt}(\cdot)$ denotes the Hamming weight and $k < \ell$ for some given k, $\mathcal{S} = \mathcal{S}_\ell$ – the symmetric group on ℓ elements, and $\Gamma_\phi(\mathbf{w}) = \phi(\mathbf{w})$.

The conditions in (1) are key to prove that $\mathbf{w} \in \mathsf{VALID}$ in ZK: The prover $\mathcal{P}$ samples $\phi \xleftarrow{\$} \mathcal{S}$ and the verifier $\mathcal{V}$ checks that $\Gamma_\phi(\mathbf{w}) \in \mathsf{VALID}$; no additional information about $\mathbf{w}$ is revealed to $\mathcal{V}$ due to the randomness of ϕ. Furthermore, to prove in ZK that $\mathbf{M} \cdot \mathbf{w} = \mathbf{v} \bmod q$ holds, $\mathcal{P}$ samples $\mathbf{r}_w \xleftarrow{\$} \mathbb{Z}_q^\ell$ to mask $\mathbf{w}$, and convinces $\mathcal{V}$ instead that $\mathbf{M} \cdot (\mathbf{w} + \mathbf{r}_w) = \mathbf{M} \cdot \mathbf{r}_w + \mathbf{v} \bmod q$.

We describe the interaction between $\mathcal{P}$ and $\mathcal{V}$ in Fig. 1. A statistically hiding and computationally binding string commitment scheme COM, e.g. the scheme in Sect. 2.1, is used.

---

1. **Commitment:** Prover $\mathcal{P}$ samples $\mathbf{r}_w \xleftarrow{\$} \mathbb{Z}_q^\ell$, $\phi \xleftarrow{\$} \mathcal{S}$ and randomness ρ_1, ρ_2, ρ_3 for COM. Then, a commitment $\mathrm{CMT} = (C_1, C_2, C_3)$ is sent to the verifier $\mathcal{V}$, where

$$C_1 = \mathsf{COM}(\phi, \mathbf{M} \cdot \mathbf{r}_w \bmod q; \rho_1), \quad C_2 = \mathsf{COM}(\Gamma_\phi(\mathbf{r}_w); \rho_2),$$
$$C_3 = \mathsf{COM}(\Gamma_\phi(\mathbf{w} + \mathbf{r}_w \bmod q); \rho_3).$$

2. **Challenge:** $\mathcal{V}$ sends a challenge $Ch \xleftarrow{\$} \{1, 2, 3\}$ to $\mathcal{P}$.
3. **Response:** Based on Ch, $\mathcal{P}$ sends RSP computed as follows:
   - $Ch = 1$: Let $\mathbf{t}_w = \Gamma_\phi(\mathbf{w})$, $\mathbf{t}_r = \Gamma_\phi(\mathbf{r}_w)$, and $\mathrm{RSP} = (\mathbf{t}_w, \mathbf{t}_r, \rho_2, \rho_3)$.
   - $Ch = 2$: Let $\phi_2 = \phi$, $\mathbf{w}_2 = \mathbf{w} + \mathbf{r}_w \bmod q$, and $\mathrm{RSP} = (\phi_2, \mathbf{w}_2, \rho_1, \rho_3)$.
   - $Ch = 3$: Let $\phi_3 = \phi$, $\mathbf{w}_3 = \mathbf{r}_w$, and $\mathrm{RSP} = (\phi_3, \mathbf{w}_3, \rho_1, \rho_2)$.

Verification: Receiving RSP, $\mathcal{V}$ proceeds as follows:

- $Ch = 1$: Check that $\mathbf{t}_w \in \mathsf{VALID}$, $C_2 = \mathsf{COM}(\mathbf{t}_r; \rho_2)$, $C_3 = \mathsf{COM}(\mathbf{t}_w + \mathbf{t}_r \bmod q; \rho_3)$.
- $Ch = 2$: Check that $C_1 = \mathsf{COM}(\phi_2, \mathbf{M} \cdot \mathbf{w}_2 - \mathbf{v} \bmod q; \rho_1)$, $C_3 = \mathsf{COM}(\Gamma_{\phi_2}(\mathbf{w}_2); \rho_3)$.
- $Ch = 3$: Check that $C_1 = \mathsf{COM}(\phi_3, \mathbf{M} \cdot \mathbf{w}_3; \rho_1)$, $C_2 = \mathsf{COM}(\Gamma_{\phi_3}(\mathbf{w}_3); \rho_2)$.

In each case, $\mathcal{V}$ outputs 1 if and only if all the conditions hold.

Fig. 1. Stern-like ZKAoK for the relation $\mathrm{R}_{\mathrm{abstract}}$.

The properties of the protocol are summarized in Theorem 1.

Theorem 1 ([33]). *Assuming that* COM *is a statistically hiding and computationally binding string commitment scheme, the protocol in Fig. 1 is a statistical* ZKAoK *with perfect completeness, soundness error 2/3, and communication cost* $\mathcal{O}(\ell \log q)$. *In particular:*

- *There exists a polynomial-time simulator that, on input* $(\mathbf{M}, \mathbf{v})$, *outputs an accepted transcript statistically close to that produced by the real prover.*
- *There exists a polynomial-time knowledge extractor that, on input a commitment* CMT *and 3 valid responses* $(\mathrm{RSP}_1, \mathrm{RSP}_2, \mathrm{RSP}_3)$ *to all 3 possible values of the challenge* Ch, *outputs* $\mathbf{w}' \in \mathsf{VALID}$ *such that* $\mathbf{M} \cdot \mathbf{w}' = \mathbf{v} \bmod q$.

The proof of the Theorem 1, which appeared in [33], employs standard simulation and extraction techniques for Stern-like protocols [28,37]. (In the full version, we also provide the proof, for the sake of completeness.)

2.3   Password Strings and Password Policies

Next, we present the models of password strings and policies, adapted from [30].

Password Strings. We consider password strings pw over the set of 94 printable characters Σ_{all} in the ASCII alphabet Σ_{ASCII}, where $\Sigma_{\mathsf{all}} = \Sigma_D \cup \Sigma_S \cup \Sigma_L \cup \Sigma_U \subset \Sigma_{\mathsf{ASCII}}$ is split into four disjoint subsets:

- The set of 10 digits $\Sigma_D = \{0, 1, \ldots, 9\}$;
- The set of 32 symbols $\Sigma_S = \{$!"#$%&'()*+,-./ :;<=>?@ [\]^_'{|} ~ $\}$;
- The set of 26 lower case letters, $\Sigma_L = \{a, b, \ldots, z\}$;
- The set of 26 upper case letters, $\Sigma_U = \{A, B, \ldots, Z\}$.

We denote by `Dict` a general dictionary containing all strings that can be formed from the characters in Σ_{all}. A password string $pw = (c_1, c_2, \ldots, c_k) \in \Sigma_{\mathsf{all}}^k \subset \mathtt{Dict}$ of length k is an ordered multi-set of characters $c_1, \ldots, c_k \in \Sigma_{\mathsf{all}}$.

Password Policies. A password policy $f = ((k_D, k_S, k_L, k_U), n_{\mathsf{min}}, n_{\mathsf{max}})$ has six components, a minimum length n_{min}, maximum length n_{max}, and integers k_D, k_S, k_L and k_U that indicate the minimum number of digits, symbols, upper-case and lower-case letters, respectively, a password string must contain. We say that $f(pw) = \mathtt{true}$ if and only if policy f is satisfied by the password string pw. For instance,

1. Policy $f = ((1, 1, 1, 1), 8, 16)$ indicates that password strings must be between 8 and 16 characters and contain at least one digit, one symbol, one lower-case and one upper-case letters.
2. Policy $f = ((0, 2, 0, 1), 10, 14)$ demands that password strings must be between 10 and 14 characters, including at least two symbols and one upper-case letter.

Remark 1. In practice, password policies typically do not specify n_{max} but we can simply fix a number that upper-bounds all reasonable password lengths.

2.4   Randomised Password Hashing and Zero-Knowledge Password Policy Check

We now recall the notions of randomised password hashing and zero-knowledge password policy check. Our presentation follows [29,30].

Randomised Password Hashing. This mechanism aims to compute some password verification information that can be used later in more advanced protocols (e.g., ZKPPC and VPAKE). In order to prevent off-line dictionary attacks, the computation process is randomised via a pre-hash salt and hash salt. More formally, a randomised password hashing scheme $\mathcal{H}$ is a tuple of 5 algorithms $\mathcal{H} = (\mathsf{Setup}, \mathsf{PreSalt}, \mathsf{PreHash}, \mathsf{Salt}, \mathsf{Hash})$, defined as follows.

- $\mathsf{Setup}(\lambda)$: On input security parameter λ, generate public parameters pp, including the descriptions of the salt spaces $\mathbb{S}_P$ and $\mathbb{S}_H$.
- $\mathsf{PreSalt}(pp)$: On input pp, output a random pre-hash salt $s_P \in \mathbb{S}_P$.
- $\mathsf{PreHash}(pp, pw, s_P)$: On input pp, password pw and pre-hash salt s_P, output a pre-hash value P.
- $\mathsf{Salt}(pp)$: On input pp, output a random hash salt $s_H \in \mathbb{S}_H$.
- $\mathsf{Hash}(pp, P, s_P, s_H)$: On input pp, pre-hash value P, pre-hash salt s_P and hash salt s_H, output a hash value $\mathbf{h}$.

A secure randomised password hashing scheme $\mathcal{H}$ must satisfy 5 requirements: *pre-image resistance, second pre-image resistance, pre-hash entropy preservation, entropy preservation* and *password hiding*.

- Pre-image resistance (or tight one-wayness in [11]): Let $pp \leftarrow \mathsf{Setup}(\lambda)$ and $\texttt{Dict}$ be a dictionary of min-entropy β. Let $Hash(\cdot)$ be a function such that $(H_i, s_{H_i}) \leftarrow Hash(\cdot)$, where $s_{H_i} \leftarrow \mathsf{Salt}(pp)$ and $H_i \leftarrow \mathsf{Hash}(pp, P_i, s_{P_i}, s_{H_i})$. Let $P_i \leftarrow \mathsf{PreHash}(pp, pw_i, s_{P_i})$ with $s_{P_i} \leftarrow \mathsf{PreSalt}(pp)$ and $pw_i \xleftarrow{\$} \texttt{Dict}$. P_i is stored by $Hash(\cdot)$ and there is a function $\texttt{Verify}(i, P)$ such that $\texttt{Verify}(i, P) = 1$ if $P = P_i$.
  For all PPT adversaries $\mathcal{A}$ running in time at most t, there exists a negligible function $\varepsilon(\cdot)$ such that

$$Pr[(i, P) \leftarrow \mathcal{A}^{Hash(\cdot)}); \texttt{Verify}(i, P) = 1] \leq \frac{\alpha t}{2^\beta t_{\mathsf{PreHash}}} + \varepsilon(\lambda)$$

  for small α and t_{PreHash}, the running time of $\mathsf{PreHash}$.

- Second pre-image resistance: For all PPT adversaries $\mathcal{A}$, there exists a negligible function $\varepsilon(\cdot)$ such that for $P' \leftarrow \mathcal{A}(pp, P, s_H)$,

$$Pr\big[(P' \neq P) \wedge \big(\mathsf{Hash}(pp, P, s_H) = \mathsf{Hash}(pp, P', s_H)\big)\big] \leq \varepsilon(\lambda),$$

  where $pp \leftarrow \mathsf{Setup}(\lambda)$, $s_P \leftarrow \mathsf{PreSalt}(pp)$, $s_H \leftarrow \mathsf{Salt}(pp)$, $P \leftarrow \mathsf{Hash}(pp, pw, s_P)$ for any $pw \in \texttt{Dict}$.

- Pre-hash entropy preservation: For all dictionaries $\texttt{Dict}$ that are samplable in polynomial time with min-entropy β and any PPT adversary $\mathcal{A}$, there exists a negligible function $\varepsilon(\cdot)$ such that for $(P, s_P) \leftarrow \mathcal{A}(pp)$ with $pp \leftarrow \mathsf{Setup}(\lambda)$ and random password $pw \xleftarrow{\$} \texttt{Dict}$,

$$Pr\big[(s_P \in \mathbb{S}_P) \wedge \big(P = \mathsf{PreHash}(pp, pw, s_P)\big)\big] \leq 2^{-\beta} + \varepsilon(\lambda).$$

- Entropy preservation: For all min-entropy β polynomial-time samplable dictionaries Dict and any PPT adversary $\mathcal{A}$, there exists a negligible function $\varepsilon(\cdot)$ such that for $(H, s_P, s_H) \leftarrow \mathcal{A}(pp)$

$$Pr\left[(s_P \in \mathbb{S}_P) \wedge (s_H \in \mathbb{S}_H \wedge H = \mathsf{Hash}(pp, pw, s_P, s_H))\right] \leq 2^{-\beta} + \varepsilon(\lambda),$$

  where $pp \leftarrow \mathsf{Setup}(\lambda)$ and $pw \overset{\$}{\leftarrow} \mathtt{Dict}$.
- Password hiding: For all PPT adversaries $\mathcal{A} = (\mathcal{A}_1, \mathcal{A}_2)$, where $\mathcal{A}_1(pp)$ outputs two equal length passwords pw_0, pw_1 for $pp \leftarrow \mathsf{Setup}(\lambda)$ and $\mathcal{A}_2(H)$ outputs a bit b' for $H \leftarrow \mathsf{Hash}(pp, P, s_P, s_H)$, where $s_H \leftarrow \mathsf{Salt}(\lambda)$, $s_P \leftarrow \mathsf{PreSalt}(\lambda)$ and $P \leftarrow \mathsf{PreHash}(pp, pw_b, s_P)$ for a random bit $b \overset{\$}{\leftarrow} \{0, 1\}$, there exists a negligible function $\varepsilon(\cdot)$ such that

$$\left|Pr[b = b'] - \tfrac{1}{2}\right| \leq \varepsilon(\lambda).$$

ZK Password Policy Check. Let $\mathcal{H} = (\mathsf{Setup}, \mathsf{PreSalt}, \mathsf{PreHash}, \mathsf{Salt}, \mathsf{Hash})$ be a randomised password hashing scheme. A password policy check (PPC) is an interactive protocol between a client and server where the password policy of the server $f = ((k_D, k_S, k_L, k_U), n_{\min}, n_{\max})$ and public parameters $pp \leftarrow \mathsf{Setup}(\lambda)$ are used as common inputs. At the end of the execution, the server accepts a hash value $\mathbf{h}$ of any password pw of the client's choice if and only if $f(pw) = \mathtt{true}$. A PPC protocol is an argument of knowledge of the password pw and ssrandomness $s_P \leftarrow \mathsf{PreSalt}(pp)$, $s_H \leftarrow \mathsf{Salt}(pp)$ used for hashing. To prevent leaking the password to the server, one additionally requires that the protocol be zero-knowledge.

More formally, a zero-knowledge PPC protocol is an interactive protocol between a prover (client) and verifier (server), in which, given $(pp, f, \mathbf{h})$ the former convinces the later in zero-knowledge that the former knows pw and randomness (s_P, s_H) such that:

$$f(pw) = \mathtt{true} \qquad \text{and} \qquad \mathsf{Hash}(pp, P, s_P, s_H) = \mathbf{h},$$

where $P \leftarrow \mathsf{PreHash}(pp, pw, s_P)$.

3　Our Constructions

To construct randomised password hashing schemes and ZKPPC protocols from concrete computational assumptions, the first challenge is to derive a password encoding mechanism that operates securely and interacts smoothly with the hashing and zero-knowledge layers. In the discrete log setting considered in [30], passwords are mapped to large integers and then encoded as elements in a group of large order. Unfortunately, this does not translate well to the lattice setting as working with large-norm objects usually reduces the security and efficiency of the construction. Therefore, a different method, which encodes passwords as small-norm objects, is desirable. In this work, we will therefore use binary vectors.

Let $\mathrm{bin}(\cdot)$ be the function that maps non-negative integers to their binary decomposition. For any character c encoded in ASCII, let $\mathtt{ASCII}(c) \in [0, 255]$ be its code. Then, we define $\mathrm{enc}(c)$ for an ASCII encoded character c and $\mathrm{enc}(pw)$ for some length-t password $pw = (c_1, \ldots, c_t) \in \Sigma^t$ as

$$\mathrm{enc}(c) = \mathrm{bin}(\mathtt{ASCII}(c)) \in \{0,1\}^8,$$
$$\mathrm{encode}(pw) = \big(\mathrm{enc}(c_1)\|\ldots\|\mathrm{enc}(c_t)\big) \in \{0,1\}^{8t}.$$

3.1   Notations, Sets and Permutations

Let m, n be arbitrary positive integers. We define the following sets and permutations:

⋄ $\mathsf{B}_{\mathsf{m}}^2$: the set of all vectors in $\{0,1\}^{2\mathsf{m}}$ whose Hamming weight is exactly m. Note that for $\mathbf{x} \in \mathbb{Z}^{2\mathsf{m}}$ and $\psi \in \mathcal{S}_{2\mathsf{m}}$ the following holds:

$$\begin{cases} \mathbf{x} \in \mathsf{B}_{\mathsf{m}}^2 & \Leftrightarrow \quad \psi(\mathbf{x}) \in \mathsf{B}_{\mathsf{m}}^2; \\ \mathbf{x} \in \mathsf{B}_{\mathsf{m}}^2 \text{ and } \psi \xleftarrow{\$} \mathcal{S}_{2\mathsf{m}}, \text{ then } \psi(\mathbf{x}) \text{ is uniform over } \mathsf{B}_{\mathsf{m}}^2. \end{cases} \qquad (2)$$

⋄ $T_{\psi,\mathsf{n}}$, for $\psi \in \mathcal{S}_{\mathsf{m}}$: the permutation that, when applied to $\mathbf{v} = (\mathbf{v}_1\|\mathbf{v}_2\|\ldots\|\mathbf{v}_{\mathsf{m}}) \in \mathbb{Z}^{\mathsf{nm}}$, consisting of m blocks of size n, re-arranges the blocks of $\mathbf{v}$ according to ψ, as follows,

$$T_{\psi,\mathsf{n}}(\mathbf{v}) = (\mathbf{v}_{\psi(1)}\|\mathbf{v}_{\psi(2)}\|\ldots\|\mathbf{v}_{\psi(\mathsf{n})}).$$

For convenience, when working with password alphabet $\Sigma_{\mathsf{all}} = \Sigma_D \cup \Sigma_S \cup \Sigma_L \cup \Sigma_U$ and password policy $f = \big((k_D, k_U, k_L, k_S), n_{\mathsf{min}}, n_{\mathsf{max}}\big)$, we introduce the following notations and sets:

⋄ $\eta_D = |\Sigma_D| = 10$, $\eta_S = |\Sigma_S| = 32$, $\eta_L = |\Sigma_L| = 26$, $\eta_U = |\Sigma_U| = 26$ and $\eta_{\mathsf{all}} = |\Sigma_{\mathsf{all}}| = 94$.

⋄ For $\alpha \in \{D, S, L, U, \mathsf{all}\}$: $\mathsf{Enc}_\alpha = \{\mathrm{enc}(w)) \mid w \in \Sigma_\alpha\}$.

⋄ SET_α for $\alpha \in \{D, S, L, U, \mathsf{all}\}$: the set of all vectors $\mathbf{v} = (\mathbf{v}_1\|\ldots\|\mathbf{v}_{\eta_\alpha}) \in \{0,1\}^{8\eta_\alpha}$, such that the blocks $\mathbf{v}_1, \ldots, \mathbf{v}_{\eta_\alpha} \in \{0,1\}^8$ are exactly the binary encodings of all characters in Σ_α, i.e.,

$$\{\mathbf{v}_1, \ldots, \mathbf{v}_{\eta_\alpha}\} = \{\mathrm{enc}(w)) : w \in \Sigma_\alpha\}.$$

⋄ $\mathsf{SET}_{n_{\mathsf{max}}}$: the set of all vectors $\mathbf{v} = (\mathbf{v}_1\|\ldots\|\mathbf{v}_{n_{\mathsf{max}}}) \in \{0,1\}^{n_{\mathsf{max}}\lceil \log n_{\mathsf{max}}\rceil}$, such that the blocks $\mathbf{v}_1, \ldots, \mathbf{v}_{n_{\mathsf{max}}} \in \{0,1\}^{\lceil \log n_{\mathsf{max}}\rceil}$ are exactly the binary decompositions of all integers in $[n_{\mathsf{max}}]$, i.e.,

$$\{\mathbf{v}_1, \ldots, \mathbf{v}_{n_{\mathsf{max}}}\} = \{\mathrm{bin}(1), \ldots, \mathrm{bin}(n_{\mathsf{max}})\}.$$

Observe that the following properties hold.

⋄ For all $\alpha \in \{D, S, L, U, \mathsf{all}\}$, all $\mathbf{x} \in \mathbb{Z}^{8\eta_\alpha}$ and all $\psi \in \mathcal{S}_{\eta_\alpha}$:

$$\begin{cases} \mathbf{x} \in \mathsf{SET}_\alpha & \Leftrightarrow \quad T_{\psi,8}(\mathbf{x}) \in \mathsf{SET}_\alpha; \\ \mathbf{x} \in \mathsf{SET}_\alpha \text{ and } \psi \xleftarrow{\$} \mathcal{S}_{\eta_\alpha}, \text{ then } T_{\psi,8}(\mathbf{x}) \text{ is uniform over } \mathsf{SET}_\alpha. \end{cases} \quad (3)$$

⋄ For all $\mathbf{x} \in \mathbb{Z}^{n_{\max}\lceil \log n_{\max}\rceil}$ and all $\psi \in \mathcal{S}_{n_{\max}}$:

$$\begin{cases} \mathbf{x} \in \mathsf{SET}_{n_{\max}} & \Leftrightarrow \quad T_{\psi,\lceil \log n_{\max}\rceil}(\mathbf{x}) \in \mathbf{x} \in \mathsf{SET}_{n_{\max}}; \\ \mathbf{x} \in \mathsf{SET}_{n_{\max}} \text{ and } \psi \xleftarrow{\$} \mathcal{S}_{n_{\max}}, \text{ then } T_{\psi,\lceil \log n_{\max}\rceil}(\mathbf{x}) \text{ is uniform over } \mathsf{SET}_{n_{\max}}. \end{cases} \quad (4)$$

3.2 Randomised Password Hashing from Lattices

We describe our randomised password hashing scheme $\mathcal{L}$ for passwords of length between two given integers $n_{\min}$ and $n_{\max}$. At a high level, our scheme maps characters of the password pw to binary block vectors, re-arranges them with a random permutation χ, and finally computes the password hash as a KTX commitment ([28], see also Sect. 2.1) to a vector storing all the information on pw and χ. The scheme works as follows,

$\mathcal{L}.\mathsf{Setup}(\lambda)$. On input security parameter λ, the algorithm performs the following steps:

1. Choose parameters $n = \mathcal{O}(\lambda)$, prime modulus $q = \widetilde{\mathcal{O}}(n)$, and dimension $m = 2n\lceil \log q\rceil$.
2. Sample matrices $\mathbf{A} \xleftarrow{\$} \mathbb{Z}_q^{n \times (n_{\max}\lceil \log n_{\max}\rceil + 8n_{\max})}$ and $\mathbf{B} \xleftarrow{\$} \mathbb{Z}_q^{n \times m}$.
3. Let the pre-hash salt space be $\mathbb{S}_P = \mathcal{S}_{n_{\max}}$ - the set of all permutations of $n_{\max}$ elements, and hash salt space be $\mathbb{S}_H = \{0,1\}^m$.
4. Output the public parameters $pp = (n, q, m, \mathbb{S}_P, \mathbb{S}_H, \mathbf{A}, \mathbf{B})$.

$\mathcal{L}.\mathsf{PreSalt}(pp)$. Sample $\chi \xleftarrow{\$} \mathcal{S}_{n_{\max}}$ and output $s_P = \chi$.

$\mathcal{L}.\mathsf{PreHash}(pp, pw, s_P)$. Let $s_P = \chi \in \mathcal{S}_{n_{\max}}$ and $t \in [n_{\min}, n_{\max}]$ be the length of password pw. The pre-hash value P is computed as follows.

1. Compute $\mathsf{encode}(pw) \in \{0,1\}^{8t}$, consisting of t blocks of length 8.
2. Insert $n_{\max} - t$ blocks of length 8, each one being $\mathsf{enc}(g)$ for some non-printable ASCII character $g \in \Sigma_{\mathsf{ASCII}} \setminus \Sigma_{\mathsf{all}}$, into the block-vector $\mathsf{encode}(pw)$ to get $\mathbf{e} \in \{0,1\}^{8n_{\max}}$.[1]
3. Apply $T_{\chi,8}$ to get $\mathbf{e}' = T_{\chi,8}(\mathbf{e}) \in \{0,1\}^{8n_{\max}}$.
4. Output the pre-hash value $P = \mathbf{e}'$.

$\mathcal{L}.\mathsf{Salt}(pp)$. Sample $\mathbf{r} \xleftarrow{\$} \{0,1\}^m$ and output $s_H = \mathbf{r}$.

$\mathcal{L}.\mathsf{Hash}(pp, P, s_P, s_H)$. Let $P = \mathbf{e}' \in \{0,1\}^{8n_{\max}}$, $s_P = \chi \in \mathcal{S}_{n_{\max}}$ and $s_H = \mathbf{r} \in \{0,1\}^m$. The hash value $\mathbf{h}$ is computed as follows,

---

[1] This hides the actual length t of the password in the ZKPPC protocol in Sect. 3.4.

1. Express the permutation χ as $\chi = [\chi(1), \ldots, \chi(n_{max})]$, where for each $i \in [n_{max}]$, $\chi(i) \in [n_{max}]$. Then, form

$$\mathbf{e}_0 = \big(\mathsf{bin}(\chi(1) - 1) \| \ldots \| \mathsf{bin}(\chi(n_{max}) - 1)\big) \in \{0, 1\}^{n_{max}\lceil \log n_{max}\rceil}.$$

2. Form $\mathbf{x} = (\mathbf{e}_0 \| \mathbf{e}') \in \{0, 1\}^{n_{max}\lceil \log n_{max}\rceil + 8n_{max}}$ and output $\mathbf{h} = \mathbf{A} \cdot \mathbf{x} + \mathbf{B} \cdot \mathbf{r} \in \mathbb{Z}_q^n$.

In the following theorem, we demonstrate that the proposed scheme satisfies the security requirements defined in Sect. 2.4.

Theorem 2. *Under the* SIS *assumption, the randomised password hashing scheme, $\mathcal{L}$, described above satisfies 5 requirements:* pre-image resistance, second pre-image resistance, pre-hash entropy preservation, entropy preservation *and* password hiding.

Proof. First, we remark that, by construction, if the pre-hash salt $s_P = \chi$ is given, then we can reverse the procedure used to extend the length t password by simply discarding any non-printable characters after applying the inverse of the permutation specified by s_P. Hence, if s_P is hidden, then due to its randomness, the min-entropy of P is larger than the min-entropy of pw. Thus, the proposed hashing scheme has the pre-hash entropy preservation and entropy preservation properties.

Next, note that $\mathbf{h} = \mathbf{A} \cdot \mathbf{x} + \mathbf{B} \cdot \mathbf{r} \bmod q$ is a proper KTX commitment of message $\mathbf{x}$ with randomness $\mathbf{r}$. Thus, from the statistical hiding property of the commitment scheme, the password hiding property holds.

Furthermore, if one can produce distinct pre-hash values P, P' that yield the same hash value $\mathbf{h}$, then one can use these values to break the computational binding property of the KTX commitment scheme. This implies that second pre-image resistance property holds under the SIS assumption.

Finally, over the randomness of matrix $\mathbf{A}$, password pw and pre-hash salt s_P, except for a negligible probability (i.e., in the event one accidentally finds a solution to the SIS problem associated with matrix $\mathbf{A}$), vector $\mathbf{A} \cdot \mathbf{x}$ accepts at least 2^β values in $\mathbb{Z}_q^n$, where β is the min-entropy of the dictionary Dict from which pw is chosen. Therefore, even if $\mathbf{A} \cdot \mathbf{x} = \mathbf{h} - \mathbf{B} \cdot s_H \bmod q$ is given, to find $P = \mathbf{e}'$, one has to perform 2^β invocations of PreHash which implies that the scheme satisfies the pre-image resistance property. □

3.3 Techniques for Proving Set Membership

In our construction of ZKPPC in Sect. 3.4, we will have to prove that a linear relation of the form

$$\sum_i (\text{public matrix } \mathbf{M}_i) \cdot (\text{binary secret vector } \mathbf{s}_i) = \mathbf{h} \bmod q$$

holds, where each secret vector $\mathbf{s}_i$ must be an element of a given set of relatively small cardinality, e.g., $\mathsf{Enc}_D, \mathsf{Enc}_S, \mathsf{Enc}_L, \mathsf{Enc}_U, \mathsf{Enc}_{all}$. Thus, we need to design suitable sub-protocols to prove set membership.

In the lattice-based world, a set membership argument system with logarithmic complexity in the cardinality of the set was proposed in [35], exploiting Stern-like protocols and Merkle hash trees. Despite its asymptotic efficiency, the actual efficiency is worse when the underlying set has small, constant size. To tackle the problems encountered here, we employ a different approach, which has linear complexity but is technically simpler and practically more efficient.

Suppose we have to prove that an n-dimensional vector $\mathbf{s}_i$ belongs to a set of m vectors $\{\mathbf{v}_1, \ldots, \mathbf{v}_m\}$. To this end, we append $m-1$ blocks to vector $\mathbf{s}_i$ to get an nm-dimensional vector $\mathbf{s}_i^\star$ whose m blocks are exactly elements of the set $\{\mathbf{v}_1, \ldots, \mathbf{v}_m\}$. At the same time, we append $n(m-1)$ zero-columns to public matrix $\mathbf{M}_i$ to get matrix $\mathbf{M}_i^\star$ satisfying $\mathbf{M}_i^\star \cdot \mathbf{s}_i^\star = \mathbf{M}_i \cdot \mathbf{s}_i$, so that we preserve the linear equation under consideration. In this way, we reduce the set-membership problem to the problem of proving the well-formedness of $\mathbf{s}_i^\star$. The latter can be done via random permutations of blocks in the framework of Stern's protocol. For instance, to prove that $\mathbf{s}_i \in \mathsf{Enc}_D$, i.e., $\mathbf{s}_i$ is a correct binary encoding of a digit, we extend it to $\mathbf{s}_i^\star \in \mathsf{SET}_D$, apply a random permutation to the extended vector, and make use of the properties observed in (3).

3.4 Zero-Knowledge Password Policy Check Protocol

We now present our construction of ZKPPC from lattices. Throughout, we use notations, sets and permutation techniques specified in Sect. 3.1 to reduce the statement to be proved to an instance of the relation R_{abstract} considered in Sect. 2.2, which in turn can be handled by the Stern-like protocol of Fig. 1.

Our protocol allows a prover $\mathcal{P}$ to convince a verifier $\mathcal{V}$ in ZK that $\mathcal{P}$ knows a password pw that hashes to a given value with randomness $\chi, \mathbf{r}$, and satisfies some policy $f = ((k_D, k_U, k_L, k_S), n_{\min}, n_{\max})$.[2] Recall that $\mathcal{V}$ demands pw must have length between $n_{\min}$ and $n_{\max}$ inclusive, contain at least k_D digits, k_S symbols, k_L lower-case and k_U upper-case letters. For simplicity, we let $k_{\mathsf{all}} = n_{\min} - (k_D + k_U + k_L + k_S)$.

The common input consists of matrices $\mathbf{A} \in \mathbb{Z}_q^{n \times (n_{\max}\lceil \log n_{\max}\rceil + 8n_{\max})}, \mathbf{B} \in \mathbb{Z}_q^{n \times m}$, hash value $\mathbf{h} \in \mathbb{Z}_q^n$ and extra information

$$\Delta = (\delta_{D,1}, \ldots, \delta_{D,k_D}, \delta_{S,1}, \ldots, \delta_{S,k_S}, \delta_{L,1}, \ldots, \delta_{L,k_L}, \ \delta_{U,1}, \ldots, \delta_{U,k_U},$$
$$\delta_{\mathsf{all},1}, \ldots, \delta_{\mathsf{all},k_{\mathsf{all}}}) \in [n_{\max}]^{n_{\min}},$$

which indicates the positions of the blocks, inside vector $P = \mathbf{e}'$, encoding k_D digits, k_S symbols, k_L lower-case letters, k_U upper-case letters and k_{all} other printable characters within pw. Revealing Δ to $\mathcal{V}$ does not harm $\mathcal{P}$, since the original positions of those blocks (in vector $\mathbf{e}$) are protected by the secret permutation χ.

The prover's witness consists of vectors $\mathbf{x} = (\mathbf{e}_0 \| \mathbf{e}') \in \{0,1\}^{n_{\max}\lceil \log n_{\max}\rceil + 8n_{\max}}$ and $\mathbf{r} \in \{0,1\}^m$ satisfying the following conditions:

---

[2] The construction we present considers the scenario where k_D, k_S, k_L, k_U are all positive. Our scheme can be easily adjusted to handle the case where one or more of them are 0.

1. $\mathbf{A} \cdot \mathbf{x} + \mathbf{B} \cdot \mathbf{r} = \mathbf{h} \bmod q$;
2. $\mathbf{e}_0 = \big(\, \mathsf{bin}(\chi(1) - 1) \, \| \ldots \| \, \mathsf{bin}(\chi(n_{\mathsf{max}} - 1)) \, \big)$;
3. $\mathbf{e}'$ has the form $(\mathbf{x}_1, \ldots, \mathbf{x}_{n_{\mathsf{max}}})$, where, for all $\alpha \in \{D, S, L, U, \mathsf{all}\}$ and all $i \in [k_\alpha]$, it holds that $\mathbf{x}_{\delta_{\alpha,i}} \in \mathsf{Enc}_\alpha$.

We first observe that, if we express matrix $\mathbf{A}$ as $\mathbf{A} = \big[\mathbf{A}_0 \mid \mathbf{A}_1 \mid \ldots \mid \mathbf{A}_{n_{\mathsf{max}}} \big]$, where $\mathbf{A}_0 \in \mathbb{Z}_q^{n_{\mathsf{max}} \lceil \log n_{\mathsf{max}} \rceil}$ and $\mathbf{A}_1, \ldots, \mathbf{A}_{n_{\mathsf{max}}} \in \mathbb{Z}_q^{n \times 8}$, then equation $\mathbf{A} \cdot \mathbf{x} + \mathbf{B} \cdot \mathbf{r} = \mathbf{h} \bmod q$ can be equivalently written as

$$\mathbf{A}_0 \cdot \mathbf{e}_0 + \sum_{\alpha \in \{D,S,L,U,\mathsf{all}\}, i \in [k_\alpha]} \mathbf{A}_{\delta_{\alpha,i}} \cdot \mathbf{x}_{\delta_{\alpha,i}} + \sum_{j \in [n_{\mathsf{max}}] \setminus \Delta} \mathbf{A}_j \cdot \mathbf{x}_j + \mathbf{B} \cdot \mathbf{r} = \mathbf{h} \bmod q. \quad (5)$$

Note that, we have $\mathbf{e}_0 \in \mathsf{SET}_{n_{\mathsf{max}}}$. We next transform the witness vectors $\mathbf{x}_1, \ldots, \mathbf{x}_{n_{\mathsf{max}}}, \mathbf{r}$ as follows,

$\diamond$ For all $\alpha \in \{D, S, L, U, \mathsf{all}\}$ and all $i \in [k_\alpha]$, to prove that $\mathbf{x}_{\delta_{\alpha,i}} \in \mathsf{Enc}_\alpha$, we append $\eta_\alpha - 1$ suitable blocks to $\mathbf{x}_{\delta_{\alpha,i}}$ to get vector $\mathbf{x}^\star_{\delta_{\alpha,i}} \in \mathsf{SET}_\alpha$.

$\diamond$ For vectors $\{\mathbf{x}_j\}_{j \in [n_{\mathsf{max}}] \setminus \Delta}$, note that it is necessary and sufficient to prove that they are binary vectors (namely, they are encoding of characters that may or may not be printable). Similarly, we have to prove that $\mathbf{r}$ is a binary vector. To this end, we let $\mathbf{y} \in \{0,1\}^{8(n_{\mathsf{max}} - n_{\mathsf{min}})}$ be a concatenation of all $\{\mathbf{x}_j\}_{j \in [n_{\mathsf{max}}] \setminus \Delta}$ and $\mathbf{z} = (\mathbf{y} \| \mathbf{r}) \in \{0,1\}^{8(n_{\mathsf{max}} - n_{\mathsf{min}}) + m}$. Then, we append suitable binary entries to $\mathbf{z}$ to get $\mathbf{z}^\star \in \{0,1\}^{2(8(n_{\mathsf{max}} - n_{\mathsf{min}}) + m)}$ with Hamming weight exactly $8(n_{\mathsf{max}} - n_{\mathsf{min}}) + m$, i.e., $\mathbf{z}^\star \in \mathsf{B}^2_{8(n_{\mathsf{max}} - n_{\mathsf{min}}) + m}$.

Having performed the above transformations, we construct the vector $\mathbf{w} \in \{0,1\}^\ell$, where

$$\ell = n_{\mathsf{max}} \lceil \log n_{\mathsf{max}} \rceil + 8(k_D \eta_D + k_S \eta_S + k_L \eta_L + k_U \eta_U) + 8 k_{\mathsf{all}} \eta_{\mathsf{all}} + 2(8(n_{\mathsf{max}} - n_{\mathsf{min}}) + m),$$

and $\mathbf{w}$ has the form:

$$\mathbf{w} = \big(\, \mathbf{e}_0 \ \| \ \mathbf{x}^\star_{\delta_{D,1}} \ \| \ \ldots \ \| \ \mathbf{x}^\star_{\delta_{D,k_D}} \ \| \ \mathbf{x}^\star_{\delta_{S,1}} \ \| \ \ldots \| \mathbf{x}^\star_{\delta_{S,k_S}} \ \| \ \mathbf{x}^\star_{\delta_{L,1}} \ \| \ \ldots \ \| \ \mathbf{x}^\star_{\delta_{L,k_L}}$$
$$\| \ \mathbf{x}^\star_{\delta_{U,1}} \ \| \ \ldots \ \| \ \mathbf{x}^\star_{\delta_{U,k_U}} \ \| \ \mathbf{x}^\star_{\delta_{\mathsf{all},1}} \ \| \ \ldots \ \| \ \mathbf{x}^\star_{\delta_{\mathsf{all},k_{\mathsf{all}}}} \ \| \ \mathbf{z}^\star \, \big). \quad (6)$$

When performing extensions over the secret vectors, we also append zero-columns to the public matrices in equation (5) so that it is preserved. Then, we concatenate the extended matrices to get $\mathbf{M} \in \mathbb{Z}_q^{n \times \ell}$ such that (5) becomes, with $\mathbf{v} = \mathbf{h} \in \mathbb{Z}_q^n$,

$$\mathbf{M} \cdot \mathbf{w} = \mathbf{v} \bmod q. \quad (7)$$

We have now established the first step towards reducing the given statement to an instance of the relation $\mathsf{R}_{\mathsf{abstract}}$ from Sect. 2.2. Next, we will specify the set VALID containing the vector $\mathbf{w}$, set $\mathcal{S}$ and permutations $\{\Gamma_\phi : \phi \in \mathcal{S}\}$ such that the conditions in (1) hold.

Define VALID as the set of all vectors $\mathbf{w} \in \{0,1\}^\ell$ having the form (6), where

$\diamond$ $\mathbf{e}_0 \in \mathsf{SET}_{n_{\max}}$;

$\diamond$ $\mathbf{x}^\star_{\delta_{\alpha,i}} \in \mathsf{SET}_\alpha$ for all $\alpha \in \{D, S, L, U, \mathsf{all}\}$ and all $i \in [k_\alpha]$;

$\diamond$ $\mathbf{z}^\star \in \mathsf{B}^2_{8(n_{\max}-n_{\min})+m}$.

It can be seen that the vector $\mathbf{w}$ obtained above belongs to this tailored set VALID. Next, let us define the set of permutations $\mathcal{S}$ as follows,

$$\mathcal{S} = \mathcal{S}_{n_{\max}} \times (\mathcal{S}_{\eta_D})^{k_D} \times (\mathcal{S}_{\eta_S})^{k_S} \times (\mathcal{S}_{\eta_L})^{k_L} \times (\mathcal{S}_{\eta_U})^{k_U} \times (\mathcal{S}_{\eta_{\mathsf{all}}})^{k_{\mathsf{all}}} \times \mathcal{S}_{2(8(n_{\max}-n_{\min})+m)}.$$

Then, for each element

$$\phi = \big(\pi, \tau_{D,1}, \ldots, \tau_{D,k_D}, \tau_{S,1}, \ldots, \tau_{S,k_S}, \tau_{L,1}, \ldots, \tau_{L,k_L}, \tau_{U,1}, \ldots, \tau_{U,k_U},$$
$$\tau_{\mathsf{all},1}, \ldots, \tau_{\mathsf{all},k_{\mathsf{all}}}, \theta\big) \in \mathcal{S},$$

we define the permutation Γ_ϕ that, when applied to $\mathbf{w} \in \mathbb{Z}^\ell$ of the form

$$\mathbf{w} = \big(\mathbf{e}_0 \parallel \mathbf{x}^\star_{\delta_{D,1}} \parallel \ldots \parallel \mathbf{x}^\star_{\delta_{D,k_D}} \parallel \mathbf{x}^\star_{\delta_{S,1}} \parallel \ldots \parallel \mathbf{x}^\star_{\delta_{S,k_S}} \parallel \mathbf{x}^\star_{\delta_{L,1}} \parallel \ldots \parallel \mathbf{x}^\star_{\delta_{L,k_L}}$$
$$\parallel \mathbf{x}^\star_{\delta_{U,1}} \parallel \ldots \parallel \mathbf{x}^\star_{\delta_{U,k_U}} \parallel \mathbf{x}^\star_{\delta_{\mathsf{all},1}} \parallel \ldots \parallel \mathbf{x}^\star_{\delta_{\mathsf{all},k_{\mathsf{all}}}} \parallel \mathbf{z}^\star\big).$$

where $\mathbf{e}_0 \in \mathbb{Z}^{n_{\max}\lceil \log n_{\max}\rceil}$, $\mathbf{x}^\star_{\delta_{\alpha,i}} \in \mathbb{Z}^{8\eta_\alpha}$ for all $\alpha \in \{D, S, L, U, \mathsf{all}\}$ and $i \in k_\alpha$, and $\mathbf{z}^\star \in \mathbb{Z}^{2(8(n_{\max}-n_{\min})+m)}$, it transforms the blocks of vector $\mathbf{w}$ as follows,

$\diamond$ $\mathbf{e}_0 \mapsto T_{\pi,\lceil \log n_{\max}\rceil}(\mathbf{e}_0)$.

$\diamond$ For all $\alpha \in \{D, S, L, U, \mathsf{all}\}$ and all $i \in k_\alpha$: $\mathbf{x}^\star_{\delta_{\alpha,i}} \mapsto T_{\tau_{\alpha,i},8}(\mathbf{x}^\star_{\delta_{\alpha,i}})$.

$\diamond$ $\mathbf{z}^\star \mapsto \theta(\mathbf{z}^\star)$.

Based on the properties observed in (2), (3), and (4), it can be seen that we have satisfied the conditions specified in (1), namely,

$$\begin{cases} \mathbf{w} \in \mathsf{VALID} \iff \Gamma_\phi(\mathbf{w}) \in \mathsf{VALID}, \\ \text{If } \mathbf{w} \in \mathsf{VALID} \text{ and } \phi \text{ is uniform in } \mathcal{S}, \text{ then } \Gamma_\phi(\mathbf{w}) \text{ is uniform in VALID}. \end{cases}$$

Having reduced the considered statement to an instance of the relation R_{abstract}, let us now describe how our protocol is executed. The protocol uses the KTX string commitment scheme COM, which is statistically hiding and computationally binding under the SIS assumption. Prior to the interaction, the prover $\mathcal{P}$ and verifier $\mathcal{V}$ construct the matrix $\mathbf{M}$ and vector $\mathbf{v}$ based on the common inputs $(\mathbf{A}, \mathbf{B}, \mathbf{h}, \Delta)$, while $\mathcal{P}$ builds the vector $\mathbf{w} \in \mathsf{VALID}$ from vectors $\mathbf{x}$ and $\mathbf{r}$, as discussed above. Then, $\mathcal{P}$ and $\mathcal{V}$ interact per Fig. 1. We thus obtain the following result, as a corollary of Theorem 1.

Theorem 3. *Under the* SIS *assumption, the protocol above is a ZKPPC protocol with respect to the randomised password hashing scheme $\mathcal{L}$ from Sect. 3.2 and policy $f = ((k_D, k_U, k_L, k_S), n_{\min}, n_{\max})$. The protocol is a statistical ZKAoK with perfect completeness, soundness error $2/3$ and communication cost $\mathcal{O}(\ell \log q)$.*

Proof. Perfect completeness, soundness error $2/3$ and communication cost $\mathcal{O}(\ell \log q)$ of the protocol follow from the use of the abstract protocol in Fig. 1. For simulation, we simply run the simulator of Theorem 1.

As for knowledge extraction, we first run the knowledge extractor of Theorem 1 to get the vector $\mathbf{w}' \in \mathsf{VALID}$ such that $\mathbf{M} \cdot \mathbf{w}' = \mathbf{v} \bmod q$. Then, we "backtrack" the transformations to extract from $\mathbf{w}'$, vectors $\mathbf{x}' = (\mathbf{e}'_0 \| \mathbf{x}'_1 \| \dots \| \mathbf{x}'_{n_{max}}) \in \{0,1\}^{n_{max}\lceil \log n_{max} \rceil + 8n_{max}}$ and $\mathbf{r}' \in \{0,1\}^m$ such that

$\diamond$ $\mathbf{A} \cdot \mathbf{x}' + \mathbf{B} \cdot \mathbf{r}' = \mathbf{h} \bmod q$;

$\diamond$ $\mathbf{e}'_0 \in \mathsf{SET}_{n_{max}}$;

$\diamond$ For all $\alpha \in \{D, S, L, U, \mathsf{all}\}$ and all $i \in k_\alpha$: $\mathbf{x}'_{\delta_{\alpha,i}} \in \mathsf{Enc}_\alpha$.

Notice that one can recover a permutation of n_{max} elements from an element of $\mathsf{SET}_{n_{max}}$. Let χ' be the permutation encoded by $\mathbf{e}'_0$. Then, by applying the inverse permutation $T^{-1}_{\chi',8}$ to $(\mathbf{x}'_1 \| \dots \| \mathbf{x}'_{n_{max}})$, we recover $\mathbf{e}' \in \{0,1\}^{8n_{max}}$. Finally, by removing potential blocks of length 8 that correspond to encodings of non-printable ASCII characters from $\mathbf{e}'$, we obtain a vector that encodes some password string pw' satisfying policy f. $\qquad\square$

Efficiency analysis. By inspection, we see that, without using the big-O notation, each round of the proposed protocol has communication cost slightly larger than

$$\ell \log q = \left(n_{max} \lceil \log n_{max} \rceil + 8(k_D \eta_D + k_S \eta_S + k_L \eta_L + k_U \eta_U) \right.$$
$$\left. + 8k_{\mathsf{all}} \eta_{\mathsf{all}} + 2(8(n_{max} - n_{min}) + m) \right) \log q.$$

Let us estimate the cost in practice. Note that the KTX commitment scheme can work with relatively small lattice parameters, e.g., $n = 256$, $\log q = 10$, $m = 5120$. For a common password policy $f = \big((1,1,1,1), 8, 16\big)$, the communication cost would be about $17\,\mathrm{KB}$. As each round has a soundness error of $2/3$, one may have to repeat the protocol many times in parallel to achieve a high level of confidence. For instance, if a soundness error of 2^{-30} is required, then one can repeat 52 times for a final cost of around $900\,\mathrm{KB}$. In practical implementations, one can exploit various optimizations (e.g., instead of sending a random vector, one can send the PRNG seed used to generate it) to reduce the communication complexity.

4   Conclusion and Open Questions

Through the use of the KTX commitment scheme [28] and a Stern-like zero-knowledge argument of set membership, we designed a lattice-based zero-knowledge protocol for proving that a committed/hashed password sent to the server satisfies the required password policy. All together, we obtain the first ZKPPC that is based on the hardness of the SIS problem which to date remains quantum resistant. Unfortunately, there are no viable VPAKE protocols from lattices that can be coupled with our ZKPPC protocol to construct a complete privacy-preserving password-based authentication and key exchange system.

Our proposed ZKPPC protocol can be employed to securely register chosen passwords at remote servers with the following security guarantees: (1) Registered passwords are not disclosed to the server until used; (2) Each registered password provably conforms to the specified password policy. Although not being ready to be deployed in practice, we view this work as the first step in designing post-quantum privacy-preserving password-based authentication and key exchange systems.

We leave several open questions as potential future work: (1) to construct a more practical lattice-based ZKPPC; (2) to develop a lattice-based VPAKE; and (3) to extend lattice-based ZKPPC to other PAKE protocols, such as two-server PAKE, where the passwords are secretly shared between two servers, of which we assume at most one to be compromisable. The third question is similar to the one asked by Kiefer and Manulis [30] and as they noted, it is a challenge even in the classical discrete logarithm setting.

Acknowledgements. We would like to thank the anonymous reviewers of ISC 2017 for helpful comments. The research is supported by Singapore Ministry of Education under Research Grant MOE2016-T2-2-014(S) and by NTU under Tier 1 grant RG143/14.

References

1. Ajtai, M.: Generating hard instances of lattice problems (extended abstract). In: STOC 1996 (1996)
2. Baum, C., Damgård, I., Larsen, K.G., Nielsen, M.: How to prove knowledge of small secrets. In: Robshaw, M., Katz, J. (eds.) CRYPTO 2016. LNCS, vol. 9816, pp. 478–498. Springer, Heidelberg (2016). doi:10.1007/978-3-662-53015-3_17
3. Baum, C., Damgrd, I., Oechsner, S., Peikert, C.: Efficient commitments and zero-knowledge protocols from ring-sis with applications to lattice-based threshold cryptosystems. Cryptology ePrint Archive, Report 2016/997 (2016)
4. Bauman, E., Lu, Y., Lin, Z.: Half a century of practice: who is still storing plaintext passwords? In: Lopez, J., Wu, Y. (eds.) ISPEC 2015. LNCS, vol. 9065, pp. 253–267. Springer, Cham (2015). doi:10.1007/978-3-319-17533-1_18
5. Bellare, M., Pointcheval, D., Rogaway, P.: Authenticated key exchange secure against dictionary attacks. In: Preneel, B. (ed.) EUROCRYPT 2000. LNCS, vol. 1807, pp. 139–155. Springer, Heidelberg (2000). doi:10.1007/3-540-45539-6_11
6. Bellovin, S.M., Merritt, M.: Encrypted key exchange: password-based protocols secure against dictionary attacks. In: IEEE Symposium on Security and Privacy (1992)
7. Bellovin, S.M., Merritt, M.: Augmented encrypted key exchange: a password-based protocol secure against dictionary attacks and password file compromise. In: ACM CCS 1993 (1993)
8. Benhamouda, F., Blazy, O., Chevalier, C., Pointcheval, D., Vergnaud, D.: New techniques for SPHFs and efficient one-round PAKE protocols. In: Canetti, R., Garay, J.A. (eds.) CRYPTO 2013. LNCS, vol. 8042, pp. 449–475. Springer, Heidelberg (2013). doi:10.1007/978-3-642-40041-4_25

9. Benhamouda, F., Camenisch, J., Krenn, S., Lyubashevsky, V., Neven, G.: Better zero-knowledge proofs for lattice encryption and their application to group signatures. In: Sarkar, P., Iwata, T. (eds.) ASIACRYPT 2014. LNCS, vol. 8873, pp. 551–572. Springer, Heidelberg (2014). doi:10.1007/978-3-662-45611-8_29

10. Benhamouda, F., Krenn, S., Lyubashevsky, V., Pietrzak, K.: Efficient zero-knowledge proofs for commitments from learning with errors over rings. In: Pernul, G., Ryan, P.Y.A., Weippl, E. (eds.) ESORICS 2015. LNCS, vol. 9326, pp. 305–325. Springer, Cham (2015). doi:10.1007/978-3-319-24174-6_16

11. Benhamouda, F., Pointcheval, D.: Verifier-based password-authenticated key exchange: new models and constructions. Cryptology ePrint Archive, Report 2013/833 (2013)

12. Cramer, R., Damgård, I., Xing, C., Yuan, C.: Amortized complexity of zero-knowledge proofs revisited: achieving linear soundness slack. In: Coron, J.-S., Nielsen, J.B. (eds.) EUROCRYPT 2017. LNCS, vol. 10210, pp. 479–500. Springer, Cham (2017). doi:10.1007/978-3-319-56620-7_17

13. del Pino, R., Lyubashevsky, V.: Amortization with fewer equations for proving knowledge of small secrets. Cryptology ePrint Archive, Report 2017/280 (2017)

14. Ding, Y., Fan, L.: Efficient password-based authenticated key exchange from lattices. In: CIS 2011 (2011)

15. Dong, C., Chen, L., Wen, Z.: When private set intersection meets big data: an efficient and scalable protocol. In: ACM CCS 2013 (2013)

16. Dong, C., Kiefer, F.: Secure set-based policy checking and its application to password registration. In: Reiter, M., Naccache, D. (eds.) CANS 2015. LNCS, vol. 9476, pp. 59–74. Springer, Cham (2015). doi:10.1007/978-3-319-26823-1_5

17. Florêncio, D., Herley, C.: Where do security policies come from? In: SOUPS 2010 (2010)

18. Furukawa, J.: Efficient and verifiable shuffling and shuffle-decryption. IEICE TFECCS **88A**(1), 172–188 (2005)

19. Gates, S.: Linkedin password hack: Check to see if yours was one of the 6.5 million leaked (2012). http://www.huffingtonpost.com/2012/06/07/linkedin-password-hack-check_n_1577184.html

20. Gennaro, R., Lindell, Y.: A framework for password-based authenticated key exchange. In: Biham, E. (ed.) EUROCRYPT 2003. LNCS, vol. 2656, pp. 524–543. Springer, Heidelberg (2003). doi:10.1007/3-540-39200-9_33

21. Gentry, C., MacKenzie, P., Ramzan, Z.: A method for making password-based key exchange resilient to server compromise. In: Dwork, C. (ed.) CRYPTO 2006. LNCS, vol. 4117, pp. 142–159. Springer, Heidelberg (2006). doi:10.1007/11818175_9

22. Gentry, C., Peikert, C., Vaikuntanathan, V.: Trapdoors for hard lattices and new cryptographic constructions. In: STOC 2008 (2008)

23. Goldreich, O., Goldwasser, S.: On the limits of non-approximability of lattice problems. In: STOC 1998 (1998)

24. Groth, J.: Evaluating security of voting schemes in the universal composability framework. In: Jakobsson, M., Yung, M., Zhou, J. (eds.) ACNS 2004. LNCS, vol. 3089, pp. 46–60. Springer, Heidelberg (2004). doi:10.1007/978-3-540-24852-1_4

25. Hunt, T.: Have i been pwned (2017). https://haveibeenpwned.com/. Accessed 7 July 2017

26. Jain, A., Krenn, S., Pietrzak, K., Tentes, A.: Commitments and efficient zero-knowledge proofs from learning parity with noise. In: Wang, X., Sako, K. (eds.) ASIACRYPT 2012. LNCS, vol. 7658, pp. 663–680. Springer, Heidelberg (2012). doi:10.1007/978-3-642-34961-4_40

27. Katz, J., Vaikuntanathan, V.: Smooth projective hashing and password-based authenticated key exchange from lattices. In: Matsui, M. (ed.) ASIACRYPT 2009. LNCS, vol. 5912, pp. 636–652. Springer, Heidelberg (2009). doi:10.1007/978-3-642-10366-7_37

28. Kawachi, A., Tanaka, K., Xagawa, K.: Concurrently secure identification schemes based on the worst-case hardness of lattice problems. In: Pieprzyk, J. (ed.) ASIACRYPT 2008. LNCS, vol. 5350, pp. 372–389. Springer, Heidelberg (2008). doi:10.1007/978-3-540-89255-7_23

29. Kiefer, F.: Advancements in password-based cryptography. PhD thesis, University of Surrey (2016)

30. Kiefer, F., Manulis, M.: Zero-knowledge password policy checks and verifier-based PAKE. In: Kutyłowski, M., Vaidya, J. (eds.) ESORICS 2014. LNCS, vol. 8713, pp. 295–312. Springer, Cham (2014). doi:10.1007/978-3-319-11212-1_17

31. Kiefer, F., Manulis, M.: Blind password registration for two-server password authenticated key exchange and secret sharing protocols. In: Bishop, M., Nascimento, A.C.A. (eds.) ISC 2016. LNCS, vol. 9866, pp. 95–114. Springer, Cham (2016). doi:10.1007/978-3-319-45871-7_7

32. Kiefer, F., Manulis, M.: Blind password registration for verifier-based PAKE. In: AsiaPKC@AsiaCCS 2016 (2016)

33. Libert, B., Ling, S., Mouhartem, F., Nguyen, K., Wang, H.: Signature schemes with efficient protocols and dynamic group signatures from lattice assumptions. In: Cheon, J.H., Takagi, T. (eds.) ASIACRYPT 2016. LNCS, vol. 10032, pp. 373–403. Springer, Heidelberg (2016). doi:10.1007/978-3-662-53890-6_13

34. Libert, B., Ling, S., Mouhartem, F., Nguyen, K., Wang, H.: Zero-Knowledge Arguments for Matrix-Vector Relations and Lattice-Based Group Encryption. In: Cheon, J.H., Takagi, T. (eds.) ASIACRYPT 2016. LNCS, vol. 10032, pp. 101–131. Springer, Heidelberg (2016). doi:10.1007/978-3-662-53890-6_4

35. Libert, B., Ling, S., Nguyen, K., Wang, H.: Zero-knowledge arguments for lattice-based accumulators: logarithmic-size ring signatures and group signatures without trapdoors. In: Fischlin, M., Coron, J.-S. (eds.) EUROCRYPT 2016. LNCS, vol. 9666, pp. 1–31. Springer, Heidelberg (2016). doi:10.1007/978-3-662-49896-5_1

36. Libert, B., Mouhartem, F., Nguyen, K.: A lattice-based group signature scheme with message-dependent opening. In: Manulis, M., Sadeghi, A.-R., Schneider, S. (eds.) ACNS 2016. LNCS, vol. 9696, pp. 137–155. Springer, Cham (2016). doi:10.1007/978-3-319-39555-5_8

37. Ling, S., Nguyen, K., Stehlé, D., Wang, H.: Improved zero-knowledge proofs of knowledge for the ISIS problem, and applications. In: Kurosawa, K., Hanaoka, G. (eds.) PKC 2013. LNCS, vol. 7778, pp. 107–124. Springer, Heidelberg (2013). doi:10.1007/978-3-642-36362-7_8

38. Ling, S., Nguyen, K., Wang, H.: Group signatures from lattices: simpler, tighter, shorter, ring-based. In: Katz, J. (ed.) PKC 2015. LNCS, vol. 9020, pp. 427–449. Springer, Heidelberg (2015). doi:10.1007/978-3-662-46447-2_19

39. Ling, S., Nguyen, K., Wang, H., Xu, Y.: Lattice-based group signatures: achieving full dynamicity with ease. In: Gollmann, D., Miyaji, A., Kikuchi, H. (eds.) ACNS 2017. LNCS, vol. 10355, pp. 293–312. Springer, Cham (2017). doi:10.1007/978-3-319-61204-1_15

40. Lyubashevsky, V.: Lattice-based identification schemes secure under active attacks. In: Cramer, R. (ed.) PKC 2008. LNCS, vol. 4939, pp. 162–179. Springer, Heidelberg (2008). doi:10.1007/978-3-540-78440-1_10

41. Lyubashevsky, V.: Lattice signatures without trapdoors. In: Pointcheval, D., Johansson, T. (eds.) EUROCRYPT 2012. LNCS, vol. 7237, pp. 738–755. Springer, Heidelberg (2012). doi:10.1007/978-3-642-29011-4_43

42. Micciancio, D., Peikert, C.: Hardness of SIS and LWE with small parameters. In: Canetti, R., Garay, J.A. (eds.) CRYPTO 2013. LNCS, vol. 8042, pp. 21–39. Springer, Heidelberg (2013). doi:10.1007/978-3-642-40041-4_2

43. Micciancio, D., Vadhan, S.P.: Statistical zero-knowledge proofs with efficient provers: lattice problems and more. In: Boneh, D. (ed.) CRYPTO 2003. LNCS, vol. 2729, pp. 282–298. Springer, Heidelberg (2003). doi:10.1007/978-3-540-45146-4_17

44. NIST: Post-quantum crypto standardization - call for proposals announcement (2016). http://csrc.nist.gov/groups/ST/post-quantum-crypto/cfp-announce-dec2016.html

45. Pedersen, T.P.: Non-interactive and information-theoretic secure verifiable secret sharing. In: Feigenbaum, J. (ed.) CRYPTO 1991. LNCS, vol. 576, pp. 129–140. Springer, Heidelberg (1992). doi:10.1007/3-540-46766-1_9

46. Peikert, C., Vaikuntanathan, V.: Noninteractive statistical zero-knowledge proofs for lattice problems. In: Wagner, D. (ed.) CRYPTO 2008. LNCS, vol. 5157, pp. 536–553. Springer, Heidelberg (2008). doi:10.1007/978-3-540-85174-5_30

47. Perlroth, N.: More than half a billion yahoo accounts have been hacked, yahoo confirms (2016). https://www.nytimes.com/2016/09/23/technology/yahoo-hackers.html

48. Regev, O.: On lattices, learning with errors, random linear codes, and cryptography. In: STOC 2005 (2005)

49. Shor, P.W.: Polynomial-time algorithms for prime factorization and discrete logarithms on a quantum computer. SIAM Review **41**(2), 303–332 (1999)

50. Stern, J.: A new paradigm for public key identification. IEEE Trans. Inf. Theor. **42**(6), 1757–1768 (1996)

51. Ur, B., Kelley, P.G., Komanduri, S., Lee, J., Maass, M., Mazurek, M.L., Passaro, T., Shay, R., Vidas, T., Bauer, L., Christin, N., Cranor, L.F.: How does your password measure up? the effect of strength meters on password creation. In: USENIX Security Symposium 2012 (2012)

Generic Forward-Secure Key Agreement Without Signatures

Cyprien de Saint Guilhem, Nigel P. Smart$^{(\boxtimes)}$, and Bogdan Warinschi

Department of Computer Science, University of Bristol, Bristol, UK
`nigel@cs.bris.ac.uk`

Abstract. We present a generic, yet simple and efficient transformation to obtain a forward secure authenticated key exchange protocol from a two-move passively secure unauthenticated key agreement scheme (such as standard Diffie–Hellman or Frodo or NewHope). Our construction requires only an IND-CCA public key encryption scheme (such as RSA-OAEP or a method based on ring-LWE), and a message authentication code. Particularly relevant in the context of the state-of-the-art of postquantum secure primitives, we avoid the use of digital signature schemes: practical candidate post-quantum signature schemes are less accepted (and require more bandwidth) than candidate post-quantum public key encryption schemes. An additional feature of our proposal is that it helps avoid the bad practice of using long term keys certified for encryption to produce digital signatures. We prove the security of our transformation in the random oracle model.

1 Introduction

Forward secrecy and authentication are the standard security requirements for authenticated key agreement protocols (AKA). They require that parties authenticate one another, and that the key derived remains secret to anyone but to the two parties involved at the time of the execution. Modern realizations rely on the Diffie–Hellman protocol which is unauthenticated and guarantees key secrecy only against passive adversaries. The stronger property is obtained via additional mechanisms which authenticate the two parties and ensure integrity of the conversation between them, even against active adversaries.

Numerous generic transformations in the literature show how to achieve full AKA active security from protocols with weaker guarantees [3,9,18,22,24,28] using simple mechanisms such as signatures, encryption, and MACs.

Such generic techniques are particularly appealing; on the one hand they enable a modular approach where the base protocol and the details of the transformation are designed and analyzed independently – in particular, if needed, the underlying protocol can be easily swapped out and replaced with a different mechanism. On the other it provide conceptual clarity for choices that are made,

This work has been supported in part by ERC Advanced Grant ERC-2015-AdG-IMPaCT.

P.Q. Nguyen and J. Zhou (Eds.): ISC 2017, LNCS 10599, pp. 114–133, 2017.
https://doi.org/10.1007/978-3-319-69659-1_7

e.g. which part of the protocol provides say, key-secrecy, and which deals with integrity/entity authentication.

In this paper we contribute to this research direction. We provide a simple generic transformation which, when applied to a certain class of passively secure key-exchange protocols, yields the most round-efficient authenticated key-agreement protocols against active adversaries to date. Besides optimal round complexity, our proposal has two interesting implications which serve as further motivation for this work. The first concerns the practicalities of existing RSA certified public keys; the second concerns security of key-agreement protocols in the post-quantum world.

Consider the instantiation of the "signed Diffie-Hellman" construction which appears, for example, in the popular TLS 1.0-1.2 ciphersuite

TLS_ECDHE_RSA_WITH_AES_128_GCM_SHA256,

using RSA signatures and elliptic curve based Diffie–Hellman. This usage is a bit of a kludge: RSA certificates in existence were issued for dual-use of RSA in both signature and encryption mode (which was needed for the earlier TLS mechanism of RSA key- transport which is still prevalent). Deploying protocols where the same keys are used for both signature and encryption would encourage a usage which is not supported by rigorous mathematical guarantees. Short of issuing new RSA keys, this type of misuse could be avoided by ensuring that existing keys are only used for encryption. We note that this is not just a theoretical concern. Attacks against deployed cryptography that reuse keys in unintended ways have been previously reported [19,20,27].

We now discuss the design of key-exchange protocols secure in the post-quantum setting. Here, a natural strategy is to consider existing designs and replace the different components with post-quantum secure versions. The underlying Diffie-Hellman constructions can be replaced by (Ring-)LWE-based variant such as NewHope [7] or Frodo [1]. For other primitives, the situation seems to be more delicate. Both for historical and technical reasons, there seems to be less confidence in proposals for post-quantum signatures th an for post-quantum encryption. Whilst lattice based encryption schemes have a strong track record, see NTRU [16] for a historic scheme or Ring-LWE [25,26] for more modern ones, the use of lattice based signature schemes is less stable. Many early schemes, such as GGH [13] and NTRUSign [15,17], were eventually broken due to issues with the distribution of the signatures [12,29]; however recently more promising lattice based candidates have been proposed such as [10]. Post-quantum signature schemes based on Merkle hash trees have also had issues related to the need to maintain a large state; again recently this issue has been overcome with the introduction of state-less hash tree based [5].

Questionable dual use of RSA keys, and the relatively slow progress of post-quantum secure signature schemes, raises the question of whether one can design a passively (forward) secure unauthenticated protocol together with authentication mechanisms that rely solely on post-quantum public key encryption schemes.

Our results. We answer this question in the positive. We propose a generic transformation which bootstraps a forward secure AKA protocol out of a two-pass passively secure unauthenticated key agreement (KA) scheme which satisfies some mild additional conditions. The transformation uses an arbitrary IND-CCA public key encryption scheme and a strongly unforgeable MAC. Below we provide a sketch of our transformation, motivate its design and discuss the additional requirements on the underlying protocol.

Consider an arbitrary such protocol Π, whose execution between parties U and V is described in Fig. 1 using the general syntax introduced by Bellare and Rogaway [4]. For example, Diffie–Hellman is an instantiation where U's ephemeral key is e_A and m_1 is g^{e_A}, V's ephemeral key is e_B (which can be deleted as soon as it is used to derive $m_2 = g^{e_B}$ and $k_B = m_1^{e_B}$), finally the computation of k_A is done by U using the equation $k_A = m_2^{e_A}$. To obtain forward secrecy, the ephemeral key data is assumed to be deleted as soon as the session keys are locally computed.

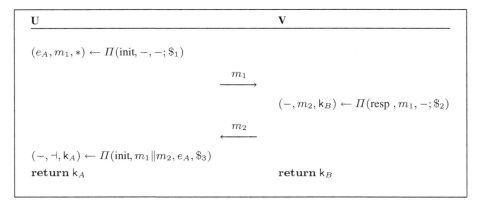

Fig. 1. An arbitrary two-round unauthenticated key agreement protocol Π.

We bootstrap this two round KA protocol into a fully authenticated one (which inherits the forward secrecy property). Our construction, presented in Fig. 2, requires a public key encryption scheme secure under chosen ciphertext attacks, a strongly unforgeable message authentication code, and two key derivation functions H_1 and H_2 which we model as random oracles.

The protocol works by wrapping the message flows, m_1 and m_2, of the KA protocol in encryptions under the long term keys of the two parties. Interestingly, the main role played by encryption here is to authenticate the parties and ensure integrity of the messages they exchange. Indeed, one can think of the first two messages of the protocol as a challenge-response exchange where U attempts to authenticate V by sending an encryption of m_1 under the public key of V and expecting to receive the same m_1 in the next flow. Similarly, the second and third flow can be interpreted as a challenge-response where V sends m_2 to U

U $(\mathsf{pk}_U, \mathsf{sk}_U)$		V $(\mathsf{pk}_V, \mathsf{sk}_V)$
$(e_U, m_1, *) \leftarrow \Pi(\mathsf{init}, -, -; \$_1)$		
$\mathsf{m}_1 \leftarrow \mathsf{Enc}_{\mathsf{pk}_V}(U \| m_1)$	$\xrightarrow{\ \mathsf{m}_1\ }$	$U \| m_1 = \mathsf{Dec}_{\mathsf{sk}_V}(\mathsf{m}_1)$
		$(-, m_2, \kappa_V) \leftarrow \Pi(\mathsf{resp}, m_1, -; \$_2)$
$m_1' \| m_2 = \mathsf{Dec}_{\mathsf{sk}_U}(\mathsf{m}_2)$	$\xleftarrow{\ \mathsf{m}_2\ }$	$\mathsf{m}_2 \leftarrow \mathsf{Enc}_{\mathsf{pk}_U}(m_1 \| m_2)$
if $m_1' \neq m_1$ **then**		
reject		
$(-, \vdash, \kappa_U) \leftarrow \Pi(\mathsf{init}, m_1 \| m_2, e_U; \$_3)$		
$\mathsf{k}_{U,1} \leftarrow H_1(\kappa_U)$		
$\mathsf{m}_3 \leftarrow \mathsf{Mac}_{\mathsf{k}_{U,1}}(U \| V)$	$\xrightarrow{\ \mathsf{m}_3\ }$	$\mathsf{k}_{V,1} \leftarrow H_1(\kappa_V)$
		if $\mathsf{Vrfy}_{\mathsf{k}_{V,1}}(U \| V, \mathsf{m}_3) = 0$ **then**
		reject
$\mathsf{k}_{U,2} \leftarrow H_2(\kappa_U \| U \| V)$		$\mathsf{k}_{V,2} \leftarrow H_2(\kappa_V \| U \| V)$
return $\mathsf{k}_{U,2}$		**return** $\mathsf{k}_{V,2}$

Fig. 2. The new AKA protocol construction.

and expects to receive a message that depends on m_2. In addition, the MAC send as the last message also ties the identities of the parties involved with this particular execution of the protocol run. The final application key is derived from the same key from Π, but in a way that decouples it from the MAC key and also incorporates the identities of the participants.

The last message flow and key derivation methodology also thwart an analogue of the (in)famous attack against the Needham-Schroeder protocol. A malicious V could reencrypt the first message for a third party W who would reply with its own encrypted m_2 for U; V could simply forward this message so U. Parties U and W would thus derive the same key for the underlying passively secure protocol. However, W will no longer accept the MAC as it will be on the wrong message ($U \| V$ as opposed to $U \| W$), thus thwarting the attack. In addition, since it depends on the participants' identities, the derived session key will also be different for U and W.

The essence of our transformation is that it attempts to ensure that an active adversary cannot interfere with the execution of the underlying protocol, i.e. that when a party accepts, it must have engaged in an execution with another honest party. Put otherwise, even an active adversary cannot force a session to accept other than by forwarding honest messages.

Using non-malleable encryption to protect the integrity of messages goes someway towards implementing this intuition. Ensuring that parties authenticate each other successfully is however not obvious, and in fact require additional properties on the underlying protocol Π. As explained above, one should think of the first two messages as a challenge-response protocol to authenticate V. Notice that for security of authentication, this requires that message m_1 of the Π has sufficient entropy; otherwise, an adversary who guesses m_1 can reply with an appropriately message which encrypts m_1 and some m_2 and get U to accept.

Similarly, one should think of the second and third messages as a challenge-response protocol that authenticates U: the last message should only be computable by some party which received m_2 and derived the MAC key from it. This intuition is valid only if m_2 actually helps determine the MAC key, which is not necessarily the case. Consider a two message protocol where, if the first message of U for V is some fixed message bad, then V sets the local key to, say, 0^n. Such a protocol may still be secure against a passive adversary as an honest execution U would never send bad. Yet, the protocol obtained by applying our transformation is not actively secure since the adversary can send the encryption of bad to V. More generally, a close look shows that the problem is that the adversary can send an appropriately crafted message m_1 which coerces the key into one which can be easily guessed (even if V behaves honestly).

The above discussion shows that we need two additional properties for our transformation to work: (i) that the first message of Π is unpredictable and (ii) that even if the first message is an arbitrary message sent by the adversary then the key derived by V is still unpredictable.

Naturally, one can ask if further subtle attacks are possible. We show that this is not the case and provide rigorous guarantees for the above intuition. We show that if the starting protocol is an arbitrary passively secure two-message protocol and satisfies the two additional security properties informally described above, then the transformation that we propose yields a full fledged forward secure key exchange protocol with mutual authentication (in the random oracle model), under standard assumptions on the encryption and MAC scheme used in the transformation.

Related work. The first generic compilers for authenticated key exchange were by Bellare, Canetti, and Krawczyk [3] later refined by Canetti and Krawczyk [9]. These works consider adversaries of different strength, but share an interesting idea of protocol design. First construct a protocol secure in a model where links between parties are authenticated (i.e. secure against passive adversaries), and then compile it into a stronger version, secure in a world with unauthenticated links, by using special-purpose *authenticators* which authenticate the sender of each message and ensure their integrity. In particular, BCK present an authenticator that uses IND-CCA2 secure encryption and MAC schemes. However, the use of authenticator replaces every message flow of the base protocols with three flows, so starting from a two-message flow protocols one obtains a stronger protocol that requires five rounds. Unfortunately the general setting of MT-authenticators of BCK works does not immediately allows for further optimisation which reduces the number of rounds.

Katz and Young [22] consider the problem of boosting passive security to active security for *group* key exchange by first exchanging nonces between parties and then authenticating each message through signatures that involve these nonces. For the case of two parties this result in a protocol with four message flows. For this type of protocols, a less efficient compiler is the one studied by Morrissey, Smart and Warinschi [28]. They show that TLScan be regarded as TLS as the successive applications of two generic transformations which bootstrap passive security to active security.

A second line of work which is related to ours is based on the observation that key encapsulation mechanisms naturally give rise to passively secure keyexchange protocols (where one party sends the parameters of a KEM scheme, and the second party sends a KEM). There are by now several constructions of key-exchange protocols (in settings which are sometimes different from ours) which start from KEMs. For example, Boyd et al. [8] construct authenticated key exchange from KEMs, meeting the eCK stronger security requirement, and Gunther et al [14] show how to add forward security to KEMs to obtain forward security when these are used as a full-key exchange protocol that enables forward secure 0-RTT. Both transformations work in the ID-based setting, use pairings and therefore are not generic.

Perhaps the closest work with ours is that of Li et al. [24] who present two transformations that bootstrap AKA protocols out of passively secure ones, one based on signatures and another based on encryption. Both transformations first execute a passively secure KA protocol and then use three additional flows to perform entity authentication (and ensure the integrity of the conversation between the two parties). Just like our proposal, the encryption-based construction of [24] can serve to avoid the two issues which we have outlined above but at an increased round-complexity cost. In essence, we avoid additional communication rounds by showing how to piggy-back entity authentication on top of the passively secure protocol.

One observations which is warranted at this point is that our transformation does not achieve key-confirmation [11] (while derived keys are secret and parties authenticate each other, one party may accept without the other party actually having derived the key), whereas some other transformations do. This was not an explicit goal, afterall the notion has only recently been formalized [11].

2   Preliminaries

We first recall some standard definitions of primitives and their A comprehensive overview of this material can be found in [21] and in the full version of this paper. We then recall basic notions of security for passive key agreement protocols and introduce two new formal definitions. Throughout this paper, we denote the security parameter by λ, represented in unary notation as 1^λ, and the empty string by $-$.

2.1 Standard Definitions

We recall briefly the informal descriptions of actively secure public-key encryption schemes (with the addition of multi-user security), strongly unforgeable message authentication codes as well as key derivation functions and the random oracle model.

Public-key encryption schemes. In this paper, we denote a public-key encryption scheme by a tuple $E = (\mathsf{Setup}, \mathsf{KGen}, \mathsf{Enc}, \mathsf{Dec})$ of $\mathsf{poly}(\lambda)$-time algorithms. We assume that such schemes correctly decrypt honestly encrypted ciphertexts with overwhelming probability.

The standard (single-user) active security notion for such schemes is that of *indistinguishability under chosen ciphertext attack*, denoted $\mathsf{IND\text{-}CCA}$. The experiment, also called game, for this setting gives an arbitrary adversary a randomly sampled public-key and, upon query of a left-right oracle, denoted $\mathsf{L\text{-}R}$, with two messages of identical lengths, returns the encryption of one of the two. Given access to a decryption oracle, the adversary's goal is to guess which of the two messages the oracle encrypts. The adversary may query either oracle several times, with the only restriction that it may not query the decryption oracle on any ciphertext output by the left-right oracle.

In the proof of security of our protocol, we make use of the multi-user security notion described in [2]. For n participants, the $n\text{-}\mathsf{IND\text{-}CCA}$ security experiment is very similar to the single-user setting. The difference is that the adversary is provided with n different public keys and may query the left-right oracle on any one of these keys. Whether it is the right or left message which is encrypted is still selected at random, but this choice remains consistent between all queries of the $\mathsf{L\text{-}R}$ oracle.

Unforgeable message authentication codes. Message authentication codes (MACs) are symmetric key primitives that allow parties sharing a secret key k to authenticate and verify messages, thus detecting eventual modification of their content. A MAC is a triple of $\mathsf{poly}(\lambda)$-time algorithms $M = (\mathsf{KGen}, \mathsf{Mac}, \mathsf{Vrfy})$ such that, given a message and a key, Mac produces a tag, and such that, given a message, a tag and a key, Vrfy verifies that the tag corresponds to the message.

The security experiment for strong unforgeability, denoted $\mathsf{MAC\text{-}sFORGE}$, generates a random key and gives the adversary access to a Mac oracle whilst recording pairs of queried messages and the tag that was returned for each. The goal of the adversary is to output a message and a tag such that the verify algorithms accepts this tag and such that this tag was never produced by the Mac oracle for this message.

Key derivation functions and the random oracle model. In cryptographic schemes such as key agreement protocols, the secret information that is exchanged often cannot be used "out of the box" to achieve other goals such as encryption or authentication. Instead, we must use a method to transfer the high entropy of the key agreement session key into a format that is more suitable. This is achieved by making use of *key derivation functions* (KDFs) which are functions with high min-entropy, i.e. an adversary has a negligible chance of correctly guessing the output computed from a given input. While in practice great care must be given to the instantiation of such a KDF, we will make use here of the *random oracle model* and assume that the KDFs we use sample their output uniformly at random from a given space. We will use two independent random oracles which we will denote by H_1 and H_2.

2.2 Passively Secure Unauthenticated Key Agreement Protocol

First, we formalise what we mean by a (simple) unauthenticated key agreement protocol and what it means for such a protocol to be passively secure. Informally we consider a protocol passively secure if an adversary cannot determine the session key from seeing a transcript. We make no usage of long term keys at this stage, as we are focusing on unauthenticated protocols. In a later section we will discuss the model for fully actively secure, and authenticated, key agreement.

Informally, a key agreement protocol is a set of instructions, executed by two parties involved in a conversation, which leads to both of them computing identical session keys. These keys are then usually used to authenticate or encrypt further communication. The most basic security notion expected of such a protocol is that an adversary who has access to the transcript of a conversation is incapable of obtaining any information regarding the final session key. Our formalisation below is inspired by the original definition of such protocols by Bellare and Rogaway [4].

Definition 1 (Unauthenticated Key Agreement Protocol). *An* unauthenticated key agreement protocol *is a pair of probabilistic* poly(λ)*-time algorithms* (Setup, Π) *such that:*

1. *The* setup *algorithm* Setup *takes as input the security parameter* 1^λ *and outputs a tuple of public parameters,* params, *required by the key agreement protocol. Amongst other information* params *specifies a message space* $\mathcal{M}$ *and a key space* $\mathcal{K}$. *We assume for convenience that* λ *is implicit in* params.
2. *The* protocol function Π *is a function that dictates which messages the participating entities should compute and send to one another. Its input and output are of the form* $(\epsilon', m, \delta, \kappa) \leftarrow \Pi(\text{params}, \rho, \tau, \epsilon; \$)$ *where the inputs are defined by:*
   - params *are the system parameters.*
   - $\rho \in \{\text{init}, \text{resp}\}$ *is the role of the entity running the function.*
   - $\tau \in \{0,1\}^*$ *is a transcript of the conversation so far.*
   - $\epsilon \in \{0,1\}^* \cup \{\perp\}$ *is ephemeral state information which needs to be passed from one party's invocation of Π to the next.*
   - $\$$ *is some randomness.*

   And the outputs of Π are given by
   - $\epsilon' \in \{0,1\}^* \cup \{\perp\}$ *is updated state ephemeral information, if any.*
   - $m \in \mathcal{M} \cup \{\perp, \dashv\}$ *is the next message to be sent in the conversation, where $\dashv$ signifies that no further message needs to be sent.*

- $\delta \in \{$accept, reject, $*\}$ indicates U's decision in the current conversation. The symbol $*$ signifies a decision has not yet been made. If $\delta =$ reject is returned then ϵ' and m are set to $\bot$ and κ must be equal to $*$.
- $\kappa \in \mathcal{K} \cup \{*\}$ is the secret session key computed, where $*$ denotes that it has not been computed yet.

We often abuse notation and use the symbol Π to denote both the protocol function and the entire protocol (Setup, Π) and we assume that params is made implicit in the use of Π. See Fig. 1 for a two round example; which will be the focus of this paper.

An unauthenticated key agreement protocol is said to be *correct* if when the messages are relayed faithfully, i.e. unmodified and in the correct order, between two participants, then they both accept and compute identical session keys, except with negligible probability over the randomness used in the algorithms.

In practice one defines a specific key agreement protocol by defining how each new input message is responded to, given the current player state ϵ. We implicitly assume that if the input state is $\bot$, then the output state and message are also $\bot$ and δ will be reject.

For such unauthenticated key agreement protocol the best security guarantee we can obtain is that of passive security. Such a protocol is said to be passively secure if a single session of the protocol does not leak any information regarding the computed session key to an arbitrary poly(λ)-time adversary $\mathcal{A}$ that only eavesdrops on the conversation. For an unauthenticated key agreement protocol Π and an adversary $\mathcal{A}$, this is formalised in the EAV-KA experiment described in Fig. 3. We denote $\mathcal{A}$'s advantage in the EAV-KA game as $\mathbf{Adv}_{\mathcal{A},\Pi}^{\mathsf{EAV\text{-}KA}}(\lambda) = \left| \frac{1}{2} - \Pr\left[\mathbf{Exp}_{\mathcal{A},\Pi}^{\mathsf{EAV\text{-}KA}}(\lambda) = 1\right] \right|$.

---

1. Two parties holding 1^λ execute protocol Π with one another. This results in a transcript tran of the entire conversation, and a key κ output by each of the parties.
2. A uniform bit $b \in \{0, 1\}$ is chosen. If $b = 0$, set $\hat{\kappa} := \kappa$, and if $b = 1$ then sample $\hat{\kappa} \leftarrow_\$ \mathcal{K}$ uniformly at random.
3. $\mathcal{A}$ is given tran and $\hat{\kappa}$, and outputs a guess bit b'.
4. The output of the experiment is defined to be 1 if $b' = b$, and 0 otherwise.

Fig. 3. The EAV-KA security experiment $\mathbf{Exp}_{\mathcal{A},\Pi}^{\mathsf{EAV\text{-}KA}}(\lambda)$.

Definition 2 (Passive KA Security). *A key agreement protocol Π is passively secure in the presence of an eavesdropper if for all probabilistic* poly(λ)-*time adversaries $\mathcal{A}$, the following conditions hold.*

1. *If messages are relayed faithfully by a benign adversary between two participant oracles, then both oracles accept holding identical session keys, and each participant's key is distributed uniformly at random over $\mathcal{K}$.*
2. *There exists a negligible function* negl(λ) *such that* $\mathbf{Adv}_{\mathcal{A},\Pi}^{EAV\text{-}KA}(\lambda) \leq$ negl(λ).

It is an easy exercise to see that our syntax captures the syntax of Diffie–Hellman, Frodo and NewHope. In addition it is another easy exercise to show that the standard unauthenticated Diffie–Hellman protocol meets our Passive KA Security definition, assuming the Decision Diffie–Hellman problem is hard. In addition it is relatively easy to check that the proofs of security of the Frodo and NewHope key agreement schemes, given in [1,7], also imply security for our Passive KA definition.

Minor Active Security Properties. We also introduce two simple active security notions relevant to KA protocols. Most well designed passive KA schemes are implicitly understood to satisfy these two notions, but we choose to make them explicit (with the definition of two new security experiments) as we shall require them later on.

The first of these formalises the notion of the first protocol message being sufficiently "unpredictable"; i.e. the adversary is not able to guess what the first message m_1 of the transcript tran is going to be. We define the M1-GUESS experiment in Fig. 4 and denote an arbitrary adversary $\mathcal{A}$'s advantage in that game as

$$\mathbf{Adv}_{\mathcal{A},\Pi}^{\text{M1-GUESS}}(\lambda) = \Pr\left[\mathbf{Exp}_{\mathcal{A},\Pi}^{\text{M1-GUESS}}(\lambda) = 1\right].$$

---

1. One party holding 1^λ computes $(\epsilon', m_1, *, *) \leftarrow \Pi(\text{params}, \text{init}, \emptyset, \bot; \$)$.
2. $\mathcal{A}$ is given 1^λ and params and outputs a guess message m_1'.
3. The output of the experiment is defined to be 1 if $m_1' = m_1$, and 0 otherwise.

Fig. 4. The M1-GUESS security experiment $\mathbf{Exp}_{\mathcal{A},\Pi}^{\text{M1-GUESS}}(\lambda)$.

The second security notion models the property that an adversary should not be able to obtain information about the final key κ even if it may choose the first protocol message. This definition applies only to two-messages KA protocols. To this intent, we define the experiment KEY-FORCE in Fig. 5 and denote an arbitrary adversary $\mathcal{A}$'s advantage as

$$\mathbf{Adv}_{\mathcal{A},\Pi}^{\text{KEY-FORCE}}(\lambda) = \Pr\left[\mathbf{Exp}_{\mathcal{A},\Pi}^{\text{KEY-FORCE}}(\lambda) = 1\right]$$

3   Forward-Secure Authenticated Key Agreement Protocols and Security Model

In this section, we focus on the formal definition of Authenticated Key Agreement (AKA) protocols and the security model which we will use. For our purposes, we reformulate slightly Kudla's BJM and mBJM models [23] which were

1. The challenger sets 1^λ and runs **Setup** to obain **params**.
2. $\mathcal{A}$ is given 1^λ and **params** and ouputs a first message m_1.
3. If $m_1 \not\in \mathcal{M}$ the experiment outputs 0. Otherwise, the challenger computes $(\bot, m_2, \delta, \kappa_0) \leftarrow \Pi(\textsf{params}, \textsf{resp}, \{m_1\}, \bot; \$)$, together with sampling $\kappa_1 \leftarrow_\$ \mathcal{K}$, from the KE key space.
4. A bit $b \leftarrow_\$ \{0, 1\}$ is chosen uniformly at random.
5. $\mathcal{A}$ is given κ_b and returns a guess $\tilde{b}$.
6. The experiment outputs 1 if and only if $\tilde{b} = b$, and 0 otherwise.

Fig. 5. The KEY-FORCE security experiment $\mathbf{Exp}_{\mathcal{A},\Pi}^{\mathsf{KEY\text{-}FORCE}}(\lambda)$.

themselves an elaboration of Bellare and Rogaway's original model [4] and of Blake-Wilson et al.'s formulation for the public-key setting [6]. In particular, we add the appropriate elements so that forward secrecy is captured by our model.

First we present the definition of a general authenticated key agreement protocol. Then we describe the execution environment of our security model which is the first step in capturing forward secrecy. Next we present the security experiment and definition for mutual authentication. Finally, we present the security experiment and definition for a secure authenticated key agreement protocol which combines both mutual authentication and secrecy of session keys. We also include a discussion regarding the security notions, including forward secrecy, that this definition of security guarantees.

3.1 AKA Protocol Definition

The key difference, between the AKA protocol we will discuss in this section and the definition of a simpler key agreement protocol from Sect. 2.2, lies in the fact that AKA protocols hope to achieve *entity authentication*. That is, the parties seek to confirm each other's identities as well as establish a secret session key. To do so, we require the introduction of long-term keying material that belongs to specific entities which we then use in the computation of the protocol messages. We therefore modify Definition 1 as follows.

Definition 3 (AKA Protocol). *An* authenticated key agreement *(AKA) protocol is a triple of probabilistic* poly(λ)-*time algorithms* (*Setup,* KGen, Π) *such that:*

1. *The* setup *algorithm* Setup *functions similarly to the eponymous algorithm of a key agreement protocol.*
2. *The* key-generation *algorithm* KGen *takes as input the public parameters* params *and an entity identifier U and outputs an entity-specific public/private key pair* $(\mathsf{pk}_U, \mathsf{sk}_U)$.
3. *The* protocol function Π *functions similarly to the function of a key agreement protocol with the following differences. It is of the form* $(\epsilon', m, \delta, \kappa) \leftarrow \Pi(\textit{params}, (U, \mathsf{pk}_U, \mathsf{sk}_U), \rho, (V, \mathsf{pk}_V), \tau, \epsilon; \$)$ *where:*

- U is the identifier of a participating entity and is the sender of a message. We write $(\mathsf{pk}_U, \mathsf{sk}_U)$ for the public/private key pair of entity U.
- V is the identifier of a participating entity and is the intended recipient of U's message. We write pk_V for the public key of V.
- All other elements are as in Definition 1.

Again *correctness* requires that whenever messages are relayed faithfully between two participants, then they both accept and compute identical session keys (except with negligible probability over the randomness used in the algorithms).

Similarly to key agreement protocols, we will usually present protocols by giving the flows of a single run. A description of the function Π can be easily inferred. Also, we will use abuse notation and write Π (or sometimes Σ) both for the protocol function and the entire protocol which includes key generation, i.e. for $(\mathsf{Setup}, \mathsf{KGen}, \Pi)$ (or sometimes $(\mathsf{Setup}, \mathsf{KGen}, \Sigma)$).

3.2 Execution Environment

In the BJM model, the challenger simulates to the adversary an execution environment which constitutes of several participants. We wish to obtain "active" security, and so we allow the adversary to be active in the running of the protocol between the different entities In particular communication between protocol participants, modelled as oracles, which are controlled by the adversary, i.e. it can choose to invoke oracles to send legitimate messages or to insert is own, as well as modify, redirect, delay or erase messages. Each oracle, at the command of the adversary, may engage in several concurrent sessions of the protocol, with the same partner or not.

Oracle Participants: As mentioned above, we model protocol participants as oracles which we assume run as probabilistic $\mathsf{poly}(\lambda)$-time algorithms. More precisely, all participating entities are grouped in a set $\mathcal{U}$ of identifiers (IDs), and each session (or "run") of the protocol is modelled by an oracle $\Pi_{U,V}^s$. This represents a participant $U \in \mathcal{U}$ believing it is engaging in a protocol session with $V \in U$ for the s-th time; we say that V is U's *intended partner*. Each participant $U \in \mathcal{U}$ possesses a public and private key pair $(\mathsf{pk}_U, \mathsf{sk}_U)$, generated by KGen, and which we assume is authenticated by some public-key infrastructure (PKI). Each oracle instance of U has access to both keys, and every oracle in the model has access to every other user's public key.

Each individual oracle $\Pi_{U,V}^s$ maintains a public transcript $T_{U,V}^s$ which it updates as follows. When it receives a message m, it records it on $T_{U,V}^s$ and then invokes the protocol function on the corresponding input. When the function produces an output, this is also recorded on $T_{U,V}^s$ before being returned to the adversary. Each oracle $\Pi_{U,V}^s$ also maintains an internal decision state $\delta_{U,V}^s$. This decision may take one of four values:

- ∗: the initial state of the oracle which indicates it has not yet reached a decision.
- accept: the oracle has successfully terminated this run of the protocol after having computed some session key $k_{U,V}^s$.
- reject: the oracle has terminated without computing a session key.
- revealed: the oracle had previously accepted and has since been revealed by the adversary, as is described below.

As indicated above, each oracle $\Pi_{U,V}^s$ maintains a variable $k_{U,V}^s$ which holds the value ∗ until the protocol returns a computed session key. Finally, each oracle is also associated a role $\rho_{U,V}^s \in \{\text{init}, \text{resp}\}$ depending on its function in the protocol session. Within this model, the adversary $\mathcal{A}$ is represented as a $\text{poly}(\lambda)$-time algorithm that interacts with the oracles via specific queries; in addition, it also has access to the public key of each participant together with the transcript of each oracle.

Oracle Queries: During a security experiment for AKA security, run by a challenger $\mathcal{C}$ simulating protocol participants as oracles to an adversary $\mathcal{A}$, the adversary can make various queries of the oracles, to which the challenger simulates the responses.

At the beginning of the experiment, $\mathcal{C}$ generates protocol-specific parameters params by running $\text{Setup}(1^\lambda)$, $\mathcal{C}$ is also responsible for generating a set of participant IDs $\mathcal{U}$, where $|\mathcal{U}| = n_P$ and $n_P = \text{poly}(\lambda)$. For each participant $U \in \mathcal{U}$, $\mathcal{C}$ then runs $\text{KGen}(\text{params})$ in order to generate a key pair $(\text{pk}_U, \text{sk}_U)$. The challenger $\mathcal{C}$ also imposes the constraint that a given participant $U \in \mathcal{U}$ can engage in at most n_S sessions with another given participant $V \in \mathcal{U}$, where $n_S = \text{poly}(\lambda)$. Therefore, the model composes of the following set of oracles $\{\Pi_{U,V}^s \mid U, V \in \mathcal{U}, s \in [n_S]\}$. Finally, $\mathcal{C}$ initialises an empty list $\Gamma \leftarrow \emptyset$ which he will use to keep track of which participant oracles have been corrupted by the adversary as is explained below. The adversary $\mathcal{A}$ is then given params, $\mathcal{U}$ and $\{\text{pk}_U\}_{U \in \mathcal{U}}$, and proceeds by making the following queries:

- **Send**$(\Pi_{U,V}^s, m)$: The requests $\mathcal{C}$ to send the message m to $\Pi_{U,V}^s$. The message is recorded on $T_{U,V}^s$ and $\mathcal{C}$ responds to the message according to the protocol, simulating user U interacting with V for the s-th time. If $m = \vdash$, then $\Pi_{U,V}^s$ initiates a new protocol run, and its role is set as $\rho_{U,V}^s \leftarrow \text{init}$. If an oracle's first received message is any message other than $\vdash$, then it sets $\rho_{U,V}^s \leftarrow \text{resp}$. Once the response to m is computed according to the protocol, it is added to $T_{U,V}^s$ before being returned to the adversary. If this response is $\dashv$, this is also recorded on the transcript.
- **Reveal**$(\Pi_{U,V}^s)$: This query is used by $\mathcal{A}$ to request the session key computed by $\Pi_{U,V}^s$. If $\delta_{U,V}^s = \text{accept}$, and hence $k_{U,V}^s$ exists, then this is output and returned to $\mathcal{A}$. Otherwise, this query returns $\perp$. If the query is successful, $\delta_{U,V}^s \leftarrow \text{revealed}$ and we say that this session has been *revealed*.
- **Corrupt**$(U, \text{pk}_U', \text{sk}_U')$: This allows $\mathcal{A}$ to request the long-term secret key of participant U and is able to replace U's key pair with one of its choice.

The challenger $\mathcal{C}$ returns sk_U to $\mathcal{A}$ and replaces $(\mathsf{pk}_U, \mathsf{sk}_U)$ with $(\mathsf{pk}'_U, \mathsf{sk}'_U)$. All oracles in the simulation are updated with the new public key, and secret key for the oracles representing U. Such a participant U is called *corrupted* and $\mathcal{C}$ updates the set $\Gamma \leftarrow \Gamma \cup \{U\}$.

3.3 Secure Mutual Authentication

Now that we have described the execution environment, we are able to define the first goal of an authenticated key exchange protocol, namely mutual authentication. This notion was first defined in the original BR model [4] using the concept of matching conversations. The concept of matching conversations is used to determine whether or not two oracles have engaged in a protocol session together (by means of the adversary relaying messages from one to the other).

Definition 4 (Matching conversation). *Suppose we are given the transcripts* $T^s_{U,U'} = \{\vdash, r_1, m_2, r_2, \ldots, m_j, r_j\}$ *and* $T^{s'}_{V,V'} = \{m'_1, r'_1, m'_2, r'_2, \ldots, m_k, r_k\}$ *such that*

- *$m'_i = r_i$ for $i \geq 1$,*
- *$m_i = r'_{i-1}$ for $i \geq 2$,*
- *for j even: $r_j = \dashv$ and $k = j - 1$,*
- *for j odd: $r_k = \dashv$ and $k = j$,*
- *$U = V'$ and $U' = V$,*

then we say that the oracles $\Pi^s_{U,U'}$ *and* $\Pi^{s'}_{V,V'}$ *have engaged in a* matching conversation. *We also sometimes say that* $\Pi^s_{U,U'}$ *and* $\Pi^{s'}_{V,V'}$ *are* matching (oracles).

Entity authentication is captured in the BR model using the **No-Matching** event which is triggered if an adversary manages to make an oracle accept without a matching oracle. Here we reformulate this as a security experiment to be consistent with the more modern way of defining security.

For an AKA protocol Π and an arbitrary $\mathsf{poly}(\lambda)$-time adversary $\mathcal{A}$, the AKA-AUTH experiment is defined in Fig. 6. The intuition behind this experiment is the same as the one behind the No-Matching event; the aim of $\mathcal{A}$ is to make an oracle accept without having perfectly relayed the messages to and from its intended partner, and to do so without corrupting either parties. We denote $\mathcal{A}$'s advantage in the AKA-AUTH security game as

$$\mathbf{Adv}^{\mathsf{AKA\text{-}AUTH}}_{\mathcal{A},\Pi}(\lambda) = \Pr\left[\mathbf{Exp}^{\mathsf{AKA\text{-}AUTH}}_{\mathcal{A},\Pi}(\lambda) = 1\right].$$

Definition 5 (Secure Mutual Authentication). *We say that an AKA protocol* $\Pi = (\mathsf{Setup}, \mathsf{KGen}, \Pi)$ *is a* secure mutual authentication *protocol if, for any* $\mathsf{poly}(\lambda)$-*time adversary* $\mathcal{A}$, *the following hold.*

- *(Matching Conversations $\Rightarrow$ Acceptance.) If two oracles* $\Pi^s_{U,V}$ *and* $\Pi^{s'}_{U',V'}$ *have matching conversation, then both oracles accept.*
- *(Acceptance $\Rightarrow$ Matching Conversations.) For all probabilistic* $\mathsf{poly}(\lambda)$-*time adversaries* $\mathcal{A}$, *there exists a negligible function* $\mathsf{negl}(\lambda)$ *such that* $\mathbf{Adv}^{\mathsf{AKA\text{-}AUTH}}_{\mathcal{A},\Pi}(\lambda) \leq \mathsf{negl}(\lambda)$.

1. Setup (1^λ) is run to obtain **params**.
2. The challenger $\mathcal{C}$ generates $\mathcal{U}$ and runs KGen(params, U) for every $U \in \mathcal{U}$ to obtain key pairs $(\mathsf{pk}_U, \mathsf{sk}_U)$.
3. $\mathcal{A}$ is given **params** and $\{\mathsf{pk}_U\}_{U \in \mathcal{U}}$ and access to the participant oracles via the **Send, Reveal** and **Corrupt** queries. Eventually, $\mathcal{A}$ outputs a chosen session $\Pi^s_{U,V}$.
4. The output of the experiment is defined to be 1 if $\delta^s_{U,V} = \mathsf{accept}$, $U, V \notin \Gamma$ and there does not exists another oracle $\Pi^{s'}_{U',V'}$ which has had a matching converstation with $\Pi^s_{U,V}$.

Fig. 6. The AKA-AUTH security experiment $\mathbf{Exp}^{\mathsf{AKA\text{-}AUTH}}_{\mathcal{A},\Pi}(\lambda)$.

3.4   Session Key Secrecy and Forward Secrecy

Given a definition for mutual authentication, we now need to provide a security definition for the main purpose of key agreement; namely agreeing a private key. The secrecy game we present in Fig. 7 can be seen as an extension of the AKA-AUTH experiment used to define mutual authentication. This is a natural progression as intuitively, it makes sense for an AKA protocol to first authenticate the entity it is conversing with before establishing a shared secret session key. The game is played between a challenger simulating the AKA protocol Π and an arbitrary poly(λ)-time adversary $\mathcal{A}$.

Before we formally define the secrecy game, we will describe it briefly here so that the following definition may be placed into some context. As explained above, the simulator $\mathcal{C}$ first sets up the participants and then allows $\mathcal{A}$ to interact with them using some of the three queries. At some point in the simulation, $\mathcal{A}$ then has to select a session on which it wishes to be *tested*. At that point, the simulator flips a coin and either returns to the adversary that session's true key or a newly randomly sampled one. The adversary then continues the game, with further access to the oracles as before. Eventually the adversary has to guess which key the simulator returned; the real one or a random one. If it guesses correctly, it wins the security game.

We allow the adversary to reveal keys of completed sessions as well as corrupt participants and therefore we must make sure that it does not ask to be tested on a session for which it could have trivially obtained the key. Sessions on which we allow the adversary to request a test are those which are called *fresh* as defined below.

Definition 6 (Fresh Session). *A protocol session, represented by an oracle $\Pi^s_{U,V}$ is called* fresh *if the following conditions hold:*

- *$\Pi^s_{U,V}$ has accepted, and therefore holds a computed session key, but has not been revealed; i.e. $\delta^s_{U,V} = \mathsf{accept}$ and $\mathsf{k}^s_{U,V} \neq *$.*
- *Neither U nor his intended partner V has been corrupted by $\mathcal{A}$; i.e. $U, V \notin \Gamma$.*
- *There does not exist an oracle $\Pi^{s'}_{U',V'}$ which matches $\Pi^s_{U,V}$ and has been revealed.*

1. Setup (1^λ) is run to obtain params.
2. The challenger $\mathcal{C}$ generates $\mathcal{U}$ and runs KGen(params, U) for every $U \in \mathcal{U}$ to obtain key pairs $(\mathsf{pk}_U, \mathsf{sk}_U)$.
3. $\mathcal{A}$ is given params and $\{\mathsf{pk}_U\}_{U \in \mathcal{U}}$ and access to the participant oracles via the **Send**, **Reveal** and **Corrupt** queries. Eventually, $\mathcal{A}$ outputs a chosen session $\Pi_{U,V}^s$.
4. If $\Pi_{U,V}^s$ is not fresh, it is rejected and $\mathcal{A}$ must submit a new one. If it is, $\mathcal{C}$ selects a bit $b \in \{0, 1\}$ at random. If $b = 0$, set $\widehat{\mathsf{k}} = \mathsf{k}_{U,V}^s$, and if $b = 1$, then sample $\widehat{\mathsf{k}} \leftarrow_\$ \mathcal{K}$ uniformly at random.
5. $\mathcal{A}$ is given $\widehat{\mathsf{k}}$, as well the same information as before, and it may continue to interact via the **Send**, **Reveal** and **Corrupt** queries with the exception that it may not reveal the session on which it chose to be tested, nor any session with a matching conversation. It may however corrupt either of the participants that took part in that session. Eventually, $\mathcal{A}$ outputs a guess bit b'.
6. The output of the experiment is defined to be 1 if $b' = b$, and 0 otherwise.

Fig. 7. The AKA-SEC security experiment $\mathbf{Exp}_{\mathcal{A},\Pi}^{\mathsf{AKA\text{-}SEC}}(\lambda)$.

Note that this definition does not require $\Pi_{U,V}^s$ to have a matching partner. The session is still considered to be fresh even if the adversary has managed to make $\Pi_{U,V}^s$ accept by generating and sending its own message. In addition an oracle only needs to be fresh at the point of it being tested; after testing the adversary can corrupt the parties in a test session; thus capturing forward secrecy. The only restriction on future operations is that it may not pass a reveal query to a test session (or an oracle with a matching conversation).

The Secrecy Experiment: Security for AKA protocols in the BJM model is defined in terms of the experiment shown in Fig. 7, run with an AKA protocol Π and an arbitrary poly(λ)-time adversary $\mathcal{A}$. We denote $\mathcal{A}$'s advantage in the AKA-SEC security game as

$$\mathbf{Adv}_{\mathcal{A},\Pi}^{\mathsf{AKA\text{-}SEC}}(\lambda) = \left| \frac{1}{2} - \Pr\left[\mathbf{Exp}_{\mathcal{A},\Pi}^{\mathsf{AKA\text{-}SEC}}(\lambda) = 1 \right] \right|$$

3.5 Full Security Definition

We finally combine both the notions of mutual authentication and session key secrecy into a single security definition. As mentioned briefly above, the most notable characteristic of our security definition for AKA protocols is that it captures the property known as *forward secrecy*. This property requires that the compromise of long-term secret keying information of entities does not allow an adversary to obtain any information regarding past session keys that these entities might have established.

This is captured in our model since the adversary is allowed, before it makes its final guess, to submit a **Corrupt** query on the entities that took part in the test session. With that possibility in mind, we still require that its advantage in the AKA-SEC experiment remains negligible. Thus, proving that an AKA protocol satisfies our definition of security also proves that it possesses forward secrecy, in which case we say it is a *forward secure AKA protocol*. Additionally, our definition also captures the usual security properties of AKA protocol such as session-key reveal secrecy and third-party compromise security.

Definition 7 (Active AKA Security). *An authenticated key agreement protocol Π is* actively secure *if for all probabilistic $\mathsf{poly}(\lambda)$-time adversaries $\mathcal{A}$, the following conditions hold.*

1. *If messages are relayed faithfully (by a benign or an active adversary) between two participant oracles, then both oracles accept holding identical session keys, and each participant's key is distributed uniformly at random over $\mathcal{K}$.*
2. *Π is a secure mutual authentication protocol.*
3. *There exists a negligible function $\mathsf{negl}(\lambda)$ such that $\boldsymbol{Adv}_{\mathcal{A},\Pi}^{AKA\text{-}SEC}(\lambda) \leq \mathsf{negl}(\lambda)$.*

4   A New AKA Protocol Construction

We now present in more detail our new construction of a secure AKA protocol. We also state the theorems that establish secrecy for keys and the level of authentication that our protocol offers. The detailed proofs are in the full version of the paper.

The construction: Let $E = (\mathsf{Setup}_E, \mathsf{KGen}_E, \mathsf{Enc}, \mathsf{Dec})$ be a public-key encryption scheme. Let $M = (\mathsf{KGen}_M, \mathsf{Mac}, \mathsf{Vrfy})$ be a message authentication code such that its key space is $\mathcal{K}_M = \{0,1\}^{l(\lambda)}$ for some polynomial function l, and its KGen_M algorithm simply selects a key from $\mathcal{K}_M$ uniformly at random. Let $\Pi = (\mathsf{Setup}_\Pi, \Pi)$ be a two-round key agreement protocol and finally, let $H_1 : \{0,1\}^* \to \{0,1\}^{l(\lambda)}$ and $H_2 : \{0,1\}^* \to \{0,1\}^{h(\lambda)}$, where h is a polynomial function, be two key derivation functions. Using these elements, we construct the AKA protocol $\Sigma = (\mathsf{Setup}_\Sigma, \mathsf{KGen}_\Sigma, \Sigma)$ where:

1. Setup_Σ takes as input the security parameter 1^λ and outputs public parameters params_Σ which contain the parameters of the encryption scheme E output by $\mathsf{Setup}_E(1^\lambda)$ and the parameters of the KA protocol Π output by $\mathsf{Setup}_\Pi(1^\lambda)$.
2. KGen_Σ takes as input params_Σ and an identifier U. It then outputs a public/private key pair for U by setting $(\mathsf{pk}_U, \mathsf{sk}_U) \leftarrow \mathsf{KGen}_E(\mathsf{params}_E)$, i.e. a normal public-key encryption scheme key pair.
3. Σ functions as specified by the protocol run described in Fig. 2. The protocol works by first wrapping the message flows, m_1 and m_2, of the unauthenticated key agreement in encryptions to each party and then sending a MAC tag on the identities under a key derived from the key agreement session key using the KDF H_1. The final AKA session key is derived from the underlying agreed key and the party identities, using a different KDF H_2.

Security of our scheme: Authentication of Bob to Alice is obtained by Bob prefixing the plaintext m_1 to his response m_2 in the second message flow m_2. In this way Alice can verify that the message m_1' that she receives is identical to the one she sent out, i.e. m_1, and therefore Bob must have decrypted it; since only Bob has Bob's decryption key. Authentication of Alice to Bob is obtained by Alice sending a valid MAC on the identities under a key derived from the underlying unauthenticated key agreement scheme. Since only Alice can decrypt Bob's message m_2, only Alice could compute the underlying key agreement session key and therefore the associated MAC key. Notice that the these forms of authentication also imply liveness of the parties. The above intuition is formalized by the following theorem.

Theorem 1. *If Π is M1-GUESS-secure and KEY-FORCE-secure, E is 2-IND-CCA-secure and M is MAC-sFORGE-secure, then Σ is a secure mutual authentication protocol.*

Finally, we show that our construction yields a protocol that guarantee key secrecy.

Theorem 2. *If Π is EAV-KA-secure, M1-GUESS-secure and KEY-FORCE-secure, E is 2-IND-CCA-secure and M is MAC-sFORGE-secure, then Σ is AKA-SEC- secure.*

References

1. Alkim, E., Ducas, L., Pöppelmann, T., Schwabe, P.: Post-quantum key exchange - a new hope. In: Holz, T., Savage, S. (eds.) 25th USENIX Security Symposium, USENIX Security 16, Austin, TX, USA, 10–12 August 2016, pp. 327–343. USENIX Association (2016)
2. Bellare, M., Boldyreva, A., Micali, S.: Public-key encryption in a multi-user setting: security proofs and improvements. In: Preneel, B. (ed.) EUROCRYPT 2000. LNCS, vol. 1807, pp. 259–274. Springer, Heidelberg (2000). doi:10.1007/3-540-45539-6_18
3. Bellare, M., Canetti, R., Krawczyk, H.: A modular approach to the design and analysis of authentication and key exchange protocols (extended abstract). In: 30th ACM STOC, pp. 419–428. ACM Press, May 1998
4. Bellare, M., Rogaway, P.: Entity authentication and key distribution. In: Stinson, D.R. (ed.) CRYPTO 1993. LNCS, vol. 773, pp. 232–249. Springer, Heidelberg (1994). doi:10.1007/3-540-48329-2_21
5. Bernstein, D.J., et al.: SPHINCS: practical stateless hash-based signatures. In: Oswald, E., Fischlin, M. (eds.) EUROCRYPT 2015. LNCS, vol. 9056, pp. 368–397. Springer, Heidelberg (2015). doi:10.1007/978-3-662-46800-5_15
6. Blake-Wilson, S., Johnson, D., Menezes, A.: Key agreement protocols and their security analysis. In: Darnell, M. (ed.) Cryptography and Coding 1997. LNCS, vol. 1355, pp. 30–45. Springer, Heidelberg (1997). doi:10.1007/BFb0024447
7. Bos, J.W., Costello, C., Ducas, L., Mironov, I., Naehrig, M., Nikolaenko, V., Raghunathan, A., Stebila, D.: Frodo: take off the ring! practical, quantum-secure key exchange from LWE. In: Weippl, E.R., Katzenbeisser, S., Kruegel, C., Myers, A.C., Halevi, S. (eds.) ACM CCS 16, pp. 1006–1018. ACM Press, October 2016

8. Boyd, C., Cliff, Y., Gonzalez Nieto, J., Paterson, K.G.: Efficient one-round key exchange in the standard model. In: Mu, Y., Susilo, W., Seberry, J. (eds.) ACISP 2008. LNCS, vol. 5107, pp. 69–83. Springer, Heidelberg (2008). doi:10.1007/978-3-540-70500-0_6

9. Canetti, R., Krawczyk, H.: Analysis of key-exchange protocols and their use for building secure channels. In: Pfitzmann, B. (ed.) EUROCRYPT 2001. LNCS, vol. 2045, pp. 453–474. Springer, Heidelberg (2001). doi:10.1007/3-540-44987-6_28

10. Ducas, L., Durmus, A., Lepoint, T., Lyubashevsky, V.: Lattice signatures and bimodal gaussians. In: Canetti, R., Garay, J.A. (eds.) CRYPTO 2013. LNCS, vol. 8042, pp. 40–56. Springer, Heidelberg (2013). doi:10.1007/978-3-642-40041-4_3

11. Fischlin, M., Günther, F., Schmidt, B., Warinschi, B.: Key confirmation in key exchange: a formal treatment and implications for TLS 1.3. In: IEEE Symposium on Security and Privacy, SP 2016, San Jose, CA, USA, 22–26 May 2016, pp. 452–469 (2016)

12. Gentry, C., Szydlo, M.: Cryptanalysis of the revised NTRU signature scheme. In: Knudsen, L.R. (ed.) EUROCRYPT 2002. LNCS, vol. 2332, pp. 299–320. Springer, Heidelberg (2002). doi:10.1007/3-540-46035-7_20

13. Goldreich, O., Goldwasser, S., Halevi, S.: Public-key cryptosystems from lattice reduction problems. In: Kaliski, B.S. (ed.) CRYPTO 1997. LNCS, vol. 1294, pp. 112–131. Springer, Heidelberg (1997). doi:10.1007/BFb0052231

14. Günther, F., Hale, B., Jager, T., Lauer, S.: 0-RTT key exchange with full forward secrecy. In: Coron, J.-S., Nielsen, J.B. (eds.) EUROCRYPT 2017. LNCS, vol. 10212, pp. 519–548. Springer, Cham (2017). doi:10.1007/978-3-319-56617-7_18

15. Hoffstein, J., Howgrave-Graham, N., Pipher, J., Silverman, J.H., Whyte, W.: NTRUSign: digital signatures using the NTRU lattice. In: Joye, M. (ed.) CT-RSA 2003. LNCS, vol. 2612, pp. 122–140. Springer, Heidelberg (2003). doi:10.1007/3-540-36563-X_9

16. Hoffstein, J., Pipher, J., Silverman, J.H.: NTRU: a ring-based public key cryptosystem. In: Buhler, J.P. (ed.) ANTS 1998. LNCS, vol. 1423, pp. 267–288. Springer, Heidelberg (1998). doi:10.1007/BFb0054868

17. Hoffstein, J., Pipher, J., Silverman, J.H.: NSS: an NTRU lattice-based signature scheme. In: Pfitzmann, B. (ed.) EUROCRYPT 2001. LNCS, vol. 2045, pp. 211–228. Springer, Heidelberg (2001). doi:10.1007/3-540-44987-6_14

18. Jager, T., Kohlar, F., Schäge, S., Schwenk, J.: Generic compilers for authenticated key exchange. In: Abe, M. (ed.) ASIACRYPT 2010. LNCS, vol. 6477, pp. 232–249. Springer, Heidelberg (2010). doi:10.1007/978-3-642-17373-8_14

19. Jager, T., Paterson, K.G., Somorovsky, J.: One bad apple: backwards compatibility attacks on state-of-the-art cryptography. In: NDSS 2013. The Internet Society, February 2013

20. Jager, T., Schwenk, J., Somorovsky, J.: On the security of TLS 1.3 and QUIC against weaknesses in PKCS#1 v1.5 encryption. In: Ray, I., Li, N., Kruegel, C. (eds.) ACM CCS 15, pp. 1185–1196. ACM Press, October 2015

21. Katz, J., Lindell, Y.: Introduction to Modern Cryptography. Chapman and Hall/CRC Press (2007)

22. Katz, J., Yung, M.: Scalable protocols for authenticated group key exchange. J. Cryptology **20**(1), 85–113 (2007)

23. Kudla, C.J.: Special signature schemes and key agreement protocols. Ph.D. thesis, Royal Holloway University of London (2006)

24. Li, Y., Schäge, S., Yang, Z., Bader, C., Schwenk, J.: New modular compilers for authenticated key exchange. In: Boureanu, I., Owesarski, P., Vaudenay, S. (eds.) ACNS 2014. LNCS, vol. 8479, pp. 1–18. Springer, Cham (2014). doi:10.1007/978-3-319-07536-5_1

25. Lindner, R., Peikert, C.: Better key sizes (and Attacks) for LWE-based encryption. In: Kiayias, A. (ed.) CT-RSA 2011. LNCS, vol. 6558, pp. 319–339. Springer, Heidelberg (2011). doi:10.1007/978-3-642-19074-2_21

26. Lyubashevsky, V., Peikert, C., Regev, O.: On ideal lattices and learning with errors over rings. In: Gilbert, H. (ed.) EUROCRYPT 2010. LNCS, vol. 6110, pp. 1–23. Springer, Heidelberg (2010). doi:10.1007/978-3-642-13190-5_1

27. Mavrogiannopoulos, N., Vercauteren, F., Velichkov, V., Preneel, B.: A cross-protocol attack on the TLS protocol. In: Yu, T., Danezis, G., Gligor, V.D. (eds.) ACM CCS 12, pp. 62–72. ACM Press, October 2012

28. Morrissey, P., Smart, N.P., Warinschi, B.: The TLS handshake protocol: a modular analysis. J. Cryptology **23**(2), 187–223 (2010)

29. Nguyen, P.Q., Regev, O.: Learning a parallelepiped: cryptanalysis of GGH and NTRU signatures. In: Vaudenay, S. (ed.) EUROCRYPT 2006. LNCS, vol. 4004, pp. 271–288. Springer, Heidelberg (2006). doi:10.1007/11761679_17

Public-Key Cryptography

A Constant-Size Signature Scheme with Tighter Reduction from CDH Assumption

Kaisei Kajita[1](✉), Kazuto Ogawa[1], and Eiichiro Fujisaki[2]

[1] Japan Broadcasting Corporation, Tokyo, Japan
{kajita.k-bu,ogawa.k-cm}@nhk.or.jp
[2] Japan Advanced Institute of Science and Technology, Ishikawa, Japan
fujisaki@jaist.ac.jp

Abstract. We present a signature scheme with the tightest security-reduction among known constant-size signature schemes secure under the computational Diffie-Hellman (CDH) assumption. It is important to reduce the security-reduction loss of a cryptosystem, which enables choosing of a smaller security parameter without compromising security; hence, enabling constant-size signatures for cryptosystems and faster computation. The tightest security reduction thus far from the CDH assumption is $\mathcal{O}(q)$, presented by Hofheinz et al., where q is the number of signing queries. They also proved that the security loss of $\mathcal{O}(q)$ is optimal if signature schemes are "re-randomizable". In this paper, we revisit the non-re-randomizable signature scheme proposed by Böhl et al. Their signature scheme is the first that is fully secure under the CDH assumption and has a compact public key. However, they constructed the scheme with polynomial-order security-reduction loss. We first constructed a new existentially unforgeable against extended random-message attack (EUF-XRMA) secure scheme based on Böhl et al.'s scheme, which has tighter security reduction of $\mathcal{O}(q/d)$ to the CDH assumption, where d is the number of group elements in a verification key. We then transformed the EUF-XRMA secure signature scheme into an existentially unforgeable against adaptively chosen-message attack (EUF-CMA) secure one using Abe et al.'s technique. In this construction, no pseudorandom function, which results in increase of reduction loss, is used, and the above reduction loss can be achieved. Moreover, a tag can be generated more efficiently than Böhl et al.'s signature scheme, which results in smaller computation. Consequently, our EUF-CMA secure scheme has tighter security reduction to the CDH assumption than any previous schemes.

Keywords: Digital signatures · CDH assumption · Trapdoor commitment · Tight security reduction

1 Introduction

1.1 Background

Digital signatures are the most elemental cryptographic primitives that guarantee authenticity of electronic documents and are analogous to pen-and-ink

© Springer International Publishing AG 2017
P.Q. Nguyen and J. Zhou (Eds.): ISC 2017, LNCS 10599, pp. 137–154, 2017.
https://doi.org/10.1007/978-3-319-69659-1_8

signatures on physical documents. In digital signatures, each signer has a pair of secret (signing) and public (verification) keys. A signer signs documents by using one secret key, and authenticity of a signature is publicly verifiable with the public key. Digital signatures are widely used in the real world. For example, it is used in transport layer security and e-commerce.

The performance of cryptographic primitives is evaluated by reduction loss to a certain difficult problem. The (security) reduction is a particular way of using a mathematical proof to ensure that a cryptographic primitive is secure. It shows that breaking the primitive is at least as difficult as breaking the difficult problem. Reduction loss is the gap in difficulty between breaking the primitive and breaking the difficult problem. When the security-reduction loss is small, it is called tight. It is important to reduce the security-reduction loss of a cryptosystem, which enables the choosing of as small a security parameter without compromising security as possible; hence, enabling small security parameters for cryptosytems, i.e., signatures and verification keys, and fast computations of signature generation and verification, etc.

1.2   Related Works

There are many digital signature schemes. Digital signatures can only be proven in the random oracle model [11] first. Then, digital signatures in the standard model are developed. With these schemes, there are two major problems used for security proof, decisional problem, i.e. the decisional Diffie-Hellman (DDH) problem, and search problem, i.e., the computational Diffie-Hellman (CDH) problem. Generically, search problems are harder than decisional problems. For example, breaking the CDH problem is harder than breaking the DDH problem. On the other hand, it is important to consider the security reduction to the hard problem. The digital signatures with security reduction to decisional problems has been extensively studied, and in constant-size signatures, its reduction loss to the DDH problem is achieved $\mathcal{O}(l)$, where l is the bit length of a message [8,12]. There are a few digital signatures secure under the hardness of search problems. Waters proposed a scheme [17] that is efficient and provably secure under the CDH assumption. Some digital signatures under CDH assumption based on Waters' signature scheme have been developed [4,5,13,15,16].

However, their reduction losses to the CDH problem are not so tight. The loss of security reductions on Waters' signature scheme is $\mathcal{O}(8(l+1)q)$, where q is the number of adversarial signature queries. The technique called programmable hash functions (PHFs) [14] improves the tightness of security reduction to $\mathcal{O}(\sqrt{l}q)$. To the best of our knowledge, the tightest security reduction to the CDH problem from a constant-size signature scheme is $\mathcal{O}(q)$, presented by Hofheinz et al. [13]. They proposed a re-randomizable signature scheme by applying an error-correcting code to Waters' signature scheme. They also proved that reduction loss of $\mathcal{O}(q)$ is optimal if signature schemes are re-randomizable. At the present time there is a tightly secure signature scheme from search problems [6]. But the signature scheme has large signature size. Concretely the signature size needs $\mathcal{O}(\kappa)$ group elements, where κ is the security parameter.

1.3   Our Contribution

We present a signature scheme with tighter security reduction than known constant-size (in the sense that the signature contains constant number of group elements or vectors) signature schemes under the CDH assumption. In this paper, we revisit the non-re-randomizable signature scheme proposed by Böhl et al. [5]. Their scheme has compact public keys at the price of loose security-reduction loss. We address that there is a trade-off between public key size and security-reduction loss in their scheme. Moreover, by removing the use of a pseudo-random generator and adopting a generic transformation from the scheme with extended random-message-attack security to that with chosen-message-attack security [1], we can obtain a signature scheme with reduction loss of $\mathcal{O}(q/d)$, where d is the number of group elements in a verification key.

2   Preliminaries

For $n \in \mathbb{N}$, $[n]$ denotes the set $\{1, \ldots, n\}$. We let $\mathsf{negl}(\kappa)$ denote an unspecified function $f(\kappa)$ such that $f(\kappa) = \kappa^{-\omega(1)}$, saying that such a function is negligible in κ. For a probabilistic polynomial-time (PPT) algorithm $\mathcal{A}$, we write $y \leftarrow \mathcal{A}(x)$ to denote the experiment of running $\mathcal{A}$ for given x, selecting inner coins r uniformly from an appropriate domain, and assigning the result of this experiment to the variable y, i.e., $y = \mathcal{A}(x; r)$. Let $X = \{X_\kappa\}_{\kappa \in \mathbb{N}}$ and $Y = \{Y_\kappa\}_{\kappa \in \mathbb{N}}$ be probability ensembles such that each X_κ and Y_κ are random variables ranging over $\{0, 1\}^\kappa$. The (statistical) distance between X_κ and Y_κ is $\mathsf{Dist}(X_\kappa, Y_\kappa) \triangleq \frac{1}{2} \cdot |\Pr_{s \in \{0,1\}^\kappa}[X = s] - \Pr_{s \in \{0,1\}^\kappa}[Y = s]|$. We say that two probability ensembles, X and Y, are statistically indistinguishable in κ, denoted as $X \overset{s}{\approx} Y$, if $\mathsf{Dist}(X_\kappa, Y_\kappa) = \mathsf{negl}(\kappa)$. Let $\mathcal{A}$ and $\mathcal{B}$ be PPT algorithms that both take as input $x \in \{0, 1\}^*$. We write $\{\mathcal{A}(x)\}_{\kappa \in \mathbb{N},\, x \in \{0,1\}^\kappa} \overset{s}{\approx} \{\mathcal{B}(x)\}_{\kappa \in \mathbb{N},\, x \in \{0,1\}^\kappa}$ to denote $\{\mathcal{A}(x_\kappa)\}_{\kappa \in \mathbb{N}} \overset{s}{\approx} \{\mathcal{B}(x_\kappa)\}_{\kappa \in \mathbb{N}}$ for every sequence $\{x_\kappa\}_{\kappa \in \mathbb{N}}$ such that $|x_\kappa| = \kappa$.

2.1   Digital Signatures

We use the standard definition of digital signature schemes [10]. A digital signature scheme is given by a triple, $\mathsf{SIG} = (\mathsf{KGen}, \mathsf{Sign}, \mathsf{Vrfy})$, of PPT Turing machines, where for every (sufficiently large) $\kappa \in \mathbb{N}$, KGen, the key-generation algorithm, takes as input security parameter 1^κ and outputs a pair of verification and signing keys, (vk, sk). The signing algorithm Sign, takes as input (vk, sk) and m and produces σ. The verification algorithm Vrfy, takes as input vk, m, and σ, and outputs a bit (i.e., verification result). For completeness, it is required that for any (vk, sk) pair generated with $\mathsf{KGen}(1^\kappa)$ and for any $m \in \{0, 1\}^*$, it holds $\mathsf{Vrfy}(vk, m, \mathsf{Sign}(sk, m)) = 1$.

Tag-Based Signatures. A tag-based signature scheme $\mathsf{SIG}_t = (\mathsf{KGen}_t, \mathsf{Sign}_t, \mathsf{Vrfy}_t)$ with message space $\mathcal{M}_\lambda$ and tag space $\mathcal{T}_\lambda$ consists of three PPT algorithms.

Key-generation $(vk, sk) \leftarrow \mathsf{KGen}_t(1^\lambda)$ takes as input a security parameter 1^λ and outputs a pair of verification and signing keys (vk, sk). The signing algorithm $\sigma \leftarrow \mathsf{Sign}_t(sk, m, t)$ computes σ on input sk, m, and tag t. The verification algorithm $\mathsf{Vrfy}_t(vk, m, \sigma, t) \in \{0, 1\}$ takes vk, m, σ, and t, and outputs a bit (i.e., verification result). For correctness, we require that for any $\lambda \in \mathbb{N}$, all $(vk, sk) \leftarrow \mathsf{KGen}_t(1^\lambda)$, $m \in \mathcal{M}_\lambda$, $t \in \mathcal{T}_\lambda$, and $\sigma \leftarrow \mathsf{Sign}_t(sk, m, t)$, $\mathsf{Vrfy}_t(vk, m, \sigma, t) = 1$.

Re-Randomizable Signatures. Intuitively, re-randomizable signatures [13] have a property that, given vk, m, and valid σ, one can efficiently generate a new σ' that is distributed uniformly over the set of all possible signatures for m under vk.

Formally, let $\mathsf{SIG} = (\mathsf{KGen}, \mathsf{Sign}, \mathsf{Vrfy})$ be a signature scheme. Let us denote the set of σ for m that can be verified correctly under vk by

$$\Sigma(vk, m) = \{\sigma \mid \mathsf{Vrfy}(vk, m, \sigma) = 1\}.$$

We say that SIG is re-randomizable if there is a PPT algorithm *Rerand* such that for all (vk, m, σ) with $\mathsf{Vrfy}(vk, m, \sigma) = 1$, the output distribution of *Rerand*(vk, m, σ) is identical to uniform distribution over $\Sigma(vk, m)$.

2.2 Trapdoor Commitments

We now define a trapdoor commitment scheme [9]. Let $\mathsf{TCOM} = (\mathsf{Gen}^{\mathsf{tc}}, \mathsf{Com}^{\mathsf{tc}}, \mathsf{TCom}^{\mathsf{tc}}, \mathsf{TCol}^{\mathsf{tc}})$ be a tuple of the following four algorithms. The $\mathsf{Gen}^{\mathsf{tc}}$ algorithm is a PPT algorithm that takes as input security parameter κ and outputs a pair of public and trapdoor keys (pk, tk). The $\mathsf{Com}^{\mathsf{tc}}$ algorithm is a PPT algorithm that takes as input pk and m, selects a random $r \leftarrow \mathsf{COIN}^{\mathsf{com}}$, where $\mathsf{COIN}^{\mathsf{com}}$ represents the internal random number 0 or 1, and outputs a $\psi = \mathsf{Com}_{pk}^{\mathsf{tc}}(m; r)$. The $\mathsf{TCom}^{\mathsf{tc}}$ algorithm is a PPT algorithm that takes as input tk and outputs $(\psi, \chi) \leftarrow \mathsf{TCom}_{tk}^{\mathsf{tc}}(1^\kappa)$. The $\mathsf{TCol}^{\mathsf{tc}}$ algorithm is a deterministic polynomial-time (DPT) algorithm that takes $(tk, \psi, \chi, \hat{m})$ and outputs $\hat{r} \in \{0, 1\}$ such that $\psi = \mathsf{Com}_{pk}^{\mathsf{tc}}(\hat{m}; \hat{r})$.

We call TCOM a trapdoor commitment scheme if the following two conditions hold.

Condition 1 *Trapdoor Collision*. *For the pk generated with $\mathsf{Gen}^{\mathsf{tc}}(1^\kappa)$, and all $m \in \{0, 1\}^{\lambda_m(\kappa)}$, the following ensembles are statistically indistinguishable in κ:*

$$\left\{ (\psi, m, r) \mid r \leftarrow \mathsf{COIN}^{\mathsf{com}}; \psi = \mathsf{Com}_{pk}^{\mathsf{tc}}(m; r) \right\}$$
$$\overset{s}{\approx} \left\{ (\psi, m, r) \mid (\psi, \chi) \leftarrow \mathsf{TCom}_{tk}^{\mathsf{tc}}(1^\kappa); r = \mathsf{TCol}_{tk}^{\mathsf{tc}}(\psi, \chi, m) \right\}.$$

Condition 2 *Computational Binding*. *For any PPT adversary $\mathcal{A}$,*

$$\varepsilon^{\mathsf{comp\text{-}bind}} = \Pr \left[\begin{array}{l} pk \leftarrow \mathsf{Gen}^{\mathsf{tc}}(1^\kappa); (m_1, m_2, r_1, r_2) \leftarrow \mathcal{A}(pk) : \\ \mathsf{Com}_{pk}^{\mathsf{tc}}(m_1; r_1) = \mathsf{Com}_{pk}^{\mathsf{tc}}(m_2; r_2) \wedge (m_1 \neq m_2) \end{array} \right] = \mathsf{negl}(\kappa).$$

2.3   Security Class of Digital Signatures

EUF-CMA. A digital signature scheme SIG is said to be existentially unforgeable against adaptively chosen-message attack (EUF-CMA) [11], if for any $\mathcal{A}$, $\mathsf{Adv}_{\mathsf{SIG},\mathcal{A}}^{\mathrm{EUF\text{-}CMA}}(\kappa) := \Pr[\mathsf{Expt}_{\mathsf{SIG},\mathcal{A}}^{\mathrm{EUF\text{-}CMA}}(\kappa) = 1] = \mathsf{negl}(\kappa)$, where $\mathsf{Expt}_{\mathsf{SIG},\mathcal{A}}^{\mathrm{EUF\text{-}CMA}}(\kappa)$ is defined in Fig. 1.

$$\boxed{\begin{array}{l} \mathsf{Expt}_{\mathsf{SIG},\mathcal{A}}^{\mathrm{EUF\text{-}CMA}}(\kappa): \\ \quad (vk, sk) \leftarrow \mathsf{KGen}(1^{\kappa}); \; (m^*, \sigma^*) \leftarrow \mathcal{A}^{\mathsf{Sign}_{sk}(\cdot)}(vk) \\ \quad \text{If } m^* \in \mathcal{Q}_m, \text{ then return } 0 \\ \quad \text{Return } \mathsf{Vrfy}(vk, m^*, \sigma^*). \end{array}}$$

Fig. 1. Experiment with EUF-CMA. $\mathsf{Sign}_{sk}(\cdot)$ is a signing oracle with respect to sk that takes m and returns $\sigma \leftarrow \mathsf{Sign}_{sk}(m)$ and records m to $\mathcal{Q}_m$, which is initially an empty list.

EUF-XRMA. A SIG is said to be existentially unforgeable against extended random-message attack (EUF-XRMA) [1] with respects to the message generator MsgGen, a PPT algorithm that takes as input a message-generation key gk and outputs m, if for any $\mathcal{A}$ and any positive integer n bounded by a polynomial in κ, $\mathsf{Adv}_{\mathsf{SIG},\mathcal{A}}^{\mathrm{EUF\text{-}XRMA}}(\kappa) := \Pr[\mathsf{Expt}_{\mathsf{SIG},\mathcal{A}}^{\mathrm{EUF\text{-}XRMA}}(\kappa) = 1] = \mathsf{negl}(\kappa)$, where $\mathsf{Expt}_{\mathsf{SIG},\mathcal{A}}^{\mathrm{EUF\text{-}XRMA}}(\kappa)$ is defined in Fig. 2, and $\mathcal{Q}_m = \{m_1, \ldots, m_n\}$.

$$\boxed{\begin{array}{l} \mathsf{Expt}_{\mathsf{SIG},\mathcal{A}}^{\mathrm{EUF\text{-}XRMA}}(\kappa): \\ \quad (vk, sk) \leftarrow \mathsf{KGen}(1^{\kappa}); \; gk \leftarrow \mathsf{Setup}(1^{\kappa}) \\ \quad \text{For } \forall i \in [n], \\ \quad\quad (m_i, w_i) \leftarrow \mathsf{MsgGen}(gk); \; \sigma_i \leftarrow \mathsf{Sign}_{sk}(m_i) \\ \quad (m^*, \sigma^*) \leftarrow \mathcal{A}(vk, \{m_i, \sigma_i, w_i\}_{i=1}^{n}) \\ \quad \text{If } m^* \in \mathcal{Q}_m, \text{ then return } 0 \\ \quad \text{Return } \mathsf{Vrfy}(vk, m^*, \sigma^*). \end{array}}$$

Fig. 2. Experiment with EUF-XRMA. The Setup algorithm is a PPT algorithm that takes as input a security parameter 1^{κ} and outputs gk.

EUF-dnaCMA. A SIG is said to be existentially unforgeable against distinct-message non-adaptively chosen-message attack (EUF-dnaCMA) [4,5], if for any $\mathcal{A}, \mathsf{Adv}_{\mathsf{SIG},\mathcal{A}}^{\mathrm{EUF\text{-}dnaCMA}}(\kappa) := \Pr[\mathsf{Expt}_{\mathsf{SIG},\mathcal{A}}^{\mathrm{EUF\text{-}dnaCMA}}(\kappa) = 1] = \mathsf{negl}(\kappa)$. $\mathsf{Expt}_{\mathsf{SIG},\mathcal{A}}^{\mathrm{EUF\text{-}dnaCMA}}(\kappa)$ is the experiment with EUF-dnaCMA and refer to [5].

EUF-dnaCMA$_{\mathsf{d}}^*$. A tag-based signature scheme SIG_t is said be EUF-dnaCMA with d-fold tag-collisions (EUF-dnaCMA$_{\mathsf{d}}^*$) [4,5], if for any $\mathcal{A}, \mathsf{Adv}_{\mathsf{SIG}_t,\mathcal{A}}^{\mathrm{EUF\text{-}dnaCMA}_{\mathsf{d}}^*}(\kappa) := \Pr[\mathsf{Expt}_{\mathsf{SIG}_t,\mathcal{A}}^{\mathrm{EUF\text{-}dnaCMA}_{\mathsf{d}}^*}(\kappa) = 1] = \mathsf{negl}(\kappa)$, where $\mathsf{Expt}_{\mathsf{SIG}_t,\mathcal{A}}^{\mathrm{EUF\text{-}dnaCMA}_{\mathsf{d}}^*}(\kappa)$ is the experiment with EUF-dnaCMA$_{\mathsf{d}}^*$ and refer to [5].

Note that we call d a tag-collision parameter; it affects key and signature sizes, and the security reduction. The d-fold tag-collisions means that the same tag t_i is chosen for d different signed messages.

2.4   Bilinear Groups

Let $\mathcal{G}$ be a PPT algorithm that, on input of a security parameter 1^κ, outputs a description of bilinear groups $(\mathbb{G}, \mathbb{G}_T, e, q, g)$ [7] such that $\mathbb{G}$ and $\mathbb{G}_T$ are cyclic groups of prime order q, g is a generator of $\mathbb{G}$, and a map $e : \mathbb{G} \times \mathbb{G} \rightarrow \mathbb{G}_T$ satisfies the following properties:

- (Bilinear:) for any $g, h \in \mathbb{G}$ and any $a, b \in \mathbb{Z}_q$, $e(g^a, h^b) = e(g, h)^{ab}$,
- (Non-degenerate:) $e(g, g)$ has order q in $\mathbb{G}_T$, and
- (Efficiently computable:) $e(\cdot, \cdot)$ is efficiently computable.

2.5   Computational Diffie-Hellman Assumption

Let g be a group generator of $\mathbb{G}$. We say that the CDH assumption [16] holds if for any PPT algorithm $\mathcal{A}$ the following advantage

$$
\begin{aligned}
&\mathsf{Adv}_{\mathcal{A}}^{CDH}(\kappa) \\
&:= Pr\big[\mathcal{A}(q, \mathbb{G}, g, g^\alpha, g^\beta) \rightarrow g^{\alpha\beta} | \alpha, \beta \xleftarrow{\$} \mathbb{Z}_q, g \xleftarrow{\$} \mathbb{G}\big] \\
&= \varepsilon^{CDH}
\end{aligned}
$$

is negligible function in the security parameter κ.

2.6   Pseudorandom Functions

For any set $\mathcal{S}$ a pseudorandom function (PRF) [3] with a range $\mathcal{S}$ is an efficiently computable function $\mathsf{PRF}^{\mathcal{S}} : \{0, 1\}^\kappa \times \{0, 1\}^* \rightarrow \mathcal{S}$. We may write $\mathsf{PRF}^{\mathcal{S}}_\kappa(x)$ for $\mathsf{PRF}^{\mathcal{S}}(\kappa, x)$ with key $\kappa \in \{0, 1\}^*$. Additionally we require that

$$
\mathsf{Adv}_{\mathsf{PRF}^{\mathcal{S}}, \mathcal{A}}^{\mathsf{prf}}(\kappa) := \Big| \Pr\big[\mathcal{A}_\kappa^{\mathsf{PRF}}(\cdot) = 1 \text{ for } \kappa \leftarrow \{0, 1\}^*\big] - \Pr[\mathcal{A}_{\mathcal{S}}^{\mathcal{U}}(\cdot) = 1] \Big| = \varepsilon^{\mathsf{PRF}}
$$

is negligible in κ where $\mathcal{U}$ is a truly uniform function to $\mathcal{S}$. We often write PRF, which is omitted from $\mathcal{S}$.

2.7   Scheme of Böhl et al.

We now revisit the signature scheme [5] proposed by Böhl et al. They present a new paradigm for the construction of efficient signature schemes secure under standard computational assumptions. First, they define a mild security for signature schemes that is much easier to achieve than full security. We consider EUF-CMA security as full security. They present efficient mildly secure schemes under the CDH assumption in pairing-friendly groups. Concretely, they construct an EUF-dnaCMA secure signature scheme by using a SIG_t, which is

EUF-dnaCMA$_d^*$ secure, and a PRF, which is a PRF. Moreover, they applied trapdoor commitment and modified the EUF-dnaCMA secure signature scheme and achieved an EUF-CMA secure signature scheme under the CDH assumption. Therefore, they constructed a full secure signature scheme generically from a mildly secure signature one. They constructed the signature scheme that is secure against non-adaptive attack by using PRFs. Pseudorandom functions affect security-reduction loss. In their security proof, they use the *confined guessing* technique. They choose an appropriately sized tag set, where their signature simulation is done.

Theorem 1. *If* PRF *is a PRF and a* SIG$_t$ *is* EUF-dnaCMA$_d^*$ *secure, then there is an* EUF-dnaCMA$_d$ *secure* SIG. *Concretely, let* $\mathcal{A}$ *be a PPT adversary against a SIG with at most* q *signature queries and having advantage* $\varepsilon := \mathsf{Adv}_{\mathsf{SIG}_t,\mathcal{A}}^{\mathrm{EUF\text{-}dnaCMA}}(\kappa)$. *Then there exists an* EUF-dnaCMA$_d^*$ *adversary* $\mathcal{A}'$ *against the* SIG$_t$ *that makes* $q'(\kappa) \leq 2 \cdot \{\frac{2 \cdot q^{d+1}}{\varepsilon(\kappa)}\}^{c/d} + l \cdot q$ *signature queries and has advantage* $\varepsilon' := \mathsf{Adv}_{\mathsf{SIG}_t,\mathcal{A}'}^{\mathrm{EUF\text{-}dnaCMA}_d^*}(\kappa)$ *and PRF distinguisher with advantage* $\varepsilon_{\mathsf{PRF}}$ *such that*

$$\varepsilon' \geq \varepsilon/2 - \varepsilon^{\mathsf{PRF}} - \frac{p'(\kappa)}{|\mathcal{M}_k|}$$

for infinitely large κ, *where* $p'(\kappa)$ *is a suitable polynomial and* $\mathcal{M}_k$ *denotes the message space.*

Lemma 1. *Let* T *be a tag set with* $|T| = n$. *Let* $t_1, \ldots, t_q$ *be* q *independent random variables taken uniformly random from* T. *Then, the probability that there exist* $d + 1$ *pairwise distinct indices* $i_1, \ldots, i_{d+1}$ *such that* $t_{i_1} = \cdots = t_{i_{d+1}}$ *is upper bounded by* $\frac{q^{d+1}}{n^d}$.

Theorem 2. *The* SIG$_t$ *is* EUF-dnaCMA$_d^*$ *secure if the CDH assumption holds in* $\mathbb{G}$. *Let* $\mathcal{A}$ *be a PPT adversary on* SIG$_t$ *with advantage* $\varepsilon := \mathsf{Adv}_{\mathsf{SIG},\mathcal{A}}^{\mathrm{EUF\text{-}dnaCMA}_d^*}(\kappa)$ *with at most* q *random messages along with signatures. Then, it can be used to solve the CDH problem with probability of at least* ε/q', *where* q' *denotes the number of distinct tags queried by* $\mathcal{A}$.

Theorem 3. *If the CDH assumption holds in* $\mathbb{G}$, *then the signature scheme with trapdoor commitments* SIG$_t^{\mathcal{B}}$ *is* EUF-CMA *secure. Let* $\mathcal{A}$ *be a PPT adversary on* $SIG_t^{\mathcal{B}}$ *with advantage* $\varepsilon := \mathsf{Adv}_{\mathsf{SIG},\mathcal{A}}^{\mathrm{EUF\text{-}dnaCMA}_d^*}(\kappa)$ *querying for* q *random messages along with signatures. Then, it can be used to solve the CDH problem with probability of at least* $\frac{2^{2+\frac{c}{d}} \cdot q^{c+\frac{c}{d}}}{\varepsilon^c d + 1 - 2\varepsilon^c d(\varepsilon_{\mathsf{PRF}} + \varepsilon^{\mathrm{comp\text{-}bind}})}$, *where* $\varepsilon_{\mathsf{PRF}}$ *and* $\varepsilon^{\mathrm{comp\text{-}bind}}$ *correspond to the advantages for breaking the* PRF *and computational binding, respectively, and* $c > 1$ *denotes a granularity parameter in which the size of tag spaces is defined by* $T^i = 2^{\lceil c^i \rceil}$.

There are some changes of notation between our signature scheme and Böhl et al.'s signature scheme. We omit these proofs. Please visit [5] for details of these proofs.

3   Proposal: Modified Mildly Secure Signature Scheme

We modify Böhl et al.'s signature scheme and reduced it to the CDH assumption more efficiently. We first construct an EUF-XRMA secure signature scheme under the CDH assumption based on Böhl et al.'s signature scheme [5].

- Böhl et al. transformed $EUF\text{-}dnaCMA_d^*$ secure signature schemes to EUF-CMA secure ones. We first construct a EUF-XRMA secure signature scheme based on theirs. Then we transform it to an EUF-CMA secure signature scheme with trapdoor commitments using Abe et al.'s technique [1]. In this way, we construct a new *non*-re-randomizable signature scheme since re-randomizable signature scheme has a property that bounds of security-reduction loss to CDH problem is $\mathcal{O}(q)$.
- We construct this signature scheme without a PRF. In an experiment with EUF-XRMA security, messages are generated by a message generator MsgGen instead of the PRF. The PRF affects security-reduction loss, but the MsgGen does not. Consequently, the security-reduction loss of our scheme improves when PRF disappears.
- In Böhl et al.'s signature scheme, the tag space is divided into $|T_j| = 2^{\lceil c^j \rceil}$. While in our construction, we make the tag space stepwise $|T_j| = 2^j$ and set a tag by using modulo operation $t^{(j)} = m \mod 2^j$, where m is generated by the MsgGen. We can choose the size of the tag set T_j adequately and prepare T_j to be as small as possible so that any q signatures can be produced from q messages.
- We evaluate the condition under which an m interlaps tag t in the signature simulation more strictly. In Böhl et al.'s Lemma 1, the probability of condition $\Pr[(d+1)\text{-fold}]$ is negligible. Since we change the parameter size of tag sets and the number of tag collisions d, we evaluate the lemma again with the parameter d, which results in exponential small $\Pr[(d+1)\text{-fold}]$.

3.1   Construction

SIG_0 is an EUF-XRMA secure signature scheme under CDH assumption and described in Fig. 3. Tag sets are generated along with the following tag-making rule. Each T_j is set as $\{0,1\}^j$ ($1 \leq j \leq l$), and each tag in T_j is determined as $t_i^{(j)} = m_i \mod 2^j$ for $1 \leq i \leq q$ by using an m. This scheme does not require a PRF, unlike that by Böhl et al. [5]. In the EUF-XRMA experiment, messages $\{m_i\}_{i=1}^n$ are generated by MsgGen uniformly. Thus, tag $t^{(j)}$ is also distributed uniformly. We assume that $\mathbb{G}$ and $\mathbb{G}_T$ are groups of prime orders and $e : \mathbb{G} \times \mathbb{G} \to \mathbb{G}_T$ is an efficiently computable non-degenerate bilinear map. We let $l = \omega(\log \kappa)$ and $d = O(\kappa)$ for public parameters.

3.2   Security Analysis

We first show the following lemma used in the security proof of SIG_0 then prove that SIG_0 is secure under the CDH assumption.

KGen(1^κ)	Sign(sk, m)	Vrfy(vk, m, σ)
set $\mathbb{G}$ *s.t.* $\lvert\mathbb{G}\rvert = p$	$r \leftarrow \mathbb{Z}/p\mathbb{Z}$	For $j := 1$ to ℓ do
$\alpha \leftarrow \mathbb{Z}_p$	$u(m) = \sum_{i=0}^{d} u_i^{m^i}$	$\quad t^{(j)} = m \mod 2^j$.
$(g, h, \{u_i\}_{i=0}^{d}, \{z_j\}_{j=1}^{l}) \leftarrow \mathbb{G}$	$T^{(j)} = \{0,1\}^j$	If $e(\sigma_0, g)$
$sk = \alpha$	$t^{(j)} = m \mod 2^j$	$\quad \neq e(u(m), g^\alpha) e(z(m)h, \sigma_1)$
$vk = (g, g^\alpha, h, \{u_i\}_{i=0}^{d}, \{z_j\}_{j=1}^{l})$	$z(m) = \prod_{j=1}^{l} z_j^{t^{(j)}}$	$\quad$ return 0
return (vk, sk)	$\sigma_0 = u(m)^\alpha (z(m)h)^r$	else
	$\sigma_1 = g^r$	$\quad$ return 1
	return $\sigma = (\sigma_0, \sigma_1)$	

Fig. 3. SIG_0: EUF-XRMA-secure signature scheme under CDH assumption

Lemma 2. *Let T be a set with $\lvert T \rvert = n$. Let $t_1, \ldots, t_q$ be q independent random variables, taken uniformly random from T. Then, let $q = O(poly(\kappa))$, $d = O(\kappa)$. For $n > \frac{e \cdot q}{d+1}$,*

$$\Pr[\exists i_1, \ldots, i_{d+1} \in [q] \mid t_{i_1} = \cdots = t_{i_{d+1}}]$$

is exponentially small in κ, where e is the base of the natural logarithm.

Proof.

$$\Pr[\exists i_1, \ldots, i_{d+1} \in [q] \mid t_{i_1} = \cdots = t_{i_{d+1}}]$$

$$= {}_q C_{d+1} \left(\frac{1}{n}\right)^d$$

$$= \frac{q!}{(q-(d+1))!(d+1)!} \left(\frac{1}{n}\right)^d$$

$$= \frac{q \cdot (q-1) \cdots (q-d)}{(d+1)!} \left(\frac{1}{n}\right)^d$$

$$\leq \frac{q^{d+1}}{(d+1)!} \left(\frac{1}{n}\right)^d \quad \cdots (*)$$

$$\leq \frac{q^{d+1}}{\sqrt{2\pi(d+1)}} \left(\frac{e}{d+1}\right)^{d+1} \left(\frac{1}{n}\right)^d \quad \cdots (**)$$

$$= \frac{e \cdot q}{\sqrt{2\pi(d+1)}(d+1)} \left(\frac{e \cdot q}{n(d+1)}\right)^d$$

where Inequation $**$ holds by Stirling's approximation

$$\sqrt{2\pi x} \left(\frac{x}{e}\right)^x \leq x! \leq e\sqrt{x} \left(\frac{x}{e}\right)^x.$$

Now, we set $n > \frac{eq}{d+1}$ then $\frac{e \cdot q}{n(d+1)} < 1$ and $\frac{e \cdot q}{\sqrt{2\pi(d+1)}(d+1)}$ is polynomial in κ.

Hence, $\Pr[\exists i_1, \ldots, i_{d+1} \in [q] \mid t_{i_1} = \cdots = t_{i_{d+1}}]$ is exponentially small in κ. $\square$

Böhl et al. assumed that d is constant and showed that the probability $\Pr[\exists i_1, \ldots, i_{d+1} \in [q] \mid t_{i_1} = \cdots = t_{i_{d+1}}]$ is bounded by $\frac{q^{d+1}}{n^d}$. However, d is not necessarily constant. When assuming $d = \mathcal{O}(\kappa)$, $(d+1)!$ in Inequation $*$, which is also in the proof of Lemma 1, cannot be ignored. Lemma 2 shows that the $(d+1)$-fold probability is exponentially small when q tags $\{t_i^{(j)}\}_{i=1}^q$ are chosen from T_j. Böhl et al. [5] bound this probability by q^{d+1}/n^d. This is a key lemma since this probability affects reduction loss. This modification makes our security reduction tighter than that of Böhl et al.'s scheme and helps reduce the vk size.

Theorem 4. *If the CDH assumption holds in $\mathbb{G}$, then SIG_0 is EUF-XRMA secure. Concretely, let $\mathcal{A}$ be a PPT adversary against SIG_0 with advantage $\varepsilon^{\text{EUF-XRMA}} := \mathsf{Adv}_{\mathsf{SIG},\mathcal{A}}^{\text{EUF-XRMA}}(\kappa)$ and let $\mathcal{A}$ have at most q random messages and their corresponding signatures. Then, another adversary $\mathcal{B}$, which can solve the CDH problem with probability of at least $\mathcal{O}(\frac{d}{q})$, can be constructed using $\mathcal{A}$.*

Proof. Suppose that there exists an $\mathcal{A}$ that has at most q random messages and corresponding signatures, and outputs a valid forged signature with probability $\varepsilon^{\text{EUF-XRMA}}$. We show that we can construct another adversary $\mathcal{B}$ that uses $\mathcal{A}$ as an internal sub-algorithm to solve the CDH problem.

Let $\varepsilon^{\text{EUF-XRMA}}$ be $\mathcal{B}$'s advantage in the EUF-XRMA experiment.

Setup. Adversary $\mathcal{B}$ receives a CDH challenge $(g, g^\alpha, g^\beta) \in \mathbb{G}^3$ as an instance of the CDH problem. It then generates q random messages $m_i \leftarrow \mathsf{MsgGen}(gk)$; $gk \leftarrow \mathsf{Setup}(1^\kappa)$ for $1 \leq i \leq q$, defines tag sets $T^{(j)} = \{0,1\}^j$, and generates tags $t_i^{(j)} \in T^{(j)}$ from message m_i,

$$t_i^{(j)} = m_i \bmod 2^j \quad \text{for } 1 \leq i \leq q, \ 1 \leq j \leq l.$$

Note that $t_i^{(j)}$ is not t_i to the j-th power, and $l = \omega(\log_2 \kappa)$. $\mathcal{B}$ chooses the challenge instance j^* such that the probability of a $(d+1)$-tag collision $\Pr[(d+1)\text{-fold}]$ is exponentially small, i.e.,

$$\Pr[\{\exists i_1, \ldots, i_{d+1}\} \subseteq [q] : t_{i_1}^{(j^*)} = \cdots = t_{i_{d+1}}^{(j^*)} \mid \forall i \in [q] : t_i^{(j^*)} \leftarrow T^{(j^*)}]$$

is exponentially small such that $|T^{(j^*)}|$ is polynomial in κ. Thus, $j^* := \lfloor \log(\frac{e \cdot q}{d+1}) \rfloor + 1$ for $|T^{(j^*)}| = \lfloor (e \cdot q/(d+1)) \rfloor + 1$ is an index that fulfills these conditions (see Lemma 2).

Adversary $\mathcal{B}$ chooses $\tilde{t} \in T^{(j^*)}$ randomly and $m_{i_1}, \ldots, m_{i_d}$ such that $t_{i_1}^{(j^*)} = \cdots = t_{i_d}^{(j^*)} = \tilde{t}$. It can choose at most d messages $m_{i_1}, \ldots, m_{i_d}$ which have the same tag $\tilde{t}$ with probability 1, except exponentially small probability according to Lemma 2. It then constructs a polynomial:

$$f(X) = \prod_{i=1}^{d}(X - m_i) = \sum_{i=0}^{d} \mu_i X^i \in \mathbb{Z}_p[X] ,$$

where coefficients $(\mu_0, \ldots, \mu_d)$ in $\mathbb{Z}_p$ and $f(X) = 1$ for $d = 0$. Note that $f(X) = 0$ for $m_i, \ldots, m_{i_d}$. Adversary $\mathcal{B}$ chooses random exponents $(r_0, \ldots, r_d, x_{z_1}, \ldots, x_{z_l}, x_h) \in \mathbb{Z}_p$, where the index $z_1, \ldots, z_l \subseteq [l]$, and defines

$$r(X) = \sum_{i=0}^{d} r_i X^i,$$

$$u(X) = (g^\beta)^{f(X)} g^{r(X)},$$

$$z(X) = (g^\beta)^{\tilde{t}} g^{\sum_{j=1}^{l} x_{z_j}^{t^{(j)}}} \mid t^{(j)} = X \mod 2^j,$$

using the instance of the CDH problem.

Adversary $\mathcal{B}$ then generates a vk. Concretely, $\mathcal{B}$ chooses $\check{t} \in T^{(j^*)}$ such that $\check{t} \neq \tilde{t}$ and generates coefficients μ_i and h as follows:

$$u_i = (g^\beta)^{\mu_i} g^{r_i} \ (i = 0, \ldots, d),$$

$$h = (g^\beta)^{-\check{t}} g^{x_h}.$$

Moreover, $\mathcal{B}$ chooses g^α from the CDH instance and generates a $vk = (g, g^\alpha, \{u_i\}_{i=0}^{d}, \{z_j\}_{j=1}^{l}, h)$.

Adversary $\mathcal{B}$ then creates q signatures $\sigma_1, \ldots, \sigma_q$ for q messages $m_1, \ldots, m_q$. Let $\hat{t}$ be a tag for a message $\hat{m}$. For $\hat{m} \in \{m_1, \ldots, m_q\}$, let $\hat{t} = \hat{m} \mod 2^{j^*}$. If $\tilde{t} \neq \hat{t}$, then $f(\hat{m}) \neq 0$ since $f(X)$ does not have $m_{i_1}, \ldots, m_{i_d}$ as a root, which maps to $\tilde{t}$. There are two cases according to the value of $\check{t}$; $\check{t} = \hat{t}$ or $\check{t} \neq \hat{t}$.

When $\hat{t} = \tilde{t}$, then $\mathcal{B}$ chooses a random $r \leftarrow \mathbb{Z}_p$ and computes a signature $\hat{\sigma} = (\hat{\sigma}_0, \hat{\sigma}_1)$ as follows:

$$\hat{\sigma}_0 = (g^\alpha)^{r(\hat{m})} (z(\hat{m})h)^r,$$

$$\hat{\sigma}_1 = g^r.$$

From the definition of SIG_0, $\hat{\sigma}_0 = u(\hat{m})^\alpha (z(\hat{m})h)^r, g^r)$. In fact,

$$\hat{\sigma}_0 = (u(\hat{m})^\alpha (z(\hat{m})h)^r, g^r)$$

$$= \left((g^\beta)^{f(\hat{m})} g^{r(\hat{m})} \right)^\alpha (z(\hat{m})h)^r.$$

In case that $\hat{t} = \tilde{t}$, $f(\hat{m}) = 0$. Then

$$\hat{\sigma}_0 = (g^\alpha)^{r(\hat{m})} (z(\hat{m})h)^r.$$

When $\tilde{t} \neq \hat{t}$, then $\mathcal{B}$ chooses a random $r \leftarrow \mathbb{Z}_p$ and computes a signature $\hat{\sigma} = (\hat{\sigma}_0, \hat{\sigma}_1)$ as follows:

Let $S = g^{\sum_{j=1}^{l} x_{z_j}^{t^{(j)}} + x_h}$, $\hat{r} = \frac{-\alpha f(\hat{m})}{\tilde{t} - \check{t}} \mod p$, $r' \leftarrow \mathbb{Z}_p$, and $r = \hat{r} + r' \mod p$.

$$\hat{\sigma}_0 = (g^\alpha)^{r(\hat{m})}(g^\beta)^{r'(\tilde{t}-\hat{t})} S^r$$
$$\hat{\sigma}_1 = g^r.$$

Note that $r \in \mathbb{Z}_p$ is uniformly distributed since r' is chosen at random. From the definition of SIG_0, $\hat{\sigma}_0 = u(\hat{m})^\alpha (z(\hat{m})h)^r, g^r)$. In fact,

$$
\begin{aligned}
\hat{\sigma}_0 &= u(\hat{m})^\alpha (z(\hat{m})h)^r \\
&= (g^{\beta f(\hat{m})+r(\hat{m})})^\alpha \{(g^\beta)^{\hat{t}} g^{\sum_{j=1}^l x_{z_j}^{t(j)}} (g^\beta)^{-\hat{t}} g^{x_h}\}^r \\
&= (g^{\beta f(\hat{m})+r(\hat{m})})^\alpha \{g^{\sum_{j=1}^l x_{z_j}^{t(j)}} (g^\beta)^{(\tilde{t}-\hat{t})} g^{x_h}\}^r \\
&= (g^\alpha)^{r(\hat{m})} (g^r)^{\sum_{j=1}^l x_{z_j}^{t(j)} +x_h} (g^{\alpha\beta})^{f(\hat{m})} (g^\beta)^{(r'-\frac{\alpha f(\hat{m})}{\tilde{t}-t^*})(\tilde{t}-\hat{t})} \\
&= (g^\alpha)^{r(\hat{m})} (g^r)^{\sum_{j=1}^l x_{z_j}^{t(j)} +x_h} (g^{\alpha\beta})^{f(\hat{m})} (g^\beta)^{r'(\tilde{t}-t^*)} (g^{\alpha\beta})^{-f(\hat{m})} \\
&= (g^\alpha)^{r(\hat{m})} (g^r)^{\sum_{j=1}^l x_{z_j}^{t(j)} +x_h} (g^\beta)^{r'(\tilde{t}-t^*)} \\
&= (g^\alpha)^{r(\hat{m})} (g^\beta)^{r'(\tilde{t}-t^*)} S^r.
\end{aligned}
$$

$\mathcal{B}$ then sends $(vk, \{m_i, \sigma_i\}_{i=1}^q)$ to $\mathcal{A}$.

Forgery. Adversary $\mathcal{A}$ receives q message and signature pairs $(m_1, \sigma_1), \ldots,$ (m_q, σ_q) from $\mathcal{B}$. After that, $\mathcal{A}$ generates a forged signature $\sigma^* = (\sigma_0^*, \sigma_1^*)$ on m^* and returns (m^*, σ^*) to $\mathcal{B}$.

Solution of CDH problem. Adversary $\mathcal{B}$ derives the solution of the CDH problem using (m^*, σ^*).

When $\mathcal{A}$ succeeds in the forgery, $m^* \notin \{m_1, \ldots, m_q\}$; hence $f(m^*) \neq 0$. Adversary $\mathcal{B}$ then calculates a tag t^* of m^*. If $t^* \neq \tilde{t}$, then it aborts; otherwise, it outputs the solution of the CDH problem $g^{\alpha\beta}$ as follows:

$$
\left(\frac{\sigma_0^*}{(g^\alpha)^{r(m^*)}(\sigma_1^*)^{(\sum_{j=1}^l x_{z_j} t(j)+x_h)}} \right)^{-f(m^*)} = g^{\alpha\beta}.
$$

The simulation of $\mathcal{B}$ is perfect, and $\mathcal{A}$ is given the same environment as a real attack.

Claim. The q signature and message pairs (m_i, σ_i) sent to $\mathcal{A}$ are valid.

Proof of Claim. Let $(m_1, \sigma_1), \ldots, (m_q, \sigma_q)$ be the message and signature pairs that $\mathcal{A}$ received. Adversary $\mathcal{A}$ verifies these signatures using $vk = (g, g^\alpha, \{u_i\}_{i=0}^d, \{z_j\}_{j=1}^l, h)$.

The pairs that $\mathcal{A}$ received are classified into two groups according to the tag of message $\hat{t} = \hat{m} \mod 2^{j^*}$. One group is $\hat{t} = \tilde{t}$ and the other is $\hat{t} \neq \tilde{t}$.

Regarding the group that has $\hat{t} = \tilde{t}$, $\hat{\sigma} = (\hat{\sigma}_0, \hat{\sigma}_1) = ((g^\alpha)^{r(\hat{m})}(z(\hat{m})h)^r, g^r)$. The signature $\hat{\sigma}$ is verified as follows:

$$
\begin{aligned}
e(\hat{\sigma}_0, g) &= e\left((g^\alpha)^{r(\hat{m})}(z(\hat{m})h)^r, g \right) \\
&= e\left((g^\alpha)^{r(\hat{m})}, g \right) e\left((z(\hat{m})h)^r, g \right) \\
&= e\left((g^\alpha)^{r(\hat{m})+\beta f(\hat{m})}, g \right) e\left((z(\hat{m})h)^r, g \right) \\
&= e\left(g^{r(\hat{m})+\beta f(\hat{m})}, g \right)^\alpha e\left((z(\hat{m})h), g \right)^r \\
&= e\left(g^{r(\hat{m})+\beta f(\hat{m})}, g^\alpha \right) e\left((z(\hat{m})h), g^r \right) \\
&= e\left(u(\hat{m}), g^\alpha \right) e(z(\hat{m})h, \hat{\sigma}_1) .
\end{aligned}
$$

Regarding the group that has $\hat{t} \neq \tilde{t}$, $\hat{\sigma} = (\hat{\sigma}_0, \hat{\sigma}_1) = ((g^\alpha)^{r(\hat{m})}$ $(g^\beta)^{r'(\tilde{t}-\hat{t})}S^r, g^r)$. The signature $\hat{\sigma}$ is verified as follows:

$$
\begin{aligned}
e(\hat{\sigma}_0, g) &= e\left((g^\alpha)^{r(\hat{m})}(g^\beta)^{r'(\tilde{t}-t^*)}S^r, g \right) \\
&= e\left((g^\alpha)^{r(\hat{m})}(g^\beta)^{(r+\frac{\alpha f(\hat{m})}{(\tilde{t}-t^*)})(\tilde{t}-t^*)}(g^r)^{\sum_{j=1}^l x_{z_j}^{t^{(j)}}+x_h}, g \right) \\
&= e\left((g^\alpha)^{r(\hat{m})+\beta f(\hat{m})}(g^r)^{\beta(\tilde{t}-t^*)+\sum_{j=1}^l x_{z_j}^{t^{(j)}}+x_h}, g \right) \\
&= e\left((g^\alpha)^{r(\hat{m})+\beta f(\hat{m})}, g \right) e\left((g^r)^{\beta(\tilde{t}-t^*)+\sum_{j=1}^l x_{z_j}^{t^{(j)}}+x_h}, g \right) \\
&= e\left(g^{r(\hat{m})+\beta f(\hat{m})}, g \right)^\alpha e\left(g^{\beta(\tilde{t}-t^*)+\sum_{j=1}^l x_{z_j}^{t^{(j)}}+x_h}, g \right)^r \\
&= e\left(g^{r(\hat{m})+\beta f(\hat{m})}, g^\alpha \right) e\left((g^\beta)^{\tilde{t}+\sum_{j=1}^l x_{z_j}^{t^{(j)}}}(g^\beta)^{-t^*+x_h}, g^r \right) \\
&= e(u(\hat{m}), g^\alpha)e(z(\hat{m})h, \hat{\sigma}_1).
\end{aligned}
$$

Both groups satisfy the equation

$$
e(\hat{\sigma}_0, g) = e\left(u(\hat{m}), g^\alpha \right) e(z(\hat{m})h, \hat{\sigma}_1) .
$$

□

Analysis. Let *success* be the event that $\mathcal{B}$ outputs a CDH solution $g^{\alpha\beta}$. In this simulation, $\mathcal{B}$ can extract $g^{\alpha\beta}$ from the forgery if $\tilde{t} = t^*$. This probability $\Pr[\tilde{t} = t^*]$ is

$$
\Pr[\tilde{t} = t^*] = \frac{1}{|T^{(j^*)}|} = \frac{1}{\lfloor \frac{e \cdot q}{d+1} \rfloor + 1} .
$$

However, if no tag $t_i^{(j^*)} \in T^{(j^*)}$ has at most d-fold collisions, $\mathcal{B}$ can not extract $g^{\alpha\beta}$ from the forgery since $f(m^*) \neq 0$. Moreover, there is a gap in tag distribution

$1/2^{\mathcal{O}(\kappa)}$ between $\bmod 2^j$ computation and uniform distribution, where $j \le d \le \mathcal{O}(\kappa)$. Hence,

$$\Pr[success] = \frac{1}{\lfloor \frac{e \cdot q}{d+1} \rfloor + 1} \varepsilon^{\text{EUF-XRMA}} - \Pr[d + 1\text{-fold}] - \frac{1}{2^{\mathcal{O}(\kappa)}}$$

$$= \mathcal{O}\left(\frac{d}{q}\right) \varepsilon^{\text{EUF-XRMA}}.$$

$\square$

4   EUF-CMA Full Security Scheme

In this section, we discuss the construction of a fully EUF-CMA secure scheme from SIG_0 by applying trapdoor commitment TCOM.

4.1   Construction

We describe SIG in Fig. 4.

$\mathsf{KGen}(1^\kappa)$	$\mathsf{Sign}(sk, m)$	$\mathsf{Vrfy}(vk, m, \sigma, r)$
set $\mathbb{G}$ s.t. $|\mathbb{G}| = p$	$r \leftarrow \mathsf{COIN}^{\text{com}}$, $s \leftarrow \mathbb{Z}/p\mathbb{Z}$	$\psi = \mathsf{Com}_{pk}^{\text{tc}}(m; r)$
$\alpha \leftarrow \mathbb{Z}_p$	$\psi = \mathsf{Com}_{pk}^{\text{tc}}(m; r)$	For $i := 1$ to ℓ do
$(g, h, \{u_i\}_{i=0}^d, \{z_j\}_{j=1}^l) \leftarrow \mathbb{G}$	$u(\psi) = \prod_{i=0}^d u_i^{\psi^i}$	$t^{(j)} = \psi \bmod 2^j$
$sk = \alpha$	For $j := 1$ to ℓ do	If $e(\tilde{\sigma}_0, g)$
$vk = (g, h, g^\alpha, \{u_i\}_{i=0}^d, \{z_j\}_{j=1}^l)$	$t^{(j)} = \psi \bmod 2^j$	$\neq e(u(\psi), g^\alpha)e(z(\psi)h, \tilde{\sigma}_1)$
$(tk, pk) \leftarrow \mathsf{Gen}^{\text{tc}}(1^\kappa)$	$z(\psi) = \prod_{j=1}^l z_j^{t^{(j)}}$	return 0
return (vk, sk, tk, pk)	$\tilde{\sigma}_0 = u(\psi)^\alpha (z(\psi)h)^s$	else
	$\tilde{\sigma}_1 = g^s$	return 1
	return $(\sigma = (\tilde{\sigma}_0, \tilde{\sigma}_1), r)$	

Fig. 4. SIG: EUF-CMA-secure signature scheme with TCOM under CDH assumption

Remark 1. One can construct TCOM such that ψ can be seen in an element in $\mathbb{Z}/p\mathbb{Z}$ (except for one element). In addition, $\psi \leftarrow \mathsf{Com}_{pk}^{\text{tc}}(m)$ is (almost) uniformly distributed over $\mathbb{Z}/p\mathbb{Z}$ for any m. The latter condition is needed to transform an EUF-XRMA secure signature scheme to an EUF-CMA secure one. Let $\mathbb{G}$ be the group defined over the super-singular elliptic curve $y^2 = x^3 + b$ on $\mathbb{F}_p$, where $p = 2 \pmod 3$. Then, there is the one-to-one encoding, called map-to-point, from $\mathbb{G}^\times (= \mathbb{G}\backslash\{\mathcal{O}\})$ to $\mathbb{Z}/p\mathbb{Z}$ [2].

Lemma 3. *The signature scheme* SIG *(Fig. 4) is non-re-randomizable.*

Proof. Let $vk = (g, g^\alpha, \{u_i\}_{i=0}^d, \{z_j\}_{j=1}^l, h)$ be a given vk, and let m and $(\sigma = (\tilde{\sigma}_0, \tilde{\sigma}_1), r)$ be valid messages for signatures, i.e., σ satisfies

$$e(\tilde{\sigma}_0, g) = e(u(\psi), g^\alpha)e(h \prod_{j=1}^l z_j^{t^{(j)}}, \tilde{\sigma}_1). \tag{1}$$

The set of all σs satisfying (1) is therefore identical to the set

$$\Sigma(vk, m) = \{(u(\psi))^{\alpha}(z(\psi)h)^s, g^s; s \in \mathbb{Z}_p, r \leftarrow \mathsf{COIN}^{\mathsf{com}}\}.$$

Consider an algorithm $Rerand$ taking as input vk, σ, and message m. We assume that $Rerand$ samples $s' \leftarrow \mathbb{Z}_p$ and returns $\sigma' = (\sigma'_0, \sigma'_1)$ distributed uniformly over $\Sigma(sk, m)$. However, since $Rerand$ cannot generate $\psi = \mathsf{Com}^{\mathsf{tc}}_{pk}(x; r); r \leftarrow \mathsf{COIN}^{\mathsf{com}}$, there is no $Rerand$ that returns the new signature σ' distributed uniformly over the set of all possible signatures for m. Hence, SIG is non-re-randomizable. □

4.2 Security Analysis

Theorem 5. *Let* $\mathsf{TCOM} = (\mathsf{Gen}^{\mathsf{tc}}, \mathsf{Com}^{\mathsf{tc}}, \mathsf{TCom}^{\mathsf{tc}}, \mathsf{TCol}^{\mathsf{tc}})$ *be a trapdoor commitment and* SIG_0 *be EUF-XRMA secure. Therefore,* SIG *is EUF-CMA secure. Concretely, let* $\varepsilon^{\mathrm{EUF\text{-}XRMA}}_{\mathsf{SIG}_0} = \mathsf{Adv}^{\mathrm{EUF\text{-}XRMA}}_{\mathsf{SIG}_0, \mathcal{A}}(\kappa)$ *be an advantage of an* EUF-XRMA *adversary for* SIG_0, $\varepsilon^{\mathrm{EUF\text{-}CMA}}_{\mathsf{SIG}} = \mathsf{Adv}^{\mathrm{EUF\text{-}CMA}}_{\mathsf{SIG}, \mathcal{A}}(\kappa)$ *be an advantage of an* EUF-CMA *adversary for* SIG, *and* $\epsilon^{\mathrm{comp\text{-}bind}}$ *be an advantage of a computational binding adversary. Then,* $\varepsilon^{\mathrm{EUF\text{-}CMA}}_{\mathsf{SIG}}$ *can be bounded by* $\varepsilon^{\mathrm{EUF\text{-}XRMA}}_{\mathsf{SIG}_0} + \varepsilon^{\mathrm{comp\text{-}bind}}$.

Proof. We construct adversaries $\mathcal{A}^{\mathrm{EUF\text{-}XRMA}}_{\mathsf{SIG}_0}$ against SIG_0 and $\mathcal{A}^{\mathrm{comp\text{-}bind}}$ against computational binding using an adversary against SIG and compare their advantages $\varepsilon^{\mathrm{EUF\text{-}XRMA}}_{\mathsf{SIG}_0}$ and $\varepsilon^{\mathrm{comp\text{-}bind}}$ with $\varepsilon^{\mathrm{EUF\text{-}CMA}}_{\mathsf{SIG}}$.

Suppose that there exists a PPT adversary $\mathcal{A}^{\mathrm{EUF\text{-}CMA}}_{\mathsf{SIG}}$ that breaks SIG in the EUF-CMA game. In the game, $\mathcal{A}^{\mathrm{EUF\text{-}CMA}}_{\mathsf{SIG}}$ receives public parameters vk, pk in the setup phase. It then uses a signing oracle q times and obtains q triples $\{(m_i, \sigma_i, r_i)\}^q_{i=1}$ of (message, signature, random), where $\sigma_i = (\tilde{\sigma}_{i_0}, \tilde{\sigma}_{i_1})$. It finally forges a signature and random pair (σ^*, r^*) for a message m^*, where $m^* \notin \{m_1, \ldots, m_q\}$.

Setup. Let $\mathcal{B}$ have the role of transmitting some data from $\mathcal{A}^{\mathrm{EUF\text{-}CMA}}_{\mathsf{SIG}}$ to $\mathcal{A}^{\mathrm{comp\text{-}bind}}$ and $\mathcal{A}^{\mathrm{EUF\text{-}XRMA}}_{\mathsf{SIG}_0}$. Adversary $\mathcal{B}$ receives $vk, pk, \{(m_i, \sigma_i, r_i)\}^q_{i=1}$, and $\{(m^*, \sigma^*, r^*)\}$ from $\mathcal{A}^{\mathrm{EUF\text{-}CMA}}_{\mathsf{SIG}}$. Adversary $\mathcal{B}$ computes $\psi_i = \mathsf{Com}^{\mathsf{tc}}_{pk}(m_i; r_i)$ for $i = 1, \ldots, q$ and $\psi^* = \mathsf{Com}^{\mathsf{tc}}_{pk}(m^*; r^*)$. Adversary $\mathcal{B}$ transmits pk, and q triples $\{(m_i, r_i, \psi_i)\}^q_{i=1}$ and a triple (m^*, r^*, ψ^*) to $\mathcal{A}^{\mathrm{comp\text{-}bind}}$, and transmits vk, q pairs $\{(\psi_i, \sigma_i)\}^q_{i=1}$ and a pair (ψ^*, σ^*) to $\mathcal{A}^{\mathrm{EUF\text{-}XRMA}}_{\mathsf{SIG}_0}$.

Breaking computational binding. Adversary $\mathcal{A}^{\mathrm{comp\text{-}bind}}$ receives pk and q triples $\{(m_i, r_i, \psi_i)\}^q_{i=1}$ and a triple (m^*, r^*, ψ^*) from $\mathcal{B}$.

In the case that $\psi^* \in \{\psi_1, \ldots, \psi_q\}$, $\mathcal{A}^{\mathrm{comp\text{-}bind}}$ can break the computational bindings. That is, let $\psi^* = \psi_j$ for $j \in \{1, \ldots, q\}$, then $\mathsf{Com}^{\mathsf{tc}}_{pk}(m^*; r^*) = \mathsf{Com}^{\mathsf{tc}}_{pk}(m_j; r_j)$ for $m^* \neq m_j$. When $\mathcal{A}^{\mathrm{comp\text{-}bind}}$ is given a pk in the computational bindings game, $\mathcal{A}^{\mathrm{comp\text{-}bind}}$ returns (m^*, r^*, m_j, r_j). This means, $\mathcal{A}^{\mathrm{comp\text{-}bind}}$ succeeds in breaking computational bindings, since $\mathsf{Com}^{\mathsf{tc}}_{pk}(m^*; r^*) = \mathsf{Com}^{\mathsf{tc}}_{pk}(m_j; r_j)$.

Let p be the probability that $\psi^* \in \{\psi_1, \ldots, \psi_q\}$. Then, the success probability of $\mathcal{A}^{\text{comp-bind}}$ is at least $p \cdot \varepsilon_{\text{SIG}}^{\text{EUF-CMA}}$. That is,

$$\varepsilon^{\text{comp-bind}} \geq p \cdot \varepsilon_{\text{SIG}}^{\text{EUF-CMA}}.$$

Breaking XRMA security of SIG$_0$. Adversary $\mathcal{A}_{\text{SIG}_0}^{\text{EUF-XRMA}}$ receives a vk, q pairs $\{(\psi_i, \sigma_i)\}_{i=1}^q$ and a pair (ψ^*, σ^*) from $\mathcal{B}$.

In the case that $\psi^* \notin \{\psi_1, \ldots, \psi_q\}$, $\mathcal{A}_{\text{SIG}_0}^{\text{EUF-XRMA}}$ can break the EUF-XRMA security of SIG$_0$. That is, σ_i for $i \in \{1, \ldots, q\}$ is a valid signature for ψ_i, and σ^* is a valid signature for ψ^*.

When $\mathcal{A}_{\text{SIG}_0}^{\text{EUF-XRMA}}$ is given a vk and $\{(\psi_i, \sigma_i)\}_{i=1}^q$ in the EUF-XRMA game, $\mathcal{A}_{\text{SIG}_0}^{\text{EUF-XRMA}}$ returns (ψ^*, σ^*). Note that $\mathcal{A}_{\text{SIG}_0}^{\text{EUF-XRMA}}$ generates valid randoms $r^* = \text{TCol}_{tk}^{\text{tc}}(\psi, w, m)$ by using a trapdoor key tk and random r as an auxiliary information w. Then $\mathcal{A}_{\text{SIG}_0}^{\text{EUF-XRMA}}$ can make a connection with commitments and messages. This means $\mathcal{A}_{\text{SIG}_0}^{\text{EUF-XRMA}}$ succeeds in the EUF-XRMA game, since $\psi^* \notin \{\psi_1, \ldots, \psi_q\}$ and σ^* is a valid signature for ψ^*.

The success probability of $\mathcal{A}_{\text{SIG}_0}^{\text{EUF-XRMA}}$ is at least $(1-p) \cdot \varepsilon_{\text{SIG}}^{\text{EUF-CMA}}$, since the probability $\psi^* \notin \{\psi_1, \ldots, \psi_q\}$ is $1 - p$. That is,

$$\varepsilon_{\text{SIG}_0}^{\text{EUF-XRMA}} \geq (1-p) \cdot \varepsilon_{\text{SIG}}^{\text{EUF-CMA}}.$$

Analysis. The inequalities $\varepsilon^{\text{comp-bind}} \geq p \cdot \varepsilon_{\text{SIG}}^{\text{EUF-CMA}}$ and $\varepsilon_{\text{SIG}_0}^{\text{EUF-XRMA}} \geq (1-p) \cdot \varepsilon_{\text{SIG}}^{\text{EUF-CMA}}$ hold from the above. Hence,

$$\varepsilon^{\text{comp-bind}} + \varepsilon_{\text{SIG}_0}^{\text{EUF-XRMA}} \geq p \cdot \varepsilon_{\text{SIG}}^{\text{EUF-CMA}} + (1-p) \cdot \varepsilon_{\text{SIG}}^{\text{EUF-CMA}}$$
$$\geq \varepsilon_{\text{SIG}}^{\text{EUF-CMA}}.$$

$\square$

5   Discussion

The reduction loss of Böhl et al.'s signature scheme is

$$\varepsilon^{\text{CDH}} \geq |\frac{1}{T^{(j^*)}}| \left(\varepsilon^{\text{EUF-CMA}} - \varepsilon^{\text{PRF}} - Pr[d+1\text{-fold}]\right),$$

where $|T^{(j^*)}|$ is the size of tag sets. In our scheme, $T^{(j^*)} = \mathcal{O}(\frac{q}{d})$ since its tag space is $|T^{(j^*)}| := \lfloor (d+1)/e \cdot q \rfloor + 1$. The advantage regarding PRF ε^{PRF} is $\frac{1}{2^{\mathcal{O}(\kappa)}}$, which is the gap between the case in which tags are chosen uniformly and that in which tags are generated as $t^j = m \mod 2^j$. In Böhl et al.'s scheme, the key lemma is as follows:

$$\Pr[d+1\text{-fold}] = \Pr[\exists i_1, \ldots, i_{d+1} \in [q] \mid t_{i_1} = \cdots = t_{i_{d+1}}] \leq \frac{q^{d+1}}{n^d}.$$

Since they assumed that the size of d is constant, the evaluation was sufficient. However, we assume $d = \mathcal{O}(\kappa)$; thus, we evaluate the probability more strictly. According to Theorems 4 and 5,

$$\varepsilon^{\text{CDH}} \geq |\frac{1}{T^{(j^*)}}| \left(\varepsilon^{\text{EUF-XRMA}} - \frac{1}{2^{\mathcal{O}(\kappa)}} - Pr[d + 1\text{-fold}] \right) \tag{2}$$

$$\geq \mathcal{O}\left(\frac{d}{q}\right) \cdot \varepsilon^{\text{EUF-XRMA}}$$

$$\geq \mathcal{O}\left(\frac{d}{q}\right) \cdot \left(\varepsilon^{\text{EUF-CMA}} - \varepsilon^{\text{comp-binding}} \right)$$

Hence,

$$\varepsilon^{\text{EUF-CMA}} \leq \mathcal{O}\left(\frac{q}{d}\right) \cdot \varepsilon^{\text{CDH}} + \varepsilon^{\text{comp-binding}}. \tag{3}$$

Computational binding is reduced to the discrete logarithm problem. The whole security-reduction loss to the CDH problem, a search problem, is $\mathcal{O}(q/d)$.

The tag set of Böhl et al.'s scheme is chosen from a sparse tag set whose size is $2^{\lfloor c^j \rfloor}$, where c is constant. Our tag set size is 2^j, which is appropriate to choose a small T^{j^*} such that $|T^{j^*}| > \frac{e \cdot q}{d+1}$. On the other hand, d is constant in Böhl et al.'s scheme, while $d = \mathcal{O}(\kappa)$ in our scheme. The size of the vk increases according to the size of d. Hence, the vk size of our scheme is larger than that of Böhl et al.'s scheme. That is, although the vk size is larger than that of Böhl et al.'s scheme, our scheme achieves a constant-size signature with tighter reduction.

6   Conclusion

The optimal security-reduction loss to CDH problem from a constant-size signature scheme is $\mathcal{O}(q)$ if signature schemes are re-randomizable. We proposed a constant-size non-re-randomizable signature scheme that is secure under the CDH assumption with tighter security-reduction than ever constant-size signature schemes. Particularly, its security reduction, $\mathcal{O}(q/d)$ is the tightest thus far.

References

1. Abe, M., Chase, M., David, B., Kohlweiss, M., Nishimaki, R., Ohkubo, M.: Constant-size structure-preserving signatures: generic constructions and simple assumptions. J. Cryptology **29**(4), 833–878 (2016). ISO 690
2. Boneh, D., Franklin, M.: Identity-based encryption from the Weil pairing. In: Kilian, J. (ed.) CRYPTO 2001. LNCS, vol. 2139, pp. 213–229. Springer, Heidelberg (2001). doi:10.1007/3-540-44647-8_13
3. Boyle, E., Goldwasser, S., Ivan, I.: Functional signatures and pseudorandom functions. In: Krawczyk, H. (ed.) PKC 2014. LNCS, vol. 8383, pp. 501–519. Springer, Heidelberg (2014). doi:10.1007/978-3-642-54631-0_29

4. Böhl, F., Hofheinz, D., Jager, T., Koch, J., Seo, J.H., Striecks, C.: Practical signatures from standard assumptions. In: Johansson, T., Nguyen, P.Q. (eds.) EUROCRYPT 2013. LNCS, vol. 7881, pp. 461–485. Springer, Heidelberg (2013). doi:10.1007/978-3-642-38348-9_28

5. Böhl, F., Hofheinz, D., Jager, T., Koch, J., Striecks, C.: Confined guessing: new signatures from standard assumptions. J. Cryptology **28**(1), 176–208 (2015)

6. Blazy, O., Kakvi, S.A., Kiltz, E., Pan, J.: Tightly-secure signatures from chameleon hash functions. In: Katz, J. (ed.) PKC 2015. LNCS, vol. 9020, pp. 256–279. Springer, Heidelberg (2015). doi:10.1007/978-3-662-46447-2_12

7. Boneh, D., Mironov, I., Shoup, V.: A secure signature scheme from bilinear maps. In: Joye, M. (ed.) CT-RSA 2003. LNCS, vol. 2612, pp. 98–110. Springer, Heidelberg (2003). doi:10.1007/3-540-36563-X_7

8. Chen, J., Wee, H.: Fully, (almost) tightly secure IBE and dual system groups. In: Canetti, R., Garay, J.A. (eds.) CRYPTO 2013. LNCS, vol. 8043, pp. 435–460. Springer, Heidelberg (2013). doi:10.1007/978-3-642-40084-1_25

9. Damgård, I.: Efficient concurrent zero-knowledge in the auxiliary string model. In: Preneel, B. (ed.) EUROCRYPT 2000. LNCS, vol. 1807, pp. 418–430. Springer, Heidelberg (2000). doi:10.1007/3-540-45539-6_30

10. Goldreich, O.: Foundation of cryptography (in two volumes: Basic tools and basic applications) (2001)

11. Goldwasser, S., Micali, S., Rivest, R.L.: A digital signature scheme secure against adaptive chosen-message attacks. SIAM J. Comput. **17**(2), 281–308 (1988)

12. Hofheinz, D.: Algebraic partitioning: fully compact and (almost) tightly secure cryptography. In: Kushilevitz, E., Malkin, T. (eds.) TCC 2016. LNCS, vol. 9562, pp. 251–281. Springer, Heidelberg (2016). doi:10.1007/978-3-662-49096-9_11

13. Hofheinz, D., Jager, T., Knapp, E.: Waters signatures with optimal security reduction. In: Fischlin, M., Buchmann, J., Manulis, M. (eds.) PKC 2012. LNCS, vol. 7293, pp. 66–83. Springer, Heidelberg (2012). doi:10.1007/978-3-642-30057-8_5

14. Hofheinz, D., Kiltz, E.: Programmable hash functions and their applications. J. Cryptology **25**(3), 484–527 (2012)

15. Hohenberger, S., Waters, B.: Realizing hash-and-sign signatures under standard assumptions. In: Joux, A. (ed.) EUROCRYPT 2009. LNCS, vol. 5479, pp. 333–350. Springer, Heidelberg (2009). doi:10.1007/978-3-642-01001-9_19

16. Seo, J.H.: Short Signatures from Diffie-Hellman, Revisited: Sublinear Public Key, CMA Security, and Tighter Reduction. IACR Cryptology ePrint Archive, 2014, 138 (2014)

17. Waters, B.: Efficient identity-based encryption without random oracles. In: Cramer, R. (ed.) EUROCRYPT 2005. LNCS, vol. 3494, pp. 114–127. Springer, Heidelberg (2005). doi:10.1007/11426639_7

Homomorphic-Policy Attribute-Based Key Encapsulation Mechanisms

Jérémy Chotard[1,2,3(✉)], Duong Hieu Phan[1], and David Pointcheval[2,3]

[1] XLIM, University of Limoges, CNRS, Limoges, France
jeremy.chotard@ens.fr
[2] DIENS, École normale supérieure, CNRS, PSL Research University, Paris, France
[3] Inria, Paris, France

Abstract. Attribute-Based Encryption (ABE) allows to target the recipients of a message according to a policy expressed as a predicate among some attributes. Ciphertext-policy ABE schemes can choose the policy at the encryption time, contrarily to key-policy ABE schemes that specify the policy at the key generation time, for each user.

In this paper, we define a new property for ABE, on top of a ciphertext-policy ABE scheme: homomorphic-policy. A combiner is able to (publicly) combine ciphertexts under different policies into a ciphertext under a combined policy (AND or OR). This allows to specify even much later the policy for a specific ciphertext: the sender encrypts, and the combiner specifies the policy, without knowing the plaintext.

More precisely, using linear secret sharing schemes (LSSS), we design Attribute-Based Key Encapsulation Mechanisms (ABKEM) with our new Homomorphic-Policy property. Technically, by exploiting a specific property in the structure of LSSS matrix, we can show that, given several encapsulations of the same keys under various policies, anyone can derive an encapsulation of the same key under any combination of the policies. As a consequence, from encapsulations under many single attributes, one can build an encapsulation under a complex policy over the attributes.

Similarly to the case of encryption with homomorphic properties, where malleability weakens confidentiality, homomorphic-policy ABE also weakens the security of an ABE when the combiner colludes with legitimate users. On the other hand, homomorphic-policy provides additional flexibility and nice features when one targets some practical application: in Pay-TV, this allows to separate the content providers that can generate the encapsulations of a session key under every attributes, this key being used to encrypt the payload, and the service providers that build the decryption policies according to the subscriptions. The advantage is that the aggregation of the encapsulations by the service providers does not contain any secret information.

1   Introduction

Attribute-Based Encryption (ABE), introduced by Sahai and Waters [16], is a generalization of some advanced primitives such as identity-based

© Springer International Publishing AG 2017
P.Q. Nguyen and J. Zhou (Eds.): ISC 2017, LNCS 10599, pp. 155–172, 2017.
https://doi.org/10.1007/978-3-319-69659-1_9

encryption [2,17] and broadcast encryption [6]. It gives a flexible way to define the target group of people who can receive the message: encryption and decryption can be based on the user's attributes. This primitive was further developed by Goyal *et al.* [9] who introduced two categories of ABE: *ciphertext-policy* attribute-based encryption (CP-ABE) and *key-policy* attribute-based encryption (KP-ABE). In a CP-ABE scheme, the secret key is associated with a set of attributes and the ciphertext is associated with an access policy over the universe of attributes: a user can decrypt a given ciphertext if he holds the attributes that satisfy the access policy underlying the ciphertext. KP-ABE is the dual to CP-ABE in the sense that an access policy is encoded into the users secret key, and a ciphertext is computed with respect to a set of attributes: the ciphertext is decryptable by a user only if the attributes in the ciphertext satisfy the user's access policy.

CP-ABE and KP-ABE consider different scenarios. In KP-ABE, the encryptor has no control over who has access to the data he encrypts. This is the key-issuer who generates and controls the appropriate keys to grant or deny access to the users. In contrast, in CP-ABE, the encryptor is able to decide who should or should not have access to the data that he encrypts. In the applications we target such as Pay-TV, this would mean that the access control is either dynamically managed by the encryptor (with a ciphertext-policy ABE) or statically managed by the key-issuer (with a key-policy ABE), while in real-life a third-party could be in charge of a dynamic policy.

Fine-Grained Access Control. Over the last few years, there has been a lot of progress in constructing secure and efficient ABE schemes from different assumptions and for different settings [1,3,4,7–10,13–16,18], to name a few. The Sahai-Waters' scheme [16] produces ciphertexts decryptable when at least k attributes overlapped between a ciphertext and a private key. While they showed that this primitive is useful for error-tolerant encryption with biometrics, the lack of expressibility limits its applicability when more general policy are required. Fine-grained access control systems [9] facilitate granting differential access rights to a set of users and allow flexibility in specifying the access rights of individual users. Several techniques are known for implementing fine-grained access control. In our work, we focus on fine-grained access control which are expressed by logic formulas and we rely on the standard Linear Secret Sharing Scheme (LSSS) access structures, first considered in the context of ABE by Goyal *et al.* [9].

1.1   Homomorphic-Policy Attribute-Based Key Encapsulation Mechanisms

In KP-ABE, the access policy is controlled at the key generation phase, while in CP-ABE, the access policy is controlled at the message encryption phase. We go a step further in this consideration by postponing the management of the access policy to a later phase and show how one can manage the access policies without knowing any secret nor the content of message.

Previous works on CP-ABE consider classical encryption: the encryptor, taking as input an access policy and a message, produces a corresponding ciphertext. The encryptor thus manages both the access policy and the encryption of the original message. This scenario is unavoidable when limiting the access policy as a single atomic attribute characterizing a user's identity (*e.g.*, identity-based encryption) or a target group of users (*e.g.*, identity-based broadcast encryption) because the encryptor needs to know the message to encrypt with the single attribute. However, in the general case, where the access policy is composed from sub-policies via AND and OR operators, the encryption of a message for the whole access policy can be computed from the ciphertexts of the sub-policies, without the knowledge of the original message.

Aiming to this scenario, where a combiner should manage the access policy without knowing to the original message, we need an additional property in ABE: the homomorphic-policy. This property weakens the security of an ABE when the combiner colludes with legitimate users. However, in our practical application (described below), there is no incentive for the combiner to break the scheme. The combiner is indeed involved in the protocol to improve on the flexibility of the access control, and even if it is corrupted, there is no harm for the system, comparing to the scenario where there is no combiner and everything is managed by a unique authority.

Considering Pay-TV, we can now separate the roles of the content provider and of the manager of the access policies (see Fig. 1, the left part): the content provider (C) encapsulates the same session key K under each attribute, encrypts the content under this session key K, and provides the encapsulation together with the encrypted content to the manager of the access policies (A). The latter broadcasts the encrypted content, but according to the access policy, it combines the appropriate encapsulations to produce a unique encapsulation, to be broadcast to the users (the recipients (R)). Each authorized user can decrypt this encapsulation (by owning attributes satisfying the access policy) and get the session key to decrypt the content.

Fig. 1. Separation of the roles: content provider (C) – access policy manager (A).

We can also envisage another case where the entities C and A are totally independent. To illustrate this, let us assume the manager (A) is a service of video conferencing (see Fig. 1, the right part), and the content provider (C) is a client that asks A to organize a meeting with the participants (P). The authorized participants are identified by several attributes. At the moment of the meeting, C secretly gives A the encapsulations of the session key K, under the various attributes, so that it can publicly distribute it according to the appropriate policy to the participants. Only the authorized participants get access to the session K

and can participate to the meeting. The manager A does not learn any secret information, and cannot eavesdrop the meeting.

As explained in the above context, the homomorphic-policy property is compatible for key encapsulation rather than for encryption. Technically, we thus need to define Attribute-Based Key Encapsulation Mechanisms (ABKEM) which encapsulate a session key for an access policy. Then, the combination of two encapsulations of the same session key under two sub-policies into an encapsulation for the composed access policy is completed via the homomorphic-policy property: if we have encapsulations of a session key K under two policies p_1 and p_2, we will be able to produce an encapsulation of the same session key K for the policies $p_1 \vee p_2$ and $p_1 \wedge p_2$. The achievement of an homomorphic-policy ABKEM is the main contribution of this paper. But of course, this is important to keep all the initial properties of an ABE scheme, and namely the collusion-resistance of the final encapsulation.

1.2   Contribution

As explained above, our main contribution is the definition and construction of Homomorphic-Policy Attribute-Based Key Encapsulation Mechanisms (HP-ABKEM). To this aim

– we focus on homomorphic policy and define attribute-based key encapsulation mechanisms (ABKEM).
– we propose homomorphic-policy methods to combine ciphertexts for AND and OR operations on policies.
– Our construction of ABKEM relies on the Lewko-Waters ABE scheme [11], which security holds in the random-oracle model. ABKEM is very convenient to be used with a Data Encapsulation Method (DEM) for practical applications which encrypt large contents or streams of data, such as the case of Pay-TV. We exploit special properties of LSSS for AND and OR operations and transforms them in an efficient way of combining the corresponding encapsulations.
– we then propose an efficient randomization method for making any ciphertext (possibly obtained from the above combinations) statistically indistinguishable from a fresh ciphertext targeting the same policy. This is important for the security of the system.

Putting altogether, our final result gives an HP-ABKEM which is as efficient as the Lewko-Waters ABE system. It is interesting that we get the homomorphic-policy property without paying an extra cost. Actually, the final encapsulation after several combinations turns out to be the same as the one the Lewko-Waters sender would have produced, hence the same security level, and namely the collusion-resistance (in the random-oracle model).

1.3 Our Technique

While the homomorphic property for two group laws over the encrypted messages (usually called *fully homomorphic* property) is quite difficult to achieve. Fortunately, achieving *homomorphic policy* seems much easier and more efficient.

Our technique exploits specific structures of the LSSS-matrix and carries them on the combination of encapsulations. The OR operation is relatively easy to get, because it essentially corresponds to a concatenation of the encapsulations. However, the AND operation does require a particular property on the LSSS-matrix, that we explain below.

Let us first briefly summarize the general method of constructing an LSSS-based ABE, adapted to an ABKEM. For any policy p, expressed as a logic formula, an LSSS-matrix $\mathbf{A} \in \mathbb{K}^{m \times n}$ is generated such that each line $x \in \{1, \ldots, m\}$ corresponds to an attribute, and from a set of attributes that satisfies the policy p, one can do a linear combination on the corresponding lines of the matrix $\mathbf{A}$ to reconstruct the vector $(1, 0, \ldots, 0)$. One then sets $\vec{v} \leftarrow (s, \$, \ldots, \$)^t$ and the share-vector $\vec{v} \leftarrow \mathbf{A} \cdot \vec{v}$ for the secret s, where the vector $\vec{v}$ is completed with random components. A linear combination that reconstructs the vector $(1, 0, \ldots, 0)$ leads to the same linear combination on the share-vector $\vec{v} = \mathbf{A} \cdot \vec{v}$ that reconstructs the secret s. One can thus encapsulate each element of the vector $\vec{v}$ so that a legitimate user can reconstruct the session key $e(g, g)^s$ in a pairing-friendly setting, thanks to the additive property of the exponents.

Now, from an encapsulation for the policy p_1 of the session key $e(g, g)^{s_1}$ and an encapsulation for the policy p_2 of the session key $e(g, g)^{s_2}$, our objective is to produce an encapsulation for the policy $p_1 \wedge p_2$ of the session key $e(g, g)^{s_1 + s_2}$. We first observe a property on the LSSS-matrix: with the LSSS-matrix $\mathbf{A}_1 \in \mathbb{K}^{m \times n}$ associated to the policy p_1 and the LSSS-matrix $\mathbf{A}_2 \in \mathbb{K}^{m \times n}$ associated to the policy p_2, the LSSS-matrix of $\mathbf{A}$ associated to a policy $p_1 \wedge p_2$ is of the following form:

$$\mathbf{A}_\wedge = \begin{bmatrix} \mathbf{A}_1^1 & \mathbf{A}_1^1 & \mathbf{A}_1^* & 0 \\ 0 & -\mathbf{A}_2^1 & 0 & -\mathbf{A}_2^* \end{bmatrix}$$

where for any $\mathbf{A}$, we denote $\mathbf{A}^1$ the first column and $\mathbf{A}^*$ the matrix $\mathbf{A}$ without the first column (i.e., $\mathbf{A} = \begin{bmatrix} \mathbf{A}^1 & \mathbf{A}^* \end{bmatrix}$).

Looking at the first and the second column of the matrix $\mathbf{A}_\wedge$, the vector $\mathbf{A}_1^1$ is repeated twice in the upper part, and in the bottom part, the corresponding block is $\begin{bmatrix} 0 & -\mathbf{A}_2^1 \end{bmatrix}$. Therefore, if we put $s_1 + s_2$ and $-s_2$ as the two first components of the vector $\vec{v}$, when combining the resulting share-vector according to the known attributes, the upper part will first lead to the secret $s_1 + s_2 - s_2 = s_1$ and the bottom part will lead to the secret $-s_2$. Consequently, in order to produce the encapsulation of $s_1 + s_2$ under $\mathbf{A}_\wedge$, we only need to combine the encapsulation of s_1 in $\mathbf{A}_1$ and the encapsulation of s_2 in $\mathbf{A}_2$. The resulting share-vector is $\mathbf{A} \cdot (s_1 + s_2, -s_2, \$, \ldots, \$)^t$. However, as one could recover individually the secret $s_1 + s_2$ and $-s_2$ with the appropriate attributes in each sub-policies, but not necessarily for the same user, a collusion attack is possible. We thus need a final randomization step to glue everything together.

1.4 Organization of the Paper

In the next section, we provide a few definitions about linear secrete sharing schemes and attribute-based encryption or key encapsulation. In Sect. 3, we describe our main contribution, with the notion of homomorphic policy. In Sect. 4, we give a concrete instantiation of homomorphic-policy attribute-based key encapsulation mechanism. It also details the security analysis.

2 Definitions

2.1 Access Structure

For any application with limited access, one needs to define the *access structure*, which precises which combinations of conditions grant access to the data or to the system.

Definition 1 (Access Structure). *Let $\mathcal{P} = \{P_1, P_2, \ldots, P_m\}$ be a set of parties (human players or attributes). An access structure in $\mathcal{P}$ is a collection $\mathbb{A} \subseteq 2^{\mathcal{P}} \setminus \{\varnothing\}$. The sets in $\mathbb{A}$ are called the authorized sets, while the others are called unauthorized sets.*

When some minimal sets of parties are required to access the system (but any superset is good too), only monotone access structures make sense, since one can always ignore any supplementary party.

Definition 2 (Monotone Access Structure). *Let $\mathcal{P} = \{P_1, P_2, \ldots, P_m\}$ be a set of parties and $\mathbb{A}$ an access structure in $\mathcal{P}$. $\mathbb{A}$ is said monotone if, for any subsets $B, C \subseteq \mathcal{P}$, if $B \subseteq C$, when $B \in \mathbb{A}$ then $C \in \mathbb{A}$.*

2.2 Linear Secret Sharing Scheme

In order to control access rights according to a monotone access structure, the use of a secret sharing scheme that spreads the secret key among several players is a classical technique. One must use a secret sharing scheme that just allows authorized sets to reconstruct the secret key. This is even better if the secret key is never fully reconstructed, but just in a virtual way to run the restricted process (such as signature or decryption).

Definition 3 (Secret Sharing Scheme). *A secret sharing scheme over a set of parties $\mathcal{P}$, for an access structure $\mathbb{A}$ over $\mathcal{P}$, allows to share a secret s among the players, with shares $\nu_1, \ldots, \nu_m$ such that:*

- *any set of parties in $\mathbb{A}$ can efficiently reconstruct the secret s from their shares;*
- *any set of parties not in $\mathbb{A}$ has no information about the secret s from their shares.*

A linear secret sharing scheme is quite appropriate to share a secret key in order to run the restricted process in a distributed way, since many cryptographic primitives have such linear properties.

Definition 4 (LSSS). *A Linear Secret Sharing Scheme over a field $\mathbb{K}$ and a set of parties $\mathcal{P}$ is defined by a share-generating matrix $\mathbf{A} \in \mathbb{K}^{m \times n}$ and a labeling map $\rho : \{1, \ldots, m\} \to \mathcal{P}$ according to the access policy $\mathbb{A}$: for any $I \subset \{1, \ldots, m\}$, anyone can efficiently find a vector $\vec{c} \in \mathbb{K}^m$ with support I such that $\vec{c}^t \cdot \mathbf{A} = (1, 0, \ldots, 0)$ if and only if $\rho(I) \in \mathbb{A}$.*

In order to share $s \in \mathbb{K}$, one chooses $v_2, \ldots, v_n \xleftarrow{\$} \mathbb{K}$ and sets $\vec{v} \leftarrow (s, v_2, \ldots, v_n)^t$, then the share-vector is $\vec{\nu} \leftarrow \mathbf{A} \cdot \vec{v}$. One would like to be able to reconstruct s from a few coordinates of this share-vector is $\vec{\nu}$. Being able to find such a vector $\vec{c}$ with support I is equivalent to reconstruct s for the players satisfying $\rho(I)$ only: $\sum_{i \in I} c_i \cdot \nu_i = \sum_{i=1}^{m} c_i \cdot \nu_i = \vec{c}^t \cdot \vec{\nu} = \vec{c}^t \cdot \mathbf{A} \cdot \vec{v} = (1, 0, \ldots, 0) \cdot \vec{v} = s$. To give an example, we can refer to the LSSS proposed by Lewko-Waters [11]. It generates the matrix $\mathbf{A}$ and the map ρ from any monotone policy p that is encoded as a boolean tree, with binary AND and OR gates. One does not need to handle NOT gates, since one only considers monotone policies. It is recalled in the full version [5]. We describe it with matrices in Sect. 4.3, with the proof in the full version [5].

2.3 Attribute-Based Key Encapsulation Mechanism

In this paper, we extend ABE to Attribute-Based Key Encapsulation Mechanism (ABKEM), where the ciphertext encapsulates a session key, later used to encrypt the payload, in a symmetric way.

Definition 5 (ABKEM). *An attribute-based key encapsulation mechanism over an attribute space $\mathfrak{A}$ is defined by four algorithms:*

- Setup(λ): *Takes as input the security parameter, and outputs the master secret key* msk *and the public key* pk;
- KeyGen(msk, id, a): *Takes as input the master secret key* msk, *the identity* id *of a player, and an attribute* $a \in \mathfrak{A}$, *to output the private decryption key* dk_{id}^a *for this attribute* a;
- Encaps(pk, p): *Takes as input the public key* pk *and a policy* p, *to output a key* K *and an encapsulation* E *of this key;*
- Decaps(dk, E): *Takes as input a decryption key and an encapsulation* E, *to output the encapsulated key* K *or* $\perp$.

A decryption key will indifferently mean a key dk_{id}^a for a specific user id and a specific attribute a, or a set dk_{id}^A of keys specific to a user id, but for many attributes $a \in A \subset \mathfrak{A}$. The correctness property is: for any $(msk, pk) \leftarrow$ Setup(λ), $dk_{id} = \{dk_{id}^a \leftarrow$ KeyGen(msk, id, a)$\}_{a \in A}$, and $(K, E) \leftarrow$ Encaps(pk, p), Decaps(dk_{id}, E) $= K$ if A satisfies the policy p. The main security property is the usual indistinguishability (IND), which should prevent collusions of adaptively chosen players, that can also get decryption keys for adaptively chosen attributes:

Definition 6 (IND for ABKEM). *Let us consider an ABKEM over an attribute space $\mathfrak{A}$. No adversary $\mathcal{A}$ should be able to break the following security game against a challenger:*

- *Initialization: the challenger runs the setup algorithm* $(\mathsf{msk}, \mathsf{pk}) \leftarrow \mathsf{Setup}(\lambda)$, *and provides* pk *to the adversary* $\mathcal{A}$;
- *Key Queries: the adversary* $\mathcal{A}$ *can ask* KeyGen-*queries, for any* id *and any attribute* a *of its choice to get* $\mathsf{dk}_{\mathsf{id}}^{\mathsf{a}}$;
- *Challenge: the adversary* $\mathcal{A}$ *provides a policy* p *to the challenger that runs* $(K, E) \leftarrow \mathsf{Encaps}(\mathsf{pk}, p)$, *and sets* $K_b \leftarrow K$ *and* K_{1-b} *as a random key, for a random bit* b. *It provides* (E, K_0, K_1) *to the adversary;*
- *Key Queries: the adversary* $\mathcal{A}$ *can again ask* KeyGen-*queries of its choice;*
- *Finalize: the adversary* $\mathcal{A}$ *outputs its guess* b' *on the bit* b.

We also define the event Cheat, which means that a user (with some identity id) owns a set of attributes A (the set of all the attributes a asked to a Key Query for id) that satisfies p: in such a case, the adversary can trivially guess b. Hence, we only allow adversaries such that $\Pr[\mathsf{Cheat}] = 0$. We then define $\mathsf{Adv}^{\mathsf{ind}}(\mathcal{A}) = |2 \times \Pr[b' = b] - 1|$, and say that an *ABKEM* is (t, ε)-*adaptively secure if no adversary* $\mathcal{A}$ *running within time* t *can get* $\mathsf{Adv}^{\mathsf{ind}}(\mathcal{A}) \geq \varepsilon$.

We stress that everything is adaptive in this definition: the identities and the attributes asked to the key queries, and the policy asked for the challenge query. However, we are in the chosen-plaintext scenario, without access to any decryption/decapsulation oracle.

3   Homomorphic-Policy

3.1   Definition

While **CP-ABE** allows to specify the policy at the encryption time, which is also the case for our definition of **ABKEM**, the sender may not be aware of the policy yet. We thus suggest to exploit an homomorphic property on the policy: we would like to allow the derivation of an encapsulation of K under a combination $p = p_1 \wedge p_2$ or $p = p_1 \vee p_2$ from the encapsulations of K under the policies p_1 and p_2 on the attributes in $\mathfrak{A}$, without knowing K (which has already been used to encrypt the payload).

With such an homomorphism on the policies, from the encapsulations of a common key K under all the attributes $\mathsf{a} \in \mathfrak{A}$, one could publicly generate an encapsulation of K under any policy on $\mathfrak{A}$: as illustrated on Fig. 2, from the encapsulations $\{E_i\}_i$ of K for the attributes $\mathfrak{A} = \{\mathsf{a}_i\}$, one can derive the encapsulation E_p of K under any policy p, encoded as a binary tree with AND ($\wedge$) and OR ($\vee$) gates. Again, we only consider monotone policies, hence the absence of NOT gates. On attributes, if one wants to consider the negation (or absence) of some attribute a, one has to define a second attribute a' that is exclusive with a, so that, if $p = (\mathsf{a})$, then $\neg p = (\mathsf{a}')$.

To achieve this goal, we just need to be able to combine two encapsulations of K under p_1 and p_2 in order to derive the encapsulation of K under $p_\vee = p_1 \vee p_2$ and under $p_\wedge = p_1 \wedge p_2$. The global encapsulation under a more general policy can then be recursively built.

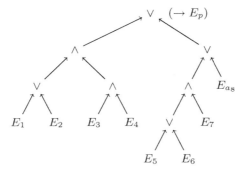

Fig. 2. Derivation of E_p from $\{E_i\}$, for $p = ((a_1 \vee a_2) \wedge (a_3 \wedge a_4)) \vee (((a_5 \vee a_6) \wedge a_7) \vee a_8)$

Definition 7 (HP-ABKEM). *An homomorphic-policy attribute-based key-encapsulation mechanism over an attribute space $\mathfrak{A}$ is an ABKEM (see Definition 5), with a more specific encapsulation algorithm and two additional algorithms for the homomorphism:*

- Encaps(pk, P): *Takes as input the public key* pk, *a list of policies* $P = (p_i)_i$, *to output a key* K *and the encapsulations* E_i *of this key under the policies* p_i*'s;*
- Combine(pk, gate, E_1, E_2): *Takes as input the public key* pk *as well as two encapsulations* E_1 *and* E_2, *and a gate* gate $\in \{\wedge, \vee\}$, *to output an encapsulation under the combination of the initial policies for* E_1 *and* E_2;
- Rand(pk, E) *Takes as input the public key* pk *as well as an encapsulation, to output a new encapsulation (of the same key under the same policy).*

The intuition behind the new Encaps algorithm is that we want to be able to encapsulate the same key K under various policies. We thus opt for an encapsulation algorithm that takes as input all the policies that will be combined later. The correctness properties are:

- if $(E_i)_i \leftarrow$ Encaps(pk, $(p_i)_i$) are common encapsulations of a key K under the p_i's, then for any i, j, $E \leftarrow$ Combine(pk, gate, E_i, E_j) is an encapsulation of the same key K, but under the policy $p = p_i$ gate p_j;
- for any encapsulation E of some key K under a policy p, $E' \leftarrow$ Rand(pk, E) follows the same distribution as a fresh encapsulation of K under the policy p.

Note that we do not expect the combination to hide the structure of the initial encapsulations. The randomization will do this work, but there is no need to do it at each step, hence the separation of the two processes: one will iteratively combine the encapsulations in order to obtain the encapsulation under the appropriate policy, and then the randomization will finalize the process. Figure 3 illustrates this fact: combining and randomizing at each step leads to exactly the same distribution of the root encapsulation as combining at each step and randomizing at the last step only.

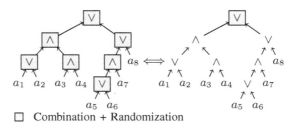

Fig. 3. Randomization process in combination

3.2 Security

As explained in the Pay-TV scenario in the introduction, we have three players: the content provider (or the sender), the manager of the access policy (or the combiner) and the receiver. We thus expect the sender to encapsulate a key K under each attribute, and to encrypt the payload under K; the combiner then generates the encapsulation of K under the appropriate policy; so that only the legitimate receivers can decapsulate and decrypt the payload.

When the adversary plays the role of the receivers, the required security notion is exactly the previous indistinguishability: given several keys for various attributes, and even several identities (to model collusions), an adversary should not be able to get any information about a key encapsulated under a policy that is not satisfies by any of the users under its control. We stress that this indistinguishability game (IND) models the resistance against the collusion of receivers. But both the sender and the combiner are considered honest.

On the other hand, the sender may not totally trust the combiner and may want to limit the risk in case the combiner would be corrupted: while the former sends K encapsulated under many attributes (or more generally many policies), the latter should not be able to distinguish K from a random key, in order to guarantee to privacy of the content encrypted under K. Hence the new indistinguishability game with multiple encapsulations ($m - \mathsf{IND}$), but without being able to get any decryption key, hence the no-key attack (NKA). Since the adversary does not have access to any decryption key, this security scenario does not allow the combiner to collude with anybody, and namely not with any receiver.

Definition 8 ($m - \mathsf{IND} - \mathsf{NKA}$ for **ABKEM**). *Let us consider an ABKEM over an attribute space $\mathfrak{A}$. No adversary $\mathcal{A}$ should be able to break the following security game against a challenger:*

- *Initialization: the challenger runs the setup algorithm* $(\mathsf{msk}, \mathsf{pk}) \leftarrow \mathsf{Setup}(\lambda)$, *and provides* pk *to the adversary* $\mathcal{A}$;
- *Challenge: the challenger runs* $(K, (E_i)_i) \leftarrow \mathsf{Encaps}(\mathsf{pk}, \mathfrak{A})$, *and sets* $K_b \leftarrow K$ *and* K_{1-b} *as a random key, for a random bit b. It provides* $((E_i)_i, K_0, K_1)$ *to the adversary;*
- *Finalize: the adversary* $\mathcal{A}$ *outputs its guess b' on the bit b.*

We then define $\mathsf{Adv}^{\mathsf{m-ind-nka}}(\mathcal{A}) = |2 \times \Pr[b' = b] - 1|$, *and say that an ABKEM is* $(t, \varepsilon)\text{-}\mathsf{m} - \mathsf{IND}$ *if no adversary* $\mathcal{A}$ *running within time* t *can get* $\mathsf{Adv}^{\mathsf{m-ind-nka}}(\mathcal{A}) \geq \varepsilon$.

We stress that now, nothing is adaptive, since the adversary cannot get decryption keys, but gets the encapsulations of the same key K under all the individual attributes. We also remain in the chosen-plaintext scenario, without access to any decryption/decapsulation oracle. In addition, since the adversary is the combiner that receives the key K encapsulated under every attribute, we do not allow any collusion with a user: any attribute would be enough to get K and break the security game.

On can note that in the real-life, such a combiner would not be a critical party since it does not know any long-term secret. Of course, it will learn ephemeral encapsulations that would allow any receiver (with attributes that satisfy the final policy or not) to decapsulate the session key and to decrypt the content. But a short-term corruption will just leak the content during a short period, and not for ever.

4   Construction

4.1   Modified Lewko-Waters Scheme

We present here a revised version of the ABE scheme from [11]. First, for the sake of simplicity, we do not exploit the decentralized version and so all the attributes are managed by the same entity (but we could keep the decentralized version). Second, for the homomorphic property, we consider a Key Encapsulation Mechanism (KEM) instead of an encryption scheme, which just encaps a session key. However, we still use an LSSS to realize the access policy and pairing techniques to ensure collusion resistance. More precisely, we use a symmetric pairing $e : \mathbb{G} \times \mathbb{G} \longrightarrow \mathbb{G}_T$, where the groups $\mathbb{G}$ and $\mathbb{G}_T$ will be of composite order $N = q_1 q_2 q_3$, with three large prime integers q_1, q_2, and q_3. Let us first describe our variant of ABKEM.

4.2   Description

- Setup(λ): One first generates a symmetric pairing $e : \mathbb{G} \times \mathbb{G} \longrightarrow \mathbb{G}_T$ for groups of composite order $N = q_1 q_2 q_3$ (of length λ). One also generates a generator g_1 of the subgroup $\mathbb{G}_1 \subset \mathbb{G}$ of order q_1 and a hash function $\mathcal{H} : \{0, 1\}^* \longrightarrow \mathbb{G}$. We also denote $G = e(g_1, g_1) \in \mathbb{G}_T$. Then, for each attribute a, the authority specifies the pair of secret/public keys, respectively $\mathsf{sk_a} = (\alpha_\mathsf{a}, y_\mathsf{a})$ and $\mathsf{pk_a} = (G_\mathsf{a} = G^{\alpha_\mathsf{a}}, g_\mathsf{a} = g_1^{y_\mathsf{a}})$. The master secret key msk is the concatenation of the $\mathsf{sk_a}$'s, and the public key pk contains N, g_1 and $\mathcal{H}$, together with the concatenation of the $\mathsf{pk_a}$'s.
- KeyGen(msk, id, a): From msk = $\{\mathsf{sk_a}\}$, id and a, the authority outputs $\mathsf{dk}_{\mathsf{id}}^{\mathsf{a}} = g_1^{\alpha_\mathsf{a}} \mathcal{H}(\mathsf{id})^{y_\mathsf{a}}$.

- Encaps(pk, P): From the public key pk and a set P of policies, one first chooses some random $s \xleftarrow{\$} \mathbb{Z}_N$ and sets the symmetric encapsulated key $K \leftarrow G^s$. Then, for each $p \in P$, we process the following encapsulation: from the LSSS matrix $\mathbf{A} \in \mathbb{K}^{m \times n}$ and the associated labeling map ρ onto the attributes describing the access structure defined by the policy p, we set $\vec{v} = (s, v_2, \dots, v_n)$ and $\vec{w} = (0, w_2, \dots, w_n)$, with $v_k, w_k \xleftarrow{\$} \mathbb{Z}_N$ for $k = 2, \dots, n$ and $\vec{r} \xleftarrow{\$} \mathbb{Z}_N^m$. We build the share vectors $\vec{\nu} = \mathbf{A} \cdot \vec{v}$ and $\vec{\omega} = \mathbf{A} \cdot \vec{w}$. Eventually, for each line $x \in \{1, \dots, m\}$ of the matrix $\mathbf{A}$, we construct the encapsulation using the keys $\mathsf{pk}_{\rho(x)} = (G_{\rho(x)}, g_{\rho(x)})$ associated to the attribute $\mathsf{a}_x = \rho(x)$ involved in the policy p:

$$E_{1,x} = G^{\nu_x} \cdot G_{\rho(x)}^{r_x} \qquad E_{2,x} = g_1^{r_x} \qquad E_{3,x} = g_1^{\omega_x} \cdot g_{\rho(x)}^{r_x}$$

The algorithm returns $E_p = \{(E_{1,x}, E_{2,x}, E_{3,x})\}_x$ for each $p \in P$.

- Decaps($\mathsf{dk}_{\mathsf{id}}, E_p$), where $\mathsf{dk}_{\mathsf{id}} = (\mathsf{dk}_{\mathsf{id}}^{\mathsf{a}})$ for the attributes owned by id: First, the user must find a vector $\vec{c} \in \mathbb{K}^m$ such that $\vec{c}^t \cdot \mathbf{A} = (1, 0, \dots, 0)$ and the support I of the non-zero components of $\vec{c}$ links to a set of attributes owned by the user. Then, for each $x \in I$, the user computes $F_x = E_{1,x} \cdot e(H(\mathsf{id}), E_{3,x})/e(\mathsf{dk}_{\mathsf{id}}^{\rho(x)}, E_{2,x})$. He finally gets K by combining with the vector $\vec{c}$: $K \leftarrow \prod_{x \in I} F_x^{c_x}$.

The latter reconstruction works since

$$\sum_{x \in I} c_x \cdot \nu_x = \sum_{x=1}^{m} c_x \cdot \nu_x = \vec{c}^t \cdot \vec{\nu} = \vec{c}^t \cdot \mathbf{A} \cdot \vec{v} = (1, 0, \dots, 0) \cdot \vec{v} = s$$

$$\sum_{x \in I} c_x \cdot \omega_x = \sum_{x=1}^{m} c_x \cdot \omega_x = \vec{c}^t \cdot \vec{\omega} = \vec{c}^t \cdot \mathbf{A} \cdot \vec{w} = (1, 0, \dots, 0) \cdot \vec{w} = 0$$

In addition, for each $x \in I$,

$$F_x = E_{1,x} \cdot e(H(\mathsf{id}), E_{3,x})/e(\mathsf{dk}_{\mathsf{id}}^{\rho(x)}, E_{2,x}) = G^{\nu_x} e(H(\mathsf{id}), g_1)^{\omega_x}.$$

And so, the final combination leads to

$$\prod_{x \in I} F_x^{c_x} = \prod_{x \in I} (G^{\nu_x} e(H(\mathsf{id}), g_1)^{\omega_x})^{c_x} = G^{\vec{c}^t \cdot \vec{\nu}} \cdot e(H(\mathsf{id}), g_1)^{\vec{c}^t \cdot \vec{\omega}} = G^s.$$

One should note that for this construction to work, the map ρ needs to be an injection. In practice, this is not a real issue, since one can simply duplicate the attributes and provide multiple keys to users.

4.3   Construction of the LSSS

In this section, we detail a construction of the LSSS, in an iterative way, from a boolean tree (with only OR and AND gates).

First, we have to start from an LSSS for a simple policy $p = (a_i)$, for some i (i.e., a unique attribute): $\mathbf{A}_i = (1)$ and $\rho(1) = i$. Then we explain how to combine two policies p_1 and p_2, represented by the LSSS's $(\mathbf{A}_1, \rho_1)$ and $(\mathbf{A}_2, \rho_2)$ respectively, into the policies $p_\wedge = p_1 \wedge p_2$ and $p_\vee = p_1 \vee p_2$ with LSSS's $(\mathbf{A}_\wedge, \rho_\wedge)$ and $(\mathbf{A}_\vee, \rho_\vee)$ respectively.

In the following, for any $\mathbf{A}$, we denote $\mathbf{A}^1$ the first column et $\mathbf{A}^*$ the matrix $\mathbf{A}$ without the first column (i.e., $\mathbf{A} = \begin{bmatrix} \mathbf{A}^1 & \mathbf{A}^* \end{bmatrix}$).

Proposition 9. *Let $(\mathbf{A}_1, \rho_1)$ and $(\mathbf{A}_2, \rho_2)$ be two LSSS's for the policies p_1 and p_2. Then we can build the LSSS's $(\mathbf{A}_\wedge, \rho_\wedge)$ and $(\mathbf{A}_\vee, \rho_\vee)$ for the policies $p_\wedge = p_1 \wedge p_2$ and $p_\vee = p_1 \vee p_2$ as follows*

$$
\mathbf{A}_\vee = \begin{bmatrix} \mathbf{A}_1^1 & \mathbf{A}_1^* & 0 \\ \mathbf{A}_2^1 & 0 & \mathbf{A}_2^* \end{bmatrix}
\qquad
\mathbf{A}_\wedge = \begin{bmatrix} \mathbf{A}_1^1 & \mathbf{A}_1^1 & \mathbf{A}_1^* & 0 \\ 0 & -\mathbf{A}_2^1 & 0 & -\mathbf{A}_2^* \end{bmatrix}
$$

If we label the rows of the matrices from 1 to $m_1 + m_2$, where $\mathbf{A}_1 \in \mathbb{K}^{m_1 \times n_1}$ and $\mathbf{A}_2 \in \mathbb{K}^{m_2 \times n_2}$, we have

$$
\rho_\wedge = \rho_\vee : x \mapsto \begin{cases} \rho_1(x), & \text{if } x \leq m_1 \\ \rho_2(x - m_1), & \text{if } x \geq m_1 + 1 \end{cases}
$$

This construction is not really new, since it was described in [12] in a more generic way. But we need this explicit description for the security analysis of our ABKEM. The correctness of this LSSS construction is provided in the full version [5]. Up to a re-ordering of the rows and columns of the matrices, this is also the same construction obtained from the algorithm presented in [5] from [11]. A comparison of the two methods is indeed proposed in the full version [5].

4.4   Homomorphic Policy

Our main goal is now to show that this iterative construction of the LSSS can be applied to our ABKEM, starting from encapsulations of the same key K under every attribute. This will follow from the homomorphic-policy property.

We recall that in the ABKEM, $\vec{\nu} = \mathbf{A} \cdot \vec{v}$ is a secret sharing of a random scalar s, while $\vec{\omega} = \mathbf{A} \cdot \vec{w}$ is a secret sharing of 0, the components ν_x and ω_x being hidden in $E_{1,x}$ and $E_{3,x}$ by $G_{\rho(x)}^{r_x}$ and $g_{\rho(x)}^{r_x}$ respectively. Because of the linear property of the LSSS, by concatenating or by adding the shares, we either obtain the OR or the AND policies of two encapsulations $E^{(1)}$ and $E^{(2)}$:

$$
\begin{array}{cc}
\textbf{Share-Vectors} & \textbf{Encapsulations} \\
\begin{bmatrix} \vec{\nu}_1 \\ \vec{\nu}_2 \end{bmatrix} & \longleftrightarrow \quad E^{(1)} \cup E^{(2)} \\
\vec{\nu}_1 + \vec{\nu}_2 & \longleftrightarrow \quad E^{(1)} \cdot E^{(2)}
\end{array}
$$

Of course, the same applies on the shares $\vec{\omega}$ of 0, but we focus on the shares $\vec{\nu}$ of the random s.

One Secret Under Two Policies. Let us be given two encapsulations $E^{(1)}$ and $E^{(2)}$ of the same secret value $K = G^s$ under the policies p_1 and p_2, represented by the LSSS $(\mathbf{A}_1, \rho_1)$ and $(\mathbf{A}_2, \rho_2)$.

The construction thus used the share-vectors $\vec{\nu}_i = (\nu_{i,1}, \ldots, \nu_{i,m_i}) = \mathbf{A}_i \cdot \vec{v}_i$, with $\vec{v}_i = (s, v_{i,2}, \ldots, v_{i,n_i})^t$, for $i = 1, 2$. Using

$$\mathbf{A}_\vee = \begin{bmatrix} \mathbf{A}_1^1 & \mathbf{A}_1^* & 0 \\ \mathbf{A}_2^1 & 0 & \mathbf{A}_2^* \end{bmatrix} \text{ and } \vec{v} = (s, v_{1,2}, \ldots, v_{1,n_1}, v_{2,2}, \ldots, v_{2,n_2})^t,$$

one gets $\vec{\nu} = \begin{bmatrix} \vec{\nu}_1 \\ \vec{\nu}_2 \end{bmatrix}$.

From attributes satisfying p_i, under the LSSS property, one can efficiently find a vector $\vec{c}_i = (c_{i,1}, \ldots, c_{i,m_i})^t \in \mathbb{K}^m$ such that $\vec{c}_i^t \cdot \mathbf{A}_i = (1, 0, \ldots, 0)$. By multiplying this vector on the appropriate half of $\vec{v}$, one can get s:

$$(c_{1,1}, \ldots, c_{1,m_1}, 0, \ldots, 0) \cdot \vec{\nu} = \vec{c}_1^t \cdot \vec{\nu}_1 = s$$
$$(0, \ldots, 0, c_{2,1}, \ldots, c_{2,m_2}) \cdot \vec{\nu} = \vec{c}_2^t \cdot \vec{\nu}_2 = s.$$

It will be used for the disjunction of policies.

Two Secrets Under Different Policies. Let us be given two encapsulations $E^{(1)}$ and $E^{(2)}$ of two secret values $K_1 = G^{s_1}$ and $K_2 = G^{s_2}$ under the policies p_1 and p_2, represented by the LSSS $(\mathbf{A}_1, \rho_1)$ and $(\mathbf{A}_2, \rho_2)$.

The construction thus used the share-vectors $\vec{\nu}_i = (\nu_{i,1}, \ldots, \nu_{i,m_i}) = \mathbf{A}_i \cdot \vec{v}_i$, with $\vec{v}_i = (s_i, v_{i,2}, \ldots, v_{i,n_i})^t$, for $i = 1, 2$. Using

$$\mathbf{A}_\wedge = \begin{bmatrix} \mathbf{A}_1^1 & \mathbf{A}_1^1 & \mathbf{A}_1^* & 0 \\ 0 & -\mathbf{A}_2^1 & 0 & -\mathbf{A}_2^* \end{bmatrix} \text{ and } \vec{v} = (s_1 + s_2, -s_2, v_{1,2}, \ldots, v_{1,n_1}, v_{2,2}, \ldots, v_{2,n_2})^t,$$

one gets again $\vec{\nu} = \begin{bmatrix} \vec{\nu}_1 \\ \vec{\nu}_2 \end{bmatrix}$. This combination will be used for the conjunction of policies, but only with the same secret. Note that the produced encapsulation must be randomized to perform the new policy, otherwise there is a colluding attack: with independent keys for each policy, two players can independently get s_1 and s_2, and can then combine them to get $s_1 + s_2$.

Two Secrets Under the Same Policy. Let us be given two encapsulations $E^{(1)}$ and $E^{(2)}$ of two secret values $K_1 = G^{s_1}$ and $K_2 = G^{s_2}$ under the same policy p, represented by the LSSS $(\mathbf{A}, \rho)$.

The construction thus used the share-vectors $\vec{\nu}_1$ and $\vec{\nu}_2$ of the random scalars s_1 and s_2 respectively under the same policy p. Then, one can see $\vec{\nu} = \vec{\nu}_1 + \vec{\nu}_2$ as a share-vector of $s = s_1 + s_2$ under the policy p, since $\vec{\nu} = \mathbf{A} \cdot (\vec{v}_1 + \vec{v}_2)$. Indeed, from attributes satisfying p, one can efficiently find a vector $\vec{c} \in \mathbb{K}^m$ such that $\vec{c}^t \cdot \mathbf{A} = (1, 0, \ldots, 0)$:

$$\vec{c}^t \cdot \vec{\nu} = \vec{c}^t \cdot \mathbf{A} \cdot (\vec{v}_1 + \vec{v}_2) = (1, 0 \ldots, 0) \cdot (\vec{v}_1 + \vec{v}_2) = s_1 + s_2.$$

This combination will be used for the randomization, with $s_2 = 0$.

4.5   Security

IND *security.* In [11], Lewko and Waters proved their ABE scheme to be indistinguishable under several assumptions in the composite-order pairing setting (we recall them in the full version [5]) and the condition that ρ is injective. This easily leads to the IND security for the above variant of ABKEM, even for adaptive KeyGen-queries. Hence, this ABKEM construction achieves the IND security level.

m $-$ IND $-$ NKA *security.* We now show that, the m $-$ IND $-$ NKA security of the modified ABKEM can also be based on the IND security of Lewko-Waters scheme.

Theorem 10. *The* IND *security level of Lewko-Waters implies the* m $-$ IND $-$ NKA *security of the modified* ABKEM.

Proof. As highlighted in the full version [5], the two security games are quite similar, the main differences appear in the challenge phase, and the lack of key-queries in the latter. If one looks at the above construction of the LSSS-matrix, for $p = a_1 \vee \ldots \vee a_k$, then $\mathbf{A} = (1, \ldots, 1)^t$ and $\vec{v} = (s, \ldots, s)^t$: from an encapsulation E of the key $K = G^s$ under the policy p, one can easily extract the encapsulations E_i of the same K, under the policies $p_i = (a_i)$ respectively: indeed, each triple $(E_{1,x}, E_{2,x}, E_{3,x})$ is a simple encapsulation of K under $a_x = \rho(x)$.

This remark is true for every conjunction $p_f = \bigvee p_i$ where the policies p_i's do not share any attribute. Note that the triples $(E_{1,x}, E_{2,x}, E_{3,x})$ involved in the decryption of a policy p_i are those associated to the attributes which appears in this policy. The choice of these triples is given by the vector c. Consequently, we can easily convert the challenger's answer from one game to another by concatenating/separating the ciphertext(s) by following this policy decomposition. Because of the lack of key-queries in the m $-$ IND $-$ NKA security game, we can just build an adversary $\mathcal{B}$ for the IND game from an adversary $\mathcal{A}$ of the m $-$ IND $-$ NKA game. More precisely, if an adversary $\mathcal{A}$ has an advantage $\mathsf{Adv}^{m-ind-nka}(\mathcal{A}) = \varepsilon$ in the m $-$ IND $-$ NKA game for the policies $(p_j)_j$, one can construct an adversary $\mathcal{B}$ with the same advantage $\mathsf{Adv}^{ind}(\mathcal{B}) = \varepsilon$ in the IND game for the policy $p_f = \bigvee p_i$.

As already noted, Lewko and Waters [11] assume a one-use restriction on attributes throughout the proof: this means that the row-labeling map ρ of the challenge ciphertext access matrix $(\mathbf{A}, \rho)$ must be injective. The reason is that, if an attribute is used twice in the access matrix, then there will appear an implicit relation between the randomnesses associated to the corresponding two lines of the matrix and the proof does not go through anymore. To overcome this issue, Lewko and Waters suggested to associate k independent attributes to any attribute a, where k is an upper-bound on the number of repetitions of an attribute in a policy. Our scheme inherently has the same limitation.

4.6   Homomorphic Policy

Let us now see how this impacts on the encapsulations, when one wants to do disjunctions and conjunctions of policies.

Disjunctions. Let us be given two encapsulations $E^{(1)}$ and $E^{(2)}$ of the same key $K = G^s$ under the policies p_1 and p_2, represented by the LSSS $(\mathbf{A}_1, \rho_1)$ and $(\mathbf{A}_2, \rho_2)$. We want to make an encapsulation of K under the policy $p_1 \vee p_2$. Using the construction of the share-vectors from Sect. 4.4, which applies on both $\vec{\nu}_1, \vec{\nu}_2$ and $\vec{\omega}_1, \vec{\omega}_2$, we know that the resulting encapsulation should use

$$\vec{\nu} = \begin{bmatrix} \vec{\nu}_1 \\ \vec{\nu}_2 \end{bmatrix} \qquad \vec{\omega} = \begin{bmatrix} \vec{\omega}_1 \\ \vec{\omega}_2 \end{bmatrix}.$$

Therefore, the resulting encapsulation is $E_{p_1 \vee p_2} = \{(E_{j,x}^{(1)}, E_{j,x}^{(2)})_{j=1,2,3}\}_{x \in \mathfrak{A}}$.

Conjunctions. Let us be given two encapsulations $E^{(1)}$ and $E^{(2)}$ of the same key $K = G^s$ under the policies p_1 and p_2, represented by the LSSS $(\mathbf{A}_1, \rho_1)$ and $(\mathbf{A}_2, \rho_2)$. We want to make an encapsulation of K under the policy $p_1 \wedge p_2$. Using the construction of the share-vectors from Sect. 4.4, which applies on both $\vec{\nu}_1, \vec{\nu}_2$ and $\vec{\omega}_1, \vec{\omega}_2$, we know that the resulting encapsulation should use

$$\vec{\nu} = \begin{bmatrix} \vec{\nu}_1 \\ \vec{\nu}_2 \end{bmatrix} \qquad \vec{\omega} = \begin{bmatrix} \vec{\omega}_1 \\ \vec{\omega}_2 \end{bmatrix}.$$

However, this will contain the key $K^2 = G^{2s}$. We thus have to use square-roots: the resulting encapsulation is $E_{p_1 \wedge p_2} = \{((E_{j,x}^{(1)})^{1/2}, (E_{j,x}^{(2)})^{1/2})_{j=1,2,3}\}_{x \in \mathfrak{A}}$.

Note that even if in the Lewko-Waters' construction there is a modulus $N = q_1 q_2 q_3$ that is hard to factor, this is the order of the group. Hence $g^{1/2} = g^\alpha$ where $\alpha = (N + 1)/2$.

As already noted, collusion is possible. But this is even worse in this case since we are using $s = s_1 = s_2$: just satisfying one of the two policies, one can recover $K^{1/2} = G^{s/2}$, which thereafter easily leads to K. We thus need to randomize the encapsulation, in order to glue together the policies.

Randomization. If one looks in details the description of the Encaps algorithm, there are 4 kinds of randomness:

– s, that defined the encapsulated key $K = G^s$;
– $v_k, w_k \xleftarrow{\$} \mathbb{Z}_N$ for $k = 2, \ldots, n$, to define $\vec{v}$ and $\vec{w}$;
– $\vec{r} \xleftarrow{\$} \mathbb{Z}_N^m$.

Let us start from any encapsulation $E^{(1)}$ of K under a policy p, with

$$E_{1,x}^{(1)} = G^{\nu_x^{(1)}} \cdot G_{\rho(x)}^{r_x^{(1)}} \qquad E_{2,x}^{(1)} = g_1^{r_x^{(1)}} \qquad E_{3,x}^{(1)} = g_1^{\omega_x^{(1)}} \cdot g_{\rho(x)}^{r_x^{(1)}}$$

for each $a_x = \rho(x)$ involved in the policy p, where $\vec{\nu}^{(1)} = \mathbf{A} \cdot \vec{v}^{(1)}$ and $\vec{\omega}^{(1)} = \mathbf{A} \cdot \vec{w}^{(1)}$. We now define a new fresh encapsulation $E^{(2)}$:

$$E^{(2)}_{1,x} = G^{\nu^{(2)}_x} \cdot G^{r^{(2)}_x}_{\rho(x)} \qquad E^{(2)}_{2,x} = g_1^{r^{(2)}_x} \qquad E^{(2)}_{3,x} = g_1^{\omega^{(2)}_x} \cdot g^{r^{(2)}_x}_{\rho(x)}$$

where $\vec{\nu}^{(2)} = \mathbf{A} \cdot \vec{v}^{(2)}$ and $\vec{\omega}^{(2)} = \mathbf{A} \cdot \vec{w}^{(2)}$, for $\vec{v}^{(2)} = (0, v'_2, \ldots, v'_n)^t$ and $\vec{w}^{(2)} = (0, w'_2, \ldots, w'_n)^t$, with $v'_k, w'_k \overset{\$}{\leftarrow} \mathbb{Z}_N$ for $k = 2, \ldots, n$, and $\vec{r}^{(2)} \overset{\$}{\leftarrow} \mathbb{Z}_N^m$. This is actually a fresh random encapsulation of $K^{(2)} = 1_{\mathbb{G}_T}$ under the policy p. It can be computed from the public key pk that contains N, g_1, and the keys $\mathsf{pk_a} = (G_a, g_a)$, for all the attributes, as would be generated a fresh encapsulation of $K = 1_{\mathbb{G}_T}$.

Eventually, the new encapsulation $E = \{(E^{(1)}_{1,x} \cdot E^{(2)}_{1,x}, E^{(1)}_{2,x} \cdot E^{(2)}_{2,x}, E^{(1)}_{3,x} \cdot E^{(2)}_{3,x})\}_x$ is a truly random encapsulation of the same K under the policy p, and so looks like a fresh encapsulation.

5   Conclusion

We proposed a new feature for ABE, with the homomorphic policy. It allows to separate the roles of the sender and the access right manager. This is a quite useful property for the Pay-TV context, since the access right manager does not have access anymore to the content payload. The distribution to the subscribers can be performed by a weakly trusted party.

Acknowledgments. This work was supported in part by the European Community's Seventh Framework Programme (FP7/2007-2013 Grant Agreement no. 339563 – CryptoCloud) and by the French ANR ALAMBIC project (ANR-16-CE39-0006).

References

1. Attrapadung, N., Libert, B., de Panafieu, E.: Expressive key-policy attribute-based encryption with constant-size ciphertexts. In: Catalano, D., Fazio, N., Gennaro, R., Nicolosi, A. (eds.) PKC 2011. LNCS, vol. 6571, pp. 90–108. Springer, Heidelberg (2011)

2. Boneh, D., Franklin, M.: Identity-based encryption from the Weil pairing. In: Kilian, J. (ed.) CRYPTO 2001. LNCS, vol. 2139, pp. 213–229. Springer, Heidelberg (2001). doi:10.1007/3-540-44647-8_13

3. Boneh, D., Gentry, C., Gorbunov, S., Halevi, S., Nikolaenko, V., Segev, G., Vaikuntanathan, V., Vinayagamurthy, D.: Fully key-homomorphic encryption, arithmetic circuit ABE and compact garbled circuits. In: Nguyen, P.Q., Oswald, E. (eds.) EUROCRYPT 2014. LNCS, vol. 8441, pp. 533–556. Springer, Heidelberg (2014). doi:10.1007/978-3-642-55220-5_30

4. Chen, C., Chen, J., Lim, H.W., Zhang, Z., Feng, D., Ling, S., Wang, H.: Fully secure attribute-based systems with short ciphertexts/signatures and threshold access structures. In: Dawson, E. (ed.) CT-RSA 2013. LNCS, vol. 7779, pp. 50–67. Springer, Heidelberg (2013). doi:10.1007/978-3-642-36095-4_4

5. Chotard, J., Phan, D.H., Pointcheval, D.: Homomorphic-policy attribute-based key encapsulation mechanisms. Cryptology ePrint Archive, Report 2016/1089 (2016). http://eprint.iacr.org/2016/1089
6. Fiat, A., Naor, M.: Broadcast encryption. In: Stinson, D.R. (ed.) CRYPTO 1993. LNCS, vol. 773, pp. 480–491. Springer, Heidelberg (1994). doi:10.1007/3-540-48329-2_40
7. Gorbunov, S., Vaikuntanathan, V., Wee, H.: Attribute-based encryption for circuits. In: Boneh, D., Roughgarden, T., Feigenbaum, J. (eds.) 45th ACM STOC, pp. 545–554. ACM Press, June 2013
8. Goyal, V., Jain, A., Pandey, O., Sahai, A.: Bounded ciphertext policy attribute based encryption. In: Aceto, L., Damgård, I., Goldberg, L.A., Halldórsson, M.M., Ingólfsdóttir, A., Walukiewicz, I. (eds.) ICALP 2008. LNCS, vol. 5126, pp. 579–591. Springer, Heidelberg (2008). doi:10.1007/978-3-540-70583-3_47
9. Goyal, V., Pandey, O., Sahai, A., Waters, B.: Attribute-based encryption for fine-grained access control of encrypted data. In: Juels, A., Wright, R.N., Vimercati, S. (eds.), ACM CCS 2006, pp. 89–98. ACM Press, October/Available as Cryptology ePrint Archive Report 2006/309, November 2006
10. Herranz, J., Laguillaumie, F., Ràfols, C.: Constant size ciphertexts in threshold attribute-based encryption. In: Nguyen, P.Q., Pointcheval, D. (eds.) PKC 2010. LNCS, vol. 6056, pp. 19–34. Springer, Heidelberg (2010). doi:10.1007/978-3-642-13013-7_2
11. Lewko, A., Waters, B.: Decentralizing attribute-based encryption. In: Paterson, K.G. (ed.) EUROCRYPT 2011. LNCS, vol. 6632, pp. 568–588. Springer, Heidelberg (2011). doi:10.1007/978-3-642-20465-4_31
12. Nikov, V., Nikova, S.: New monotone span programs from old. Cryptology ePrint Archive, Report 2004/282 (2004). http://eprint.iacr.org/2004/282
13. Okamoto, T., Takashima, K.: Fully secure unbounded inner-product and attribute-based encryption. In: Wang, X., Sako, K. (eds.) ASIACRYPT 2012. LNCS, vol. 7658, pp. 349–366. Springer, Heidelberg (2012). doi:10.1007/978-3-642-34961-4_22
14. Ostrovsky, R., Sahai, A., Waters, B.: Attribute-based encryption with non-monotonic access structures. In: Ning, P., di Vimercati, S.D.C., Syverson, P.F. (eds.) ACM CCS 2007, pp. 195–203. ACM Press, October 2007
15. Rouselakis, Y., Waters, B.: Practical constructions and new proof methods for large universe attribute-based encryption. In: Sadeghi, A.-R., Gligor, V.D., Yung, M. (eds.) ACM CCS 2013, pp. 463–474. ACM Press, November 2013
16. Sahai, A., Waters, B.: Fuzzy identity-based encryption. In: Cramer, R. (ed.) EUROCRYPT 2005. LNCS, vol. 3494, pp. 457–473. Springer, Heidelberg (2005). doi:10.1007/11426639_27
17. Shamir, A.: Identity-based cryptosystems and signature schemes. In: Blakley, G.R., Chaum, D. (eds.) CRYPTO 1984. LNCS, vol. 196, pp. 47–53. Springer, Heidelberg (1985). doi:10.1007/3-540-39568-7_5
18. Yamada, S., Attrapadung, N., Hanaoka, G., Kunihiro, N.: A framework and compact constructions for non-monotonic attribute-based encryption. In: Krawczyk, H. (ed.) PKC 2014. LNCS, vol. 8383, pp. 275–292. Springer, Heidelberg (2014). doi:10.1007/978-3-642-54631-0_16

Watermarking Public-Key Cryptographic Functionalities and Implementations

Foteini Baldimtsi[1], Aggelos Kiayias[2], and Katerina Samari[3(✉)]

[1] George Mason University, Fairfax, USA
foteini@gmu.edu
[2] University of Edinburgh and IOHK, Edinburgh, UK
Aggelos.Kiayias@ed.ac.uk
[3] National and Kapodistrian University of Athens, Athens, Greece
ksamari@di.uoa.gr

Abstract. A watermarking scheme for a public-key cryptographic functionality enables the embedding of a mark in the instance of the secret-key algorithm such that the functionality of the original scheme is maintained, while it is infeasible for an adversary to remove the mark (unremovability) or mark a fresh object without the marking key (unforgeability). Cohen et al. [STOC'16] has provided constructions for watermarking arbitrary cryptographic functionalities; the resulting schemes rely on indistinguishability obfuscation (iO) and leave two important open questions: (i) the realization of both unremovability and unforgeability, and (ii) schemes the security of which reduces to simpler hardness assumptions than iO.

In this paper we provide a new definitional framework that distinguishes between watermarking cryptographic functionalities and implementations (think of ElGamal encryption being an implementation of the encryption functionality), while at the same time provides a meaningful relaxation of the watermarking model that enables both unremovability and unforgeability under minimal hardness assumptions. In this way we can answer questions regarding the ability to watermark a *given* implementation of a cryptographic functionality which is more refined compared to the question of whether a watermarked implementation functionality exists. Taking advantage of our new formulation we present the first constructions for watermarking public key encryption that achieve both unremovability and unforgeability under minimal hardness assumptions. Our first construction enables the watermarking of *any public-key* encryption *implementation* assuming only the existence of one-way functions for private key detection. Our second construction is at the functionality level and uses a stronger assumption (existence of identity-based encryption (IBE)) but supports public detection of the watermark.

F. Baldimtsi—Part of the work performed while at the National and Kapodistrian University of Athens.

A. Kiayias—Work partly performed at the National and Kapodistrian University of Athens, supported by ERC project CODAMODA #259152. Work partly supported by H2020 Project #653497, PANORAMIX.

K. Samari—Research supported by ERC project CODAMODA, # 259152..

P.Q. Nguyen and J. Zhou (Eds.): ISC 2017, LNCS 10599, pp. 173–191, 2017.
https://doi.org/10.1007/978-3-319-69659-1_10

1   Introduction

Watermarking digital objects like pictures, video or software is usually achieved by embedding a special piece of information, the *mark*, into the object so that it is difficult for an adversary to remove it without damaging the object itself, or to introduce a fresh and legible mark. At the same time, the embedding of the mark should not result to a significantly different object, or an object with different functionality. Watermarking in practice is particularly useful, and widely applied, in order to protect content creators against illegal use and distribution of copyrighted digital objects. A plethora of watermarking schemes exists in the literature [1,13,26,27] (and references therein), most of them focusing on watermarking "static" objects while lacking a rigorous theoretical analysis and provable secure constructions.

The first formal security definitions for watermarking objects were given by Barak et al. [3,4] and by Hopper et al. [16]. Barak et al. [3,4] proposed definitions for software watermarking and showed impossibility relations between program obfuscation and watermarking, while Hopper et al. [16] defined watermarking of perceptual objects without providing any constructions. Nishimaki [22], inspired by the work of [16], extended their definitions to formalize watermarking of *cryptographic functions/circuits* and defined the security properties to be: correctness, functionality-preserving, unremovability and unforgeability.

Watermarking cryptographic functions has various real-life applications. Consider for instance the case of VPN clients. An organization might wish to distribute VPN clients to its employees where every employee has a public/secret-key pair. Watermarking the VPN client restricts the employees from sharing their clients since, due to the unremovability and unforgeability property, given any client one could detect to whom does this client belongs to (assuming the ID of the user is embedded in the watermark).

Nishimaki [22] provided the first construction of a cryptographic watermarking. While proven secure, the scheme is still vulnerable to a general obfuscation attack described in [4]; Cohen et al. [10] (merged result of [11,24]) gave a watermarking scheme for puncturable PRFs [7,8,18] which avoids the impossibility result of [4] by allowing statistical correctness, i.e. the marked PRF is allowed to behave differently in a negligible fraction of inputs, comparing to the initial one. The construction suggested in [10] is based on the assumption that indistinguishability obfuscation (iO) exists, allows for public key detection and it provably satisfies the unremovability property.

Our results. Our contributions are both in definitional and constructional level. We start by rethinking the definitional framework for watermarking public-key cryptographic functionalities. We approach cryptographic watermarking, by making a relaxation and refinement to the model considered in previous works, which we argue maintains all the relevant to practice features that the previous formulations enjoyed, and moreover can be very suitable for some real world scenarios due to its more refined nature. Previous approaches [10,11,22,24] considered a watermarking definition where the marking algorithm would take as input a *specific* unmarked program/circuit and would output the marked version of it, i.e., a program that *preserves the functionality* of the one given as input to Mark. The origins of this thinking are in the work of [16], that dealt with the cryptographic formalization of watermarking in general.

An important observation that motivates our modeling is that limiting the interaction between the marking system and the recipient of the object in the above fashion is unnecessarily restrictive. In most, if not all, applications of public-key cryptography, the actual details of the decryption or signing program are not relevant to its user, only its functionality is (which encompasses its correctness and security properties). For instance, in the VPN scenario we described above, the organization (i.e. the marking system) is often the one to sample a key K_U for its client and provide it along with the VPN client. Thus we argue that in practice, any interaction between the marking system and the recipient that results in the sampling of a decryption or signing program would be sufficient for an application of watermarking. Following the above reasoning, we propose a new version of watermarking definitions where the Mark algorithm does not take a specific program as input[1] but instead it partitions[2] the exponential space of available secret-key program instances into *marked* and *unmarked* (taking advantage of the marking key) and whenever queried it samples and returns a program from the *marked* space. This extends to the case of embedding a watermark in the form of a message *msg*, in which setting, the space is partitioned further labeled by the different messages that may be embedded.

In our model, we define watermarking for public-key cryptographic *functionalities* as well as cryptographic *implementations*. Distinguishing between the two is a further refinement of the definitional framework and relevant from a real world point of view. Specifically, in all previous works the focus was in the watermarking of a cryptographic functionality, in the sense of constructing a *new* scheme (say, public-key encryption or digital signature) for which one can argue the basic properties of watermarking (unremovability, unforgeability, functionality preserving) or watermarking a circuit directly. In other words, the starting point was the cryptographic functionality and the solution was a specific construction realizing it or the starting point was a fixed program. While this is sensible as in the first case it permeates the way cryptographic primitives are proposed and realized in general and in the second it resembles the definition of obfuscation, for the case of watermarking it appears also important to be able to watermark a *specific cryptographic implementation* of a functionality, which is a probability distribution ensemble of programs (with each sample containing both code and keys). In plain words, a marking service may want to watermark,

---

[1] In [6] a similar relaxation of the marking algorithm is given, in the sense that the algorithm does not receive as input a specific circuit to be marked, but instead samples a key to be marked and returns it together with the marked circuit. However, their watermarking model is restricted to watermarking PRFs only.

[2] This partition of the space to marked and unmarked programs is the reason why the impossibility result of [4] does not apply in our setting – applying iO to a marked program in our model would not remove the marking.

say, ElGamal public-key encryption because this particular implementation of public-key encryption is the one that is standardized, backwards compatible, or sufficiently efficient for the context within which the cryptographic system is used. This of course can be achieved by watermarking a circuit implementing ElGamal decryption but definitionally this can be relaxed and the objective, can be seen to lie in between the objectives of designing a watermarked public-key encryption and watermarking arbitrary circuits.

Following the above we formulate secure watermarking both for the case of functionalities and implementations, focusing on the public-key setting. We also validate our model by showing that watermarking a given implementation of a functionality is a stronger notion than merely watermarking a functionality (i.e., producing a watermarked implementation of the functionality). Note that, existing work in formalizing watermarking is either done for circuit classes [10] or even more restricted, for pseudorandom functions [20]. Our definition is more general, encompasses any public-key cryptographic functionality and implementation and is consistent to existing work. Cohen et al. [10] attempted to provide *specific* definitions for watermarking public-key cryptographic primitives, i.e. "Watermarkable Public Key Encryption and "Watermarkable Signature Scheme". Our definitional framework is more general and encompasses any public-key cryptographic functionality and implementation and is consistent with theirs for these functionalities. Thus, any construction that is described in their model for watermarkable encryption and signatures will be syntactically compliant and secure in our more general model as well.

Once we set our new definitional model we present two constructions. In Sect. 5 we propose a scheme for watermarking cryptographic implementations, precisely a watermarking scheme for watermarking *any* public key encryption implementation. This construction works for private detection of watermarked programs. It assumes a shared state of logarithmic size in the security parameter between the Mark and Detect algorithms while the running time of the detection algorithm depends on the number of marked programs so far. We stress that these relaxations to the notion of watermarking do not appear to hurt the applicability of the scheme in a real world setting, where e.g., an organization wishes to issue watermarked versions of cryptographic algorithms (embedded in VPN clients). In such scenarios private detection is the default requirement and given that detection of malicious clients happens with much lower frequency compared to marking, a detection process with linear running time to the number of clients can be reasonable. Countering these downsides, our construction enjoys security against *both* unremovability and unforgeability attacks, actually achieving *unconditional* unremovability for any public-key encryption implementation. Moreover, the only assumption needed for unforgeability is the existence of one-way functions (that we utilize as a facilitator for a PRF function). This suggests that the security of watermarking comes essentially "for free" since the security of the underlying public-key encryption would imply the existence of one-way functions already.

Our second construction achieves watermarking for the public key encryption *functionality*. It is based in identity-based encryption (IBE) [5], also assumes a shared state of logarithmic size in the security parameter between the Mark and Detect but, as opposed to our first construction, it allows for public key detection of the watermark. This is the *first* construction in the literature for watermarking a cryptographic functionality with public-key detection when only based on standard assumptions (i.e. without using iO).

In a high level, both our constructions exploit the notion of a PRF [15], to create a compact "dictionary" of marked objects that is subsequently scanned and compared with the adversarial implementation. Our proposed constructions are simple and use well-known building blocks and are secure under minimal standard assumptions. Despite their simplicity, our schemes require a very careful analysis in order to comply with the complex security properties of watermarking. Finally, we would like to note that we view the simplicity of our constructions as an advantage, and a testament to the fact that rethinking and performing small relaxations to the model of watermarking public-key functionalities can allow for quite substantial improvements, both in terms of efficiency and security assumptions, that remain relevant to practice.

Related Work and Comparison to Our Model. One of the earliest works related to software watermarking is due to Naccache et al. [21] that considered the problem of "copyrighting" public-key encryption schemes in a setting that is akin to traitor tracing [9]; implementations are fingerprinted and the detection mechanism should be collusion resilient. Note that this type of fingerprinting an object is distinct from the one we consider here. Indeed, watermarking is about establishing the ownership of a certain object whereas fingerprinting is about controlling its distribution. A number of heuristic methods for software watermarking were later presented in [12]. Another related notion is leakage-deterring public key cryptography as defined in [19]. The idea there is that some personal information is embedded to the public key of a user such that, if she decides to share her secret key (or a partial working implementation of her decryption function) the recipient can extract the private information embedded in the public key. This notion is different from watermarking since it focuses on *private* information embedding in a cryptosystem that remains hidden unless the secret key is shared. Privacy is not an issue in watermarking thus construction techniques are technically and conceptually different. Finally, leakage deterring schemes require the embedded information to be of high entropy while in watermarking it is meaningful, depending on the application, to embed arbitrary messages or even not include a message at all.

In [3,4], Barak et al. provide a formal definition for software watermarking and explore its relation with iO. The authors provide an impossibility result showing that if a marked circuit has exactly the same functionality as the original one, then under the assumption of indistinguishability obfuscation (iO), watermarking is impossible. Note that the definition of watermarking is not included in original version [3] and is only added in the more recent full version [4].

Nishimaki, [22] (cf. also [23]), inspired by the definitions of watermarking given in [16] (for static objects), suggests a new model for watermarking cryptographic functions modeling both notions unremovability and unforgeability and proposes a watermarking scheme for Lossy Trapdoor functions [25]. The construction is vulnerable, in light of the impossibility result of [4], to an obfuscation attack, i.e., the application of iO to a marked circuit which would effectively remove the mark. It should be noted that [22] circumvents the impossibility result by considering more restricted adversaries whose outputs in the security games should preserve the format of the original functions but, naturally, this leaves open the question of considering general adversaries.

More recently, Cohen et al. [10] motivated by the fact that the iO impossibility result does not hold if a marked circuit is *approximately* close to the original unmarked one (they formulate this as statistical correctness), they propose a watermarking scheme for any puncturable PRF family. This scheme relies on iO, features public key detection and satisfies unremovability without placing any restriction to the adversarial strategy. Based on this scheme and the constructions given by Sahai and Waters [28] for public key encryption and signatures, Cohen et al. [10] describe how to construct "Watermarkable Public-key Encryption" and "Watermarkable Signatures". Both constructions rely on iO. Furthermore, the definitions for these primitives do not consider the notion of unforgeability, however there are some preliminary results related to this notion in [11] (but they are not conclusive).

Boneh et al. [6] provide a watermarking construction for a class of PRFs, called private programmable PRFs, as an application of private constrained PRFs. Their construction achieves unremovability and unforgeability in the private key setting (i.e. private key detection), but relies on iO.

Concurrently to our work, Kim and Wu [20] suggest a watermarking scheme for a family of PRFs based on standard lattice assumptions. In particular, they first introduce a new primitive called private translucent PRFs for which they give a lattice-based construction. Based on that, they provide a construction for a watermarkable family of PRFs that allows private key detection.

Apart from the differences in our definitional models, we also highlight the following differences between [10,20] and our work. We achieve watermarking of both public key encryption implementations and functionalities instead of only constructing watermarkable instances of public-key cryptographic functionalities (as done by [10]). Our first construction takes advantage of a small shared state while at the same time being very efficient during marking; in fact it is as efficient as the underlying public-key cryptographic implementation and does not require any additional intractability assumptions. Our second construction for watermarking PKE functionalities is the first to achieve both unforgeability and unremovability with public detection which is an open problem in the setting of both [10,20].

2   Preliminaries

Notation. We first set the notation to be used throughout the paper. By $\lambda \in \mathbb{N}$ we denote the security parameter and by $\mathsf{negl}(\cdot)$ a function negligible in some parameter. The left arrow notation, $x \leftarrow \mathcal{D}$, denotes that x is chosen at random from a distribution $\mathcal{D}$. *PPT* stands for probabilistic polynomial time. C will always denote an unmarked algorithm/circuit and $\widetilde{C}$ a watermarked one.

Relations between circuits. In this paragraph we define some notions of "closeness" between circuits which are crucial in defining properties of a watermarking scheme like unforgeability and unremovability as we will see later. These notions are defined with respect to a distribution $\mathcal{D}$ over an input space X.

Definition 1 (ρ-closeness). *We say that two circuits C_1, C_2 are ρ-close with respect to distribution $\mathcal{D}$ over a space X if they agree on at least ρ-fraction of the inputs chosen according to $\mathcal{D}$. Namely,*

$$\Pr_{x \leftarrow \mathcal{D}}[C_1(x) = C_2(x)] \geq \rho.$$

We denote ρ-closeness by $C_1 \sim_{\rho, \mathcal{D}} C_2$.

Definition 2 (γ-farness). *We say that two circuits C_1, C_2 are γ-far with respect to a distribution $\mathcal{D}$ over a space X, if they agree on at most $(1 - \gamma)$-fraction of the inputs chosen according to $\mathcal{D}$. Namely,*

$$\Pr_{x \leftarrow \mathcal{D}}[C_1(x) = C_2(x)] \leq 1 - \gamma.$$

We denote γ-farness by $C_1 \nsim_{\gamma, \mathcal{D}} C_2$.

2.1   Defining Cryptographic Objects

We now define the notions of cryptographic functionalities and implementations. The goal of the cryptographic functionality definition is to capture cryptographic objects (such as: an encryption scheme, a pseudorandom function, etc.) in an abstract ideal way, focusing on the properties it should satisfy (one could think of this as the ideal functionality of a cryptographic scheme). On the other hand, the notion of a cryptographic implementation is used to describe a *specific* implementation of a cryptographic functionality (i.e. the ElGamal encryption scheme [14] is an implementation of the encryption functionality).

Definition 3 (Cryptographic functionality). *A cryptographic functionality $\mathcal{C}_{\mathcal{F}}$ consisting of m algorithms[3], $(C_1, \ldots, C_m)$, is defined by a set of n properties and their corresponding probabilities $(G_{\mathcal{A}}^{\mathsf{prop}_i}, \pi_{\mathsf{prop}_i})_{i=1}^{n}$. Each property $G_{\mathcal{A}}^{\mathsf{prop}_i}$ is described in a game fashion: it receives as input m algorithms (that constitute an instance of a candidate implementation of the functionality) and interacts with any PPT adversary $\mathcal{A}$ that attempts to "break" the desired property.*

---

[3] We consider protocols to also be described as a set of algorithms.

Remark 1. In a more complex definition we could associate each property with a parameter $t_i(\lambda)$ which would define the running time of the adversary. For simplicity, in Definition 3, we opt to define all the properties with respect to PPT adversaries. However, some properties may also hold for super-polynomial adversaries (e.g. correctness-related properties).

Example. Consider the public key encryption functionality as an example, which can be defined as a pair of algorithms $\langle \mathsf{Enc}, \mathsf{Dec} \rangle$ that should satisfy the properties of *correctness* and *IND-CPA security*. As we explain in the full version [2], correctness can be defined as a security game where an adversary is challenged to provide an encryption of a message M which is decrypted to a message different than M. The IND-CPA security property is defined in the standard way. Corresponding to our definitions, the games will receive as input the encryption/decryption algorithms for a specific key pair. Given that the definition of a cryptographic functionality describes the "ideal" scenario, correctness would always hold with probability 0 (perfect correctness) while in IND-CPA property the adversary would have probability of success of exactly $1/2$.

Definition 4 (Cryptographic Implementation). *Let $\mathcal{C}_\mathcal{F}$ be a cryptographic functionality with m algorithms and n properties $(G_\mathcal{A}^{\mathsf{prop}_i}, \pi_{\mathsf{prop}_i})_{i=1}^n$. An implementation of the cryptographic functionality $\mathcal{C}_\mathcal{F}$ consists of an $(m+1)$-tuple of algorithms/protocols $(\mathsf{Gen}, C_1, \ldots, C_m)$ such that, for every security parameter λ and each property prop_i for $i \in \{1, \ldots, n\}$ and for any corresponding PPT adversary $\mathcal{A}$, it holds that:*

$$\Pr\left[\begin{array}{l} (k_1, \ldots, k_m) \leftarrow \mathsf{Gen}(1^\lambda): \\ G_\mathcal{A}^{\mathsf{prop}_i}(C_1(k_1, \cdot), \ldots, C_m(k_m, \cdot)) = 1 \end{array}\right] \leq \pi_{\mathsf{prop}_i} + \mathsf{negl}(\lambda).$$

In Definition 4 we consider *single-instance* properties. This means that the input of the property game is a specific instance of the implementation's algorithms under a fixed key. One could also define *multi-instance* properties, where the corresponding game would receive as inputs multiple versions of the algorithms all under different keys.

3 Watermarking Cryptographic Functionalities

We now define the notion of watermarking cryptographic functionalities. The main idea of our definition follows [4,6,10,20] however notice that: (1) we define watermarking of a *functionality* rather than a circuit class, (2) our marking algorithm is not given a *specific* algorithm/circuit to mark but selects and outputs only an instance of the functionality being marked (i.e. the tuple of the corresponding algorithms), and last (3) our definition allows for a shared public state between the Mark and Detect algorithms. In this section we will refer to the algorithms of a cryptographic functionality as circuits.

3.1 Syntax of a Watermarking Scheme

Let $\mathcal{C}_{\mathcal{F}}$ be a cryptographic functionality with m algorithms/circuits and n properties $(G_{\mathcal{A}}^{\mathsf{prop_i}}, \pi_{\mathsf{prop_i}})_{i=1}^n$ and let $\{\mathcal{M}_\lambda\}_{\lambda \in \mathbb{N}}$ denote the message space (of the messages to be embedded on the watermarked scheme), where λ is a security parameter. The entities that are involved in a watermarking scheme are a set of clients, and a "marking service", MarkService.

Definition 5 (Watermarking Scheme). *A stateful watermarking scheme for a cryptographic functionality $\mathcal{C}_{\mathcal{F}}$, consists of three probabilistic polynomial time algorithms $\langle$WGen, Mark, Detect$\rangle$ whose input/output behavior has as follows:*

- *WGen : On input 1^λ, it outputs public parameters param and a pair of keys (mk, dk), where mk is the marking key and dk is the detection key. It also initializes a public variable* state *which can be accessed by all the parties.*
- *Mark : On input mk, param, a message $msg \in \mathcal{M}_\lambda$ (which is sent by a client to the* MarkService*) and current* state*, the marking algorithm outputs a tuple of circuits $(\widetilde{C}_1, C_2, \ldots, C_m)$, an efficiently sampleable and representable distribution $\mathcal{D}$ on the inputs of the circuit $\widetilde{C}_1$[4], and the updated state* state'*.*
- *Detect : On input dk, param,* state *and a circuit C_1', it outputs a message msg' or* unmarked*.*

Despite the fact that the marking service outputs a tuple of circuits (as many as the algorithms of $\mathcal{C}_{\mathcal{F}}$), only one circuit among them is considered marked. By convention, this would be the first circuit in a tuple produced by the Mark algorithm. It is trivial to extend this definition for the case where more than one circuits are considered marked. The Detect algorithm, as in previous definitions, will run on input any circuit C_1'. Also, note that a *stateless* watermarking scheme could be described by setting the variable state to be empty string.

Remark 2. Notice that a new feature of our definition of watermarking is that the Mark algorithm outputs a distribution $\mathcal{D}$ on the inputs of marked circuit. This distribution is relevant to our definitions of closeness and farness between circuits (cf. Definitions 1 and 2) and essentially defines on which inputs we expect that circuits are similar or not.

3.2 Security Model

For our security model, we define oracles Challenge, Detect and Corrupt in Fig. 1. The Challenge oracle calls the Mark algorithm, and returns to the client a tuple of all output circuits except the one that is considered marked (i.e. the first one) along with an index i that shows how many times the Mark algorithm is invoked so far. The Corrupt oracle outputs the whole tuple of circuits generated

---

[4] The marking algorithm, Mark, can output the distribution $\mathcal{D}$ in the form of an algorithm that samples inputs for the circuit $\widetilde{C}_1$.

ChallengeOracle$(msg, \cdot)$:

1. $i \leftarrow i + 1$;
2. $((\widetilde{C}_1^i, C_2^i, \ldots, C_m^i), \mathcal{D}_i, \mathsf{state}') \leftarrow$ $\mathsf{Mark}(param, mk, msg, \mathsf{state})$;
3. $\mathsf{Marked} \quad\leftarrow\quad \mathsf{Marked} \quad \cup$ $\{(i, (\widetilde{C}_1^i, C_2^i, \ldots, C_m^i), \mathcal{D}_i, msg)\}$;
4. Set $\mathsf{state} \leftarrow \mathsf{state}'$;
5. Return $(i, (C_2^i, \ldots, C_m^i), \mathcal{D}_i, \mathsf{state})$;

CorruptOracle(i):

1. Retrieve $(i, (\widetilde{C}_1^i, \ldots, C_m^i), \mathcal{D}_i, msg_i)$ from Marked;
2. $\mathsf{Corrupted} \quad\leftarrow\quad \mathsf{Corrupted} \quad \cup$ $\{(i, (\widetilde{C}_1^i, C_2^i, \ldots, C_m^i), \mathcal{D}_i, msg_i)\}$;
3. Return $((\widetilde{C}_1^i, \ldots, C_m^i), \mathcal{D}_i)$;

DetectOracle(C):

1. $msg \leftarrow \mathsf{Detect}(dk, param, C, \mathsf{state})$;
2. Return msg ;

Fig. 1. The Challenge, and Detect and Corrupt oracles.

by the Mark algorithm for a specific i and works for queries the indices of which were previously returned the Challenge oracle. The Detect oracle runs the Detect algorithm with input a given circuit. Finally, given that state is public, we assume that all oracles have access to it.

Remark. Notice that for marked (but not corrupted tuples) the adversary does not have access to the marked circuit $\widetilde{C}_1$. This might be restrictive for certain schemes and properties. Consider for instance the case of CCA security for a public key encryption scheme. Then, the marked algorithm would be the decryption one. Although the adversary should not receive Dec_{sk}, he should still be able to query it on ciphertexts of his choice. Thus, we could define one more oracle name QueryOracle that would take as input an index i and an input x and would return the output of the i-th watermarked circuit produced by ChallengeOracle.

Comparing our security model with previous work. In the security model of [10], [20] (note that [20] is specific to PRFs), the adversary has access to both marking and challenge oracles. Their marking oracle receives as input an unmarked circuit and returns the corresponding marked one, while the challenge oracle samples a circuit and returns it marked without revealing the sampled, unmarked one. In the security model of [6], the marking oracle receives a message as input, and returns an unmarked PRF key and a marked circuit embedded with this message. Note that [6,20] give only definitions for PRFs and not circuit classes in general. Although the security model of [6] seems closer to our model, the existence of a marking oracle, as this is defined in [10,20] and [6], does not comply with our model. The Mark algorithm in our case neither takes as input an unmarked circuit nor returns an unmarked circuit together with the marked one as output. Another difference with the model of [6,10,20] is that our challenge oracle does not return the marked circuit of the tuple, i.e. the first one by convention. The corrupt oracle is the one that returns the marked cicruit for a previously sampled marked instance of a functionality or implementation. Notice that our challenge oracle does not play any important role for functionalities with a single algorithm like a PRF but it is crucial for multi-algorithm functionalities. For example, in the public-key encryption functionality if the decryption function, i.e. a secret key, is the one which is marked, it is reasonable that the adversary should be given the corresponding public key.

3.3 Security Properties

Next, we define the properties that should be satisfied by a watermarking scheme.

We start by detection correctness which informally states that a valid water-marked circuit should be detected as such with a non-negligible probability. Our definition guarantees that any update on the state, after each execution of Mark, does not affect the detection correctness of previously marked circuits.

Definition 6 (Detection Correctness). *We say that a watermarking scheme satisfies detection correctness if for any PPT adversary $\mathcal{A}$ against the security game described in Fig. 2, it holds that:*

$$\Pr[G^{\mathsf{det-corr}}(1^\lambda) = 1] \leq \mathsf{negl}(\lambda).$$

The next property we define is ρ-unremovability. Informally, an adversary after querying the Challenge and Corrupt oracles, should not be able to output a circuit that is ρ-close to any of the queried ones, and at the same time is unmarked or is marked under a different (than the original) mark. In Fig. 3 we first describe the unremovability security game and then we provide the definition below.

$$G^{\mathsf{det-corr}}_{\mathcal{A}}(1^\lambda):$$

1. The Challenger runs $\mathsf{WGen}(1^\lambda)$ which outputs $(param, (mk, dk), \mathsf{state})$. It gives $param$ to the adversary $\mathcal{A}$. $\mathcal{A}$ has also access to the public variable state. If detection is public, $\mathcal{A}$ also receives dk from the Challenger. The Challenger initializes the sets Marked and $\mathsf{Corrupted}$ as empty and $i \leftarrow 0$.
2. $\mathcal{A}$ makes queries to $\mathsf{DetectOracle}$, $\mathsf{ChallengeOracle}$ and $\mathsf{CorruptOracle}$.
3. $\mathcal{A}$ outputs an index j.
4. Output 1 iff $\left(j, (\widetilde{C}^j_1, \cdot), \mathcal{D}_j, msg\right) \in \mathsf{Marked}$ and $\mathsf{Detect}(dk, param, \widetilde{C}^j_1, \mathsf{state}) \neq msg$.

Fig. 2. The Detection-Correctness game

Definition 7 (ρ-Unremovability). *We say that a watermarking scheme satisfies the ρ-unremovability property if for any PPT adversary $\mathcal{A}$ against the security game described in Fig. 3, it holds that*

$$\Pr[G^{\mathsf{unrmv}}_{\mathcal{A}}(1^\lambda, \rho) = 1] \leq \mathsf{negl}(\lambda).$$

$G_{\mathcal{A}}^{\mathsf{unrmv}}(1^\lambda, \rho)$:

1. The Challenger runs $\mathsf{WGen}(1^\lambda)$ which outputs $(param, (mk, dk), \mathsf{state})$. It gives $param$ to the adversary $\mathcal{A}$. $\mathcal{A}$ has also access to the public variable state. If detection is public, $\mathcal{A}$ also receives dk from the Challenger. The Challenger initializes the sets Marked and $\mathsf{Corrupted}$ as empty and $i \leftarrow 0$.
2. $\mathcal{A}$ makes queries to $\mathsf{DetectOracle}$, $\mathsf{ChallengeOracle}$ and $\mathsf{CorruptOracle}$.
3. $\mathcal{A}$ outputs a circuit C^*.
4. The game outputs 1 iff there exists $\left(j, (\widetilde{C}_1^j, \cdot), \mathcal{D}_j, msg\right) \in \mathsf{Marked}$ such that $C^* \sim_{\rho, \mathcal{D}_j} \widetilde{C}_1^j$ and $\mathsf{Detect}(dk, param, C^*, \mathsf{state}) \neq msg$.

Fig. 3. The ρ-Unremovability game

$G_{\mathcal{A}}^{\mathsf{unforge}}(1^\lambda, \gamma)$:

1. The Challenger runs $\mathsf{WGen}(1^\lambda)$ which outputs $(param, (mk, dk), \mathsf{state})$. It gives $param$ to the adversary $\mathcal{A}$. $\mathcal{A}$ has also access to the public variable state. If detection is public, $\mathcal{A}$ also receives dk from the Challenger. The Challenger initializes the sets Marked and $\mathsf{Corrupted}$ as empty and $i \leftarrow 0$.
2. $\mathcal{A}$ makes queries to $\mathsf{DetectOracle}$, $\mathsf{ChallengeOracle}$ and $\mathsf{CorruptOracle}$.
3. $\mathcal{A}$ outputs a circuit C^*.
4. The game outputs 1 iff
   (a) For all $\widetilde{C}_1^j$ such that $\left(j, (\widetilde{C}_1^j, \cdot), \mathcal{D}_j, msg\right) \in \mathsf{Corrupted}$ it holds that $C^* \not\sim_{\gamma, \mathcal{D}_j} \widetilde{C}_1^j$.
   (b) $\mathsf{Detect}(dk, param, C^*, \mathsf{state}) \neq \mathsf{unmarked}$.

Fig. 4. The γ-Unforgeability game

We then define γ-unforgeability which informally states that an adversary, after receiving marked circuits through oracle queries, should not be able to output a marked circuit that is γ-far from the received, marked ones. Note that $\mathcal{A}$ only receives marked circuits through the Corrupt oracle, thus if he manages to forge a circuit that is close to a marked (but not corrupted one) he should still win the game. The unforgeability security game is described in Fig. 4.

Definition 8 (γ-Unforgeability). *We say that a watermarking scheme satisfies γ-unforgeability if for any PPT adversary $\mathcal{A}$ against the security game defined in Fig. 4 it holds that*

$$\Pr[G_{\mathcal{A}}^{\mathsf{unforge}}(1^\lambda, \gamma) = 1] \leq \mathsf{negl}(\lambda).$$

Finally, we define the functionality property-preserving notion. Informally, this notion captures the requirement that a watermarked cryptographic functionality $\mathcal{C}_{\mathcal{F}}$ should preserve the properties of the original (non-marked) functionality. In other words, the probability that an adversary $\mathcal{A}$ breaks a property prop_i of a watermarked functionality should be less or equal to the probability that an adversary breaks the same property for the non-watermarked functionality (plus a negligible factor). We define functionality property-preserving with the aid of the game in Fig. 5. In that game, the adversary $\mathcal{A}$ decides the instance of the algorithms for which they will play the security property game $G_{\mathcal{A}}^{\mathsf{prop}_j}$, choosing among the watermarked ones he received by the ChallengeOracle. Note that $\mathcal{A}$ cannot pick an instance that has previously corrupted. If the selected instance was a corrupted one, then the security property prop_j could have been trivially broken by $\mathcal{A}$.

$\underline{G_{\mathcal{A}}^{\mathsf{wm-prop}_j}(1^\lambda)}$:

1. The Challenger runs $\mathsf{WGen}(1^\lambda)$ which outputs $(param, (mk, dk), \mathsf{state})$. It gives $param$ to the adversary $\mathcal{A}$. $\mathcal{A}$ has also access to the public variable state. If detection is public, $\mathcal{A}$ also receives dk from the Challenger. The Challenger initializes the sets Marked and Corrupted as empty and $i \leftarrow 0$.
2. $\mathcal{A}$ can make queries to DetectOracle, the ChallengeOracle and the CorruptOracle.
3. $\mathcal{A}$ chooses i such that $(i, (\widetilde{C}_1^i, C_2^i, \ldots, C_m^i), \mathcal{D}_i, msg) \in$ Marked \ Corrupted and sends i to the Challenger.
4. Then, the Challenger runs the game $G_{\mathcal{A}}^{\mathsf{prop}_j}$ with $\mathcal{A}$ but on input $(\widetilde{C}_1^i, C_2^i, \ldots, C_m^i)$ (notice that only challenger knows $\widetilde{C}_1^i$).
5. The game $G_{\mathcal{A}}^{\mathsf{wm-prop}_j}(1^\lambda)$ outputs whatever $G_{\mathcal{A}}^{\mathsf{prop}_j}$ outputs.

Fig. 5. The Functionality property-preserving game for a property prop_j.

Definition 9 (Functionality Property-preserving). *A watermarking scheme is property-preserving for a cryptographic functionality $C_{\mathcal{F}}$ with m algorithms and n properties $(G_{\mathcal{A}}^{\mathsf{prop}_j}, \pi_{\mathsf{prop}_j})_{j=1}^n$ if for any PPT adversary $\mathcal{A}$ against the security game defined in Fig. 5, and for any property prop_j, it holds that*

$$\Pr[G_{\mathcal{A}}^{\mathsf{wm-prop}_j}(1^\lambda) = 1] \le \pi_{\mathsf{prop}_j} + \mathsf{negl}(\lambda).$$

Note 1. There may be property games where the adversary is not given all the circuits $C_2^i, \ldots, C_m^i$ but only a subset of them. We could give an alternative definition capturing such cases, however we omit it for simplicity reasons. We also described property-preserving for the scenario when $\mathcal{A}$ is not given the marking key mk. One could also consider an alternative, stronger definition, where $\mathcal{A}$ has mk, marks objects by himself and then for a state of his choice, runs the security game for the particular property using the algorithms returned by Mark in the chosen state.

4   Watermarking Cryptographic Implementations

Let $(\mathsf{Gen}, C_1, \ldots, C_m)$ be an implementation of a cryptographic functionality $\mathcal{C}_\mathcal{F}$. The syntax of a watermarking scheme for cryptographic implementations is exactly the same with the syntax for cryptographic functionalities. The reason is that in practice the Mark algorithm of the watermarking scheme acts as (replaces in a sense) the Gen algorithm of a cryptographic implementation and outputs an instance of the implementation algorithms under a specific key. What differentiates these two definitions is only the property-preserving notion. The rest of the security properties (detection correctness, ρ-unremovability, γ-unforgeability) remain the same as in Sect. 3.

In order for a watermarked implementation to be property-preserving it needs to hold that the watermarked implementation preserves the properties of the non-watermaked one, which in turn preserves the properties of the corresponding cryptographic functionality it implements. Notice that, when we watermark a cryptographic implementation we naturally want to achieve multi-instance security for the properties of the implementation (multi-instance versions of security definitions are encountered in the literature for various types of cryptographic functionalities, i.e. [17]). This arises by the fact that the $\mathsf{ChallengeOracle}$ is called multiple times by the adversary, who thus receives multiple instances of implementations and then chooses for which one he will attempt to break the property of the implementation. Therefore we first define the multi-instance version of the security game for a property prop_i in Fig. 6. The $\mathsf{MultiInstanceOracle}$ called in the game is identical to the $\mathsf{ChallengeOracle}$ but instead of calling the Mark algorithm it calls the key generation algorithm Gen of the implementation and stores all the created instances of generated algorithms to a set $\mathsf{Instances}$. The security game $G_S^{\mathsf{prop}_j}$ is defined as in the previous definition.

$G_\mathcal{A}^{\mathsf{mi-prop}_j}(1^\lambda):$

1. Set $i \leftarrow 0$.
2. $\mathcal{A}$ can make queries to $\mathsf{MultiInstanceOracle}$ and the $\mathsf{CorruptOracle}$.
3. $\mathcal{A}$ chooses i such that $(i, (C_1^i, C_2^i, \ldots, C_m^i), \mathcal{D}_i, msg) \in \mathsf{Instances} \setminus \mathsf{Corrupted}$ and sends i to the Challenger.
4. Then, $\mathcal{A}$ runs with the Challenger the game $G_\mathcal{A}^{\mathsf{prop}_j}$ but on input $(C_1^i, C_2^i, \ldots, C_m^i)$.
5. The game $G_\mathcal{A}^{\mathsf{mi-prop}_j}(1^\lambda)$ outputs whatever $G_\mathcal{A}^{\mathsf{prop}_j}$ outputs.

Fig. 6. The multi-instance security game for a property prop_j.

Definition 10 (Implementation Property-preserving). *We say that a watermarking scheme satisfies implementation property-preserving with error* ε

for a cryptographic implementation $(\mathsf{Gen}, C_1, \ldots, C_m)$ *if for any p.p.t. adversary* $\mathcal{S}$ *there is a PPT adversary* $\mathcal{A}$ *such that*

$$\left| \Pr[G_{\mathcal{S}}^{\mathsf{wm-prop}_j}(1^\lambda) = 1] - \Pr[G_{\mathcal{A}}^{\mathsf{mi-prop}_j}(1^\lambda) = 1] \right| \leq \varepsilon.$$

Proposition 1. *If a watermarking scheme is implementation property-preserving, it is also functionality property-preserving, i.e. Definition 10 implies Definition 9, when ε is negligible to the security parameter.*

5   A Watermarking Scheme for Implementations of PKE

We describe a construction of an efficient watermarking scheme for a cryptographic implementation of a public key encryption scheme. One could view our construction as a compiler that takes as input an existing public key encryption scheme and converts it into a watermarked public key encryption scheme.

Public key detection via linear size state vs secret-key detection via logarithmic size state. Given that our definition of a watermarking scheme (Definition 5) allows for a public state one could design a watermarking scheme for an implementation of a public key encryption scheme by assuming a state with size linear to the number of markings. Specifically, assume that the shared state is represented as a public table which can be accessed by both the Marking Service and any party that runs Detect algorithm. For any marking request, Mark generates a fresh pair of keys (pk, sk) using the key generation algorithm of the public key encryption scheme that is being watermarked. Then, it stores the generated public key pk to the state table and outputs $(\mathsf{Enc}_{pk}, \mathsf{Dec}_{sk})$. Thus, state will hold all the public keys generated by Mark so far. Now, how does Detect work given the public state? When Detect receives as input a (decryption) algorithm/circuit C, it will check for any public key stored in the public table state, whether the circuit can decrypt correctly a number of ciphertexts which is above a certain threshold.

Such a construction could be proven to be a secure watermarking scheme for public key encryption however the use of a state that grows linearly to the number of markings is not very appealing in practice especially for implementations where the public keys are large. We overcome this problem by focusing on private detection watermarking. In Fig. 7, we suggest a watermarking scheme with logarithmic state and private key detection where the same key is being used for both marking and detection.

Overview of our construction. Our proposed construction is given in Fig. 7 and assumes a state of logarithmic size (in the security parameter). We use a PRF function F with a random key K and set marking and detection keys equal to K and state to be a counter of the number of markings so far. Whenever, Mark is run it will compute (pk, sk) by running $F(K, \mathsf{state} + 1)$, set $\mathsf{state} = \mathsf{state} + 1$ and output $\mathsf{Enc}_{pk}, \mathsf{Dec}_{sk}$. In order for the detection algorithm to correctly identify

---

- WGen: On input 1^λ, it chooses uniformly at random a key K for a pseudo-random function $F : \mathcal{K} \times \{0,1\}^n \to \{0,1\}^\ell$. It outputs $mk = dk = K$ and initializes the public variable state $\leftarrow 0$.
- Mark: On input K, state, marked, compute $i = \text{state} + 1$ and run $\text{Gen}(1^\lambda)$ with randomness $F(K, i)$. The output is a public-secret key pair (pk_i, sk_i) and the algorithm returns a pair of circuits $(\text{Enc}_{pk_i}, \text{Dec}_{sk_i})$. Set as $\mathcal{D}_i$ the distribution of the ciphertexts that correspond to plaintexts chosen uniformly from the plaintext space. Then, set state $\leftarrow$ state $+ 1$.
- Detect: On input K, a circuit C and state, for $i = 1$ to state:
  - Run $\text{Gen}(1^\lambda)$ with randomness $F(K, i)$ (as the Mark algorithm does) in order to obtain (pk_i, sk_i).
  - Choose $k = \lambda/\rho$ plaintexts uniformly at random and encrypt them under pk_i, i.e. compute the ciphertexts $c_1, \ldots, c_k$.
  - For $j = 1$ to k check whether $C(c_j) = m_j$. If this is true for at least $\lambda/2$ ciphertexts, return marked.
  Otherwise, return unmarked.

Fig. 7. Watermarked Public Key Encryption Implementation

whether a decryption circuit C is marked or not, it will first re-generate all possible key pairs by running $F(K, i)$ for every $i \leq$ state. Then, for each produced pk_i it will check whether an encryption of a random plaintext under it, can be correctly decrypted with C. As it turns out by our security analysis it is not enough to check for a single plaintext, in fact, it will check the decryptions of λ/ρ randomly selected plaintexts.

A note about state. Note that the state information in our construction is public and it should be immutable for the system to work in practice. A potential solution for storing the state would be by using a public bulletin board or a blockchain system. For example, every time the state is updated, the marking service signs it and posts a new transaction in the blockchain with the new state and the signature. Even though storing information in the blockchain is an expensive operation, our scheme, with its logarithmic size state, is suitable for a blockchain deployment. We leave a detailed analysis under a formal blockchain security model for future work.

Security analysis of our construction. In our analysis we consider key-generation algorithms which create their random tape by choosing keys uniformly at random. This aligns with the key generation algorithms of all the well-known encryption schemes. We provide below the security theorem for our construction.

Theorem 1. *Let $\langle \text{Gen}, \text{Enc}, \text{Dec} \rangle$ be an implementation of the Public Key Encryption functionality that has plaintext space of exponential size (in the security parameter) and satisfies (multi-instance) perfect correctness[5] and*

---

[5] Our proofs could also be extended for implementations which have a negligible decryption error.

- WGen(1^λ): Run IBE.Setup(1^λ) which outputs $(msk, \mathsf{IBE.param})$. Set $mk = msk$, $param = \mathsf{IBE.param}$, $dk = \mathsf{IBE.param}$, and initialize state $\leftarrow 0$.
- Mark: On input $mk, param$, compute $i = \mathsf{state} + 1$ and set $id_i = i$. Run IBE.Extract($msk, f(param, id_i)$) which outputs a secret key sk_i for the identity id_i. Return to the Client $(\mathsf{Dec}_{sk_i}, \mathsf{Enc}_{pk_i})$. Set as $\mathcal{D}_i$ the distribution of the ciphertexts that correspond to plaintexts chosen uniformly from the plaintext space. Set state $\leftarrow$ state $+ 1$.
- Detect: On input dk and a circuit C, for $i = 1$ to state:
  - Compute $pk_i = f(param, id_i)$.
  - Choose $k = \lambda/\rho$ plaintexts uniformly at random from the the plaintext space and encrypt them under pk_i. We denote the corresponding ciphertexts as $c_1, \ldots, c_k$.
  - If for at least $\lambda/2$ plaintexts it holds that $C(c_i) = m_i$ then return marked
  Otherwise return unmarked.

Fig. 8. Watermarked Public Key Encryption Functionality from IBE

(multi-instance) IND-CPA security. Let $F : \mathcal{K} \times \{0,1\}^n \leftarrow \{0,1\}^\ell$ be a pseudorandom function, where $\mathcal{K}$ is the key space. Then, the scheme in Fig. 7 is a watermarking scheme for the implementation $\langle \mathsf{Gen}, \mathsf{Enc}, \mathsf{Dec} \rangle$. Namely, it satisfies Detection Correctness, Implementation property-preserving with error ε_{prf}, ρ-Unremovability and $(1 - \rho/3)$-Unforgeability, where ε_{prf} is the security of the PRF and ρ is a parameter with $\rho \geq \frac{1}{\mathsf{poly}(\lambda)}$.

Due to lack of space, the proof of Theorem 1 is provided in the full version of the paper [2].

6   Watermarking PKE Funtionality from IBE

Finally, we present a watermarking scheme for the public key encryption functionality. Our construction relies on identity-based encryption (IBE) [5] and will allow for public detection of the watermark. The state, as before, will be of logarithmic size to the security parameter.

Assuming an IBE scheme, one can construct a watermarking scheme for the public-key encryption functionality based on the following idea: The private marking key equals the master secret key of the IBE scheme. Then, the marking service (i.e., the Mark algorithm of the watermaking scheme), when invoked, sets $pk_i = f(param, id_i)$ for some deterministic function f[6] and then runs the private key generator of IBE, IBE.Extract($msk, f(param, id_i)$), to get the corresponding sk_i. The identities, id_i, are not given as input to Mark, instead, each identity is the next value of a counter that keeps the number of keys generated so far

---

[6] In standard IBE the *id* of the user (i.e. email address or other unique identifier) serves as *pk*. Here, since *id*'s are just a short counter value one might want to extend them in some deterministic way - else f could also the identity function.

(which is stored at state). Detection works in a similar way to our construction in Sect. 5: try every possible public key (since by state you know the number of keys generated) and check if the given decryption circuit is watermarked by checking if for any of these public keys it correctly decrypts ciphertexts. We present our construction in Fig. 8. The security analysis of this construction shares many insights with that of Sect. 5 and will be further discussed in the full version of the paper [2].

References

1. Adelsbach, A., Katzenbeisser, S., Veith, H.: Watermarking schemes provably secure against copy and ambiguity attacks. In: ACM Workshop on Digital Rights Management (2003)
2. Baldimtsi, F., Kiayias, A., Samari, K.: Watermarking public-key cryptographic functionalities and implementations. IACR Cryptology ePrint Archive (2017)
3. Barak, B., Goldreich, O., Impagliazzo, R., Rudich, S., Sahai, A., Vadhan, S., Yang, K.: On the (Im)possibility of obfuscating programs. In: Kilian, J. (ed.) CRYPTO 2001. LNCS, vol. 2139, pp. 1–18. Springer, Heidelberg (2001). doi:10.1007/3-540-44647-8_1
4. Barak, B., Goldreich, O., Impagliazzo, R., Rudich, S., Sahai, A., Vadhan, S.P., Yang, K.: On the (im)possibility of obfuscating programs. J. ACM 59(2) (2012)
5. Boneh, D., Franklin, M.K.: Identity-based encryption from the weil pairing. SIAM J. Comput. 32(3) (2003)
6. Boneh, D., Lewi, K., Wu, D.J.: Constraining pseudorandom functions privately. In: Fehr, S. (ed.) PKC 2017. LNCS, vol. 10175, pp. 494–524. Springer, Heidelberg (2017). doi:10.1007/978-3-662-54388-7_17
7. Boneh, D., Waters, B.: Constrained pseudorandom functions and their applications. In: Sako, K., Sarkar, P. (eds.) ASIACRYPT 2013. LNCS, vol. 8270, pp. 280–300. Springer, Heidelberg (2013). doi:10.1007/978-3-642-42045-0_15
8. Boyle, E., Goldwasser, S., Ivan, I.: Functional signatures and pseudorandom functions. In: Krawczyk, H. (ed.) PKC 2014. LNCS, vol. 8383, pp. 501–519. Springer, Heidelberg (2014). doi:10.1007/978-3-642-54631-0_29
9. Chor, B., Fiat, A., Naor, M.: Tracing traitors. In: Desmedt, Y.G. (ed.) CRYPTO 1994. LNCS, vol. 839, pp. 257–270. Springer, Heidelberg (1994). doi:10.1007/3-540-48658-5_25
10. Cohen, A., Holmgren, J., Nishimaki, R., Vaikuntanathan, V., Wichs, D.: Watermarking cryptographic capabilities. In: STOC (2016)
11. Cohen, A., Holmgren, J., Vaikuntanathan, V.: Publicly verifiable software watermarking. IACR Cryptology ePrint Archive (2015)
12. Collberg, C.S., Thomborson, C.D.: Watermarking, tamper-proofing, and obfuscation-tools for software protection. IEEE Trans. Software Eng. 28(8) (2002)
13. Cox, I.J., Miller, M.L., Bloom, J.A., Honsinger, C.: Digital Watermarking, vol. 1558607145. Springer, Heidelberg (2002)
14. ElGamal, T.: A public key cryptosystem and a signature scheme based on discrete logarithms. In: Blakley, G.R., Chaum, D. (eds.) CRYPTO 1984. LNCS, vol. 196, pp. 10–18. Springer, Heidelberg (1985). doi:10.1007/3-540-39568-7_2
15. Goldreich, O., Goldwasser, S., Micali, S.: How to construct random functions (extended abstract). In: FOCS (1984)

16. Hopper, N., Molnar, D., Wagner, D.: From weak to strong watermarking. In: Vadhan, S.P. (ed.) TCC 2007. LNCS, vol. 4392, pp. 362–382. Springer, Heidelberg (2007). doi:10.1007/978-3-540-70936-7_20

17. Katz, J.: Analysis of a proposed hash-based signature standard. In: Chen, L., McGrew, D., Mitchell, C. (eds.) SSR 2016. LNCS, vol. 10074, pp. 261–273. Springer, Cham (2016). doi:10.1007/978-3-319-49100-4_12

18. Kiayias, A., Papadopoulos, S., Triandopoulos, N., Zacharias, T.: Delegatable pseudorandom functions and applications. In: CCS (2013)

19. Kiayias, A., Tang, Q.: How to keep a secret: leakage deterring public-key cryptosystems. In: CCS (2013)

20. Kim, S., Wu, D.J.: Watermarking cryptographic functionalities from standard lattice assumptions. In: Katz, J., Shacham, H. (eds.) CRYPTO 2017. LNCS, vol. 10401, pp. 503–536. Springer, Cham (2017). doi:10.1007/978-3-319-63688-7_17

21. Naccache, D., Shamir, A., Stern, J.P.: How to copyright a function? In: Imai, H., Zheng, Y. (eds.) PKC 1999. LNCS, vol. 1560, pp. 188–196. Springer, Heidelberg (1999). doi:10.1007/3-540-49162-7_14

22. Nishimaki, R.: How to watermark cryptographic functions. In: Johansson, T., Nguyen, P.Q. (eds.) EUROCRYPT 2013. LNCS, vol. 7881, pp. 111–125. Springer, Heidelberg (2013). doi:10.1007/978-3-642-38348-9_7

23. Nishimaki, R.: How to watermark cryptographic functions. IACR Cryptology ePrint Archive (2014)

24. Nishimaki, R., Wichs, D.: Watermarking cryptographic programs against arbitrary removal strategies. IACR Cryptology ePrint Archive (2015)

25. Peikert, C., Waters, B.: Lossy trapdoor functions and their applications. In: STOC (2008)

26. Podilchuk, C.I., Delp, E.J.: Digital watermarking: algorithms and applications. IEEE Sig. Process. Magazine **18**(4) (2001)

27. Potdar, V.M., Han, S., Chang, E.: A survey of digital image watermarking techniques. In: INDIN. IEEE (2005)

28. Sahai, A., Waters, B.: How to use indistinguishability obfuscation: deniable encryption, and more. In: STOC (2014)

Authentication

Contactless Access Control Based on Distance Bounding

Handan Kılınç$^{(\boxtimes)}$ and Serge Vaudenay

EPFL, Lausanne, Switzerland
handan.kilinc@epfl.ch

Abstract. Contactless access control systems are critical for security but often vulnerable to relay attacks. In this paper, we define an integrated security and privacy model for access control using distance bounding (DB) which is the most robust solution to prevent relay attacks. We show how a secure DB protocol can be converted to a secure contactless access control protocol. Regarding privacy (i.e., keeping anonymity in strong sense to an active adversary), we show that the conversion does not always preserve privacy but it is possible to study it on a case by case basis. Finally, we provide two example protocols and prove their security and privacy according to our new models.

Keywords: Access control · Distance bounding · RFID · NFC · Relay attack · Mafia fraud · Distance hijacking · Privacy

1 Introduction

Access control (AC) is a mechanism assuring that a system or a place can be accessed only by authorized users. AC is in the center of our daily lives. We use it to unlock smartphones, unlock and start cars, enter buildings or databases. Authentication in the AC systems based on two factors: The first one is a password, PIN code or biometric information such as fingerprints and retinal scans. The second one is a (contactless) card where authentication is done without contact via this card. With the development of the technology, the usage of contactless AC is becoming common because it is more convenient than carrying various keys, using PIN codes or using biometric information. However, the full security model for contactless AC has not been studied adequately. In this paper, we focus on contactless AC. So, whenever we use AC, we refer to contactless one.

A report from Smart Card Alliance [1] lists the main components of an access control system (tags, readers, controllers, database) and their security requirements which are however informal. Wongsen et al. [33] proposed an access control protocol between doors and mobile units (e.g. smartphone), but the protocol lacks any security proof. Some access control systems such as OPACITY [2] and PLAIN [14] mutually authenticate and establish a shared key between the terminal and card. The security analysis of PLAIN in [14] is far from being formal. OPACITY [2] was partly analyzed by Dagdelen et al. [7] where their security

© Springer International Publishing AG 2017
P.Q. Nguyen and J. Zhou (Eds.): ISC 2017, LNCS 10599, pp. 195–213, 2017.
https://doi.org/10.1007/978-3-319-69659-1_11

model is based on the key agreement security model of Bellare and Rogaway [4]. Hence, most of the previous works do not have a comprehensive security analysis. Moreover, **none of them consider relay attacks in their security analysis**. Figures 1 and 2 show real world relay attack scenarios. Unfortunately, these type of attacks are easily implementable [12,13,16,17,24,28], so they violate access control.

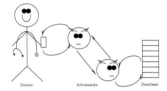

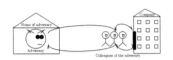

Fig. 1. The adversaries retrieve information from a hospital database by relaying the messages between the database reader and the doctor's card. Here, the doctor is far-away from the database. Arrows show that receiving or sending messages.

Fig. 2. The adversary who is an employee of the company accesses to the door of the company which shows that he arrived his job although he is at home. Here, the adversary can use one of his colleagues who is just next to the door. Arrows show that receiving or sending messages.

The other problem in contactless AC is to address privacy. Informally, if an AC protocol is private then it is hard for an outside observer to identify or recognize a party who wants to access a system. Some previous works [7,8,14] touched on privacy. PLAID [14] claims to be private (with an informal definition) but Degabriele et al. [8] show that it is weaker than what it claims. Dagdelen et al. [7] give two privacy related definitions: identity hiding and untraceability. The problem in their privacy model is that it only considers the interaction between the card and the reader. In reality, this may not be enough because the other interactions or outputs of the other components (i.e., controller, database) of an AC system can violate the privacy.

As a result, a formal security model which covers relay attacks has not been designed for AC. In addition to this, a formal privacy model which considers whole AC system is missing. In the literature, a powerful solution for relay attacks is distance bounding (DB) [6]. It relies on the limited celerity of communication signals. DB is typically an authentication protocol with the condition that a user who authenticates is close enough to a reader. Privacy has also been extensively studied in DB [3,15,18,20,23,26,29,34].

By considering these critical issues, we design the first security and privacy model of an access control system which encompasses the propagation time of communication. Intuitively, in our definitions, we mix DB and access control based on a database of privileges. However, mixing both is not so straightforward when it comes to prove the security in a generic composition. Current AC protocols [2,14] do not consider malicious users in their security models while DB considers malicious users (e.g., as in Fig. 2). Therefore, the natural composition of them does not necessarily achieve the security level we need for AC protocols[1]. In addition, we can show that an AC protocol which is constructed based on a private DB protocol does not achieve privacy in AC. All these reasons obviously show the need for complete security and privacy models in AC.

Our Contribution:

- We first define **an integrated security model for AC** including identification, access control, and distance bounding by using the same components as defined in [1].
- We define **a new privacy model for AC** which includes the time of the communication. To the best of our knowledge, the time of the communication has not been considered for defining a privacy model before. Our new model covers all the previously defined privacy related definitions for access control such as identity hiding and untraceability.
- We give **a framework that clarifies how to use a secure DB** to construct a secure AC in our new security model. Basically, we show how to transform a man-in-the-middle (MiM), distance fraud (DF) and distance hijacking (DH) secure DB protocol into a secure AC scheme with proximity check. We also formally prove the security of this transformation.
- We show that the same framework can be used to achieve privacy in AC with restrictions on the database of AC system: The framework achieves privacy if the database is trivial meaning it is empty, or it includes all possible relations. We give a counterexample protocol that clearly shows why the framework does not work for non-trivial databases. This shows that **privacy in distance bounding is not always preserved when transformed into an access control system** which unfolds the need for a new model for AC.
- We construct a specific AC scheme by using a secure and private DB protocol Eff-pkDB [21] and prove its security and privacy with database.

2 Definitions from Previous Work

In this section, we give some definitions and results about public-key DB which we integrate into our new security and privacy model for AC. This section is helpful to understand the DB related notions that we use in the next section.

Definition 1 (Public key DB Protocol [31]). *A public key distance bounding protocol is a two-party probabilistic polynomial-time (PPT) protocol and it consists of a tuple $(\mathcal{K}_P, \mathcal{K}_V, V, P, B)$. Here, $(\mathcal{K}_P, \mathcal{K}_V)$ are the key generation algorithms of P and V, respectively. The output of $\mathcal{K}_P$ is a secret/public key pair*

---

[1] A malicious user can behave maliciously in an AC protocol and retrieve some information which may help him to attack the DB protocol which is composed with this AC protocol.

$(\mathsf{sk}_P, \mathsf{pk}_P)$ *and similarly the output of* $\mathcal{K}_V$ *is a secret/public key pair* $(\mathsf{sk}_V, \mathsf{pk}_V)$. *P is the proving algorithm,* V *is the verifying algorithm where the inputs of* P *and* V *are from* $\mathcal{K}_P$ *and* $\mathcal{K}_V$. *B is the distance bound.* $P(\mathsf{sk}_P, \mathsf{pk}_P, \mathsf{pk}_V)$ *and* $V(\mathsf{sk}_V, \mathsf{pk}_V)$ *interact with each other. At the end of the protocol,* $V(\mathsf{sk}_V, \mathsf{pk}_V)$ *outputs a final message* Out_V *and have* pk_P *as a private output. If* $\mathsf{Out}_V = 1$, *then* V *accepts. If* $\mathsf{Out}_V = 0$, *then* V *rejects.*

A public-key DB protocol is correct if and only if under honest execution, whenever the distance between V *and* P *is less than* B, *then* V *always outputs* $\mathsf{Out}_V = 1$ *and* pk_P.

In symmetric DB, we have one key generation algorithm $\mathcal{K}$ and the input of P and V is a secret key generated by $\mathcal{K}$.

Now, we explain the security games which are designed for the threats of DB: mafia fraud and distance hijacking from [31]. These games address security in concurrent settings. So, they consist of multi-party settings which informally means that the parties run multiple times their algorithms during the games. An **instance** of a party is each new execution of its algorithm.

In mafia fraud, a man-in-the-middle (MiM) adversary between a verifier and a far-away honest prover tries to make the verifier accept. Formally, it is defined as follows:

Definition 2 (Mafia fraud (MiM security)) [31]. *The game begins by running the key setup algorithms* $\mathcal{K}_V$ *and* $\mathcal{K}_P$ *which output* $(\mathsf{sk}_V, \mathsf{pk}_V)$ *and* $(\mathsf{sk}_P, \mathsf{pk}_P)$, *respectively. The adversary receives* pk_V *and* pk_P. *The game consists of several verifier instances including a distinguished one* $\mathcal{V}$, *honest prover's instances and adversary's instances. The adversary wins if* $\mathcal{V}$ *outputs* $\mathsf{Out}_V = 1$ *and* pk_P *when no close prover instance to* $\mathcal{V}$ *exists. A DB protocol is MiM-secure if, for any such game, the probability of an adversary to win is negligible.*

In a nutshell, the adversary interacts or sees multiple new executions of P and V at any location to make only one of the verifier instances $(\mathcal{V})$ accept when no instance of P is close.

In distance hijacking (DH), a far-away malicious prover uses some honest and active provers who are close to the verifier to make the verifier grant privileges to the far-away prover. The distance hijacking security implies also the **distance fraud (DF)** security which provides security against a malicious and far-away prover who wants to authenticate himself (without using any other close party).

Definition 3 (Distance hijacking [31]). *The game consists of several verifier instances including a distinguished one* $\mathcal{V}$, *instances of honest prover* P' *and instances of malicious prover* P. *The game begins by running the key setup algorithms* $\mathcal{K}_V, \mathcal{K}_P$ *and malicious setup* $\mathcal{K}_P^*(\mathsf{pk}_V, \mathsf{pk}_{P'})$ *of* P. *P lets one of the instance of* P' *run the time critical phase of DB with* $\mathcal{V}$. *The malicious prover* P *wins if* $\mathcal{V}$ *outputs* $\mathsf{Out}_V = 1$ *and* pk_P *when* P's *instance is far away from* $\mathcal{V}$. *A DB protocol is DH-secure if, for any such game, the probability of an adversary to win is negligible.*

The above definition is specific to a class of protocols which have a clearly identified time critical phase. Here, the time critical phase corresponds to a challenge/response exchange phase where the verifier calculates the round trip time of sending challenge and receiving response. Essentially, by letting an honest P' run this phase in the game, P tries to succeed to show himself close to the verifier. Again, we have many instances in this game.

The another security model in DB is for terrorist fraud (TF) [9]. Informally, TF adversary tries to authenticate himself while he is far-away from the verifier by getting help from his close accomplice. However, a trivial attack of TF-adversary could consist of giving his secret key to his accomplice who would execute DB with this key. So, usual definitions for TF [5,10,11,22] exclude this particular attack explicitly. We do not integrate TF-security in our AC security model because we think that this exclusion is arbitrary. In practice, we do not see why this attack would be excluded or how it would be prevented.

In the next definition, we give the privacy model by Hermans et al. [18] which has been used in many DB protocols [19,21,30,31]. In this model, the adversary tries to distinguish provers. It can corrupt provers and learn their secret keys. The model is also called strong private. The details are given below:

Definition 4 (Privacy in DB [18]**).** *The privacy game is the following: Pick $b \in \{0, 1\}$ and let the adversary $\mathcal{A}$ play with the following oracles:*

- **CreateP**(ID) $\rightarrow P_i$: *It creates a new prover identity of ID and returns its identifier P_i.*
- **Launch**() $\rightarrow \pi$: *It launches a new protocol with the verifier V_j and returns the session identifier π.*
- **Corrupt**(P_i) : *It returns the current state of P_i. Current state means the all the values in P_i's current memory. It does not include volatile memory (i.e., the short term state in an interactive session).*
- **DrawP**(P_i, P_j) $\rightarrow vtag$: *It draws either P_i (if $b = 0$) or draws P_j (if $b = 1$) and returns the virtual tag reference $vtag$. If one of the provers was already an input of DrawP $\rightarrow vtag'$ query and $vtag'$ has not been released, then it outputs $\emptyset$.*
- **Free**($vtag$) : *It releases $vtag$ which means $vtag$ can no longer be accessed.*
- **SendP**($vtag, m$) $\rightarrow m'$: *It sends the message m to the drawn prover and returns the response m' of the prover. If $vtag$ was not drawn or was released, nothing happens.*
- **SendV**(π, m) $\rightarrow m'$: *It sends the message m to the verifier in the session π and returns the response m' of the verifier. If π was not launched, nothing happens.*
- **Result**(π) $\rightarrow b'$: *It returns a bit that shows if the session π is accepted by the verifier (i.e. the message Out_V).*

In the end of the game, the adversary outputs a bit b''. If $b'' = b$, then $\mathcal{A}$ wins. Otherwise, it loses.

A DB protocol is strong private *if for all PPT adversaries, the advantage of winning the privacy game is negligible.*

3   Security and Privacy Model of AC

We first introduce the components of an access control system (ACS). In our definitions, for simplicity, we do not consider the user who may give PIN code or a biometric data to authenticate himself (this would be a parallel protocol). The components of an access control system are tag, reader, database and controller. Controller and database are in the secure area of ACS where it is not possible to tamper or access.

Tags (Access Cards): They hold personalized data which is used for identification and authentication. In ACS, each tag T generates a secret/public key pair $(\mathsf{sk}_T, \mathsf{pk}_T)$. They also store the public key of the controllers that are responsible for the doors[2] that T can access.

Reader: A reader is an interface between a tag and a door. We can consider them as transmitters. They communicate with the tags. Each reader R has a location loc_R which is important as the tag can be granted if the tag proves that it is close enough to the reader.

Database: It contains information about tags and their rights. It stores a list of $(\mathsf{pk}_T, loc_R, req)$ triplets meaning that the tag with pk_T is allowed to make the service request req on a reader at location loc_R. For instance, a service request can be the opening of a door. The database is in the secure area.

The database is not necessarily a list of triplets. It can also be a predicate deciding if a triplet belongs to it or not. A database is ***trivial*** if it is empty or if it contains all possible triplets.

For simplicity, we consider that the content of the database is static in what follows.

Controller: It controls access authentication. All controllers can be connected with multiple readers. Depending on the data they receive from its one of readers and the database, they give the final decision for the authorization.

More generally, the access control is relative to a service (such as opening a door) in a given location. The tag T of public key pk_T requests a service req to a reader at location loc_R and its corresponding controller checks if the privilege $(\mathsf{pk}_T, loc_R, req)$ exists in the database. T stores req and it can change req later on. All controllers stay in the secure area.

Definition 5 (Access Control (AC)). *AC consists of a distance bound B, a database $DataB$, a controller C, a reader R, and a tag T, the key generation algorithms:* Gen_C *generating* $(\mathsf{sk}_C, \mathsf{pk}_C)$ *for a controller C and* Gen_T *generating* $(\mathsf{sk}_T, \mathsf{pk}_T)$ *for a tag T. $C, R,$ and T run the algorithms* $\mathcal{C}(\mathsf{sk}_C, \mathsf{pk}_C, DataB, B), \mathcal{R}(loc_R)$ *and* $\mathcal{T}(\mathsf{sk}_T, \mathsf{pk}_T, \mathsf{pk}_C, req)$, *respectively. In the end of the protocol, C outputs either* $\mathsf{Out}_C = 1$ *and private output* $\mathsf{POut}_C = (\mathsf{pk}_T, loc_R, req)$ *if the authentication succeeds or* $\mathsf{Out}_C = 0$ *if it fails. R also publicly outputs* $\mathsf{Out}_R = \mathsf{Out}_C$.

---

[2] Door is a representation of the system or service that a user desires to access.

Definition 6 (Correctness of AC). *An AC is correct, if for all loc_R, req and for all sets of keys generated by Gen_C and Gen_T, if*

- *T requests service req to R at location loc_R,*
- *T is within a distance at most B from loc_R and*
- *$(\mathsf{pk}_T, loc_R, req)$ is in DataB,*

then

$$\Pr[\mathsf{Out}_C = 1 \wedge \mathsf{POut}_C = (\mathsf{pk}_T, loc_R, req)] = 1$$

3.1 Security

In this section, we give the formal security model for an access control system.

Adversarial and Communication Model: Each party (readers, controllers, tags, adversaries) has polynomially many instances. An instance of a party corresponds to a protocol execution with this party at a given location and time. Each instance of our model is as follows:

- All parties in AC are limited by the speed limit (speed of light) for communication, which simply says that a message sent at time t by a party X cannot arrive to a party Y at time t' which is less than $t + d(X, Y)$ (d is a metric which shows the time of flight distance between X and Y).
- Readers are all honest. They are connected to their corresponding controllers with a secure and an authenticated channel.
- Controllers are all honest. They are the only components of the ACS which can access the database.
- **Tags are all honest.** However, they can receive special signals [32]. There can be only one activatable instance of each tag at a time. The special signal $\mathsf{Activate}(T, req)$ activates the only activatable instance of T with a specified input req[3]. After receiving this signal, further activation signals are ignored by this instance. An instance can be terminated by one of the following signals: $\mathsf{Terminate}(T)$ and $\mathsf{Move}(T, loc')$. $\mathsf{Terminate}(T)$ terminates the instance execution, but it remains "active". The special signal $\mathsf{Move}(T, loc')$ orders to terminate and move the tag to loc'. It means that the instance becomes inactive and that only one unused instance of T at location loc' can be activated. The terminated instance sends a special signal Go which, when received by this unused instance at location loc', will make it activatable (Go signals cannot be sent by malicious participants; they are here only to enforce that a tag cannot move faster than a signal propagation). After, it may receive another $\mathsf{Activate}(T, req')$ as a new instance of the same tag at location loc'. **This models the tags being at a single location and moving (as influenced by the adversary) to run other instances.** Besides, it models that instances of the same tag cannot be run concurrently.

---

[3] This can also correspond to a user who is the owner of T to input whatever requests he wants into his tag.

- **Adversaries create the database.** So, they can generate fake relations $(\tilde{pk}_T, ., .)$ where $\tilde{pk}_T$ and its corresponding secret key $\tilde{sk}_T$ are generated by an adversary. Instances which could hold some $\tilde{sk}_T$ are called **fake tags**. In addition, adversaries can change the destination of messages (except for special signals) between a tag and a reader. We assume that they have very special hardware which can intercept a message and change its destination without any delay. Similarly, they can update a message and send it to the same destination with this hardware without any delay. So, if a party X sends a message at time t_1, and the adversary reads or updates the message at time t_2 and sends it to a party Y at time t_3, then the arrival of the message to Y is still bounded by $t_1 + d(X, Y)$ because $t_3 - t_2 \geq 0$.
  Except for the communication between readers and controllers, the adversary instances see all communication.

Definition 7 (AC-Security). *The game begins by setting up the components of the ACS. The security game is as follows given the security parameter n:*

- *Run $\mathsf{Gen}_C(1^n) \rightarrow (\mathsf{sk}_C, \mathsf{pk}_C)$ for the controller and run $\mathsf{Gen}_T \rightarrow (\mathsf{sk}_{T_i}, \mathsf{pk}_{T_i})$ for each tag T_i and give the public key pk_C and pk_{T_i}'s to the adversary.*
- *The adversary creates instances of T_i at chosen locations. Each instance can start after activation and run $\mathcal{T}(\mathsf{sk}_{T_i}, \mathsf{pk}_{T_i}, \mathsf{pk}_C, req)$ only once.*
- *The adversary creates instances of readers at chosen locations loc_{R_k}. They run $\mathcal{R}(loc_{R_k})$ once activated by an incoming message. They communicate with an instance of C over a secure channel[4]. There is a distinguished instance of a reader R. We denote by loc_R its location.*
- *The adversary sets $DataB$.*
- *The adversary creates instances of himself (fake tags). These instances run independently and communicate.*

All messages follow our communication model. The game ends when the distinguished instance R (and its corresponding instance C) outputs some value Out_R. An AC protocol is secure, if for any such game, the adversary wins with a negligible probability. $\mathcal{A}$ wins the game if $\mathsf{Out}_R = 1$ and $\mathsf{POut}_C = (\mathsf{pk}_T, loc_R, req)$ for some pk_T and req satisfying at least one of the following conditions:

1. *$(\mathsf{pk}_T, loc_R, req) \notin DataB$,*
2. *$\mathsf{pk}_T \in \{\mathsf{pk}_{T_i}\}_{i=1}^t$ and no active instance of the honest tag holding pk_T is close to loc_R during the execution of the AC protocol with C and R,*
3. *$\mathsf{pk}_T \notin \{\mathsf{pk}_{T_i}\}_{i=1}^t$ and no fake tag is close to loc_R during the execution with C and R.*

where t is the number of public keys generated by Gen_T in setup.

---

[4] For simplicity, we assume that the instance C of the controller is at the same location as R_k but the time of communication between R_k and C should have no influence on the result. The difference between C and R_k only makes sense for practical reasons.

Remarks:

- In the third condition, we need that no fake tag is close to loc_R to prevent the trivial attacks where a far away fake tag can give its secret key to a close by fake tag. Without this condition, the adversary would always win. This would however exclude all TF-attacks as well.
- If $\mathsf{pk}_T \notin \{\mathsf{pk}_{T_i}\}_{i=1}^t$, the security definition includes DH (and also DF).
- If $\mathsf{pk}_T \in \{\mathsf{pk}_{T_i}\}_{i=1}^t$, then the security definition corresponds to MF. It includes impersonation attacks, relay attacks and other forms of man-in-the-middle attacks as well since MF covers all of them.

In practice, the controllers are connected to multiple readers. So, it is not possible for them to check if a tag is close. Therefore, readers are the components that can give this decision.

Before proceeding the next part, we show that the natural composition of access control and distance bounding does not always achieve the security in Definition 7. Assume that we have a MiM, DF and DH secure symmetric DB protocol $DB = (\mathcal{K}, P, V, B)$. As an AC protocol, we have an AC protocol OPACITY [2][5]. In the natural composition, first the parties run OPACITY with a minor change and then DB (the reader runs V, the tag runs P with the secret key K). The change in OPACITY is as follows: the reader sends K at the end of the OPACITY protocol. Clearly, the modified version of OPACITY is still secure AC in the security model of Dagdelen et al. [7] since K is completely independent parameter. Unfortunately, this composition is not secure in Definition 7 since an adversary can win AC-game with satisfying the second condition. However, when we look the modified OPACITY and DB separately in their own security models, they are secure. Therefore, the generic composition of AC and DB is not straightforward.

3.2 Privacy

Privacy is also important in access control protocols. The definition of privacy we provide uses the same adversarial and communication model that we use for security. It also covers the identity hiding and untraceability with the corruption of tags. Informally, identity hiding means given an execution of protocol the adversary should not output the public key of the tag and untraceability means the adversary should not decide if two executions belong to the same tag or not.

Definition 8 (AC-Privacy). *The privacy game has the same setting as the game in Definition 7. We first decide to play the right r or the left ℓ game. Differently than the security model, each active tag instance can be paired with an another tag instance by an adversary. The pairing happens with the signal* $\mathsf{Draw}(T_i, T_j, k)$ *which pairs T_i and T_j by giving an index k, if the conditions below are satisfied:*

---

[5] OPACITY is basically a key agreement protocol where the authentication of a tag is done with this key.

- T_i *and* T_j *are at the same location,*
- T_i *and* T_j *have the same access privileges,*
- *neither* T_i *nor* T_j *is already paired and*
- *k is greater than the index of previous* Draw *signal to both* T_i *and* T_j.

A tag instance can be paired to itself as well. The adversary lets $vtag = (T_i, T_j, k)$ *be a virtual tag. All messages (and special signals) can only have a virtual tag as a destinator. If we are in game* ℓ, *then vtag simulates* T_i *and if we are in game* r, *vtag simulates* T_j. *The signal* Free(T_i, T_j, k) *breaks the pair if it exists. The adversary can corrupt a tag* T_i *(and actually all tags) by receiving* sk$_{T_i}$ *during the setup.*

In the end, the adversary decides if vtag simulates game r *or game* ℓ. *If the decision of the adversary is correct, then the adversary wins.*

If an AC protocol is private, the advantage of a polynomial time adversary in this game is bounded by a negligible probability.

The most important distinction of our definition is that we consider "communication time which leaks the proximity of a party" in our privacy definition contrarily previous work related to privacy [18, 29]. To the best of our knowledge, it has not been taken into account before for a privacy model. It is reasonable to consider the location of a user as a privacy leakage for the protocols where the communication time influences the output such as DB.

Since Mitrokotsa et al. [25] showed that location privacy is nearly impossible to achieve, we cannot prevent this leakage. So, our privacy game has the condition of being at the same location which is necessary to avoid the adversary to trivially distinguish the left or right game by checking the communication time.

Besides, the condition of having the same access privileges is necessary to prevent the adversary to determine the left or right game by seeing the accepting or the rejecting message by a controller.

4   Distance Bounding in Access Control

In this section, instead of designing a new AC protocol, we give a conceivable framework that converts a DB protocol into an AC protocol. We prove in Theorem 1 that, after conversion, the AC protocol achieves AC-security (in Definition 7) assuming that the DB protocol is MiM and DH secure. However, we show that we cannot always achieve AC-Privacy with this framework, even though the DB protocol is (strong) private according to Definition 4. Therefore, we prove in Theorem 2 that the AC protocol which is converted from a private DB achieves privacy, if $DataB$ is trivial. The details are in the following subsections.

4.1   Secure AC with Secure DB

If we have a public-key DB protocol $(\mathcal{K}_P, \mathcal{K}_V, P, V, B)$, we can construct an AC protocol with $(\mathsf{Gen}_C, \mathsf{Gen}_T, \mathcal{C}, \mathcal{T}, DataB, B)$ with the framework below:

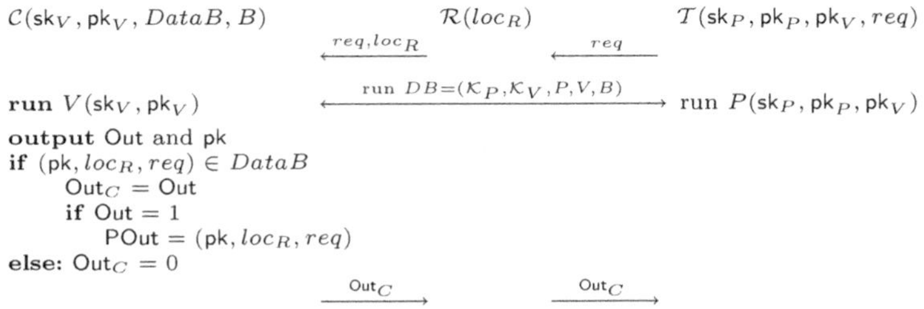

$\mathcal{C}(\mathsf{sk}_V, \mathsf{pk}_V, DataB, B)$ $\qquad\qquad$ $\mathcal{R}(loc_R)$ $\qquad\qquad$ $\mathcal{T}(\mathsf{sk}_P, \mathsf{pk}_P, \mathsf{pk}_V, req)$

$\qquad\qquad\qquad\qquad\xleftarrow{\quad req, loc_R \quad}\qquad\qquad\xleftarrow{\quad req \quad}$

$\qquad\qquad\qquad\qquad\xleftarrow{\quad \text{run } DB=(\mathcal{K}_P,\mathcal{K}_V,P,V,B) \quad}$

run $V(\mathsf{sk}_V, \mathsf{pk}_V)$ $\qquad\qquad\qquad\qquad\qquad\qquad\qquad$ run $P(\mathsf{sk}_P, \mathsf{pk}_P, \mathsf{pk}_V)$

output Out and pk

if $(\mathsf{pk}, loc_R, req) \in DataB$

$\qquad$ Out$_C$ = Out

$\qquad$ **if** Out = 1

$\qquad\qquad$ POut = $(\mathsf{pk}, loc_R, req)$

else: Out$_C$ = 0

$\qquad\qquad\qquad\qquad\xrightarrow{\quad \text{Out}_C \quad}\qquad\qquad\xrightarrow{\quad \text{Out}_C \quad}$

Fig. 3. The framework to convert a DB protocol to an AC protocol

- We match the key generation algorithms: $\mathsf{Gen}_C = \mathcal{K}_V$, $\mathsf{Gen}_T = \mathcal{K}_P$. So, $(\mathsf{sk}_C, \mathsf{pk}_C) = (\mathsf{sk}_V, \mathsf{pk}_V)$ and $(\mathsf{sk}_T, \mathsf{pk}_T) = (\mathsf{sk}_P, \mathsf{pk}_P)$.
- We create $DataB$ according to the access privileges of tags using the keys.
- $\mathcal{T}(\mathsf{sk}_P, \mathsf{pk}_P, \mathsf{pk}_V, req)$ uses $P(\mathsf{sk}_P, \mathsf{pk}_P, \mathsf{pk}_V)$ as a subroutine. $\mathcal{T}$ outputs req and then run $P(\mathsf{sk}_P, \mathsf{pk}_P, \mathsf{pk}_V)$.
- Whenever $\mathcal{R}(loc_R)$ is activated with req, it sends req and loc_R to $\mathcal{C}$.
- $\mathcal{C}(\mathsf{sk}_V, \mathsf{pk}_V, DataB, B)$ runs $V(\mathsf{sk}_V, \mathsf{pk}_V)$ as a subroutine jointly with $\mathcal{R}(loc_R)$. When V reaches the part where challenge/response is necessary to determine the distance to loc_R, $\mathcal{R}$ steps in to check if the responses arrive on time and are correct.

  Here, $\mathcal{C}$ may give all necessary input(s) to $\mathcal{R}$ so that $\mathcal{R}$ can check the responses. Alternatively, $\mathcal{C}$ may only give the challenges, and $\mathcal{R}$ only determines if the responses arrive on time. Then, if they arrive on time, $\mathcal{R}$ can send the responses to $\mathcal{C}$ so that $\mathcal{C}$ can check if the responses are correct. The only restriction is that **$\mathcal{R}$ has to decide if the responses arrive on time.**
- When $V(\mathsf{sk}_V, \mathsf{pk}_V)$ outputs Out and the private output pk_P: If $(\mathsf{pk}_P, loc_R, req) \in DataB$ and Out = 1, it publicly outputs Out$_C$ = 1 and privately outputs POut$_C$ = $(\mathsf{pk}_P, loc_R, req)$. Otherwise, it outputs Out$_C$ = 0. In both cases, $\mathcal{R}$ outputs Out$_R$ = Out$_C$. The framework is in Fig. 3.

An example protocol in Fig. 4 is constructed using this framework. Before, we prove that the framework achieves AC security if DB is MiM and DH secure.

Theorem 1. *Assuming that a DB protocol with $(\mathcal{K}_P, \mathcal{K}_V, P, V, B)$ is MiM-secure and DH-secure, then an AC protocol with using this DB protocol with the framework as described in Fig. 3 is secure according to Definition 7.*

Proof. Assume that there exists an adversary $\mathcal{A}$ which wins the game in Definition 7 where the output of the game is Out$_R$ = 1 and POut$_C$ = $(\mathsf{pk}_{T_i}, loc_R, req)$, then we can construct an adversary which wins MiM-game or DH-game.

Apparently, $\mathcal{A}$ can win the AC-game with either second or third condition because C outputs Out$_C$ = 0 if given $(\mathsf{pk}_{T_i}, loc_R, req) \notin DataB$ (the first winning condition) which makes impossible to win with the first condition.

Winning with the second condition: If $\mathsf{pk}_{T_i} \in \{\mathsf{pk}_{T_k}\}_{k=1}^{t}$ and no instance of the tag with pk_{T_i} is close to loc_R during the execution of the AC protocol with C and R, then we can construct an adversary $\mathcal{B}$ which wins MiM-game (Definition 2) of DB protocol with $(\mathcal{K}_P, \mathcal{K}_V, P, V)$.

$\mathcal{B}$ receives pk_V and pk_P from MiM-game. Then, it randomly picks $i \in \{1, ..., t\}$ where t is the number of (honest) tags needing to be simulated. The public key pk_{T_i} which will be used to simulate the ith tag T_i is pk_P. Here, T_i will have a role as a prover on MiM-game. For the rest of the tags, $\mathcal{B}$ generates $t-1$ secret/public key pairs $(\mathsf{sk}_{T_j}, \mathsf{pk}_{T_j})$ with using $\mathsf{Gen}_T(1^n)$ which are the secret/public keys of T_j's. After, it sends pk_V as the controller's public key and $\mathsf{pk}_{T_1}, ..., \mathsf{pk}_{T_{i-1}}, \mathbf{pk}_P, \mathsf{pk}_{T_{i+1}}, ..., \mathsf{pk}_{T_t}$ as the tags' public-keys in AC-game to $\mathcal{A}$. Remark that pk_V and pk_P are indistinguishable since they are generated with the same key generation algorithms of controllers and tags, respectively.

At some moment, $\mathcal{B}$ receives $DataB$ from $\mathcal{A}$. If $(\mathsf{pk}_P, ., .) \notin DataB$, then $\mathcal{B}$ loses MiM-game since in this case, there will be no chance that $\mathcal{A}$ wins the AC-game with this tag. Otherwise, it locates instances of T_i (which corresponds to P's instances in MiM-game) on the locations that $\mathcal{A}$ decides. $\mathcal{B}$ simulates the instances of AC-game as follows:

- Instances of T_j's where $T_j \neq T_i$: For the signals $\mathsf{Move}(T_j, loc)$ and $\underline{\mathsf{Terminate}(T_j)}$, $\mathcal{B}$ just simulates. When it receives the signal $\mathsf{Activate}(T_j, req)$, it simulates by running the algorithm $\mathcal{T}(\mathsf{sk}_{T_j}, \mathsf{pk}_{T_j}, \mathsf{pk}_V, req)$. Remark since $\mathcal{B}$ knows each sk_{T_j}, it can run $\mathcal{T}$.
- Instances of T_i: For the signals $\mathsf{Move}(T_i, loc)$ and $\mathsf{Terminate}(T_i)$, $\mathcal{B}$ moves the corresponding instance of P in the MiM-game to loc and halts the corresponding instance of P in the MiM-game, respectively. Whenever it receives the signal $\mathsf{Activate}(T_i, req)$, it first outputs req and then runs (activates) the corresponding instance of P in the MiM-game. Whatever the instance of P in MiM-game outputs, $\mathcal{B}$ outputs the same.
- Instances of controller and reader: Whenever $\mathcal{A}$ activates $\mathcal{R}$ (via sending req) so that $\mathcal{C}$, $\mathcal{B}$ runs an instance of V.

In the end, if $\mathcal{A}$ picks a reader instance R which sees $\mathsf{pk}_{T_j} = \mathsf{pk}_P$ as a distinguished one, $\mathcal{B}$ wins with the success probability below. Otherwise, $\mathcal{B}$ loses MiM-game since V has to output $\mathsf{Out}_V = 1$ and pk_P in MiM-game.

$$\Pr[\mathcal{B} \text{ wins}] \geq \Pr[\mathcal{A} \text{ wins} \wedge \text{Condition 2}] \times \frac{1}{t}$$

Winning with the third condition: If $\mathsf{pk}_T \notin \{\mathsf{pk}_{T_i}\}_{i=1}^{t}$ and no instance of the adversary is close to loc_R during the execution with R, then we can construct an adversary $\mathcal{B}'$ which wins DH-game. The reduction is very similar to the previous one except we replace P with an honest prover P'.

$$\Pr[\mathcal{B}' \text{ wins}] \geq \Pr[\mathcal{A} \text{ wins} \wedge \text{Condition 3}] \times \frac{1}{t}$$

In the end, we have

$$\Pr[\mathcal{B} \text{ wins}] + \Pr[\mathcal{B}' \text{ wins}] \geq \Pr[\mathcal{A} \text{ wins}] \times \frac{1}{t}.$$

Since we know that the success probability of $\mathcal{B}$ in MiM and $\mathcal{B}'$ in DH game is negligible, then the success probability of $\mathcal{A}$ is negligible as well.   □

Now, we give an example AC protocol (Eff-AC) in our framework by converting the public-key DB protocol Eff-pkDB [21] which is one of the most efficient public-key distance bounding protocols.

Eff-AC: We use Eff-pkDB with its variant. Its variant uses a key agreement protocol Nonce-DH [21] (based on random oracle and Gap Diffie Hellman (GDH) [27]) to agree on a secret S and a symmetric-key DB OTDB [31] to run with S. We stress that this is only an example of the generic construction of Eff-pkDB. In particular, we could replace NonceDH by another key agreement protocol which is D-AKA secure [21] and possibly eliminate the random oracle assumption.

The public parameters for the key generation algorithms Gen_C ($\mathcal{K}_V$) and Gen_T ($\mathcal{K}_P$) are a group G of prime order q and its generator g. Gen_C and Gen_T pick sk_C and sk_T from $\mathbb{Z}_q$, and set $\mathsf{pk}_C = g^{sk_C}$ and $\mathsf{pk}_T = g^{sk_T}$, respectively. Eff-AC works as follows:

The tag has the input $\mathsf{sk}_T, \mathsf{pk}_T, \mathsf{pk}_C, req$, the controller $\mathcal{C}$ has the input $\mathsf{sk}_C, \mathsf{pk}_C, B, DataB$ and the reader $\mathcal{R}$ has the input loc_R. $\mathcal{T}$ sends req to R and R sends it along with loc_R to C . Then, C, R and $\mathcal{T}$ run Eff-pkDB. Here, $\mathcal{T}$ runs the proving algorithm of Eff-pkDB, and $\mathcal{C}$ and $\mathcal{R}$ run the verifying algorithm of Eff-pkDB, jointly. The details of these algorithms are as follows: First, $\mathcal{T}$ picks a random value N from $\{0,1\}^n$ and sends N and pk_T. After $\mathcal{C}$ receives them, it computes $S = H(g, \mathsf{pk}_T, \mathsf{pk}_C, \mathsf{pk}_T^{sk_C}, N)$. Meanwhile, $\mathcal{T}$ also computes $S = H(g, \mathsf{pk}_T, \mathsf{pk}_C, \mathsf{pk}_C^{sk_T}, N)$. After, $\mathcal{C}$ gives S and B to R so that $\mathcal{R}$ runs the challenge phase. Until this part corresponds to the Nonce-DH protocol. Then, OTDB [31] is run by $\mathcal{R}$ and $\mathcal{T}$ as follows:

$\mathcal{R}$ picks a value $N_R \in \{0,1\}^{2n}$ and sends it to $\mathcal{T}$. Then, $\mathcal{R}$ and $\mathcal{T}$ compute $X = N_R \oplus S$ before n-round challenge phase begins. In each round i, $\mathcal{R}$ picks a challenge Q_i and starts the timer. In response, $\mathcal{T}$ sends W_i which is the $2i + Q_i^{th}$ bit of X. When $\mathcal{R}$ receives it, it stops the timer. After the challenge phase, if all responses are correct and arrive on time (i.e. with in less than $2B$), then $\mathcal{R}$ sets $\mathsf{Out} = 1$. Then, $\mathcal{R}$ sends Out to $\mathcal{C}$. This is the end of of Eff-pkDB.

$\mathcal{C}$ sets $\mathsf{Out}_C = \mathsf{Out}$. If $\mathsf{Out} = 1$, $\mathcal{C}$ checks if $\mathcal{C}$ has the access privilege by checking if $(\mathsf{pk}_T, loc_R, req) \in DataB$. If it is in $DataB$, it privately outputs $\mathsf{POut}_C = (\mathsf{pk}_T, loc_R, req)$. Otherwise, it sets $\mathsf{Out}_C = 0$. Finally, C sends Out_C to $\mathcal{R}$ and $\mathcal{R}$ outputs it as Out_R.

Since Eff-pkDB is MiM and DH-secure [21], **Eff-AC which uses Eff-pkDB with the framework in Fig. 3 is AC-secure thanks to Theorem 1.**

Remark: The security proof of Eff-pkDB [21] is also valid for a variant where the verifier generates an ephemeral $(\mathsf{sk}_C, \mathsf{pk}_C)$ pair and sends pk_C to the prover.

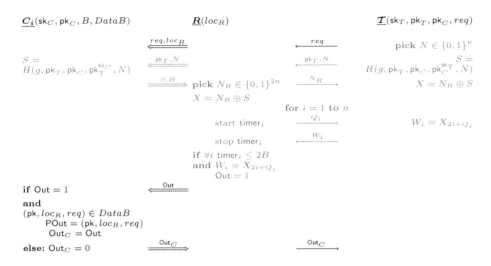

Fig. 4. Eff-AC. Double arrow shows that the communication is secure and authenticated while sending the message above it. The gray colored parts are Eff-pkDB.

So, tags do not even need to store pk_C in this variant of Eff-pkDB. Therefore, a variant of Eff-AC with an ephemeral key is secure thanks to Theorem 1. This variant is very desirable for practical reasons because we can allow many controllers and the tag does not need to store all the corresponding keys.

4.2 Private AC with Private DB

The difficulty in proving privacy in an AC protocol which uses a private DB protocol comes from the fact that $DataB$ must discriminate tags. This fact may leak information about identities. In DB, the output of V does not depend on pk_P. Hence, the private output of the verifier (pk_P) plays no role in the privacy game of Definition 4. We show here a generic privacy preservation result with our framework, but only for a trivial $DataB$. Trivial $DataB$ makes $POut_C$ play no role in AC. We cannot prove the same result for an arbitrary database. Remember, a database is *trivial* if it is empty or if it contains all possible triplets.

Theorem 2. *Assuming that DB protocol with $(\mathcal{K}_P, \mathcal{K}_V, P, V, B)$ is private according to Definition 4, then an AC protocol with using this DB protocol with the framework as described in Fig. 3 is private* **when DataB is trivial** *based on Definition 8.*

Proof. Assuming that there exists an adversary $\mathcal{A}$ breaking the privacy in AC with a trivial $DataB$, then we can construct an adversary $\mathcal{B}$ that breaks the privacy of DB.

$\mathcal{B}$ simulates the communication model of AC for $\mathcal{A}$, except the subroutines P and V for honest participants. For each message and signal that $\mathcal{B}$ receives for tags, it works as follows:

- *Receiving a signal* Draw(T_i, T_j, k): It checks the necessary conditions to be paired. If they are satisfied, it calls the Draw oracle in the privacy game of DB with the inputs T_i, T_j. In respond, the Draw oracle sends *vtag*. $\mathcal{B}$ stores the information that *vtag* corresponds to (T_i, T_j, k).
- *Receiving a signal* Free(T_i, T_j, k): It retrieves the corresponding *vtag* to (T_i, T_j, k). If it exists, it calls the oracle Free with the input *vtag* in the privacy game of DB.
- *Receiving a signal* Activate *or* Move: It simulates them.
- *Receiving a message m:* It retrieves *vtag* and calls the oracle SendP in the privacy game of DB with the input $(vtag, m)$. Then, it receives a respond m' from the SendP oracle and sends m' to $\mathcal{A}$.

To simulate a reader receiving m, $\mathcal{B}$ behaves as follows:

- If it is the first time and $m = req$, $\mathcal{B}$ calls the Launch oracle to get a session identifier π. Then, it calls SendV with π and receives an empty message m'.
- Otherwise, it calls the oracle SendV with the input (π, m) and receives m'.

If m' is not the final message, it sends m' to $\mathcal{A}$. Otherwise, $m' = \text{Out}_V$. In this case, $\mathcal{B}$ assigns $b = 0$ if $DataB$ is empty and $b = 1$ if it is not empty (meaning that it has all possible relations). In the end, it sends $\text{Out}_C = \text{Out}_V \wedge b$ to $\mathcal{A}$. The simulation is perfect. So, $\mathcal{A}$ and $\mathcal{B}$ have the same advantage. $\qquad\square$

Why only for trivial DataB: We can show that Theorem 2 does not work for all $DataB$ with the following counterexample.

Assume that we have a private DB $(\mathcal{K}_P, \mathcal{K}_V, P, V, B)$. From DB, we can construct another private protocol DB' $(\mathcal{K}_P, \mathcal{K}_V, P', V', B)$ where P' and V' work as defined below:

$P'(\mathsf{sk}_P, \mathsf{pk}_P, \mathsf{pk}_V):$ $V'(\mathsf{sk}_V, \mathsf{pk}_V)$

receive *flag*   **send** 0
if *flag* $= 1$ **and** pk_P is odd   **run** $V(\mathsf{sk}_V, \mathsf{pk}_V)$
  $\mathcal{K}_P \rightarrow (\mathsf{sk}'_P, \mathsf{pk}'_P)$
  $(\mathsf{sk}_P, \mathsf{pk}_P) \leftarrow (\mathsf{sk}'_P, \mathsf{pk}'_P)$
run $P(\mathsf{sk}_P, \mathsf{pk}_P, \mathsf{pk}_C)$

Clearly, DB' is still private because the only change is to remove the identity of the prover by replacing the secret and public keys with some random keys. (We recall that pk_P as a private output of V plays no role in Definition 4.)

Now, let's consider the conversion of DB' to an AC protocol with the framework. The adversary can break the privacy of the AC protocol as follows: He first picks two tags T_1 and T_2 which have public keys with different parities and moves them at the same location. It also creates a $DataB = \{(\mathsf{pk}_{T_1}, loc_R, req), (\mathsf{pk}_{T_2}, loc_R, req)\}$. Then, it pairs (T_1, T_2) with the signal Draw$(T_1, T_2, 0)$ and activates the pair. It sends a message $flag = 1$ to $vtag = (T_1, T_2, 0)$ (by replacing the message $flag = 0$ which comes from a reader R). Then, it lets C, R and $vtag$ execute the protocol. In the end, R outputs Out_R. Depending on the parity, the adversary can find out the left or right game with probability 1 (e.g., if pk_{T_1} is odd and $\mathsf{Out}_R = 1$, it means right game (T_2) is simulated).

In addition, even by weakening Definition 8 such that the adversary does not create a database and it is not allowed to pair tags (instead, the game does), we achieve **no** privacy. In this case, the advantage of the adversary with this attack would be $\frac{1}{2}$: If the paired parities' public keys have the same parity, then the attack does not give any more advantage than the privacy game of DB' gives. If they have different parity, the adversary wins with probability 1.

Even though we cannot use our framework to achieve privacy with **all** private DB protocols, we can still have private AC using our framework with **some** DB protocols where one of them is Eff-pkDB^p [21]. Now, we describe Eff-AC^p which is converted from Eff-pkDB^p.

Eff-AC^p (See Fig. 5): It is very similar to Eff-AC. Differently here, the secret/public key pair of C consists of two parts: $(\mathsf{sk}_C, \mathsf{pk}_C) = ((\mathsf{sk}_{C_1}, \mathsf{sk}_{C_2}), (\mathsf{pk}_{C_1}, \mathsf{pk}_{C_2}))$ where $(sk_{C_1}, \mathsf{pk}_{C_1})$ is used for the encryption and $(\mathsf{sk}_{C_2}, \mathsf{pk}_{C_2})$ is used for Nonce-DH (key agreement protocol). The only change on T is that it sends the encryption of (pk_T, N) and on C is that it retrieves pk_T, N by decrypting the encryption with sk_{C_1}. The rest is the same with Eff-AC.

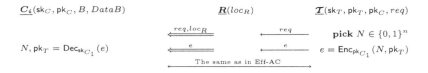

Fig. 5. Eff-AC^p

Theorem 3. *Eff-AC^p is a private access protocol in the random oracle model according to Definition 8, assuming that the cryptosystem is IND-CCA secure and Gap Diffie-Hellman (GDH) problem [27] is hard.*

Note that the same result applies to the generic construction of Eff-pkDB^p [21], i.e., not only the one based on GDH and the random oracle. We could indeed replace Nonce-DH by another key agreement protocol which is D-AKA^p secure [21].

Proof (sketch): We adapt the proof from the privacy proof of Eff-pkDB^p [21].

We define games Γ_i^b below and the success probability of an adversary is p_i^b.

Γ_0^b : It is the same game that we defined in Definition 8 where $b = \ell$ meaning we are in the left-game or $b = r$ meaning we are in the right-game.

Γ_1^b : We reduce Γ_0^b to Γ_1^b where we simulate the controller instances without decrypting the ciphertext that is sent by a *vtag*. Because of the correctness of the cryptosystem, $p_1^b = p_0^b$.

Γ_2^b : We reduce Γ_1^b to Γ_2^b where $vtag$ is simulated by encrypting a random value instead of (pk_T, N). We can easily show $p_2^b - p_1^b$ is negligible by using the IND-CCA security of the cryptosystem.

We reduce Γ_2^ℓ to Γ_2^r where we replace all secret/public keys $(\mathsf{sk}_\ell, \mathsf{pk}_\ell)$ which are the keys of the tag in the left-side in $vtag$ by replacing secret/public keys $(\mathsf{sk}_r, \mathsf{pk}_r)$ of its paired tag. Using D-AKA^p security of Nonce-DH (Theorem 7 in [21]), we can show that $p_2^\ell - p_2^r$ is negligible.

Remark that if pk_ℓ and pk_r are kept in a plaintext and used by the controller, the replacing pk_ℓ with pk_r make the same Out_C result due to our assumption which says the paired tags have the same access privileges.

So, $p_0^\ell - p_0^r$ is negligible. $\hfill\square$

5 Conclusion

In this paper, we designed a security model for AC which considers the whole interaction between components. The security model integrates the model of DB since the distance of the tag is important to detect the relay attacks. In our model, we preserve the security against adversaries which can be a tag or not. We also let the adversaries construct the database. We constructed a privacy model for AC which includes time of communication as well.

We gave a simple framework which securely transforms a DB to an AC. We proved a similar result for privacy assuming that $DataB$ is trivial. We showed why the theorem does not work for other types of database. Finally, we constructed two AC protocols Eff-AC and Eff-AC^p which are adapted from existing public-key distance bounding protocols Eff-pkDB and Eff-pkDB^p [21], respectively. We proved their security and privacy in our security and privacy models.

References

1. Alliance, S.C.: Using smart cards for secure physical access. Smart Card Alliance Report, 54 (2003)
2. Alliance, S.C.: Industry technical contributions: OPACITY (2013)
3. Avoine, G., Dysli, E., Oechslin, P.: Reducing time complexity in RFID systems. In: Preneel, B., Tavares, S. (eds.) SAC 2005. LNCS, vol. 3897, pp. 291–306. Springer, Heidelberg (2006). doi:10.1007/11693383_20
4. Bellare, M., Rogaway, P.: Entity authentication and key distribution. In: Stinson, D.R. (ed.) CRYPTO 1993. LNCS, vol. 773, pp. 232–249. Springer, Heidelberg (1994). doi:10.1007/3-540-48329-2_21
5. Boureanu, I., Vaudenay, S.: Optimal proximity proofs. In: Lin, D., Yung, M., Zhou, J. (eds.) Inscrypt 2014. LNCS, vol. 8957, pp. 170–190. Springer, Cham (2015). doi:10.1007/978-3-319-16745-9_10
6. Brands, S., Chaum, D.: Distance-bounding protocols. In: Helleseth, T. (ed.) EUROCRYPT 1993. LNCS, vol. 765, pp. 344–359. Springer, Heidelberg (1994). doi:10.1007/3-540-48285-7_30

7. Dagdelen, Ö., Fischlin, M., Gagliardoni, T., Marson, G.A., Mittelbach, A., Onete, C.: A cryptographic analysis of OPACITY. In: Crampton, J., Jajodia, S., Mayes, K. (eds.) ESORICS 2013. LNCS, vol. 8134, pp. 345–362. Springer, Heidelberg (2013). doi:10.1007/978-3-642-40203-6_20

8. Degabriele, J.P., Fehr, V., Fischlin, M., Gagliardoni, T., Günther, F., Marson, G.A., Mittelbach, A., Paterson, K.G.: Unpicking PLAID. In: Chen, L., Mitchell, C. (eds.) SSR 2014. LNCS, vol. 8893, pp. 1–25. Springer, Cham (2014). doi:10.1007/978-3-319-14054-4_1

9. Desmedt, Y.: Major security problems with the "unforgeable" (Feige-) Fiat-Shamir proofs of identity and how to overcome them. In: Congress on Computer and Communication Security and Protection Securicom, pp. 147–159. SEDEP, Paris (1988)

10. Dürholz, U., Fischlin, M., Kasper, M., Onete, C.: A formal approach to distance-bounding RFID protocols. In: Lai, X., Zhou, J., Li, H. (eds.) ISC 2011. LNCS, vol. 7001, pp. 47–62. Springer, Heidelberg (2011). doi:10.1007/978-3-642-24861-0_4

11. Fischlin, M., Onete, C.: Terrorism in distance bounding: modeling terrorist-fraud resistance. In: Jacobson, M., Locasto, M., Mohassel, P., Safavi-Naini, R. (eds.) ACNS 2013. LNCS, vol. 7954, pp. 414–431. Springer, Heidelberg (2013). doi:10.1007/978-3-642-38980-1_26

12. Francillon, A., Danev, B., Capkun, S.: Relay attacks on passive keyless entry and start systems in modern cars. In: NDSS (2011)

13. Francis, L., Hancke, G., Mayes, K., Markantonakis, K.: Practical NFC peer-to-peer relay attack using mobile phones. In: Ors Yalcin, S.B. (ed.) RFIDSec 2010. LNCS, vol. 6370, pp. 35–49. Springer, Heidelberg (2010). doi:10.1007/978-3-642-16822-2_4

14. C.A. Government's Department of Human Services (DHS). Protocol for lightweight authentication of identity (PLAID) (2010)

15. Ha, J.H., Moon, S.J., Zhou, J., Ha, J.C.: A new formal proof model for RFID location privacy. In: Jajodia, S., Lopez, J. (eds.) ESORICS 2008. LNCS, vol. 5283, pp. 267–281. Springer, Heidelberg (2008). doi:10.1007/978-3-540-88313-5_18

16. Hancke, G.P.: A practical relay attack on ISO 14443 proximity cards. Technical report, University of Cambridge Computer Laboratory, vol. 59, pp. 382–385 (2005)

17. Hancke, G.P.: Practical attacks on proximity identification systems. In: 2006 IEEE Symposium on Security and Privacy, pp. 328–333. IEEE (2006)

18. Hermans, J., Pashalidis, A., Vercauteren, F., Preneel, B.: A new RFID privacy model. In: Atluri, V., Diaz, C. (eds.) ESORICS 2011. LNCS, vol. 6879, pp. 568–587. Springer, Heidelberg (2011). doi:10.1007/978-3-642-23822-2_31

19. Hermans, J., Peeters, R., Onete, C.: Efficient, secure, private distance bounding without key updates. In: WiSec, Proceedings of the Sixth ACM Conference on Security and Privacy in Wireless and Mobile Networks, pp. 207–218 (2013)

20. Juels, A., Weis, S.A.: Defining strong privacy for RFID. ACM Trans. Inf. Syst. Secur. (TISSEC) 13(1), 7 (2009)

21. Kılınç, H., Vaudenay, S.: Efficient public-key distance bounding protocol. In: Cheon, J.H., Takagi, T. (eds.) ASIACRYPT 2016. LNCS, vol. 10032, pp. 873–901. Springer, Heidelberg (2016). doi:10.1007/978-3-662-53890-6_29

22. Kim, C.H., Avoine, G., Koeune, F., Standaert, F.-X., Pereira, O.: The swiss-knife RFID distance bounding protocol. In: Lee, P.J., Cheon, J.H. (eds.) ICISC 2008. LNCS, vol. 5461, pp. 98–115. Springer, Heidelberg (2009). doi:10.1007/978-3-642-00730-9_7

23. Li, Y., Deng, R.H., Lai, J., Ma, C.: On two RFID privacy notions and their relations. ACM Trans. Inf. Syst. Secur. (TISSEC) 14(4), 30 (2011)

24. Markantonakis, K.: Practical relay attack on contactless transactions by using NFC mobile phones. Radio Freq. Identif. Syst. Secur. RFIDsec **12**, 21 (2012)
25. Mitrokotsa, A., Onete, C., Vaudenay, S.: Location leakage in distance bounding: why location privacy does not work. Comput. Secur. **45**, 199–209 (2014)
26. Ng, C.Y., Susilo, W., Mu, Y., Safavi-Naini, R.: RFID privacy models revisited. In: Jajodia, S., Lopez, J. (eds.) ESORICS 2008. LNCS, vol. 5283, pp. 251–266. Springer, Heidelberg (2008). doi:10.1007/978-3-540-88313-5_17
27. Okamoto, T., Pointcheval, D.: The gap-problems: a new class of problems for the security of cryptographic schemes. In: Kim, K. (ed.) PKC 2001. LNCS, vol. 1992, pp. 104–118. Springer, Heidelberg (2001). doi:10.1007/3-540-44586-2_8
28. Roland, M., Langer, J., Scharinger, J.: Applying relay attacks to Google Wallet. In: 2013 5th International Workshop on Near Field Communication (NFC), pp. 1–6. IEEE (2013)
29. Vaudenay, S.: On privacy models for RFID. In: Kurosawa, K. (ed.) ASIACRYPT 2007. LNCS, vol. 4833, pp. 68–87. Springer, Heidelberg (2007). doi:10.1007/978-3-540-76900-2_5
30. Vaudenay, S.: On privacy for RFID. In: Au, M.-H., Miyaji, A. (eds.) ProvSec 2015. LNCS, vol. 9451, pp. 3–20. Springer, Cham (2015). doi:10.1007/978-3-319-26059-4_1
31. Vaudenay, S.: Private and secure public-key distance bounding. In: Böhme, R., Okamoto, T. (eds.) FC 2015. LNCS, vol. 8975, pp. 207–216. Springer, Heidelberg (2015). doi:10.1007/978-3-662-47854-7_12
32. Vaudenay, S.: Sound proof of proximity of knowledge. In: Au, M.-H., Miyaji, A. (eds.) ProvSec 2015. LNCS, vol. 9451, pp. 105–126. Springer, Cham (2015). doi:10.1007/978-3-319-26059-4_6
33. Wognsen, E.R., Karlsen, H.S., Calverley, M., Follin, M.N., Thomsen, B., Huttel, H.: A secure relay protocol for door access control. In: Proceedings of the Xii Brazilian Symposium on Information and Computer System Security. SBC-Sociedade Brasileira de Computação (2012)
34. Yang, A., Zhuang, Y., Wong, D.S., Yang, G.: A new unpredictability-based RFID privacy model. In: Lopez, J., Huang, X., Sandhu, R. (eds.) NSS 2013. LNCS, vol. 7873, pp. 479–492. Springer, Heidelberg (2013). doi:10.1007/978-3-642-38631-2_35

Improving Gait Cryptosystem Security Using Gray Code Quantization and Linear Discriminant Analysis

Lam Tran[1,3(✉)], Thang Hoang[2], Thuc Nguyen[3], and Deokjai Choi[1(✉)]

[1] ECE, Chonnam National University, Gwangju, South Korea
dchoi@jnu.ac.kr
[2] EECS, Oregon State University, Corvallis, OR, USA
hoangmin@oregonstate.edu
[3] FIT, Ho Chi Minh University Of Science, Ho Chi Minh, Vietnam
{thlam,ndthuc}@fit.hcmus.edu.vn

Abstract. Gait has been considered as an efficient biometric trait for user authentication. Although there are some studies that address the task of securing gait templates/models in gait-based authentication systems, they do not take into account the low discriminability and high variation of gait data which significantly affects the security and practicality of the proposed systems. In this paper, we focus on addressing the aforementioned deficiencies in inertial-sensor based gait cryptosystem. Specifically, we leverage Linear Discrimination Analysis to enhance the discrimination of gait templates, and Gray code quantization to extract high discriminative and stable binary template. The experimental results on 38 different users showed that our proposed method significantly improve the performance and security of the gait cryptosystem. In particular, we achieved the False Acceptant Rate of $6 \times 10^{-5}\%$ (i.e., 1 fail in 16983 trials) and False Rejection Rate of 9.2% with 148-bit security.

Keywords: Gait authentication · Biometric cryptosystem · Biometric template protection · Fuzzy commitment scheme

1 Introduction

Gait has been considered as an efficient modality for recognizing individual via human motion [2]. The growth of microelectromechanical technology has opened a new approach for implementing gait authentication systems (e.g., [3,7,8,11–13, 25,31,33,34,36]), in which the gait signals are collected by inertial-sensors. This technique permits implicit user authentication and therefore, offers significant usability advantages compared with password or other biometric systems [13] which require the user to perform explicit gesture to be authenticated. Several inertial-sensors based gait authentication schemes have been proposed in the literature (e.g., [3,7,13,25,31,33]). Despite their merits, all these studies rely on traditional pattern recognition approaches, where the extracted gait templates

© Springer International Publishing AG 2017
P.Q. Nguyen and J. Zhou (Eds.): ISC 2017, LNCS 10599, pp. 214–229, 2017.
https://doi.org/10.1007/978-3-319-69659-1_12

or models are stored locally without confidentiality protection, which might pose security and privacy issues to the user once such raw data are compromised by the attacker (e.g., via malware) [19].

To address the privacy concern of biometric data, several studies leveraging Biometric Cryptosystem (BCS) [28] have been proposed [11,14,15,21,23,27]. One of the most common techniques that has been recently used to protect biometrics templates is Fuzzy Commitment Scheme (FCS) [18], where a binary string is extracted from the biometric templates and then, binded with a crypto-graphic key encoded by Error Correcting Code (ECC) [22] before being written to the storage (e.g., [11,14,15,27]). Despite the fact that such schemes offer an elegant strategy to protect the privacy of biometric templates, they did not take into account the characteristic of behavioral biometric modalities such as gait, which is well-known to be low discriminative and highly unstable. As described in [20], these issues can significantly degrade the security and performance of the FCS-based system (e.g., key length, False Acceptant Rate (FAR), False Rejection Rate (FRR)), where a low discriminative extracted binary string might result in a high FAR while an unstable one can lead to high FRR and low security. Thus, it is vital to develop a method that can extract high discriminative and stable strings from the gait templates to improve the security and performance of gait cryptosystem.

In this paper, we propose methods to address the aforementioned deficiencies to improve the security and performance of inertial-sensor based gait cryptosystem as follows:

- First, we handle the problem of low discriminability and high variation of gait data by adopting Linear Discriminant Analysis (LDA) [32]. As the traditional LDA is incompatible with FCS (see Sect. 3.3), we propose a modification of LDA to *(i)* improve the discriminability of gait data from different users, *(ii)* reduce the variation of gait data from the same user, *(iii)* maintain the high feature dimension of gait data to extract a long enough binary string to be used in FCS (Sect. 3.3).
- Second, we propose Gray code [9] quantization scheme, which can offer strong capability of error toleration, to quantize the gait templates after LDA pro-jection to binary template (Sect. 3.4).
- Third, we design a method that can determine the reliability of each compo-nents in the extracted binary template (Sect. 3.5). Highly reliable components will be selected to form the final binary string input for FCS.
- Last, we conduct a comprehensive experiment to analyze the efficiency of the proposed techniques and perform security analysis in details to evaluate the security of our system against different attacks. We achieved $6 \times 10^{-5}\%$ FAR (i.e., 1 fail in 16983 trials), 9.2% FRR at 148-bit security. This experimental result indicated that the proposed methods significantly improve not only the security but also the performance of the gait cryptosystem compared with other state-of-the-art works (Sect. 4).

2   Preliminaries

2.1   Notations

Given a matrix $\mathbf{M}$, $\mathbf{M}[i,j]$ denotes accessing the cell indexing at row i and column j. $|\mathbf{M}|$ denotes the determinant of matrix $\mathbf{M}$. Given two matrices $\mathbf{A}$ and $\mathbf{B}$ having the same number of rows, $\mathbf{C} = [\mathbf{A}\ \mathbf{B}]$ denotes that matrix $\mathbf{C}$ is formed by concatenating $\mathbf{A}$ and $\mathbf{B}$ horizontally. $\mathbf{C} = \begin{bmatrix} \mathbf{A} \\ \mathbf{B} \end{bmatrix}$ means $\mathbf{C}$ is formed by vertically concatenating two matrices $\mathbf{A}$ and $\mathbf{B}$ having the same number of columns. Given an $m \times n$ matrix $\mathbf{M}$, we denote the mean vector of $\mathbf{M}$ as $\overline{\mathbf{m}} = (\overline{m}_1, \ldots, \overline{m}_j, \ldots, \overline{m}_n)$ where $\overline{m}_j = \frac{1}{m} \sum_{i=1}^{m} \mathbf{M}[i,j]$. Given an n-dimensional vector $\mathbf{x} = (x_1, \ldots, x_j, \ldots, x_n)$, we denote the mean of $\mathbf{x}$ as $\bar{x} = \frac{1}{n} \sum_{j=1}^{n} x_j$. $\lceil \cdot \rceil$ is the ceiling operator. $|x|$ means the absolute value of variable x. We denote $\oplus$ as the bitwise XOR operator and $||$ as binary string concatenation operator. $\alpha \gg t$ means logical right shifting α by t bits. $H : \{0,1\}^* \rightarrow \{0,1\}^n$ is a secure cryptographic hash function, where n is the length of hash value.

2.2   The Fuzzy Commitment Scheme

Fuzzy Commitment Scheme (FCS) is a generic BCS framework proposed by Juels and Wattenberg [18], which leverages Error Correcting Code (ECC) [22] to handle the variation of biometric data. The key idea of FCS is to express an n-bit witness ω (i.e., biometric template) in term of a codeword $c \in \mathcal{C}$ of length n and an offset $\delta \in \{0,1\}^n$ such that $\omega = c \oplus \delta$ where $\mathcal{C}$ is an error correcting codebook. FCS operates in two phases as sketched in Fig. 1.

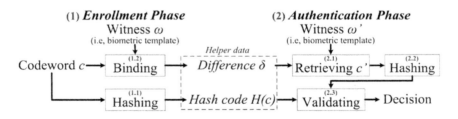

Fig. 1. The Fuzzy Commitment Scheme [18].

1. **Enrollment phase**: A codeword $c \in \mathcal{C}$ is selected randomly and its hash value $H(c)$ is calculated (step 1.1). Meanwhile, c is sealed to δ by the biometric template ω (step 1.2). The hash value $H(c)$ and δ are stored as helper data for authentication while c and ω are discarded.
2. **Authentication phase**: Given a biometric template ω', the estimated codeword c' is retrieved using the helper data δ (step 2.1). Then, its hash value $H(c')$ is calculated (step 2.2). Finally, $H(c')$ is matched with $H(c)$ to give the final verification decision (step 2.3).

As discussed in [18], each codeword c in $\mathcal{C}$ has two parts as information part of length k $(k < n)$ and redundancy part of length $(n - k)$. The ratio between the amount of two parts in c is a trade-off between security strength and the resilience. The system is more secure when the information part is extended. In contrast, the system provides higher capability of resilience when the redundancy part is lengthened.

2.3   Fisher's Linear Discriminant Analysis

Linear Discriminant Analysis (LDA) is a data dimensional reduction technique that reserves as much as possible the discrimination information between different classes. Assuming that a training dataset $\mathbf{X}$ includes D classes L_i, each having N_i templates. LDA finds $\mathbf{W}$ to transform $\mathbf{X}$ to $\mathbf{Y}$ as $\mathbf{Y} = \mathbf{W}^T\mathbf{X}$ so that the intra-class variation is minimized and inter-class discrimination is maximized in $\mathbf{Y}$.

Let $\bar{\mathbf{x}}$ be the mean vector of $\mathbf{X}$ and $\bar{\mathbf{x}}_i$ be the mean vector of templates of class L_i. The within-class scatter matrix $\mathbf{S}_w$ and between-class scatter matrix $\mathbf{S}_b$ are calculated by:

$$\mathbf{S}_w = \sum_{i=1}^{D}\sum_{j=1}^{N_i}(\mathbf{x}_{ij} - \bar{\mathbf{x}}_i)(\mathbf{x}_{ij} - \bar{\mathbf{x}}_i)^\top, \tag{1}$$

$$\mathbf{S}_b = \sum_{i=1}^{D} N_i(\bar{\mathbf{x}}_i - \bar{\mathbf{x}})(\bar{\mathbf{x}}_i - \bar{\mathbf{x}})^\top, \tag{2}$$

where $\mathbf{x}_{ij}$ is the template j of class L_i. The projection matrix $\mathbf{W}$ is the result of the maximization problem using the Fisher's criterion [6] as:

$$J\left(\mathbf{W}\right) = \frac{|\mathbf{W}^\top\mathbf{S}_b\mathbf{W}|}{|\mathbf{W}^\top\mathbf{S}_w\mathbf{W}|}. \tag{3}$$

The optimization task of (3) is equivalent to the following generalized eigenvalue problem described in [32] as: $\mathbf{S}_b\mathbf{w}_i = \lambda_i\mathbf{S}_w\mathbf{w}_i$, where $\mathbf{w}_i$ and λ_i $(1 \leq i \leq D - 1)$ respectively are the eigenvector and eigenvalue of $\mathbf{S}_w^{-1}\mathbf{S}_b$. When $\mathbf{S}_w$ is nonsingular, the optimal $\mathbf{W}$ is the one whose columns are the eigenvectors corresponding to at most $(D - 1)$ largest eigenvalues of $\mathbf{S}_w^{-1}\mathbf{S}_b$.

3   The Proposed Gait Cryptosystem

In this section, we first present the general architecture of our proposed inertial-sensor-based gait authentication cryptosystem. We introduce overall steps of data (pre)processing to extract gait templates collected from the inertial sensor data. Finally, we present the main techniques which adopt LDA and Gray code quantization along with a reliability extraction method to enhance the security and performance of the gait cryptosystem.

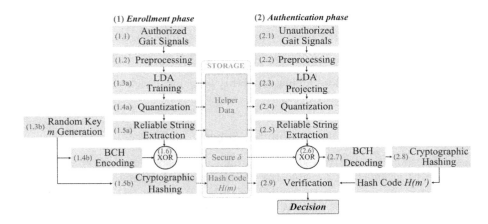

Fig. 2. The architecture of the inertial-sensor based gait cryptosystem.

3.1 Overall of System Architecture

We present in Fig. 2 the specification of our proposed inertial-sensor based gait authentication system which follows the Fuzzy Commitment Scheme as follows.

1. **Enrollment**: First, we collect the training gait data (step 1.1) from inertial sensor, and perform data (pre)processing to extract gait templates (step 1.2). We then apply LDA training (step 1.3a) to the extracted gait templates, followed by a Gray code-based quantization (step 1.4a) and reliable string extraction (step 1.5a) to obtain a discriminative and stable binary string. Concurrently, we generate a key m randomly (step 1.3b) and then encode it into a BCH codeword (step 1.4b). Meanwhile, we calculate the hash value of m (denoted as $H(m)$) (step 1.5b). Finally, we bind the binary string with the codeword to get the secure δ (step 1.6). We store the hash value $H(m)$ and δ along with some auxiliary data in steps 1.3a–1.5a as helper data for using in authentication phase.
2. **Authentication**: Given gait data to be verified, we extract a stable binary string by using the stored helper data (steps 2.1–2.5). We retrieve an estimated BCH codeword by binding the new extracted binary string with the stored secure δ (step 2.6). We then decode the estimated codeword to get the secret key m' (step 2.7), and calculate its hash code $H(m')$ (step 2.8). Finally, we match $H(m')$ with $H(m)$ to verify the authenticating user (step 2.9).

Notice that our general framework is inspired and extended from [11]. In this paper, we mainly focus on improving the security and performance of the gait cryptosystem, wherein we introduce two additional steps including LDA and Gray code quantization to enhance the discriminability of gait data. Hence, we present in following sections how to implement such vital steps in details, and refer the readers to [11] for detailed presentations of other (pre)processing steps.

3.2   Data Preprocessing and Feature Extraction

We leverage the methods proposed in [12] for gait data preprocessing. Specifically, we address the disorientation problem using the data additionally collected from orientation sensor, and mitigate the noise in gait signals by adopting the Daubechies orthogonal wavelet with level 2. We represent each sampling of gait signals as $\mathbf{a} = (a_X, a_Y, a_Z)$, where a_X, a_Y, a_Z are acceleration values captured in X, Y, Z dimensions, respectively. Subsequently, we divide the gait data into consecutive of gait-cycle-based segments where each gait cycle is defined as a time period between two times of ground contacting of a same foot while walking. Hence, each gait cycle $\mathbf{C}_i$ contains t acceleration samples as $\mathbf{C}_i = [\mathbf{a}_{i1} \ldots \mathbf{a}_{ij} \ldots \mathbf{a}_{it}]$. We then form the gait pattern by concatenating 4 consecutive gait cycles in a way that two consecutive gait patterns overlap with each other by 2 gait cycles as $\mathbf{P}_i = [\mathbf{C}_{2i-1} \ldots \mathbf{C}_{2(i+1)}]$. For each $\mathbf{P}_i$, we extract features in both time and frequency domain as described in [12] to form a gait template $\mathbf{x}_i = (x_{i1}, \ldots, x_{ij}, \ldots, x_{iM}) \in \mathbb{R}^M$, where x_{ij} denotes the feature j extracted from pattern $\mathbf{P}_i$, and M is the total number of features being extracted.

3.3   Improving the Discriminability of Gait Data

We observe that gait is more noisy and less discriminative than other biometric traits. Hence, instead of directly using the gait templates for further processing, we adopt LDA to enhance the inter-class discriminability and reduce the intra-class variation.

LDA Training: In the enrollment phase, we form a data matrix $\mathbf{G}$ including N gait templates $\mathbf{x}_i$ of the genuine user as $\mathbf{G} = \begin{bmatrix} \mathbf{x}_1 \ldots \mathbf{x}_i \ldots \mathbf{x}_N \end{bmatrix}^\top \in \mathbb{R}^{N \times M}$, and the data matrix $\mathbf{I}$ including N' gait templates $\mathbf{x}_i'$ of all other users $\mathbf{I} = \begin{bmatrix} \mathbf{x}_1' \ldots \mathbf{x}_i' \ldots \mathbf{x}_{N'}' \end{bmatrix}^\top \in \mathbb{R}^{N' \times M}$. We form the dataset $\mathbf{M} = \begin{bmatrix} \mathbf{G} \\ \mathbf{I} \end{bmatrix} \in \mathbb{R}^{(N+N') \times M}$. We label the templates in $\mathbf{M}$ with two classes including genuine and impostor. We use $\mathbf{M}$ as the data for LDA training to find the projection matrix for transforming gait templates.

However, the traditional LDA has a dimensional limitation as described in [32] which makes it incompatible to the gait cryptosystem. Specifically, with D as the number of classes, there are $(D-1)$ eigenvectors $\mathbf{w}_i$ of $\mathbf{S}_w^{-1}\mathbf{S}_b$ that have the corresponding eigenvalues λ_i satisfying $\lambda_i > 0$, where $\mathbf{S}_w$ and $\mathbf{S}_b$ are calculated by (1) and (2), respectively. Then, LDA will form a projection matrix $\mathbf{W}$ by using at most $(D-1)$ eigenvectors. Thus, the data dimension after LDA projection will be at most $(D-1)$. In current system, with $D = 2$, the dimension of data after LDA projection is 1 which is insufficient for extracting to a reliable string because the it is required to have the same length with BCH codeword for binding (Fig. 2, step 1.6). Therefore, we modify the process of LDA as follows.

First, instead of using $\mathbf{M}$ for LDA training, we separate $\mathbf{M}$ into S submatrices $\mathbf{M}_i$ $(1 \leq i \leq S)$, each having K columns, and apply LDA to each $\mathbf{M}_i$ independently to get a projection matrix $\mathbf{W}_i$. Specifically, we calculate the within-class scatter matrix $\mathbf{S}_w^{(i)}$ and between-class scatter matrix $\mathbf{S}_b^{(i)}$ of each dataset $\mathbf{M}_i$. Then, we factorize the matrix $(\mathbf{S}_w^{(i)})^{-1}\mathbf{S}_b^{(i)}$ to a set of K eigenvectors $\mathbf{w}_l^{(i)}$ and corresponding eigenvalues $\lambda_l^{(i)}$ $(1 \leq l \leq K)$. Second, instead of using at most $(D-1)$ eigenvectors $\mathbf{w}_l^{(i)}$ corresponding to $(D-1)$ largest eigenvalues $\lambda_l^{(i)}$ to form $\mathbf{W}_i$ as described in Sect. 2.3, we use all eigenvectors $\mathbf{w}_l^{(i)}$ as

$$\mathbf{W}_i = [\mathbf{w}_1^{(i)} \ldots \mathbf{w}_l^{(i)} \ldots \mathbf{w}_K^{(i)}]. \tag{4}$$

$\mathbf{W}_i$ is used to transform gait data in sub-space i in both enrollment and authentication phase. We store all projection matrices $\mathbf{W}_i$ as helper data.

LDA Projection: Given S projection matrices $\mathbf{W}_i$, we determine the LDA projection $\mathbf{G}'$ of $\mathbf{G}$ by *(i)* determining $\mathbf{G}_i \in \mathbb{R}^{N \times K}$ for each sub-space $1 \leq i \leq S$; *(ii)* calculating the projection of $\mathbf{G}_i$ as $\mathbf{G}'_i = \mathbf{W}_i^\top \mathbf{G}_i$ for each $\mathbf{G}_i$; *(iii)* forming $\mathbf{G}'$ as:

$$\mathbf{G}' = [\mathbf{G}'_1 \ldots \mathbf{G}'_i \ldots \mathbf{G}'_S] \in \mathbb{R}^{N \times M}. \tag{5}$$

We also transform matrix $\mathbf{I}$ to $\mathbf{I}'$ using $\mathbf{W}_i$ similar to transforming $\mathbf{G}$ as above. Then, we use $\mathbf{G}'$ and $\mathbf{I}'$ for quantization and reliable binay string extraction as will be described in the following sections.

3.4   Gray Code Quantization

In order to reduce the natural variation of gait data, we use N templates in matrix $\mathbf{G}'$ (5) for quantization to construct a binary gait template. We determine $\bar{\mathbf{g}}' \in \mathbb{R}^M$ as the mean vector of matrix $\mathbf{G}'$ and use $\bar{\mathbf{g}}'$ to generate a binary gait template as follows.

First, we normalize each component $\bar{g}'_j$ in $\bar{\mathbf{g}}'$ such that $\bar{g}'_j \in [0,1]$, for $1 \leq j \leq M$. Note that all the min, max values (represented as min, max vectors) extracted in the normalization process will be stored as the helper data. Let Ψ be a system parameter that specifies the number of bits representing one real-valued component in quantization. Then, we divide the range value $[0,1]$ to 2^Ψ continuous subranges which are called as quanta. Hence, the range of each quantum is $\phi = \frac{1}{2^\Psi}$. Consequently, we map each quantum to a unique Ψ-bit string. The normalized value of $\bar{g}'_j$ may variate in two continuous quanta at different times of sampling. So the mapping between the set of quanta and set of Ψ-bit strings should be well-arranged so that any two binary strings corresponding to two continuous quanta differ to each other in one bit. Gray code [9] is a good candidate for this requirement as it is a technique for designing a binary numeral system in which two successive strings have only one different bit. Given a normalized value of $\bar{g}'_j$, the quantum index i_j is defined such that $i_j\phi < \bar{g}'_j \leq (i_j + 1)\phi$. Then we calculate the corresponding Ψ-bit string ω_j following Gray code system as [5]:

$$\omega_j = B(\Psi, i_j) \oplus (B(\Psi, i_j) \gg 1), \tag{6}$$

where $B(\Psi, i_j)$ is the representation of i_j in Ψ-bit string.

Finally, from all ω_j, we form the binary gait template ω which is the quantized template of $\bar{\mathbf{g}}'$ as:

$$\omega = (\omega_1, \dots, \omega_j, \dots, \omega_M). \tag{7}$$

3.5 Reliable Binary String Extraction

In this section, we propose a method to extract highly reliable components in the binary gait template. By reliability, we mean the one having low variation in enrolled users' templates and high discriminability between templates of enrolled user and other users.

Given a binary gait template ω, we select R reliable components ω_j to form the reliable string $\omega \in \{0, 1\}^n$ which will be used to bind with codeword c. The value of R is determined based on two other predefined parameters including the codeword length n and the number of Gray code quantization bits Ψ as $R = \lceil \frac{n}{\Psi} \rceil$.

We use $\mathbf{I}'$ and $\mathbf{G}'$ in (5) for estimating the reliability of each component. We propose a formula to calculate the reliability φ_j of each component ω_j of as:

$$\varphi_j = \frac{1}{2} \left(1 + \mathsf{erf} \left(\frac{\frac{1}{N'} \sum_{i=1}^{N'} \left| \mathbf{I}'[i,j] - \bar{g}'_j \right|}{\sqrt{2\sigma_j^2}} \right) \right), \tag{8}$$

where erf denotes the Gaussian Error Function [1], $\bar{g}'_j$ is the component j of mean vector $\bar{\mathbf{g}}'$ in Sect. 3.4, and the variance σ_j^2 of component j is calculated as:

$$\sigma_j^2 = \frac{1}{N-1} \sum_{i=1}^{N} \left(\mathbf{G}'[i,j] - \bar{g}'_j \right)^2. \tag{9}$$

In (8), the numerator of expression inside the erf function measures the discriminability of component j between enrolled user and other users. The denominator measures the variation of component j of enrolled user. Let $\mathbf{p} = (p_1, \dots, p_j, \dots, p_M) \in \mathbb{N}^M$ be the vector containing the index of components that follows the descending order of reliability, $\varphi_{p_j} \geq \varphi_{p_{j+1}}$. We use first R components of $\mathbf{p}$ to extract the reliable components in ω to form the final reliable string ω as:

$$\omega = \omega_{p_1} || \omega_{p_2} || \dots || \omega_{p_R}. \tag{10}$$

Note that we store the first R components in $\mathbf{p}$ as helper data to extract reliable components in the authentication phase.

4 Experiments

4.1 Configurations and Results

We used the dataset in [12] for the experimental analysis of the proposed system. The dataset contains gait signals of 38 users. We extracted the gait signals to

10224 gait templates using the process in Sect. 3.2. For the empirical analysis, we built an authentication models for each user. In each model, we considered one user as the genuine and the others are impostors. In the enrollment phase for each user, we formed the matrix $\mathbf{G}$ containing $N = 100$ gait templates of the genuine user and $\mathbf{I}$ containing $N' = 100 \cdot 37 = 3700$ templates of the impostors; and the remaining data is used in authentication phase to verify the built model (12 templates for each time of attempting). In the LDA training step, we divided the original data space into $S = 15$ sub-spaces as explained in Sect. 3.3. We selected BCH codeword lengths of 255 and 511 bits. We analyzed the system with different values of quantization bit Ψ and key length k to understand the impact of such parameters. We used False Acceptant Error Rate (FAR) and False Rejection Error Rate (FRR) as the standard metrics to evaluate the performance of our proposed system. Finally, we analyzed the security of our system against various attacks.

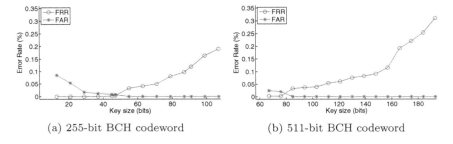

(a) 255-bit BCH codeword   (b) 511-bit BCH codeword

Fig. 3. The FRR and FAR at different key length of codeword 255, 511 and 4-bit Gray code quantization.

With 4-bit Gray code quantization, we have the optimal result. Figure 3 displays the FAR and FRR with different key lengths and BCH codewords. At 255-bit codeword and 87-bit key, the system achieves 0% FAR and 9.8% FRR. With the 511-bit codeword and 148-bit key, the FRR is 9.2% and FAR is $6 \times 10^{-5}\%$ (i.e., 1 fail in 16983 trials). Under different attacks, the security of the system is 87 and 148 bits according to 255-bit and 511-bit codeword, respectively (analyzed in Sect. 4.4).

4.2   The Impact of LDA Projection

We used Normalized Euclidean distance [35] to analyze the impact of LDA projection on the discriminability of gait template. Figure 4a displays the Normalized Euclidean distance distribution of gait template before LDA projecting. We can see that the overlapping area of the intra-class and inter-class is substantial which reflects the naturally low discrimination of gait data. After applying the modified LDA, the overlapping area reduces significantly as shown in Fig. 4b. This contrast illustrates the effectiveness of the modified LDA presented

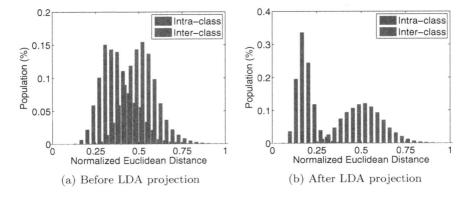

(a) Before LDA projection   (b) After LDA projection

Fig. 4. The normalized Euclidean distance distribution of gait templates before and after LDA projection.

in Sect. 3.3. The LDA projection step plays an important role since it enhances the data discriminability, and therefore, significantly improves the system performance.

4.3 The Impact of Gray Code Quantization

We used the Normalized Hamming distance [35] to analyze the impact of Gray code quantization. As gait signals are unstable, a specific component of gait template can have different values at each time of sampling. However, if these values still belong to the same quantum, the system will result in the same binary string. The use of Gray code quantization can minimize the error bits when these values fall into different quanta. So, adopting Gray code provides higher capability of error tolerance to enhance the performance.

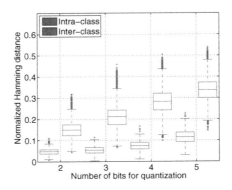

Fig. 5. The Hamming distance distribution when using different values of Ψ for Gray code quantization.

The number of quantization bits Ψ is a trade-off between the FAR and FRR values of the system. The quantum range ϕ decreases as Ψ increases and vice versa. Given that Ψ is small, (thus ϕ is large), it is likely that the same binary string can be extracted from two different gait templates. As a result, the inter-class and intra-class Hamming distance are decreased as illustrated in Fig. 5. This results in the increase of the FAR, and the decrease of the FRR. Figure 6 displays the comparison of Hamming distance distribution between the cases of using 4-bit natural binary code and 4-bit Gray Code quantization. When using Gray code (Figs. 6c and d), the intra-class Hamming distance is much smaller compared with using natural binary code (Figs. 6a and b). Table 1 gives a comparison of 3-bit and 4-bit Gray code quantizations in terms of FRR, FAR at the same codeword length and key length. We can see that when $\Psi = 3$, the FRR is lower while FAR is higher than that of $\Psi = 4$, respectively.

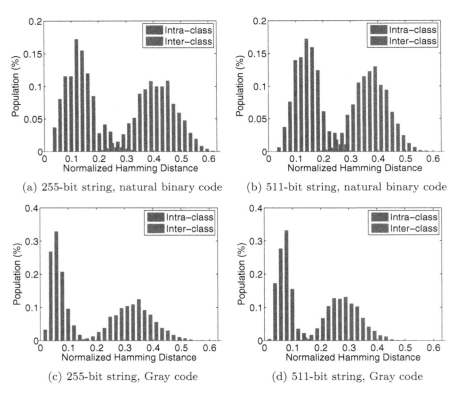

(a) 255-bit string, natural binary code   (b) 511-bit string, natural binary code

(c) 255-bit string, Gray code   (d) 511-bit string, Gray code

Fig. 6. The Hamming distance distribution of 255-, 511-bit reliable strings when using natural binary code and Gray code with 4-bit quantization.

Table 1. The system performance pertaining to codeword length n, key length k and number of quantization bits Ψ

$\Psi = 3$				$\Psi = 4$			
n (bits)	k (bits)	FAR (%)	FRR (%)	n (bits)	k (bits)	FAR (%)	FRR (%)
255	79	0.4	1.9	255	79	6×10^{-5}	8.1
	87	0.3	2.3		87	0	9.8
	91	0.3	2.8		91	0	12.0
511	139	0.65	0.93	511	139	11×10^{-5}	8.3
	148	0.56	1.17		148	6×10^{-5}	9.2
	157	0.38	1.4		157	6×10^{-5}	11.5

4.4 Security Analysis

In this section, we analyze the system security against several statistical attacks. The typical attack is brute force the random key. As the proposed key lengths are 87 and 148 bits for 255-bit and 511-bit codewords, the security strength against key brute force attack are 87 and 148 bits, respectively.

We analyze whether an attacker can exploit information from the helper data including projection matrices $\mathbf{W}_i$, the min, max vectors for normalization, the reliable components index $\mathbf{p}$, secured δ and hash code $H(m)$. The min, max vectors contain statistical information from the whole dataset, and therefore, is not user-specific. Thus, the min, max vectors do not reveal information about genuine user. The reliable component index vector $\mathbf{p}$ only contains the information about the discriminability and stability of gait templates. Such indexes does not reveal information about biometric template, thus it cannot be used to revert to biometric template. With the hash code $H(m)$, the attacker cannot revert to m with a non-negligible probability, given that the cryptographic hash function H is secure.

LDA projection matrices are not user-specific since they only reflect the information about the dataset population. Additionally, the projection matrix is formed by eigenvectors λ of $S_w^{-1}S_b$. From λ, we cannot revert to $S_w^{-1}S_b$ without knowing the corresponding eigenvalues, which are immediately discarded after the LDA training phase. Thus, from the stored eigenvectors, we cannot revert to $S_w^{-1}S_b$ and obtain original biometric templates of the enrolled user.

Using the secure δ, in order to get the key m, the attacker can guess a string ω' that is close enough to ω hidden in δ. The distance strictly depends on the error correcting capability of BCH code and the uncertainty of ω which depends on the quantization method. We use entropy to measure the uncertainty of ω. We calculate the entropy of each bit in ω by the formula in [29] as:

$$H(\omega_i) = -p_i \log_2(p_i) + (1 - p_i) \log_2(1 - p_i), \tag{11}$$

where $p_i = \Pr(\omega_i = 1)$ is the probability of bit i getting value 1 due to quantization. The entropy E of reliable string ω is calculated by summarizing entropy of all components as $E = \sum_{i=1}^{n} H(\omega_i)$. According to the Gray code quantization, the probability of a bit i receiving value 1 is $p_i = 0.5$. Then, the system achieves the entropy E of 250 and 500 for codeword 255 and 511, respectively. The strength of system security against this attack is measured by Sphere-packing bound according to [10] as:

$$C_{SB} \geq \frac{2^E}{\sum_{i=0}^{t} \binom{E}{i}} \simeq \frac{2^E}{\binom{E}{t}}, \tag{12}$$

where t is the error correcting capability. For two proposed key lengths of 255-bit and 511-bit codewords, the error correcting capability t is 26 and 53 bits as in [22], respectively, so the system achieves C_{SB} as 2^{133} and 2^{269}.

Further more, we analyzed the system under statistical attack that is performed based on the distribution of inter-class Hamming distance of extracted reliable string. Specifically, the adversary can extract the reliable string ω' from his own gait signal. Then, with the inter-class Hamming distance as h, he knows that he can guess the string ω of enrolled user by searching for all ω satisfying $d_{H(\omega',\omega)} = h$. Additionally, by utilizing the error correcting capability of BCH code as t, he only needs to search for all ω such that $d_{H(\omega',\omega)} = h - t$ in order to retrieve key m from secure δ. Let $d = h - t$, then the cost of this attack is

$$C_{ST(h)} = \binom{n}{d} = \frac{n!}{d!(n-d)!}. \tag{13}$$

We assume that h follows the Gaussian distribution. We estimate the mean μ_h and variance σ_h of h in Fig. 6. Then, we analyze $C_{ST(h)}$ with h at $(\mu_h - 2\sigma_h)$ and $(\mu_h + 2\sigma_h)$ using (13). With 4-bit quantization, the security strength are 108 and 235 bits corresponding to codeword 255 and 511 bits, respectively.

In summary, as the attack on error correcting capability and Hamming distance are more costly than doing brute force on key, the system security is 87 and 148 bits according to 255-bit and 511-bit codewords, respectively.

5   Related Work

Biometric Cryptosystems (BCS) are techniques for securing biometric templates, and also provide approaches to integrate biometrics and existing security solutions (i.e., symmetric cryptography, password-based authentication) by releasing biometric-dependent key [28]. BCS techniques are classified into two main approaches, namely key binding and key generation. In the key binding approach, biometric templates are used to hide/retrieve a pre-specified secret key which can be selected by the user or randomly generated. Fuzzy Commitment [18] and Fuzzy Vault [17] are cryptographic primitives that offer key binding function. On the other hand, the key generation approach directly generates secret key from biometric templates. The cryptographic primitive supporting this approach is Fuzzy Extractor - Secure Sketch [4].

As the concerns of security and privacy have increased tremendously recently, the BCS techniques were widely applied to various biometric traits such as face [21], iris [27], fingerprint [14,23], speech [15], gait [11] and achieved promising results. Most of studies followed the key binding scheme [11,14,15,27]. For example, the authors in [27] proposed an Adaptive FCS to secure the iris-code and achieved 0% FAR and FRR of 4.92% with 128 bits security. Having to note that, as the great variation of biometric templates in nature, the task of directly generating stable and high-entropy secret key from biometric template is challenging [16,24]. Several studies on key generation on biometric samples have been proposed [21,30].

A number of studies also proposed methods to protect gait templates (e.g., [11,26,34]). In [11], the authors applied FCS to secure inertial sensors based gait signals. In [26], the authors proposed a two-factor authentication scheme named Gait-hashing. They used hash code generated from camera-based gait data and random vectors stored in token for authenticating user, and achieved EER of 10.8%. The authors in study [34] proposed Key-gait which was a scheme for generating shared secret key between two legitimate devices using gait signal captured from wearable sensors, and can generate 128-bit key with 98.3% probability.

6   Conclusion

In this paper, we addressed the problems of inter-class's low discrimination and intra-class's high variance of nature gait data, which have not been received much attention in the privacy-preserving gait authentication community. We proposed a method that applied LDA to increase the discrimination of gait data, and adopted the Gray code quantization to extract a highly stable binary template. Finally, we proposed a strategy to extract a reliable binary string from the stable binary template, which is used as an efficient input for FCS. The achieved results showed that our proposed system enhances not only the security but also the performance of the system, compared with other state-of-the-art works.

Acknowledgments. This research was supported by Korea NRF-2017R1D1A 1B03035343 project.

References

1. Andrews, L.: Special functions of mathematics for engineers (1992)
2. Cutting, J.E., Kozlowski, L.T., et al.: Recognizing friends by their walk: gait perception without familiarity cues. Bull. Psychon. Soc. **9**(5), 353–356 (1977)
3. Derawi, M., Bours, P.: Gait and activity recognition using commercial phones. Comput. Secur. **39**, 137–144 (2013)
4. Dodis, Y., Reyzin, L., Smith, A.: Fuzzy extractors: how to generate strong keys from biometrics and other noisy data. In: Cachin, C., Camenisch, J.L. (eds.) EUROCRYPT 2004. LNCS, vol. 3027, pp. 523–540. Springer, Heidelberg (2004). doi:10.1007/978-3-540-24676-3_31

5. Doran, R.W.: The gray code. J. UCS **13**(11), 1573–1597 (2007)
6. Fisher, R.A.: The use of multiple measures in taxonomic problems. Ann. Eugenics **7**, 179–188 (1936)
7. Frank, J., Mannor, S., Pineau, J., Precup, D.: Time series analysis using geometric template matching. IEEE Trans. Pattern Anal. Mach. Intell. **35**(3), 740–754 (2013)
8. Gadaleta, M., Rossi, M.: Idnet: Smartphone-based gait recognition with convolutional neural networks. arXiv preprint arXiv:1606.03238 (2016)
9. Gray, F.: Pulse code communication, 17 March 1953. US Patent 2,632,058
10. Hao, F., Anderson, R., Daugman, J.: Combining crypto with biometrics effectively. IEEE Trans. Comput. **55**(9), 1081–1088 (2006)
11. Hoang, T., Choi, D., Nguyen, T.: Gait authentication on mobile phone using biometric cryptosystem and fuzzy commitment scheme. Int. J. Inf. Secur. **14**(6), 549–560 (2015)
12. Hoang, T., Choi, D., Nguyen, T.: On the instability of sensor orientation in gait verification on mobile phone. In: 2015 12th International Joint Conference on e-Business and Telecommunications (ICETE), vol. 4, pp. 148–159. IEEE (2015)
13. Hoang, T., Vo, V., Nguyen, T., Choi, D.: Gait identification using accelerometer on mobile phone. In: 2012 International Conference on Control, Automation and Information Sciences (ICCAIS), pp. 344–348. IEEE (2012)
14. Imamverdiyev, Y., Teoh, A.B.J., Kim, J.: Biometric cryptosystem based on discretized fingerprint texture descriptors. Expert Syst. Appl. **40**(5), 1888–1901 (2013)
15. Inthavisas, K., Lopresti, D.: Speech biometric mapping for key binding cryptosystem. In: Biometric Technology for Human Identification VIII (SPIE Defense, Security, and Sensing), Orlando, FL, p. 80291P–1 (2011)
16. Jain, A.K., Nandakumar, K., Nagar, A.: Biometric template security. EURASIP J. Adv. Sig. Process. **2008**, 113 (2008)
17. Juels, A., Sudan, M.: A fuzzy vault scheme. Des. Codes Crypt. **38**(2), 237–257 (2006)
18. Juels, A., Wattenberg, M.: A fuzzy commitment scheme. In: Proceedings of the 6th ACM conference on Computer and communications security, pp. 28–36. ACM (1999)
19. Kaur, H., Khanna, P.: Biometric template protection using cancelable biometrics and visual cryptography techniques. Multimedia Tools Appl. **75**(23), 16333–16361 (2016)
20. Kelkboom, E.J., Breebaart, J., Buhan, I., Veldhuis, R.N.: Maximum key size and classification performance of fuzzy commitment for gaussian modeled biometric sources. IEEE Trans. Inf. Forensics Secur. **7**(4), 1225–1241 (2012)
21. Lim, M.-H., Teoh, A.B.J., Toh, K.-A.: An efficient dynamic reliability-dependent bit allocation for biometric discretization. Pattern Recogn. J. **45**(5), 1960–1971 (2012)
22. Morelos-Zaragoza, R.H.: The art of error correcting coding. Wiley, New York (2006)
23. Morse, M., Hartloff, J., Effland, T., Schuler, J., Cordaro, J., Tulyakov, S., Rudra, A., Govindaraju, V.: Secure fingerprint matching with generic local structures. In: Proceedings of the IEEE Conference on Computer Vision and Pattern Recognition Workshops, pp. 84–89 (2014)
24. Natgunanathan, I., Mehmood, A., Xiang, Y., Beliakov, G., Yearwood, J.: Protection of privacy in biometric data. IEEE Access **4**, 880–892 (2016)
25. Nickel, C., Busch, C.: Classifying accelerometer data via hidden markov models to authenticate people by the way they walk. IEEE Aerosp. Electron. Syst. Mag. **28**(10), 29–35 (2013)

26. Ntantogian, C., Malliaros, S., Xenakis, C.: Gaithashing: a two-factor authentication scheme based on gait features. Comput. Secur. J. **52**, 17–32 (2015)
27. Rathgeb, C., Uhl, A.: Adaptive fuzzy commitment scheme based on iris-code error analysis. In: 2010 2nd European Workshop on Visual Information Processing (EUVIP), pp. 41–44. IEEE (2010)
28. Rathgeb, C., Uhl, A.: A survey on biometric cryptosystems and cancelable biometrics. EURASIP J. Inf. Secur. **2011**(1), 3 (2011)
29. Shannon, C.E., Weaver, W., Burks, A.W.: The mathematical theory of communication (1951)
30. Sheng, W., Chen, S., Xiao, G., Mao, J., Zheng, Y.: A biometric key generation method based on semisupervised data clustering. IEEE Trans. Syst. Man Cybern. Syst. **45**(9), 1205–1217 (2015)
31. Sun, H., Yuao, T.: Curve aligning approach for gait authentication based on a wearable accelerometer. Physiol. Meas. **33**(6), 1111 (2012)
32. Theodoridis, S., Koutroumbas, K.: Pattern recognition, 4th edn. (2009)
33. Trung, N.T., Makihara, Y., Nagahara, H., Sagawa, R., Mukaigawa, Y., Yagi, Y.: Phase registration in a gallery improving gait authentication. In: 2011 International Joint Conference on Biometrics (IJCB), pp. 1–7. IEEE (2011)
34. Xu, W., Javali, C., Revadigar, G., Luo, C., Bergmann, N., Hu, W.: Gait-key: A gait-based shared secret key generation protocol for wearable devices. ACM Trans. Sens. Netw. (TOSN) **13**(1), 6 (2017)
35. Xu, Z., Xia, M.: Distance and similarity measures for hesitant fuzzy sets. Inf. Sci. **181**(11), 2128–2138 (2011)
36. Zhao, Y., Zhou, S.: Wearable device-based gait recognition using angle embedded gait dynamic images and a convolutional neural network. Sensors **17**(3), 478 (2017)

Attacks

Low-Level Attacks in Bitcoin Wallets

Andriana Gkaniatsou[(✉)], Myrto Arapinis, and Aggelos Kiayias

School of Informatics, University of Edinburgh, Edinburgh, UK
a.e.gkaniatsou@sms.ed.ac.uk, marapini@inf.ed.ac.uk,
aggelos.kiayias@ed.ac.uk

Abstract. As with every financially oriented protocol, there has been a great interest in studying, verifying, attacking, identifying problems, and proposing solutions for Bitcoin. Within that scope, it is highly recommended that the keys of user accounts are stored offline. To that end, companies provide solutions that range from paper wallets to tamper-resistant smart-cards, offering different level of security. While incorporating expensive hardware for the wallet purposes is though to bring guarantees, it is often that the low-level implementations introduce exploitable back-doors. This paper aims to bring to attention how the overlooked low-level protocols that implement the hardware wallets can be exploited to mount Bitcoin attacks. To demonstrate that, we analyse the general protocol behind LEDGER Wallets, the only EAL5+ certified against side channel analysis attacks hardware. In this work we conduct a throughout analysis on the Ledger Wallet communication protocol and show how to successfully attack it in practice. We address the lack of well-defined security properties that Bitcoin wallets should conform by articulating a minimal threat model against which any hardware wallet should defend. We further use that threat model to propose a lightweight fix that can be adopted by different technologies.

1 Introduction

Bitcoin is currently considered to be the most successful cryptocurrency, with an estimated average daily transaction value of US$200K. As it is becoming the most widely adopted digital currency, there is substantial resource and research investment into the security of the Bitcoin protocol and its transactions. Bitcoin is based on public key cryptography, which requires users to digitally sign their payments to prove ownership. Therefore, a salient aspect of Bitcoin is the wallet key management: loss of the private keys effectively means loss of funds; exposure of the public keys conveys privacy loss.

Online wallets are popular with Bitcoin users, as they are offered as a service that is faster and safer than running the Bitcoin client locally. User accounts are hosted on remote servers and accessed through third-party Web services; wallets either store the keys also in remote servers, or locally in the user's web client (typically a web browser). The user accesses his wallet through web-based authentication mechanisms and all cryptographic operations take place server-side, typically in the Cloud. Although this approach is popular among Bitcoin

© Springer International Publishing AG 2017
P.Q. Nguyen and J. Zhou (Eds.): ISC 2017, LNCS 10599, pp. 233–253, 2017.
https://doi.org/10.1007/978-3-319-69659-1_13

users, certain security issues arise as the user's private keys can be exploited by the host. For instance, in 2013 the StrongCoin web-hosted wallet transferred without user consent bitcoins from their servers to a different service, OzCoin, as it was claimed to be stolen [7]. Online wallets are also common targets for *Distributed Denial of Service* (DDoS) attacks, *e.g.*, BitGo and `blockchain.info` in June 2016. Such examples raised concerns about the reliability of such wallets and created the trend for *cold storage* and *cryptographic tokens*, with most major companies having integrated their software wallets with hardware devices.

Hardware wallets aim to offer a secure environment for key management and transaction signing. When a user requests a payment, the wallet's API creates the corresponding Bitcoin transaction and sends it to the hardware to be signed. The hardware signs the transaction and returns the signature together with the corre-

Table 1. Bitcoin Hardware Wallets Characteristics

Wallet	Secure element	HID	Encrypted channel
LEDGER *HW.1*	Smart card	×	×
LEDGER *Nano*	Smart card	×	×
LEDGER *Nano S*	Smart card	✓	×
Trezor	Microcontroller	✓	×
KeepKey	Microcontroller	✓	×
Digital BitBox	Microcontroller	✓	✓

sponding public key to the API, which is then pushed it to the network. In that way the sensitive signing keys do not ever leave the secure environment of the hardware wallet. The Bitcoin wallets currently in the market incorporate either microcontrollers or smart-cards. As of April 2017, the hardware wallet options suggested by `bitcoin.org` are the three LEDGER wallets, which are based on smart-cards; or *Trezor*, *Digital Bitbox* and *Keepkey*, which are based on microcontrollers. All wallets offer two versions: (*a*) a plain USB dongle, or (*b*) a USB Human Interface Device (HID) with an embedded screen for the user to verify and confirm the transaction. The main differences between current hardware wallets are shown in Table 1. Currently, apart from Digital BitBox, none of the wallets uses a secure communication channel. Offering a tamper resilient cryptographic memory is not enough on its own to guarantee against transaction attacks. Unauthorised access to the signing oracle of the wallet is not much different from plain access to the keys themselves, as both allow the funds to be stolen. Processing a Bitcoin request involves the communication between the hardware wallet and third-party systems. The lack of a general threat model for the Bitcoin wallets and well-defined specifications of that communication leads to proprietary implementations. As previous studies on different protocols have shown (*e.g.*, [8,10,13]), such practice often results in insecure low-level implementations that are prone to *Man-in-the-Middle* (MitM) attacks.

All hardware wallets implement a payment protocol similar to the following. The API broadcasts to the device the input funds and the payment details and requests the transaction signature If the device supports a second factor verification mechanism for the payment, it will sign the transaction only after the user's approval. If the device does not support such mechanism, it will sign it immediately. Although most Bitcoin wallets claim to secure the transactions by enforcing the user's validation of the payment data, the success rate of transaction attacks is analogous to the user error rate. The validation/comparison of hashes by the user, is a common technique *e.g.*, device pairing, self-signed certificates with HTTPS *etc.*. The usability aspects of hash comparison in security protocols and the effects of human errors have been studied before. For example, in [30] the authors conclude that the compare-and-confirm method (the user has to confirm a checksum presented on the device's screen) for a 4-digit string has 20% failure rate, whereas the work in [17] concludes that comparison of the Base32[1] hashes has an average 14% failure rate. Such studies focus on low entropy hashes and suggest that raising the entropy would result in bigger error rates. They conclude such techniques cannot provide strong security guarantees. Thus, a transaction attack on an HID wallet depends on the user's ability to identify the tampered data.

In this paper we stress the importance of securing the low-level communication of Bitcoin hardware wallets. We show that by taking advantage of that communication layer it is possible to propagate the attacks directly to the underlying Bitcoin transactions. The attacks we address are general and target any low-level communication with hardware wallets. Applying them in practice is a matter of adapting them to the corresponding hardware implementation. The security of microcontrollers has been extensively examined, and a number of fault and side-channel attacks have been found, *e.g.*, [4,12,20,21]. Therefore, we focus on smart-card based wallets, which provide guarantees against physical and interdiction attacks and have traditionally been used for key management and cryptographic operations. As of April 2017, LEDGER is the only company offering smart-card solutions. The LEDGER wallets are EAL5+ certified and are advertised as the most secure, tamper-proof and trustworthy devices for managing Bitcoin transactions.[2]

We consider client-side security and not security in the Bitcoin network, although a single wallet attack may escalate. Attacking Bitcoin at the network level is immensely expensive as it requires great computational resources. General attacks on Bitcoin wallets that could be applied to several users simultaneously are a much cheaper, easier and efficient way to gain access to multiple accounts. The LEDGER API is available on the *Chrome Web Store*, making it the ideal target for massively attacking users.

Our Contributions and Roadmap. To the best of our knowledge our work is the first to: (i) stress the importance of securing Bitcoin transactions and preserving the account's privacy at the wallet level, (ii) consider a minimal threat model for hardware Bitcoin wallets, and (iii) address the security issues originating in low-level communication of Bitcoin devices, by showcasing practical attacks. We provide a thorough analysis of the LEDGER wallets by extracting their protocols, analysing them and showing practical attacks. We propose a lightweight and

---

[1] Base32 hashes are a total of 25 bit entropy and consist of five characters with 32 possible character mappings. A Bitcoin address has 160 bit entropy.

[2] See http://goo.gl/KhtWXc, http://goo.gl/sbYXzh, http://goo.gl/hOU5jB.

user-friendly fix which is general enough to be adapted to all wallets regardless the hardware technology. As, the LEDGER protocols are not publicly available, we reverse-engineered the communication protocol and abstracted its implementations. In Sect. 3 we present and analyse the protocols that we extracted. In Sect. 4 we articulate a general purpose threat model for Bitcoin wallets and show how we have successfully mounted the identified attacks on LEDGER wallets. To that end, in Sect. 4 we propose a lightweight and easily adaptable fix that requires minimal changes.

2   Background

Bitcoin is a *Peer-to-Peer* (P2P) payment system that utilises public-key cryptography and consists of addresses and transactions. A transaction may have multiple inputs and outputs and is formed by digitally signing the hash of the transaction from which specific funds are transferred. The signature and the corresponding public key are sent to the network for verification. Upon successful validation, the funds are transferred to the stated addresses. Assuming a user u with a private/public key pair (sk_u, pk_u), let x_u be the recipient address, generated by hashing pk_u; let y_u be the hash of transaction t_u that transferred the funds to x_u. The transaction that further transfers b funds to some address z_p is the signature Sig_u of y_u, b and z_p using private key sk_u: $Sig_{sk_u}(y_u, b, z_p)$. Once a transaction is formed, it is broadcast to the network to be validated for: (a) outputs not exceeding inputs, (b) the user's ownership of the funds by verification of the signature with the corresponding pk_u.

Table 2. The transaction block.

	v: version	4 bytes
Inputs	ic: input count	1 byte
	$txid_i$: previous transaction id (hash)	variable length
	pc: previous output index	4 bytes
	$sigL$: script signature length	1 byte
	$scriptSig$: script signature	variable length
	s: sequence	4 bytes
Outputs	oc: output count	1 byte
	$amount_t$: value	8 bytes
	l: script length	1 byte
	$addr_p$: scriptPubKey	variable length
	bt: block lock time	4 bytes

Transactions in Bitcoin are expressed in a scripting language known as the *Bitcoin raw* protocol, which defines the conditions on the inputs and the outputs. According to [6], a transaction is defined in blocks of bytes. Table 2 presents the specific structure of a transaction block and the abbreviations that we will use in the next Sections: v is a fixed constant that defines the block format version; ic is a counter for the inputs; $txid_i$ is the reference to the previous transaction whose outputs will fund the current transaction; pc is a reference to the outputs of $txid_i$ that will be used; $sigL$ is the length of the signature; $scriptSig$ is the signature of the current transaction with the private key that correspond to the previous transaction outputs; s is a fixed constant that defines the end of the inputs declaration; oc is a counter for the outputs of the current transaction; $amount_t$ corresponds to the amount to be spent and l to the length of the destination public key; $addr_p$ is the recipient public key for $amount_t$.

Upon payment, the wallet must access the previous transactions and the available funds. Memory limitations and absence of access to the network, make it difficult for hardware wallets to track previous transactions. Segregated Witnesses (SegWit) solve that problem by including the value of the inputs in the signature of the transaction: hardware wallets then hash the inputs and sign that hash.

Key Management of Hardware Wallets. Currently all hardware wallets implement a *Hierarchical Deterministic* (HD) wallet of BIP32, which generates a new key-pair for each address request [32]. HD wallets derive fresh private keys from a common master key pair $\{sk_m, pk_m\}$. For the creation of a new wallet a 128- to 512-bit seed s, a sequence of random numbers, is generated. The master private key sk_m is generated by a function $sk_m = hash(s)$ where $hash(s)$ is the SHA256 hash of s. Then, given the master key pair (sk_m, pk_m), the wallet generates and maintains a sequence of children private $sk_1, sk_2, ...$ and public $pk_1, pk_2, ..$ keys from the master private key sk_m. A key sk_i is derived by the function $sk_i = sk_m + hash(i, pk_m) \pmod{n}$, $pk_i = pk_m + hash(i, pk_m)N$ or equally $sk_i N$ with i denoting the index of the key, and $hash$ being the HMAC-SHA512 function. Children public keys pk_i can be derived only by knowing the master public key pk_m and the index i.

Related Work. Previous work on attacking Bitcoin has exposed malleability attacks, where the adversary forces the victims to generate a transaction to an address controlled by her. When a victim broadcasts the transaction to the network, the adversary obtains a copy of that transaction that she modifies by tampering the signature without invalidating it. That modification results in a different transaction identifier (hash). The adversary then broadcasts the tampered transaction to the network, resulting in the same transaction being in the network under two different hashes. As a single transaction can only be confirmed once, only one of these two transactions will be included in a block and the other will be ignored. The attack is successful if the attacker's modified version is accepted. Although this attack is not new, it was given great attention after the malleability attack on MtGox [11], the first and one of the largest Bitcoin exchanges, in 2014. Since then different malleability attacks and solutions have been proposed, e.g., [11,31]. Double spending is another class of attacks on Bitcoin transactions, where the user spends the same coin twice. The feasibility of double spending attacks by using hashrate-based attack models was studied in [24,26]. It was shown that the attack is successful whenever the number of confirmations of a dishonest transaction is greater than the number of confirmations of the honest one. In [19] the authors exploit non-confirmed transactions to implement double spending attacks on fast payments, and [26] shows how such attacks coupled with high computational resources can have a higher success rate. Apart from the attacks that target transactions, privacy has also been targeted. Though privacy is a concern of the original specification [24] the public nature of Bitcoin renders strong privacy difficult to achieve. For instance, by tracing the flow of coins it is possible to identify their owner [15]. Likewise, [1] studied how transaction behaviour can be linked with a single account.

All the aforementioned attacks do not tackle the wallet layer. They all assume the wallet implementation to be secure. As many malware attacks have gained publicity *e.g.*, [5,18,25] or the malware attack on the Bitstamp wallet that costed US$5M [16], the importance of protecting Bitcoin wallets has been repeatedly stressed out [28]. [3] proposes a *super-wallet* as a solution to malware, in which the funds are split across multiple devices using cryptographic threshold techniques. The importance of ensuring wallet security is also presented in [29] where the authors formally analyse the authentication properties of the *Electrum* wallet. The authors of [2,22] argue that Bitcoin wallets be tamper-resistant and propose cryptographic tokens as a countermeasure to malware attacks. Our work exploits Bitcoin transactions at the wallet level. Instead of attacking the Bitcoin raw protocol directly, we show the importance of the protocols connected to the Bitcoin implementations. Attacking such protocols overrides any security restrictions that expensive hardware additions may add, and can be equally harmful to attacking the Bitcoin raw protocol itself.

3   Ledger Wallet Implementation

The low-level communication layer of LEDGER wallets, defined by the APDU layer, is crafted to implement the Bitcoin raw protocol. The communication consists of a series of raw hexadecimal command-response pairs between the API and the hardware: the API retrieves data or requests the hardware to execute a specific operation via APDU commands; whereas the hardware responds to that request via APDU responses. For example, in the following sequence:

command	e04800001f058000002c800000008000000000000000000000000c040406060 20000000001
response	3044022033128d0d576487e2e0c5892c0915564a6a5f119e698c033262d660 527943a16d022009caa037703d9a3dbf7eec4cecca08bf33b3b9a18ef929a 810f8faf6ab0f1c7a01

command retrieves the signature (*response*) over some transaction data. The LEDGER protocols are closed-source and there does not exist any information on how the Bitcoin specifications are translated into the APDU layer. A large part of our work has been to reverse-engineer the APDU layer and extract the implemented protocol. This was achieved by creating a man-in-the-middle sniffer[3] sitting on top of the Ledger API, capable of recording and interfering with the communication during any active sessions with the dongle. To abstract the protocol from the actual implementation and to infer the dongle's operations we ran

---

[3] Due to the sensitivity of the application we have not made our code publicly available. However, it can be made available to reviewers upon request.

a series of sessions on three different Nano dongles and one Nano S[4], compared the APDU command-response pairs, analysed the exchanged data and mapped it to the Bitcoin raw protocol (see Appendix A.1 for an example session). We concluded that during an active session four protocols may be executed:

(*a*) *Dongle Alive*: the initial communication when the dongle is plugged-in.
(*b*) *Setup*: wallet configuration and generation of the master keypair $\{sk_m, pk_m\}$.
(*c*) *Login*: user authentication to the dongle, and *vice versa*.
(*d*) *Payment*: processing of a payment transaction.

The *Dongle Alive* and *Login* protocols run once each time the dongle is connected to an active API. The *Payment* protocol repeats each time the user requests a payment. To proceed to a payment the user is not required to re-authenticate. The *Setup* protocol is executed once for initialising the wallet and each time an account restore is required; user authentication is its prerequisite. The dongle communicates with the API only when one of the four protocols are executed or when a firmware update is requested.

Commands Used During the Communication. Wallet communication consists of raw messages between the API and the dongle. To make the analysis readable we present the command-response messages in the form of $c(p_1, p_2, \ldots, p_n)$ $\rightarrow r_{1,2}, \ldots, r_m$, which denotes that the API sends command c with parameters $p_1, p_2, \ldots, p_n, n > 0$ to the dongle; and the dongle responds with $r_1, r_2, \ldots, r_m, m \geq 0$. If $m = 0$ the dongle either replies with OK (success) or error (failure). Table 3 lists the communication primitives used to describe the protocols.

Keys that Appear During the Communication. We conclude that LEDGER wallets manage the following key types:

(*i*) $\{sk_{att}, pk_{att}\}$: predefined attestation keys, used for the dongle's firmware authentication and for setting up third-party hardware,
(*ii*) $\{sk_m, pk_m\}$: the master keypair from which all keys are derived,
(*iii*) $\{sk_i, pk_i\}$ pairs: transaction related keys, *i.e.*, keys$\{sk_r, pk_r\}$ for receiving funds and $\{sk_c, pk_c\}$ for transferring the change of a transaction. All keys, besides pk_r, are generated and stored dongle-side.
(*iv*) pk_{kp}: a symmetric key for the encryption/decryption of the wallet's key-pool. As most Bitcoin wallets do, LEDGER software maintains a key-pool of 100 randomly generated addresses: each time the wallet requires a new address it picks one from the key-pool which is then refilled. Based on the original Bitcoin client (*i.e.*, the Satoshi client) the key-pool gets encrypted (AES-256-CBC) with an entirely random master key [27]. This master key is encrypted with AES-256-CBC with another key derived from a SHA-512-hashed passphrase. In the original implementation, the user provides that passphrase when generating that key and each time he wishes to proceed to a transaction. LEDGER wallets use pk_{kp} as a passphrase to generate that encryption key.

---

[4] The protocol of Nano S is very similar to that of Nano, thus it was not necessary to test it in a different dongle.

Table 3. API commands and their meaning.

command	meaning
get_firmware_version() $\rightarrow fV$	returns the dongle's firmware version fv
get_wallet_public_key($bipDer_i$, $findex_i$, $lindex_i$) $\rightarrow pk_i$	given the number of bip derivations $bipDer_i$, the first index $findex_i$, the last index $lindex_i$, returns the public key pk_i
get_device_attestation($blob$) $\rightarrow \{Sig_{att}, attId, attDer, frwVer,$ $modes, currentMode\}$	returns the signature Sig_{att} of $blob$ which is the concatenated byte-string of firmware version $frmwVer$, with the private key sk_{att} the verification key parameters $attId, attDer$, the operation modes $modes$, the current mode $currentMode$ and $frmwVer$
verify(pin) $\rightarrow$ OK	sends the user's pin to the dongle; if correct, the dongle replies OK
set_operation_mode($secFac$, $opMode$)$\rightarrow$ OK	sets the second factor authentication $secFac$ to true/false and the wallet operation mode $opMode$ to standard/relax/developer
sign($bipDer_i$, $findex_i$, $lindex_i$, m) $\rightarrow$ OK	initialises the signature of the message m with the private key sk_i that corresponds to ($bipDer_i$, $findex_i$, $lindex_i$)
sign(pin) $\rightarrow Sig_m$	returns the signature Sig_m of message m with key the private key sk_i if the pin it provides is correct
setup($pin, seed, genKey$) $\rightarrow$ OK	sets up a new user's pin, stores a new $seed$ and requests from the dongle to generate, $genKey$, a new $3DES_2$ key
set_keyboard($chars, typeConf$) $\rightarrow$ OK	sets up the keymap characters $chars$ and the typing behaviour $typeConf$
get_trusted_input(X) $\rightarrow \{Sig_t , oi, amount_t\}$	given X, where X is the raw structure (Table 2) for each previous output, returns the signature of each previous output Sig_t, the output index oi and $amount_t$ of the previous transaction t
untrusted_hash_transaction_ input_start($Sig_t, oi, amount$) $\rightarrow$ OK	streams the inputs, Sig_t, oi and $amount_t$ to the dongle using the raw structure (Table 2)
untrusted_hash_transaction_ input_finalize($addr_p, amount_p,$ $fees_p, bipDer_c, findex_c, lindex_c$) $\rightarrow \{c, addr_p, amount_p, fees_p,$ $pk_c, secFC\}$	streams the outputs, payment address $addr_p$, payment amount $amount_p$, $fees_p$, and selects the key pk_c to which the change will be sent based according to its BIP32 parameters $bipDer_c, findex_c, lindex_c$. The command returns the change c, the change key pk_c, dongle's confirmation of add_p, $amount_p$, $fees_p$, and the characters of the address $secFC$ to be authenticated by the user
untrusted_hash_sign ($bipDer_i$, $findex_i$, $lindex_i$, $secFR$) $\rightarrow Sig_p$	returns the signature Sig_p of the transaction p with key sk_i given its BIP32 parameters $bipDer_i, findex_i, lindex_i$, iff $secFR$ is correct

(v) $\{sk_{auth}, pk_{auth}\}$: signature/verification keypair for the dongle-API authentication.

LEDGER dongles do not follow the common smart-card file structure: instead of supporting dedicated and elementary files, the keys are stored in a tree-like structure starting from the master key-pair and are referenced according to the corresponding BIP32 derivation parameters: (1) the number of derivations $bipDer$, (2) the first derivation index $findex$ and (3) the last derivation index, $lindex$.

Dongle Alive Protocol. *Ledger Nano:* The protocol consists of four message requests with which the API checks the integrity of the dongle's firmware through an attestation check: the API requests the dongle to sign a random $blob$ concatenated with the firmware version $frmwVer$ under a manufacturer key sk_{att}. The exact steps are: (a) The API retrieves the dongle's firmware version $frmwVer$. (b) The API retrieves pk_{att}. (c) The API sends $blob$ to the dongle and retrieves the signature Sig_{att} of the $blob$ concatenated to the firmware version $frmwVer$,

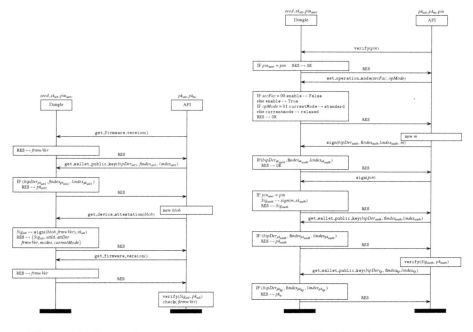

Fig. 1. The Nano alive protocol.   **Fig. 2.** The Nano login protocol.

the id of the attestation key $attId$, $frmwVer$ and the operation $modes$ and $currentMode$. (d) The API retrieves again $frmwVer$ and verifies Sig_{att}. The state transition diagram of the protocol can be found in Fig. 1.

Ledger Nano S: The API retrieves pk_{att}, the dongle's firmware version $frmwVer$ in plaintext, sets the currency and retrieves the keys pk_{auth}, pk_{kp}. The Nano S protocol does not include the attestation authentication.

Login Protocol. *Ledger Nano:* The Login Protocol (Fig. 2) establishes an authenticated session by which the user gains access to the dongle and, consequently, to the wallet. In contrary to Nano S in which no communication is involved (the user authenticates directly from the device's surface), the protocol consists of six messages, with the main operations being: (a) user pin verification, (b) dongle authenticity verification via a signature check, and (c) retrieval of wallet-related keys. The API also enables or disables second-factor authentication for payments and configures the wallet's operation modes. The supported modes are: (i) *standard*, the default, which allows standard Bitcoin scripts (addresses staring with 1) or P2PSH scripts (addresses staring with 3) and a single change address. At the beginning of the transaction the user is shown the amount to pay, the change, and any fees. (ii) *relaxed*, which allows arbitrary outputs to be authorised. At the beginning of a transaction the user is shown the amount to pay. (iii) *server*, allowing arbitrary outputs to be authorised but the transactions are controlled by a number of parameters.*e.g.*, maximum total

of transactions. (*iv*) *developer*, allowing arbitrary data to be signed. The steps of
the protocol are: (*a*) The API sends the user's *pin* to the dongle. (*b*) Upon *pin*
verification the API sets the second factor authentication (*SecFac*) and wallet
operation (*opMode*) modes. (*c*) The API requests the dongle to sign a random
message m with key sk_{auth} and retrieves Sig_{auth} by sending *pin*. (*d*) The API
retrieves pk_{auth} and verifies Sig_{auth}. (*e*) The API retrieves pk_{kp}.

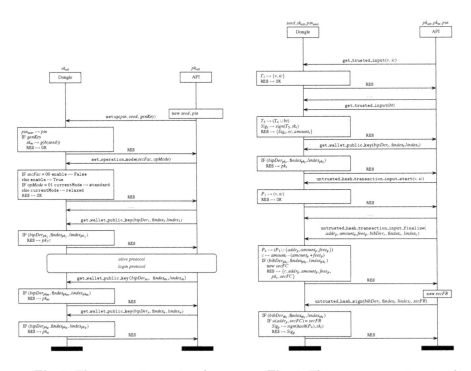

Fig. 3. The nano setup protocol.   **Fig. 4.** The nano payment protocol.

Setup Protocol. *Ledger Nano:* The setup process begins API-side. After select-
ing a PIN, the user is given a 24-word passphrase which corresponds to the
wallet's seed. After the user has confirmed the correct passphrase by providing
the words that the API has requested, API-side initialisation is done. Then, the
dongle-side setup begins. The main operations of the *Setup* protocol (due to
space limitation Fig. 3 presents only the exchanged messages that are exploited
by our attacks), are: user pin and seed initialisation, and the keyboard and
operations mode setup. During initialisation, the API also retrieves the master
public key pk_m, and the first derived public key pk_1. The message flow is the
following: (*a*) The API sets up a new *pin* and *seed* and requests the generation
of $\{sk_m, pk_m\}$. (*b*) The API requests from the dongle to sign $frmwVer$ concatenated to a random *blob* using the key sk_{att}. (*c*) The API verifies the *pin*.

(d) The API retrieves pk_1. (e) The *Dongle Alive Protocol* takes place. (f) The *Login Protocol* takes place. (g) The API retrieves pk_m and some extra unidentified key k_u.

Ledger Nano S: Initialisation is performed dongle-side. The user is shown the 24-word mnemonic and the first time the dongle connects to the API, it sends pk_m.

Payment Protocol. Both Ledger Nano and Nano S use a second factor authentication mechanism to ensure that transactions are not tampered, with both implementations requiring the user's confirmation of the payment address. In Ledger Nano the second factor authentication is of the form of a challenge-response, based on a 58-character-pairs security card the user is provided with. Each time the dongle is requested to process a payment, it presents the user with a challenge $secFC$ consisting of four indexes of the payment address. The user responds to that challenge with the corresponding characters from the security card, $secFR$. Only if $secFR$ is correct, will the dongle continue processing the transaction. Nano S also requires user interaction to process a transaction: before signing the transaction it displays part of the payment address, the payment amount and the fees on its screen. Only if the user confirms the transaction data by pressing the OK button, the dongle will sign the signature.

LEDGER implements a proprietary *Segregated Witness* by enforcing the API to send a detailed description of the inputs before the payment processing: the API forms a pseudo transaction block which has only the inputs, and sends it to the dongle, through a set of trusted_input commands. The dongle parses the block (bytewise concatenation) and returns its signature Sig_i. When the API creates the actual transaction, it will use Sig_i to define the corresponding input.

Ledger Nano: The protocol, shown in Fig. 4, is as follows: (a) The API sends to the dongle the available funds through sets of get_trusted_input commands. The inputs are sent in the form of pseudo transactions (following the specification in Table 2): one for each input. The number of get_trusted_input command sets is equal to the addresses ($t_i, i \geq 1$) with available funds. When the dongle has successfully received block t for a given input, it signs it and returns the signature Sig_t, the output index and the amount. (b) The API retrieves pk_t for input t. (c) The API creates the actual transaction block (Table 2), requested by the user, by sending the inputs Sig_t through sets of untrusted_hash_transaction_input_start commands, each set corresponding to a single input. Then, outputs, *i.e.*, the payment address $addr_p$, the payment amount $amount_p$, the fees $fees_p$ and the change key pk_c parameters ($bipDer_c$, $findex_c, lindex_c$), are sent via a untrusted_hash_transaction_input_finalize command. (d) The dongle calculates the remaining balance c, selects the authentication bytes $secFC$ sends back to the API a confirmation of the payment details, c, pk_c and $secFC$. (e) The API requests from the dongle to sign the transaction with sk_t by sending the user's validation code, $secFR$. (f) The dongle checks $secFR$ against $secFC$ and $addr_p$ and, if it is correct, it computes and returns the transaction signature Sig_t.

Ledger Nano S: The *Payment* proceeds as presented in Fig. 4 with a few differences: (*a*) The API starts the transaction by retrieving the balance address, pk_c, via a get_wallet_public_key command. (*b*) The API sends pk_c back to the dongle via the untrusted_hash_transaction_input_finalize command. (*c*) There is no second factor authentication asked by the dongle, or sent by the API.

4   Attacks

A Bitcoin wallet should provide high levels of security and privacy for the user, while also being easy to use. We therefore consider a wallet to be secure when it provides: (*a*) guarantees against tampering, (*b*) a secure environment for transaction processing, and (*c*) account privacy.

Our threat model assumes perfect cryptography and considers an adversary who has complete control over the communication layer: he can eavesdrop and manipulate the communication by deleting, inserting and altering the messages. We define the categories of possible threats to any Bitcoin wallets shown in Table 4.

Table 4. Attack categories

a. Direct wallet attacks	b. Transaction attacks
a.1 access to the master private key sk_m;	b.1 tamper the payment amount;
a.2 access to the key pool encryption key;	b.2 tamper the payment address;
a.3 unauthorised access to the wallet;	b.3 denial of service.
a.4 alter the wallet security properties.	**c. Account privacy attacks**
	c.1 account traceability.

4.1   Attacks in Practice

We show how we were able to perform attacks from the APDU layer, by bypassing the restrictions of the API. Some attacks are passive, *i.e.*, they only require observing the communication channel; while others are active *i.e.*, involve relaying and altering the exchanged messages. Some example traces of the attacks can be found in Appendix.

a.1: Access to Master Private Key sk_m**.** Access to the wallet's seed s is synonymous to having access to sk_m. During the *Setup* protocol execution we were able to sniff s which was sent in plaintext from the API to the dongle. By using the BIP32 derivation function we regenerated sk_m and all children keys. The API having access to s and transmission of s in plaintext defeats the purpose of cold storage. The attacker may gain access to the *Setup* protocol, and consequently to s, by forcing the dongle's reinitialisation. *Mounting Attack a.1:* Given a valid pin p, a replay of the session {verify(p') → error, verify(p') → error, verify(p') → error} in which $p' \neq p$ results into the dongle entering a lock state and forcing re-initialisation. The attacker has now access to the *Setup* protocol and can either acquire s or inject his own seed s_a.

a.2: Access to Key-Pool Encryption Key. Unauthorized access to key-pool implies loss of privacy and account traceability as the adversary gains insight on the addresses that the account uses/has used. During a *Login* session the passphrase that is used to create the key-pool key, which is the key pk_{kp}, is transmitted in plaintext after a `get_wallet_public_key` command.

a.3: Unauthorised Access to the Wallet. A general requirement in Bitcoin wallets is to be used only by users that have the credentials, *e.g.*, the pin. Our analysis showed that at each *Login* protocol execution the pin is sent in plaintext, (though only in the LEDGER Nano case), via a `verify` command, making the pin vulnerable to eavesdropping.

a.4: Alter the Wallet Security Properties. A second factor authentication mechanism secures each transaction: the user has to verify random characters of the payment address. The following attack changes the security parameters of the dongle and disables that mechanism. *Mounting Attack a.4:* Perform the following steps: (*a*) Replay a legit *Setup* session, {`setup`(*p*, *s*) → OK, . . . , `set_operation_mode`(*enable*, *standard*) → OK, . . . } (Fig. 3), and apply the substitutions (↦):

`set_operation_mode`(enable ↦ disable, standard ↦ relaxed). (*b*) In each *Login* session, (Fig. 2), replay the communication by applying the substitutions (↦):

`set_operation`(enable ↦ disable, standard ↦ relaxed). (*c*) In each *Payment* session, (Fig. 4), replay the communication and apply the substitutions (↦): (i) in `untrusted_transaction_input_hash_finalize`: `response`(*c*, $addr_p$, $amount_p$, pk_c, no ↦ *secFC*) where no is the card's response that no second authentication is required, and *secFC* are four random characters of the payment address $addr_p$. (ii) `untrusted_has_sign`(*sk_params*, *secFR* ↦ no) where *secFR* is the user's input to *secFC* and no declares that no secondary authentication took place.

a.4: Learning the Security Card. If the second factor authentication mechanism is enabled, each transaction requires the user's input according to a security card. The dongle requests four characters of the payment address to be verified by providing their mappings of the security card (58 hexadecimal characters that encode the letters A–W, a–w and the numbers 0–9). Each *Payment* session can reveal four new mappings. For this, 1. the adversary alters *secFC* ↦ *secFC′* in favour of the character mappings he does not yet know but that will allow him to correctly compute the response to the challenge, 2. the adversary returns to the dongle the correct *secFR* according to the original challenge *secFC*. In this way the adversary will learn four new characters in each *Payment* protocol execution. And so, after 15 legitimate user initiated payments, the attacker will have learned all characters of the security card.

b.1–b.2: Transaction Attacks. Given a *Payment* session an adversary can (*a*) redirect the payment destination: $addr_p$ and (*b*) tamper the payment amount: $amount_p$ by altering the exchanged messages. *Mounting attack b.1–b.2:* (*a*) to redirect the payment destination apply the following substitutions (↦): `untrusted_transaction_input_hash_finalize`($addr_p$ ↦ $addr'_p$, $amount_p$, $fees_p$, pk_c *parameters*)→`response`(*c*, $addr_a$ ↦ $addr_p$, $amount_p$, pk_c, *secFC*).

In the command data the original payment address $addr_p$ is substituted by the attacker's add'_p. The response is also relayed so that it contains the original address.

(*b*) to tamper the payment amount one should apply the following substitutions ($\mapsto$): `untrusted_ transaction_input_hash_finalize`($addr_p$, $amount_p \mapsto$ $amount'_p$, $fees_p$, pk_c *parameters*) $\rightarrow$ `response`($c' \mapsto c$, $addr_p$, $amount'_p \mapsto$ $amount_p$, pk_c, $secFC$). In the command data the original payment amount $amount_p$ is substituted by the attacker's $amount'_p$ whereas in the response data $amount'_p$ is changed back to $amount_p$ and the remaining funds c' is changed to the amount that would result after the original payment amount. This attack combined with either of the two a.4-type attacks allows an attacker to have any transaction signed by the dongle, even without knowledge of the PIN or the master secret key.

b.3: Denial of Service. DoS attacks that target specific Bitcoin Wallet users have become viral, *e.g.*, the DoS attacks on the BitGo wallets that left many users unable to use their funds. Such attacks target the wallet's server and consist of sending a huge amount of requests. Though out of our scope, in the LEDGER wallet side of things, DDoS attacks could also be mounted from the APDU layer by tampering the transaction data in a way that either the dongle cannot interpret, or that the transaction cannot be verified.

c.1: Account Traceability. Bitcoin is associated with anonymity and is often used by users who want their actions to be unlinkable. Each transaction results to the generation of a new key to avoid reusability of old addresses. In HD wallets, like LEDGER, all public keys are derived from the master public key pk_m with the formula $pk_i = f(pk_m + hash(i, pk_m))$ where i is the child key index and f the generator function. As such, access to pk_m equals to access to all pk_i keys and thereby the account becomes traceable. pk_m can be obtained by eavesdropping a *Setup* session (which can be enforced with Attack 4.1) as in both Nano and Nano S is transmitted in plaintext. However, the account's activities are also traceable by just eavesdropping the *Payment* sessions: at least one pk_r (an address with available funds) and probably one change address pk_c (if their available change) are revealed.

Generality of the Attacks. The purpose of our work is to show that it is possible to attack Bitcoin hardware wallets via the low-level communication. The threat model we present is hardware/software independent and applicable to all available Bitcoin wallets. The attacks on the LEDGER wallets aim to prove that Bitcoin transactions are vulnerable, even if tamper-resistant hardware such as smart-cards are incorporated. Our work showcases how the API restrictions can be bypassed by relaying the hardware communication. The same attacks, adapted to meet the criteria of each hardware, can be applied to every wallet that does not use a secure communication channel *i.e.*, Trezor and Keepkey. All hardware wallets follow the same abstraction of the *Payment* protocol; any plaintext communication is prone to attacks b.1-b.2. Although they incorporate a second factor authentication mechanism by enforcing the user's verification of the payment data, previous studies have shown that a significant average of 15% of such verification is usually erroneous.

The privacy issues we address for the LEDGER wallets is an aspect that reflects to all BIP32 wallets, especially to those that do not communicate in a secure way. Currently, all hardware wallets[5] transmit the public keys (including the master public key) in the clear: eavesdropping a single session reveals at least two public keys: the address with available funds and the address that the remaining balance will be sent to. Also, whenever the hardware connects to a fresh API, the master public key pk_m is sent in the clear. Access to that key implies access to all children public keys, which makes eavesdropping that single session sufficient to track the account's transactions. In any case, whether the adversary has access to pk_m or to its children pk_i the flow of the funds of the given account is linkable.

5   A Lightweight Fix of the Protocols

The LEDGER wallets, as all other hardware wallets not using a secure communication channel, fail to prevent MitM attacks. All transaction data is sent in the clear, making the wallet vulnerable to attacks and account linkability. Encrypting the entire communication would be an obvious solution to that. However, such strategy requires computational power, and possible changes to the security architecture of the current wallets. Additional delays to the transaction processing would be another trade-off. Instead we propose the symmetric encryption of specific communication parts: those that are prone to attacks with respect to our threat model. Table 5 summarises what LEDGER wallet data need to be protected to defend against which attacks. Our fix consists of three components: 1. the secure pre-setup phase, 2. the authentication and session key establishment protocol, 3. encryption of sensitive parts.

Table 5. LEDGER data and the corresponding attacks.

Data	a.1	a.2	a.3	a.4	b.1	b.2	b.3	c.1
s	✓	✓	✓	✓	✓	✓	✓	✓
pin	×	×	✓	×	×	×	×	×
$secFC, secFR$	×	×	×	✓	×	✓	✓	×
$opMode$	×	×	×	✓	×	✓	✓	×
$addr_p, amount_p, fees_{p,c}, pk_c$	×	×	×	×	✓	✓	✓	✓
$pk\_\{m, m+1.., m+n\}$	×	✓	×	×	×	×	×	✓

Secure Environment for the PIN Exchange. The PIN needs to be entered in the hardware before the initialisation of the wallet as the PIN is then used to derive the cryptographic keys to protect the interactions between the dongle and the API. This process must proceed in a secure offline environment. This can be achieved either by entering the PIN directly on the trusted user interface of the device (if it is an HID wallet); or by setting up the PIN on an air-gapped machine, e.g. using a live OS on a USB stick which will ensure that the OS has and will never be connected to the Internet.

---

[5] Apart from Digital BitBox whose specifications are not available publicly.

Authentication and session key establishment. This protocol gets executed every time the API establishes a new session with the dongle. It is responsible for the API/hardware authentication and the establishment of a fresh session key. A new session is established whenever the hardware connects to an active API. For the key establishment we propose Password Authenticated Key Exchange by Juggling protocol (j-PAKE) [14] which allows bootstrapping high entropy keys from the low-entropy user's PIN. In that way, we avoid storing secret data API side, ensure that fresh keys are used in each session and guarantee the user's presence at that session. In addition, the j-PAKE protocol allows zero knowledge proof of the PIN which satisfies the authentication prerequisites of the session. Finally j-PAKE provides guarantees against off-line and on-line dictionary attacks and it satisfies the forward secrecy and known-key security requirements. J-PAKE, like the Diffie-Hellman key exchange, uses ephemeral values but proceeds in an additional round in which combines them with the user's PIN and makes certain randomisation vectors vanish.

Encryption of sensitive data. Once the session key is established slightly modified versions of the four LEDGER protocols (*Alive, Login, Setup,* and *Payment*) can be executed. The four new protocols are derived from the original Ledger protocols as follows. First a session identifier is established for each execution of each of these protocols. This will be generated dongle side, and transmitted to the API in plaintext. The session identifier does not need to be confidential, but will need to be fresh and generated by the dongle to avoid replay attacks. Then dongle and API execute the original protocol but encrypting under the current session key the sensitive data identified previously (Table 5). The computed ciphertexts will all include the established session identifier. A Message Authentication Code (MAC) is further computed and concatenated to the chiphertext. The other party will then be able to decrypt and verify the encrypted parts.

6   Discussion

Although the security of financial related hardware in other areas has always attracted a lot of attention, eg., the Chip and PIN systems [23], Bitcoin-related hardware has not been extensively studied before (apart from [9]). Relying on the high levels of security that the Bitcoin protocol offers is not enough to guarantee safe transactions. Lack of a standard that defines the properties of the Bitcoin wallets leads to security misconceptions and ad-hoc implementations that hide vulnerabilities. Our work, to the best of our knowledge, is the first effort to address security aspects of Bitcoin wallets and stress the importance of securing the implementations of low-level communications. We chose to analyse smart-card based wallets as they are perceived to be the most secure and tamper resilient means for key management. However, the core idea of the attacks is general and applies to other hardware wallets of different technology.

In this paper we extract and analyse the protocols that are hidden behind the LEDGER wallets, the only available smart-card based solutions. Our work

includes the analysis of both standard and HID dongles. We identify and cate-
gorise all possible vulnerabilities for Bitcoin wallets and we introduce a general
threat model. We then use that model to analyse the LEDGER protocols. Our
work concluded that the LEDGER implementations are vulnerable to a set of
attacks that target the wallet itself as well as the Bitcoin transactions. Finally,
we propose a lightweight fix, based on the j-PAKE protocol, which can easily
be adapted by any wallet and efficiently prevents any active or passive attack.
Attacking the LEDGER wallets is just an example, whereas the same methodology
can be easily adopted in other technologies. Our work does not aim at proving
the specific wallets insecure, but rather to showcase the importance of ensuring
a secure low-level implementation even if the higher levels provide guarantees.

A   Appendix

A.1   Example Communication Trace

As an example, we provide the trace that was generated for the following transaction:

Transaction Id	92d30a91b45d6ab528af12f3a9c0701e01f67348a257ed50362439a2ee8274e7
Input addresses	1 113biVTVQk73Eem1UYYn9YcrPVrxp6xeVc
	2 15DpocdQpwXeUp9Ccf2Nz9AQ9jKp9U5VdZ
Payment address	1GocNQ4Q8BtzacpHQiGLWk9vNppoq6Lh8W
Payment amount	0.00813844
Change address	1PmXm9UcAgDBp5i3SvqD3SfdKChfWthH4W

We only provide the traces of the commands of Fig. 4 so as not to overwhelm.

1. get_trusted_input: e04200000900000010100000001
2. response: 9000
3. get_trusted_input: e04280000400000000
4. response: 32008ed5f038879105a5778cdacee02ca43f21bcbbd66cd647add
   3db69dd3222b9c3968d0000000078710d00000000009132801b579e659b
5. get_wallet_public_key: e040000015058000002c800000008000000000000
   0000000000c
6. response: 410441ec4b255d40010284f117d8105456a268cd9536ca5ca3d30
   16bf6d21902e5dc4bf9b224b5cb2379b5c2b4a47044862d42c6e5b14daf229
   39fec8023c83ac5192231313362695654565166b373345656d315559596e39
   5963725056727870367865566663da55cec9398694400832d6af2426c057addc
   73438efa016f6f9232735ee6b1a8
7. get_wallet_public_key: e040000015058000002c800000008000000000000
   00100000012

8. `response:` `41043f07a649a72651f10d5728b7f848ee879fb3b263ddd653b51`
`b563a051f138fa3e35f5f6d794a2621fbf0493d6af5c2b300734086fa0ebbe`
`411f11017b1989bdd22313544706f636451707758655570394363366324e7a`
`394151396a4b7039553556645a9bf32153ef7f646d1d1991382932bc915d67`
`1ddc3640ef8da3eb54877191e559`

9. `untrusted_hash_transaction_input_start:` e0440000050100000002

10. `response:` 9000

11. `untrusted_hash_transaction_input_finalize:` e0460200482231476f634
e5134513842747a616370485169474c576b39764e70706f71364c683857000
000000000d6d80000000000000004508058000002c8000000080000000000000000
100000013

12. `response:` 4502d8d60000000000001976a914ad5a8ba5325b4b836c49b097
97cbb83744a7a2f588ac146b0c00000000001976a914f9bebf6735e688877
e409cd494ad820b344dd76e88ac03040405121e47646f813e5dfd4fbc72e66
98cc40a67a980bccbe7881c2e40ac6fec4fbcda20d980ec3a67445e48dad87
0ee58d006745fdf953138be5fb0570e679f512c36ed

13. `untrusted_hash_sign:` e04800001f058000002c800000008000000000000000
00000000c04040606020000000001

14. `response:` 3044022033128d0d576487e2e0c5892c0915564a6a5f119e698c
033262d660527943a16d022009caa037703d9a3dbf7eec4cecca08bf33b3b9
a18ef929a810f8faf6ab0f1c7a01

A.2   Active Attacks

a.4: Alter the Wallet Security Properties. The attack requires sending the wrong pin p' three consecutive times and then tampering the `set_operation` command. A sample trace with the breakdown of the steps and their corresponding commands is given in Table 6; we underline the important pieces of the exchange.

Table 6. Attack a.4: Trace of disabling the second factor authentication during *Setup*

Steps	APDU traces
Block the dongle	• `verify(p')`: 0220000043<u>3333333</u>
	• `verify(p')`: 0220000043<u>3333333</u>
	• `verify(p')`: 0220000043<u>3333333</u>
Replay a Setup Session	• `setup(p, s)`: e02000004c020a0005043<u>1343234</u> 00408c3937fafb22e5f4979e90afe0b912cc05d 92b9910c622887f61b30d9814f714df2dd5ada8cc5cd663e998dec1cc55915377352cf6949a20ba4440 39219efd6900
	• `set_keyboard`: e028000077000000000000000000000000000760f00d4ffffffc7000000782c1e342 0212224342627252e362d3738271e1f2021222324252633333362e37381f0405060708090a0b0c0d0e0f 101112131415161718191a1b1c1d2f3130232d350405060708090a0b0c0d0e0f1011121314151617181 91a1b1c1d2f313035
	• `get_device_attestation`: e0c200000861255ccee7f8c72d
	• `set_operation`: <u>e02600000102</u>
	...

b.1–b.2:   Transaction   Attacks.   The   structure   of   `untrusted_hash_transaction_input_finalize` is: and the structure of the response data that

command	e046020048
length of payment address	22
payment address $addr_p$	314e3371757233596565334b664e74 436a4677756e346f366f4c32447868 6747796f
payment amount $amount_p$	0000000000005305
fees $fees_p$	0000000000001d60
change address BIP32 parameters	058000002c800000008000000000000 0001000000
second authentication status (true/false)	02

payment amount $amount_p$	03b1000000000000
hash160 of $addr_p$	f1253f0463e5877c5e8bb3f34e7abfb335023ee1
change c	0553000000000000
hash160 change address $addr_c$	e6e44d66125327341d6abb71e0702a4ea0537437

we are interested in is:

Depending on the attack we want to perform the corresponding data part needs to be altered. For example, to change the payment address from 163WPEe THjvFsUfx1UbDPXK92eRmqXQrGA to 113biVTVQk73Eem1UYYn9YcrPVrxp6xeVc, we tamper the original command:
e04602004822<u>31363357504565544486a7646735566783155624450584b3932655 26d715851724741</u>00000000000027100000000000001a9a058000002c80000000 8000000000000000100000000 to the command:
e04602004822<u>3131336269565456516b373345656d315559596e395963725056 727870367865566630</u>00000000000027100000000000001a9a058000002c80000000 8000000000000000100000000
where we underline the relevant parts; similarly for the response.

Learning the Security Card. The attacker gains access to the keycard mappings, $secFR$, via the untrusted_hash_sign command, *e.g.*, e04800001f 058000002c800000008000000000000000000000000104<u>0f090a02</u>0000000001.

References

1. Androulaki, E., Karame, G.O., Roeschlin, M., Scherer, T., Capkun, S.: Evaluating user privacy in bitcoin. In: Sadeghi, A.-R. (ed.) FC 2013. LNCS, vol. 7859, pp. 34–51. Springer, Heidelberg (2013). doi:10.1007/978-3-642-39884-1_4
2. Bamert, T., Decker, C., Wattenhofer, R., Welten, S.: BlueWallet: the secure bitcoin wallet. In: Mauw, S., Jensen, C.D. (eds.) STM 2014. LNCS, vol. 8743, pp. 65–80. Springer, Cham (2014). doi:10.1007/978-3-319-11851-2_5
3. Barber, S., Boyen, X., Shi, E., Uzun, E.: Bitter to better — how to make bitcoin a better currency. In: Keromytis, A.D. (ed.) FC 2012. LNCS, vol. 7397, pp. 399–414. Springer, Heidelberg (2012). doi:10.1007/978-3-642-32946-3_29

4. Biham, E., Shamir, A.: Differential fault analysis of secret key cryptosystems. In: Kaliski, B.S. (ed.) CRYPTO 1997. LNCS, vol. 1294, pp. 513–525. Springer, Heidelberg (1997). doi:10.1007/BFb0052259

5. Bitcoin ewallet vanishes from internet. http://www.tribbleagency.com/?p=8133

6. Bitcoin Protocol Documentation. https://en.bitcoin.it/wiki/Protocol%5F documentation

7. Bitcoinmagazine (2013). https://bitcoinmagazine.com/articles/ozcoin-hacked-stolen-funds-seized-and-returned-by-strongcoin-1366822516

8. Bozzato, C., Focardi, R., Palmarini, F., Steel, G.: APDU-level attacks in PKCS#11 devices. In: Monrose, F., Dacier, M., Blanc, G., Garcia-Alfaro, J. (eds.) RAID 2016. LNCS, vol. 9854, pp. 97–117. Springer, Cham (2016). doi:10.1007/978-3-319-45719-2_5

9. Datko, J., Quartier, C., Belyayev, K.: Breaking bitcoin hardware wallets. In: DEF-CON (2017)

10. De Koning Gans, G., De Ruiter, J.: The smartlogic tool: analysing and testing smart card protocols. In: 2012 IEEE Fifth International Conference on Software Testing, Verification and Validation (ICST), pp. 864–871 (2012)

11. Decker, C., Wattenhofer, R.: Bitcoin transaction malleability and MtGox. In: Kutyłowski, M., Vaidya, J. (eds.) ESORICS 2014. LNCS, vol. 8713, pp. 313–326. Springer, Cham (2014). doi:10.1007/978-3-319-11212-1_18

12. Genkin, D., Shamir, A., Tromer, E.: RSA key extraction via low-bandwidth acoustic cryptanalysis. In: Garay, J.A., Gennaro, R. (eds.) CRYPTO 2014. LNCS, vol. 8616, pp. 444–461. Springer, Heidelberg (2014). doi:10.1007/978-3-662-44371-2_25

13. Gkaniatsou, A., McNeill, F., Bundy, A., Steel, G., Focardi, R., Bozzato, C.: Getting to know your card: reverse-engineering the smart-card application protocol data unit. In: Proceedings of the 31st Annual Computer Security Applications Conference, pp. 441–450 (2015)

14. Hao, F., Ryan, P.: J-PAKE: authenticated key exchange without PKI. In: Gavrilova, M.L., Tan, C.J.K., Moreno, E.D. (eds.) Transactions on Computational Science XI. LNCS, vol. 6480, pp. 192–206. Springer, Heidelberg (2010). doi:10.1007/978-3-642-17697-5_10

15. Herrera-Joancomartí, J.: Research and challenges on bitcoin anonymity. In: Garcia-Alfaro, J., Herrera-Joancomartí, J., Lupu, E., Posegga, J., Aldini, A., Martinelli, F., Suri, N. (eds.) DPM/QASA/SETOP -2014. LNCS, vol. 8872, pp. 3–16. Springer, Cham (2015). doi:10.1007/978-3-319-17016-9_1

16. Higgins, S. (2015). http://www.coindesk.com/unconfirmed-report-5-million-bitstamp-bitcoin-exchange

17. Hsiao, H.-C., Lin, Y.-H., Studer, A., Studer, C., Wang, K.-H., Kikuchi, H., Perrig, A., Sun, H.-M., Yang, B.-Y.: A study of user-friendly hash comparison schemes. In: Annual Computer Security Applications Conference, ACSAC 2009, pp. 105–114. IEEE (2009)

18. Huang, D.Y., Dharmdasani, H., Meiklejohn, S., Dave, V., Grier, C., McCoy, D., Savage, S., Weaver, N., Snoeren, A.C., Levchenko, K.: Botcoin: monetizing stolen cycles. In: 21st Annual Network and Distributed System Security Symposium, NDSS 2014, San Diego, California, USA, 23–26 February 2014

19. Karame, G.O., Androulaki, E., Capkun, S.: Double-spending fast payments in bitcoin. In: Proceedings of the 2012 ACM Conference on Computer and Communications Security, CCS 2012, pp. 906–917 (2012)

20. Kocher, P., Jaffe, J., Jun, B.: Differential power analysis. In: Wiener, M. (ed.) CRYPTO 1999. LNCS, vol. 1666, pp. 388–397. Springer, Heidelberg (1999). doi:10. 1007/3-540-48405-1_25

21. Kocher, P.C.: Timing attacks on implementations of Diffie-Hellman, RSA, DSS, and other systems. In: Koblitz, N. (ed.) CRYPTO 1996. LNCS, vol. 1109, pp. 104–113. Springer, Heidelberg (1996). doi:10.1007/3-540-68697-5_9

22. Lim, I.-K., Kim, Y.-H., Lee, J.-G., Lee, J.-P., Nam-Gung, H., Lee, J.-K.: The analysis and countermeasures on security breach of bitcoin. In: Murgante, B., Misra, S., Rocha, A.M.A.C., Torre, C., Rocha, J.G., Falcão, M.I., Taniar, D., Apduhan, B.O., Gervasi, O. (eds.) ICCSA 2014. LNCS, vol. 8582, pp. 720–732. Springer, Cham (2014). doi:10.1007/978-3-319-09147-1_52

23. Murdoch, S.J., Drimer, S., Anderson, R.J., Bond, M.: Chip and PIN is broken. In: 31st IEEE Symposium on Security and Privacy, S&P 2010, Berleley/Oakland, California, USA, 16–19 May 2010, pp. 433–446 (2010)

24. Nakamoto, S.: Bitcoin: a peer-to-peer electronic cash system. http://bitcoin.org/ bitcoin.pdf

25. Poulsen, K.: New malware steals your bitcoin (2011). https://www.wired.com/ 2011/06/bitcoin-malware

26. Rosenfeld, M.: Analysis of hashrate-based double spending. CoRR, abs/1402.2009 (2014)

27. The Bitcoin Wiki. https://en.bitcoin.it/wiki/Wallet%5Fencryption

28. The Bitcoin Wiki (2014). https://en.bitcoin.it/wiki

29. Turuani, M., Voegtlin, T., Rusinowitch, M.: Automated verification of electrum wallet. In: Clark, J., Meiklejohn, S., Ryan, P.Y.A., Wallach, D., Brenner, M., Rohloff, K. (eds.) FC 2016. LNCS, vol. 9604, pp. 27–42. Springer, Heidelberg (2016). doi:10.1007/978-3-662-53357-4_3

30. Uzun, E., Karvonen, K., Asokan, N.: Usability analysis of secure pairing methods. In: Dietrich, S., Dhamija, R. (eds.) FC 2007. LNCS, vol. 4886, pp. 307–324. Springer, Heidelberg (2007). doi:10.1007/978-3-540-77366-5_29

31. Wuille, P.: Dealing with maellability. Online specification for BIP62 (2014)

32. Wuille, P.: Hierarchical deterministic wallets. Online specification for BIP32 (2017)

Improving Password Guessing Using Byte Pair Encoding

Xingxing Wang[1], Dakui Wang[2(✉)], Xiaojun Chen[1,2], Rui Xu[1,2], Jinqiao Shi[1,2], and Li Guo[1,2]

[1] School of Cyberspace Security, Beijing University of Posts and Telecommunications, Beijing, China
xingxingwang@bupt.edu.cn
[2] Institute of Information Engineering, Chinese Academy of Science, Beijing, China
{wangdakui,chenxiaojun,xurui,shijinqiao,guoli}@iie.ac.cn

Abstract. Recent many password guessing algorithms based on the Probabilistic Context-Free Grammars (PCFGs) model brought significant improvements in password cracking. These algorithms analyzed common semantic patterns (letter semantic patterns, date patterns, keyboard patterns etc.) from passwords and modeled the construction process of passwords by using PCFGs. However, there still left a large fraction of integral segments in passwords which seem no semantics. Can those segments be deeply analyzed and help to make further improvements on password cracking? Motivated by this challenge, this paper employs Byte Pair Encoding (BPE) algorithm for password segmentation, extracting those non-semantical patterns which are frequently used in passwords subconsciously by people. Based on the segmentation, we propose a BPE-PCFGs model to generate password guesses. Furthermore, we also utilize the existing common semantic patterns and BPE patterns to construct a new Rich-BPE-PCFGs password generator. Experimental results on large-scale password sets show that our Rich-BPE-PCFGs model can obtain a 2.36%–37.56% improvement over the original PCFGs model, which is a good complement to existing password guessing algorithms.

Keywords: Password guessing · Byte pair encoding · PCFGs

1 Introduction

Password authentication is still the most widely used authentication method among online websites. And Text-based passwords still occupy an important position in the foreseeable future [1], because of their simplicity for remembering and implementing. However, there exists the "security and usability" dilemma on text-based passwords. For example, many users tend to choose very simple passwords such as "123456", "helloworld", but these passwords are vulnerable to be guessed. Additionally, based on recent researches, the Zipf's law perfectly exists in user-generated passwords. That is to say, a small faction of common

© Springer International Publishing AG 2017
P.Q. Nguyen and J. Zhou (Eds.): ISC 2017, LNCS 10599, pp. 254–268, 2017.
https://doi.org/10.1007/978-3-319-69659-1_14

strings, such as "123", "asd", appear frequently in user-generated passwords. This fact makes passwords predictable by employing some state-of-the-art techniques. So the analysis of patterns in user-generated passwords helps researchers design more efficient password guessing algorithms, which can be used to improve the success rate of password cracking or measure the strength of passwords.

Security of user-generated passwords has attracted the researchers' attention for a long time. Many password guessing algorithms have been developed and used in practice. At first, brute-force algorithms [2] and other algorithms based on a big dictionary with a few mingling rules [3,4] are designed to crack passwords. These algorithms limit the guessing ability and reduce the guessing success rate. In recent years, the Probabilistic Context-Free Grammars (PCFGs) model proposed by Weir et al. [5] is widely used in password guessing. They divided passwords into three kinds of patterns, namely, L-pattern, D-pattern and S-pattern, which stand for letter strings, digital strings and strings composed of special characters. Then based on these patterns, they provided a password generation algorithm, which significantly improved the efficiency of password guessing. Following Weir's work, several deeper analytical methods about the pattern of passwords have been proposed. Veras et al. [6] utilized Natural Language Processing (NLP) techniques to segment, classify, and generate semantic patterns from passwords. Additionally, the date pattern [7] in D-pattern, the keyboard pattern [8,9] and even the personal information pattern [10,11] are analyzed successively. The password guessing algorithms based on above patterns have improved the success rate of password guessing greatly.

Still, the above patterns in passwords depend on people's priori knowledge and experience. For example, we know that the date will exist in a few common styles, such as "YYYYMMDD", "MMDD", "MMDDYYYY", so we can extract the date pattern from passwords by using regex matching. We can extract the letter-semantics pattern from passwords based on vocabulary. The keyboard pattern is also done with the similar idea. However, due to the wish to make passwords secret, there are still many integral segments frequently used to create passwords that could not be classified by above semantic patterns. Those integral segments seem no semantics. Can we analyze those segments deeply and help to make further improvements on password cracking?

Motivated by this problem, this paper mainly studies those integral segments statistically. As Byte Pair Encoding (BPE) [12] can find strings frequently appearing in a text, we employ the BPE algorithm [13] to extract non-semantical patterns which are frequently used in passwords. And then we provide the PCFGs model based on BPE-patterns and construct the responding password generator. Furthermore, we combine our BPE-patterns with the proposed semantic patterns, such as date patterns and letter patterns, to implement a new method called Rich-BPE-PCFGs to model the creation process of passwords. The Rich-BPE-PCFGs algorithm under 50,000 BPE merge operations is able to guess 2.36%–37.56% more passwords than original PCFGs within 100 million guesses on Chinese password sets and English password sets.

In summary, the contributions we make in this paper are as follows:

- We employ the Byte Pair Encoding algorithm to password segmentation, extracting frequently used segments in password.
- In order to explore the impact of the BPE segmentation on password structures, we utilize some new password patterns based on BPE segmentation and generate password guesses using these patterns.
- We propose a new model, called Rich-BPE-PCFGs, by incorporating new L-patterns and D-patterns into the grammars of PCFGs. A large number of experimental results show that our algorithm can guess 2.36%–37.56% more passwords than the original PCFGs method.

This paper is organized as follows: In Sect. 2, we discuss related work. Section 3 presents how to apply the BPE algorithm to extract password patterns and subsequently proposes a new Rich-BPE-PCFGs model. The details of comparative experiments and analysis of experimental results are presented in Sect. 4. Section 5 concludes with respected to this work and discusses our future work.

2   Related Work

Byte pair encoding (BPE) is a simple form of data compression, in which the most common pair of consecutive bytes of data is replaced with a byte that does not occur within that data. A table of the replacements is required to rebuild the original data. The algorithm was first proposed by Gage et al. [12]. The following researches about BPE are almost focus on applying the method in different fields, such as the compressed pattern matching and the machine translation. Potential advantages of BPE from a view point of the compressed pattern matching have been shown in Shibata et al. [14]. Senrich et al. [13] have applied the BPE algorithm in the field of Neural Machine Translation. They used BPE as a kind of word segmentation techniques, which can find out the subword units in words. However, In the field of security, there is almost no application of BPE.

Using the grammar theory to model symbol strings originating from word in computational linguistics is of great help to understand the structure of natural languages. The Probabilistic Context-Free Grammars (PCFGs) method has been used in many areas, such as RNA structure prediction, protein sequence analysis and security. In security field, Weir et al. [5] are the first to apply PCFGs in password cracking, which is considered to be the state-of-the-art technique to password cracking [15, 16]. They derived grammars from training real world password sets and then generated guesses in probability order. After Weir's work, the following researches about the PCFGs in password cracking are almost focus on how to making better password segmentation based on certain patterns. Bonneau et al. [17] explored the distribution characteristics of passwords and introduced a new pattern of adjacent keys, which occupy 11% of passwords in CSDN. Chou et al. [18] developed a platform to identify frequently used password patterns and proposed a model to generate passwords in decreasing order of probability based on a variation of Weir's algorithm [5,19]. Veras et al. [6] utilized Natural Language Processing techniques for segmentation based on a source corpus, semantic classification using WordNet and generalization of semantic patterns from passwords. Li et al. [9] presented the first large-scale empirical study on Chinese web passwords and developed new patterns like keyboard, Chinese pinyins and dates based on PCFGs. Houshmand et al. [8] incorporated keyboard patterns and multiword patterns into PCFGs and achieved a 55% improvement over the original PCFGs. Li et al. [10] introduced a new kind of patterns about personal information, which is significant to targeted guessing. Regrettably, there is still no research about statistical method, for example, BPE, applied on the password segmentation. So our work is the first to introduce BPE as a password segmentation method in security area.

3   Password Guessing on PCFGs with BPE

In this section, we show how to apply the BPE algorithm [13] to the PCFGs model for improving the effect of password guessing. Firstly, we describe the BPE scheme and propose a password segmentation method based on BPE. Secondly, we present a new password guessing model, called BPE-PCFGs, on the basis of the BPE password segmentation. Finally, we discuss a new concept of Rich-PCFGs, and combining it with the BPE password segmentation, we propose the other new password guessing model, which is called Rich-BPE-PCFGs model.

3.1   Password Segmentation Method Based on BPE

Byte Pair Encoding (BPE) is a simple dictionary encoding compression method, which utilizes a single byte that does not appear in the data to replace the most frequent adjacent bytes iteratively [12]. For example, given a data

$$T_0 = bcabebcfbca,$$

the pair "bc" occurs 3 times, which is most frequent, so we replace it with "X" and obtain the new data

$$T_1 = XabeXfXa.$$

Then the most frequent pair is "Xa", so we substitute "Y" for "Xa" and the data becomes

$$T_2 = YbeXfY.$$

Apparently, this data could not be compressed by BPE as there is no pair of bytes which appear more than once. So, using BPE algorithm, we can compress the data "bcabebcfbca" with "YbeXfY" and obtain the corresponding Replacement table

$$X = bc,$$

$$Y = Xa.$$

Note that using BPE, we can find the frequent segments, for example, "bca" in the data "bcabebcfbca". So we consider applying the BPE algorithm to password analysis for finding out the frequently used password segments. Firstly, as the algorithm (i.e. Learn BPE operations) in [13] does not consider pairs crossing word boundaries, we adapt this algorithm to count the most frequent pair in the password set iteratively. Then we apply the BPE pairs back to the dataset and finally obtain the segmentation of each password. Figure 1 shows a simple example of BPE segmentation operations. We first split every password into a sequence of characters, then find frequent pairs iteratively through merge operations, shown in Fig. 1(a). Figure 1(b) shows the result of password segmentation according to the pairs from the previous step.

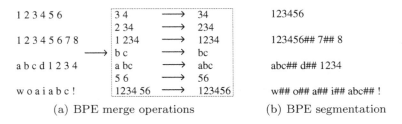

| (a) BPE merge operations | (b) BPE segmentation |

Fig. 1. The BPE segmentation from the password set {"123456", "12345678", "abcd1234", "woaiabc!"} ("##" is the separator unused in the dataset.)

3.2   BPE-PCFGs Password Guessing Model

3.2.1   Probabilistic Context-Free Grammars

Context-Free Grammars arise in Natural Language Processing where they are used to characterize the structure of sentences according to grammar rules. The generation of a sentence can be described as a set of productions from the start symbol. And Probabilistic Context-Free Grammars (PCFGs) simply assign a probability distribution to the productions.

A Probabilistic Context-Free Grammar in passwords is defined as $G = (V, \Sigma, S, R, P)$, where

(1) V is a set of variables. Each element $v_i \in V$ is a non-terminal or a variable. Non-terminals represent the semantical patterns in passwords.
(2) Σ is the set of terminals, disjoint from V. Each element $w_i \in \Sigma$ denotes a segment of grammar G. A password is made up of some w_i.
(3) S is the start variable and $S \in V$.
(4) R is a set of production rules from V to $(V \cup \Sigma)^*$, where the asterisk represents the Kleene star which means "zero or more". For each $r_i \in R$, it has the form:

$$v_i \to \eta_1 \eta_2 \ldots \eta_n,$$

where $v_i \in V$ and $\eta_j \in V \cup \Sigma$ for $i = 1 \ldots n$.

(5) P is the set of conditional probability of every rule. For any $v_i \in V$, P satisfies the constraint

$$\forall i, \sum_{v_i \to \eta_j \in R} P(v_i \to \eta_j) = 1.$$

In the guesses generation phase, we substantially improve the PCFGs model and generate password guesses in non-increasing probability order. The method is to declare a priority queue, which is similar to the one in "NEXT" FUNCTION detailed in [5] that can generate a next guess in non-increasing order, for each base structure. The method selects the one with the max probability from all queues until the guess number meets our experimental needs.

3.2.2 The BPE-PCFGs Model

The original PCFGs model is based on 3 password segmentation patterns. They are the letter-only pattern (L-pattern), the digit-only pattern (D-pattern) and the symbol-only pattern (S-pattern). For example, the password "abclove123" would define the structure L_7D_3, but in real world, the "abclove" may be two frequently used segments, "abc" and "love", which is what Weir's approach cannot find. In order to deal with this situation, we use the result of BPE segmentation to support detection of relevant patterns and generate guesses using the PCFGs model. During training, we define and learn the following four patterns of passwords. The information of our patterns is shown in Table 1.

Table 1. BPE patterns

Pattern	Description	Example
L_B_n	Letter pattern from letter-only segments of BPE segmentation	chen
D_B_n	Digital pattern from digit-only segments of BPE segmentation	163
S_B_n	Special pattern from symbol-only segments of BPE segmentation	@
M_B_n	Patterns not in above all patterns	.com

The BPE-structure is the composition of several BPE-patterns. In our training phrase, we automatically derive BPE-Structures from the password set segmented by BPE segmentation operations. Figure 2 gives an example about the generation of a BPE-structure from a password after segmented. As we can see, assuming the password "chen@163.com" becomes "chen## @## 163## .com" after BPE segmentation, it would define the BPE-structure $L\_B_4S\_B_1D\_B_3M\_B_4$, where the subscript number is the length of the observed substring.

The probability of a BPE structure S is computed as:

$$P(S) = \frac{count(S)}{N},$$

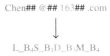

Fig. 2. The generation of BPE-Structures

Where *count(S)* denotes the number of occurrences of the structure S, and N is the number of passwords in the dataset.

In the training phase, we also learn all terminals of different BPE patterns from the training set and calculate their probability distributions. For example, the probability is assigned to the terminal "163" is

$$P(\text{"163"}|D\_B_3) = \frac{count(\text{"163"})}{count(D\_B_3)}.$$

We need to store the probability distributions of all BPE-Structures and all terminals of each pattern, preparing for the next password guessing phrase. Based on the probability distributions, we model them using the PCFGs model and generate guesses.

3.3 Rich-BPE-PCFGs Password Guessing Model

3.3.1 The Rich-PCFGs Model

In practice, we can employ a dictionary to segment passwords when analyzing the semantic characteristic of passwords. Also we can use some dictionaries to classify these segments, such as Chinese Pinyins, English words or names. These categories (we call them patterns) can enrich the semantic analysis of passwords, so we call this kind of PCFGs as Rich-PCFGs model.

Li et al. [9] showed that digit-only and letter-only passwords occupy 53.36%, 10.79% among Chinese users, and instead account for 15.80%, 43.91% respectively among English users on average. So in this paper, we use dictionaries and regular expressions to extend the categories of L-patterns and D-patterns.

In Weir's work, the L-pattern is simply replaced by dictionary words (also called alpha dictionary) of that length. This does not take the distribution of letter-only strings and language circumstances in passwords into account. Considering Chinese Pinyins, English words and names, we develop an algorithm taking a compilation of some dictionaries and using reverse maximum matching as the primary criterion for searching candidate segmentations. To improve the searching efficiency, we use Trie (also called prefix tree) to identify whether Chinese Pinyins, English words and names are included in passwords. In our method, we construct some Tries, which are based on different dictionaries, including Chinese names (downloaded from special Pinyin names library [20] of the Sogou Pinyin input method), English names (from the U.S. Social Security Administration [21]), Chinese Pinyins (containing 413 Pinyin syllables), English words and phrases (bigrams and trigrams of COCA introduced in Rafael et al. [6]

and the Merriam-Websters Collegiate Dictionary as the unigrams). The different categories of L-structures are described in Table 2.

Table 2. Categories of L-patterns

Category	Description	Example
L-CN-NAME	Pinyin of Chinese name	zhaozhiwei
L-CN-NAME-AB	Pinyin abbr. of Chinese name	zzw
L-CN-NAME-F	Pinyin of first name	zhiwei
L-CN-NAME-S	Pinyin of second name	zhao
L-CN-PINYIN	Other Pinyins	cuo
L-EN-NAME	English name	lency
L-EN-PHRASE	English phrase	ihearyou
L-EN-WORD	English word	certainly
L	Other L-patterns	aht

Li et al. [9] discussed the usage of dates in passwords but only six date formats were considered. We define and use 30 regular expressions to identify dates which are in the range from 1900 to 2016 in different formats. For instance, *19830126* may be interpreted as *January 26, 1983* and thus would be identified as *D-YYYYMMDD*. In addition, we also define and implement several other patterns of digital segments in passwords, shown in Table 3.

Table 3. Categories of D-patterns

Category	Description	Example
D-CONTINUOUS	Continuous digits of at least 3 numbers	123456
D-LEAP	Fixed interval between adjacent digits	2468
D-REPEAT0	Repeating one digit	111
D-REPEAT1	Repeating two or more digits	123123
D-DATE	D-YYYYMMDD etc.	19830126
D	Other D-patterns	437091

3.3.2 The Rich-BPE-PCFGs Model

We add the BPE word segments as a dictionary to the training phase of PCFGs. The specific steps are as follows:

- Based on L-patterns we define, we add a new pattern called L-BPE. We extract the pure letter segments in BPE segmentation as an input dictionary. Then we construct a Trie to identify whether a letter segment meets the L-BPE pattern.

- Based on D-patterns we propose, we add a new pattern called D-BPE. We extract the pure digital segments in BPE segmentation as an input dictionary. Then we construct a Trie to identify whether a digital segment meets the D-BPE pattern.
- We assign the L-BPE pattern and D-BPE pattern a minimum priority in their respective patterns (L-pattern and D-pattern). In detail, for a password segment, we firstly identify whether it conforms the L-patterns (except L) shown in Table 2 or D-patterns (except D) shown in Table 3. If not, we determine whether it meets the L-BPE pattern or D-BPE pattern. Certainly, if not satisfying any pattern, the segment would belong to L pattern or D pattern.
- We construct Probabilistic Context-Free Grammars using all patterns, including L-BPE, D-BPE and patterns in Tables 2 and 3. Finally, we generate password guesses in non-increasing probability order and plot guess-number graphs to compare different approaches.

4   Experimental Evaluation

In this section, we describe our experimental setups, including the datasets we use and choices of training sets and test sets. Then we present the experimental result under different BPE merge operations and comparatively evaluate our three models (i.e., BPE-PCFGs, Rich-PCFGs and Rich-BPE-PCFGs) with the original PCFGs model. Finally, we make quantitative analysis on our experimental results.

4.1   Introduction of Our Datasets

We use eight different leaked password sets, including four from Chinese sites and four from English sites, which are downloaded from public websites. The four Chinese datasets are from CSDN, dodonew, 178 and 7k7k. The CSDN is the largest IT community and service platform in China, and has leaked 6.4 million account information in 2011. The dodonew, as an entertainment website, leaked about 16 million passwords in 2011. The 178 and 7k7k are two gaming websites. The 178 dataset includes 9 million accounts, and the 7k7k includes 8.2 million. The four English datasets are from 000webhost, rockyou, xato and gmail. The 000webhost is a virtual hosts manufacturer, and has leaked more than 15 million accounts information in 2015. The rockyou, a popular social website in America, leaked 32 million passwords in 2009. The xato is a synthesised security website, leaking about 10 million accounts. The gmail, a free webmail service provider, leaked 5 million account information. These 8 datasets have more than 100 million passwords totally. The basic information about these datasets is shown in Table 4.

Taking the language and size of the dataset into account, we choose the CSDN, dodonew and 178 as our training sets, 7k7k as a test dataset. Similarly, we choose the 000webhost, rockyou and xato as training sets and gmail as a test set. Table 5 lists the 6 scenarios used in this paper.

Table 4. Information of our password sets

	Service type	Language	Amount
CSDN	IT community	Chinese	6413607
dodonew	entertainment	Chinese	15996857
178	game	Chinese	9049201
7k7k	game	Chinese	8201663
000webhost	web hosting	English	15232337
rockyou	social site	English	32585010
gmail	email	English	4909866
xato	security	English	9997946

Table 5. Training and test set for each experimental scenario

Experimental scenario	Training set	Test set
#1: CSDN→7k7k	CSDN	7k7k
#2: dodonew→7k7k	dodonew	7k7k
#3: 178→7k7k	178	7k7k
#4: 000webhost→gmail	000webhost	gmail
#5: rockyou→gmail	rockyou	gmail
#6: xato→gmail	xato	gmail

4.2   Experimental Results

To explore the influence of the number of BPE merge operations on password guessing, we conduct two groups of experiments under different number of BPE merge operations, one for the BPE-PCFGs model and the other for Rich-BPE-PCFGs model. We choose 10,000, 50,000 and 100,000 merge operations as the comparison parameter for our experiments. Figure 3 shows that with the increase of number of BPE merge operations, our BPE-PCFGs model can guess more passwords, especially when guessing passwords from English websites. The model under 50,000 BPE merge operations can gain a improvement of 60.83%, 19.08% and 21.09% compared with 10,000 merge operations when attacking gmail. When the number of merge operations is 100,000, comparing with 50,000, there are less than 14% improvement when attacking gmail. The improvement is quite modest (less than 3%) when cracking 7k7k, with the increase of the number of BPE merge operations.

The observations made above similarly apply to the Rich-BPE-PCFGs model, shown in Fig. 4. And the proportion of improvements among different number of BPE merge operations is much limited. So, Considering above experimental results and the time consumption of BPE segmentation, we choose 50,000 BPE merge operations for our further experiments.

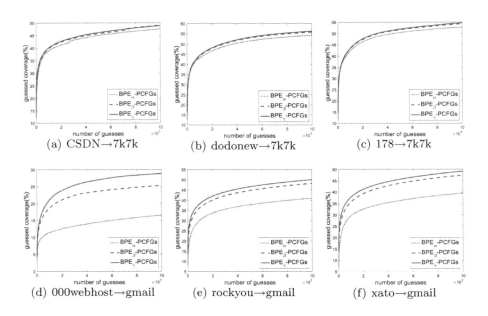

Fig. 3. BPE-PCFGs for different number of BPE merge operations ($\alpha = 10{,}000$, $\beta = 50{,}000$, $\gamma = 100{,}000$)

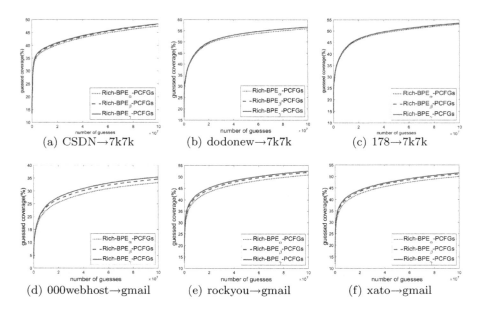

Fig. 4. Rich-BPE-PCFGs for different number of BPE merge operations ($\alpha = 10{,}000$, $\beta = 50{,}000$, $\gamma = 100{,}000$)

The segmentation after 50,000 BPE merge operations is adapted in our experiments to discuss the impact of BPE patterns to the PCFGs on password guessing. Experimental results are shown in Fig. 5.

Figures 5(a)–(c) show guessing results within 100 million guesses when attacking 7k7k, a Chinese website. We can see that the BPE-PCFGs model clearly outperforms PCFGs. The average improvements of BPE-PCFGs over PCFGs are 9.10% for CSDN, 14.01% for dodonew and 33.24% for 178. We also compare the Rich-BPE-PCFGs model with Rich-PCFGs model. Figure 5(a)–(c) demonstrate that the Rich-BPE-PCFGs model can obtain a higher success rate of 5.42% for CSDN, 4.57% for dodonew, 4.20% for 178 on average.

Figures 5(d)–(f) show guessing results when attacking gmail, a English website. We can see that the Rich-BPE-PCFGs model still performs better than Rich-PCFGs. The proportion of improvements is 8.03% for 000webhost, 6.19% for rockyou, 5.93% for xato on average. But the BPE-PCFGs model performs worse than PCFGs, which may be due to the small guess number. In order to prove when guessing number is large enough, the BPE-PCFGs model can perform better than PCFGs. We make another group of experiments using probability-threshold graphs. The experimental results are shown in Fig. 6.

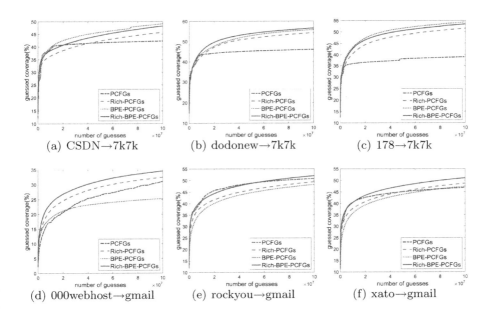

(a) CSDN→7k7k   (b) dodonew→7k7k   (c) 178→7k7k

(d) 000webhost→gmail   (e) rockyou→gmail   (f) xato→gmail

Fig. 5. Experiment results for our models under 50,000 BPE merge operations

In Fig. 6, we can see that when the guessing number is large enough, the BPE-PCFGs model can achieve almost 100% guessing coverage, but the PCFGs model only achieves less than 70% guessing coverage. The results are similar when

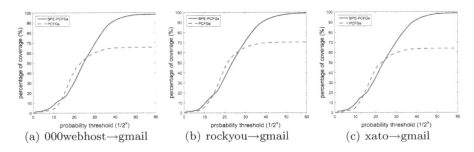

Fig. 6. Prob. threshold graph for comparing BPE-PCFGs model with PCFGs; A point (x, y) on a curve means that y percent of passwords in the dataset have probability at least $\frac{1}{2^x}$.

attacking gmail in our experiments. We can obtain these experimental results because the BPE-PCFGs model is able to make L-patterns and D-patterns into smaller units. And this group of experiments can prove the BPE-PCFGs model performs better than PCFGs when the guessing number is fully large.

Results of the Rich-BPE-PCFGs model compared with BPE-PCFGs under 10,000 and 100,000 BPE merge operations are similar to above, shown in Table 6.

Table 6. The improvement percentage of the Rich-BPE-PCFGs model among different number of BPE merge operations compared with BPE-PCFGs

	#1	#2	#3	#4	#5	#6
10,000	3.94%	3.18%	3.25%	3.40%	3.57%	3.45%
100,000	6.08%	4.64%	4.32%	10.68%	7.66%	7.18%

Based on above statistical analysis, we can see that our Rich-BPE-PCFGs model under 50,000 BPE merge operations is able to crack 2.36%–37.56% more passwords than the original PCFGs model within 100 million guesses. The result is better among Chinese websites.

5   Conclusion and Future Work

In this paper, we take advantage of the BPE algorithm to find segments frequently used in passwords and propose two new password guessing models, i.e. the BPE-PCFGs and Rich-BPE-PCFGs. The BPE-PCFGs model is based on the BPE password segmentation patterns, and the Rich-BPE-PCFGs model is based on dictionaries composed of BPE segments and other vocabularies. Experimental results show that our approach, the BPE-PCFGs model, under 50,000 BPE merge operations, outperforms the PCFGs model that has been considered to be the state-of-the-art model by 15.95%–39.71% among Chinese websites within 100 million guesses. Compared with the Rich-PCFGs model, the Rich-BPE-PCFGs model can also obtain a higher success rate of 5.42% for CSDN, 4.57% for dodonew, 4.20% for 178 on average, and similar results when attacking the English website, gmail.

We believe that the Rich-BPE-PCFGs model is very useful but also partially limiting. The model only adds the pure letter and digital segments based on original patterns, not considering more other possible segments in the BPE segmentation and the deeper association between the BPE segmentation and password semantics. Our Future work is to explore the semantics hidden in the BPE segmentation of passwords and try to combine the BPE segmentation with new patterns, for example, the personal information.

References

1. Herley, C., Van Oorschot, P.: A research agenda acknowledging the persistence of passwords. IEEE Secur. Priv. **10**(1), 28–36 (2012)
2. Paar, C., Pelzl, J.: Understanding Cryptography: A Textbook for Students and Practitioners. Springer, Heidelberg (2010)
3. JohntheRipper: Password cracking wordlist. http://www.openwall.com/wordlists/
4. WikiPedia: Dictionary attack. https://en.wikipedia.org/wiki/Dictionary_attack
5. Weir, M., Aggarwal, S., De Medeiros, B., Glodek, B.: Password cracking using probabilistic context-free grammars. In: 2009 30th IEEE Symposium on Security and Privacy, pp. 391–405. IEEE (2009)
6. Veras, R., Collins, C., Thorpe, J.: On semantic patterns of passwords and their security impact. In: NDSS (2014)
7. Veras, R., Thorpe, J., Collins, C.: Visualizing semantics in passwords: the role of dates. In: Proceedings of the Ninth International Symposium on Visualization for Cyber Security, pp. 88–95. ACM (2012)
8. Houshmand, S., Aggarwal, S., Flood, R.: Next gen PCFG password cracking. IEEE Trans. Inf. Forensics Secur. **10**(8), 1776–1791 (2015)
9. Li, Z., Han, W., Xu, W.: A large-scale empirical analysis of Chinese web passwords. In: USENIX Security Symposium, pp. 559–574 (2014)
10. Li, Y., Wang, H., Sun, K.: A study of personal information in human-chosen passwords and its security implications. In: IEEE INFOCOM 2016-The 35th Annual IEEE International Conference on Computer Communications, pp. 1–9. IEEE (2016)
11. Wang, D., Zhang, Z., Wang, P., Yan, J., Huang, X.: Targeted online password guessing: an underestimated threat. In: Proceedings of the 2016 ACM SIGSAC Conference on Computer and Communications Security, pp. 1242–1254. ACM (2016)
12. Gage, P.: A new algorithm for data compression. C Users J. **12**(2), 23–38 (1994)
13. Sennrich, R., Haddow, B., Birch, A.: Neural machine translation of rare words with subword units (2015). arXiv preprint: arXiv:1508.07909
14. Shibata, Y., Kida, T., Fukamachi, S., Takeda, M., Shinohara, A., Shinohara, T., Arikawa, S.: Byte pair encoding: a text compression scheme that accelerates pattern matching. Technical report DOI-TR-161, Department of Informatics, Kyushu University (1999)

15. Kelley, P.G., Komanduri, S., Mazurek, M.L., Shay, R., Vidas, T., Bauer, L., Christin, N., Cranor, L.F., Lopez, J.: Guess again (and again and again): measuring password strength by simulating password-cracking algorithms. In: 2012 IEEE Symposium on Security and Privacy (SP), pp. 523–537. IEEE (2012)

16. Zhang, Y., Monrose, F., Reiter, M.K.: The security of modern password expiration: an algorithmic framework and empirical analysis. In: Proceedings of the 17th ACM Conference on Computer and Communications Security, pp. 176–186. ACM (2010)

17. Bonneau, J.: The science of guessing: analyzing an anonymized corpus of 70 million passwords. In: 2012 IEEE Symposium on Security and Privacy (SP), pp. 538–552. IEEE (2012)

18. Chou, H.C., Lee, H.C., Yu, H.J., Lai, F.P., Huang, K.H., Hsueh, C.W.: Password cracking based on learned patterns from disclosed passwords. IJICIC **9**(2), 821–839 (2013)

19. Weir, C.M.: Using probabilistic techniques to aid in password cracking attacks. The Florida State University (2010)

20. Pinyin, S.: Chinese Pinyin names in sogous list (2015). http://pinyin.sogou.com/dict/detail/index/34816

21. SSA: Popular baby names. U.S. social security administration (2013). http://www.ssa.gov/oact/babynames/limits.html

How to Make Information-Flow Analysis Based Defense Ineffective: An ART Behavior-Mask Attack

Xueyi Yang[1,2,3], Limin Liu[2,3(✉)], Lingchen Zhang[2,3], Weiyu Jiang[2,3], and Shiran Pan[1,2,3]

[1] School of Cyber Security, University of Chinese Academy of Sciences, Beijing, China
[2] State Key Laboratory of Information Security, Institute of Information Engineering, Chinese Academy of Sciences, Beijing, China
liulimin@iie.ac.cn
[3] Data Assurance and Communication Security Research Center, Chinese Academy of Sciences, Beijing, China

Abstract. Android permission mechanism cannot resist permission abuse, the key of malware detection is to expose its malicious behavior. Although plentiful transformation attacks are used to bypass malware detection, the latest information-flow analysis based defenses claim that they can identify malicious flows with high accuracy. Nevertheless, in this paper, we expose a new attack surface known as Behavior-Mask attack in Android Runtime (ART), which can bypass most known information-flow analysis based defenses in practice. Our attack techniques can be utilized to hide Android applications' actual behavior by only executing some irrelevant Java code in the normal way. We corrupt few runtime data through a small piece of JNI code to hijack the control flow and data flow of Java code dynamically in ART environment. Further, we implement an automatic development framework to demonstrate the viability of Behavior-Mask attack. We analyze the existing defenses on Android and traditional desktop operating systems, and put forward some new ideas for the design and implementation of future defenses against the proposed attack.

Keywords: Android · ART · Confusion · Java · Transformation · Code reuse

1 Introduction

Android is the most popular mobile operating system with a market share of 86.8% in 2016Q3 [17]. The popularity of Android incurs endless attacks for collecting privacy data or gaining economic benefits [7]. Although Android designs its permission mechanism to reduce privacy and security risks [9], malwares can still abuse their legal permissions in an unreasonable way without users' understanding to execute malicious operations [38]. In fact, previous research has

© Springer International Publishing AG 2017
P.Q. Nguyen and J. Zhou (Eds.): ISC 2017, LNCS 10599, pp. 269–287, 2017.
https://doi.org/10.1007/978-3-319-69659-1_15

shown that more than 70% of the permission usages of Android apps are not perceived by users [38]. In order to reduce the threats of malware, abundant malware detection techniques are proposed to discover and prevent malicious behavior.

To defeat detection, code obfuscation plays an important role in malicious software development. Traditional obfuscation techniques [28] adopted by attackers are obfuscating code to conceal attackers' purposes or attackers' logic, such as call indirections and code reordering. However, these obfuscation can be easily detected by traditional static analysis techniques [29]. Some attackers complicate obfuscation by splitting malicious flows into components [14,37], Java Native Interfaces (JNIs) [1], or framework callbacks [4]. In order to resist these three types of complicated obfuscation techniques, detectors reconstruct the application behavior more precisely by considering those implicit information-flow transitions. Dynamically loading/decrypting data/code or reflection is another useful way to conceal attackers' purposes [25,28]. Static analysis can only detect the existence of these attacks, but cannot expose the purposes of malware [25]. Consequently, dynamic analysis techniques such as dynamic taint analysis is an effective way to detect the potential information-flow hidden by this kind of attack [31].

Our work focuses on code-reuse-based obfuscation on android application [34], which completes attackers' expected behavior by misusing existing code chunks in binary-level. However, the complicated attack process may cause system exceptions in the end and attackers' expected behavior is completed in JNI. Certainly, this type of obfuscation can be prevented by the similar defense techniques on traditional desktop systems such as Address Space Layout Randomization (ASLR) [30]. As a result, researchers claim that they can identify malicious flows with an accuracy about 94% [3]; most common mobile anti-malwares with information-flow analysis [20,21] has reported a large number of mobile malwares every year.

The attack technique in this paper performs in ART [13], the newly introduced managed runtime (Android version above 4.4). One of the most significant differences between ART and Dalvik is that ART executes binary code directly while Dalvik interpretively executes DEX (Dalvik EXecutable) byte-code. However, the single binary code only includes low-level semantics (e.g., loading or jumping), and runtime ensures the high-level Java semantics (e.g., sending SMS message by calling *sendTextMessage*) by maintaining plenty of data structures as the identity information of Java objects and methods. Dalvik verifies current method's access permissions when it interprets any *INVOKE* opcode. Unfortunately, in ART, above verifications have not been implemented into all method calls. These vulnerabilities increase the flexibility of attackers and increase the difficulty of detection.

In this paper, we present a new transformation attack technique known as Behavior-Mask, which can bypass existent information-flow analysis based defenses. Behavior-Mask attack exploits above vulnerabilities to misuse the high-level semantics of existing code in new ART environment. Behavior-Mask attack can hijack control-flow of any standard Java code via one JNI method including additional a minimum of 11 lines of assembly code. This attack code locates and corrupts little critical runtime data, which describes the objects and methods used in hijacked Java code.

Furthermore, we implement a development framework to generate necessary code for attacks. We implement several prototypes of Behavior-Mask attack for several kinds of program behavior by hand or by the framework, and evaluate their effectiveness and performance overhead. The evaluation results show that apps using our attack techniques achieve an improving imperceptibility than that with known transformation techniques. This demonstrates that Behavior-Mask attack can bypass most android information-flow analyses and only incurs the negligible overhead in Application Package (APK) file size, installation time, CPU, and memory usage. In addition, the evaluation results show that the source-code-based-only defenses, which do not consider the divided semantics precisely to be prone to attacks, should be reassessed. We discuss the limitations of Behavior-Mask attack and how to resist this attack with attack code detection, program behavior detection, and reinforce of execution environment.

In summary, our main contributions can be summarized as follows:

– We discover a new attack surface in ART runtime, separating the high-level semantics of Java code without enough security review. This attack surface facilitates the construction of malicious high-level payloads and opens the door for various transformation attacks.
– We present Behavior-Mask attack, an efficient transformation attack technique against Android applications running in ART environment. With Behavior-Mask attack technique, we demonstrate the limitations of a range of information-flow analysis based defenses from the state of the art.
– We implement an attack development framework, performing binary analysis and generating the basic necessary code automatically. The framework has proved the high-efficiency and wide applicability of our attack.
– We show the necessity for information-flow analysis to consider program semantics carefully and precisely, such as the whole flow analysis with JNI and runtime in binary level. In addition, we provide some new ideas for resisting Behavior-Mask attack to inspire subsequent researchers.

The rest of this paper is organized as follows. Section 2 introduces the preliminaries of Java semantics's infrastructure provided by ART environment. In Sect. 3, we present the design and working principle of Behavior-Mask attack. In Sect. 4, we show an automation implementation and some implementation details of Behavior-Mask attack. In Sect. 5, we evaluate the effectiveness and performance overhead of Behavior-Mask attack. In Sect. 6, we discuss the limitation of our attack, and possible defensive schemes. The related work and conclusion are presented in Sects. 7 and 8.

2   Technical Background

In this section, we briefly introduce the new Android runtime (ART runtime) and the necessary background for a better understanding of Behavior-Mask attack.

2.1 Android ART Runtime

Android 4.4 KitKat introduced Android Runtime (ART) as a new runtime environment, which entirely compiles application's byte-code into binary code. Since Android 5.0, ART became the only runtime option to replace Dalvik, a process virtual machine with trace-based just-in-time (JIT) compilation to run DEX byte-code. To maintain backward compatibility, ART uses DEX byte-code which is the same input as Dalvik. DEX byte-code is supplied by standard .dex files as part of APK files. Meanwhile, ART's new compiler dex2oat generates .oat file rather than .odex file which is used by Dalvik.

Oat file format is a customized ELF file format with two core sections: oat data section and oat exec section. Oat data section comprises complete original dex files and data that describes all these dex files, classes and methods. Oat exec section comprises native code of all the methods.

As the new compiler is designed from scratch, there exist considerable differences between versions regarding ART's on-device compiler dex2oat and its generated native code. In the following sections, we use ARM32 device with Android 6.0(Marshmallow) as the default subject to explain our work, and we illustrate the differences between versions when necessary.

2.2 ART Addressing Modes

Two primary addressing modes used to invoke a Java method in the ART generated native code are named multilevel indirect vtable addressing mode and multilevel indirect list addressing mode in this paper. Since ART use C++ class *art::mirror::ArtMethod* to describe Java method, the last step of those two addressing modes is locating the native code of method from the field *entry_point_from_quick_compiled_code_* of class *ArtMethod*. Naturally, the difference between these two addressing modes are the paths locating the *ArtMethod* reference of callee method.

As shown in the left of Fig. 1, in multilevel indirect vtable addressing mode, there is a virtual method table behind each Java class instance and the callee method's class instance can be resolved by the field *declaring_class_* of *art::mirror::Object*. As shown in the right of Fig. 1, in multilevel indirect list addressing mode, there is a resolved method reference list maintained by the thread and the list is resolved by the field *dex_cache_resolved_methods_* of *Art-Method*.

In the third step of those two addressing modes, there is one critical offset of callee method reference to class instance's beginning or resolved method list's beginning. This offset value in the two modes is the tag of method and is written in the native code used to invoke the method. Hence, the tag of each method is determined when the application is installed.

However, ART realizes method call by the two addressing modes without enough security reviews such as the necessary DEX byte-code verification for method signature and argument type.

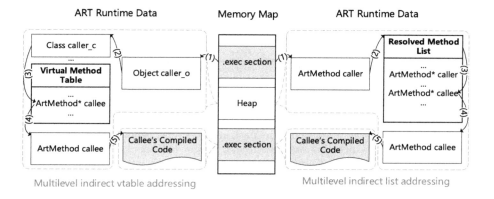

Fig. 1. Two primary addressing modes used for calling a Java method

3 Behavior-Mask Attack

In this section, we present Behavior-Mask attack, a transformation attack that misuses the actual high-level semantics of fixed code. With Behavior-Mask attack technique, an application could exhibit different behavior by executing the same Java code with the same initial values. In other words, both legitimate and malicious behavior could be realized by the same code.

3.1 Motivating Example

In the example shown in Fig. 2, an attacker's target is to steal a user's location information. To this end, attacker inserts target code to a benign app such as a pedometer app, which requires access to the user's location information and network for legitimate reasons. However, direct abuses of these privileges to send the user's location over the network, target behavior implemented by target code, can be easily detected by common information-flow analysis systems.

In Behavior-Mask attack, instead of malicious target code, an attacker could insert mask code which implements seemingly benign data operation into the pedometer app. The execution of mask code could complete mask behavior without attack or could complete target behavior after attack code was executed. The new malware's source code doesn't comprise the feasible information-flow which might result in location information leakage, moreover, it doesn't contain any API which could be exploited for completing target behavior.

In the following content of this section, a simple example which is constituted by the first line of mask and target code of the real-world example is used to illustrate our attack. The necessary variable definitions and method prototype are shown in Fig. 4(a). And the assembly code of mask code which is shown in Fig. 4(b) includes the following functions: preparing arguments, invoking callee method, and transmitting return value.

Mask Code

1. m1.object = jsonObject.opt(str1);
2. m2.double = m1.object.optDouble(null);
3. m3.double = m1.object.optDouble(null, 0);
4. m4.str = Double.toString(m2.double) + Double.toString(m3.double);
5. m5.object = myEmptyMethod(int1, int2);
6. m6.object = JSONObject.wrap(m5a.object);
7. m6a.jsonArray.remove(m4a.jsonArray.length());

Target Code

1. t1.location = locationManager. getLastKnownLocation(provider);
2. t2.latitude = t1.location.getLatitude();
3. t3.longitude = t1.location.getLongitude();
4. t4.str = Double.toString(t2.latitude) + Double.toString(t3.longitude);
5. t5.socket = new Socket(distanceName, distancePort);
6. t6.outputSteam = t5.socket.getOutputStream();
7. t6.outputSteam.write(t4.str.getBytes());

Fig. 2. A real-world example of Behavior-Mask attack. (Mask behavior: Obtaining data from *jsonObject* and Operating *m6a.jsonArray*; Target behavior: Obtaining personal location information from *myLocationManager* and sending it into *distanceName*)

3.2   Attack Design

As shown in Fig. 3, the target code is replaced by the mask code which is crafted by attackers. Little critical runtime data is corrupted to redirect the accesses of objects and methods used in mask code to the corresponding ones used in target code. As introduced in Sect. 2, the high-level semantics is dependent on various data structures that are maintained to describe Java objects and methods by ART runtime, and binary code only comprises the low-level semantics without understanding of Java object and method. Thus, although the high-level semantics of mask code and target code might be completely unrelated, mask code comprises the necessary low-level semantics of target code.

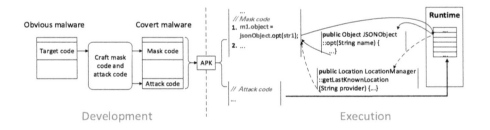

Fig. 3. A brief work flow of Behavior-Mask attack

The primary challenges for Behavior-Mask attack are (1) The suitable runtime data that is effective in controlling the high-level program semantics need to be identified. (2) The corruption of runtime data is stealthy to runtime and will not cause any system exception. (3) The attack should locate all needed runtime data efficiently and does not require additional input information.

Behavior-Mask attack misuses app's high-level semantics via implementing covert data transformation and control-flow hijack. Covert data transformation between arbitrary object fields is realized by redirecting their memory space. Two object fields could share the same memory to transfer data or exchange their memory in order to restore in the future. Control-flow hijack for any Java code including call instruction is realized by rebinding the method call. The method call of mask method could be bound to target method's instance and code. The attack code used for implementing the two goals could be placed in any normal non-static JNI method without any extra parameter.

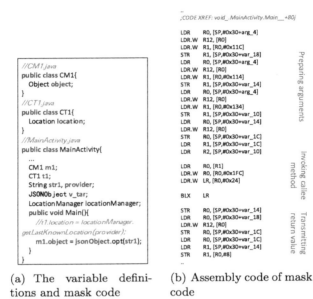

(a) The variable definitions and mask code

(b) Assembly code of mask code

Fig. 4. The simple example which is constituted by the first line of mask and target code of the real-world example

3.3   Covert Data Transformation via Object Fields Redirecting

As shown in Fig. 4(b), $MainActivity.Main$ prepares callee method's arguments by locating the variables $jsonObject$ and $str1$ on the heap and storing them in the top of stack. It also transmits the return value of callee method to $m1.object$. Those processes provide the following semantics:

$$R1 \Leftarrow [SP + 0x14] \Leftarrow [this + 0x114] \quad // \text{ pass } jsonObject$$
$$R2 \Leftarrow [SP + 0x20] \Leftarrow [this + 0x134] \quad // \text{ pass } str1$$
$$R0 \Rightarrow [SP + 0x1C] \Rightarrow [[this + 0x11C] + 0x8] \quad // \text{ return to } m1.object$$

Behavior-Mask attack allows data to flow between object fields regardless of compiler settings or calling conventions. As a result, the execution of the code used to locate mask method's arguments could obtain target method's arguments. Behavior-Mask attack realizes this goal by redirecting the memory of different object fields. For the simple example, a intuitional attack can be described as follows:

$$[this + 0x114] \Leftarrow [this + 0x118] \quad // \text{ redirect } jsonObject \text{ to } locationManager$$
$$[this + 0x134] \Leftarrow [this + 0x130] \quad // \text{ redirect } str1 \text{ to } provider$$
$$[this + 0x11C] \Leftarrow [this + 0x138] \quad // \text{ redirect } m1 \text{ to } t1$$

In order to realize the aforesaid redirections, *this* object and the above fields's offsets should be resolved. Hijacking *this* object is the start of every Behavior-Mask attack. 4 indirect reference tables such as the local indirect reference table are used by ART to maintain the state of Java objects. The reference of *this* can be located in those indirect reference tables by the two default arguments of any non-static JNI method. Even if there is a complicated path between attacker concerned field and *this* pointer, the field also can be located stepwise by understanding the memory layout rules of Java object.

Memory Layout of Java Object. Java data types are divided into eight basic value types and reference types. All reference types are inherited from *Java.Lang.Object* whose size is 8 bytes. For any reference the class member fields are arranged starting from the 9th byte and according to the following rules.

Ordering rules of member fields can be divided into three layers:

Top: Reference fields are ahead of value fields. Value fields are ordered by their size such as 64-bit, 32-bit, 16-bit, and 8-bit.

Middle: Value fields with the same size arranged as an inherent order: reference, boolean, byte, char, short, int, long, float, double, void.

Bottom: The fields with the same type are sorted by their DEX field indexes.

The memory layout of object *this* is shown in the left of Fig. 5.

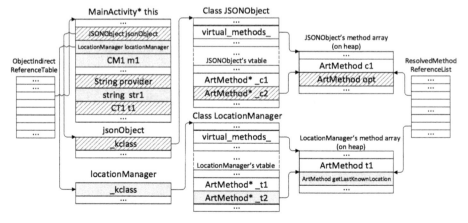

Fig. 5. Layouts of attack exploited memory in the simple example. *The critical data exploited for mask code is marked with shaded stripe and critical data used for target code is marked with shadow.*

3.4 Hijacking Control-Flow via Method Call Rebinding

As shown in Fig. 4(b), *MainActivity.Main* invokes callee method by locating *JSONObject::opt* and branching into its code. ART generated binary code locates a Java method by the two primary addressing modes, multilevel indirect vtable addressing mode and multilevel indirect list addressing mode. In our simple example, callee method *JSONObject::opt* is located by multilevel indirect vtable addressing mode and its method tag is *0x1FC*. The assembly code used for locating callee method's code provides the following semantics:

$$LR \Leftarrow [[[jsonObject] + 0x1FC] + 0x24]$$

Behavior-Mask attack allows a method call would be rebound to another irrelevant method. As a result, the execution of the code used to locate mask method could obtain target method. In our example, after the fields *jsonObject* has been redirected to the memory of *locationManager* as we introduced in Sect. 3.3, the attacker corrupts class *LocationManager*'s virtual method reference table and rebinds the method reference of the above method to target method *getLastKnownLocation*. The semantics of the rebinding process is shown below:

$$[[locationManager] + 0x1FC] \Leftarrow [[locationManager] \\ + (getLastKnownLocation's\ tag)]$$

Accordingly, when the tag of target method is equal to the tag of mask method, the process of hijacking control-flow will be completed without any additional attack code. We summarize the usage rules of the two primary addressing modes in order to design method call for attack.

Usage Scenarios of Two Primary Addressing Mode. The usage scenarios of the two addressing modes can be differentiated by whether dynamic binding is needed. We design the following three conditions for a Java method call. ART uses multilevel indirect list addressing mode to address the method if this method matches one of the three conditions or uses multilevel indirect vtable addressing mode otherwise.

(1) The method is a direct method. Direct methods comprise static, private, and ⟨*init*⟩ methods.
(2) Class of the method is not a derived class and cannot be inherited. The class does not extend from any class and not implement any interface. The class or the method has the keyword *Final*.
(3) Dynamic binding is no longer needed in the optimization of method call. If the caller object reference is a local variable, the callee method can be determined at compile time.

4 An Automatic Development Framework of Behavior-Mask Attack

The flow that developing a covert malware by Behavior-Mask attack techniques comprises six steps that are shown in Fig. 6. (1) Syntax analysis. (2) Hunting usable mask method. (3) Designing object mask. (4) Designing method mask. (5) Generating attack code. (6) Redeploying application.

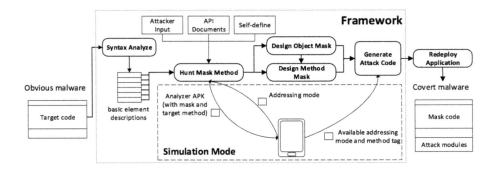

Fig. 6. The work flow of developing Behavior-Mask attack

Since implementation of an actual behavior always includes many lines of code and Behavior-Mask attack is based on binary-level analysis, Behavior-Mask attack is cumbersome and hard to perform by hand. Hence, we build a framework for the automation of first five steps to generate all necessary code of Behavior-Mask attack. The sixth step is not automated since attackers are allowed to arrange attack code and triggering conditions freely.

This framework can work in two modes: simulation mode and general mode. In simulation mode, we use some additional Android ART environments for accurate analysis of binary code and runtime information. In general mode, we need to perform the similar analysis in the exporting attack code.

4.1 Syntax Analyzing Target Code and Hunting Usable Mask Method

Firstly, framework divides target code into a series of snippets and tidies the method information and variable information for each snippet of target code.

For each target method, framework hunts a usable mask method from three sources: developer's input, Android official API reference documentation [12] or a new self-define. To identify useful mask method, framework applies two filters on all potential mask method: (1) The size of return value and the total size of parameters of mask method can't be less than the one of target method. (2) If target method's return value is a reference, the return value of mask method must be a reference whose type is inheritable from the type of target's return value such as the universal type **java.lang.Object**.

In some early system versions of Android, a handful of methods are addressed in immediate addressing mode by ART such as Android framework method *MediaCodec.queueInputBuffer* in Android 5.0.0. This kind of method is noneffective when they are appointed as mask methods. In simulation mode, our framework prepares an "analyzer" application which will be installed into Android devices to output enough addressing information. In general mode, we can't discover this kind of method without ART environment.

4.2 Design of Data Container Class and Implementation of Covert Data Transformation

We design a public class (*DataContainer*) that comprises two fields: a type *TargetDataContainer* field and a type *MaskDataContainer* field. The two fields contain all target variables and mask variables in a specific form to ensure the correct corresponding relationships of memory layouts. We use some auxiliary data transformation code to clone data between the original variables and the temporary variables in the front and the behind of mask code.

4.3 Design of Method Container and Implementation of Hijacking Control-Flow

In the final malware, one line of code invoking a container method replaces a series lines of target code. The container method comprises all mask code that uses the variables of type *MaskDataContainer* field. In simulation mode, method rebinding can be performed by the sufficient addressing information that we have analyzed aforehand. In general mode, the corresponding analysis work should be performed in attack code.

5 Evaluation

In this section we evaluate the effectiveness of Behavior-Mask attack by usual anti-malware applications and some excellent information-flow analysis systems. We also evaluate our attack's performance overhead for APK's size, installation time, CPU usage and memory usage.

In our experiment, we use a SAMSUNG Galaxy Nexus mobile phone to test our experimental apps. Our test phone runs the Google official Android firmware, Marshmallow 6.0.1 with the kernel version 3.0.101. Our backend detection server has 32 eight-core 2.00 GHz CPUs and 144 GB memory. The experimental apps are created by Android Studio 2.3.1 with Gradle 2.2.3 and Android 6.0.1 SDK.

5.1 Effectiveness

We extract the 5 kinds of common malicious behavior shown in Table 1 from some business reports [11] and research work [33]. We build a sample set for each common malicious behavior from the 5560 samples in Drebin [3] dataset. For each common malicious behavior, we design three experimental sample groups.

Group-A: 10 malware samples randomly selected from the sample set. Group-B: one malware produced with our framework. Group-C: one blank app that only introduces the necessary permissions of malicious behavior.

Table 1. 5 kinds of common malicious behavior

Label	Description
SENDSMS	Send SMS messages to premium-rate numbers
STEALSMS	Steal personal information from SMS
STEALCONTACT	Steal the contact information
TRACKLOCATION	Send user's location information continuously
STEALPHONEINFO	Steal phone information

Table 2. Evaluation results

(a) Result of SENDSMS

Analysis Tools	Group-A	Group-B	Group-C
Anti-Malwares	8+28	8+0	8
FlowDroid	1	0	0
DroidSafe	1	0	0
DroidChain	1	0	0
Amandroid	1	0	0
PRIMO	1	0	0

(b) Result of average

Analysis Tools	Group-A	Group-B	Group-C
Anti-Malwares	x+22.3	x+0	x
FlowDroid	0.9	0	0
DroidSafe	0.96	0	0
DroidChain	0.86	0	0
Amandroid	0.92	0	0
PRIMO	0.94	0	0

Anti-Malware Application Test. Anti-malware analysis is a very common way used by smartphone users to detect malware. Most anti-malware applications are declared to use various information-flow analysis techniques [20,21]. VirusTotal [35] is a free online service that enables the identification of kinds of malicious content by antivirus engines and website scanners. We perform anti-malware detection for our samples by VirusTotal, which supports 58 Android anti-malware engines until April 2017.

Information-Flow Analysis Systems Test. We also perform our evaluation with 5 publicly available information-flow analysis systems from academia. Some well-known systems haven't been used, because they do not support ART such as *TaintDroid* [10] or are unavailable such as *TaintART* [31].

Most Android information-flow analysis systems focused on Android Inter-Component Communication (ICC) mechanism [16]. *FlowDroid* [4] is such a static taint analysis tool that considers data branches between Android components, such as Lifecycle-aware and static fields. *DroidSafe* [14] is also a good platform for information-flow analysis, but it requests more system resources to be performed for some larger Android apps. *DroidChain* [36] exposes program behavior by API call chain. *Amandroid* [37] focuses on inter-component control flow. *PRIMO* [22] combines static analysis with probabilistic models.

Results. Due to space constraints, we show the statistical results of one common behavior and an average of 5 kinds of common malicious behavior in Table 2. The element value means the detection ratio for malwares. For row Anti-Malwares, we show the sum of all anti-malwares' detection ratio.

Table 2(a) illustrates that *SENDSMS* as a kind of simple behavior is detected with a very high probability. Table 2(b) illustrates the average detection accuracy of those chosen detection tools achieves 92.4%. Particularly, more than 27 anti-malwares identify all the samples in Group-A. Nevertheless, none of the detection tools can distinguish between the malware developed by Behavior-Mask attack techniques and the corresponding blank app. In summary, Behavior-Mask attack can evade those known Android information-flow analysis.

5.2 Performance

As the benchmark, Group-D for each kind of common malicious behavior is an application with one activity and necessary permissions. The malicious code used to implement the malicious behavior is appended in the activity's method: **onCreate**. For the malicious code, we implement Behavior-Mask attack manually and automatically to build two new malware in Group-E and Group-F.

APK's Size and Installation Time. Table 3 illustrates the APK's size for each group. In fact, a large proportion of the cost depends on the additional JNI libraries, rather than the additional Java mask code and JNI attack code. The overhead for APK's size introduced by Behavior-Mask attack is less than 0.8% in the aspect of APK's size, which is negligible for developers.

Figure 7 illustrates the installation time for each group. We install experimental apps by ADB tool. We record the time (t0) of a system log message (*Calling main entry com.android.commands.pm.Pm*), and the time (t1) of another system log message (*Finishing install immediately*). t1-t0 represents the installation time. The average of all experiment results shows that Behavior-Mask attack incurs at most 0.93% overhead for installation time, which is unnoticeable by normal users. Moreover, the overhead is difficult to be separated from environmental error.

CPU and Memory Usage Overhead. We perform the CPU usage overhead evaluation by monitoring the growth rate of CPU used time in user-mode and kernel-mode, which is comprised in **/proc/[pid]/stat** and **/proc/stat**. In order to improve the accuracy of detection, target behavior is carried out 50 times at 20 ms interval. We acquire the CPU used time every 100 ms and calculate the increment with the last acquired. Figure 8 illustrates that the results of *TRACKLOCATION*'s samples. The results demonstrate the indistinguishability of different sample groups and Behavior-Mask attack introduces negligible CPU usage overhead. The evaluation for other kinds of common malicious behavior don't change our evaluation conclusion of Behavior-Mask attack's CPU usage overhead.

We perform the memory usage overhead evaluation by monitoring the maximum value of virtual memory resident set size (VmRSS), which is comprised in **/proc/[pid]/status**, at runtime for each experimental application. VmRSS represents the memory occupied by application. Figure 9 illustrates that the VmRSS values of Behavior-Mask attack implemented by handwork and framework are nearly the same at run time, and they introduce at most 0.26% overhead about 68 kB.

Table 3. Comparison of APK's size

Label	D	E	F	E-OH	F-OH
SENDSMS	1463	1471	1474	0.52%	0.73%
STEALSMS	1466	1473	1477	0.47%	0.75%
STEALCONTACT	1466	1474	1477	0.55%	0.75%
TRACKLOCATION	1465	1473	1476	0.54%	0.75%
STEALPHONEINFO	1465	1472	1475	0.48%	0.68%

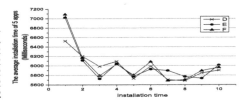

Fig. 7. Comparison of installation time

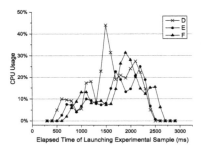

Fig. 8. Comparison of CPU usage

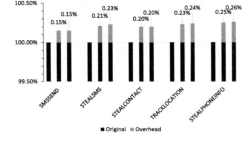

Fig. 9. Comparison of memory usage

6 Discussion

6.1 Limitation

ART implements byte-code verification for runtime type safety when every method returns. Hence, if Behavior-Mask attack refers to a return value with a reference type, the type of target return value must be derived from the type of mask return value such as the common base type *Java.Lang.Object*. Nevertheless, this limitation does not affect the caller object and the arguments of every method.

Since the floating-point operation involves some special content such as additional registers, the whole Behavior-Mask attack can't be carried out between a floating-point field and a non-floating-point field. In the real-world example shown in Fig. 2, we applied this principle.

6.2   Preventing Behavior-Mask Attack

In this section, we discuss different defense concepts to prevent Behavior-Mask attack. Sources of those concepts are not only the existing mature Android defense solutions, but also the defense techniques on the traditional operating systems.

Based on our presentation for Behavior-Mask attack, we could fight against attack in three aspects: (1) Detecting attack code; (2) Detecting unexpected behavior; (3) Reinforcing the execution environment. A single defense technique could not fight against all Behavior-Mask attacks effectively, but a solution that combines a variety of defense techniques could find some traces of the attack in a great probability.

(1) Detecting attack code

A crafted attack module includes only 11 assembly instructions, so it is hard to reveal the patterns of attack code. A perfect information-flow analysis approach, which considers JNI and ART environment in binary-level as the defenses in C++ [26], is considered to reveal attack effectively. However implementing such information-flow analysis scheme is still a hard work.

(2) Detecting unexpected behavior

(a) Dynamic monitoring on server side: All service requests based on ICC will be intercepted by this kind of defense, and malware can't recognize that it is monitored [32]. While this kind of defense needs root privilege, and it has a non-ignorable performance cost. Above all it can't reveal the whole complex behavior.

(b) DEX byte-code verification based on binary code instrumentation: As the existed DEX byte-code verification in Android such as the type verification of return value, more verifications such as method's signature and parameter types are proposed to be implemented. This kind of defense should be provided by the ART compiler. Nevertheless it still exists the possibility of Behavior-Mask attack if the verification code is indirectly invoked, or the inline verification code will result in the bloated system and program.

(3) Reinforcing the execution environment

(a) Constant addressing mode: Behavior-Mask attack corrupts the data used in multilevel indirect addressing modes. Hence, a straightforward approach to prevent Behavior-Mask attack is to use immediate addressing mode and relative addressing mode for invoking methods only. However, those constant addressing modes can only be used for the invocations that don't need dynamic binding.

(b) CFI: CFI (Control Flow Integrity) is one kind of well-developed defense technique used against code reuse attack in traditional desktop operating systems. The basic idea of CFI [2] is to limit the indirect call or return to some specific addresses. Some C++ aware CFI approaches restrict and identify the allowed vcall sites and vtables such as *VTint* [39]. According to this idea, in ART all the content of resolved method list and vtable for each class could be kept in the read-only memory. We also verify the beginning of resolved method list in each Java object and the beginning of vtable in each Java class. Nevertheless, this approach can't use lazy load mode and can't prevent the crafted Behavior-Mask attack that only needs once covert data transformation. Of course, precise source code semantics based CFI may prevent Behavior-Mask attack.

(c) Randomization of code and data structure: Randomizing method reference and Java object layouts, such as inserting randomly sized padding in resolved method list, and Java object's instance, are effective to destroy the understanding of the layouts that Behavior-Mask attack try to resolve in advance. However, Behavior-Mask attack could choose to analyze the layouts in attack code when attack is performed. In this case, it still reduces the difficulty of exhibiting patterns of the bloated attack code.

7   Related Work

In this section, we discuss the previous work related to Android transformation techniques and malicious behavior detection.

Christodorescu et al. [8] firstly gave a formal definition for obfuscation and presented some sample obfuscation transformations. [19,28] summarized lots of Android transformation attack techniques, such as reflection, function outlining, and inlining. Further, researchers reveal more Android malware evasion techniques based on Android system characteristics. As a complement, [25] introduced four kinds of dynamic code loading techniques and corresponding analysis techniques.

Petsas et al. [24] proposed three heuristics to discover if malware is running on an emulated or an actual device, thereby deciding whether to perform malicious behavior or not. *Boxify* [5] also pointed out that a malware could simply refrain from activating any malicious behavior to fool many dynamic analyzing approaches if malware recognized that it is being analyzed or sandboxed.

Permission abuse is a common behavior in Android malware. H. Peng et al. [23] proposed a permission-based probabilistic generative model for ranking risks for Android apps. *Juxtapp* [15] performed feature hashing on the opcode sequence to detect malicious code reuse. DroidAPIMiner [1] extracted Android malware features at the API level. Drebin [3] took a hybrid approach and considered both Android permissions and sensitive APIs as feature. Mu Zhang et al. [40] used contextual API dependency as feature to reflect essential behavior. Common Android application behavior analysis techniques usually extract feature sets from both manifest file and byte-code file. AutoCog [27] analyzed the consistency of the description in app market and application's permissions, AUTOREB [18] tried to understand application's behavior by application's reviews in app market. PRIMO [22] combined static analysis with probabilistic models. ARTist [6] and TaintART [31] are committed to build dynamic analysis by compiler instrumentation in ART. In our work, we proposed a new transformation technique in new Android ART environment. It makes semantic analysis based on byte-code-level hard to take effect.

8   Conclusion

In this paper, we introduce Behavior-Mask attack, a novel transformation attack technique based on ART, which can bypass almost all existing Android information-flow analysis based defenses. We discuss the technical details of Behavior-Mask attack and implement a development framework for generating necessary code for attack automatically. We believe that our work is contribute to the ongoing research on designing practical and secure defenses which can resist new Android malwares in ART and precisely abstract Android application's behavior. We think that Java-level semantics need to be taken into account in binary-level as a valuable guide for the design and implementation of future Android defenses in ART environment.

Acknowledgments. We thank the anonymous reviewers of ISC 2016 for their invaluable suggestions and comments. The work is supported by a grant from the National Natural Science Foundation of China (No. 61402470).

References

1. Aafer, Y., Du, W., Yin, H.: DroidAPIMiner: mining API-level features for robust malware detection in android. In: Zia, T., Zomaya, A., Varadharajan, V., Mao, M. (eds.) SecureComm 2013. LNICST, vol. 127, pp. 86–103. Springer, Cham (2013). doi:10.1007/978-3-319-04283-1_6
2. Abadi, M., Budiu, M., Erlingsson, U., Ligatti, J.: Control-flow integrity. In: CCS 2005, pp. 340–353. ACM (2005)
3. Arp, D., Spreitzenbarth, M., Hubner, M., Gascon, H., Rieck, K.: Drebin: effective and explainable detection of android malware in your pocket. In: NDSS (2014)
4. Arzt, S., Rasthofer, S., Fritz, C., Bodden, E., Bartel, A., Klein, J., Le Traon, Y., Octeau, D., McDaniel, P.: Flowdroid: precise context, flow, field, object-sensitive and lifecycle-aware taint analysis for android apps. ACM SIGPLAN Not. **49**(6), 259–269 (2014)

5. Backes, M., Bugiel, S., Hammer, C., Schranz, O., von Styp-Rekowsky, P.: Boxify: full-fledged app sandboxing for stock android. In: USENIX Security 2015, pp. 691–706 (2015)
6. Backes, M., Bugiel, S., Schranz, O., von Styp-Rekowsky, P., Weisgerber, S.: Artist: the android runtime instrumentation and security toolkit. arXiv preprint arXiv:1607.06619 (2016)
7. Bitdefender: Bitdefender android malware threat report h2 2015 (2015). http://download.bitdefender.com/resources/files/News/CaseStudies/study/85/Android-Malware-Threat-Report-H2-2015.pdf
8. Christodorescu, M., Jha, S.: Testing malware detectors. ACM SIGSOFT Softw. Eng. Notes **29**(4), 34–44 (2004)
9. Dimitriadis, A., Efraimidis, P.S., Katos, V.: Malevolent app pairs: an android permission overpassing scheme. In: CF 2016, pp. 431–436. ACM (2016)
10. Enck, W., Gilbert, P., Han, S., Tendulkar, V., Chun, B.-G., Cox, L.P., Jung, J., McDaniel, P., Sheth, A.N.: Taintdroid: an information-flow tracking system for realtime privacy monitoring on smartphones. ACM Trans. Comput. Syst. (TOCS) **32**(2), 5 (2014)
11. F-Secure: F-secure threat report 2015 (2015). https://www.f-secure.com/documents/996508/1030745/nanhaishu_whitepaper.pdf
12. Google: Android APIs (2016). https://developer.android.com/reference/
13. Google: Art (android runtime) (2016). https://source.android.com/devices/tech/dalvik/index.html
14. Gordon, M.I., Kim, D., Perkins, J.H., Gilham, L., Nguyen, N., Rinard, M.C.: Information flow analysis of android applications in DroidSafe. In: NDSS (2015)
15. Hanna, S., Huang, L., Wu, E., Li, S., Chen, C., Song, D.: Juxtapp: a scalable system for detecting code reuse among android applications. In: Flegel, U., Markatos, E., Robertson, W. (eds.) DIMVA 2012. LNCS, vol. 7591, pp. 62–81. Springer, Heidelberg (2013). doi:10.1007/978-3-642-37300-8_4
16. Hoffmann, J., Rytilahti, T., Maiorca, D., Winandy, M., Giacinto, G., Holz, T.: Evaluating analysis tools for android apps: status quo and robustness against obfuscation. Technical report TR-HGI-2016-003, Horst Grtz Institute for IT-Security. ACM (2016)
17. IDC: Smartphone OS market share, 2016 Q2 (2015). http://www.idc.com/prodserv/smartphone-os-market-share.jsp
18. Kong, D., Cen, L., Jin, H.: Autoreb: automatically understanding the review-to-behavior fidelity in android applications. In: Proceedings of the CCS 2015, pp. 530–541. ACM (2015)
19. Linares-Vásquez, M., Holtzhauer, A., Bernal-Cárdenas, C., Poshyvanyk, D.: Revisiting android reuse studies in the context of code obfuscation and library usages. In: MSR 2014, pp. 242–251. ACM (2014)
20. McAfee: Mcafee labs threats report first quarter 2016 (2016). http://www.mcafee.com/us/resources/reports/rp-quarterly-threats-may-2016.pdf
21. Norton: Good, bad, and sneaky: do you really know what your apps are doing? (2014). http://now.symassets.com/content/dam/norton/global/pdfs/whitepapers/NMI_Whitepaper_Consumer_Version_Fall_2014_D2-Google-Play.pdf
22. Octeau, D., Jha, S., Dering, M., McDaniel, P., Bartel, A., Li, L., Klein, J., Le Traon, Y.: Combining static analysis with probabilistic models to enable market-scale android inter-component analysis. ACM SIGPLAN Not. **51**(1), 469–484 (2016)
23. Peng, H., Gates, C., Sarma, B., Li, N., Qi, Y., Potharaju, R., Nita-Rotaru, C., Molloy, I.: Using probabilistic generative models for ranking risks of android apps. In: CCS 2012, pp. 241–252. ACM (2012)

24. Petsas, T., Voyatzis, G., Athanasopoulos, E., Polychronakis, M., Ioannidis, S.: Rage against the virtual machine: hindering dynamic analysis of android malware. In: EuroSec 2014, p. 5. ACM (2014)
25. Poeplau, S., Fratantonio, Y., Bianchi, A., Kruegel, C., Vigna, G.: Execute this! analyzing unsafe and malicious dynamic code loading in android applications. In: NDSS, vol. 14, pp. 23–26 (2014)
26. Prakash, A., Hu, X., Yin, H.: vfGuard: strict protection for virtual function calls in COTS C++ binaries. In: NDSS (2015)
27. Qu, Z., Rastogi, V., Zhang, X., Chen, Y., Zhu, T., Chen, Z.: Autocog: measuring the description-to-permission fidelity in android applications. In: CCS 2014, pp. 1354–1365. ACM (2014)
28. Rastogi, V., Chen, Y., Jiang, X.: DroidChameleon: evaluating android anti-malware against transformation attacks. In: AISA CCS 2013, pp. 329–334. ACM (2013)
29. Rastogi, V., Chen, Y., Jiang, X.: Catch me if you can: evaluating android anti-malware against transformation attacks. IEEE Trans. Inf. Forensics Secur. 9(1), 99–108 (2014)
30. Sun, M., Lui, J.C.S., Zhou, Y.: Blender: self-randomizing address space layout for android apps. In: Monrose, F., Dacier, M., Blanc, G., Garcia-Alfaro, J. (eds.) RAID 2016. LNCS, vol. 9854, pp. 457–480. Springer, Cham (2016). doi:10.1007/978-3-319-45719-2_21
31. Sun, M., Wei, T., Lui, J.: Taintart: a practical multi-level information-flow tracking system for android runtime. In: CCS 2016, pp. 331–342. ACM (2016)
32. Sun, M., Zheng, M., Lui, J., Jiang, X.: Design and implementation of an android host-based intrusion prevention system. In: ACSAC 2014, pp. 226–235. ACM (2014)
33. Tam, K., Khan, S.J., Fattori, A., Cavallaro, L.: Copperdroid: automatic reconstruction of android malware behaviors. In: NDSS (2015)
34. Tang, X., Liang, Y., Ma, X., Lin, Y., Gao, D.: On the effectiveness of code-reuse-based android application obfuscation. In: Hong, S., Park, J.H. (eds.) ICISC 2016. LNCS, vol. 10157, pp. 333–349. Springer, Cham (2017). doi:10.1007/978-3-319-53177-9_18
35. VirusTotal: Virustotal (2016). https://www.virustotal.com/en/about/
36. Wang, Z., Li, C., Guan, Y., Xue, Y.: Droidchain: a novel malware detection method for android based on behavior chain. In: CNS 2015, pp. 727–728. IEEE (2015)
37. Wei, F., Roy, S., Ou, X., et al.: Amandroid: a precise and general inter-component data flow analysis framework for security vetting of android apps. In: CCS 2014, pp. 1329–1341. ACM (2014)
38. Wijesekera, P., Baokar, A., Hosseini, A., Egelman, S., Wagner, D., Beznosov, K.: Android permissions remystified: a field study on contextual integrity. In: USENIX Security 2015, pp. 499–514 (2015)
39. Zhang, C., Song, C., Chen, K.Z., Chen, Z., Song, D.: Vtint: protecting virtual function tables' integrity. In: NDSS (2015)
40. Zhang, M., Duan, Y., Yin, H., Zhao, Z.: Semantics-aware android malware classification using weighted contextual API dependency graphs. In: CCS 2014, pp. 1105–1116. ACM (2014)

Privacy

Harvesting Smartphone Privacy Through Enhanced Juice Filming Charging Attacks

Weizhi Meng[1(✉)], Fei Fei[2], Wenjuan Li[1,2], and Man Ho Au[3]

[1] Department of Applied Mathematics and Computer Science,
Technical University of Denmark, Kongens Lyngby, Denmark
weme@dtu.dk
[2] Department of Computer Science, City University of Hong Kong,
Hong Kong, China
[3] Department of Computing, The Hong Kong Polytechnic University,
Hong Kong, China
csallen@comp.polyu.edu.hk

Abstract. The increasingly high demand for smartphone charging in people's daily lives has apparently encouraged much more public charging stations to be deployed in various places (e.g., shopping malls, airports). However, these public charging facilities may open a hole for cyber-criminals to infer private information and data from smartphone users. Juice filming charging (JFC) attack is a particular type of charging attacks, which is capable of stealing users' sensitive information from both Android OS and iOS devices, through automatically monitoring and recording phone screen during the whole charging period. The rationale is that phone screen can be leaked through a standard micro USB connector, which adopts the Mobile High-Definition Link (MHL) standard. In practice, we identify that how to efficiently extract information from the captured videos remains a challenge for current JFC attack. To further investigate its practical influence, in this work, we focus on enhancing its performance in the aspects of extracting texts from images and correlating information, and then conducting a user study in a practical scenario. The obtained results demonstrate that our enhanced JFC attack can outperform the original one in collecting users' information at large and extracting sensitive data with a higher accuracy. Our work aims to complement existing results and stimulate more efforts in defending smartphones against charging threats.

Keywords: Mobile privacy and security · Android and iOS · Charging threat · OCR technology · Juice filming charging attack

1 Introduction

With the rapid development, smartphones have become one of the most commonly adopted devices for millions of people. International Data Corporation

---

W. Meng — The author was previously known as Yuxin Meng.

P.Q. Nguyen and J. Zhou (Eds.): ISC 2017, LNCS 10599, pp. 291–308, 2017.
https://doi.org/10.1007/978-3-319-69659-1_16

(IDC) reported that shipments grew 5.3% from 344.7 million in the second quarter of 2016, and that vendors shipped a total of 362.9 million smartphones worldwide in the third quarter of 2016 [9]. The number of phone users is predicted to increase from 1.5 billion in 2014 to around 2.5 billion in 2019. Nowadays, the majority of smartphones can act as a personal assistant, i.e., allowing to run various applications that help users view Office documents, access an address book or use GPS. Due to these capabilities, people are likely to store their personal and private data on the phones, and are often using smartphones in their daily lives (e.g., video-chatting with friends), which greatly increase the demand of recharging their mobile devices.

To meet this requirement, more and more public charging stations are being deployed for smartphone users. As an example, Singapore Power (SP) had planned to deploy up to 200 free mobile charging stations in various busy locations including hospitals, tertiary institutions, libraries and supermarkets [30]. Each charging station is expected to be equipped with 10 individual slots, including multiple charging connectors like mini or micro USBs, which can fit most mobile phones and tablets. Generally, these public charging facilitates can greatly benefit smartphone users in their daily lives; however, public stations may also expose a big threat on smartphone privacy and security, since we are not sure that these charging facilities are not maliciously controlled by cyber-criminals (e.g., station developers, Government agencies). As a result, there is a great need to pay more attention to charging threats [10, 24].

In literature, Lau *et al.* [11] presented a malicious charging station named *Mactans*, which could harm a phone through injecting any malicious applications to collect users' secrets on iOS6 devices. Spolaor *et al.* [29] then designed a proof-of-concept application called *PowerSnitch*, and showed how an adversary could leverage a maliciously controlled charging station to exfiltrate data from Android smartphones via a USB charging cable by using power consumption in the form of power bursts. These two attacks are only effective on either iOS or Android devices. Meng *et al.* [20,21] developed a more scalable charging attack, called juice filming charging (JFC) attack, which can steal users' private information from both Android OS and iOS devices, through automatically recording phone screen (including users' inputs) during the charging period. All the interactions and screen information can be captured in the back-end as long as people keep charging their phones to the JFC charger. It is worth noting that JFC attack does not need to install any piece of applications or require any permission from users; thus, it may cause a large number of victims in practice.

Motivations and Contributions. JFC attack can work in an intelligent way by integrating Optical Character Recognition (OCR) technology in processing the recorded videos [21]. However, we perform a study and identify that how to efficiently extract information from the captured videos remains a challenge for current JFC attack. When a large amount of videos are recorded, it is very time-consuming and expensive for manual analysis. Therefore, it is very important for JFC attack to extract users' private information in an intelligent and accurate way. Motivated by this, in this work, we focus on JFC attack and attempt to enhance its performance in the aspects of extracting texts from images and correlating information. We further enable JFC chargers to upload recorded videos to a cloud environment and extract information from the captured videos in a centralized server. In the evaluation, we conduct a user study in a practical environment to investigate the practical influence of the improved attack. The contributions of our work can be summarized as below.

- We conduct a study to explore the practical performance of JFC attack and identify its limitation in accurately extracting users' private information from the collected videos. We then describe a technical way of improving the accuracy of information extraction from videos.
- In addition, our study identifies that information correlation is also a challenge for current JFC attack. To mitigate this issue, we present a compact but efficient approach for correlating information in terms of user credentials (e.g., unlock pattern, social networking account), as well as introduce how to launch JFC attack with a cloud environment.
- To investigate the practical influence of JFC attack on smartphone users' privacy, we further conduct a user study in a practical scenario. Experimental results demonstrate that the enhanced JFC attack can outperform the original one in both extracting and correlating users' private information. Our effort demonstrates the potential damage of charging attack and attempts to stimulate more research in this area.

Organization of the paper. Section 2 introduces the background of JFC attack including its features and setup details. Section 3 identifies the limitations of current JFC attack and describes how to enhance its performance in the aspects of information extraction and correlation. In Sect. 4, we collaborate with an IT center and perform a user study in a real scenario. We further discuss how to defend JFC attack in Sect. 5 and review related research studies in Sect. 6. Finally, we conclude this work in Sect. 7.

2   Background of JFC Attack

JFC attack was developed to steal users' private data through automatically video-capturing smartphone screen when the phone is awake or users are interacting with their phones during the whole charging period [20]. This attack does not require to install any part of applications or ask for any permissions from smartphone users. By integrating with OCR technology [21], JFC attack can provide various features as below:

- *It is easy to implement but quite efficient.* After installing the driver, JFC attack can be launched by any computing devices even some small devices like RaspberryPi.
- *It does not need to install any additional applications or components on phones.* This attack does not require to install any pieces of applications on phone's side.

- *It does not need any permissions.* This attack does not need to request any permissions from smartphone users.
- *With less user awareness.* It is a kind of passive attacks, which causes less user attention in real scenarios.
- *It cannot be detected or notified by any current anti-malware software.* Existing anti-malware software are not aware of JFC attack; thus, they cannot detect or notify users about this threat.
- *It can be scalable and effective in both Android OS and iOS devices.* As compared to malicious applications (malware), JFC attack is more effective as it can work in both Android phones and iPhones.
- *It can automatically process collected videos and extract secrets using OCR technology.* After collecting the videos, JFC chargers can automatically extract text from the videos and store data into files.

Threat model. We adopt the basic assumptions that phone charging is a common requirement from smartphone users, and that most users would not treat public chargers as highly sensitive or dangerous. These assumptions have been approved in relevant studies (e.g., [21]) that most smartphone users would charge their phones in public places such as airports, subways, shopping malls and so on. Charging attacks can be classified as *public* and *private*. The former is mainly related to public charging facilities like the charging stations provided in an airport, while the latter is mostly relevant to private charging facilities like a private charger from friends.

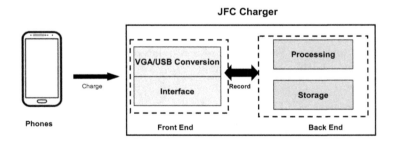

Fig. 1. The high-level implementation of JFC attack.

Basic idea. The original idea of JFC attack is from the observation that no permission would be asked when plugging phones to a projector, while the projector can display the phone screen. In addition, there are no compelling notifications on the screen when the device is being plugged, or the indicators are very small. Based on these observations, JFC attack is developed to automatically video-record phone screen by using a VGA/USB interface during the charging period. This attack reveals that the display of phone screen can be leaked through a standard micro USB connector, which adopts the Mobile

High-Definition Link (MHL) standard. For iPhones, the lighting connector is used. For Android phones, this is usually done through the micro-USB port. The micro-USB (available on most Android devices) can also involve connectors with MHL connectivity.

Real setup. The high-level implementation of JFC attack is depicted in Fig. 1. When users charge their phones to the JFC charger, their phone screens could be video-captured by the charger in the back-end and stored for later use, i.e., extracting private data from the recorded videos. To implement JFC attack, it is important to choose an appropriate VGA/USB interface, but actually there are many alternatives online. In the previous studies (e.g., [20, 21]), a hardware interface named *VGA2USB* was adopted to implement JFC attack.[1] It is particularly a full-featured VGA/RGB frame grabber, which can send a digitized video signal from VGA to USB.

Figure 2 shows two examples of setting up JFC attack in practice, where Fig. 2(a) shows how to launch JFC attack on an Android phone and Fig. 2(b) describes the implementation of JFC attack on an iPhone. It is found that the connected iPhone screen can be displayed in the computer end. It is not hard to imagine that all screen information would be captured by JFC charger, including users' inputs such as typed passwords, PIN code, chatting history, etc.

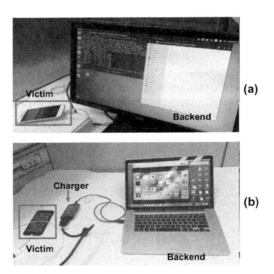

Fig. 2. Two examples of real setup for JFC attack using VGA2USB: (a) an Android phone, and (b) an iPhone.

Collected private information. The recorded videos contain the phone screen or the inputs from smartphone users; thus, various information can be extracted.

---

[1] http://www.epiphan.com/products/vga2usb/.

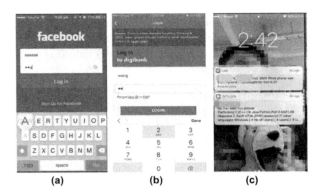

Fig. 3. Three examples of captured screen information: (a) Facebook account, (b) Bank account login, and (c) LINE and Outlook messages.

Figure 3 gives three examples of captured screen information via JFC attack, in which each of them is relevant to sensitive and private information of smartphone users. In particular, Fig. 3(a) shows the captured inputs for Facebook including the accounts and input passwords, Fig. 3(b) presents the captured screen for bank login including account name and input passwords, and Fig. 3(c) shows the captured messages from LINE chat and Outlook message. These examples demonstrate that JFC attack has a potential to become a big threat for smartphone privacy and security.

OCR technology. By integrating with OCR technology, JFC attack can process the collected videos automatically, e.g., video analysis and information extraction. There are two major phases [21]: *device checking* and *OCR processing*. The source code for Phase1 and Phase2 are presented in Fig. 4.

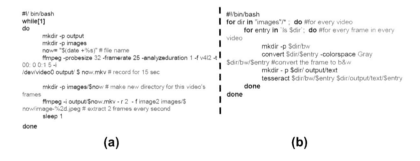

Fig. 4. The code for (a) Phase1 and (b) Phase2.

- **Phase1 - Device Checking.** This phase allows the JFC charger to decide when to start the recording process. The Ephiphan frame grabber enables a

VGA device to send input through the USB. On Linux, Ephiphan devices expose the Video4Linux (V4L) API, hence the V4L API can provide a real time stream of the display of the device whenever a device is connected to the machine. The machine can periodically check the presence of a new V4L capable USB connected device. If such a device is found, the stream is piped into a file. After 15 s of device detection, the machine can automatically pause to evaluate whether the device is still connected. If connected, it continues streaming the screen contents into a file. Otherwise, it would go back into waiting mode. It is worth noting that the time of device detection can be tuned according to specific requirements.

- **Phase2 - Optical Character Recognition (OCR).** This phase allows the JFC charger to process the collected videos using OCR technology, i.e., extracting texts from the collected videos. Since OCR may take a while, it is not done synchronously with the first phase. While the machine is running at *Phase1*, the OCR code can simultaneously process the video frames and check for new frames. Then all the text files extracted from the same video can be merged into one (i.e., removing duplicate words and sorting the remaining words in alphabetical order).

3   Enhanced JFC Attack

3.1   Accuracy of Information Extraction

The current JFC attack utilizes tessract project[2] to construct an OCR engine, which can extract text from the images. However, it is found that direct processing of the image did not yield accurate results. For example, a wide variety of colours that the text is simply not recognizable by the OCR engine.

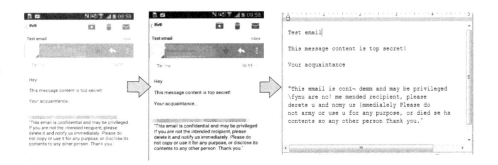

Fig. 5. Information extraction by current JFC attack: converting an image to greyscale.

To mitigate this issue, Meng *et al.* [21] employed an approach of converting the images to greyscale before running it through the OCR engine, which yield a

---

[2] https://code.google.com/p/tesseract-ocr/.

better OCR output. An example is shown in Fig. 5. However, we identify that the resulting accuracy by this approach is still not high enough in practical usage. For example, the accuracy of OCR in Fig. 5 is about 89%, whereas some words cannot be recognized properly, i.e., "This email is confidential and may be privileged. If you are not the intended recipient, please delete it or notify us immediately" may be recognized as "This email is con..demm and may be privileged. fynu are no! me mended recipient, please derete u and nomy us mmedialely".

To investigate this issue, we conduct a study by validating the existing OCR technology using 10 videos collected from [21]. Each video is around 200 M and contains 700 - 900 frames. Figure 6 shows the extraction accuracy and the specific number of frames. It is found that the average accuracy is generally below 90% and would be not high enough in practice.

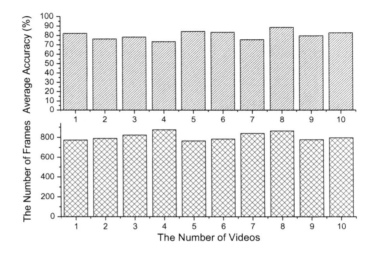

Fig. 6. The average accuracy and the number of frames.

3.2   Improvement for Information Extraction

Based on the results above, it is found how to accurately extract information from the collected videos remains a challenge for current JFC attack. To improve the attack effectiveness and the accuracy of information extraction, we adopt an engineering approach with three steps from image processing[3], including *image revision*, *image conversion* and *image clearance*.

- *Step1 - Image revision.* The main purpose of this step is to resize the image with variable height and width.

---

[3] https://github.com/tesseract-ocr/tesseract/wiki/ImproveQuality.

– *Step2 - Image conversion.* This step is similar to current JFC attack, which converts the image to grayscale format (black and white) before running it through the OCR engine.
– *Step3 - Image clearance.* This step aims to make an image clearer by removing the noise pixels.

```
Image Revision.
Input bitmap;
double nWidthFactor = (double) temp.Width / (double)newWidth;
double nHeightFactor = (double) temp.Height / (double)newHeight;
for (int x = 0; x < bmap.Width; ++x)
        for (int y = 0; y < bmap.Height; ++y)
do          // Blue
            bp1 = (byte)(nx * color1.B + fx * color2.B);
            bp2 = (byte)(nx * color3.B + fx * color4.B);
            nBlue = (byte)(ny * (double)(bp1) + fy * (double)(bp2));
            // Green
            bp1 = (byte)(nx * color1.G + fx * color2.G);
            bp2 = (byte)(nx * color3.G + fx * color4.G);
            nGreen = (byte)(ny * (double)(bp1) + fy * (double)(bp2));
            // Red
            bp1 = (byte)(nx * color1.R + fx * color2.R);
            bp2 = (byte)(nx * color3.R + fx * color4.R);
            nRed = (byte)(ny * (double)(bp1) + fy * (double)(bp2));

Image Clearance.
for (var x = 0; x < bmap.Width; x++)
        for (var y = 0; y < bmap.Height; y++)

do
            var pixel = bmap.GetPixel(x, y);
            if (pixel.R < 162 && pixel.G < 162 && pixel.B < 162)
                bmap.SetPixel(x, y, Color.Black);
            else if (pixel.R > 162 && pixel.G > 162 && pixel.B > 162)
                bmap.SetPixel(x, y, Color.White);
```

Fig. 7. The code for image revision and clearance.

Fig. 8. The accuracy of extracting information using enhanced JFC attack.

The final goal of these steps is to better recognize textual information from an image. The code for image revision and image clearance can be referred to Fig. 7, while the code for image conversion is the same as exiting JFC attack (see details in [21]). To validate the performance, we process the same videos above by means of the three-step approach, and the results are depicted in Fig. 8. The experimental results show that the average accuracy can increase to above 90% (close to 95%) as compared to the results shown in Fig. 6, demonstrating that the three-step approach is effective to enhance JFC attack in extracting users' private information.

3.3 Information Correlation

The current JFC attack can merge all the text files from the same video into one text file by removing duplicate words and sorting the remaining words in alphabetical order, whereas there is no information correlation process to link data from different videos. In such case, information could be burst when collecting videos after a period of time. In practice, JFC chargers can be deployed with a cloud as shown in Fig. 9, where a centralized server can help collect the videos recorded by each charger and extracts the information from videos. Under this architecture, JFC attack has a potential to collect a large amount of private information from smartphone users.

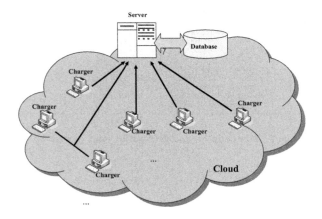

Fig. 9. Enhanced JFC attack with a cloud and centralized server.

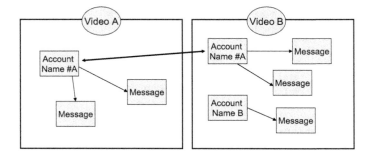

Fig. 10. An example of information correlation.

With the increasing number of videos, there is a need to correlate information from different videos and enhance the attack performance. To achieve this goal, we adopt a compact but efficient approach of indexing and linking information according to user's credentials, e.g., account names. An example is given in Fig. 10: if two identical account names are detected, then the corresponding information can be correlated (e.g., chatting history). The process of information correlation can be conducted in the back-end or in a cloud environment.

4   User Study

There are not many studies exploring the practical influence of JFC attacks in literature. In this work, we collaborated with an IT center (with over 250 personnel) in South China, and perform a user study to investigate the effectiveness of our advanced JFC attack in a practical environment.

Deployment. Before the study, we seek approval from the IT center to deploy up to 10 JFC chargers in one main dining & lobby room, where the JFC chargers can keep uploading the recorded videos to a cloud in the back-end. After uploading the videos, the chargers can delete the relevant videos to save disk space for new recorded videos and activate the attack for a long time. The centralized server has a maximum storage capacity of 100 T, where one-minute video usually requires 30 M space.

Table 1. Extracted user private information in the deployed environment.

User information	User information	User information
Android unlock pattern	PIN for iPhones	Gmail account and content
Other email account (e.g., 126, 163)	Other email content	Social networking account (e.g., Wechat, QQ)
Bank account	Social networking chat history (e.g., Wechat, QQ)	Visited website content
Email passwords (web-login)	Personal photos	Phone number list
Installed mobile applications	Settings	Bank message

Data Collection and Results. To protect users' privacy, we also seek users' approval and all data were handled by the IT center (we only collected statistics from the data). At least one IT administrator helped monitor the whole process and ensured all steps to comply with the relevant policies.

The JFC charger was implemented for two weeks excluding weekends (i.e., from Monday to Friday). The opening hours of the center are from 7am to 10pm; thus, we mainly recorded the information from 7am to 10pm. Figure 11

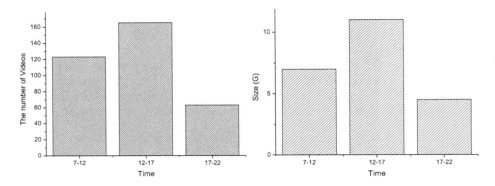

Fig. 11. The average number of collected videos for each day.

Fig. 12. The average size of collected videos for each day.

depicts the average number of recorded videos: the JFC chargers can collect more than 350 videos each day where the highest number of videos would be captured during the period of 12-17pm. This is because most people had their meals at that time and have the need to charge their phones in the room. From these collected videos, we can extract a large amount of private information about users, as summarized in Table 1, such as Android unlock pattern, PIN for iPhones, Email Account and content, social networking chat history, visited website, personal photos and so on.

Intuitively, each video has a different length and size, where a longer-time-frame video has a potential to leak more private information about a smartphone user. Figure 12 depicts the average size of collected videos for each environment. Generally, JFC chargers could collect around 22.5 G data each day. The accuracy of information extraction between the original and the advanced JFC attack is depicted in Fig. 13. It is found that the advanced attack could achieve an accuracy of 93% as compared to an accuracy of 82% achieved by the original attack setup. Overall, the advanced attack could provide a minimum accuracy over 88% while the original one could only reach a minimum accuracy of 75%.

In the study, we employ *hit rate* and *error rate* to measure the performance of JFC attack, which can be defined as below.

$$Hit\ rate = \frac{The\ number\ of\ correct\ correlation}{The\ total\ number\ of\ correlation} \tag{1}$$

$$Error\ rate = \frac{The\ number\ of\ incorrect\ correlation}{The\ total\ number\ of\ correlation} \tag{2}$$

It is revealed that the advanced JFC attack could achieve an average hit rate of 92% and an error rate of 3.3%. These errors are mainly caused by unclear texts due to inaccurate extraction. On the whole, our study validates that JFC attack can make a large impact on smartphone privacy and security. A large amount of private information could be identified through further enhancing JFC attack in the aspects of information extraction and correlation.

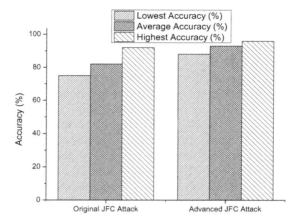

Fig. 13. The accuracy between the original and the advanced JFC attack.

5   Further Discussion

This work presents an advanced JFC attack by improving its performance in accurately extracting and correlating users' private information. In the study, we show that the JFC attack can capture phone screen in the back-end and threaten smartphone privacy. After launching JFC attack after a period of time, a large amount of data can be recorded to dig out users' private information. Our user study in a practical environment demonstrates that JFC attack has a potential to cause a large number of victims. It is worth noting that this attack can be further enhanced by integrating more advanced techniques in the aspects of both extracting and correlating secrets from videos.

Defence. The root cause of JFC attack is that Android OS and iOS devices allow screen mirroring without granting explicit permissions. To defend against this kind of attacks, there is a need to deploy additional security mechanisms and increase user awareness.

– *Disabling automate screening.* This is the most direct and easiest way to defend against JFC attack, by disabling automatic screening function. For example, the phones can disable automatically outputting screen information, and ask users to choose such function when they have the need. However, disabling screen output by default is effective, but may decrease usability, i.e., when there is a need to display phone screen for many times, users have to click the display button again and again. In this case, an alternative is to make notifications and ask for permission. Recall that when connecting iPhones to a computer, the phone will prompt a notification asking whether the user trusts the computer or not. The smartphone could do the same action to warn users before the display of phone screen. This strategy can increase user awareness especially for novice, but can provide much flexibility for advanced users.

- *Securing Charger.* To protect data leakage against JFC attack, one potential solution is to use a safe charger such as USB Condom [31]. This USB is able to prevent accidental data exchange when the device is plugged into another device with a USB cable, through cutting off the data pins in the USB cable and only allowing the power pins to connect in practice. However, this solution does not work for particular charging attacks like PowerSnitch [29], which can leak information via analyzing power consumption.
- *Employing biometrics.* It is feasible to reduce the impact of JFC attack by integrating biometrics, since JFC attack is unable to capture these secrets without a screen-input. For example, behavioral biometrics can be added to the process of inputting PIN code and unlock patterns (i.e., building a fingerprint-based unlocking mechanism). Several behavioral-based authentication methods can be referred to [5–7,12,16,17,19,27].
- *Educating users.* Until particular patches or control policies are updated by vendors, JFC attacks are difficult to defend by current security mechanisms (e.g., [18]). Therefore, similar to other area like spam detection [13], user education is a necessary action to raise users awareness and attention.

6   Related Work

As smartphones have become a major target for cyber-criminals, privacy leakage is a big concern for smartphone users. There is a line of research and practical studies on how to infer mobile users' private information and data through malware, side channels and physical access attacks.

Smartphone malware. Malicious applications are a big threat on smartphones [4]. Lin *et al.* [14] found that the ADB capability could be exposed to any party with the INTERNET permission on the same device. They then built *Screenmilker*, an application that can monitor the screen and pick up a user's password when the user is typing in real-time. Xing *et al.* [32] evaluated the Android updating mechanism and found Pileup flaws, through which a malicious application could strategically declare a set of privileges and attributes on a low-version operating system, and wait until it is able to escalate its privileges on the new system. By exploiting the Pileup vulnerabilities, their application can not only acquire a set of newly added system and signature permissions, but also determine their settings. Andriesse and Bos [1] introduced a code hiding approach for trigger-based malware, which can conceal malicious code inside spurious code fragments. A summary of malware research can be referred to a survey [25].

Accelerometer side channel. Most popular malware utilized side channel to steal information on mobile devices. Cai and Chen [3] presented a side channel on touchscreen smartphones with only soft keyboards. They identified that when users clicked on the soft keyboard, especially when he/she holds the phone by hand rather than placing it on a fixed surface, the phone vibration on touchscreens are highly correlated to the keys being typed. They conducted a study and showed that they were able to infer correctly more than 70% of the keys typed on a number-only soft keyboard on a phone. Marquardt *et al.* [15] also demonstrated that an application with access to accelerometer readings on a modern mobile phone can use side channel to recover text entered on a nearby keyboard. They showed that by characterizing consecutive pairs of keypress events, up to 80% of typed content can be recovered. Schlegel *et al.* [28] designed *Soundcomber*, a stealthy Trojan with innocuous permissions that can sense the context of its audible surroundings to automatically extract a small amount of targeted private information such as credit card and PIN numbers from both tone- and speech-based interaction with phone menu systems.

Han *et al.* [8] presented that accelerometer readings can be used to infer the trajectory and starting point of an individual who is driving, and pointed out that current smartphone operating systems allow any application to observe accelerometer readings without requiring special privileges. Thus, accelerometers can be used to locate a device owner within a 200 m radius of the true location. Owusu *et al.* [23] described how a background application can use the accelerometer as a side channel to spy on keystroke information during sensitive operations, e.g., account login. They could successfully break 59 out of 99 passwords by using only accelerometer measurements logged during text entry. Miluzzo *et al.* [22] presented *TapPrints*, a framework for inferring the location of taps on touchscreens using motion sensor data with up to 90% and 80% accuracy.

Physical side channel. These attacks are mainly based on physical objects, like oily residues left on the touchscreen or the screen reflection from nearby objects. Aviv *et al.* [2] first explored the feasibility of smudge attacks on touchscreens with different lighting angles and light sources. They indicated that the pattern could be partially identifiable in 92% and fully in 68% of the tested lighting and camera setups. Zhang *et al.* [33] presented a fingerprint attack against tapped passwords via a keypad, which could reveal more than 50% of the passwords. For the screen reflection, Raguram *et al.* [26] showed that automatic reconstruction of text typed on a mobile device's virtual keyboard is feasible via compromising reflections, i.e., those of the phone in the user's sunglasses. By means of the footage captured in realistic environments (e.g., on a bus), their approach could reconstruct fluent translations of recorded data in almost all of the test cases.

Charging attacks. To our knowledge, Lau *et al.* [11] designed an early charging attack named *Mactans*. They particularly deployed a malicious charger using BeagleBoard to conduct malware injection on smartphones during the charging period. However, their attacks require users to unlock the phone screen and install developer licenses in advance. Spolaor *et al.* [29] described how an adversary could leverage a malicious charging station to exfiltrate smartphone data via a USB charging cable using power consumption. They designed *PowerSnitch*, an application that could send out bits of data in the form of power bursts by manipulating the power consumption of the device's CPU. One limitation of this attack is that users have to pre-install a small application on their phones.

Meng *et al.* [20,21] developed JFC attacks, which can record screen information during the whole charing period, without the need to ask for any permission or phone unlock action. It is worth noting that any current anti-malware software is not aware of such threat. To launch this attack, an additional hardware of VGA/USB interface is needed, which is not hard to obtain online. Thus, charging attacks are highly deployable in real scenarios.

7   Conclusion

As compared with malicious applications (malware), charging threats are often ignored by the literature. With the increasing adoption of public charging stations, we argue that charging attacks may become a big concern for users' privacy. Juice filming charging (JFC) attack is one specific kind of charging attacks, which can steal users' private data from both Android OS and iOS devices, through automatically monitoring and recording screen information during the charging period.

In real-world deployment, we identify that information extraction and correlation are still challenges for current JFC attack. To investigate the practical influence of this attack, in this work, we focus on JFC attack and try to enhance its performance in the aspects of extracting and correlating textual information from the captured videos. In the evaluation, we conduct a user study with an IT center. The results demonstrate that the enhanced JFC attack can collect users' information at large and extract private data with a higher accuracy (i.e., over 90%) than the original one. Our work validates that JFC attack may cause a large number of victims, which should be given more attention.

Acknowledgments. We would like to thank all anonymous reviewers for their helpful comments in improving the paper. This work was partially supported by National Natural Science Foundation of China (61602396).

References

1. Andriesse, D., Bos, H.: Instruction-level steganography for covert trigger-based malware. In: Dietrich, S. (ed.) DIMVA 2014. LNCS, vol. 8550, pp. 41–50. Springer, Cham (2014). doi:10.1007/978-3-319-08509-8_3
2. Aviv, A.J., Gibson, K., Mossop, E., Blaze, M., Smith, J.M.: Smudge attacks on smartphone touch screens. In: Proceedings of the 4th USENIX Conference on Offensive Technologies (WOOT), pp. 1–7 (2010)
3. Cai, L., Chen, H.: TouchLogger: inferring keystrokes on touch screen from smartphone motion. In: Proceedings of the 6th USENIX Conference on Hot Topics in Security (HotSec), pp. 1–6 (2011)
4. Dagon, D., Martin, T., Starner, T.: Mobile phones as computing devices: the viruses are coming! IEEE Pervasive Comput. **3**(4), 11–15 (2004)
5. De Luca, A., Hang, A., Brudy, F., Lindner, C., Hussmann, H.: Touch me once and i know its you!: implicit authentication based on touch screen patterns. In: Proceedings of the 2012 ACM Annual Conference on Human Factors in Computing Systems (CHI), pp. 987–996 (2012)

6. Feng, T., Liu, Z., Kwon, K.-A., Shi, W., Carbunary, B., Jiang, Y., Nguyen, N.: Continuous mobile authentication using touchscreen gestures. In: Proceedings the 2012 IEEE Conference on Technologies for Homeland Security (HST), pp. 451–456 (2012)

7. Frank, M., Biedert, R., Ma, E., Martinovic, I., Song, D.: Touchalytics: on the applicability of touchscreen input as a behavioral biometric for continuous authentication. IEEE Trans. Inf. Forensics Secur. 8(1), 136–148 (2013)

8. Han, J., Owusu, E., Nguyen, L., Perrig, A., Zhang, J.: ACComplice: location inference using accelerometers on smartphones. In: Proceedings of the 4th International Conference on Communication Systems and Networks (COMSNETS), pp. 1–9, New York, NY, USA (2012)

9. IDC, Smartphone Momentum Still Evident with Shipments Expected to Reach 1.2 Billion in 2014 and Growing 23.1% Over (2013), http://www.idc.com/getdoc.jsp? containerId=prUS24857114

10. Juice Jacking Vulnerability for iOS, https://www.infotransec.com/news/juice-jacking-vulnerability-ios

11. Lau, B., Jang, Y., Song, C.: Mactans: Injecting malware into iOS devices via malicious chargers. Blackhat, USA (2013)

12. Li, L., Zhao, X., Xue, G.: Unobservable Re-authentication for Smartphones. In: Proceedings of the 20th Annual Network and Distributed System Security Symposium (NDSS), pp. 1–16 (2013)

13. Li, W., Meng, W.: An empirical study on email classification using supervised machine learning in real environments. In: Proceddings of the 2015 IEEE International Conference on Communications (ICC), pp. 7438–7443. IEEE (2015)

14. Lin, C.-C., Li, H., Zhou, X., Wang, X.: Screenmilker: how to milk your android screen for secrets. In: Proceedings of Annual Network and Distributed System Security Symposium (NDSS), pp. 1–10 (2014)

15. Marquardt, P., Verma, A., Carter, H., Traynor, P.: (sp)iPhone: decoding vibrations from nearby keyboards using mobile phone accelerometers. In: Proceedings of ACM Conference on Computer and Communications Security (CCS), pp. 551–562. ACM, New York (2011)

16. Meng, Y., Wong, D.S., Schlegel, R., Kwok, L.: Touch gestures based biometric authentication scheme for touchscreen mobile phones. In: Kutyłowski, M., Yung, M. (eds.) Inscrypt 2012. LNCS, vol. 7763, pp. 331–350. Springer, Heidelberg (2013). doi:10.1007/978-3-642-38519-3_21

17. Meng, Y., Li, W., Kwok, L.-F.: Enhancing click-draw based graphical passwords using multi-touch on mobile phones. In: Janczewski, L.J., Wolfe, H.B., Shenoi, S. (eds.) SEC 2013. IAICT, vol. 405, pp. 55–68. Springer, Heidelberg (2013). doi:10.1007/978-3-642-39218-4_5

18. Meng, W., Li, W., Kwok, L.F.: EFM: enhancing the performance of signature-based network intrusion detection systems using enhanced filter mechanism. Comput. Secur. 43, 189–204 (2014)

19. Meng, W., Wong, D.S., Furnell, S., Zhou, J.: Surveying the development of biometric user authentication on mobile phones. IEEE Commun. Surv. Tutorials 17, 1268–1293 (2015)

20. Meng, W., Lee, W.H., Murali, S.R., Krishnan, S.P.T.: Charging me and i know your secrets! towards juice filming attacks on smartphones. In: Proceedings of the Cyber-Physical System Security Workshop (CPSS), in Conjunction with AsiaCCS 2015. ACM (2015)

21. Meng, W., Lee, W.H., Murali, S.R., Krishnan, S.P.T.: JuiceCaster: towards automatic juice filming attacks on smartphones. J. Netw. Comput. Appl. **68**, 201–212 (2016)

22. Miluzzo, E., Varshavsky, A., Balakrishnan, S., Choudhury, R.R.: TapPrints: your finger taps have fingerprints. In: Proceedings of MobiSys, New York, NY, USA , pp. 323–336 (2012)

23. Owusu, E., Han, J., Das, S., Perrig, A., Zhang, J.: ACCessory: password inference using accelerometers on smartphones. In: Proceedings of the 12th Workshop on Mobile Computing Systems & Applications (HotMobile), pp. 1–6. ACM, New York (2012)

24. Ossmann, M., Osborn, K.: Multiplexed Wired Attack Surfaces. Black Hat USA (2013), https://media.blackhat.com/us-13/US-13-Ossmann-Multiplexed-Wired-Attack-Surfaces-WP.pdf

25. Peng, S., Yu, S., Yang, A.: Smartphone malware and its propagation modeling: a survey. IEEE Commun. Surv. Tutorials **16**(2), 925–941 (2014)

26. Raguram, R., White, A.M., Goswami, D., Monrose, F., Frahm, J.-M.: iSpy: automatic reconstruction of typed input from compromising reflections. In: Proceedings of the 18th ACM Conference on Computer and Communications Security (CCS), pp. 527–536, ACM, New York (2011)

27. Sae-Bae, N., Memon, N., Isbister, K., Ahmed, K.: Multitouch gesture-based authentication. IEEE Trans. Inf. Forensics Secur. **9**(4), 568–582 (2014)

28. Schlegel, R., Zhang, K., Zhou, X., Intwala, M., Kapadia, A., Wang, X.: Soundcomber: a stealthy and context-aware sound Trojan for smartphones. In: Proceedings of the 18th Annual Network and Distributed System Security Symposium (NDSS), San Diego, CA, USA, pp. 17–33 (2011)

29. Spolaor, R., Abudahi, L., Moonsamy, V., Conti, M., Poovendran, R.: No free charge theorem: a covert channel viaUSB charging cable on mobile devices. In: Proceedings of the 15th International Conference on Applied Cryptography and Network Security (ACNS), pp. 84–102 (2017)

30. Singapore Power to provide 200 free mobile phone charging stations for SG50 (2015), http://www.straitstimes.com/singapore/singapore-power-to-provide-200-free-mobile-phone-charging-stations-for-sg50

31. The Original USB Condom, http://int3.cc/products/usbcondoms

32. Xing, L., Pan, X., Wang, R., Yuan, K., Wang, X.: Upgrading your android, elevating my malware: privilege escalation through mobile OS updating. In: Proceedings of the 2014 IEEE Symposium on Security and Privacy, Berkeley, CA, USA, pp. 393–408 (2014)

33. Zhang, Y., Xia, P., Luo, J., Ling, Z., Liu, B., Fu, X.: Fingerprint attack against touch-enabled devices. In: Proceedings of the 2nd ACM Workshop on Security and Privacy in Smartphones and Mobile Devices (SPSM), pp. 57–68. ACM, New York (2012)

A Differentially Private Encryption Scheme

Carlo Brunetta[(✉)], Christos Dimitrakakis, Bei Liang,
and Aikaterini Mitrokotsa

Chalmers University of Technology, Gothenburg, Sweden
{brunetta,chrdimi,lbei,aikmitr}@chalmers.se

Abstract. Encrypting data with a semantically secure cryptosystem guarantees that nothing is learned about the plaintext from the ciphertext. However, querying a database about individuals or requesting for summary statistics can leak information. *Differential privacy* (DP) offers a formal framework to bound the amount of information that an adversary can discover from a database with private data, when statistical findings of the stored data are communicated to an untrusted party. Although both encryption schemes and differential private mechanisms can provide important privacy guarantees, when employed in isolation they do not guarantee full privacy-preservation.

This paper investigates how to efficiently combine DP and an encryption scheme to prevent leakage of information. More precisely, we introduce and instantiate *differentially private encryption schemes* that provide both DP and confidentiality. Our contributions are five-fold, we: *(i)* define an encryption scheme that is **not** correct with some probability α_{m_1,m_2} *i.e.*, an α_{m_1,m_2}-correct encryption scheme and we prove that it satisfies the DP definition; *(ii)* prove that combining DP and encryption, is equivalent to using an α_{m_1,m_2}-correct encryption scheme and provide a construction to build one from the other; *(iii)* prove that an encryption scheme that belongs in the DP-then-Encrypt class is at least as computationally secure as the original base encryption scheme; *(iv)* provide an α_{m_1,m_2}-correct encryption scheme that achieves both requirements (*i.e.*, DP and confidentiality) and relies on Dijk *et al.*'s homomorphic encryption scheme (EUROCRYPT 2010); and *(v)* perform some statistical experiments on our encryption scheme in order to empirically check the correctness of the theoretical results.

Keywords: Differential privacy · Encryption · Homomorphic encryption

1   Introduction

The Internet has evolved into a powerful platform interconnecting billions of users and has changed the way we do business, communicate with our friends, and perform our financial transactions. In this new communication paradigm, we leave our digital fingerprints everywhere: medical records, financial records, web search histories, and social network data. There is no doubt that the privacy

© Springer International Publishing AG 2017
P.Q. Nguyen and J. Zhou (Eds.): ISC 2017, LNCS 10599, pp. 309–326, 2017.
https://doi.org/10.1007/978-3-319-69659-1_17

implications of this increased connectivity can lead to oppressive electronic data surveillance.

Let us consider a real-world scenario: a company sells electricity to different customers in large geographical areas. The company owns and distributes a smart-metering grid [6] in order to offer the lowest price possible for its customers. Alice, that wants to pay as less as possible for her electrical consumption, signs a contract with the company by providing her personal information and accepts to install in her home different *sensors* that will measure the electrical consumption during the day and transmit this data to the electricity company. The company collects data from all its customers in an entire geographical region and, by performing statistical analysis on the collected data, is able to optimize the electrical supply distribution. Alice worries that her data may be used in a malicious way and wants to get guarantees that her privacy will be respected. She is aware that by analysing the data of her power consumption, someone may deduce private information such as when she is at home and what habits she may have. She wants her personal information to be confidential (encrypted) when they are used by a third party but she accepts that the company may use her data for statistical analysis in order to optimise the supply distribution.

This particular problem might raise different privacy concerns that we categorize into two classes, as represented in Fig. 1:

– An *individual privacy breach* can be described as the act of deducing private information for an individual from some public information.
  In this case, the electricity company can deduce Alice's habits just by observing her power consumption measurements.
– A *group privacy breach* can be defined as the act of deducing a single individual private information from public statistical information of groups of people.
  Let us suppose that the electricity company offers an open-source interface where everyone can query and obtain statistical information about the company's customers. The only limitation is that the statistics are not computed if the sample of customers is lower than five people.
  Eve wants to find out Alice's habits for malicious reasons. To achieve that she checks on every social network and finds out that Alice is a *student* and she lives in a *one-room apartment*. Eve starts querying the company's database by asking for the *"average daily power consumption of a student that lives in an one-room apartment"* and does not obtain any information because the sample is too small. Then, Eve asks for the *"average daily consumption of people that live in an one-room apartment"* and the *"average daily consumption of people that live in an one-room apartment that are **not** students"*. Thus, Eve can deduce some approximation of Alice's habits by computing the difference between the two values and obtain the *"average daily consumption of a student that lives in an one-room apartment"* in which Alice is contained.

In this paper, we do not deal with the problem of inferring some private information about an individual (such as habits) from other private data, such as consumption, from a trusted third party (*e.g.*, a company). However, we care

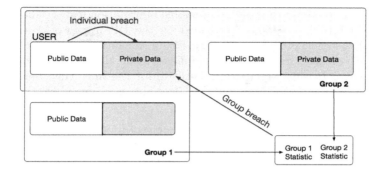

Fig. 1. Individual and group privacy breaches.

about inferring private information from publicly available data published by a third party (*e.g.,* the billing information). To protect against either of the two types of privacy breaches, different notions of privacy and methodologies that preserve privacy have been defined in the literature such as *t-closeness* [11], *k-anonymity* [5], *ℓ-diversity* [8]. However, these notions of privacy have been proven to be weak, since even when they are employed information leakage and de-anomyization attacks can still be performed.

Differential privacy (DP) introduced by Dwork *et al.* [3], addresses the problem of learning as little as possible about an individual, while learning useful information about a population. It offers a formal framework that can be used to bound the amount of info that an adversary can discover from a database that contains private data, when statistical findings of the stored data are communicated to an untrusted party. More precisely, DP assumes the existence of a data aggregator, who is publishing statistics about a population. In other words, DP is a formalism that allows statistical analysis of private datasets while minimizing a group privacy breach. Informally, by employing a *DP-mechanism* to respond to a query, we are publishing noisy statistics about a dataset. The amount of noise should depend on the sensitivity of the queried statistic to the input, *i.e., "how much the query result would change if one single entry is changed or removed?"*. This means that if the query result will change a lot, we have to introduce more noise in order to *"hide"* the influence of the changed/removed entry in the query result. Otherwise, a drop in the query result will reveal partial information on the modified entry.

Complementary, a *semantically secure encryption* scheme guarantees the *confidentiality* of the encrypted information *i.e.,* no-one can decrypt and obtain the original message of a ciphertext. As a plus, an *homomorphic encryption* scheme [9,12] allows the computation of particular functions on the encrypted data. Informally, we can encrypt our messages and then compute a particular function on the ciphertext and obtain a new ciphertext that will be decrypted to the function computed on the original plaintext messages.

The solution required to avoid any possible information leakage should guarantee privacy breach *resistance* (provided by the DP framework) **and** confidentiality of the encrypted data (provided by a semantically secure encryption scheme). Each of these frameworks, if employed alone, does not provide full privacy guarantees. In this paper, we investigate for the first time, how we may achieve both differential privacy and confidentiality and introduce the concept of a differentially private encryption scheme.

Related Work: Privacy-preservation has received a lot of attention in the literature and multiple semantically secure crypto systems as well as differential private mechanisms have been proposed. However, existing work on encrypted computation and differential privacy has proceeded mainly in isolation. In order to avoid all possible information leakage, while guaranteeing both *confidentiality* and *differential privacy*, the most common solution is to process the plaintext data in a DP-mechanism and then encrypt the result using a secure homomorphic encryption scheme. The ciphertext will guarantee confidentiality until the decryption phase, while the plaintext message will satisfy the DP definition. In the literature, it is possible to find different solutions [1,7,10] that use this paradigm: a DP-mechanism and an encryption scheme; used sequentially. We will define these solutions that combine a *DP-framework* and an *Encryption-framework* as an element in the DP-then-Encrypt class (formally defined in Definition 5). Our solution has as a starting point Dwork *et al.*'s definition of an α-correct encryption scheme [4] *i.e.,* an encryption scheme that can *wrongly decrypt* (or encrypt) a message with some probability bounded by α. Dwork *et al.* [4] defined an algorithm that takes an α-correct encryption scheme and returns a new encryption scheme, built using the α-correct one, that is correct (or almost-correct). We provide a more detailed definition of α-correctness, where we are interested in the precise probability of encrypting a message m_1 and obtaining a message m_2. Our definition is the first result that provides sufficient conditions for an α-correct encryption scheme in order to achieve ϵ-DP. In order to build a concrete instantiation of a differentially private encryption scheme, we rely on Dijk *et al.*'s [2] homomorphic public-key encryption scheme over the integers.

Our Contributions: Our main idea is defining the class Encrypt+DP that contains all the encryption schemes that are differential private and achieve privacy and confidentiality *atomically*, as represented in Fig. 2. As a starting point, we define an α_{m_1,m_2}-correct encryption scheme (Definition 4) that will permit an encryption scheme to be **not** correct, *i.e.,* the decryption of the encryption of a specific message m_1 can be a different message m_2 with probability α_{m_1,m_2}. From this definition, we prove that an α_{m_1,m_2}-correct 1-bit encryption scheme satisfies the Dwork's DP definition [3] with $\epsilon(\alpha_{m_1,m_2})$-DP, *i.e.,* the DP parameter ϵ will be strongly related to the probabilities α_{m_1,m_2} of the encryption scheme. Then, we prove in Proposition 2 that the more general N-element encryption scheme achieves $\epsilon(\alpha_{m_1,m_2})$-DP.

Furthermore, we formally define the DP-then-Encrypt and Encrypt+DP classes. As our main result, we prove in Proposition 4 that the two classes are

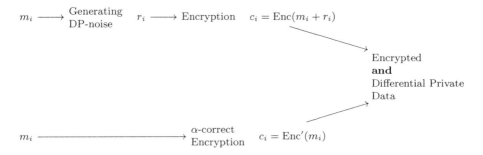

Fig. 2. The difference between the DP-then-Encrypt (on the top) and our solution (at the bottom).

equivalent and provide a construction to switch between them. This means that our solution of an α_{m_1,m_2}-correct encryption scheme can be re-written with a DP-then-Encrypt encryption scheme.

As the second main contribution, in Lemma 1, we reduce the security of a DP-then-Encrypt encryption scheme to the security of the correct encryption scheme framework. The considered security-computational model is built around a non-interactive adversary that has access only to the public key and a particular ciphertext and it guesses the original plaintext. This security model is a necessary condition in order to satisfy more complex security models like $IND - CPA$, $IND - CCA$, etc.

The last contribution is a concrete $\alpha_{m,m}$-correct encryption scheme inside Encrypt+DP. We modify the Dijk *et al.* [2] integer homomorphic encryption scheme and we show how to compute the probability $\alpha_{m,m}$. As a final point, we exploit the structure of the scheme and obtain the correspondent DP-then-Encrypt encryption scheme that relies on Dijk *et al.*'s homomorphic encryption scheme.

Paper Organisation: The paper is organised as follows. In Sect. 2, we describe the notation used throughout the paper and the definitions we are based on. In Sect. 3, we give our definition of α_{m_1,m_2}-correct encryption schemes and prove that it has $\epsilon(\alpha_{m_1,m_2})$-DP. In Sect. 4, we show the equality between our framework, Encrypt+DP, and the DP-then-Encrypt. The proof will sketch an algorithm that transforms a correct encryption scheme into an α_{m_1,m_2}-correct encryption scheme. We define the security-hardness model and prove the security-hardness of a DP-then-Encrypt encryption scheme with respect to the corresponding base (correct) encryption scheme. In Sect. 5, we provide an instantiation of an $\alpha_{m,m}$-correct encryption scheme starting from Dijk *et al.*'s [2] encryption scheme and we prove its security.

2   Preliminaries

In this section, we will define the notation used in the paper and the basic definitions of the notions we employ in the rest of the paper.

2.1 Notation

We always denote with $\mathcal{M}$ the message-space. We denote with $\mathcal{K} = \mathcal{K}_{sk} \times \mathcal{K}_{pk}$ the key-space where $\mathcal{K}_{sk}$ is the secret-key-space and $\mathcal{K}_{pk}$ is the public key-space and with $\mathcal{C}$ the ciphertext-space. $\mathbb{N}$ is the set of natural numbers (*i.e.*, integers $z \geq 0$). Then we define intervals with $[a, b] = \{a, a+1, \cdots, b\}$ and $(a, b) = [a, b] \setminus \{a, b\}$. We denote with $\mathbb{1}_A$ the identity function on the set A. We define with the symbol $\simeq$, a *probabilistic* equality between functions, *i.e.*, $f(x) \simeq g(x)$ means $\mathbb{P}(f(x) = g(x)) = p$ for some $p \in [0, 1]$. We denote with $\mathrm{negl}(n)$ a negligible function. We denote with $a(\mathrm{mod}\ n)$ the modulo n of a in the interval $\left(-\frac{n}{2}, \frac{n}{2}\right]$. We denote with U_A the uniform distribution over the set A. We denote M times the cartesian product of a set A as A^M and the range of a function f with domain X as $\mathrm{Rg}(f) := \{f(x) : x \in X\}$. For a set X, we define with $\mathcal{P}(X)$ the power-set of X, *i.e.*, the set of all the subset of X.

2.2 Basic Definitions

In order to define differential privacy, we will define a data-set:

Definition 1 (Dataset). *A dataset D is defined on an alphabet A so that either $D \in A^n$ for a fixed dataset size n, or $D \in A^*$ with $A^* = \bigcup_{i=0}^{\infty} A^i$ being the union of all product sets of A.*

Definition 2 (ϵ-differential privacy [3]). *A randomized function $\mathcal{Q}$ is ϵ-differentially private if for all data-sets D_1 and D_2 differing on at most one element, i.e., the ℓ_0-distance between D_1 and D_2 is at most 1, and all $S \subseteq Rg(\mathcal{Q})$, it holds*

$$\mathbb{P}(\mathcal{Q}(D_1) \in S) \leq \exp(\epsilon) \cdot \mathbb{P}(\mathcal{Q}(D_2) \in S)$$

Remark 1. For finite ϵ, we must have that the distribution of a DP-mechanism has always the same range, *i.e.*, for every $D_0, D_1 \subset \mathcal{M}$ it holds $\mathrm{Rg}(\mathcal{Q}(D_0)) = \mathrm{Rg}(\mathcal{Q}(D_1))$.

In our construction, we will use messages as databases and we will always use the ℓ_0-distance; for two different messages m, m', the distance is always 1.

Below we provide Dwork *et al.*'s [4] definition of an α-correct (public-key) encryption scheme:

Definition 3 (Dwork *et al.*'s α-correct public-key encryption scheme [4]). *Let (G, E, D) be any public-key encryption scheme and $\alpha : \mathbb{N} \to [0, 1]$ an arbitrary function.*

(a) *(G, E, D) is all-keys α-correct if for every pair (sk, pk) generated by G on input 1^λ, it holds that $\mathbb{P}(D_{sk}(E_{pk}(m)) \neq m) \leq 1 - \alpha(\lambda)$, where the probability is taken over the choice of $m \in U_n$, and over the random coins of E and D.*

(b) *(G, E, D) is almost-all-keys α-correct if with probability $1 - \mathrm{negl}(\lambda)$ over the random coins of G used to generate (sk, pk) on input 1^λ, it holds that $\mathbb{P}(D_{sk}(E_{pk}(m)) \neq m) \leq 1 - \alpha(\lambda)$ where the probability is taken over the choice of $m \in U_n$ and over the random coins of E and D.*

(c) (G, E, D) is almost-all-keys perfectly correct if with probability $1 - \mathrm{negl}(\lambda)$ over the random coins of G used to generate $(\mathrm{sk}, \mathrm{pk})$ on input 1^λ, it holds that $\mathbb{P}(D_{\mathrm{sk}}(E_{\mathrm{pk}}(m) \neq m) = 0$, where the probability is taken over the choice of $m \in U_n$ and over the random coins of E and D.

3   Our Definition of α_{m_1, m_2}-Correct Encryption Scheme

In this section, we define an α_{m_1, m_2}-correct encryption scheme and compare it to the Dwork *et al.*'s Definition 3. Then, we prove that an α_{m_1, m_2}-correct encryption scheme satisfies the definition of differential privacy with respect to the function $\mathcal{Q} := D \circ E \simeq \mathbb{1}_\mathcal{M}$. We start by presenting and describing the main constructions and properties for the case of a 1-bit encryption scheme, as the simplest example possible, and after that we generalize the result to an N-element encryption scheme.

3.1   Definition

Our goal is to formally define the possibility that an encryption scheme can wrongly decrypt a message with some well defined probability.

Definition 4 (α_{m_1, m_2}-correctness encryption scheme). *Let (G, E, D) be an encryption scheme defined over $(\mathcal{M}, \mathcal{K}, \mathcal{C})$ as*

- **Generation algorithm:** *let $\lambda \in \mathbb{N}$ be a security parameter. G is defined as a probabilistic algorithm that given a security parameter 1^λ, returns a key-pair $(\mathrm{sk}, \mathrm{pk}) \in \mathcal{K}$.*
- **Encryption algorithm:** *let $m \in \mathcal{M}$, $\mathrm{pk} \in \mathcal{K}_{\mathrm{pk}}$ and $c \in \mathcal{C}$. E is defined as an algorithm that takes as input a public key pk and a message m, and returns a ciphertext c.*
- **Decryption algorithm:** *let $m \in \mathcal{M}$, $\mathrm{sk} \in \mathcal{K}_{\mathrm{sk}}$ and $c \in \mathcal{C}$. D is defined as an algorithm that given a secret key sk and a ciphertext c, returns a plaintext m.*

(G, E, D) is said to be an α_{m_1, m_2}-correct encryption scheme if, for all $m_1, m_2 \in \mathcal{M}$, a fixed $\lambda \in \mathbb{N}$ and a fixed key-pair $(\mathrm{sk}, \mathrm{pk}) \leftarrow G(1^\lambda)$, it holds

$$\alpha_{m_1, m_2}((\mathrm{sk}, \mathrm{pk})) := \mathbb{P}(D(\mathrm{sk}, E(\mathrm{pk}, m_1)) = m_2)$$

If for all $m \in \mathcal{M}$ it holds $\alpha_{m, m} = 1$, then (G, E, D) is said to be a correct encryption scheme.

In simple words, in an α_{m_1, m_2}-*correct encryption scheme*, the probability of encrypting m_1 and decrypting into m_2 using the key-pair $(\mathrm{sk}, \mathrm{pk})$ is equal to α_{m_1, m_2}.

Remark 2. From the definition above, it is easy to see that every encryption scheme is an α_{m_1, m_2} encryption scheme.

Remark 3. The $\alpha_{m_1,m_2}((\text{sk},\text{pk}))$ values are strongly connected with the choice of (sk,pk). We will abuse notation and drop the key-pair since in our arguments, we will always fix some key-pair (sk,pk).

Remark 4. Our α_{m_1,m_2}-correctness (Definition 4) and Dwork *et al.*'s definition (Definition 3) describe the same encryption schemes.

Proof. – *Our definition $\Rightarrow$ Dwork* et al.*'s definition:*
Let (G, E, D) be any α_{m_1,m_2}-correct public-key encryption scheme. Let us consider

$$\alpha = \max_{m \in \mathcal{M}, (\text{sk},\text{pk}) \in \mathcal{K}} \alpha_{m,m}((\text{sk},\text{pk}))$$

Let $(\text{sk},\text{pk}) \in \mathcal{K}$ be any possible random key and $m \in \mathcal{M}$ any possible random message.

$$1 - \mathbb{P}(D_{\text{sk}}(E_{\text{pk}}(m)) \neq m) = \mathbb{P}(D_{\text{sk}}(E_{\text{pk}}(m)) = m) = \alpha_{m,m}((\text{sk},\text{pk})) \leq \alpha$$

And so, we have that (G, E, D) is an α-correct encryption scheme in Dwork *et al.*'s Definition 3.
– *Our definition $\Leftarrow$ Dwork* et al.*'s definition:* Follows directly from Remark 2 □

Dwork *et al.*'s definition describes a global upper bound on the correctness probability of an encryption scheme, while our definition defines the precise values of α_{m_1,m_2} of the encryption scheme.

3.2   Construction of an α_{m_1,m_2}-Correct 1-bit Encryption Scheme

Fix $\mathcal{M} = \{0, 1\}$. Let (G, E, D) be an α_{m_1,m_2}-correct encryption scheme defined over $(\mathcal{M}, \mathcal{K}, \mathcal{C})$. Let us fix a key pair $(\text{sk},\text{pk}) \hookleftarrow G(1^\lambda)$ and let $\mathcal{Q}(m) = D(\text{sk}, E(\text{pk}, m))$. It holds:

$$\text{Rg}(\mathcal{Q}) = \{0, 1\} \qquad D_0 = \{0\}, D_1 = \{1\}$$
$$S \in \mathcal{P}(\text{Rg}(\mathcal{Q})) = \{\emptyset, \{0\} = S_0, \{1\} = S_1, \{0, 1\} = \mathcal{M}\}$$
$$\mathcal{Q}(m) = D(\text{sk}, E(\text{pk}, m)) \simeq m \qquad \forall_{m_1,m_2 \in \mathcal{M}} \mathbb{P}(\mathcal{Q}(m_1) = m_2) = \alpha_{m_1,m_2}$$

Proposition 1. *An α_{m_1,m_2}-correct 1-bit encryption scheme such that for all $m_1, m_2 \in \mathcal{M}$ it holds that $\mathbb{P}(D(\text{sk}, E(\text{pk}, m_1)) = m_2) = \alpha_{m_1,m_2}$, achieves $\epsilon(\alpha_{m_1,m_2})$-differential privacy where*

$$\epsilon(\alpha_{m_1,m_2}) := \inf \left\{ \epsilon : \begin{array}{cc} e^\epsilon \geq \frac{\alpha_{0,0}}{\alpha_{1,0}} , & e^\epsilon \geq \frac{\alpha_{0,1}}{\alpha_{1,1}} \\[2mm] e^\epsilon \geq \frac{\alpha_{1,0}}{\alpha_{0,0}} , & e^\epsilon \geq \frac{\alpha_{1,1}}{\alpha_{0,1}} \end{array} \right\}$$

Proof. Let us prove that any α_{m_1,m_2}-correct encryption scheme satisfies the ϵ-DP definition.
    From the Definition 2, we can state that $\mathbb{P}(\mathcal{Q}(D_i) \in S_j)$ means that we encrypt the bit i and we decrypt it into the bit j. We can impose the DP definition in all possible cases in order to study the differential privacy coefficient ϵ:

- If $S = \emptyset$, all the probabilities are 0, and so the ϵ-DP definition holds for every $\epsilon \in \mathbb{R}$ since $0 \leq 0$
- If $S = \{0, 1\} = \mathcal{M}$, all the probabilities are 1, and so the ϵ-DP definition holds since $1 \leq e^\epsilon$ and $\epsilon \geq 0$
- If $S = \{0\} = S_0$:
  - $\mathbb{P}(\mathcal{Q}(D_0) \in S_0) \leq e^\epsilon \, \mathbb{P}(\mathcal{Q}(D_1) \in S_0)$ becomes $\alpha_{0,0} \leq e^\epsilon \alpha_{1,0} \implies e^\epsilon \geq \frac{\alpha_{0,0}}{\alpha_{1,0}}$
  - $\mathbb{P}(\mathcal{Q}(D_1) \in S_0) \leq e^\epsilon \, \mathbb{P}(\mathcal{Q}(D_0) \in S_0)$ becomes $\alpha_{1,0} \leq e^\epsilon \alpha_{0,0} \implies e^\epsilon \geq \frac{\alpha_{1,0}}{\alpha_{0,0}}$
- If $S = \{1\} = S_1$:
  - $\mathbb{P}(\mathcal{Q}(D_1) \in S_1) \leq e^\epsilon \, \mathbb{P}(\mathcal{Q}(D_0) \in S_1)$ becomes $\alpha_{1,1} \leq e^\epsilon \alpha_{0,1} \implies e^\epsilon \geq \frac{\alpha_{1,1}}{\alpha_{0,1}}$
  - $\mathbb{P}(\mathcal{Q}(D_0) \in S_1) \leq e^\epsilon \, \mathbb{P}(\mathcal{Q}(D_1) \in S_1)$ becomes $\alpha_{0,1} \leq e^\epsilon \alpha_{1,1} \implies e^\epsilon \geq \frac{\alpha_{0,1}}{\alpha_{1,1}}$

We can conclude that for every $\alpha_{m_1,m_2} \in [0, 1]$, we achieve ϵ-DP where ϵ has to be in the convex solution set $\mathcal{E}(\alpha_{m_1,m_2})$ defined as:

$$\text{for } \alpha_{m_1,m_2} \in [0, 1] \qquad \mathcal{E}(\alpha_{m_1,m_2}) := \left\{ \epsilon : \begin{array}{cc} e^\epsilon \geq \frac{\alpha_{0,0}}{\alpha_{1,0}} & e^\epsilon \geq \frac{\alpha_{0,1}}{\alpha_{1,1}} \\ e^\epsilon \geq \frac{\alpha_{1,0}}{\alpha_{0,0}} & e^\epsilon \geq \frac{\alpha_{1,1}}{\alpha_{0,1}} \end{array} \right\}$$

from which we can define the curve

$$\epsilon(\alpha_{m_1,m_2}) = \inf \mathcal{E}(\alpha_{m_1,m_2})$$

that defines the minimum ϵ such that the ϵ-DP definition holds for the encryption scheme.   □

Proposition 1 is a special case of Proposition 2.

3.3   Construction of an α_{m_1,m_2}-Correct N-Elements Encryption Scheme

Let $\#\mathcal{M} = N$ be the message space with uniform distribution of being transmitted, i.e., for all $m \in \mathcal{M}$, $\mathbb{P}(M \in \{m\}) = \frac{1}{\#\mathcal{M}}$. Fix a key-pair (sk, pk) and then for all $m_1, m_2 \in \mathcal{M}$ it holds

$$\alpha_{m_1,m_2} = \mathbb{P}(D(\text{sk}, E(\text{pk}, m_1)) = m_2 \mid m_1)$$

Proposition 2. *An N-element α_{m_1,m_2}-correct encryption scheme such that for all $m_1, m_2 \in \mathcal{M}$ it holds that $\mathbb{P}(D(\text{sk}, E(\text{pk}, m_1)) = m_2) = \alpha_{m_1,m_2}$. Then, the encryption scheme achieves $\epsilon(\alpha_{m_1,m_2})$-differential privacy where*

$$\epsilon(\alpha_{m_1,m_2}) := \inf \left\{ \epsilon \,\middle|\, \forall D_0, D_1 \in \mathcal{M}, \ S \subseteq \mathcal{M}. \ \frac{\sum_{m_2 \in S} \alpha_{D_0,m_2}}{\sum_{m_2 \in S} \alpha_{D_1,m_2}} \leq e^\epsilon \right\}$$

Proof. Let $\mathcal{Q} = D \circ E$ and $S \subseteq \mathcal{M}$ as before. Then, $\mathbb{P}(\mathcal{Q}(D_0) \in S) = \sum_{m_2 \in S} \alpha_{D_0,m_2}$.

Imposing the DP definition, we have that for all $D_0, D_1 \in \mathcal{M}$ such that the two elements are different and for every $S \subseteq \mathcal{M}$ it holds:

$$\mathbb{P}(\mathcal{Q}(D_0) \in S) \le e^\epsilon \, \mathbb{P}(\mathcal{Q}(D_1) \in S) \implies \sum_{m_2 \in S} \alpha_{D_0, m_2} \le e^\epsilon \left(\sum_{m_2 \in S} \alpha_{D_1, m_2} \right)$$

We can manipulate the equation and obtain $\frac{\sum_{m_2 \in S} \alpha_{D_0, m_2}}{\sum_{m_2 \in S} \alpha_{D_1, m_2}} \le e^\epsilon$

We define the convex set

$$\mathcal{E}(\alpha_{m_1, m_2}) := \left\{ \epsilon \,\middle|\, \forall D_0, D_1 \in \mathcal{M}, S \subseteq \mathcal{M} . \frac{\sum_{m_2 \in S} \alpha_{D_0, m_2}}{\sum_{m_2 \in S} \alpha_{D_1, m_2}} \le e^\epsilon \right\}$$

The value $\epsilon(\alpha_{m_1, m_2}) = \inf \mathcal{E}(\alpha_{m_1, m_2})$ will satisfy the DP-definition. $\square$

3.4   Fix ϵ, Find α_{m_1, m_2}

The parameters ϵ and α_{m_1, m_2} are dependent one from the other since for all $D_0, D_1 \in \mathcal{M}$ and for all $S \subseteq \mathcal{M}$, it holds

$$\frac{\sum_{m_2 \in S} \alpha_{D_0, m_2}}{\sum_{m_2 \in S} \alpha_{D_1, m_2}} \le e^\epsilon \tag{1}$$

The goal of finding the best α_{m_1, m_2} that achieves a fixed ϵ-DP depends on practical requirements and conditions that we want to impose on the probabilities α_{m_1, m_2}, i.e., "*maximizing the difference between two different messages*" or "*having a specific probability distribution*".

For completeness, we will provide a simple solution in a particular case.

Proposition 3. *Let α_{m_1, m_2} be the probabilities of an N-element encryption scheme, where for all $m \in \mathcal{M}$, it holds $\alpha_{m,m} = \alpha$ and for all $m' \in \mathcal{M}$ with $m' \neq m$, it holds $\alpha_{m,m'} = \beta < \alpha$. If $\alpha \ge (N-1)\beta$, then the scheme achieves $\log\left(\frac{\alpha}{\beta}\right)$-DP.*

Proof. In order to prove the thesis, we have to find the D_0, D_1, S that maximize the left side of Eq. (1). We can consider the polynomials $f_\alpha(x) = \alpha + x\beta$ and $f_\beta(x) = \beta + x\alpha$. From the hypothesis, we have that $f_\alpha(x) \ge f_\beta(x)$ for all $x \in \mathbb{R}$ and $x \ge 0$. In particular, this is true for the integer values between 0 and $N-1$. Since $\frac{f_\alpha(x)}{f_\beta(x)}$ is a decreasing function for all $x \in \mathbb{R}$ and $x \ge 0$, we can conclude that for $i \in [0, N-1]$ integers, it holds:

$$\frac{\alpha}{\beta} = \frac{f_\alpha(0)}{f_\beta(0)} \ge \frac{f_\alpha(i)}{f_\beta(i)} \ge \frac{f_\alpha(i+1)}{f_\beta(i+1)} \ge \cdots \ge \frac{f_\alpha(N-1)}{f_\beta(N-1)}$$

$$\frac{\beta}{\alpha} = \frac{f_\beta(0)}{f_\alpha(0)} \le \frac{f_\beta(i)}{f_\alpha(i)} \le \frac{f_\beta(i+1)}{f_\alpha(i+1)} \le \cdots \le \frac{f_\beta(N-1)}{f_\alpha(N-1)} = \frac{(N-1)\beta}{(N-2)\beta + \alpha} \tag{2}$$

From Eq. (2) and since $\frac{\alpha}{\beta} \geq \frac{\beta}{\alpha}$ from the hypothesis, we have

$$\frac{(N-1)\beta}{(N-2)\beta + \alpha} \leq \frac{\alpha}{(N-2)\beta + \alpha} \leq \frac{\alpha}{\beta}$$

and, in Eq. (1)

$$\frac{\sum_{m_2 \in S} \alpha_{D_0, m_2}}{\sum_{m_2 \in S} \alpha_{D_1, m_2}} \leq \frac{\alpha}{\beta} \leq e^\epsilon \tag{3}$$

We can so conclude that the minimal ϵ for which the equation holds is $\log\left(\frac{\alpha}{\beta}\right)$ and so the N-element encryption scheme will achieve $\log\left(\frac{\alpha}{\beta}\right)$-DP. □

4 Equality Between DP-then-Encrypt and Encrypt+DP

In this section, we define the two main methods of combining an encryption scheme with a differential private mechanism: *(i)* the DP-then-Encrypt and *(ii)* the Encrypt+DP. We then prove a proposition on the equivalence between the DP-then-Encrypt and the Encrypt+DP classes. After this, we prove that combining a differential privacy framework with a correct encryption scheme is at least as computationally secure as the relying encryption scheme.

Definition 5. *Define the* DP-then-Encrypt *class as the set of all the encryption schemes (G', E', D') such that*

$$G'(1^\lambda) := G(1^\lambda) \qquad E'(\mathrm{pk}, m) := E(\mathrm{pk}, \mathcal{Q}(m)) \qquad D'(\mathrm{sk}, c) := D(\mathrm{sk}, c)$$

for some (G, E, D) correct encryption scheme on $(\mathcal{M}, \mathcal{K}, \mathcal{C})$ and $\mathcal{Q} \simeq \mathbb{1}_\mathcal{M}$ a DP-mechanism.

It is trivial that $D'(\mathrm{sk}, E'(\mathrm{pk}, m)) = \mathcal{Q}(m)$.

Definition 6. *Define the* Encrypt+DP *class as the set of all the α_{m_1, m_2}-correct encryption schemes $(\hat{G}, \hat{E}, \hat{D})$ on $(\mathcal{M}, \mathcal{K}, \mathcal{C})$. From the Proposition 2, we have that $(\hat{G}, \hat{E}, \hat{D})$ is $\epsilon(\alpha_{m_1, m_2})$-DP and it holds $\hat{D}(\mathrm{sk}, \hat{E}(\mathrm{pk}, m)) \simeq \mathbb{1}_\mathcal{M}(m)$.*

In a nutshell, the DP-then-Encrypt class contains all the different combinations of the identity map as a DP-mechanism and a correct encryption scheme. On the other hand, the Encrypt-then-DP achieves the identity map as a DP-mechanism directly in the α_{m_1, m_2}-correct encryption scheme used.

In order to prove the equality between the two classes, we define a *probability "permutation"* as:

Definition 7. *Let $m_1, m_2 \in \mathcal{M}$. Let us denote a* probability "permutation" *π as the random variable on $\mathcal{M}$ with measure probability of the event "permute the message m_1 into the message m_2" defined as $\mathbb{P}(\pi(m_1) = m_2) = \alpha_{m_1, m_2}$.*

Remark 5. Let π be a probability permutation. Then, π is a DP-mechanism. This means it is a $\epsilon(\alpha_{m_1,m_2})$-DP mechanism (or it achieves ∞-DP).

Proposition 4. *The* DP-then-Encrypt *class is equivalent to the* Encrypt+DP *class.*

Proof.

- DP-then-Encrypt $\subseteq$ Encrypt+DP

  Let (G', E', D') be a DP-then-Encrypt *encryption scheme. Let us fix a key pair* $(\mathrm{sk}, \mathrm{pk}) \hookleftarrow G'(1^\lambda)$. *Trivially using Remark 2, there exists an $\alpha_{m_1,m_2} \in [0,1]$ such that for all $m_1, m_2 \in \mathcal{M}$ it holds:*

  $$\mathbb{P}((D'(\mathrm{sk}, E'(\mathrm{pk}, m_1)) = m_2) = \mathbb{P}(\mathcal{Q}(m_1) = m_2) = \alpha_{m_1,m_2}$$

  From the Definition 4, (G', E', D') is an α_{m_1,m_2}-correct encryption scheme and so from Proposition 2, we have that (G', E', D') is contained in the class Encrypt+DP *of Definition 6.*

- DP-then-Encrypt $\supseteq$ Encrypt+DP

  Let $(\hat{G}, \hat{E}, \hat{D})$ be an α_{m_1,m_2}-correct encryption scheme such that $\hat{D}(\mathrm{sk}, \hat{E}(\mathrm{pk}, m)) \simeq \mathbb{1}_{\mathcal{M}}(m)$. For every $m_1, m_2 \in \mathcal{M}$, we define the random variable $\pi : \mathcal{M} \to \mathcal{M}$ as

  $$\mathbb{P}(\pi(m_1) = m_2) := \mathbb{P}(\hat{D}(\mathrm{sk}, \hat{E}(\mathrm{pk}, m_1)) = m_2) = \alpha_{m_1,m_2}$$

  π is a probability permutation as in Definition 7 and for Remark 5, we have that π is a DP-mechanism.

  Let us define $(\hat{G}, E, D)$ a correct encryption scheme such that:
  - *$\hat{G}$ is the same key generator as the α_{m_1,m_2}-correct encryption scheme*
  - *$E : \mathcal{K} \times \mathcal{M} \to \mathcal{C}$ is an encryption algorithm*
  - *$D : \mathcal{K} \times \mathcal{C} \to \mathcal{M}$ is a decryption algorithm*

  and for all $(\mathrm{sk}, \mathrm{pk}) \hookleftarrow \hat{G}(1^\lambda)$, it holds that for all $m \in \mathcal{M}$

  $$\mathbb{P}(D(\mathrm{sk}, E(\mathrm{pk}, m)) = m) = 1$$

  We can claim that E, D always exist and we can consider any injective function $\phi : \mathcal{M} \to \mathcal{C}$ with left inverse ϕ^{-1}. Let us define:

  $$E(\mathrm{pk}, m) := \phi(m) \qquad D(\mathrm{sk}, c) := \phi^{-1}(c)$$

  For $(\hat{G}, E, D)$, we have

  $$\mathbb{P}(D(\mathrm{sk}, E(\mathrm{pk}, m)) = m) = \mathbb{P}(\phi^{-1}(\phi(m)) = m) = \mathbb{P}(m = m) = 1$$

  In order to conclude, we need to prove that $(\hat{G}, E, D)$ with π as in Definition 5, acts like an encryption scheme (G', E', D') that is contained in the Encrypt+DP *class of Definition 6. Fix a key pair $(\mathrm{sk}, \mathrm{pk}) \hookleftarrow \hat{G}(1^\lambda)$:*

  $$\begin{aligned}
  \mathbb{P}(\hat{D}(\mathrm{sk}, \hat{E}(\mathrm{pk}, m_1)) = m_2) &= \alpha_{m_1,m_2} \\
  &= \mathbb{P}(\pi(m_1) = m_2) \\
  &= \mathbb{P}(\phi^{-1}(\phi(\pi(m_1))) = m_2) \\
  &= \mathbb{P}(D(\mathrm{sk}, E(\mathrm{pk}, \pi(m_1))) = m_2) \\
  &= \mathbb{P}(D'(\mathrm{sk}, E'(\mathrm{pk}, m_1)) = m_2) \qquad \square
  \end{aligned}$$

We will now define a concept of *security-hardness* with respect to an adversary without specifying the computational model used.

Definition 8. *The adversary $\mathcal{A}$ for an encryption scheme (G, E, D) is an algorithm that takes the public key[1] and a ciphertext and it outputs a guess m' for the message m.*

$$\mathcal{A} : \mathcal{K}_{\mathrm{pk}} \times \mathcal{C} \to \mathcal{M} \qquad \mathcal{A}(\mathrm{pk}, E(\mathrm{pk}, m)) \mapsto m'$$

An encryption scheme (G, E, D) is said to be security-hard *with respect to the adversary $\mathcal{A}$ (in some computational model) if*

$$\mathbb{P}(\mathcal{A}(\mathrm{pk}, E(\mathrm{pk}, m)) = m) \leq \frac{1}{\#\mathcal{M}} + \mathrm{negl}$$

Informally, we defined the simplest adversary possible whose goal is to guess the correct decryption of a ciphertext given all the public information possible. In order to obtain a general result, we do not impose any complexity-hardness assumption. The security-hardness adversary is a weaker adversary with respect to the ones from $\mathrm{IND - CPA}, \mathrm{IND - CCA}$ (and so on). On the other hand, for an encryption scheme, being security-hard is a necessary condition in order to achieve any security requirement: the security-hardness adversary can be used as a distinguisher in a more structured security model.

Lemma 1. *Let (G, E, D) be a correct encryption scheme which is security-hard. Let $\mathcal{Q} \simeq \mathbb{1}_{\mathcal{M}}$ DP-mechanism. Then the combination of $\mathcal{Q}$ with (G, E, D), which is in the* DP-then-Encrypt *class, is security-hard. In other word, the security-hardness of the combination $\mathcal{Q}$ with (G, E, D) is at least computationally hard as the security-hardness of (G, E, D).*

Proof. We have to show and prove:

1. Reduce every instance of a (G, E, D) correct encryption scheme to an instance in the DP-then-Encrypt class.
2. We prove the lemma by contradiction and *Reductio ad absurdum*: If there exists an adversary $\mathcal{A}$ with non-negligible advantage for the DP-then-Encrypt instance, there will exist an adversary $\mathcal{B}$ with non-negligible advantage for the (G, E, D) correct encryption scheme. Let us suppose that there exists $\mathcal{A}$ with non-negligible advantage, and let us suppose that all $\mathcal{B}$ have negligible advantage. Then we prove that it is a contradiction, and so we conclude.

The reduction is trivial: we can just consider as the instance in the DP-then-Encrypt class, (G, E, D) encryption scheme with the deterministic identity map as the DP-mechanism.

For a fixed key $(\mathrm{sk}, \mathrm{pk}) \leftarrow G(1^{\lambda})$, suppose there exists an adversary $\mathcal{A}$ for the DP-then-Encrypt scheme, it means $\mathcal{A}(m) := \mathcal{A}(\mathrm{pk}, E(\mathrm{pk}, \mathcal{Q}(m)))$ will output

---

[1] It is possible to give a pure symmetric key encryption scheme definition but we do not need it.

the guess m' and the guess will be correct with probability $\frac{1}{\#\mathcal{M}} + \delta$ with $\delta > 0$ non-negligible. Formally $\mathbb{P}(\mathcal{A}(\mathrm{pk}, E(\mathrm{pk}, \mathcal{Q}(m))) = m) = \frac{1}{\#\mathcal{M}} + \delta$

Let us suppose that for all the adversaries $\mathcal{B}$ of the original scheme such that $\mathcal{B}(m) := \mathcal{B}(\mathrm{pk}, E(\mathrm{pk}, m))$, we have $\mathbb{P}(\mathcal{B}(\mathrm{pk}, E(\mathrm{pk}, m)) = m) = \frac{1}{\#\mathcal{M}} + \epsilon$ where $\epsilon > 0$ is negligible.

From the probability independence between the DP-mechanism $\mathcal{Q}$ and the encryption scheme (G, E, D) we have

$$\frac{1}{\#\mathcal{M}} + \delta = \mathbb{P}(\mathcal{A}(m) = m) = \mathbb{P}(\mathcal{B}(m) = m \mid \mathcal{Q}(m) = m)$$

$$= \mathbb{P}(\mathcal{B}(m) = m)\,\mathbb{P}(\mathcal{Q}(m) = m)$$

$$\leq \mathbb{P}(\mathcal{B}(m) = m) = \frac{1}{\#\mathcal{M}} + \epsilon$$

Absurd. So there exists an adversary $\mathcal{B}$ with non-negligible advantage.[2] □

5 Example of an α_{m_1,m_2}-Correct Homomorphic Encryption Scheme

In this section, we introduce a variation of the Dijk's *et al.* public key integer homomorphic encryption scheme [2] by only introducing a new parameter ξ that will be used to increase the noisy randomness of the encryption scheme. Then, we show how to compute the probabilities α_{m_1,m_2} that will prove that the scheme is α_{m_1,m_2}-correct. At the end, we show the connection between the original and the modified scheme and prove the security-hardness of the modified one.

Definition 9 (Variation of the Dijk *et al.* public key homomorphic encryption scheme). *Let $\mathcal{M} = \{0,1\}$ and let γ, η, ρ, τ be the four parameters defined in the original scheme such that all the security constraints hold. Let ξ be an additional parameter required for the variation.*

Let (G, E, D) be defined as:

- *$G(1^\lambda)$: randomly pick $p \in [2^{\eta-1}, 2^\eta)$ and p odd.*
  For the public key, for all $i \in 0..\tau$ sample

$$x_i \in \mathcal{D}_{\gamma,\rho}(p) = \left\{ pq + r : q \in U\left(\mathbb{Z} \cap \left[0, \frac{2^\gamma}{p}\right)\right), r \in U(\mathbb{Z} \cap (-2^\rho, 2^\rho)) \right\}$$

  and relabel so that x_0 is the greatest. Restart until x_0 is odd and $(x_0(\mathrm{mod}\ p)) \in (-\frac{p}{2}, \frac{p}{2}]$ is even.
  Define $\mathrm{pk} := \{x_0, \ldots, x_\tau\}$ as the public key and $\mathrm{sk} := p$ as the secret key.
- *$E(\mathrm{pk}, m)$: choose at random $S \subseteq [1, \tau]$ and a random integer $r \in (-2^{\rho'+\xi}, 2^{\rho'+\xi})$. The difference with respect to the original scheme is that ξ is present in the interval-bounds exponents. Output the ciphertext $c = \left(m + 2r + 2\sum_{i \in S} x_i\right)(\mathrm{mod}\ x_0)$*

---

[2] Take for example adversary $\mathcal{A}$.

- $D(p, c)$: *output* $(c(\mathrm{mod}\ p))(\mathrm{mod}\ 2)$

In order to prove that the scheme achieves some α-correctness with $\alpha \neq 1$, fix a random S and observe that

$$m + 2r + 2\sum_{i \in S} x_i = m + 2r + 2\sum_{i \in S} pq_i + r_i$$

$$= m + 2\left(r + \sum_{i \in S} r_i\right) + p \cdot 2\sum_{i \in S} q_i = m + 2R + pQ$$

where $Q \in \mathbb{Z}$ and R will be contained in a subset of the integers

$$A_S := \left(-(\#S \cdot 2^\rho + 2^{\rho' + \xi}), (\#S \cdot 2^\rho + 2^{\rho' + \xi})\right) \subseteq \mathbb{Z}$$

For this reason, for a fixed S, we can reduce the computation of $\alpha_{m,m}$ as a combinatorial problem:

$$\alpha := \frac{\# \left\{r : r \in \left(-2^{\rho' + \xi}, 2^{\rho' + \xi}\right) \mid |2\left(r + \sum_{i \in S} r_i\right)| < \frac{p}{2}\right\}}{\#S \cdot 2^{\rho+1} + 2^{\rho' + \xi + 1}}$$

For the right parameter ξ, we can obtain that the encryption scheme is an $\alpha_{m,m}$-correct encryption scheme.

Remark 6. It is important to notice that using a different S will change the probability $\alpha_{m,m}$. You can think of it as *using a different public key* for the encryption algorithm.

Consider a fixed S and the function $\lfloor x \rceil$ = closest integer to x. We can compute $\Delta = 2 \cdot \sum_{i \in S} r_i$ and if we consider ξ as the bound for the noise r, we can define the function

$$F(\tilde{\xi}, \Delta) = \frac{\int_{-\tilde{\xi} + \Delta}^{\tilde{\xi} + \Delta} \left\lfloor \frac{x}{p} \right\rceil (\mathrm{mod}\ 2)\ dx}{2 \cdot \tilde{\xi}} \in [0, 1]$$

that represents the correctness probability. We have the trivial properties

$$F(\tilde{\xi}, 0) = \frac{1}{2} \qquad \lim_{\xi \to \infty} F(\tilde{\xi}, \Delta) = \frac{1}{2} \tag{4}$$

In order to prove that our modified scheme is secure, we reduce the security-hardness of our scheme to the security of the original Dijk *et al.*'s encryption scheme. From the Proposition 4 on the class equality between Encrypt+DP and DP-then-Encrypt we will transform our modified scheme into the Dijk *et al.*'s encryption scheme in the DP-then-Encrypt class.

Remark 7. We can observe that r is randomly picked from $\left(-2^{\rho'+\xi}, 2^{\rho'+\xi}\right)$. We will now consider a random $r' \in (-2^{\rho'}, 2^{\rho'})$ and rewrite $r = r' + \hat{r}$ for some $\hat{r} \in \mathbb{Z}$. At this point, we can rewrite the general encrypted message as

$$m + 2r + 2\sum_{i \in S} x_i = m + 2(r' + \hat{r}) + 2\sum_{i \in S} x_i = (m + 2\hat{r}) + 2r' + 2\sum_{i \in S} x_i \quad (5)$$

where r' and x_i are regular values from the original encryption scheme. During the decryption phase, we will obtain:

$$\left(m + 2r + 2\sum_{i \in S} x_i\right)(\bmod\ p)(\bmod\ 2) =$$

$$\text{Eq. (5)} = \left((m + 2\hat{r}) + \left(2r' + 2\sum_{i \in S} x_i\right)\right)(\bmod\ p)(\bmod\ 2)$$

$$\text{Original scheme's values} = (m + 2\hat{r})(\bmod\ p)(\bmod\ 2)$$

$$= m \oplus (2\hat{r}(\bmod\ p)(\bmod\ 2))$$

From this equality, the message m can be decrypted in a different message $\hat{m}$ just by looking at the value $\hat{r}$.

This is exactly a DP-then-Encrypt scheme, where we can define a probability permutation π as in Definition 7 with $\mathbb{P}(\pi(m_1) = m_2) = \alpha_{m_1,m_2}$ and the original Dijk's encryption scheme.

Remark 8. As in the Remark 6, changing S will change the probability permutation π since the probability α will change. For this reason, the random subset S, the probability permutation π, the probability α and the new parameter ξ are dependent one from the others.

Proposition 5. *Given an $\alpha_{m,m}$-correct public key modified Dijk et al.'s encryption scheme with fixed parameters $(\rho, \rho', \eta, \gamma, \tau, \xi)$.*
Any adversary $\mathcal{A}$ with non-negligible advantage ϵ on the $\alpha_{m,m}$-correct encryption scheme can be converted into an adversary $\mathcal{B}$ with non-negligible advantage ϵ on the original Dijk et al.'s encryption scheme with parameter $(\rho, \rho', \eta, \gamma, \tau)$.

Proof. Follows from Lemma 1. □

5.1   Implementation and Statistics

In order to empirically study the dependency between the parameters ξ, α and ϵ, we implemented the modified Dijk *et al.*'s encryption scheme of Sect. 5 in Sage. Considering $\lambda = 10$ as a general security parameter, we started from the scheme with parameters:

$$\rho = \lambda \qquad \rho' = 2 \cdot \lambda \qquad \eta = \lambda^2 \qquad \gamma = \lambda^5 \qquad \tau = \lambda \qquad \xi = 0$$

and then we consider the k-th variation where we add a factor of $\tilde{\xi}_k = \frac{k \cdot p}{10}$ to the noise interval $2^{\rho'} + \tilde{\xi}_k$. In Fig. 3a and b, we have the measured value for α and ϵ with respect to k. For every $k \in [1, 30]$, we tested λ different choice of S, we executed $N = 100$ experiments and retrieved an empirical value for α. In order to obtain the ϵ, we just took the $\epsilon = \sup\left\{\frac{\alpha}{1-\alpha}, \frac{1-\alpha}{\alpha}\right\}$. We tested different random keys S and the empirical difference between the plots is barely visible, but it can easily be described as a *"really small translation of the plot to the left or right"*. In the chosen key used for the test, if we want to have a $\alpha = 0.8$ correctness probability, we have to use $\tilde{\xi}_4 = \frac{2 \cdot p}{5}$ and the scheme will have $\epsilon = 1.38$ -DP.

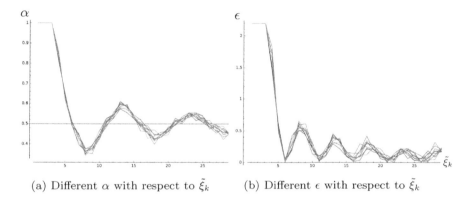

(a) Different α with respect to $\tilde{\xi}_k$ (b) Different ϵ with respect to $\tilde{\xi}_k$

Fig. 3. Empirical measurements of α and ϵ from the implementation.

6   Conclusions and Future Work

This paper bridges concepts in cryptography and differential privacy and we propose the first differentially private encryption scheme. More precisely, we show how to constructively combine differential privacy with an encryption framework in a single scheme, contained in the Encrypt+DP class, and vice versa. This construction is not limited to homomorphic encryption schemes and can be used in order to define an encryption scheme that can guarantee both privacy and confidentiality.

So far we have only examined this link in an abstract way. An open question is the trade-off between α_{m_1,m_2}-correctness and $\epsilon(\alpha_{m_1,m_2})$-DP for specific homomorphic operations, with a particular attention to the *bootstrap* procedure. This might lead to interesting practical applications, such as faster, α-correct homomorphic encryption schemes with differential privacy guarantees.

Acknowledgment. This paper was partially funded by the VR project "PRECIS: Privacy and Security in Wearable Computing devices" and the STINT project "Secure, Private and Efficient Healthcare with Wearable Computing".

References

1. Beimel, A., Nissim, K., Omri, E.: Distributed private data analysis: on simultaneously solving how and what. arXiv:1103.2626 [cs], March 2011
2. Dijk, M., Gentry, C., Halevi, S., Vaikuntanathan, V.: Fully homomorphic encryption over the integers. In: Gilbert, H. (ed.) EUROCRYPT 2010. LNCS, vol. 6110, pp. 24–43. Springer, Heidelberg (2010). doi:10.1007/978-3-642-13190-5_2
3. Dwork, C.: Differential Privacy, vol. 4052, July 2006. https://www.microsoft.com/en-us/research/publication/differential-privacy/
4. Dwork, C., Naor, M., Reingold, O.: Immunizing encryption schemes from decryption errors. In: Cachin, C., Camenisch, J.L. (eds.) EUROCRYPT 2004. LNCS, vol. 3027, pp. 342–360. Springer, Heidelberg (2004). doi:10.1007/978-3-540-24676-3_21
5. El Emam, K., Dankar, F.K.: Protecting privacy using k-anonymity. J. Am. Med. Inform. Assoc. **15**(5), 627–637 (2008). http://www.ncbi.nlm.nih.gov/pmc/articles/PMC2528029/
6. Erkin, Z., Troncoso-Pastoriza, J.R., Lagendijk, R., Pérez-Gonzáez, F.: Privacy-preserving data aggregation in smart metering systems: an overview. IEEE Signal Process. Mag. **30**(2), 75–86 (2013)
7. Garcia, F.D., Jacobs, B.: Privacy-friendly energy-metering via homomorphic encryption. In: Cuellar, J., Lopez, J., Barthe, G., Pretschner, A. (eds.) STM 2010. LNCS, vol. 6710, pp. 226–238. Springer, Heidelberg (2011). doi:10.1007/978-3-642-22444-7_15
8. Gehrke, J., Kifer, D., Machanavajjhala, A.: ℓ-Diversity. In: van Tilborg, H.C.A., Jajodia, S. (eds.) Encyclopedia of Cryptography and Security, pp. 707–709. Springer, US (2011). doi:10.1007/978-1-4419-5906-5_899
9. Gentry, C.: A fully homomorphic encryption scheme. Ph.D. thesis, Stanford University (2009)
10. Ji, Z., Lipton, Z.C., Elkan, C.: Differential privacy and machine learning: a survey and review. arXiv:1412.7584 [cs], December 2014
11. Li, N., Li, T., Venkatasubramanian, S.: t-closeness: privacy beyond k-anonymity and l-diversity. In: 2007 IEEE 23rd International Conference on Data Engineering, pp. 106–115, April 2007
12. Meissen, R.: A Mathematical Approach to Fully Homomorphic Encryption. Ph.D. thesis, Worcester Polytechnic Institute (2012)

Mobile Security

Droid Mood Swing (DMS): Automatic Security Modes Based on Contexts

Md Shahrear Iqbal$^{(\boxtimes)}$ and Mohammad Zulkernine

School of Computing, Queen's University, Kingston, ON, Canada
{iqbal,mzulker}@cs.queensu.ca

Abstract. Smartphones are becoming ubiquitous and we use them for different types of tasks. One problem of using the same device for multiple tasks is that each task requires a different security model. To address this problem, we introduce Droid Mood Swing (DMS), an operating system component that applies different security policies to detected security modes automatically. DMS uses a context manager that tracks the context of the phone from the available sensors. DMS then determines the security mode from the contexts and can impose a number of security measures, namely fine-grained permissions, an intent firewall, a context-aware SD card filesystem, and a permission verification system. The permission verification system uses machine learning techniques to detect suspicious apps and anomalous permission requests. DMS also provides an API that enables third-party developers to make their apps behave differently in different modes. DMS is designed especially for end users and does not compromise the usability of the phone. Device vendors will be able to control configurations (a switching logic and security policies) of the modes through DMS. We implement DMS using the Android Open Source Project (AOSP) and evaluate it in terms of portability, functionality, security, and operational overheads. The evaluation results show that DMS offers a more secure smartphone operating system without incurring any noticeable overhead.

Keywords: Context-dependent security · Smartphone security and privacy · Android security · Mobile malware

1 Introduction

Smartphones are already an integral part of our daily life. People use their smartphones for tasks that require different levels of security, e.g., writing emails, surfing the web, listening to music, watching videos, playing games, performing financial transactions, and creating reports. Companies now allow BYOD (Bring Your Own Device) policy, which lets the employees bring and use their own smartphones for accessing confidential business resources. As a result, companies want the security of their resources and the ability to manage their devices remotely. To address the problem, researchers proposed isolated environments [24,39] (e.g., using virtualization techniques) on the device with different

© Springer International Publishing AG 2017
P.Q. Nguyen and J. Zhou (Eds.): ISC 2017, LNCS 10599, pp. 329–347, 2017.
https://doi.org/10.1007/978-3-319-69659-1_18

controllable security properties. However, we observe a lack of research proposing similar solutions for end users. Users also have their own set of apps for personal use and they do not want to compromise their privacy due to malware or apps provided by their workplaces. Moreover, with the advent of the internet of things (IoT), people are expected to use their smartphones to control other devices (smart TVs, smart fridges, etc.) and new smartphone payment services (e.g., Google Wallet and Apple Pay) require extra security measures.

Despite all the threats, the security model of smartphone operating systems distributed to the normal users is changing at a slow pace. Since a single device is being used by mostly security unaware users, we strongly believe that automatic detection of the device context and switching to different security modes to protect user resources are now a necessity.

In this paper, we propose Droid Mood Swing (DMS), a system that applies fine-grained access control to the detected security mode. To detect the security mode, DMS uses Flamingo [23] that maintains a cache of security contexts and parameters to be used by operating system components and third-party applications. For example, if the user is using the camera app inside his or her home, the phone will switch to a mode where captured resources will be saved securely. It is designed in a way so that device vendors can manage the modes and their configurations. We define a number of security modes that cover almost all the necessary tasks of a regular user. A language is also developed to automate the process of configuring different modes. Each mode will have a configuration file which describes the access control policies of the mode.

DMS can apply fine-grained access control which consists of the Zone-Droid [22] tool and a number of security measures (called "restrictions" in this paper). ZoneDroid realizes the concept of application zones to sandbox a group of applications. Each zone has policies to control the behavior of the apps. However, in ZoneDroid, users have to customize zones and policies by themselves and there was no concept of security contexts. In this paper, we automate the process of configuring each mode to reduce user involvement, thus improving usability.

In particular, this paper makes the following contributions:

- We propose DMS that can switch to multiple security modes based on the detected context and applies fine-grained access control to satisfy the security requirements of each mode.
- We develop several restrictions to facilitate access control, namely an intent firewall (IPC restriction), a context-aware SD card filesystem (file access restriction), and a permission verification system (permission restriction).
- We develop a configuration language to automate the process of configuring ZoneDroid and restrictions without requiring any input from users.
- We provide an API for app developers so that apps can be programmed to behave correctly in different security modes and honor the security policies of each mode.

To implement DMS, we use the open source Android operating system. However, the concept of DMS is not restricted to any particular smartphone operating system. All operations of DMS are completely transparent to users. We also evaluate DMS in terms of performance and storage overhead and show that they are negligible.

In today's highly connected environment, a system like DMS can considerably improve the security of a regular user. Device vendors (Samsung, Google, OnePlus, Asus, Sony, etc.) can use DMS to manage security modes and ensure the safety of device resources.

The remainder of the paper is organized as follows. Section 2 provides the necessary technical background on Android permission model. We illustrate the design and operation of DMS in Sect. 3. We evaluate DMS in Sect. 4 and describe the related work in Sect. 5. Finally, we conclude in Sect. 6 with a little discussion on the limitations and future work.

2   Background

Security in the smartphone ecosystem begins from the application market so that malware cannot enter the device through markets. Most markets review submitted applications and provide a mechanism to sign them. Smartphone operating systems also provide a layered approach towards protection. Normally, they consist of a lower level kernel and a middleware. For example, Apple iOS uses the darwin kernel and a middleware written in C.

2.1   Android Security

Android is a Linux-based open source operating system and consists of the Linux kernel (with over 250 patches for Android [1]), a Java middleware (called the Android framework), and stock applications (phone, contacts, etc.). Android security is mainly built upon a permission-based mechanism which restricts accesses to device resources. In this subsection, we provide a description of the permission model of Android Marshmallow which introduced a new enforcing technique.

Permissions in Android. Android uses permissions to protect system components, APIs, and resources. A permission is simply a unique text string. There are more than hundred permissions [2] defined in the Android operating system. In addition to the Android defined permissions, application developers can declare customized permissions to protect their resources.

A permission can be associated with one of the following four protection levels [3]: normal, dangerous, signature, signature-Or-System. According to `developer.android.com`, normal permissions are low-risk permissions and dangerous permissions are for sensitive resources. Normal permissions are given at install time and cannot be revoked by the user. However, for dangerous permissions, users are notified at runtime. An application can continue only when the user allows the requested permission. More importantly, now users can revoke dangerous permissions later.

In Android, each application is assigned a unique user id (UID). Based on the UID, the kernel provides the application sandboxing. In addition, Android permission mechanism enforces access control in two levels. In one level, the `system_server` process (in Android framework) ensures that the calling component has the necessary permission. In another level, a number of permissions are enforced by the underlined Linux's discretionary access control (DAC). We call these permissions "granted permissions".

When an application process is created by the activity manager, it maps the granted permissions to the corresponding groups. The group IDs are then passed to the `zygote` process which forks itself and sets appropriate group IDs. `Zygote` is a daemon which is started by the `system init` and responsible for the creation of new processes. These permissions are given to the virtual machine process and dynamic permission checks will not occur for some of these permissions. As an example, the INTERNET permission in Android is mapped to the Linux `inet` user group and consequently, internet access is controlled by the underlying Linux kernel.

3   DMS Architecture and Operation

This section describes the architecture and operation details of DMS. One of the goals of DMS is to make the smartphone operating system security-aware. DMS does this without creating multiple personas or compartments. In many of the related research, creating separate compartments for abstracting data and apps is common. However, in our opinion, those approaches require far more user involvement. DMS switches to different security modes based on the detected context. Once a mode is activated, DMS can restrict certain app behaviors to protect resources. Here, data and apps are not isolated. Rather, we modify the filesystem and other OS components to deny access intelligently. The overhead of doing so is much less in comparison to other compartmentalization techniques. DMS does not require any input from users. A description of different components of DMS along with its architecture is given in the following subsections.

3.1   DMS Architecture

The architecture of DMS is presented in Fig. 1. DMS Manager is the controller of DMS and connects with vendors to get configuration files. To switch modes, it uses context information from the Flamingo context manager [23]. Flamingo defines a smartphone's security context as the degree of threat to the device's resources. It uses different phone sensors to determine the context and a number of security parameters. Flamingo exports these parameters and manages a cache to reduce power consumption (by avoiding redundant recalculation).

Based on the configuration, the DMS Manager uses the ZoneDroid Manager to modify zones and policies. All changes are written to an SQLite database named DMS.db. To implement features of DMS, we modify a number of operating system components. The components call the DMS Manager before performing their intended tasks. DMS also has a native service which communicates with other native components (e.g., the SD card filesystem) and performs actions that require root privileges (e.g., issues iptables command).

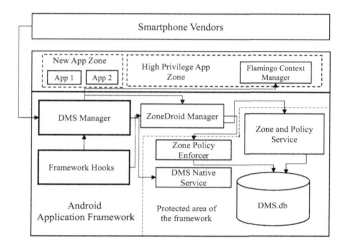

Fig. 1. The architecture of DMS.

3.2   DMS Security Modes

Each security mode is a unique combination of zones, policies, rules, and restrictions. Restrictions are components (that can be activated or deactivated) to restrict certain phone features. Below, we define these terms.

Definition 1 (Security Mode). *A mode* $m = (L_m, Z, T, s)$ *is defined by a label* L_m, *a set of zones* Z, *a set of Restrictions* T, *and a security level* s. *A configuration function* $f_{mc}(m, s) : M \to C$ *maps the mode and the security level to a unique configuration, where* M *is the set of modes and* C *is the set of configurations.*

Definition 2 (Zone). *A zone* $z = (L_z, P, A)$ *is defined by a label* L_z, *a set of policies* P, *and a set of Applications* A. *An application in the device can be assigned to only one zone at any given time. The zone policy enforcer function* f_{zpe} *defines the complete set of conditions under which an application in zone* z *is allowed to call another component or system API.*

Definition 3 (Policy). *A policy* p *is a set of rules* R *that defines the conditions under which an application is granted a number of permissions. A policy checker function* $f_{pc}(o)$ *is defined as* $r_1 \wedge r_2 \wedge r_3 \wedge \cdots \wedge r_n \to \{permit, deny\}$, *where* o *is a permission and* n *is the number of rules in the policy. In the case of a conflict, the rule with the deny will prevail.*

Definition 4 (Rule). *A rule r takes the form (o, V, e), where for a permission o, we can denote a set of attributes and values and an action e. Here, V is a set of 2-tuples of the form < attribute, value >.*

For example, the rule (SEND_SMS, {<TIME, 8AM_TO_5PM>, <PHONENO, N>}, DENY) restricts apps in a zone to send SMSs to the number N from 8AM to 5PM.

Default security modes. Default security modes of DMS are based on security contexts detected by Flamingo. Flamingo detects the following contexts: home, office, and outdoor. Moreover, in the home context, the phone can be in two subcontexts (context within another context), namely casual and private. In the office context, the phone detects whether the user is in a meeting. In addition, Flamingo identifies another two subcontexts (side-loaded, financial) and a number of security parameters. The parameters are *Location, Place-type, Type-of-user-activity, Is-moving, In-use, Is-locked, Type-of-active-app, Is-side-loaded, Network-type, Is-network-encrypted, Is-camera-on, Is-mic-on, Is-storage-encrypted*, and *Number-of-trusted-devices.* Based on the context, subcontexts, and parameters, DMS provides the following security modes:

Home-casual. In this mode, the smartphone is located in user's home. DMS blocks all dangerous permissions for office apps (camera, mic, etc.).

Home-private. DMS switches to this mode whenever a user turns on the camera or the mic inside his or her home. Files saved in this mode will be denied access from any other mode.

Home-financial. DMS activates this mode when the user opens a financial app. DMS restricts unencrypted network and inter-process communication in this mode.

Office-casual. DMS activates this mode when the location of the phone is office. All dangerous permissions are blocked for personal apps.

Office-private. DMS switches to this mode if the *In-meeting* security parameter is true. All background sensor accesses are blocked in this mode.

Office-financial. Similar to the Home-financial mode.

Outdoor-casual. If the smartphone is not in office or home, DMS activates the outdoor-casual mode.

Outdoor-financial. Similar to the Home-financial mode. In addition, if the *Place-type* is a place with a point of sale (POS) terminal (grocery stores, malls, restaurants, etc.) and an NFC payment app is active, DMS blocks all network accesses (internet, NFC, Bluetooth) to other apps. Inter-process communication is also restricted.

3.3   Fine-Grained Permissions

DMS uses ZoneDroid [22] that provides an efficient solution to control a group of applications easily. Each zone provides a certain level of privileges. By default, DMS creates the following zones: New, Trusted, Untrusted, High privilege, Office, and Restricted (for malware). The separation of application zones is analogous to the separation of industrial and residential areas in a smart city [21] where each area has their own security policies and a person has to adhere to the policies based on his or her location. It is worth mentioning that all system apps go to the Trusted app zone and all newly installed apps go to the New app zone. Users have to move them to either the Trusted zone or the Untrusted zone. Users should also keep in mind that default policies are liberal for apps in the Trusted and High Privilege zone (e.g., antiviruses).

DMS can deny permissions based on the following three attributes: time, phone number, and folder location. Attributes and their values become members of the set V. The set V and a decision to allow or deny make a permission fine-grained. Each fine-grained permission forms a rule r and a number of rules (R) constitute a policy p as described in the previous Subsection. We list a sample policy with four rules in Listing 3.1. The policy denies access to location, contacts, and all folders other than FOLDER1 from 10PM to 8AM. It also restricts sending SMSs to phone number N.

DMS zone operations. Using ZoneDroid, DMS can create/edit/delete zones, policies, and rules. For example, DMS can create a new zone, rename a zone, or move apps from one zone to another. It can create a new policy with multiple rules, or edit/add/delete rules in an existing policy. DMS can also disable a zone. Disabling a zone will block all the apps that belong to the zone from executing.

```
{ACCESS_FINE_LOCATION,{<TIME,10PM_8AM>},DENY}
{READ_CONTACTS,{<TIME,10PM_8AM>},DENY}
{SEND_SMS,{<TIME,ALWAYS>,<PHONENO,N>},DENY}
{WRITE_EXTERNAL_STORAGE,{<TIME,10PM_8AM>,<FLOC,FOLDER1>},ALLOW}
```

Listing 3.1. A policy with four rules.

3.4   Context-Aware Filesystem

We modify the Android SD card filesystem (written in C) to make it context-aware. Android uses FUSE [5] to emulate FAT on SD card. The modified filesystem connects with the DMS native service using an abstract Unix domain socket to get the value of the current mode. It then writes the information in the extended attribute of the underlying ext4 filesystem. If file access restriction is enabled, the SD card will deny access to files that are not created in the current mode.

3.5   Inter-process Communication (IPC) Firewall

A technique is developed to allow blocking of all inter-process communications to and from a zone and to and from any particular app. In Android, all intents pass through an intent firewall to allow custom rules for IPC to be applied. We modify the file and now the intent firewall consults with DMS before allowing any intent if IPC restriction is enabled. This restriction can be useful in a scenario where a benign app has vulnerabilities that other malicious apps can exploit via IPC.

3.6   Restrict Network

DMS can block communications to and from the internet per application, per zone or per mode. For example, if the current network is detected as insecure by Flamingo, a mode can block part of the system from communicating with the internet. DMS native service implements the network blocking mechanism by issuing iptables rules.

3.7   Permission Verification

The permission verification system allows DMS to block anomalous permissions. The steps of the permission verification are as follows:

1. DMS collects information from Google Play and the VirusTotal [34] website and applies machine learning classification to detect suspicious (probably malicious) apps and anomalous permission requests. VirusTotal is a website that analyzes applications by more than 60 well-known antiviruses and gives a score that tells how many antiviruses have recognized the app as malicious.
2. DMS separates the collected information based on app categories. For example, in Google Play, there are more than 50 categories. Some examples are Education, Personalization, Lifestyle, Entertainment, Music & Audio, and Travel & Local.
3. DMS trains a classifier for each category that predicts the suspiciousness of new apps. Here, DMS considers an app suspicious if its VirusTotal score is more than 0.
4. DMS also determines the permissions that are not in the set of top 30 most used permissions of the non-suspicious apps. These are the anomalous permission requests.

Features. DMS uses permissions and review scores as features for the classifiers. Permission usage is a good way to cluster well-behaved applications and used in the existing literature [20]. The feature review score is calculated from the actual review score from the app market (which is an average) and the number of reviews as a low review count may bias the classifier. To normalize this impact, we use the following formula [12] to calculate the score:

$$review\ score = Ps + 5(1 - P)(1 - e^{\frac{-q}{Q}})$$

Here, s is the review score and q is the number of reviews. After some experiments, we use $P = 0.7$ and $Q = 5,000$ as these values give a satisfactory feature importance for the review score.

Classifiers. DMS can use most of the common classifiers for supervised learning. In this work, we investigate the following classifiers: Naive Bayes, Support Vector Machine (SVM) with Radial Basis Function (RBF) kernel, Decision Tree, K-Nearest Neighbors, and Random Forest [13]. To compare the effectiveness of the classifiers, we report the precision, recall, and F_1 score.

```
 1    CHECK SWITCHING-CONDITION:
 2        IF SECURITY-PARAM IS TRUE/FALSE
 3        MESSAGE USER"SWITCHING TO MODE MODE-NAME NOT POSSIBLE, SECURITY-
              PARAM IS TRUE/FALSE"
 4
 5    SCOPE MODE-NAME:
 6        RESTORE ORIGINAL
 7        UPDATE
 8        CREATE ZONE: ZONE-NAME
 9        DELETE ZONE: ZONE-NAME
10        DISABLE ZONE: ZONE-NAME
11        MOVE APPS: FROM ZONE-NAME1 TO ZONE-NAME2: ALL
12        MOVE APPS: FROM ZONE-NAME1 TO ZONE-NAME2: ALL EXCEPT CURRENT
13        APPLY POLICY:
14            ZONE ZONE-NAME1:
15                {READ_CONTACTS,{<TIME_ALWAYS>,DENY}
16                {GET_ACCOUNTS,{<TIME_ALWAYS>,DENY}
17            ZONE ZONE-NAME2:
18                POLICY: POLICY-NAME1
19        RESTRICT IPC ZONE-NAME3
20        RESTRICT IPC ZONE-NAME4 APP-NAME1, APP-NAME2
21        RESTRICT FILE-ACCESS
22        RESTRICT NETWORK IF SECURITY-PARAM IS TRUE/FALSE
23        RESTRICT PERMISSION
```

Listing 3.2. Examples of actions in the DMS configuration language.

3.8   DMS Configuration Language

The configuration language can describe a set of actions to be performed when switching modes. It supports creating/deleting/disabling zones, moving applications between zones, and applying a set of policies to any zone. It can describe which restrictions should be activated on the current mode and the conditions of switching the mode. We demonstrate some actions in Listing 3.2.

3.9   DMS Developer API

DMS provides an API for the developers. Using the API, app developers can determine the policies and restrictions of the current mode and make their apps behave accordingly.

4   Evaluation

In this section, we describe the evaluation results of DMS. First, we evaluate the classifiers for the permission verification system. Then, we evaluate DMS in terms of portability, functionality, security, and operational overheads. We implement DMS by modifying the Android Open Source Project (Marshmallow version 6.0.1 r17 MMB29V). We deploy the resulted operating system to a Google Nexus 5. It has Qualcomm MSM8974 Snapdragon 800 CPU (Quadcore 2.3 GHz), Adreno 330 GPU with 2 GB memory, and the following sensors: accelerometer, gyroscope, magnetometer, light, proximity, pressure, and GPS.

4.1 Evaluation of the Classifiers for the Permission Verification System

To detect anomalous permission requests and suspicious apps, we need an appropriate permission request classifier. The classifier should identify most of the suspicious apps (maximize the recall) and also needs to be reasonably accurate (low false positives). To select the best classifier, we calculate the effectiveness of the classifiers on the ground truth dataset.

Ground truth. We select 14,674 apps from the androzoo [7] Android database. All the apps belong to the PERSONALIZATION category. PERSONALIZATION is one of the top 10 categories in Google Play and androzoo has the highest number of suspicious apps in this category. Among 14,674 apps, 10,316 apps are benign (VirusTotal score is 0) and 4,358 apps are suspicious (VirusTotal score is more than 5).

To build the dataset, we write a `node.js` script to visit the selected apps in Google Play. We collect the details and permission list of all the apps. From the app details, we only consider the application review score and the review count. We then divide the dataset into two parts: Training and Testing. Some details on the ground truth dataset are listed in Table 1.

Table 1. Number of mobile apps selected for the ground truth dataset.

Number of Apps	Training	Testing
Benign	7,000	3,316
Suspicious	3,000	1,358
Total	10,000	4,674

Select the appropriate classifier. From the ground truth dataset, we generate the features and then use the selected classifiers (described in Subsect. 3.7) to classify an app as either benign or suspicious. Table 2 shows the comparison of the precision, recall and F_1 score of the various classifiers.

In the ground truth data, RandomForest has the highest average precision and recall of 0.91 and 0.91. It also has the highest F_1 score of 0.91. NaiveBayes and SVM have poor recall values compared to other classifiers. In conclusion, we decide to use the Random Forest classifier.

Discussion on machine learning. DMS permission verification system is used to perform a second-level verification from the user if the sought permission is from an app which is either classified as suspicious or the permission is in the anomalous permission list. If turned on, DMS blocks unusual permissions and notifies the user. If the user wants, he or she can allow the permission and let the app perform its task. The type of the problem (i.e., providing suggestions to users) encouraged us to use machine learning techniques and the results of machine learning algorithms are often much more accurate than human-crafted rules. It gives us a quick overview on the nature of the apps and anomalous

Table 2. Performance of different machine learning classifiers. For each classification algorithm, we report the precision, recall, F_1 score, and support.

Algorithm	Class	Precision	Recall	F_1 Score	Support
NaiveBayes	0	0.95	0.04	0.08	3,316
	1	0.30	0.99	0.46	1,358
	avg/total	0.76	0.32	0.19	4,674
SVM	0	0.86	0.96	0.91	3,316
	1	0.86	0.63	0.73	1,358
	avg/total	0.86	0.86	0.86	4,674
DecisionTree	0	0.93	0.93	0.93	3,316
	1	0.84	0.83	0.83	1,358
	avg/total	0.90	0.90	0.90	4,674
15kNN	0	0.93	0.93	0.93	3,316
	1	0.83	0.82	0.83	1,358
	avg/total	0.90	0.90	0.90	4,674
RandomForest	0	0.94	0.94	0.94	3,316
	1	0.85	0.85	0.85	1,358
	avg/total	0.91	0.91	0.91	4,674

permissions. Here, the chosen Random Forest classifier correctly classifies 85% of the suspicious apps.

4.2   Portability

Other than the Google Nexus lines of devices, all manufacturers ship their own versions of Android. They provide a custom experience of Android which requires modifications to the AOSP project. The modifications required for implementing DMS components can be applied to the AOSP project easily. Notably, DMS uses the modified permission mechanism of Android which was introduced in version 6.0. As a result, DMS can only be implemented in Android version 6.0 and above. However, this does not impact the execution of apps that are developed for older versions of Android.

4.3   Functionality

Security mode switching. To test the effectiveness of DMS, we move the phone to home, office, and outdoor. Also, a banking app is used as a financial app. DMS successfully detects the eight modes described in Subsection 3.2 and applies mode configurations. No applications are crashed (including the open one) during a mode switch. This is because changes in the zone configuration are applied directly to the DMS.db database and restrictions are enforced in the framework layer of Android. However, an already allowed permission may be rejected in the new mode. Applications that are built for Android version 6.0 and above handle the case gracefully and often ask for the permission again. Users can decide to click on the "Do not ask again" checkbox to prevent further permission requests.

Fine-grained permissions and restrictions. We develop a simple application performing the following sensitive operations: initiate network connections, access user's photos, access the contact list, and access the camera. We install the app in the Untrusted zone. We observe that when the app opens the phone's camera inside the home, the phone switches to the *Home-private* mode. All the images taken in this mode are saved securely via the context-aware filesystem. The app cannot send them over the internet as networks are restricted in this mode. As soon as the app closes the camera, the phone switches to the *Home-casual* mode and the app has no longer access to the images taken. Also, in the *Home-private* mode, IPC is restricted for apps inside the Untrusted zone. As a result, the app cannot share the captured images via IPC to other apps that can leak the images. When the app tries to access the phone's contact list, DMS blocks the request and notifies the user. We then move the phone to an outside cafe (where the network is open and unencrypted) and try to open the banking app. DMS gracefully blocks the internet for the app and notifies the user.

4.4   Security Analysis

DMS adds an additional layer of security on top of Android's middleware. Modification to the SD card filesystem ensures the security of the external storage. In this subsection, we discuss some of the attacks on smartphone middleware and how DMS improves the scenario.

Assumptions. We completely trust the Android kernel and middleware. We consider a strong adversary whose goal is to access the sensitive user data as well as to use the device as a victimized attacker.

Over-privileged third-party apps, libraries, and sensory malware. Many third-party apps ask unnecessary permissions to access device information which threatens user privacy [6]. Developers also use third-party software development kits (analytics, social networking, etc.) and ad-libraries without knowing the details of their code. Unfortunately, Android always grants a full set of permissions to third-party libraries. Unintended accesses to users' private data by the complex and often obfuscated libraries make it hard for developers to estimate their correct behavior [31].

Sensory malware try to use the data collected from the phone's sensor to infer different important information (user password, location history, etc.) [16,25,38].

DMS always maintains two zones of newly installed apps and untrusted apps. Apps in these zones must adhere to the policies of the zones in different security modes. As a result, asking more permissions will not yield any benefit until the user moves the applications to the trusted zone. Sensory malware are also deemed ineffective as DMS rejects their requests to access sensors from the Untrusted zone.

Confused deputy and collusion attacks. In confused deputy attacks, malware leverage unprotected interfaces of benign apps. For example, a malicious app can use the vulnerable service of a fancy SMS app by a novice developer and send SMSs through it without having the SMS permission [15, 40]. In a collusion attack, two malicious apps are involved. Individually, their permission sets are not malicious. However, they collude using covert or overt channels to gain a permission set which can be used to perform unintended tasks [26, 29]. In both the cases, DMS can be effective if such applications are sent to a zone where IPC is restricted between apps and zones. However, users' knowledge about the apps is necessary in this case.

Being a victimized attacker. Internet users are often victimized by malicious attackers. Some attackers infect and use innocent users' devices (by making them a part of a botnet) to launch large-scale attacks without the users' knowledge. Similar to the desktop computers, smart devices (Android phones, TVs, etc.) can also be a part of such botnets and help launch large-scale low-noise attacks (e.g., DDoS, click-fraud, spam). They often perform their malicious task when the device is not busy (in the night). In the existing version of Android, users can not block internet access (it is a permission with protection level normal). However, DMS can block internet access to a zone (containing untrusted apps) when the device is not being used (e.g., from 11PM to 7AM).

4.5   Operational Overheads

In this subsection, we evaluate DMS in terms of performance and storage usage. We also evaluate the overhead of the SD card filesystem. In each case, we show that there is a very little to negligible overhead.

Table 3. Individual test scores from the AnTuTu benchmarking app.

Test Group	Score	
	Stock	DMS
3D	8,640.8	8,726.2
UX	17,949.8	18,007.6
CPU	16,143.4	16,922.8
RAM	5,249.8	6,823.2
Total	47,983.8	50,479.8

Performance. We quantify performance using the popular AnTuTu benchmarking app [4] available from Android markets. The app tests CPU and memory performance, 2D/3D graphics, Disk I/O, Multitasking, etc. It gives a score for each test which can be used to compare relative performance between devices.

The benchmarking app runs concurrently with the standard set of Android apps that launched at boot. Based on the official Android source code (6.0.1), these apps are launcher, contacts (and its provider process), photo gallery, dialer, MMS, and settings.

All numbers from the benchmarking app are averaged over 5 runs. Table 3 shows the comparison of scores resulted from the app. The score of the stock version is slightly lower due to the higher number of Google services running in it compared to the DMS version. However, the score differences are not really significant and it is clear that performance is not hampered by activating DMS.

The main runtime overhead results from the zone policy enforcement mechanism. Every time Android checks for a permission, our hook in the `checkPermission` function of the package manager will execute the zone policy enforcer function f_{zpe}. Here, in Fig. 2, we measure the actual running time of the policy enforcer function. For this experiment, we use a policy denying all the dangerous permissions as a worst-case scenario. In a total of 456 calls, the average running time was 7.91ms and the standard deviation was 5.71ms. As we understand, the occasional spikes in the running time are the result of the high CPU usage during that time. However, this delay will vary mode to mode as each mode may have different policies. Overall, an 8ms delay (in the worst-case) in the `checkPermission` function will not be noticeable by users.

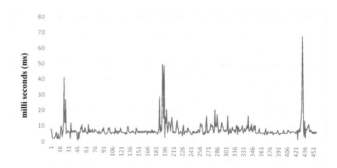

Fig. 2. Running time of the DMS policy enforcer function F_{zpe} in milliseconds.

Storage usage. We modify a few system files in the Android framework. However, this does not result in a change (in terms of size) in the final operating system size. Also, the DMS.db database contains only textual information and nowadays, most devices are equipped with 16 or more gigabytes of storage space. Hence, DMS's storage requirement can be fulfilled by modern smartphones.

SD card overhead. The socket communication between the filesystem and the DMS native service introduces a delay in file operations. Every time an app creates a file or tries to open a file, the filesystem connects to the native service to acquire information about the current mode. To measure the overhead, we execute a shell script that creates, edits, and deletes files.

We run the script a number of times (writing 10, 100, and 1,000 files) and find that the overhead is negligible up to 100 files. No app will access more than

Table 4. Overhead of the context-aware SD card filesystem.

# of files	SD card fs	modified SD card fs
	time in seconds	
10	0.11	0.18
100	1.27	1.80
1,000	8.9	15.44

a few files in a real-world scenario. Table 4 shows the comparison of time resulted from running the shell script.

5 Related Work

Researchers proposed different types of extensions to enhance the security of the smartphone operating systems. Several papers analyzed the Android permission model [8,19,27,36,37] and identified some of its shortcomings. Their study highlights that the permission model was coarse-grained and not very user customizable. In response, researchers proposed different types of extensions to the permission mechanism of Android. Most of the solutions proposed in the literature (e.g., [14,17,18,28,35]) require modification to the Android framework and/or the underlying Linux kernel. In contrast, a number of solutions [9–11] proposed an alternative approach that integrates security policy enforcement into the application layer. DMS belongs to the former category.

Lange et al. [24] implemented a generic operating system framework for secure smartphones called L4Android. Their framework hosts multiple virtual machines to separate secure and non-secure applications. Each VM hosts its own version of Android. L4Android mainly focuses on the security of the sensitive applications (e.g., financial and work-related apps). Moreover, it relies on the hardware virtualization support, which is not yet practical for smartphones. In contrast, DMS is designed for end users to provide a more secure phone to protect their resources (photos taken, location history, etc.).

Conti et al. [17] proposed CRePE that can enforce fine-grained policies based on the context of the phone. Similarly, Schreckling et al. [30] introduced a real-time user-defined policy enforcement framework for Android. The main drawback of these frameworks is that they require a lot of user control for their operation. In [33], Vecchiato et al. showed that the majority of the users neglect important and basic security configurations in Android. In DMS, security modes will be managed automatically. However, there will be options to modify the configurations for advanced users.

Smalley et al. [32] implemented the mandatory access control (MAC) in Android. They showed that the mandatory access control is able to thwart some of the well-known malware attacks reported in the literature. DMS differs significantly from MAC as it does not associate access control with the operating system users (normally apps in Android). DMS changes access control policies based on the detected security context and applies policies to a group of apps (the zones).

Zhauniarovich et al. [39] proposed a system called Moses that supports multiple security profiles on smartphones. Moses is based on the old permission model of Android and only supports a handful of restrictions and contexts. It creates a completely different persona for each context. DMS supports a comprehensive power-efficient security context manager and enables automatic switching to security modes. DMS uses the new permission model of Android that Google introduced in Android Marshmallow (version 6.0). DMS ensures security and privacy through smart restrictions without creating multiple personas. As a result, DMS is more resource efficient and users do not have to maintain separate app profiles for each persona. Moreover, Moses is designed from a perspective where corporates can create and manage security profiles. DMS's security modes are automatic and designed to protect the resources of end users.

6   Conclusion

In this paper, we present the design and implementation of Droid Mood Swing (DMS), an automated security mode management system for smartphones. DMS uses existing Android's permission model to implement a more secure and usable operating system. DMS can control application groups (called zones) through configuration files provided by device vendors. Application zones are a way to create app containers without any virtualization techniques which are heavy on hardware. Security modes are activated based on the security context of the phone to protect device resources in different use cases. DMS also implements an intent firewall, a context-aware file system, and a permission verification system. DMS enables users to use a single device for multiple types of tasks securely. All operations of DMS are completely transparent to users.

Our implementation of DMS on a real device (Nexus 5) showed its effectiveness and minimal impact on user experience. DMS automatically takes security actions like restrict network, restrict IPC, restrict file access, and deny sending SMSs to a phone number. The permission verification system is able to identify 85% of the suspicious apps and ask users for additional verifications. Our security analysis proves DMS's effectiveness against over-privileged third-party apps and libraries. DMS is also effective against confused deputy and collusion attacks. In the worst case, DMS's policy checking incurs an 8 ms delay and the delay caused by the SD card filesystem is minimal.

One limitation of DMS is that device vendors control modes and security policies which may be unacceptable by some users (for privacy reasons). In our opinion, for the general users, it is a good compromise to ensure security. Moreover, all these modes and configurations are editable by advanced users. We continue to work on the anonymization of the data sent from the device to maintain user privacy.

Acknowledgment. This work is partially supported by the Natural Sciences and Engineering Research Council of Canada (NSERC) and the Canada Research Chairs (CRC) program.

References

1. Android kernel features. http://elinux.org/Android_Kernel_Features. Accessed 03 Aug 2017
2. Android permission. http://developer.android.com/reference/android/Manifest.permission.html. Accessed 30 Aug 2016
3. Android permission categories. http://developer.android.com/guide/topics/manifest/permission-element.html. Accessed 09 Nov 2015
4. Antutu benchmark. http://www.antutu.com/en/index.shtml. Accessed 09 Feb 2016
5. Filesystem in userspace. https://en.wikipedia.org/wiki/Filesystem_in_Userspace. Accessed 09 Mar 2017
6. Report: Android and iOS apps both leak private data, but one is definitely worse for the enterprise. http://www.techrepublic.com/article/report-android-and-ios-apps-both-leak-private-data-but-one-is-definitely-worse-for-the-enterprise/. Accessed 09 Mar 2017
7. Allix, K., Bissyandé, T.F., Klein, J., Le Traon, Y.: Androzoo: Collecting millions of android apps for the research community. In: Proceedings of the 13th International Conference on Mining Software Repositories, pp. 468–471. ACM (2016)
8. Andriotis, P., Sasse, M.A., Stringhini, G.: Permissions snapshots: assessing users' adaptation to the Android runtime permission model. In: Proceedings of the International Workshop on Information Forensics and Security (WIFS). IEEE (2016)
9. Backes, M., Bugiel, S., Hammer, C., Schranz, O., von Styp-Rekowsky, P.: Boxify: Full-fledged app sandboxing for stock Android. In: Proceedings of the 24th USENIX Security Symposium, pp. 691–706. USENIX (2015)
10. Backes, M., Gerling, S., Hammer, C., Maffei, M., von Styp-Rekowsky, P.: AppGuard – enforcing user requirements on android apps. In: Piterman, N., Smolka, S.A. (eds.) TACAS 2013. LNCS, vol. 7795, pp. 543–548. Springer, Heidelberg (2013). doi:10.1007/978-3-642-36742-7_39
11. Bianchi, A., Fratantonio, Y., Kruegel, C., Vigna, G.: Njas: Sandboxing unmodified applications in non-rooted devices running stock Android. In: Proceedings of the 5th Annual ACM CCS Workshop on Security and Privacy in Smartphones and Mobile Devices, pp. 27–38. ACM (2015)
12. Bogaerts, M.: Algorithm to calculate rating based on multiple reviews (using both review score and quantity). https://math.stackexchange.com/questions/942738/algorithm-to-calculate-rating-based-on-multiple-reviews-using-both-review-score, 23 September 2014. Accessed 09 Sep 2017
13. Breiman, L.: Random forests. J. Mach. Learn. **45**(1), 5–32 (2001)
14. Bugiel, S., Davi, L., Dmitrienko, A., Fischer, T., Sadeghi, A.R.: Xmandroid: A new Android evolution to mitigate privilege escalation attacks. Technical report TR-2011-04, Technische Universität Darmstadt (2011)
15. Bugiel, S., Davi, L., Dmitrienko, A., Fischer, T., Sadeghi, A.R., Shastry, B.: Towards taming privilege-escalation attacks on Android. In: Proceedings of the Network and Distributed System Security Symposium (NDSS). The Internet Security (2012)

16. Cai, L., Chen, H.: Touchlogger: Inferring keystrokes on touch screen from smartphone motion. In: Hot topics in security (HotSec) 2011, p. 9 (2011)
17. Conti, M., Nguyen, V.T.N., Crispo, B.: CRePE: context-related policy enforcement for android. In: Burmester, M., Tsudik, G., Magliveras, S., Ilić, I. (eds.) ISC 2010. LNCS, vol. 6531, pp. 331–345. Springer, Heidelberg (2011). doi:10.1007/978-3-642-18178-8_29
18. Enck, W., Gilbert, P., Chun, B.G., Cox, L.P., Jung, J., McDaniel, P., Sheth, A.N.: Taintdroid: An information-flow tracking system for realtime privacy monitoring on smartphones. In: Proceedings of the 9th USENIX Conference on Operating Systems Design and Implementation, pp. 393–407. USENIX Association (2010)
19. Felt, A.P., Chin, E., Hanna, S., Song, D., Wagner, D.: Android permissions demystified. In: Proceedings of the 18th ACM Conference on Computer and Communications Security, pp. 627–638. ACM (2011)
20. Gorla, A., Tavecchia, I., Gross, F., Zeller, A.: Checking app. behavior against app. descriptions. In: Proceedings of the 36th International Conference on Software Engineering, pp. 1025–1035. ACM (2014)
21. Iqbal, M.S., Zulkernine, M.: Sam: A secure anti-malware framework for smartphone operating systems. In: Proceedings of the IEEE Wireless Communications and Networking Conference (WCNC 2016), pp. 1–6. IEEE (2016)
22. Iqbal, M.S., Zulkernine, M.: Zonedroid: Control your droid through application zoning. In: Proceedings of the 11th International Conference on Malicious and Unwanted Software (MALCON), pp. 113–120. IEEE (2016)
23. Iqbal, M.S., Zulkernine, M.: Flamingo: A framework for smartphone security context management. In: Proceedings of the 32nd ACM Symposium on Applied Computing (ACM SAC), pp. 563–568. ACM (2017)
24. Lange, M., Liebergeld, S., Lackorzynski, A., Warg, A., Peter, M.: L4Android: a generic operating system framework for secure smartphones. In: Proceedings of the 1st ACM Workshop on Security and Privacy in Smartphones and Mobile Devices, pp. 39–50. ACM (2011)
25. Lin, C.C., Li, H., Zhou, X.y., Wang, X.: Screenmilker: How to milk your Android screen for secrets. In: Proceedings of the Network and Distributed System Security Symposium (NDSS) (2014)
26. Marforio, C., Ritzdorf, H., Francillon, A., Capkun, S.: Analysis of the communication between colluding applications on modern smartphones. In: Proceedings of the 28th Annual Computer Security Applications Conference, pp. 51–60. ACM (2012)
27. Nauman, M., Khan, S., Zhang, X.: Apex: extending Android permission model and enforcement with user-defined runtime constraints. In: Proceedings of the 5th ACM Symposium on Information, Computer and Communications Security, pp. 328–332. ACM (2010)
28. Russello, G., Conti, M., Crispo, B., Fernandes, E.: Moses: supporting operation modes on smartphones. In: Proceedings of the 17th ACM Symposium on Access Control Models and Technologies, pp. 3–12. ACM (2012)
29. Schlegel, R., Zhang, K., Zhou, X.y., Intwala, M., Kapadia, A., Wang, X.: Soundcomber: a stealthy and context-aware sound trojan for smartphones. In: Proceedings of the Network and Distributed System Security Symposium (NDSS), vol. 11, pp. 17–33 (2011)
30. Schreckling, D., Köstler, J., Schaff, M.: Kynoid: real-time enforcement of fine-grained, user-defined, and data-centric security policies for Android. Inf. Secur. Tech. Rep. 17(3), 71–80 (2013)

31. Seo, J., Kim, D., Cho, D., Kim, T., Shin, I.: Flexdroid: Enforcing in-app privilege separation in android. In: Proceedings of the Network and Distributed System Security Symposium (NDSS), pp. 1–53 (2016)
32. Smalley, S., Craig, R.: Security enhanced (se) Android: Bringing flexible mac to Android. In: Proceedings of the 20th Annual Network and Distributed System Security (NDSS) Symposium, vol. 310, pp. 20–38 (2013)
33. Vecchiato, D., Vieira, M., Martins, E.: Risk assessment of user-defined security configurations for Android devices. In: 27th International Symposium on Software Reliability Engineering (ISSRE), pp. 467–477. IEEE (2016)
34. VirusTotal: Virustotal is a free service that analyzes suspicious files and urls and facilitates the quick detection of viruses, worms, trojans, and all kinds of malware (2017). https://www.virustotal.com/. Accessed 03 Aug 2017
35. Wang, X., Sun, K., Wang, Y., Jing, J.: Deepdroid: Dynamically enforcing enterprise policy on Android devices. In: Proceedings of the 22nd Annual Network and Distributed System Security Symposium (NDSS 2015) (2015)
36. Wei, X., Valler, N.C., Madhyastha, H.V., Neamtiu, I., Faloutsos, M.: Characterizing the behavior of handheld devices and its implications. Comput. Netw. **114**, 1–12 (2017)
37. Xu, W., Zhang, F., Zhu, S.: Permlyzer: Analyzing permission usage in android applications. In: Proceedings of the 24th International Symposium on Software Reliability Engineering (ISSRE), pp. 400–410. IEEE (2013)
38. Xu, Z., Bai, K., Zhu, S.: Taplogger: Inferring user inputs on smartphone touchscreens using on-board motion sensors. In: Proceedings of the 5th ACM conference on Security and Privacy in Wireless and Mobile Networks, pp. 113–124. ACM (2012)
39. Zhauniarovich, Y., Russello, G., Conti, M., Crispo, B., Fernandes, E.: Moses: supporting and enforcing security profiles on smartphones. IEEE Trans. Dependable Secure Comput. **11**(3), 211–223 (2014)
40. Zhou, Y., Jiang, X.: Dissecting Android malware: characterization and evolution. In: Proceedings of the IEEE Symposium on Security and Privacy (SP), pp. 95–109. IEEE (2012)

T-MAC: Protecting Mandatory Access Control System Integrity from Malicious Execution Environment on ARM-Based Mobile Devices

Diming Zhang[1,2(✉)], Liangqiang Chen[1], Fei Xue[1], Hao Wu[1],
and Hao Huang[1(✉)]

[1] Department of Computer Science and Technology,
Nanjing University, Nanjing, Jiangsu, China
`diming.zhang@gmail.com, hhuang@nju.edu.cn`
[2] School of Computer Science and Engineering, Jiangsu University of Science and
Technology, Zhenjiang, Jiangsu, China

Abstract. Mobile security has become increasingly important in mobile computing, hence mandatory access control (MAC) systems have been widely used to protect it. However, malicious code in the mobile system may have significantly impact to the integrity of these MAC systems by forcing them to make the wrong access control decision, because they are running on the same privilege level and memory address space. Therefore, for a trusted MAC system, it is desired to be isolated from the malicious mobile system at runtime. In this paper, we propose a trusted MAC isolation framework called T-MAC to solve this problem. T-Mac puts the MAC system into the enclave provided by the ARM TrustZone so as to avert the direct impact of the malicious code on the access decision process. In the meanwhile, T-MAC provides a MAC supplicant client which runs in the mobile system kernel to effectively lookup policy decisions made by the back-end MAC service in the enclave and to enforce these rules on the system with trustworthy behaviors. Moreover, to protect T-MAC components that are not in the enclave, we not only provide a protection mechanism that enables TrustZone to protect the specific memory region from the compromised system, but establish a secure communication channel between the mobile system and the enclave as well. The prototype is based on SELinux, which is the widely used MAC system, and the base of SEAndroid. The experimental results show that SELinux receives enough protection, and the performance degradation that ranges between 0.53% to 7.34% compared to the original by employing T-MAC.

Keywords: Trust · Mandatory access control · Isolation · ARM TrustZone

1 Introduction

With mobile devices, attack vectors are amplified as they are designed as open and programmable network devices that can provide a large number of

P.Q. Nguyen and J. Zhou (Eds.): ISC 2017, LNCS 10599, pp. 348–365, 2017.
https://doi.org/10.1007/978-3-319-69659-1_19

information services, including instant messaging, email, financial transaction and so on. Numerous threats that aim at getting illegal access rights to sensitive data in applications may breach mobile devices for monetary gain have become a severe security problem in mobile computing. Currently, the mandatory access control (MAC) has been employed by the mobile system kernel to build a stronger protection [3,4,13,19,22]. However, the attacks that compromise the kernel would breach these security services as well, because they run on the same privilege level and memory address space with the kernel.

The isolation is a feasible option for elimination of this ripple effect. Currently, either separating the entire MAC system as a distinct system process with a smaller attack surface (*i.e.*, small Trusted Computing Base) [4] or using hypervisor-assisted isolation mechanism [13] is used to solve this problem. However, the former cannot provide enough protection if the kernel is compromised. While the latter may cause heavy performance overhead and additional security problems in practice. To solve these problems, we propose a trusted isolation framework for MAC systems, which is called T-MAC, by using ARM TrustZone. ARM TrustZone technology [1] is a security extension enables the ARM-based devices to create an enclave, which is also named "secure world", to isolate the sensitive data from the normal world rich execution environment (REE). T-MAC puts the MAC system into the secure world trusted execution environment (TEE), which can prevent adversaries from the normal world to change the policy decision behaviors by modifying the MAC's execution environment variables. In the T-MAC architecture, much of the communication between the kernel and the migrated MAC system is based on the cross-world calling from a MAC supplicant client, which runs in the normal world as a front-end part of T-MAC. The main job for the MAC supplicant client is to receive requests from the kernel, forward them to the secure world and send back the results. Lowest level of cross-world calling builds on ARM Secure Monitor Call (SMC) instruction. Whenever an SMC instruction invokes, it will cause a switching to the monitor mode of the secure world, which can verify whether the call is safe or not. Thus, T-MAC provides the required capabilities to do effective monitoring and protection for the policy decision process of the migrated MAC system.

To protect T-MAC front-end components hosted by the REE, in the meanwhile, we create a memory protection mechanism to enable TrustZone to protect the specific memory regions of the normal world. We prevent unauthorized writes to the kernel code by replacing operations writing to critical CPU registers, such as *SCTLR, TTBRs, and TTBCR* with the SMC instruction. By instrumenting the mobile system kernel like this, page tables, a.k.a. memory translation tables, cannot be directly modified by the kernel, but all the page table update operations are routed through the secure world to check their legitimacy. Furthermore, T-MAC prevents the physical memory double mapping to avoid bypassing the memory protection mechanism. Thus, the security of the front-end components in the kernel code are guaranteed, even though they are on the same privilege level and memory address space as the mobile system. Additionally, due to the cross-world design, T-MAC needs security guarantee for the communication channel by encrypting these transmitted data on the world-shared memory. In our design, the private key is stored in the secure world permanently making sure that adversaries cannot acquire it to unseal these data, or create a malicious process with crafted arguments to intrude upon the secure world to grab its vulnerabilities.

It is also notable that the performance overhead may particularly be of great concern in the mobile devices that are mostly restricted by severe resource constraints. Although the TrustZone hardware-assisted isolation does not cause significant system-wide performance degradation compared to other software-based solutions, the processor still needs to perform context switches to the secure world before accessing the isolated resources, so that frequently access to the secure world will inevitably impact on the overall performance. Hence, T-MAC uses an access vector cache (AVC) to minimize the performance impact caused by the TrustZone-based isolation mechanism. The AVC is a submodule of the MAC supplicant client, it allows the MAC supplicant client to cache access decisions made by the back-end isolated MAC service in the secure world in order to minimize the performance overhead, because the MAC supplicant client does not usually need to perform additional lookups outside of that cache.

Briefly speaking, we migrate the MAC system to the secure world, and establish a series of protection mechanisms to protect the rest part in the normal world. Compared to other feasible solutions, our design not only diminishes the performance overhead caused by isolation, but also reduces the MAC system's attack surface so as to make all specific attacks which are known or unknown against the MAC system itself invalid. T-MAC does not have to trade off isolation and effectiveness. In summary, our contributions in this paper are:

- We design a feasible trusted framework for MAC systems by using ARM TrustZone technology. Our method provides the most secure and effective hardware isolation feature so as to protect the security of the MAC systems.
- We provide a series of techniques that enable TrustZone to protect the portion of T-MAC components hosted by the normal world, and guarantee the security of the communication channel between the two worlds in TrustZone by encrypting transmitted data on the world-shared memory. These security mechanisms enlarge the scope of protection provided by TrustZone.
- To evaluate T-MAC, we implement the prototype based on SELinux, which is the widely used MAC system, and the base of SEAndroid on the mobile. The experimental results show that SELinux receives enough protection, and the system's performance degradation is no more than 8% at most compared to the original by employing the T-MAC.

The remainder of this paper is organized as follows. Section 2 introduces the background knowledge. Section 3 discusses threat model and assumptions. Section 4 presents T-MAC design in detail. Section 5 describes our implementation based on SELinux. Section 6 discusses our experimental evaluation. Section 7 summarizes related work. Section 8 concludes this paper.

2   Background

This section describes a summary of the MAC knowledge, and the TrustZone security extension supported by ARM architecture, both of them are the key technologies used in the design of T-MAC.

2.1   Mandatory Access Control

Numerous active MAC framework can trace its origin back to a security architecture developed from Flask [16], such as security-enhanced Linux (SELinux) built by National Security Agency (NSA), TrustedBSD MAC framework and OpenSolaris FMAC. The Flask security architecture describes the interactions between subsystems which enforce security decisions and a subsystem that makes those decisions, it is a flexible access control security architecture which is designed to provide a security framework for MAC systems to support dynamic security policies, for example, role-based access control, multi-level security policies, and multi-category policies.

MAC is a security mechanism that restricts the level of control that users or subjects have over the objects that they create. Unlike in a discretionary access control (DAC), where users have full access control over their own files, directories, etc., MAC adds additional security contexts to all file system objects. Users and processes must have the appropriate access right to these categories before they can interact with these objects. However, adversaries can provoke unusual modifications to the MAC system behavior by tampering its execution state variables, such as some critical CPU registers. Moreover, due to the current monolithic kernel design, a MAC system is hard to guarantee its security thoroughly. The malicious code, such as kernel-level rootkits, can embed itself into the compromised kernel and stealthily inflicts damages with full, and unrestricted control to the MAC resources, like policies. Therefore, we design T-MAC to solve this problem in this paper.

2.2   ARM TrustZone Security Extension

ARM TrustZone security extension is a system-wide security approach to enable the system to operate in both the normal and secure world in a time-sliced fashion. It is a hardware-assisted security extension that introduces the notion of privilege separation to build a TEE. Diverse extensions are integrated across the system to separate the two worlds and ensure the confidentiality and integrity of the secure world. The secure world has a higher privilege than the normal world, therefore it can freely access the resources in the normal world such as CPU registers, memory, and peripherals, but not vice versa. In addition, the highest privileged mode, called the monitor mode, is added alongside the existing privileged modes to coordinate and arbitrate between normal world and secure world. Both two worlds are able to enter the monitor mode by issuing an SMC instruction.

The normal and secure worlds have their own CPU modes, ARM TrustZone uses an NS bit in the secure configuration register (SCR) to control and indicate whether a CPU is executing in the normal world or the secure world. This bit is also used by TrustZone components to manage access to resources (*i.e.*, memory and peripherals) out of the CPUs. TrustZone memory adaptor (TZMA) and TrustZone Address Space Controller (TZASC) partition the memory address corresponding to DRAM and SRAM into several memory regions, each of which is marked as either non-secure or secure. Similarly, the device privilege is configured in the TrustZone Protection Controller (TZPC) that dedicates one bit to each independent device, in order to enforce a security policy with regard to peripherals such that the secure world can configure and access peripherals in an explicit way.

3   Threat Model and Assumptions

This section describes the threat model and assumptions pertaining to the design and implementation of T-MAC.

3.1   Threat Model

Threat models for mobile devices involve three main vectors. The first vector includes attacks from rogue users. The second vector involves attacks from rogue applications. The third vector includes internet-borne attacks. The attacks of these vectors are able to exploit vulnerabilities existing in the mobile system so as to compromise the kernel. Hence, adversaries can use attacks that aim to execute malicious code inside the mobile system to: (1) escalate the privilege of user space application, (2) inject malicious code into the kernel-space or (3) modify privileged code binaries in memory. After breaching the system, they may try to compromise the MAC system in the kernel and tamper with policies at runtime.

Meanwhile, adversaries may compromise the communication channel by owning the privilege of the system kernel, so that they can access and modify the data on the world-shared memory. Furthermore, the malicious process may attempt to subvert the TEE in the secure world by making arbitrary system calls with crafted arguments, even though the mobile system is not compromised. Because common authentication framework of the ARM TrustZone can be as simple as checking the universally unique identifier (UUID) of the requester, adversaries can easily bypass such an authentication by using the crafted data structure related to the UUID. With this capability, adversaries may try to access sensitive data and system resources such as memory, cache, and registers belonging to the secure world.

3.2   Assumptions

We assume the ARM-based architecture supports the TrustZone security extension, and believe the trusted boot in our design. The secure world provided by ARM TrustZone are trusted. We also assume that the components of T-MAC running in the secure world will not leak its data intentionally. The adversaries can launch multi-vector software attacks so that they can freely access system resources in the normal world. In other words, the mobile system can be compromised, and the compromised mobile system can be manipulated to attack any kernel module. However, the adversaries will not be able to access anything such as memory, cache, and registers in the secure world, which benefits from the ARM TrustZone. In addition, vulnerabilities like CVE-2016-7545 which can bypass the MAC system due to bugs of its code are out of our scope. We only focus on threats from malicious execution environment in the normal world, except for attacks that trick the kernel control flow. We also do not consider memory attacks such as bus monitoring attacks and cold boot attacks [5,11]. The denial-of-service (DoS) attacks are not in the scope of our adversary model, either. Naturally, hardware attacks such as JTAG and physical side-channel attacks are beyond our work as well.

4   Design

In this section, we describe the design of T-MAC. First, we introduce the architecture overview of T-MAC. Second, we present memory protection mechanism provided by T-MAC. Third, we describe the secure communication mechanism used by T-MAC. These three parts make up T-MAC so as to build a comprehensive protection framework.

4.1   T-MAC Architecture

Figure 1 provides an overview of our architecture. T-MAC is based on ARM TrustZone security extensions. Compared to the *Baseline*, the architecture components of T-MAC are across worlds: a back-end MAC service hosted in the secure world and a front-end MAC supplicant client serving in the normal world.

As we mentioned in Sect. 2.1, most MAC systems are derived from the Flask security architecture. The core component of the Flask-based MAC system is the security server (SS) that provides policy decisions based on policies. Therefore, we migrate the SS to the secure world in order to protect it from vulnerabilities in the normal world. In our architecture, we use the back-end MAC service to host the MAC system components. In the simplest implementation, the back-end MAC service is required to provide security policy decisions, to maintain the security policy logic and policy-independent data (*i.e.*, security context and security identifier map), and to manage the AVC of the MAC supplicant client. The back-end MAC service also provides functionality for loading and changing policies. Moreover, the SS is also benefit from providing its own caching mechanism to hold the results of access computations. This can prove advantageous because the SS can improve its response time by using cached results. Meanwhile, the security policy is stored in the secure world for security as well. All the MAC system components hosted by the back-end MAC service are isolate from the normal world so that adversaries are unable to directly launch attacks against them.

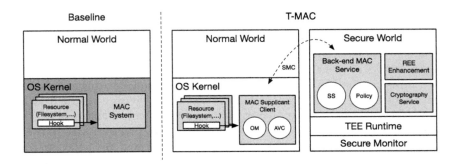

Fig. 1. T-MAC architecture.

The MAC supplicant client is responsible to route access control requests to the back-end MAC service, to cache policy decisions and to enforce security policy decisions in the normal world. The object manager (OM) in the client is used to enforce security policy decisions. The MAC supplicant client provides three primary elements for the OM. First, the architecture provides interfaces for retrieving policy decisions from the SS in the back-end MAC service. Second, the architecture provides the OM the ability to register to receive notifications of changes to the security policy. Third, the architecture provides an AVC module that allows the OM to access the policy decisions cached in the AVC to reduced the performance overhead. Since the MAC supplicant client is not built in the secure world, T-MAC provides Rich Execution Environment Enhancement (REEE) mechanism for the components running in the normal world to enhance the security of T-MAC across two worlds. In addition, the communication channel between the normal world and the secure world is also secured due to our design is across world. In the Sects. 4.2 and 4.3, we describe the design of these protection mechanisms in detail.

4.2   Rich Execution Environment Enhancement

To protect the portion in the normal world, T-MAC separates the mobile system virtual address into 3 distinct ranges: user memory, the kernel code, and the kernel *const_map_mem*. The *const_map_mem* is used to describe the physical memory which is constantly mapped by the kernel. The kernel allocates memory from the *const_map_mem* regions when it needs to create new objects like page tables. The user space memory regions are mapped as Privileged eXecute Never (PXN). The kernel code memory regions are mapped as read-only. The kernel *const_map_mem* is mapped as non-executable privileged memory, indicating that it cannot be accessed by user processes. Meanwhile, REEE records the state of every page of the physical memory. Whenever a new virtual address to physical address mapping is going to be built, the EEE service checks the new access permission given to the physical page against the saved state to verify that there is no violation to the memory protection. The physical memory state is saved in an array named the *phystate*, each entry of this array corresponds to a 4KB physical page. The *phystate* determines physical pages of whom need to be protected. The *phystate* marks physical pages which are used by kernel code or page tables as protected. Any request to build a writable mapping to the protected physical pages must be rejected by REEE. Similarly, mapping a physical page which is already mapped writeable to user space will be rejected either (Fig. 2).

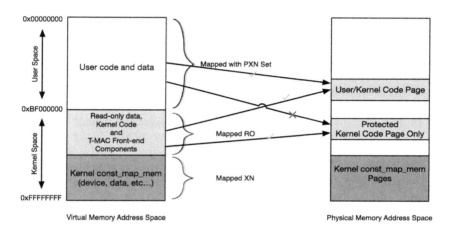

Fig. 2. Normal world virtual memory layout and mapping principle.

Furthermore, we intercept all modifications to the protected page tables by depriving the kernel from its own capability to modify page tables. We replace operations writing to critical CPU registers, such as *SCTLR, TTBRs, and TTBCR* with the SMC instruction. Then, modifications to protected page tables are obliged to request appropriate operations from the secure world. This is achieved by modifying the access permission in the page table entry so that the memory hosting the modified page tables become read-only region. Such a process begins when the mobile system performs initialization and is mandatory during each modify operation to the protected page table. If a page table is read-only to the kernel, usually, write to a read-only page is ended in a descriptor indicating a lack of permissions. When a page fault occurs, the page fault handler in the kernel will then generally pass a segmentation fault to the offending process, indicating that the update was invalid. The code of the page fault handler is part of the kernel. Its job is to analyze the cause of the fault and to do something about it. Therefore, we can replace the conventional page fault handler by SMC instruction so that it is able to make specific page faults trap

into the secure world. The key point here is that TZASC and other bus peripherals can grant access for the secure world to read/write normal world memory.
In addition, important to note that intercepting page table modifications does
not need the kernel in a safe state even though the trap relies on the kernel
to send the request for page table modification from the secure world. Since
the read-only page tables are non-writable to the kernel, it is not possible for a
compromised kernel to skip this mechanism without TrustZone knowledge.

Therefore, T-MAC components such as the MAC supplicant client which is
a module installed in the kernel space and stored in a certain memory region
can be protected based on the mechanism mentioned above, we can guarantee
the security by modifying their *const_map_mem* mapping to be read-only.

4.3   Security Cross-World Communication

The Weakness of Communication Channel for TrustZone: When the normal
world requests resources from the secure world, a communication channel is
required for messaging between the two worlds. The channel simply use a block
of world-shared memory area that is not secure as it is used by both normal and
secure world.

To protect the shared data, T-MAC provides a crypto service built in the
secure world. We use public-key cryptography to encrypt the data which will be
transmitted to the secure world. The key pair are generate in the secure world.
The public key is sent to the MAC supplicant client to encrypt the shared data,
and the private key is only saved in the secure world for decryption. Therefore,
adversaries cannot steal the private key, and the data in the shared memory
can be sent to the secure world safely. Additionally, the integrity of the MAC
supplicant client will be checked by the secure world, as long as it builds the
session to the back-end MAC service. If the verification is invalid, the secure
world will reject the further requests of it and reboot the device. Thus, we can
guarantee that adversaries cannot breach the secure world by exploiting the
insecure communication way.

5   Implementation

5.1   Trusted Execution Environment

The secure world is controlled by a thinner, safer software stack that is responsible for providing TEE for hosting security services. In our design, the TEE
consists of TrustZone secure monitor layer and the secure world runtime layer.

The TrustZone secure monitor layer consists of drivers providing the low-level
ARM TrustZone hardware features responsible for interrupt handling, world
switching, and isolation protection. This layer provides three secure isolation
guarantee: CPU isolation, memory isolation, and I/O device isolation. In brief,
the principle of this monitor is to switch resources that are needed in both worlds.
All secure states, including CPU, memory, and I/O device saved by the monitor

must be saved into a region of memory that belongs to secure world, so that the normal world cannot tamper with it.

The secure world runtime layer is designed as a small and tight monolithic kernel that provides secure memory management, thread model and sharing facilities to manage the service threads, and serve their system resource requirements. This layer uses a couple of threads to be able to support running jobs in parallel. Notice that the secure world runtime layer does not provide any interface to load dynamic application into the secure world from the outside for security considerations.

5.2   SELinux and Kernel Instrumentation

SELinux uses the Linux security Module (LSM) in the Linux kernel to achieve mandatory access control in the REE. The main components of SELinux are the SELinuxFS, object-managers, access vector cache, security server, and security policy. We move security server, security policy, and configuration files to the secure world, and keep the SELinuxFS, object managers, and the access vector cache staying in the normal world. We build a back-end MAC service trusted application to host the security server and the security policy in order to make them work properly in the TEE. The object managers and the access vector cache are merged into the MAC supplicant process. The SELinuxFS is an extension module of the filesystem. Both the MAC supplicant process and the SELinuxFS are stored in the kernel code memory region, hence, we mark their memory regions as protected so as to secure their integrity even though the REE is compromised.

The Inter-Process Communication (IPC) is the original way of communication between the SELinux components. By employing the T-MAC architecture, the IPC is replaced by the Remote Procedure Call (RPC) which is responsible to cross-world communication. The MAC supplicant process in the REE can invoke the back-end service in the TEE. In our prototype, the RPC is based on GlobalPlatform TEE Client API in the REE and GlobalPlatform TEE Internal API in the TEE, which are the industry standard.

In the current prototype, we directly modify the source code of the kernel to place hooks upon modifying page tables and upon writing to critical CPU registers. The hooks execute an SMC instruction to switch to the secure world. We use a command ID which is placed in a general purpose register upon the SMC call to differentiate the SMC instructions called by kernel hooks from those requesting the back-end MAC service. Whenever the execution switches to the secure world, the security monitor checks that register value to determine the call type. In addition to kernel instrumentation, we use a binary analysis tool to ensure that all critical CPU registers writes are replaced by hooks, which is a basic requirement for REE execution environment enhancement as discussed in Sect. 4.2. Additionally, if the kernel code is not available, we also can insert an SMC instruction in place of the page table exception handler to implement the hooks. Therefore, every page fault would execute an SMC instruction to switch the secure world.

5.3   Secure Booting

Before T-MAC working properly, two booting phases are required on the device. The first phase stage is the secure world initialization. T-MAC components in the secure world is loaded into the secure world as long as the TEE boots up and remains in the secure world memory until the system powers off or restarts. Figure 3 shows the secure boot sequence. Firstly, after power on, the hardware platform loads the secure bootloader from the secure ROM to the memory of the secure world. Then, the secure bootloader initializes the ARM images of TrustZone Secure Monitor layer and secure world runtime layer in an orderly manner, and loads images of trusted service from the secure non-volatile storage into the memory of the secure world. Finally, the secure bootloader switches the primary CPU state from the secure to the non-secure so as to finish the first phase. The second phase stage is the normal world initialization. After the primary processor switching from the secure state to the non-secure state, it launches the non-secure bootloader to initialize the REE in the normal world. The last step of secure boot is initializing the T-MAC components in the normal world. The most important work of the normal world part initialization is to interact with the back-end MAC service, which is already running in the secure world, for object labeling. Then the booting finished. Notice that the system will panic if any step fails. The booting in our implementation is trusted, it prevents malicious firmware from running on the memory by authenticating all firmware images up to and including the normal world bootloader.

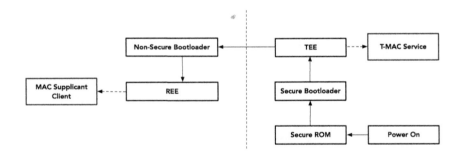

Fig. 3. The secure boot sequence of the prototype.

6   Evaluation

In this section, we present the evaluation on our prototype. First, we use a micro-benchmark to measure the execution time required for a full context switching to and from the secure world. Second, we use a set of benchmarking tools to evaluate the overhead caused by employing T-MAC. Third, we use some real world exploits to test the effectiveness of our design, and describe the security analysis about T-MAC from multiple vectors.

6.1   Platform

Performance evaluation was performed on the Hikey board. The board is built around the HiSilicon Kirin 620 SOC whose microarchitecture is the Cortex-A53 with a 64-bit ARMv8-A instruction set. This board has 8 physical cores clocked at 1.2 GHz, 2 GB of SDRAM, 8 GB eMMC storage on board, 2.4 GHz 802.11 b/g/n Wi-Fi for network and 4 UART expansion interfaces for program debugging. There are two reasons that we choose the Hikey board as the target board. Firstly, the Kirin 620 SOC utilized by the board is designed by Huawei. In our point of view, this SOC has large amount of successful cases in commercial use and its datasheets are in more detail than products made by other companies. Secondly, Google supports Hikey as an Android reference board. This mean that the basic Android kernel source and board support files for Hikey are sufficient to provide favorable working conditions for the following evaluation work. In addition, the mobile system, which runs in the normal world, is Debian based on Linux kernel 4.4 in our evaluation.

6.2   Overhead of World Switching

Our first experiment is a micro-benchmark to measure the execution time required for a full context switching to and from the secure world. To enable a more accurate analysis, we use cycle counters and ARM cycle count register (CCNT) to ensure consistency across multiple CPUs in the analysis of micro-benchmark cases. Instruction barriers were utilized before and after taking timestamps to avoid out-of-order execution or pipelining from skewing our measurements.

The *SMC-In* micro-benchmark is to measure costs of the switch from the normal world to the secure world by directly issuing the SMC instruction. The *SMC-Out* micro-benchmark is for the opposite direction. The experimental results show that the cost of *SMC-In* was 2941 cycles and the cost of *SMC-Out* was 2256 cycles, indicating that the number of cycles of a full round trip of switch was around 5200 cycles. Exactly what needs to be saved and restored for each switch depends on the hardware design and the software mechanism used for inter-world communications. In our experiment design, the full context switch consists of saving register state to memory and restoring the new context's state from memory to registers. The involving registers include all general purpose registers and any coprocessor registers (*e.g.* NEON and VFP). Although the cost of a full context switch is very expensive, we noticed that a full context switch is not necessary upon every occasion. Because an SMC driven world switch can carry a message payload in some of the processor registers, for instance, partial general purpose registers are not saved and restored during switching since those are used to pass parameters. Therefore, switch time varies between hundreds to thousands cycles.

6.3   Performance Impact on Mainstream Benchmarking

Our second measurement is to use popular benchmarks to evaluate the performance overhead of TEE-perf implementation. We measured the performance with widely used mobile benchmark tools: AnTuTu, BaseMark and Geekbench. In the meanwhile, we also utilized other synthetic workload benchmark tools: CF-bench, IOZone, GFXBench and LMbench.

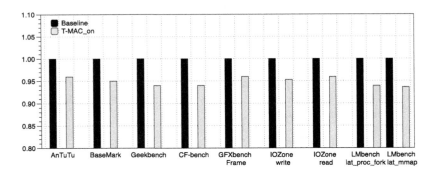

Fig. 4. Mainstream benchmarking results.

To investigate the performance impact on the system, we tested the two cases: *Baseline* and *T-MAC_on*. Note that the performance of *Baseline* represents the performance of applications when SELinux is running in the REE, while the performance of *T-MAC_on* represents the performance of applications when T-MAC is employed by SELinux.

Figure 4 provides the experimental results. In the figure, 1 represents the performance of the *Baseline*, and higher values indicate lower latency or higher throughput. When the T-MAC is employed, overall performance is degraded slightly. As shown in the experimental results, T-MAC shows a low overhead that ranges between 0.53% to 7.34%. The results are expected because these benchmarks involves a comprehensive evaluation of the overall system performance, which includes CPU, memory, and I/O. T-MAC adds overhead to a small portion of these operations.

6.4   Latency of Application Loading Time

User application loading time is an important aspect of the performance of mobile devices since it impacts user experience. Therefore, the second measurement is to measure the impact of loading Linux user space applications.

To simulate the real feelings, the process of loading time measurement was done by using a Canon EOS 5D Mark III to record a video for displaying the open process, and the exact time spent in loading an app to display on the screen was extracted from the video by playing it back. Twice measurements were done

Table 1. APP loading time (in seconds)

Application	Baseline		T-Mac		Extra Cost	
	1st	2nd	1st	2nd	1st	2nd
Firefox	1.58	1.26	1.81	1.38	0.23	0.12
Calculator	1.01	0.72	1.26	0.86	0.25	0.14
Calendar	0.98	0.64	1.11	0.75	0.13	0.11
Disk Utility	1.13	0.93	1.36	1.08	0.23	0.15
Search	1.03	0.47	1.28	0.58	0.25	0.11
Contacts	1.04	0.48	1.25	0.51	0.21	0.03
Gallery	1.12	0.72	1.38	0.83	0.26	0.11
Chess	1.11	0.88	1.33	1.01	0.22	0.13
Advanced Setting	0.99	0.81	1.22	0.89	0.23	0.08

by us for one application. The first measurement was for creating a fresh process, including making the policy decision, loading the binary code from the storage device to memory and displaying for the first time. The second measurement was made when the first measurement was finished and the target application was closed.

The results of the measurement are listed in Table 1, the extra cost indicates the overhead added by T-MAC. It is observed that there exists an obvious difference between two measurements. The overhead in the first loading is higher than that of the second loading. For further investigation, we found that the high overhead in the first measurement is because there is no corresponding policy decisions cached in the AVC. While most of latency caused in the second measurement is due to kernel just executes the application process and displays it on the screen.

6.5   Security Analysis

T-MAC passed through rigorous testing and evaluation that validate the effectiveness of its protection. We tested T-MAC using the real world exploits, including CVE-2007-5495, CVE-2007-5496, CVE-2015-1815, and an attack called "troubleshooter" published in Github. We also wrote our own attack code that writes to the physical memory using the */dev/mem* interface. Exploiting this vulnerability allows a user space process to trick the kernel into maliciously modifying its own memory hosting T-MAC front-end components. We use these exploits to trick the kernel to write the protected memory region, page tables and parts of its data. All of these attacks failed because the protected memory region is mapped read-only. We also failed to modify the page tables to change the protected kernel memory's read-only access permission.

In the end, we analyze the security of T-MAC by discussing how it defeats security threats. We summarize these threats by the attack surface they target.

Attacks Against TrustZone: T-MAC is based on the ARM TrustZone technology, therefore all its security properties are contingent on the security of

TrustZone. Recent reports [18,21] showed that any user space application is able to execute shellcode in the secure world. These attacks require two basic conditions: (1) the normal world TrustZone driver accepts malformed *ioctl* command will allow installed application the execute arbitrary code in the kernel. (2) the secure world runtime layer has the mistake in input structure bound check may lead to an arbitrary code execution vulnerability in the secure world. As we mentioned in Sect. 5.1, the secure world runtime layer does not provide the public interface for the applications running in the normal world to load any executable code into the secure world. All applications running in the secure world are loaded by the secure bootloader and launched by the secure world runtime layer. There is no application dynamic loading feature in our TEE design. Therefore, we can guarantee that the basic conditions of attacks against TrustZone do not exist in our system.

Attacks Against the Sensitive Data in the Secure World: Since the policy decisions are made in the secure world, the malicious code in the normal world has no privileges to access or modify any resources of the security server directly at runtime. The access policy set used in the security server are stored on the secure non-volatile storage. They are loaded into the secure world memory region by the secure bootloader when the system starts up. Therefore, the adversaries is unable to access the secure world part of T-MAC from either the non-volatile storage or the secure memory except for the hardware attacks. In addition, the adversaries may try to tamper with the control flow of security server. But, due to the code of security server runs in the secure world, the attacks cannot modify its code. Moreover, since all the secure interrupts are triggered in the secure world, the adversaries cannot intercept the workflow of the secure world part through interrupts. Although a world-shared memory region that can be modified by the mobile system, T-MAC provides the cryptography method to protect the security of communication channel between two worlds. Therefore, we can guarantee that the information to and from the secure world is safe.

Attacks Against Protected Data in the Normal World: In the normal world, the components of T-MAC is loaded in to the protected memory region. As mentioned in Sect. 4.2, the protected memory region is also protected by the secure world that prevents the protected memory region from being modified by the REE. Another threat to the normal world is control flow attacks. Since T-MAC does not aim to protect the entire kernel data, some kinds of kernel attacks can intercept the kernel control flow. The control flow attacks, such as return-oriented programming [12] and a kernel integer overflow can lead to malicious behavior without the change of the kernel. A lot of recent researches [10,25] show that these attacks are difficult to prevent unless we use orthogonal techniques [6–8,27]. Therefore, the control flow attacks against the kernel are considered out of the scope of the paper. Nevertheless, T-MAC guarantees that the control flow attacks cannot damage its protected region in the normal world or subvert the secure world.

7   Related Work

There are two main research directions that target isolation mechanism: hypervisor-based and hardware-based methods.

Hypervisor-assisted isolation methods are widely researched and applied. They use virtualization technology to provide high privilege and isolation for protecting security services. Nevertheless, hypervisors have security challenges of their own. They are expected to do more tasks for system resource management and distribution. Their source codes are too big to ensure safety. Therefore, a number of vulnerabilities in hypervisors increase the risks of attacks on isolated security services. It is difficult to ensure the absence of exploitable vulnerabilities in hypervisors that could be utilized to disable security checks and access sensitive data. Hence, they become subject to many vulnerabilities. The proposition of dedicating the entire virtualization layer to hosting security services will help decrease the risks by reducing the complexity of the code, but it is an unpractical solution because virtualization methods incur performance overhead on mobile devices which are already suffering from resource restrictions.

Hardware-based methods use a different type of hardware protection. Realizing the security threats to hypervisors, current hardware platforms introduce a novel secure and isolated execution environment, which is called the "secure world". Examples of the secure world include Intel TXT, AMD SVM and ARM TrustZone. In mobile computing, ARM is the most widely used instruction set architecture in terms of quantity produced, with over a hundred billion ARM processors produced as of 2017. Therefore, There are many researches [2,9,14,15,17,20,23,24,26,28,29] have managed to use TrustZone to protect their sensitive code and data of applications in an isolated execution environment against a potentially compromised mobile system. Most of them focus on building a thinner, more secure environment dedicated to process sensitive data, such as cryptography and authentication. In this paper, we provide an isolation mechanism to the MAC system by migrating it to the TrustZone secure world. In addition, we present techniques that focus on data integrity outside the secure world and on performance optimization to make T-MAC a real world solution.

8   Conclusion

We introduced T-MAC, a framework that provides MAC system real-time protection based on the ARM TrustZone security extension. T-MAC puts the MAC system into the secure world, and provides a supplicant client in the normal world to link the migrated MAC system in the secure world. T-MACuses memory protection mechanism to prevent attacks that aim at modifying the supplicant service in the normal world and uses secure communication channel to guarantee the security of transmitted data. Hence, it is safe from attacks that compromise the normal world operating system. Moreover, T-MAC does not have to trade off isolation and effectiveness due to our performance optimization.

Acknowledgments. This work was supported by the National Science Foundation of China grants No. 61321491, and in part by Commission of Economy and Information Technology grants the project of the security protection foundation of operating system based on hardware resource isolation mechanism.

References

1. Arm, A.: Security technology-building a secure system using TrustZone technology. ARM Technical White Paper (2009)
2. Azab, A.M., Ning, P., Shah, J., Chen, Q., Bhutkar, R., Ganesh, G., Ma, J., Shen, W.: Hypervision across worlds: real-time kernel protection from the ARM Trust-Zone secure world. In: Proceedings of the 2014 ACM SIGSAC Conference on Computer and Communications Security, pp. 90–102. ACM (2014)
3. Bugiel, S., Heuser, S., Sadeghi, A.R.: Towards a framework for android security modules: extending SE android type enforcement to android middleware. Cased. nr. Technical report, TUD-CS-2012-0231, 05 December 2012
4. Bugiel, S., Heuser, S., Sadeghi, A.R.: Flexible and fine-grained mandatory access control on Android for diverse security and privacy policies. In: USENIX Security, pp. 131–146 (2013)
5. Carbone, R., Bean, C., Salois, M.: An in-depth analysis of the cold boot attack. DRDC Valcartier, Defence Research and Development, Canada, Technical report (2011)
6. Cheng, Y., Zhou, Z., Miao, Y., Ding, X., Deng, H., et al.: ROPecker: a generic and practical approach for defending against ROP attack (2014)
7. Criswell, J., Dautenhahn, N., Adve, V.: KCoFI: complete control-flow integrity for commodity operating system kernels. In: 2014 IEEE Symposium on Security and Privacy (SP), pp. 292–307. IEEE (2014)
8. Davi, L., Dmitrienko, A., Egele, M., Fischer, T., Holz, T., Hund, R., Nürnberger, S., Sadeghi, A.R.: MoCFI: a framework to mitigate control-flow attacks on Smartphones. In: NDSS, vol. 2, p. 27 (2012)
9. Ge, X., Vijayakumar, H., Jaeger, T.: Sprobes: enforcing kernel code integrity on the TrustZone architecture. arXiv preprint arXiv:1410.7747 (2014)
10. Göktas, E., Athanasopoulos, E., Bos, H., Portokalidis, G.: Out of control: overcoming control-flow integrity. In: 2014 IEEE Symposium on Security and Privacy (SP), pp. 575–589. IEEE (2014)
11. Halderman, J.A., Schoen, S.D., Heninger, N., Clarkson, W., Paul, W., Calandrino, J.A., Feldman, A.J., Appelbaum, J., Felten, E.W.: Lest we remember: cold-boot attacks on encryption keys. Commun. ACM **52**(5), 91–98 (2009)
12. Hund, R.: Return-oriented rootkits. In: SPRING-SIDAR Graduierten-Workshop über Reaktive Sicherheit, 14–15 September 2009, Stuttgart, Deutschland (2010)
13. Lee, S.M., Suh, S.B., Jeong, B., Mo, S.: A multi-layer mandatory access control mechanism for mobile devices based on virtualization. In: 2008 5th IEEE Consumer Communications and Networking Conference, CCNC 2008, pp. 251–256. IEEE (2008)
14. Li, W., Li, H., Chen, H., Xia, Y.: AdAttester: secure online mobile advertisement attestation using TrustZone. In: Proceedings of the 13th Annual International Conference on Mobile Systems, Applications, and Services, pp. 75–88. ACM (2015)

15. Pirker, M., Slamanig, D.: A framework for privacy-preserving mobile payment on security enhanced ARM TrustZone platforms. In: 2012 IEEE 11th International Conference on Trust, Security and Privacy in Computing and Communications (TrustCom), pp. 1155–1160. IEEE (2012)

16. Ray, S., Stephen, S., Peter, L., Mike, H., Dave, A., Jay, L.: The flask security architecture: system support for diverse security policies, pp. 123–140 (1999)

17. Reineh, A.A., Petracca, G., Uusilehto, J., Martin, A.: Enabling secure and usable mobile application: revealing the nuts and bolts of software TPM in todays mobile devices. arXiv preprint arXiv:1606.02995 (2016)

18. Rosenberg, D.: QSEE TrustZone kernel integer over flow vulnerability. In: Black Hat Conference (2014)

19. Sadeghi, A.R.: Mobile security and privacy: the quest for the mighty access control. In: Proceedings of the 18th ACM Symposium on Access Control Models and Technologies, pp. 1–2. ACM (2013)

20. Santos, N., Raj, H., Saroiu, S., Wolman, A.: Using ARM TrustZone to build a trusted language runtime for mobile applications. In: ACM SIGARCH Computer Architecture News, vol. 42, pp. 67–80. ACM (2014)

21. Shen, D.: Exploiting TrustZone on Android. Black Hat US (2015)

22. Smalley, S., Craig, R.: Security enhanced (SE) Android: bringing flexible MAC to Android. In: NDSS, vol. 310, pp. 20–38 (2013)

23. Sun, H., Sun, K., Wang, Y., Jing, J.: TrustOTP: transforming Smartphones into secure one-time password tokens. In: Proceedings of the 22nd ACM SIGSAC Conference on Computer and Communications Security, pp. 976–988. ACM (2015)

24. Sun, H., Sun, K., Wang, Y., Jing, J., Wang, H.: TrustICE: hardware-assisted isolated computing environments on mobile devices. In: 2015 45th Annual IEEE/IFIP International Conference on Dependable Systems and Networks (DSN), pp. 367–378. IEEE (2015)

25. Vogl, S., Pfoh, J., Kittel, T., Eckert, C.: Persistent data-only malware: function hooks without code. In: NDSS (2014)

26. Yang, B., Yang, K., Qin, Y., Zhang, Z., Feng, D.: DAA-TZ: an efficient DAA scheme for mobile devices using ARM TrustZone. In: Conti, M., Schunter, M., Askoxylakis, I. (eds.) Trust 2015. LNCS, vol. 9229, pp. 209–227. Springer, Cham (2015). doi:10.1007/978-3-319-22846-4_13

27. Zhang, C., Wei, T., Chen, Z., Duan, L., Szekeres, L., McCamant, S., Song, D., Zou, W.: Practical control flow integrity and randomization for binary executables. In: 2013 IEEE Symposium on Security and Privacy (SP), pp. 559–573. IEEE (2013)

28. Zhang, N., Sun, H., Sun, K., Lou, W., Hou, Y.T.: CacheKit: evading memory introspection using cache incoherence. In: 2016 IEEE European Symposium on Security and Privacy (EuroS&P), pp. 337–352. IEEE (2016)

29. Zhang, N., Sun, K., Lou, W., Hou, Y.T.: Case: cache-assisted secure execution on ARM processors. In: 2016 IEEE Symposium on Security and Privacy (SP), pp. 72–90. IEEE (2016)

Enforcing ACL Access Control on Android Platform

Xiaohai Cai[1,2,3], Xiaozhuo Gu[2,3(✉)], Yuewu Wang[2,3], Quan Zhou[2,3], and Zhenhuan Cao[4]

[1] University of Chinese Academy of Sciences, Beijing, China
[2] Institute of Information Engineering, CAS, Beijing, China
guxiaozhuo@iie.ac.cn
[3] Data Assurance and Communication Security Research Center, CAS, Beijing, China
[4] Gansu Information Center, Lanzhou, China

Abstract. Android is an operating system with Linux kernel running on smartphone. Part of system resources are provided in the form of APIs offered by system service. Access permission to these resources for application is controlled in Android middleware according to app's UID. Since any application can run native code such like C/C++ and bypass the permission check in framework layer, Linux kernel uses UGO (user-/group/others) access control to protect resource in Android. However, UGO enforces control through group instead of UID, system is unable to authorize a specific app to access resources according to its UID. Thus, some weaknesses remain, such as malicious code may have the privilege to access privacy data and operate the important system peripherals by native code. In this paper, we present an ACL (Access Control List) based access control mechanism to Android system, which can provide fine-grained access control according to the UID of application in file system of Android. This ACL based access control mechanism enables the fine-grained policy may be enforced reliably and prevents some attacks that access resources by native code directly, such as transplantation attack. We make a customized system at both the kernel layer and the framework layer. We develop an entire prototype and verify the compatibility, effectiveness and performance overhead of our system. The result shows it can effectively prevent the abnormal access through C/C++ code. The customized system has a negligible impact on performance overhead and also offers a stable operating environment for applications.

Keywords: Android permission mechanism · Access Control List · Transplantation attack · Fine-grained

1 Introduction

Android introduces UID-based permission mechanism [2] to protect the resources in system. Each application is allocated a unique UID when it is installed.

© Springer International Publishing AG 2017
P.Q. Nguyen and J. Zhou (Eds.): ISC 2017, LNCS 10599, pp. 366–383, 2017.
https://doi.org/10.1007/978-3-319-69659-1_20

System services provide APIs with a permission check for applications about accessing part of related resources. A request with the string of requested permission and caller's UID will be examined whether the app is granted to the resource. Since any application can run native code [6] and bypass the permission check in framework layer, system files and device files like socket can be accessed directly, Android enforce a discretionary access control (DAC) to protect resources.

Linux kernel uses UGO which is based on group instead of UID to enforce DAC. Hence, system is unable to authorize a specific app to access resources according to its UID. Different from mechanism in middleware, the user in resource group has the same permission to object and this coarse-grained permission mechanism remains some weaknesses. For example, malware can take a photo secretly by using native code to call camera driver directly. According the data from IDC [8], Android dominated the smartphone market with a share of 86.8% in 2016Q3. In such environment, the weakness of Android permission mechanism can be a great threat.

Lots of extensions have been proposed to refine the Android permission model. Most enforcements attempt to address access control at the Android middleware layer. [16,19] inspect permission through IPC call chain. [10,17,22] track the flow of tainted data to notify the user whether the data is gained by apps in an illegal way. However, all of these works were based on the original permission mechanism and provided no solution for underlying UGO access control. Following works [12–14,26] involve the Linux DAC mechanism to make an enforcement. [12,13] are relied on TOMOYO Linux [9] which is based on the UID of application and data file to ensure the files of application are not accessed by at kernel layer. And our work has also improve the DAC access control at kernel layer.

In this paper, we present a new access control based on ACL, which provides a fine-grained access control according to the UID of application. The system we present enables user to create a fine-grained policy to resources and prevents some attacks which access resources by native code directly, such as transplantation attack. We make a customized system at both the kernel layer and the framework layer. ACL is a list of permissions attached to an object and it specifies which user or system process are granted access to objects as well as the operations allowed. The key challenge is how to support ACL in low-level platform since there is no prior work for reference. In our system, ACL is supported in kernel layer and a system library is provided. We reset the features of Linux kernel and recompile a new kernel for Android. Linux ACL related code is transplanted from Linux to Android, we modify the code and add a library into system library. Besides, we implement an API for other components to call through embedding a hook at *zygote* and *system_server* which are critical process in Android. And we also achieve an ACL control center for users.

In summary, we make the following contributions in this paper.

- We present a novel access control enforcement based on ACL to enforce fine-grained control on system resources. Even though ACL is a feature in Linux and Android is based on Linux kernel, it is not supported in Android so far. We enable ACL in kernel and achieve an ACL library which is missing in Android. ACL support in Android has no prior work to reference so this is a challenging work.

- An entire system based on ACL kernel support is achieved on Android 5.1.1 platform. The system enable user configure their own policy to control application access resource according to his own requirement. We create a new service to provide API that is used to execute ACL command for the only granted application or process. User has the capacity to dynamically grant application the access to a specified resource at permission center as well as gain the permission of the object.
- We develop a prototype and verify the effectiveness of our system against transplantation attack. The result shows it can effectively prevent the abnormal access of malicious application through native code. The customized system has a negligible effect on performance overhead and also offers a stable operating environment for applications.

The rest of the paper is organized as follows. Section 2 introduces necessary background knowledge. Section 3 presents the system design of our scheme. Section 4 shows the prototype implementation of our system. Section 5 presents the evaluation. Section 6 describes related works. Finally, we conclude this paper in Sect. 7.

2   Background

2.1   Access Control List

An access control list (ACL), with respect to a computer file system, is a list of permissions attached to an object. (An object can be a file, process, event, or anything else having a security descriptor.) ACL provides an additional, more flexible permission mechanism for file systems.

UGO uses 9 bits to identify the privileges of user, group and others. The most common privileges include the ability to read a file (or all the files in a directory), to write to the file, and to execute the file. If the file's privileges are rwxr--r--, that means file owner can read, write and execute the file, the group that file owner belongs to and others besides mentioned above have the only permission to read the file. However, suppose there are two users need to be given different access rights, respectively, UGO would fail to effectuate this goal, but ACL can make it come true.

An ACL specifies which user or system process are granted access to objects, as well as what operations are allowed on given objects. Each entry in a typical ACL specifies a subject and an operation. For instance, if a file object has an ACL that contains two entries: Alice: read, write; Bob: read, this would give Alice permission to read and write the file and Bob to only read it. Thus, ACL can assign multiple users and groups different access policies to a certain object.

2.2   Permission Mechanism in Android

Android permission mechanism is used to protect system resources and it contains two layers. One is application-level and another is kernel-level.

Android defines a series of important permissions to protect system resources, such as SMS, contacts, etc. At the beginning of app installation, all permission requests will be presented to user, if user agrees to the requests, the granted permissions will be stored in the PMS (*PackageManagerService*).

Android replaces an authorization hooks (*checkPermission ()* method) in AMS (*ActivityManagerService*). When app accesses a resource by system API, a permission check request with a string of applied permission and the PID (process identifier) of caller will be sent to *system_server*, *checkPermission ()* method will be called to check if the permission is granted to this app and then return the result back.

Android is a Linux-based open source software stack. Each application in Android is allocated a unique user and group identifier (UID and GID respectively) when it is installed and the relevant process is assigned these identifiers. Android makes each app run in an isolated process space like Linux multi-users system does and Linux kernel provides enforcement. In order to control the app and system resources, Android relies on Linux DAC. DAC allows resource owners to authorize apps to access system resources and files in filesystem directly. When the holder acquiesces in the permission, the UID of app will be added in group which pertains the object.

2.3   Transplantation Attack

In Android system, most system resources, like GPS, Camera, etc. are accessed through system services, such as LocationManager service, Camera service. When an app wants to obtain the resources above, app needs to send a request to relevant system service though IPC (Inter-Process Communication). After receiving request from app, service asks *system_server* to check if the app has the permission to access resource. If yes, service will call the system library (.so) loaded in system service process to interact with hardware driver and return the result back.

By embedding malicious code into install package and repackaging it, malware can copy system libraries from system service process space to its own process space, and directly access the hardware driver, or software resources through these libraries, this modus operando is donated "transplantation attack". We know that before application calls API to gain the system resource, a permission check will be performed and user will be reminded if any application makes a visit at the same time. If attack is successfully enforced, system service process would not be necessary when malware wants to access system resources. As a result, most of security enhancements will be bypassed in Android especially middleware enforcements.

One type of transplantation attack [27] can take picture passing by API auditing on user's smartphone. Figure 1 shows the normal photo taking workflow and how transplantation attack applies to camera. When an app takes a photo, the app will send a request to *MediaService* where the Camera Service runs. Then *MediaService* asks *system_server* to make an API auditing and check the permission. The code of photo taking exists in the form of .so library and it runs in *MediaService*. If the caller process belongs to the camera group, camera driver can be accessed directly by libhardware.so and libcamera.so. Transplantation attack transplants the needed .so libraries from *MediaService* process to malicious app process, so in app process, app can visit */dev/video0*, */dev/video2*, */dev/video3*, etc., to take pictures directly.

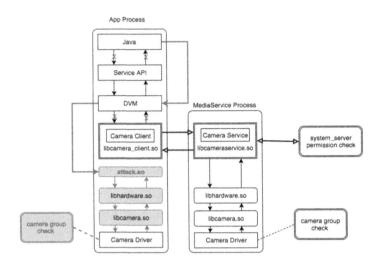

Fig. 1. Transplantation attack applied to CameraService

3   System Design

The system targets at enforcing fine-grained resource access control on system files, including device descriptors and database files (contacts, call history). The essence of transplantation attack is duplicating system libraries from system service process space to malware process space, so that malicious software can address to hardware driver or file resource directly. However, some prerequisites are required for the implementation of transplantation attack. To access the driver of hardware and system file, app's identifier UID must be in the group which object owner belongs to.

This system can set each app's access permission for given object and it is a new way to against transplantation attack. The system consists of three parts: ACL Control Center, ACL Service and ACL Support, as shown in Fig. 2.

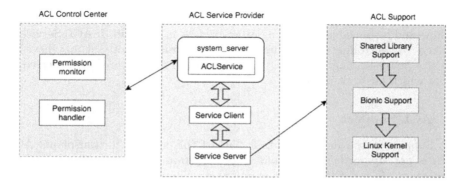

Fig. 2. System architecture

3.1   ACL Control Center

ACL Control Center is responsible for interacting with users, and it has two main modules: Permission monitor and Permission handler. Android is made up of files in kernel because it is based on Linux. ACL control center allows user to make customized policy for system files according to security requirements or user's own needs. Permission monitor acquires the resources access permission of which application can access in real-time. In addition to this, it records all the operations that performed on the specific file, such as disabling read and write permissions for an app, or forbidding some groups to fetch the file. Permission handler dynamically controls the access of resources through sending a command to ACL Service Provider, after successfully receiving the result from ACL Service, it feeds the result back to the user.

3.2   ACL Service Provider

ACL Service Provider is composed of three subcomponents: ACLService, Service Client and Service Server, all of them are running in framework layer.

ACLService. We structure a new service named ACLService which runs in *system_server* and it provides APIs to ACL Control Center for getting and setting the access control permissions of a specific resource. This service will apply a permission to protect the system resource. In order to call the interfaces without fail, ACL Control Center will apply for the permission, only when user grants the permission can control center or other application use the APIs.

Service Client. Service client plays the role of communicating with server via socket and runs in *Process* process. Service client runs in *Process* because there exists a reusable-architecture of socket between *Process* and *Zygote*. To reduce overhead of the initiation of new connection and the amount of work, we finally choose this scheme.

Service Server. Service server serves to receive messages from service client and after that calls libacl.so to operate the command. Service Server is executed as a root user because it runs in *Zygote* process which is the first Dalvik virtual machine and responsible for forking other process in Android. If ACL Service is in charge of controlling the resource access permission directly, it may have an excessive power leading to misuse the authority. So this feature is transferred to *Zygote* which has root privilege.

3.3   ACL Support

ACL Support is the most important part of this system, it transplants ACL which is not supported in Android at present from Linux into Android. This module is made up of three main components: Shared Library Support, Bionic Support and Linux Kernel Support.

Shared Library Support. Shared library and bionic are included in the Android userspace software stack. None of the prior work could be reused for Android so we have to implant ACL related source code and recompile it for Android. This module will provide a shared library entitled as libacl.so or libacl.a for framework layer's call, in general, libacl.so is used most often. It contains several native functions that are used to convert file's extended attributes into acl entries and vice versa.

Bionic Support. Bionic is Android C/C++ library, libc is GNU/Linux and other Unix-like system based library. Libc is much bigger and slower than bionic, as a consequence, Android uses bionic as its own basic library. Though it is different from libc, bionic still possesses functions related xattrs and then makes a system call to set extended attributes.

Linux Kernel Support. Even though Android is based on Linux kernel which supports ACL settings, the use of ACL in Android is still not supported because of the simplification of linux kernel. ACL needs filesystem to provide support for access permission, and the storage of permission can be provided through the use of extended attributes on files. In this module, we modify some kernel build configurations and recompile the kernel to in favor of ACL.

4   Implementation

In this section, we implement a system prototype and describe the implementation details of some critical components.

4.1   Kernel Configuration

Android is based on Linux kernel, in order to reduce the runtime memory, Google has cut some features that are not used frequently, including ACL. In *AOSP* (Android Open Source Project), there exists a shrinking and compiled kernel, so we can do nothing to change it.

In our scheme, we recompile a new kernel of paired *AOSP* [3] version. In Linux kernel source code, the code about Linux features are all kept, but the features of issued kernel depend on a configuration file. We reset the values concerned about ACL in file .config, and Table 1 lists the arguments changed before and after. From the table we can see that the properties modified are related to file system, like *EXT4* and *TMPFS*. Android device is using *EXT4* as its file system. Compiler finally derives a boot image *booting.img* in accordance with an amended profile. After replacing a new kernel, ACL attribute will be one of the file extended attributes in *EXT4*, and the information of ACL is stored in inode which is a file node and used for logging all file and directory information.

Table 1. Configuration of kernel before and after

Before	After
# CONFIG_EXT4_FS_POSIX_ACL is not set	CONFIG_EXT4_FS_POSIX_ACL=y
# CONFIG_FS_POSIX_ACL is not set	CONFIG_FS_POSIX_ACL=y
# CONFIG_TMPFS_POSIX_ACL is not set	CONFIG_TMPFS_POSIX_ACL=y
# CONFIG_NFSD_V3_ACL is not set	CONFIG_NFSD_V3_ACL=y

4.2   Shared Library Support

Android is divided into four layers, they are: Application layer, Application framework layer, Libraries & Android runtime layer and Linux kernel layer from top to bottom. Section 4.1 occurs in Linux kernel layer, and this section is focus on Libraries & Android runtime layer. This section works on transplanting ACL code from Linux to *AOSP*, the code will be compiled into a shared library and then collected into Android C/C++ libraries that can be used by different components in the Android system.

In Linux, most softwares and packages can be installed by command. But in Android, no complete setup package is provided for Android installing, so we have to make a transplantation from Linux to Android and achieve a customized Android system-image.

At first we download 'libacl' code which should run on Linux from the open source community [1]. Because the differences of system architecture between Linux and Android, we should make an alteration to the code, including adding missing code, removing useless code, and integrating scattered code. We put 'libacl' source code to the path: *MYAOSP/system/core/*.

We efface the files except libacl and include directories since the rest is beyond requisite function, like some executing commands: man, setfacl, chacl, etc. In libacl directory, there are many .c files and header files mixed together, we make a new directory dedicate to containing the needed header files using for compiling. The number of remaining .c files is a bit much and each file carries only one function, basing on the role of each function plays, we divide these files into three categories, and create three new files to refactor the source code, as list in Table 2. The functions in *posix_functions.c* are following the standards by the IEEE Computer Society [20] which are used to maintain compatibility between operating systems and provide common APIs for other application. This file involves 29 files once were in libacl, *libacl_functions.c* has 11 files and *internal_functions.c* has 6. *Internal_functions.c* is responsible for transforming strings between ACL and file extended attributes as well as internal calling. *Libacl_functions.c* is the wrapper for underlying code and offers operations about ACL such as checking if an ACL is valid.

Table 2. Integration of files

New file name	Function number	Role
posix_functions.c	29	Portable Operating System Interface of UNIX
libacl_functions.c	11	Wrapper for underlying code
internal_functions.c	6	Internal functions about file system

For compiling the source code successfully, we add a makefile for Android. During the whole process of compilation, there are some missing file headers or C files needed to be included and some variable types which are not supported in Android should be revised in accordance with compile log. After compiling with success, libacl.so becomes a part of system library in the path */system/lib*, the new system is a customized one that can favor ACL settings.

4.3   ACL Service Provider

System_server servers as the eldest son of *Zygote* process, plays a significant role in Android. Many important system service such as *ActivityManagerService*, *PowerManagerService*, *PackageManagerService* are provided in *system_server* server process. We implemented ACL as an extra system service in *system_server*.

We add ACLService in *system_server* process for reason explained below. ACL setting operation need root privilege and to be implemented in *Zygote* process. *System_server* process is an interface of Android application to *Zygote*. After *Zygote* starting, the first thing it ready to do is registering a socket to make itself a server, and then waiting for the notification of creating process from *system_server*. There is an existing socket between *Zygote* and *system_server*. Implementing ACLService in *system_server* may simplify the communication with *Zygote* and have a higher efficiency than other schemes.

Figure 3 shows the profile of ACLService provider. Firstly, we add ACLService in *system_server* and register it into *system_server*, and then intercept *Zygote* to inject our own socket communication code so that it can serve as an ACL setting server. ACLService code in *system_server* plays the part of a client and sends access permission to *Zygote*. But there still exists a problem: how to start a new socket between *Zygote* and *Process*. Injecting code to send a new message in *Process* is moderately easy compare to handling message in *Zygote*.

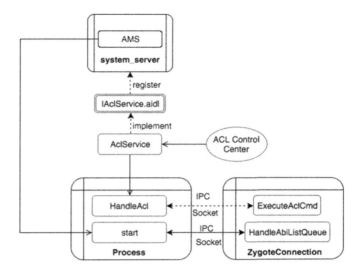

Fig. 3. Structure of service provider

In this part, what need to do is packing a wrapper function using existing way to start communication. All that left is altering command parameters in communication.

As for *Zygote*, we have to analyze the clear procedure of socket establish, and try to locate the appropriate position to insert the code about dealing with the message received from *Process*. As mentioned above, the first thing *Zygote* process does after the creation is registering a socket, so we start from this and trace the following behaviors. Through tracing the code, we find a key function *"runSelectLoop"* in ZygoteInit. This function is used to receive and handle the request from client named *ActivityManagerService* in loops. Inside the loop, function *serverSocket.accep()* means when there comes a connection, the server accepts it and establishes a connection. There is a ZygoteConnection queue in *Zygote*, after establishing the connection, ZygoteConnection will be placed in the queue and wait to be handled. The entrance that we are looking for eventually is function *runOnce* which achieved in ZygoteConnection. By carefully analyzing, a branch is caught in function runOnce, as shown in Listing 1.1. Line 5 is a branch, it judges whether the parameter is true, and then next to another execution. So a new branch which contains wrapper function can be injected here as line 9 does. If the request with a unique parameter we customized, *Zygote* will follow an expected flow: *ExecuteAclCmd*. In this inserted channel, we imbed the code of specifying access permission on given object.

Listing 1.1. Imbed code in *runOnce*

```
 1 boolean runOnce () throws ZygoteInit.MethodAndArgsCaller {
 2     ......
 3     try {
 4         parsedArgs = new Arguments(args);
 5         if (parsedArgs.abiListQuery) {
 6             return handleAbiListQuery();
 7         }
 8         // imbed hook here
 9         if (parsedArgs.execShell != null) {
10             return ExecuteAclCmd(parsedArgs.execShell);
11         }
12     } catch (IOException ex) {
13         logAndPrintError(newStderr, "Exception creating
14             pipe", ex);
15     }
16     ......
17 }
```

4.4 SEAndroid Configuration

Android introduced a set of security mechanism based on SELinux and this is known as SEAndroid [26]. SEAndroid adopts MAC to Android and enforces mandatory policy between subjects and objects. A policy contains subject(domain), object(type) and operation permissions and this defines which subject can operate which object with a series of permissions, such as read, write, setattr.

Table 3 shows the added strategies in zygote context and system_server context, respectively. We assign *Zygote* to perform ACL enforcement in Sect. 4.3, and the enforcement will execute some extended attribute operations like setattr, getattr on files. Each important system process has its own permission policy file which is contained a set of policies. There are no rules for *Zygote* to execute the setattr and getattr to system data file and device file. Hence, system will deny related actions. Therefore, Table 3 shows the rules added in zygote.te to make these behaviors legal. Section 4.3 also hooks a new service ACLService in *system_server* and this service will be forbidden by SEAndroid as well because the lack of strategy. As a result, we have to increase a new policy for *system_server* context at mean time as Table 3 displays.

4.5 Access Permission Checking

In our prototype, there generally will be four checks if any app or process wants to access the resources in the kernel, such like file and device. As shown in Fig. 4, the first one is general error checking, for example, to see whether the accessed object is existing, whether the access parameter is correct, and so on. After general error check finishing, the original permission check will be performed.

Table 3. Added SEAndroid configuration of Zygote and system_server

Domain	Policy	File name
zygote	allow zygote system_data_file:file setattr	zygote.te
zygote	allow zygote video_device:chr_file setattr	zygote.te
system_server_service	aclService u:object_r:system_server_service:s0	service_context

In other words, the original permission check is DAC check which is based on the Linux UID/GID security check. Only when original permission check passed, can ACL permission check begin to work. ACL permission check will determine whether the access list of object contains access permission of subject according to its UID. The last step is SELinux checks, that is, security checks based on security contexts and security policies.

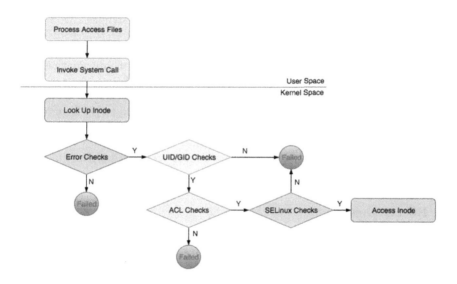

Fig. 4. Procedure of access permission check

Sections 4.1 and 4.2 implement the support of Android kernel, Sect. 4.3 achieves a service of controlling ACL permission dynamically. Generally, the resources that require to be dynamic controlled have already authorized to be accessed by some applications, and we increase the access control base on this. Meanwhile, SELinux check has no effect on the previous inspection because the subject originally has the permission of the resource.

5   Evaluation

This section makes an evaluation for our prototype system compared to a pristine build of the corresponding AOSP version. The AOSP images were built from the 5.1.1_r14 tag for the Nexus 6 devices, using the prebuilt kernel provided by AOSP for shamu device. Device Nexus 6 had Snapdragon 805 CPU (2.7 GHZ, quad-core) and 3 GB RAM. The images were used to supply the baseline for each set of results. The system we present was built from the same AOSP version for the same device, using a kernel built from 3.10[10]. We evaluate our prototype system in following aspects:

(i) Verify the stability of the custom system through running various Apps on prototype system;
(ii) Verify the effectiveness of run-time ACL access permission control of the object in our system and the resistance of transplantation attack;
(iii) evaluate the overall performance of the prototype system.

5.1   Stability

We downloaded 100 popular Apps belonging to various categories from *Google Play* [4] for experiment and chose Google *Monkey* [5] as testing tool because Monkey could be easily run on any version of physical devices. Monkey would send pseudo-random user events to designated application automatically and help test whether the app would be crashed.

At the beginning, we manually checked the stability of some apps. Then randomly selected 25 applications from apps we downloaded to perform Monkey, and made a script to send 500 pseudo-random events to each application. Luckily, we found that no app was crashed during the whole procedure. We draw a conclusion that the system we present has almost no effect on system stability and is compatible for app.

5.2   Effectiveness

We chose some important resources to evaluate the effectiveness of our system. As shown in Table 4, the resources contained system databases (contacts and sms) and device files such as camera device and socket. Host app applied all the permissions of following resources in *AndroidManifest.xml*. Application visited network by creating a socket, we set the privilege bits --- to one of the socket device files to close the access permission for holder app, then a message 'net::ERR_NAME_NOT_RESOLVED' was displayed for us and log contained a record: permission denied. Different from socket, some resources are accessed by calling APIs, the UID of access user would be the UID of system service which is responsible to provide API to access the resource. So we shutdown the group privileges and inspected the result. Table 4 shows the final result.

Most applications called APIs to gain the object in a normal way, but we could't make sure that there was no application calling native code to access

Table 4. Effectiveness result of some important system resources

Detail	Location	Result
Address book	/data/data/com.android.providers. contacts/databases/contacts2.db	Success
SMS	/data/data/com.android.providers. telephony/databases/mmssms.db	Success
Front camera device	/dev/video3	Success
Back camera device	/dev/video2	Success
Socket	/dev/socket/dnsproxyd	Success

the resource directly. To evaluate the effectiveness of preventing transplantation attack, we applied ACL to a malicious app with camera transplantation attack and set it inaccessible to front camera device according to its UID. A message "mm_camera_open: cannot open control fd of '*/dev/video3*' (Permission denied)" was found in log and this attack was not executed properly after the ACL permission setting.

5.3 Overall Performance

To measure the performance overhead of the system we present, we run three well-known benchmarks which are hot in Google Play Store: AnTuTu, Geekbench4 and CF-Bench. Each benchmark was performed 10 times both on original AOSP and built on the same device.

Antutu would comprehensively test all aspects of a device, including UX, GPU, RAM, CPU, I/O and more. Each item was individually assessed and given a score. Table 5 shows result for 10 runs of AnTuTu. The average and standard deviation of each aspect are displayed. 3D, CPU, and RAM test were not affected by our system because they had no system calls and usage of file extended attributes. UX test included I/O, file reading and file writing, so this evaluation could be affected and may have a small overhead because of the check of ACL permission. We could see the overheads were 262.4 in UX and 413.3 in total and they were negligible and both within on standard deviation of the *AOSP* result.

The scores and results of Geekbench4 and CF-Bench are shown in Table 6. Each row represents one result of one benchmark, including the average of some particular scores, the average of overall score in respective system, the overhead and percentage of overhead it costs. CF-bench is designed to evaluate CPU and memory for multi-core devices and test both native as well managed code performance. Geekbench4 includes single-core, multi-core and GPU tests, it executes CPU tests modeling real-world tasks and applications, GPU Compute tests measuring the processing power of device's GPU.

From the table we can see that the overhead produced by our system in CF-Bench is less than 1.29% and 4.14% in GeekBench4, all of it is negligible to the

Table 5. Antutu benchmarking

	AOSP		Our system	
	Mean	SD	Mean	SD
Total Score	70866.1	774.51	70452.8	957.86
3D Score	16823.3	706.48	16596.7	712.70
UX Score	24690.3	285.17	24427.9	423.33
CPU Score	22203	288.63	22088.2	367.93
RAM Score	7149.5	156.58	7310	230.35

Table 6. Overall performance evaluated in Geekbench4 and CF-Bench

Benchmark	AOSP	Our system	Over	Over. (%)
CF-Bench:Native	49682.2	49649.4	32.8	0.01%
CF-Bench:Java	27514.8	27159.2	355.6	1.29%
CF-Bench:Overall	36381.2	36155.6	225.6	0.62%
GeekBench4:Single-Core	1029.4	1017	12.4	1.20%
GeekBench4:Multi-Core	2932.6	2842.8	89.8	3.06%
GeekBench4:GPU	3967.2	3802.8	164.4	4.14%

system. So we can draw a conclusion that our system has little impact on overall performance.

6   Related Work

This section provides an overview of the related work. There are a lot of Android security enforcements proposed to improve the security of Android, whereas most enforcements attempt to address access control at the Android middleware layer. Section 6.1 describes the research efforts in enhancing the security at the Android middleware layer. Solutions based on Linux DAC mechanism are present in Sect. 6.2.

6.1   Android Middleware Layer Enforcements

Apex [23] allows user to select parts of permissions to grant to an application during the installation. Kirin [18] checks the permission of applications for indications of malicious activities, user can refuse to install the application when it is inconformity with security policies. Saint [24] is a policy-based application management system aimed to control how apps interact with each other. Quire [16] provides developers with new interfaces to acquire IPC call chain which relies on AIDL instrumentation. Felt et al. [19] proposed IPC inspection to prevent permission re-delegation attacks through intersecting the permissions of all the applications in the IPC call chain. But the scheme is inflexible to allow intentional permission re-delegations.

Taintdroid [17] proposes dynamic taint analysis to control the data flow between applications. It tracks the flow of tainted data and notifies the user if the data leaves the device through an illegal way. In [10,22], taint tracking makes the system trace sensitive information, enterprise data possible, and can enforce policies for those data.

[11,15,23] use context to dynamically configure app's permissions. In [10], special context is a necessary condition to generate security notifications. In [22], the context is used to taint data generated in predefined environments.

6.2 Kernel Layer Enforcements

So far, most of the security extensions are aim at Android middleware layer access control, and do not involve the Linux DAC mechanism. But the realization of middleware access control depends on the kernel layer control to ensure the access control can not be bypassed.

[7,14,25,26] introduce SELinux into Android to reinforce the security of Android underlying operating system. FlaskDroid [14] uses boolean variables to instantiate the policy which is based on the extension of SEAndroid mandatory access control. This considerably diminishes the effect of root exploits. However, the delegation of rights or permissions in accordance to a hierarchy is not supported.

TrustDroid [13], XManDroid SELinux [12] and SELinux [26] provide MAC at both middleware layer and kernel layer, but TrustDroid and XManDroid are relied on TOMOYO Linux [9] which is based on the UID of application and data file to ensure the files of application not be accessed by other applications rather than SELinux in kernel layer. SELinux implements SELinux at kernel layer. Either TOMOYO Linux or SELinux changes the file access control in the Linux level, from the original DAC into MAC.

7 Conclusions and Future Work

In this paper, we present a system which introduces ACL access control mechanism. ACL provides a run-time fine-grained access control and prevent the leakages through native code such as transplantation attack. This paper implements kernel and C library support where they are barely existing, besides, a service and a permission control center are offered. The kernel based on Linux is recompiled according to a new configuration file which contains ACL features. After replacing a kernel, the system we customized is supporting ACL extended attribute in filesystem. Because of the cut of system, some system libraries are missing, the code about libacl is transplanted to this system and a system library *libacl.so* is added to make a system call and interact with filesystem. *Zygote* process is intercepted to imbed a hook, by doing this, a low overhead communication can be established between *Zygote* and *Process*. When an application is given an ACL permission set to a resource, system would check the origin permission at first, if passed, then ACL permission check would be executed. Finally, the performance overhead imposed by our system is evaluated in three benchworks and each result shows the overhead can be negligible.

The scheme we implement aims at the control of access to system resources such as device files and system files. However, Android uses Fuse [21] which is a user-space pseudo filesystem to provide flexibility in managing the internal storage space and maintain host compatibility. Thus, some file extended attributes are not supported in sdcard. In our future work, we intend to introduce ACL to Fuse filesystem in Android to achieve a fine-grained access control of shared resources in sdcard like DCIM.

Acknowledgements. This research was supported by National Natural Science Foundation of China (Grant No. 61602475), National Key Research and Development Program of China (Grant No. 2016YFB0800102) and National Cryptographic Foundation of China (Grant No. MMJJ20170212).

References

1. ACL open source community. http://savannah.nongnu.org/projects/acl
2. Android permissions. https://developer.android.com/guide/topics/security/permissions.html
3. AOSP. https://source.android.com/
4. Google play. https://play.google.com/store
5. Monkey. https://developer.android.com/studio/test/monkey.html
6. Security and permissions. http://developer.android.com/guide/topics/security/security.html
7. Security-enhanced linux. http://www.nsa.gov/research/selinux
8. Smartphone OS market share. http://www.idc.com/promo/smartphone-market-share/os
9. Tomoyo linux home page. http://tomoyo.sourceforge.jp/
10. Ahmed, M., Ahamad, M.: Protecting health information on mobile devices. In: Second ACM Conference on Data and Application Security and Privacy, CODASPY 2012, San Antonio, TX, USA, pp. 229–240, 7–9 February 2012
11. Bai, G., Gu, L., Feng, T., Guo, Y., Chen, X.: Context-aware usage control for android. In: Jajodia, S., Zhou, J. (eds.) SecureComm 2010. LNICST, vol. 50, pp. 326–343. Springer, Heidelberg (2010). doi:10.1007/978-3-642-16161-2_19
12. Bugiel, S., Davi, L., Dmitrienko, A., Fischer, T., Sadeghi, A.-R., Shastry, B.: Towards taming privilege-escalation attacks on android. In: 19th Annual Network and Distributed System Security Symposium, NDSS 2012, San Diego, California, USA, 5–8 February 2012
13. Bugiel, S., Davi, L., Dmitrienko, A., Heuser, S., Sadeghi, A.-R., Shastry, B.: Practical and lightweight domain isolation on android. In: SPSM 2011, Proceedings of the 1st ACM Workshop Security and Privacy in Smartphones and Mobile Devices, Co-located with CCS 2011, Chicago, IL, USA, pp. 51–62, 17 October 2011
14. Bugiel, S., Heuser, S., Sadeghi, A.-R.: Flexible and fine-grained mandatory access control on android for diverse security and privacy policies. In: Proceedings of the 22nd USENIX Security Symposium, Washington, DC, USA, pp. 131–146, 14–16 August 2013

15. Conti, M., Crispo, B., Fernandes, E., Zhauniarovich, Y.: Crêpe: a system for enforcing fine-grained context-related policies on android. IEEE Trans. Inf. Forensics Secur. **7**(5), 1426–1438 (2012)
16. Dietz, M., Shekhar, S., Pisetsky, Y., Shu, A., Wallach, D.S.: QUIRE: lightweight provenance for smart phone operating systems. In: Proceedings of the 20th USENIX Security Symposium, San Francisco, CA, USA, 8–12 August 2011
17. Enck, W., Gilbert, P., Chun, B.-G., Cox, L.P., Jung, J., McDaniel, P.D., Sheth, A.: Taintdroid: an information flow tracking system for real-time privacy monitoring on smartphones. Commun. ACM **57**(3), 99–106 (2014)
18. Enck, W., Ongtang, M., McDaniel, P.D.: On lightweight mobile phone application certification. In: Proceedings of the 2009 ACM Conference on Computer and Communications Security, CCS 2009, Chicago, Illinois, USA, pp. 235–245, 9–13 November 2009
19. Felt, A.P., Wang, H.J., Moshchuk, A., Hanna, S., Chin, E.: Permission redelegation: attacks and defenses. In: Proceedings of the 20th USENIX Security Symposium, San Francisco, CA, USA, 8–12 August 2011
20. Grünbacher, A.: POSIX access control lists on linux. In: Proceedings of the FREENIX Track: 2003 USENIX Annual Technical Conference, San Antonio, Texas, USA, pp. 259–272, 9–14 June 2003
21. Jeong, S., Won, Y.: Buffered FUSE: optimising the android IO stack for user-level filesystem. IJES **6**(2/3), 95–107 (2014)
22. Kodeswaran, P.A., Nandakumar, V., Kapoor, S., Kamaraju, P., Joshi, A., Mukherjea, S.: Securing enterprise data on smartphones using run time information flow control. In: 13th IEEE International Conference on Mobile Data Management, MDM 2012, Bengaluru, India, pp. 300–305, 23–26 July 2012
23. Nauman, M., Khan, S., Zhang, X.: Apex: extending android permission model and enforcement with user-defined runtime constraints. In: Proceedings of the 5th ACM Symposium on Information, Computer and Communications Security, ASIACCS 2010, Beijing, China, pp. 328–332, 13–16 April 2010
24. Ongtang, M., McLaughlin, S.E., Enck, W., McDaniel, P.D.: Semantically rich application-centric security in android. Secur. Commun. Netw. **5**(6), 658–673 (2012)
25. Shabtai, A., Fledel, Y., Elovici, Y.: Securing android-powered mobile devices using selinux. IEEE Secur. Priv. **8**(3), 36–44 (2010)
26. Smalley, S., Craig, R.: Security enhanced (SE) android: bringing flexible MAC to android. In: 20th Annual Network and Distributed System Security Symposium, NDSS 2013, San Diego, California, USA, 24–27 February 2013
27. Zhang, Z., Liu, P., Xiang, J., Jing, J., Lei, L.: How your phone camera can be used to stealthily spy on you: transplantation attacks against android camera service. In: Proceedings of the 5th ACM Conference on Data and Application Security and Privacy, CODASPY 2015, San Antonio, TX, USA, pp. 99–110, 2–4 March 2015

Software Security

Nightingale: Translating Embedded VM Code in x86 Binary Executables

Xie Haijiang[1,2], Zhang Yuanyuan[1(✉)], Li Juanru[1], and Gu Dawu[1]

[1] Shanghai Jiao Tong University, Shanghai, China
yyjess@sjtu.edu.cn
[2] Keen Security Lab of Tencent, Shanghai, China

Abstract. Code protection schemes nowadays adopt language embedding, a technique in which a customized language is built within a general-purpose one, often referred to as the host language, to obfuscate original code through transforming it into a customized form with which the analyst is not familiar. The transformed code is then interpreted by a so-called Embedded VM. This type of transformation does increase the cost of code comprehending and maintaining, and introduces extra runtime overhead.

In this paper, we conduct an in-depth study on embedded VM based code protection and propose a de-obfuscation approach that aims to recover the original code form. Our approach first pinpoints the interpretation procedure and partitions handlers of the embedded VM, and then employs a VM-state based handler translating, which represents the VM-state-updated behaviors of handlers. Finally, the translated operations of each handler is optimized and transformed into host code. After this process, we can obtain a clear and runtime efficient code representation. We build NIGHTINGALE, a binary translation tool, to fulfil this de-obfuscation automatically with x86 binary executables. We test our approach on the latest commercial code obfuscators, embedded domain-specific languages and a set of home brewed obfuscation schemes. The results demonstrate that this kind of obfuscated code can be simplified with host language effectively.

Keywords: Code obfuscation · Virtual machine interpreter · Code protection

1 Introduction

Embedded languages are programming languages designed to be used from within another program. Compared with its host language, an embedded language is usually more flexible with clear and simple syntax. For instance, the

This work was partially supported by the Key Program of National Natural Science Foundation of China (Grants No. U1636217), the Major Project of the National Key Research Project (Grants No. 2016YFB0801200), and the Technology Project of Shanghai Science and Technology Commission under Grants No. 15511103002.

P.Q. Nguyen and J. Zhou (Eds.): ISC 2017, LNCS 10599, pp. 387–404, 2017.
https://doi.org/10.1007/978-3-319-69659-1_21

Windows operating system provides the *WindowsScriptingHost* API for programs to load and execute scripts written in WSH language. While this hybrid programming style significantly extends the feature of the host language and attains success with many concrete examples (e.g., C and Lua), it may also increase the comprehension complexity and runtime overhead if the embedded language is not familiar to code maintainer and user. For that reason more and more code protection schemes use custom embedded language to impede program analysis and reverse engineering efforts. This type of protection is especially popular with the malware developers, who aim to hide the behavior and character of their program and shield away from the scanning of Anti-Virus software. A prevailing implementation technique for those protection schemes is to design a simple virtual machine. It transforms original code fragment (functions or basic blocks) into bytecode corresponding to this VM, and then simulates it in host language by interpreting the bytecode. Code diversity is also introduced to generate different VMs to frustrate automatic analysis. As a result, it is usually more difficult to analyze and understand such protected code with analysis techniques and tools of host languages.

Difficulties of comprehending embedded obfuscated code mainly comes from comprehending the definition of embedded language and the embedded language VM. In the VM obfuscated executable, instead of analyzing original program code, it is the VM interpreter that requires to analyze. The analysis should first recover the structure of the used VM (e.g., program counter variable, the fetch/decode/execute loop, and instruction buffer) and then understand the obfuscated code. Once the structure is well defined, the syntax and semantics of the target instruction set can be derived with static and dynamic analyses. Previous studies on VM de-obfuscation [3,13,19,20], however, mainly concentrate on comprehending obfuscated code with traditional program analysis and do not consider the characteristic of it. For instance, they are trying to recover high-level syntactic structure (e.g., Control Flow Graph) of the obfuscated code, or employ heavyweight symbolic execution to recover the syntax and semantics of VM bytecode. These analyses usually provide less help when understanding the VM interpreter. As a result, although traditional binary code analysis techniques are well-developed to handle commodity programs, they are sometimes too ideal to comprehend obfuscated code. If the target of the analysis is the embedded language rather than the n host language, a more basic problem is to conduct an embedded language disassembling (or translating) to help understand it.

Methodology. To tackle this challenge, this paper presents a heuristic approach to fulfil embedded language translation. It is profitable to translate the bytecode from the embedded language to the host language. This not only helps comprehend the semantics of the code with simplicity, but also reduces the runtime overhead because the execution in host language is generally more efficient than the interpretive style of the embedded language. Our proposed approach relies on the assumption that *each handler of the embedded language's VM interpreter could be translated into a set of simple operations in host language*, and our target is to automated this inverse procedure and achieve binary code translation.

Main issues of this translation work include: (1) how to pinpoint the interpretation and comprehend handlers, (2) how to translate one handler using the host instructions, (3) how to simplify useless code inserted, and (4) how to replace original obfuscated code. To pinpoint the interpretation procedure, we mainly rely on the feature of how a part of the program is driven by data buffer to identify the VM. Then, a concept of VM-state, which is the core memory operated by the VM, is used to slice code of handlers and build the concise description of each handler. After that, the re-expressed instructions are further optimized to generate a simpler alternative function of the obfuscated code stub. Finally, we use dynamic instrumentation to patch the VM interpreter and replace it with our translated code.

Two properties of embedded VM based obfuscation are leveraged to support our translation. First, most of the embedded bytecode is a transformation of existing program code. Thus it is feasible to re-express it with the original instruction set. This often becomes an important prerequisite for effective de-obfuscation. Second, to communicate with host languages, the embedded code generally uses data structures conforming to host language to pass parameters to and from the host program to the interpreter. For instance, an x86 assembly function will still use stack to pass the parameters even if it is obfuscated.

The core insight of our work is to leverage an abstract **VM-state** to represent the heavily obfuscated operations. Abstractly, the VM-state is the set of intermediate buffer of the VM interpreter, which could be defined through a program analysis of the interpretation. Then the behavior of the VM interpreter is defined by how the VM-state is updated. Through this way different behaviors of various VM interpreters can be expressed in a unified way.

We design and implement an embedded language translator, NIGHTINGALE, to execute automated obfuscated code extraction and translation. NIGHTINGALE mainly makes use of dynamic analysis to employ the obfuscated code extraction. It monitors certain execution that contains a VM interpretation and extracts handlers of the interpreter. When the handler is extracted, an offline analysis is executed to translate and simplify the corresponding embedded code. Finally, the simplified code in host language is dynamically inserted into the program to replace the original obfuscated one.

Evaluation. To evaluate the effectiveness of our approach, we conduct a series of empirical studies on several code obfuscators. To the best of our knowledge, most previous studies on code de-obfuscation only focus on two mainstream obfuscator manufacturers. While those code obfuscators covers a large portion of obfuscated programs, there are still many custom obfuscators used by different software products in the wild. Our evaluation also considers them and conducts an in-depth analysis on some novel obfuscation measures adopted. In detail, we collect five obfuscated samples from online Capture The Flag (CTF) contests as well as our home brewed sample obfuscated by the popular *VMProtect* obfuscator as one of the most famous obfuscators. We then use NIGHTINGALE to analyze these samples and translate their embedded code stubs. While other works try to compare the similarity of recovered code structure with the original one, our validation is simple: we only observe if our rewritten code is able to fulfil the same transformation as the obfuscated one for multiple inputs. If this input-output relationship preserves, it is believed that the translation works. Besides, analysts will get a more comprehensible expression of the program.

Contributions. This paper makes the following contributions:

- We propose an obfuscated code translating approach for code comprehension. Our translating approach adopts a embedded language disassembling methodology and simplifies the obfuscated code. It not only helps understanding the obfuscated code but also improves the execution efficiency to some extent.
- We propose a VM-state analysis to deal with different VM implementations and express the behavior of handlers based on this VM-state. The VM-state based behavior expression is helpful when performing binary translating because it is defined using host language, and is able to be integrated into host program as a patch of the VM code.
- We implement NIGHTINGALE, a binary translating tool to fulfil the task of code de-obfuscation. Our evaluation shows different VM implementations can be analyzed and translated by NIGHTINGALE with a unified analysis style.

2   Preliminaries

2.1   Basic Concept

Figure 1 depicts a concrete example of VM code embedding. The non-obfuscated program, a Windows x86 or x64 executable, is generated with normal compilation process and the layout of the executable follows standard Windows PE file format. After a VM-based code obfuscation (i.e., a code transformation process), part of the original code is wiped and replaced as control flow transitions to lately inserted code section defined in this paper as a *VM stub*. In Fig. 1, original code of *func_A* and *func_B* is replaced as *vm_func_A* and *vm_func_B*. Notice that *vm_func_A* and *vm_func_B* are not typical binary code functions. Instead, they are composed of the header in the original Code section and a series of bytecode placed at the VM section. Then the VM core is responsible for executing the bytecode in the VM section. A typical header (control flow transition) of VM stub can be a simple branch instruction in code section:

```
00401000|push ebp
00401001|mov ebp, esp
00401003|sub esp, 0x8
00401006|push 0x4020f4
0040100b|jmp 0x4a4a97
```

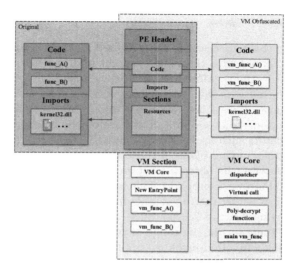

Fig. 1. An instance of VM code embedding

The last *jmp* instruction in this example leads the control flow to the entry point of the VM stub in VM sections, which consists of mainly a VM bytecode buffer and a VM interpreter.

To fulfil the same functionality as the original code, the obfuscator will generate a segment of VM bytecode through analyzing and transforming the original instructions. For instance, if there exists an *add* instruction in original code and the code interpreter also contains an instruction that fulfils addition operation, the obfuscator will then generate a corresponding VM bytecode instruction. The VM bytecode buffer is basically the transformed results of original code with the form of a customized instruction set architecture (ISA). However, not all of the original instructions can be replaced by an alternative VM bytecode. Particular instruction in host language may be complex and the obfuscator may use a set of alternative VM bytecode instructions to replace it. In this manner, the embedded VM code executes within the host language execution environment and always tries to keep the same semantics to prove the reliability.

In the scenario of VM based code obfuscation, the VM interpreter is generally the implementation of a lightweight code interpreter written in host language. Different VMs adopt different designs of ISA and corresponding bytecode handlers. Some VMs are stack machines while some are register machines. However, both implementations follow the common design principle of code interpreter and each consists of basic components such as a *bytecode decoder*, an *execution scheduler*, and numerous *bytecode handlers*, which are core components that determine the ISA of the VM and fulfil the main functionality.

2.2   Assumptions

One assumption in this paper is that the VM used for code obfuscation is a simple interpreter compared with those heavyweight interpreters (e.g., interpreters of Ruby, Lua, and Python). Moreover, we assume that the protected code are simple data transformations that mainly contain plain instructions. This is reasonable because most obfuscators, according to our observation, only deal with those plain instructions. Our assumption is base on the observation of common commercial obfuscators such as *VMProtect* and *ExeCryptor*. The obfuscation is often employed through using SDKs of those obfuscators to transform only part of their code. Otherwise, the obfuscation process may fail or the generated executable may not able to work properly. This indicates that these automated VM obfuscators only deal with relatively simple instructions to prove the stability.

Another important feature is that most obfuscators would not recursively obfuscate invoked functions in the range of protected code. That is, if the protected code contains a function invoking, obfuscators generally do not obfuscate this invoked function. Instead, they just replace the invoking instruction (call or jmp) with a vague stub that does not obviously expose the target function's address.

For commercial VM obfuscators, although we do not know their accurate work mechanisms, we can send a home brewed sample to them and obtain the obfuscated version (these obfuscators provides trial versions). This also helps understand the used bytecode instructions and handlers.

3   VM Code Translating

3.1   Overview

In this paper we aim at translating the embedded VM code, which is mainly generated by automated code obfuscator, into the form of host language of the program. As the embedded code can be seen as an alternative transformation P' that replaces the original transformation P. The target is to recover the original transformation P as much as possible. However, state-of-the-art obfuscators can add various layers of transformations and heavily complicate the process of reverse engineering the semantics of binary code. In most cases it is unpractical to obtain a complete understanding of the underlying logic of a program. Thus we do not pursuit a perfect recovery because this can be seen as a form of decompilation and it is not expected to have a perfect solution to the problem. Our solution is instead to present a generic and practical translation scheme that reveals the state transition of VM code. Concentrating on VM code restricts the scope of the analysis, and helps analyst focus on collect high-level information and identify interesting parts of the obfuscated code. Particularly, in this paper we do not consider the unpacking and anti-analysis code issues. We mainly focus on how to comprehend the structure of embedded VM and how to translate embedded VM bytecode into host language expression.

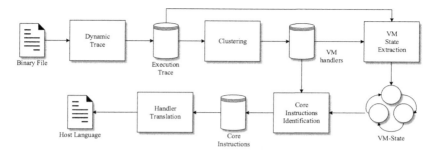

Fig. 2. VM code translating process

Figure 2 depict the entire translating process, which consists of five phases. At the very beginning, the binary code executable is analyzed to first collect execution trace and pinpoint the interpretation procedure. Then, the interpretation procedure is partitioned into different smaller procedures corresponding to VM bytecode handlers. The third phase then extracts and composes a VM-state through synthesizing each handler's behavior. After acquiring the definition of the VM-state, the operation of each handler can be expressed in a new form of host language instructions, and this new representation could be further simplified using traditional program optimization techniques. Finally, to complete the translation, the VM code is replaced by those simplified code through a dynamic binary code instrumentation. In the following, we introduce the details of each phase.

3.2 Interpretation Pinpointing

We propose a handler partition approach, which relies on the analysis of indirected branch semantics. Embedded VM code in host program often executes with a relatively lightweight interpreter, and pinpointing its interpretation process is crucial for the translating. Some studies assume that the VM code and interpreter are placed into a separated section of the executable. Although this corresponds to most commercial VM obfuscators such as VMProtect and Themida, it is not always true for those customized VM obfuscators. Some VM interpreters are embedded into the program during the development stage, hence are located within the same code section as the host code. In this situation, a more generic pinpointing approach is required.

We propose a pinpointing approach based on the feature that the execution of the interpreter is driven by the VM code placed beforehand. A VM interpreter often contains a code dispatching mechanism that responds for choosing the next executing instruction after the interpretation of current bytecode instruction is finished. This code dispatching mechanism can be implemented with a *decode-and-dispatch* style or with a *threaded interpretation* style [14]. For the decode-and-dispatch interpreter, there exists one particular indirect branch instructions (e.g., call eax) that transits the control flow to different handlers.

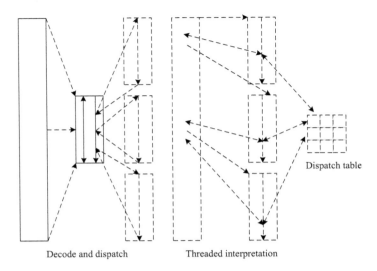

Fig. 3. Two types of interpretation

For the threaded interpretation, the indirect branch instructions may be contained in different handlers (see Fig. 3). However, both kinds of indirect branch instructions, as we called dispatching instructions, are driven by the VM code. Hence for both implementations, we first collect all indirect branch instructions in the execution trace. Then how those concrete control flow transitions are influenced by the input data (from external input or be directly coded in the program) are extracted through a data dependency analysis. The data dependency analysis mainly calculates which part of the input data determines the final indirect branching with a basic data flow analysis against the execution trace. The input data that influences the branching is labeled as the data source. After the analysis, these indirect branch instructions are clustered according to the data source that influence them. The clustering is based on the metric of data source's distance. A basic K-means clustering is adopted here, intending to group those instructions that are influenced by data source with closed distance. According to our observation, the VM code is generally placed in a continuous buffer in data section, or hard coded in code section. If instructions are driven by similar data that is from a small region in memory, it is very possible that the data represents the VM code and the clustered instructions indicate the existence of the interpretation. Another observation is that the embedded VM code has generally been placed during the program generation stage. Thus the buffer of VM bytecode should be placed before the execution of the program. We leverage this property to classify VM bytecode interpreter and the state machine of network protocol, which possesses similar data-driven behavior but the data source is often determined during the execution (i.e., received from the network).

After pinpointing the code dispatching part of the interpretation, the next step is to partition the entire execution trace into individual operation of bytecode instruction handler. We directly use the code dispatching part as the splitter to partition the execution trace, and consider each partitioned segment as a handler. Notice that a handler is not necessarily implemented as a function. Thus a partitioning with the granularity of assembly function is not feasible for this application.

3.3   VM-State Analysis

The key insight of our approach is to recover the format of VM-state, which contains the virtual context of the VM during the interpretation. In general, a VM-state is a set of memory buffer and registers that represents the context of the current VM execution and is maintained by the VM. However, because our analyzed VM is embedded into a host program and the VM itself is implemented using the host language, its VM-state is also expressed using the host memory and registers and is not easily distinguished from the host program's context. Moreover, we expect that the VM-state can still be defined using host language so that in the later translating we can utilize this expression to rewriting the interpretation. To this end, our VM-state analysis is a reverse engineering effort to recover basic format of the VM-state. Since we do not know the virtual ISA beforehand, it is infeasible to define a fixed abstraction of this state beforehand. For instance, if the VM is a stack machine, it often uses a memory buffer to simulate its own virtual stack and manages its own stack *push* and *pop* operations. However, if the VM is a register machine, the abstraction may vary significantly. Hence, our analysis only define a VM as the program that manipulates a memory buffer with relative pointers. Take a virtual *push* operation as an example, our analysis gives the result of a memory write operation only. In this way, we aim to express different VMs in a unified style.

The VM-state reverse engineering starts from analyzing memory and registers updating of each handler in a trace. Now that the aforementioned handler partitioning has already defined the range of each handler, in this phase we concern about how each handler update memory and registers and among the updated content, which part is the used by the following operations. This can be done by a simple data citation analysis: the memory and registers updating of one handler is first recorded and then the following handlers' operations are checked to see which part of those memory buffers and registers is cited in at least one following handler's operation. If the particular memory buffer or register is cited, it is labeled as a *critical* context, otherwise it is labeled as a *forgiving* context. Then we analyze every handler to acquire each one's critical context, and merge them to generate the VM-state. In addition, how each handler manipulates the element in the VM-state is also recorded so that we can define data member of the VM-state with a finer granularity. After this phase the VM-state is extracted from the host program context and the handlers are expected to be translated into host language.

3.4   Handler Translating

Handler translating is the core phase of the entire VM code translating process. It translates variously implemented handlers into a unified form based on the definition of VM-state. That is, one handler's operation is translated as an expression consisted of basic calculation and VM-state elements. For instance, if a handler originally fulfils an add operation on two abstract registers, then the translation results may be:

```
VM-state.buffer[0:4] =
    VM-state.buffer[0:4] + VM-state.buffer[4:8]
```

As the operation of one handler is represented as the operation on the VM-state, it provides a clear description of the handler's behavior with the help of the VM-state. Moreover, it tackles the issue of implementation diversity issue. Even the VM obfuscator adopts code diversity technique to change same handler in different implementations, our analysis is still able to recover the semantics with the VM-state representation.

The detailed handler translating starts from a value-based backward code slicing [3] that resects irrelevant instructions in the handler. It keeps those instructions related to VM-state updating in the handler, which can be employed by a standard slicing approach. Then the remained instructions are transformed into a expression. This expression is generated according to the input and the output of the handler, and illustrates the semantics of the input and the output. Because we can define the input and the output using VM-state, the expression is obviously consists of the relevant VM-state elements.

3.5   Code Simplification

The VM-state based expression of handler may still be complex even if the code slicing removes irrelevant instructions. The reasons for this complexity include the VM obfuscator's implementation is not efficient, or the VM obfuscator intentionally uses a combination of operations to fulfil a simple operation. For instance, some VM obfuscators would use NOR and NAND operations only to emulate every arithmetic operations. To improve the execution efficiency of our translated code, a further code simplification is required.

Our code simplification relies on state-of-the-art code compilation tools to perform code optimization. We first translate every handler in the concrete execution trace to output a VM-state operation sequence. This VM-state operation sequence represents the specific transformation executed by the VM interpretation. Then we rewrite this sequence as a single function using commodity program language so that it can be compiled by state-of-the-art code compilation tools. In our work we use C programming language to rewrite this sequence and use LLVM as the optimization tool. We can compile this single function as a static or a dynamic lib and it could be linked latterly.

3.6   Dynamic Patching

The final step of our translating is to replace the embedded code with a more clear and efficient form. As the embedded code has already been translated and encapsulated into a static or dynamic lib. We can link this lib and use the alternative function to replace the VM stub.

Our dynamic patching is implemented through dynamic code instrumentation. We use popular code instrumentation tools such as Intel's PIN to rewrite the binary code. For a VM stub, we instrument an alternative stub before its entry point to replace its functionality. The control flow is then directed to the new translated function implemented in our lib. And after the execution of this function as a replacement, the alternative stub directly leads the control flow to the invoker of VM stub.

Notice that our translated function is generated by a dynamic analysis phase, which means it may suffer from code coverage problem. The translated function may only able to perform a partial transformation of the original one. However, our observation indicates that most VM stubs are simple transformations with few or no branches. This guarantees our patching works most of the time.

4   Empirical Evaluation

We implement NIGHTINGALE, a binary translation tool, to fulfil this de-obfuscation automatically with x86 and x64 binary executables. NIGHTINGALE consists of an execution trace recording module, an offline program analysis module, and a code patching module. The execution trace recording module and the code patching module are based on Intel's PIN instrumentation framework (900+ LOC) [8], and the offline program analysis module is written in Python (2900+ LOC). In this section we report our empirical study using NIGHTINGALE on five different obfuscators including the state-of-the-art VM obfuscator–*VMProtect 3.0*, and four VM obfuscators from different CTF contests that introduce special code obfuscation techniques (all of the samples from CTF contests can be found online).

4.1   Analysis Results

The chosen samples cover mainstream implementation styles of VM obfuscation and the diversity of each sample is significant for analysis. **Foodie-VM** is a simple VM from *0CTF 2015* CTF contest. It is implemented in C and adopts a standard decode-and-dispatch model. **BCTF-VM** is a C++ implemented VM adopting standard decode-and-dispatch interpretation model. It contains basic arithmetic operations (*add*, *sub*, *mul*, and *div*), logic operations (*xor*, *and*), and virtual stack operations (*push*, *pop*). **Paris-VM** is an obfuscation sample from the *PlaidCTF 2014* CTF contest, which utilizes exception-driven and data-driven implicit control flow manipulating to hide the execution path. **DonnBeach-VM** is an obfuscation sample from the *Hack.lu 2012* CTF contest, which utilizes Intel's MMX instruction set to fulfil a simple AES encryption (2 rounds). The overall experiment results are listed in Table 1.

Table 1. Features of different VMs and the analysis results

VMs	Type	Host language	Handlers	VM-state
VMProtect	Threaded interpretation	C++	138	53 units, 156 bytes
BCTF-VM	Decode-and-dispatch	C++	19	59 units, 448 bytes
Foodie-VM	Decode-and-dispatch	C	6	104 units, 260 bytes
Paris-VM	Data-control	C++	20	7 units, 440 bytes
DonnBeach-VM	Decode-and-dispatch	C	16	8 units, 64 bytes

VMProtect. VMProtect adopts a threaded interpretation style rather than the classic decode-and-dispatch style used in previous versions. Each handler of its interpreter contains a decode stub at the end of its procedure and calculates next handler in situ, which increases the difficulty of handler partitioning. However, using our indirect branch instruction clustering, NIGHTINGALE still successfully extracts the handler related decoding and dispatching instructions and partitions the handlers from the entire execution trace.

BCTF-VM. For BCTF-VM, because of the C++ implementation style, static program analysis does not recognize the caller and callee relationship of dispatching procedure. Our approach solves this issue through dynamic analysis and successfully recognizes all handlers in the execution trace. The recovered VM-state contains 59 memory units and because this VM does not insert any interfering instructions, the backward slicing only resect a few instructions. We can pinpoint handler with method proposed in Sect. 3.2.

Foodie-VM. Handlers of Foodie-VM generally include core functionality and a decode procedure to determine next handler. The extracted VM-state include 104 memory units, and with value-based backward slicing and handler translating, the result is partially showed in Fig. 6. We then compare this recovered result with the original source code of the VM and find it corresponds to original design well.

DonnBeach-VM. The analysis of DonnBeach-VM finds the dispatcher–an obvious indirect branch instruction at 0x40522F driven by buffer_0x405000, and handlers are easily partitioned due to its decode-and-dispatch interpretation style. However, the VM-state of this obfuscator is hard to be analyzed due to the MMX instructions such as palignr mmx7, mmx7, 0x7. To handle this situation we add an extra MMX instruction analysis to NIGHTINGALE so that it could parse these handlers. As the handlers are parsed, the VM-state of this obfuscator is finally defined as an 8×8 byte array, which reflects the eight MMX registers (each register is 128-bit). Also notice that in the host language (x86 Assembly) there is no corresponding instruction for those SIMD operations, e.g., an 128-bit xor operation, we manually add some template functions to fulfil such operations.

Paris-VM. Paris-VM is the most special sample in our analysis. It uses three continuous memory buffers plus four independent bytes to store the VM-state. Instead of using either threaded interpretation or decode-and-dispatch interpretation, this VM executes every handler in each iteration. Only one handler is effective in each iteration and this is determined by the current VM bytecode. Each handler first executes its own functionality and then performs a calculation according to the VM bytecode. Only if the result corresponds to particular handler, the updating of VM-state could be preserved. Otherwise, state updating of those ineffective handlers is restored from a mirror VM-state maintained by the VM.

4.2   Case Studies

VMProtect 3.0. In our experiment we use VMProtect 3.0, the latest version of VMProtect software (until 2015.08), to protect a sample program. VMProtect inserts many interfering instructions in the handler to obscure the semantics from being comprehended. Using our VM-state analysis proposed in Sect. 3.3, we obtain a VM-state containing 53 units and according to relevant operations of those 53 units, crucial instructions in this handler can be determined. After the backward slicing with the information collected we obtain optimized handlers and the simplification effect is shown in Fig. 4

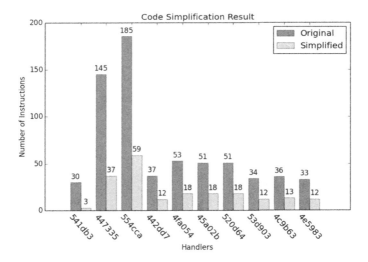

Fig. 4. Handler simplification of VMP handlers

We use one of the handlers to illustrate our analysis. The original handler fulfils the functionality of poping two data elements from the virtual stack (VMProtect uses *ebp* to store the virtual stack's header pointer). Then those two elements are stored into *eax* and *ecx* register respectively. Finally a calculation

((!eax) & (!ecx)), i.e., a *NOR* logic computation is executed and the results of calculation and flag register modification are pushed into the virtual VM stack. In addition, the decode procedure, which fetches a 4-byte VM code and uses *ret* instruction to transit to next handler, is attached at the end.

Then we execute the handler translating on this result to obtain the translated code in Fig. 5. It shows the top 10 handlers with the most simplification degree. The translated code is expressed in C and is able to be compiled (the decode part of VM-state is omitted). We then integrated the entire translated code of the execution trace to replace the original VM stub. The execution displays that our code updates the status of the program with the same semantics.

```
1   ...
2
3   void handler_NOR()
4   {
5       /* Pop 2 data from VM Stack */
6       // 0x44ae3c: mov eax, dword ptr [ebp];
7       (eax.r32[0]) = vm_state[22];
8       // 0x44ae47: mov ecx, dword ptr [ebp+0x4]
9       (ecx.r32[0]) = vm_state[24];
10
11      /* NOR */
12          // 0x44ae51: not eax
13      (eax.r32[0]) = (~(eax.r32[0])) & 0xffffffff;
14      // 0x44ae55: not ecx
15      (ecx.r32[0]) = (~(ecx.r32[0])) & 0xffffffff;
16      // 0x44ae5d: and eax, ecx
17      (eax.r32[0]) = (eax.r32[0]) & (ecx.r32[0]);
18
19      /* Push Result to VM Stack */
20      //44ae5f: mov dword ptr [ebp+0x4], eax
21      vm_state[24] = (eax.r32[0]);
22
23      // Push Flag to VM Stack
24      // 0x44ae6b: pushfd
25      (esp.r32[0]) = (esp.r32[0]) - 0x4;
26      // 0x44ae76: pop dword ptr [ebp]
27      *(unsigned int *)(esp.r32[0]) = eflags.r32[0];
28      vm_state[22] = *(unsigned int *)((esp.r32[0]));
29      (esp.r32[0]) = (esp.r32[0]) + 0x4;
30
31      /* Fetch next handler offset */
32      // 0x44ae8e: mov eax, dword ptr [esi]
33      (eax.r32[0]) = (*(unsigned int *)((esi.r32[0])));
34
35          /* Offset Decryption
36              Calculating next Handler address */
37      ...
38  }
```

Fig. 5. A translated handler of VMProtect obfuscated code

Foodie-VM. Foodie-VM is a VM that simulates an online shellcode battle between two players. The authors have released the source code so we can verify the de-obfuscation result, especially the recovered VM-state with the original

```
 1   // MOVri source code
 2   int32_t vm(Ins *code, uint32_t code_size, char *input)
 3   {
 4       ...
 5       for (i = 0; i < code_size && executing == VM_EXECUTING; ++i)
 6       {
 7           Ins ins = read_mem(ctx->memory, ctx->pc);
 8           Opcode op = get_opcode(ins);
 9           ctx->pc++;
10           switch(op)
11           {
12               ...
13               case MOVri:
14                   reg0 = get_reg_idx(ins, 0);
15                   if (reg0 == ERR_REG_IDX)
16                       executing = VM_STOP;
17                   else
18                       ctx->reg[reg0] = (Reg)get_imm(ins);
19                   break;
20               ...
21           }
22       }
23       ...
24   }
```

(a) Source code of Foodie-VM

```
 1   // Result of Handler Translating
 2   void MOVri()
 3   {
 4       ...
 5       // Fetch Immediate from VM bytecode
 6       eax.r32[0] = (*(unsigned short *)((ebp.r32[0]) + 0x8));
 7       eax.r32[0] = (eax.r32[0]) & 0x3ff;
 8
 9       // Get VM Context address
10       ecx.r32[0] = vm_state[11];
11
12       // Update VM Register with Immediate
13       vm_state[18] = (eax.r16[0]);
14       ...
15       // Update VM PC
16       edx.r16[0] = vm_state[17];
17       edx.r16[0] = (edx.r16[0]) + 0x1;
18       vm_state[17] = (edx.r16[0]);
19       ...
20   }
```

(b) Translated handler of MOVri operation

Fig. 6. Comparison between original code and translated handler of Foodie-VM

structure. We got 104 memory units from the VM-State Analysis. After value-based backward slicing and handler Translating, all of the vm bytecode handlers were successfully translated. Figure 6 lists one bytecode named *MOVri*, which fulfils the function of moving one immediate into VM register that specified in the operand component of the bytecode (we only reserve the key part of the source code and translating result).

In the result of handler translating, new code fetches 4 bytes whose memory address is specified in *ebp.r32[0]* (line 6 of Fig. 6b) and stores the fetched data to *vm_state[18]* (line 13 of Fig. 6b). The corresponding operations in source code are listed at line 19 of Fig. 6a, which indicate the assignment from immediate operand of VM bytecode to the VM register *reg0*. Finally, *vm_state[17]* increases by one (line 16–18 in Fig. 6b), which corresponds to ctx->pc++ in source code. From the result analysts could infer that *vm_state[17]* is the VM's virtual PC after observing all of the handlers since most of handlers have to update the VM's virtual PC during execution. Thus, our translated results will be helpful to accelerate the process of reverse engineering.

5   Related Work

Code obfuscation is an active and practical field of code protection. Although the theoretic proof of impossibility of perfect obfuscation has been provided by Barak *et al.* [1] in 2012. There are still numerous code obfuscation schemes and most of them are ad hoc implemented. These schemes can be classified into two categories. Schemes in the first category mainly work with source code only, and cover many programming languages include C, C++, Java and C#. Among them, the Obfuscator-LLVM [7] (OLLVM) project is a recently emerged obfuscation scheme that takes advantage of the feature of LLVM-IR to help obfuscate. It is initiated in June 2010 by the information security group of the University of Applied Sciences and Arts Western Switzerland of Yverdon-les-Bains (HEIG-VD). As it works at the Intermediate Representation (IR) level, Obfuscator-LLVM compatible with all programming languages and target platforms currently supported by LLVM. Thus it is widely deployed by many applications on different ISAs.

The second category of code obfuscation schemes could manipulate binary code and are frequently used by commercial software and malware. Two famous obfuscation software providers, VMProtect Software [17] and Oreans Technologies [9], release a vast majority of publicly known obfuscators such as *VMProtect, Themida, WinLicense,* and *Code Virtualizer*). Other binary code obfuscators such EXEcryptor [16] and SafeEngine [12] may even be more complex, but are not so popular and less used mainly due to their compatibility issues.

To the best of our knowledeg, the work of Sharif *et al.* [13] proposed the first generic de-obfuscation approach against VM based code obfuscation. They mainly relies on abstract variable analysis and binding to recognize VPC (virtual pc of the emulator) and re-construct the CFG. Their work provides a clear definition of the VM analyzed. However, their analysis relies on the assumption of certain VM structure and only focuses on recovering structure (CFG) of the VM bytecode. This is less meaningful for VM based code obfuscation because a VM stub is generally transformed from a relatively simple function or basic block. It is the bytecode's definition rather than the structure that gives the information of the obfuscation code. Yadegari *et al.* [20] also propose a generic de-obfuscation approach. The advantage of their proposed approach is that it does not make any assumptions about the nature of the obfuscation scheme, but instead using semantics-preserving program transformations to simplify away obfuscation code. Although the proposed code simplification technique is effective, the main target of their approach is still the CFG and the approach does not provide any concrete bytecode definition.

Coogan *et al.* [3] proposed a semantics-based approach to de-obfuscate common commercial obfuscators. However they make a strong assumption that requires the involving of system calls to help analyzing. This assumption is not valid for many VM stubs and thus their approach is not universal. Rolf Rolles gives a well-defined de-obfuscation procedure on unpacking virtualization obfuscators in [10] and proposes a semantics-based methods in [11]. However these work lacks details on handling many obfuscator variants and do not scale.

Specific de-obfuscation tools corresponding to particular version of obfuscators are frequently developed. VMSweeper is a plugin of popular Ollydbg debugger that helps decompile VM code of Code Virtualizer (Oreans Technology) and VMProtect (VMProtect Software). Oreans UnVirtualizer is also an Ollydbg plugin that focus on analyzing Code Virtualizer. In response to LLVM-IR based obfuscation, de-obfuscation technique [5] against OLLVM is also proposed. This technique utilize Miasm [2], a Python open source reverse engineering framework, to deal with specific cases of Control Flow Flattening, Bogus Control Flow, and Instructions Substitution. Besides, there are works concentrating on particular aspects of de-obfuscation. Using symbolic execution to help de-obfuscate VM stub is a promising strategy and many studies have been proposed [6,15,19]. Other de-obfuscation techniques include using probable-plaintext attacks to de-obfuscate malware [18] and simplifying obfuscated machine Code [4].

For famous code obfuscator, corresponding analysis tools are able to deal with fixed pattern and recover the obfuscated code with necessary manual effort. However, as the obfuscators change or evolve, these tools are immediately not available. This becomes an endless arms race and the designers of VM obfuscator have the advantage of adopting "security by obscurity" strategy. Moreover, for those obfuscators in the wild, there is no known effective de-obfuscation tool to analyze them. As a result, our automated and universal analysis is more profitable.

6   Conclusion

In this paper we study the VM based obfuscation and propose a binary translation approach to simplify the embedded VM stub in a host program. Our approach differs from most recent de-obfuscation schemes for its VM-state analysis, which is a universal analysis against various VM implementations. Based on the VM-state a clear expression of VM handler is generated and translated into host language. This translated code can replace the VM stub and fulfil same functionality, and is easily to understand and more efficient. Experiments on five different VMs illustrate the feasibility of our approach.

References

1. Barak, B., Goldreich, O., Impagliazzo, R., Rudich, S., Sahai, A., Vadhan, S., Yang, K.: On the (im)possibility of obfuscating programs. J. ACM **59**(2), 1–6 (2012)
2. CEA IT Security. Miasm: Reverse engineering framework in Python. https://github.com/cea-sec/miasm
3. Coogan, K., Lu, G., Debray, S.: Deobfuscation of virtualization-obfuscated software: a semantics-based approach. In: Proceedings of the 18th ACM Conference on Computer and Communications Security (CCS) (2011)
4. COSEINC. COSEINC OptiCode: Deobfuscate Machine Code. http://opticode.coseinc.com/
5. Gabriel, F.: Deobfuscation: recovering an OLLVM-protected program. http://blog.quarkslab.com/deobfuscation-recovering-an-ollvm-protected-program.html
6. Guillot, Y., Gazet, A.: Automatic binary deobfuscation. J. Comput. Virol. **6**(3), 261–276 (2010)
7. Junod, P., Rinaldini, J., Wehrli, J., Michielin, J.: Obfuscator-LLVM - software protection for the masses. In: Proceedings of the IEEE/ACM 1st International Workshop on Software Protection (SPRO) (2015)
8. Luk, C.K., Cohn, R., Muth, R., Patil, H., Klauser, A., Lowney, G., Wallace, S., Reddi, V.J., Hazelwood, K.: Pin: building customized program analysis tools with dynamic instrumentation (2005)
9. Oreans Inc. Oreans Technology: Software Security Defined. http://www.oreans.com/
10. Rolles, R.: Unpacking virtualization obfuscators. In: Proceedings of the 3rd USENIX Workshop on Offensive Technologies (WOOT) (2009)
11. Rolles, R.: The case for semantics-based methods in reverse engineering. In: RECON (2012)
12. Safengine.com. Safengine Protector. http://safengine.com/
13. Sharif, M., Lanzi, A., Giffin, J., Lee, W.: Automatic reverse engineering of malware emulators. In: Proceedings of the 30th IEEE Symposium on Security and Privacy (SP). IEEE (2009)
14. Smith, J., Nair, R.: Virtual Machines: Versatile Platforms for Systems and Processes. Elsevier, Amsterdam (2005)
15. Souchet, A.: Obfuscation, breaking kryptonite's: a static analysis approach relying on symbolic execution. http://doar-e.github.io/blog/2013/09/16/breaking-kryptonites-obfuscation-with-symbolic-execution/
16. StrongBit Technology. EXECryptor - bulletproof software protection. http://www.strongbit.com/execryptor.asp
17. VMProtect Inc. VMProtect Software Protection. http://vmpsoft.com/
18. Wressnegger, C., Boldewin, F., Rieck, K.: Deobfuscating embedded malware using probable-plaintext attacks. In: Stolfo, S.J., Stavrou, A., Wright, C.V. (eds.) RAID 2013. LNCS, vol. 8145, pp. 164–183. Springer, Heidelberg (2013). doi:10.1007/978-3-642-41284-4_9
19. Yadegari, B., Debray, S.: Symbolic execution of obfuscated code. In: Proceedings of the 22nd ACM Conference on Computer and Communications Security (CCS) (2015)
20. Yadegari, B., Johannesmeyer, B., Whitely, B., Debray, S.: A generic approach to automatic deobfuscation of executable code. In: Proceedings of the 36th IEEE Symposium on Security and Privacy (SP) (2015)

Run-Time Verification for Observational Determinism Using Dynamic Program Slicing

Mohammad Ghorbani and Mehran S. Fallah[(✉)]

Amirkabir University of Technology, 424 Hafez Ave., Tehran, Iran
{Mohammadghorbani,msfallah}@aut.ac.ir

Abstract. Information flow security states that secret information should not affect what is publicly observable. Such a requirement is usually expressed as a noninterference policy, which in general stipulates that the executions of a program must be indistinguishable to public observers when the program runs on inputs that differ only in secret values. When applied to multithreaded programs, an appropriate noninterference policy should specifically care about the nondeterministic behavior of programs resulting from the fact that the underlying scheduler is not known a priori. Observational determinism is such a policy that we aim to enforce in multithreaded programs. To do so, we first elaborate on how the inputs that are equivalent to public observers may lead to different public outputs. This, in turn, helps us propose a run-time verification mechanism based on threaded program dependence graphs and dynamic program slicing to prevent what causes the policy to be violated. The proposed mechanism is provably sound and is more permissive than analogous static mechanisms. It is also shown that the mechanism prevents illegal information flows when programs run in environments with different thread schedulers.

Keywords: Concurrent programs · Dynamic program slicing · Information flow security · Run-time verification · Observational determinism

1 Introduction

Information flow security is usually expressed as a noninterference policy. Such policies, in general, demand that runs of a secure program on inputs that differ only in secret (high) values be indistinguishable to public (low) observers, who can only observe public (low) values [1]. The enforcement of such a policy in multithreaded programs is more challenging than that in sequential programs because, in multithreaded programs, a variable may be defined in one thread and be used in another thread. In addition, a multithreaded program may run in an environment with a scheduler that is not known a priori. Thus, an appropriate information flow policy for such programs should be independent of the scheduler the program runs on.

There are a number of suggestions for an appropriate information flow policy for multithreaded programs among which observational determinism [2] has received great attention. This policy requires a program to be deterministic in the view of public observers. If all possible runs of a multithreaded program on low-equivalent inputs are indistinguishable to low observers, the program is deterministic in the view of low

© Springer International Publishing AG 2017
P.Q. Nguyen and J. Zhou (Eds.): ISC 2017, LNCS 10599, pp. 405–416, 2017.
https://doi.org/10.1007/978-3-319-69659-1_22

observers and satisfies observational determinism. This policy indeed formulates a scheduler-independent information flow policy.

One promising mechanism for information flow control is the use of data and control dependence graphs in identifying possible paths of information flows from secret to public variables [3]. Indeed, one should find those parts of a program, also known as a slice, that potentially influence the amounts calculated at a point of interest. Given a program dependence graph (PDG) and a slicing criterion, which is a node on the PDG, a slice for the node consists of all nodes from which there is a path to the slicing criterion. A noninterference policy can in general be enforced if the slice for any statement creating publicly observable values does not include the statements or expressions that depend on secret values [4–6].

Incorporating the concept of dependence analysis into multithreaded programs has led to so-called threaded PDGs (tPDGs) [7, 8]. In addition to the types of edges an ordinary PDG has, threaded PDGs also include edges to reflect the possibility of parallel execution and edges to address intransitive data dependence among threads. To employ tPDGs in the run-time verification of observational determinism, we also define two relations on the nodes of a tPDG. A node N_1 that defines a variable x in a thread is said to have a data conflict with any node N_2 defining or using x in another thread, provided the two threads can run concurrently. Moreover, any pair of nodes representing the commands that output values on public channels in concurrent threads are said to be in output conflict with each other.

By using tPDGs, we devise a mechanism that applies program slicing to enforcing observational determinism in multithreaded programs. To achieve a higher precision, however, we make use of dynamic slices instead of static ones. Indeed, among the nodes of the tPDG located in the slice for a given slicing criterion, we only consider the nodes that have already traversed in the current run of the program together with the untaken nodes controlled by secrets conditionals. Slicing criteria for enforcing observational determinism are outputs on public channels.

Whenever the program is going to execute a public output command, the proposed mechanism investigates if there exist data and control paths from the nodes defining secret variables to this output command in the corresponding dynamic slice. The mechanism suppress the execution of the output command if there exist such paths of information. The mechanism also checks that there are no pairs of nodes with data conflict relation in the dynamic slice of the public output command. If such nodes occur in the slice, the mechanism suppresses the output command. The mechanism also suppresses any public output that is in output conflict with some other output commands in the tPDG of the program. We evaluate the proposed mechanism by applying it to example multithreaded programs which run on different thread schedulers. We also give a formal proof of the soundness of the proposed mechanism.

This paper goes on as follows: Sect. 2 defines some basic concepts. In Sect. 3, we devise a run-time verification mechanism for observational determinism. Section 4 is on the verification of the proposed mechanism. Section 5 concludes the paper.

2 Preliminaries

A program slice consists of parts of a program that potentially affect the value of variables as well as the mere execution of the command at a particular point of the program [9–12]. Program slicing is to find such parts of the program given a so-called slicing criterion, which is a pair C of a point P of interest and a subset V of variables therein. A slice for C is a subset of commands in the original program. Static slicing is to find such a subset of commands irrespective of the actual path taken at run-time. A dynamic slice, on the contrary, does not include those commands not executed at run-time. By dynamic slicing, one can analyze programs more accurately [13]. Notice that program slicing may be based on abstract interpretation where properties of values, i.e., abstract values, are considered in lieu of concrete values at slicing criteria [14].

A program dependence graph (PDG) is a directed graph whose nodes represent statements or expressions of a program and edges represent data and control dependence among the nodes. PDGs are extended to threaded programs [7, 8] in which case they are called threaded PDGs or tPDGs for short. In addition to control and data dependencies, these graphs also encode so-called interference dependence among the nodes. A node N_2 of one thread is said to be interference dependent on a node N_1 of another thread if a variable used in N_2 is defined in N_1, provided the two threads can run concurrently.

Given the PDG of a sequential program, a slicing criterion is a node of the graph and the corresponding slice consists of all the nodes of the PDG having a path to the slicing criterion. Indeed, paths on PDGs reflect dependencies because data and control dependence are transitive relations. Paths on tPDGs, however, may not necessarily reflect dependencies among the nodes, since interference dependence is not transitive. Throughout this paper, we make use of the algorithms presented in [7, 8] to find the slices of multithreaded programs.

A noninterference policy in general states that the runs of a program on the same public (low) inputs should be the same in the view of public observers [1]. That is, any change in secret (high) inputs has no effect on public outputs of the program. An important instantiation of this concept for concurrent programs is known as observational determinism [2]. This policy is an appropriate formulation of information flow security for nondeterministic systems and demands that programs be deterministic in the view of public observers. Because the scheduling policy of the environment is not known a priori, a multithreaded program is indeed a nondeterministic system. Thus, observational determinism stipulates that low observers can learn nothing about high inputs no matter which scheduler the environment employs.

One may make use of PDGs for enforcing information flow policies in sequential programs [15–18]. It is known that if there is no path from a node N_1 to another N_2 on the PDG of a given program, no information flows from N_1 to N_2—we exclude the flows that result from side channels. This indicates that PDGs can be used in run-time verification for information flow policies [19–22]. In particular, PDGs may convey the lattice of security labels so that a number of flow relations, which are required for security, can be derived [16]. A run-time mechanism using dynamic slicing has also been devised for enforcing information flow policies in sequential programs [17].

A tool for analyzing information flow control in Java bytecode has also been introduced which derives PDGs from program texts and employs program slicing to enforce noninterference [23].

3   Dynamic Program Slicing for Enforcing Observational Determinism

We propose a run-time mechanism that uses tPDGs to enforce observational determinism. The mechanism computes dynamic slices and prevents illegal flows at run-time. Attackers are assumed to know the program, the low inputs to the program, and the values the program outputs on public channels.

The programming language we consider in this paper is a While language that supports multithreaded programming. For the sake of simplicity, it is assumed that programs do not include nested threads. Moreover, threads exchange information through shared memories. Every program begins with a block of input commands. The input block may be followed by a sequence of non-input commands that run sequentially. To create threads, one may put a number of threads $\{c\}$, separated by commas, between *cobegin* and *coend*. The command $input_L(var)$ reads a value from an input channel with security label L and stores it in the variable *var*. Similarly, $output_L(var)$ outputs the value of variable *var* on an output channel whose security label is L. Security labels are assumed to make a lattice $(\{L, H\}, \leq)$ where $L \leq H$. The syntax of the language is shown in Fig. 1.

$Program \ni P$ ::= *begin input; tstr end*
$C \ni c$ ::= *skip* | *var = exp* | *c; c* |
while b do c endw | *if b then c else c* endif| $output_L(exp)$ | $output_H(exp)$| λ
$Bool \ni b$ ::= *true* | *false* | *exp == exp*| *exp $\geq$ exp* |*exp < exp* | $\neg b$ | $b_1 \wedge b_2$ | $b_1 \vee b_2$
$OP \ni op$ ::= $*$ | $\backslash$ | $+$ | $-$
$Exp \ni exp$ ::= *exp op exp*| $n \in \mathbb{Z}$ | *var*
$Var \ni var$ ::= x | y | ... | w
$Input \ni input$ ::= $input_L(var)$ | $input_H(var)$ | *input; input*
$TStructure \ni tstr$ ::= *cobegin tdef coend* | *tstr; tstr* | *c* | λ
$TDefine \ni tdef$ ::= $\{c\}$ | *tdef, tdef*

Fig. 1. Syntax of the multithreaded while language.

Definition 1. An event is defined to be a triple $(type, label, val)$ where $type \in \{I, O\}$ indicates the type of the event which is either input (I) or output (O), *label* is the security label of the corresponding channel, and *val* is the value read form or written to the channel. A trace of a program is a sequence of events the program can generate at run-time. A low event is defined to be an event whose label is L. A low observable behavior of a program is a subsequence of a trace t of that program, denoted by t_L, obtained by removing high events from t.

Notice that any trace of any program of our multithreaded While language begins with a fixed number of input events. It is also worth noting that the sequence of events a program generates is obtained from the semantics of the language. Here, we assume the standard semantics of While languages [15, 24]. The root of the nondeterministic behavior of programs is in the way the unknown thread scheduler determines which thread should be run at a given step of a computation, see [25–27] for how one may model the interaction between a program and an unknown scheduler in the language semantics.

Definition 2. A program is said to satisfy observational determinism if for every pair t and u of traces of that program, $t_L = u_L$ holds whenever $t_L^{in} = u_L^{in}$, where t_L^{in} is the subsequence of t consisting of low input events.

Definition 3. A node N_1 in the tPDG of a multithreaded program defining a variable in a thread is said to have data conflict with another node N_2 in another thread if N_2 defines or uses that variable and the two threads can run concurrently. Two nodes in different threads are said to have output conflict if the nodes represent the commands that output public values and the threads can run concurrently.

We present a run-time verification mechanism for observational determinism. The mechanism makes use of the tPDG of the target program and the nodes marked at run-time to decide whether an output command should be suppressed. The proposed mechanism indeed derives the dynamic slice of low output commands from the tPDG of the program as well as the actions the program takes at run-time. In this way, the mechanism is able to guarantees that

- the target program never outputs the low values that depend on high inputs,
- data conflicts have no effect on low outputs, and
- the program never runs the commands having output conflict.

The first point above ensures that implicit and explicit flows do not leak high information. The second and the third guarantee that the value and the order of public outputs do not depend on the underlying scheduler. Figure 2 gives a high-level description of how the proposed mechanism uses tPDGs to enforce these requirements. The mechanism can indeed be thought of as an algorithm (program) that runs in parallel with the target program. It is assumed that each thread has its own program counter, which keeps track of the commands of the thread that have already been executed. If the mechanism decides not to execute the command of the current thread, the program counter of that thread is incremented without the execution of that command. Notice that the scheduler selects a thread for execution after the execution of an instruction. The following are the functions used in Fig. 2.

- *MarkAsExecuted(PC)*: marks as executed the node of the tPDG represented by *PC*.
- *DynamicSlice(PC)*: calculates the dynamic slice for the slicing criterion represented by *PC*.
- *eval(e)*: returns the value of expression e.
- *MarkRegionAsExecuted(PC, b)*: gets a program counter and a Boolean value and marks as executed the nodes representing the branch of the control structure not taken in case the value of the condition part is *b*.
- *StatementAt(PC)*: returns the statement *PC* points to.

```
//Verify observational determinism using tPDGs
//PC_Thread[Num] is the program counter of the thread NUM

INPUTS:
    1. A tPDG with data and output conflict relations
    2. Secret = the set of secret variables
while (not end of program) do
  Num = Get the thread number from the scheduler();
  MarkAsExecuted(PC_Thread[Num]);
  Case statementAt(PC_Thread[Num]) do
    output:
        if (PC_Thread[Num] is in output-conflict relation) then
            PC_Thread[Num] = PC_Thread[Num] + 1; //NOP
            Continue; // Go to while statement
        endif
        if (DynamicSlice(PC_Thread[Num]) ∩ Secret != Ø) then
            PC_Thread[Num] = PC_Thread[Num] + 1;
            Continue;
        endif
         List = EnterDC(DynamicSlice(PC_Thread[Num]));
        If (List != Ø)
            PC_Thread[Num] = PC_Thread[Num] + 1;
            Continue;
        endif
    if(e):
        if (DynamicSlice(PC_Thread[Num]) ∩ Secret != Ø) then
            MarkRegionAsExecuted(PC_Thread[Num],not eval(e));
        endif
    while(e):
        if (DynamicSlice(PC_Thread[Num]) ∩ Secret != Ø) then
            if (eval(e) == false) then
                MarkRegionAsExecuted(PC_Thread[Num],true);
            endif
        endif
  endCase
  execute(PC_Thread[Num]);
  PC_Thread[Num] = PC_Thread[Num] + 1;
Wend
```

Fig. 2. A run-time verification mechanism for observational determinism based on tPDGs and dynamic program slicing.

- *EnterDC(DynamicSlice(PC))*: returns the nodes having data conflict with the nodes in the dynamic slice of the slicing criterion represented by *PC*.

The mechanism described in Fig. 2 operates as follows: it marks as executed any statement on the tPDG of the program before executing the statement. To control information flow, the mechanism conducts specific run-time analyses of output commands and control structures. For an output command in the current thread, the mechanism first checks that its corresponding node on the tPDG is not in output conflict relation to any other output command of the program. Then, the mechanism verifies that there is no explicit or implicit information flow from secret variables to this output command. Moreover, it is checked that no node in the tPDG of the program is in data conflict relation to some node in the dynamic slice of this output command. If the verification fails in any of the stages above, the mechanism suppresses the execution of the output command and goes to the next command to be executed. It is worth noting that the mechanism may also replace such an output command with some other commands [15]. The mechanism marks the untaken branch of a conditional statement whenever there exists a secret variable in the dynamic slice of the node representing the condition part of the statement.

4 Verifying the Proposed Mechanism

To illustrate how effective the proposed mechanism is, we apply it to the program of Fig. 3 in environments with different schedulers. We also give a formal proof of the soundness of the mechanism. In what follows, it is assumed that all threads are within a main thread and each thread has its own program counter. The threads of a program are numbered with natural numbers and the main thread is numbered 0. The thread numbered i is denoted by T_i and its program counter is noted PC_i. The tPDG of the program of Fig. 3 is shown in Fig. 4. The mechanism is applied to the program where the environment employs a round-robin or a FIFO scheduler and the results are given in Tables 1 and 2. Notice that nodes N_{11} and N_{16} are in output conflict relation to each other and N_{14} are in data conflict relation to N_{11}. There are no other pairs in output conflict and data conflict relations associated with the tPDG of the program.

```
                    begin
    1                   inputH(h1);
    2                   inputH(h2);
    3                   inputL(l1);
    4                   inputL(l2);
                        cobegin {
    5                       l1 = 2;
    6                       if (h1 >= 0) then
    7                           Skip;
    8                           Skip;
    9                           Skip
                                            else
    10                          Skip
                            endif;
    11                      outputL (l1)
                            }, {
    12                      while (h2 < 0) do
    13                          h1 = h1 + 1
                            endw;
    14                      l1 = 3;
    15                      l2 = 4;
    16                      outputL (l2)
                            }
                        coend
                    end
```

Fig. 3. A program of the multithreaded while language.

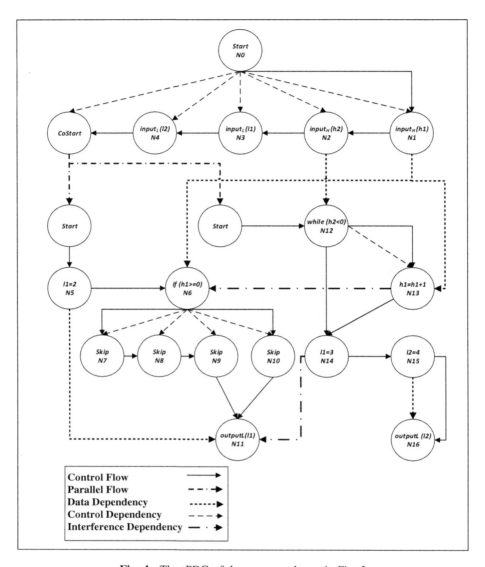

Fig. 4. The tPDG of the program shown in Fig. 3

Table 1 gives the result of executing the program of Fig. 3 in the presence of the proposed run-time mechanism and in an environment with a round-robin scheduler. The inputs are $h1 = 1$, $h2 = 2$, $l1 = 1$, and $l_2 = 2$. The secret variables are those that occur at lines 1 and 2. Thus, the set of secret variables is $Secret = \{1, 2\}$. For the sake of simplicity, we take PC_i to be equal to the line numbers the program counter points to. The action $execute(PC_i)$ denotes executing the command PC_i refers to. By $mark(PC_i)$, we mean the mechanism marks as executed the corresponding node on the given tPDG. Moreover, $slice(PC_i)$ is the result of computing the dynamic slice for the

Table 1. The result of executing the program shown in Fig. 3 using the proposed mechanism where the run-time environment uses a round-robin scheduler.

Secret = $\{1,2\}$, Inputs: h1 = 1, h2 = 2, l1 = 1, l2 = 2

PC₁	PC₂	T	Memory	Mechanism's actions	After execution
5		T_1	[h1 = 1, h2 = 2, l1 = 1, l2 = 2]	execute (5)	l1 = 2 PC₁ = 6
	12	T_2	[h1 = 1, h2 = 2, l1 = 2, l2 = 2]	slice(12) = {2}, mark (13), execute(12)	PC₂ = 14
6		T_1	[h1 = 1, h2 = 2, l1 = 2, l2 = 2]	slice(6) = {1, 13}, mark(10), execute(6)	PC₁ = 7
	14	T_2	[h1 = 1, h2 = 2, l1 = 2, l2 = 2]	execute (14)	l1 = 3 PC₂ = 15
7		T_1	[h1 = 1, h2 = 2, l1 = 3, l2 = 2]	execute (7)	PC₁ = 8
	15	T_2	[h1 = 1, h2 = 2, l1 = 3, l2 = 2]	execute (15)	L2 = 4 PC₂ = 16
8		T_1	[h1 = 1, h2 = 2, l1 = 3, l2 = 4]	execute (8)	PC₁ = 9
	16	T_2	[h1 = 1, h2 = 2, l1 = 3, l2 = 4]	slice(16) = {15}	END T_2
9		T_1	[h1 = 1, h2 = 2, l1 = 3, l2 = 4]	execute (9)	PC₁ = 11
11		T_1	[h1 = 1, h2 = 2, l1 = 3, l2 = 4]	slice(11) = {5, 14}	END T_1

node represented by PC_i. It is also assumed that one command is executed in every quantum of the scheduler. As seen, output command at lines 11 and 16 are not executed, and thus, a low observer sees no output when the program runs under the proposed mechanism. As seen in Table 2, the same holds when the program runs in an environment with a FIFO scheduler. This demonstrates that the proposed mechanism can enforce observational determinism.

4.1   Proof of Soundness

We prove that the proposed mechanism is sound for observational determinism. That is, by using the mechanism, for every program of the multithreaded While language, a low observer sees the same sequence of low events irrespective of the high inputs to the program and the thread scheduler employed by the run-time environment.

Lemma 1. Let t and u be two traces of program P and $t_L^{in} = u_L^{in}$. Then, the position of a low output event produced by a specific output command in P is the same in t_L and u_L whenever P runs in the presence of the proposed mechanism.

Proof. Suppose that e is a low output event at position i of t_L which results from the execution of an output command c at a specific line of P. This occurs if c is not in

Table 2. The result of executing the program shown in Fig. 3 using the proposed mechanism where the run-time environment uses a FIFO scheduler.

Secret = {1,2}, Inputs:h1 = 1, h2 = 2, l1 = 1, l2 = 2					
PC_1	PC_2	T	Memory	Mechanism's actions	After execution
5		T_1	[h1 = 1, h2 = 2, l1 = 1, l2 = 2]	execute (5)	L1 = 2 PC_1 = 6
6		T_1	[h1 = 1, h2 = 2, l1 = 2, l2 = 2]	slice(6) = {1, 13}, mark (10), execute(6)	PC_1 = 7
7		T_1	[h1 = 1, h2 = 2, l1 = 2, l2 = 2]	execute(7)	PC_1 = 8
8		T_1	[h1 = 1, h2 = 2, l1 = 2, l2 = 2]	execute (8)	PC_1 = 9
9		T_1	[h1 = 1, h2 = 2, l1 = 2, l2 = 2]	execute (9)	PC_1 = 11
11		T_1	[h1 = 1, h2 = 2, l1 = 2, l2 = 2]	slice(11) = {5,14}	PC_1 = 12 END T_1
	12	T_2	[h1 = 1, h2 = 2, l1 = 2, l2 = 2]	slice(12) = {2}, mark(13), execute (12)	PC_2 = 14
	14	T_2	[h1 = 1, h2 = 2, l1 = 2, l2 = 2]	execute (14)	PC_2 = 15 l1 = 3
	15	T_2	[h1 = 1, h2 = 2, l1 = 3, l2 = 4]	execute (15)	PC_2 = 16 l2 = 4
	16	T_2	[h1 = 1, h2 = 2, l1 = 3, l2 = 4]	slice(16) = {15}	END T_2

output conflict relation to any other nodes of the tPDG of P. Also, assume that e' is an event at position j of u which occurs when c is executed. If $i \neq j$, it has been possible for c to run concurrently with some other output commands of P. This means that c is in output conflict relation to some other output command, which is a contradiction.

Lemma 2. Let e be a low output event in a trace t of program P that is executed in the presence of the proposed mechanism. Then, the same event e occurs in any trace u with $u_L^{in} = t_L^{in}$.

Proof. Because e occurs in t in the presence of the proposed mechanism, the command c producing e does not depend on high variables. Moreover, there exists no node on the tPDG of P that is in data conflict to any node the dynamic slice of c. Similarly, c is not in output conflict to any node of the tPDG of P. Thus, e occurs in any other trace u with $u_L^{in} = t_L^{in}$.

Theorem 1. The proposed mechanism is sound for observational determinism.

Proof. It is immediate form Lemmas 1 and 2.

5   Conclusion

This paper proposes a run-time verification mechanism for observational determinism. The mechanism is based on modified dynamic slices of multithreaded programs. The proposed mechanism indeed ensures a fixed order of execution for the nodes whose execution leads to low observable outputs. In doing so, the mechanism prevents any race on public outputs. It also guarantees that there is no explicit or implicit flow from high to low information resulting from the sequential or concurrent execution of commands. We prove that the proposed mechanism is sound and give examples showing how the mechanism prevents illegal flows when programs run on different thread schedulers. Extending the ideas presented in this paper to the languages supporting classes, objects, and other features of modern languages deserves future research. Another challenging problem is to modify the mechanism so that it can suppress fewer output commands.

References

1. Goguen, J. A., Meseguer, J.: Security policies and security models. In: IEEE Symposium on Security and Privacy, p. 11. IEEE (1982)
2. Zdancewic, S., Myers, A.C.: Observational determinism for concurrent program security. In: 16th Proceedings on Computer Security Foundations Workshop, pp. 29–43. IEEE (2003)
3. Johnson, A., Waye, L., Moore, S., Chong, S.: Exploring and enforcing security guarantees via program dependence graphs. In: Proceedings of the 36th ACM SIGPLAN Conference on Programming Language Design and Implementation, pp. 291–302. ACM (2015)
4. Abadi, M., Banerjee, A., Heintze, N., Riecke, N.G.: A core calculus of dependency. In: Proceedings of the 26th ACM SIGPLAN-SIGACT Symposium on Principles of Programming Languages, pp. 147–160. ACM (1999)
5. Bergeretti, J.F., Carré, B.A.: Information-flow and data-flow analysis of while-programs. ACM Trans. Program. Lang. Syst. (TOPLAS) 7(1), 36–61 (1985)
6. Robschink, T., Snelting, G.: Efficient path conditions in dependence graphs. In: Proceedings of the 24th International Conference on Software Engineering, pp. 478–488. ACM (2002)
7. Krinke, J.: Advanced slicing of sequential and concurrent programs. In: Proceedings of the 20th IEEE International Conference on Software Maintenance, pp. 464–468. IEEE (2004)
8. Krinke, J.: Advanced slicing of sequential and concurrent programs. PhD thesis, University of Passau (2003)
9. Weiser, M.: Program slices: formal, psychological, and practical investigations of an automatic program abstraction method, PhD thesis, University of Michigan (1979)
10. Weiser, M.: Programmers use slices when debugging. Commun. ACM 25(7), 446–452 (1982)
11. Weiser, M.: Program slicing. IEEE Trans. Softw. Eng. 10(4), 352–357 (1984)
12. Tip, F.: A survey of program slicing techniques. Technical report, Amsterdam, The Netherlands (1994)
13. Korel, B., Laski, J.: Dynamic program slicing. Inf. Process. Lett. 29(3), 155–163 (1988)
14. Mastroeni, I., Zanardini, D.: Abstract program slicing: an abstract interpretation-based approach to program slicing. ACM Trans. Comput. Logic (TOCL) 18(1), 7 (2017)
15. Afshin, L., Fallah, M.S.: Rewriting-based enforcement of noninterference in programs with observable intermediate values. J. Univers. Comput. Sci. 22(7), 956–991 (2016)

16. Hammer, C., Snelting, G.: Flow-sensitive, context-sensitive, and object-sensitive information flow control based on program dependence graphs. Int. J. Inf. Secur. **8**(6), 399–422 (2009)
17. Cavadini, S., Cheda, D.: Run-time information flow monitoring based on dynamic dependence graphs. In: 3th International Conference on Availability, Reliability and Security, pp. 586–591. IEEE (2008)
18. Hammer, C.: Experiences with PDG-based IFC. In: Massacci, F., Wallach, D., Zannone, N. (eds.) ESSoS 2010. LNCS, vol. 5965, pp. 44–60. Springer, Heidelberg (2010). doi:10.1007/978-3-642-11747-3_4
19. Horwitz, S., Prins, J., Reps, T.: On the adequacy of program dependence graphs for representing programs. In: Proceedings of the 15th ACM SIGPLAN-SIGACT Symposium on Principles of Programming Languages, pp. 146–157. ACM (1988)
20. Hammer, C.: Information flow control for Java: A comprehensive approach based on path conditions in dependence graphs. PhD Thesis, Univ-Verlag Karlsruhe (2009)
21. Ranganath, V.P., Amtoft, T., Banerjee, A., Hatcliff, J., Dwyer, M.B.: A new foundation for control dependence and slicing for modern program structures. ACM Trans. Program. Lang. Syst. (TOPLAS) **29**(5), 27 (2007)
22. Wasserrab, D., Lohner, D., Snelting, G.: On PDG-based noninterference and its modular proof. In: Proceedings of the ACM SIGPLAN Fourth Workshop on Programming Languages and Analysis for Security, pp. 31–44. ACM (2009)
23. Graf, J., Hecker, M., Mohr, M.: Using JOANA for information flow control in Java programs-a practical guide. In: Software Engineering (Workshops), pp. 123–138 (2013)
24. Giacobazzi, R., Mastroeni, I.: A proof system for abstract non-interference. J. Logic Comput. **20**(2), 449–479 (2009)
25. Iranmanesh, Z., Fallah, M.S.: Specification and static enforcement of scheduler-independent noninterference in a middleweight java. Comput. Lang. Syst. Struct. **46**, 20–43 (2016)
26. Terauchi, T.: A type system for observational determinism. In: 21th Computer Security Foundations Symposium, pp. 287–300. IEEE (2008)
27. Huisman, M., Worah, P., Sunesen, K.: A temporal logic characterisation of observational determinism. In: 19th Computer Security Foundations Workshop. IEEE (2006)

Automated Analysis of Accountability

Alessandro Bruni, Rosario Giustolisi$^{(\boxtimes)}$, and Carsten Schuermann

IT University of Copenhagen, Copenhagen, Denmark
rosg@itu.dk

Abstract. A recent trend in the construction of security protocols such as voting and certificate management systems is to make principals *accountable* for their actions. Whenever some principals deviate from the protocol's prescription and cause the failure of a goal of the system, accountability ensures that the system can detect the misbehaving parties who caused that failure. Accountability is an intuitively stronger property than *verifiability* as the latter only rests on the possibility of detecting the failure of a goal. A plethora of accountability and verifiability definitions have been proposed in the literature. Those definitions are either very specific to the protocols in question, hence not applicable in other scenarios, or too general and widely applicable but requiring complicated and hard to follow manual proofs.

In this paper, we advance formal definitions of verifiability and accountability that are amenable to automated verification. Our definitions are general enough to be applied to different classes of protocols and different automated security verification tools. Furthermore, we point out formally the relation between verifiability and accountability. We validate our definitions with the automatic verification of three protocols: a secure exam protocol, Google's Certificate Transparency, and an improved version of Bingo Voting. We find through automated verification that all three protocols satisfy verifiability while only the first two protocols meet accountability.

1 Introduction

In the real world, disputes among principals can be resolved with trials. A judge or jury will decide on a trial according to the evidence presented by the parties. In the digital world, even if the design of a security protocol is sound, dishonest principals may still attempt attacks that cause protocol functional failures. Similarly to real-world protocols, principals should be able to raise disputes in which a judge blames principals who caused the failure according to the evidence. This notion is known as *accountability* and ensures that (i) failures are detectable and (ii) misbehaving principals can be blamed. Accountability is a stronger notion than *verifiability* as the latter only requires that the failure of a protocol's goal can be detectable [1]. Thus, security protocols should be designed to provide adequate evidence to enable accountability. In so doing, principals are discouraged to misbehave, fostering minimal intentional protocol failures.

© Springer International Publishing AG 2017
P.Q. Nguyen and J. Zhou (Eds.): ISC 2017, LNCS 10599, pp. 417–434, 2017.
https://doi.org/10.1007/978-3-319-69659-1_23

Contribution. The goal of this paper is to fully mechanise the analysis of verifiability and accountability in security protocols. We propose definitions based on the existence of an accountability test that decides whether a principal should be blamed for the failure of a protocol's goal. We conveniently adapt a generic definition of protocol advanced by Küsters et al. [2] to specify the soundness and completeness conditions for accountability tests that can be checked by automated security protocol tools. We show that verifiability is a necessary condition for accountability and our treatment of accountability is general enough to apply to different tools and protocols. Then, we validate our definitions in three different case studies with two different tools. The first case study is about a secure exam protocol, and we check accountability with ProVerif [3]. The second case study concerns Google's Certificate Transparency, and we prove accountability with AIF-ω [4]. The third case study considers an improved version of Bingo Voting, which is analysed again with ProVerif.

Outline. The paper is organised as follows. Section 2 discusses some related work. Section 3 details our definitions of verifiability and accountability. Section 4 validates the definitions in a secure exam protocol. Section 5 details the formal analysis of Google's Certificate Transparency. Section 6 analyses verifiability and accountability in Bingo Voting. Finally, Sect. 7 concludes the paper.

2   Related Work

In this paper we define an accountability test, which can be used to decide if a protocol is accountable, meaning if it has the capability to single out reliably the parties (if any) that are compromised and behaving dishonestly. A precondition for our accountability test is verifiability that is designed to detect if something went wrong in the first place. The hallmark characteristic of our accountability and verifiability definitions is that they are mechanizable in the symbolic model. The definition of our criterion is formalism and tool independent, which sets it apart from related projects, which we discuss briefly below.

Our work builds on the work by Küsters et al. [2] who define notions of accountability and verifiability in the symbolic and computational models. The symbolic definitions aim at precisely describing the assessment of the level of accountability that a protocol provides. This comes at the cost of definitions that may not be amenable to automated analysis as the verification approach would heavily depend on the accountability property under consideration. Differently, our definitions are explicitly adapted for checking accountability with automated security protocol tools. To aid the reader familiar with Küsters et al. work in comparing our work to theirs, we revisit in this paper the example of Bingo Voting, whose analysis was supported with manual proofs in Küsters et al.'s work.

Milner et al. [5] focus on a provably sound detection of misuse of secrets. Their work has yielded new insights into detecting the misuse of a Certification Authorities key on the Internet and contributed to the broader area of Certificate

Transparency. Again, to aid the reader familiar with this work to compare their results to ours, we demonstrate how to mechanise this argument in AIF-ω [4].

Jagadessan et al. [6] proposed a framework that deals with the general notion of accountability but cannot deal with cryptography. Bella and Paulson [7] advanced a computer-assisted analysis of accountability of the Zhou-Gollman non-repudiation protocol [8]. Similarly, Abadi and Blanchet [9] analysed accountability for a certified email protocol. The definitions proposed in these works are not general but specific to the protocols in question.

The notion of verifiability has been extensively studied in voting [1,10]. The notion of *individual verifiability* signifies that voters can verify that their votes have been handled correctly, namely "cast as intended", "recorded as cast", and "counted as recorded" [11,12]. The notion of *universal verifiability* has been introduced to express the concept in which auditors can verify the correctness of the tally using only public information [11,13,14]. Kremer et al. [10] formalised both individual and universal verifiability in the applied pi-calculus. They also introduced the requirement of *eligibility verifiability*, which expresses that auditors can verify that each vote in the election result was cast by a registered voter, and there is at most one vote per voter. Smyth et al. [15] used ProVerif to check verifiability in three voting protocols. They express the requirements as reachability properties. Similarly, Dreier et al. [16] checked in ProVerif soundness and completeness conditions for verifiability-tests in three auction protocols. In this paper, we also analyse two security protocols in ProVerif. However, our definitions of verifiability and accountability are constrained neither to the applied pi-calculus nor ProVerif.

Guts et al. [17] defined *auditability* as the quality of a protocol, which stores a sufficient number of pieces of evidence, to convince an honest judge that specific properties are satisfied. Auditability is a weaker notion of accountability and expresses the same concept of universal verifiability: anyone, even an outsider without a private knowledge about the protocol execution, can verify that the system relies only on the available pieces of evidence.

3 Definitions

We begin our formal treatment with the formal definition of a protocol, following roughly the exposition of Küsters et al. [2]. Our definitions differ from theirs to support better the mechanisation effort discussed below.

Definition 1 (Protocol). *A protocol is a tuple* $P = \langle \mathsf{Ch}, \mathsf{A}, \Pi, \mathsf{G} \rangle$ *such that:*

- $\mathsf{Ch} = \{ch_1, \ldots, ch_n\}$ *is a set of* channels;
- $\mathsf{A} = \{\alpha_1, \ldots, \alpha_n\}$ *is a set of* principals;
- Π *is the set of* programs *run by the principals;*
- G *is the set of* goals *that the protocol aims to meet.*

Given a set of primitive operations, for example, for sending and receiving messages on channels, encrypting and decrypting messages using keys, etc. we refer to sequences of such operations as *programs*. The set of all such programs is denoted by Π, with the intention that for each run of the protocol each principal $\alpha_i \in \mathsf{A}$ is expected to running one and only one such program $\pi_{\alpha_i} \in \Pi$. We write r for a *run* of the protocol. Each run produces a trace. A *witness trace*, which we denote with t, is a run of the protocol from the point of the view of a principal and serves as input and evidence for the verifiability and accountability tests. We do not distinguish between input and output channels. Instead, we introduce predicates $g \in G$ that range over traces and distinguish the traces that achieve the *goal* of a protocol from those that do not. As we shall see later, verifiability and accountability definitions are pivoted on protocol's goal. Thus, we detail its treatment here to obtain clearer definitions later.

For each set of goals G, we define Π^G as the set of all tuples $\{\pi_{\alpha_i}\}_{\alpha_i \in \mathsf{A}}$, where each such tuple defines one program for each respective principal, that converge towards satisfying all the goal defined within G, when running in parallel, as $(\pi_{\alpha_1} | \pi_{\alpha_2} | \dots | \pi_{\alpha_n})$. For instance, let us consider two principals, Alice and Bob, who will communicate over some channel. The goal g of this protocol is that Bob eventually receives some message. Let us consider the protocol consisting of two programs $(\pi^1_{\text{Alice}}, \pi^1_{\text{Bob}})$ that Alice and Bob are expected to run. The first program consists of π^1_{Alice} that sends one message while the other π^1_{Bob} expects to receive some message. Now, let us assume that Alice runs a different program π^2_{Alice} that sends two messages. Although Alice runs a program that deviates from the original protocol prescription, the tuple of programs $(\pi^2_{\text{Alice}}, \pi^1_{\text{Bob}})$ still clearly converges towards the goal. Consequently, $(\pi^1_{\text{Alice}}, \pi^1_{\text{Bob}}) \in \Pi^g$ as well as $(\pi^2_{\text{Alice}}, \pi^1_{\text{Bob}}) \in \Pi^g$. We say that both programs $\pi^1_{\text{Alice}}, \pi^2_{\text{Alice}}$ are *goal-convergent*. The specification of goals is left to the specific formalism adopted by the chosen tool.

The introduction of the set Π^G is useful to clarify the notion of *misbehaviour*. A principal may run a program that deviates from the original protocol prescription, but if such deviation is irrelevant for the purpose of achieving the goal, the principal should not be considered as a misbehaving entity. This notion of misbehaviour contrasts from the usual interpretation that a principal misbehaves if she runs any program that differs from the expected one. However, our interpretation is necessary for accountability as in a dispute a judge should never blame a principal who runs a goal-convergent program.

Having seen the definition of a protocol, we can specify the definition of *verifiability test* as follows.

Definition 2 (Verifiability Test). *A verifiability test* $\mathtt{vt}(\mathcal{T}, \mathtt{g}) : \mathtt{bool}$ *is an efficient and terminating algorithm such that:*

- $\mathcal{T}$ *is a set of witness traces;*
- $\mathtt{g}$ *is a goal in* G.

The verifiability test should return $\mathtt{true}$ if, according to the evidence, a protocol run met the goal. It should return $\mathtt{false}$ otherwise. In other words, the verifiability test returns $\mathtt{true}$ if it accepts the set of witness traces, and $\mathtt{false}$ otherwise. Definition 3 formalises the concept of verifiability.

Definition 3 (g-verifiability). *A Protocol P is* g-verifiable *if P admits a verifiability test* vt *that meets the following conditions:*

1. *(soundness)* $\text{vt}(\mathcal{T}, g) : \text{true} \implies g$ *holds in* $r(P)$;
2. *(completeness)* g *holds in* $r(P) \implies \text{vt}(\mathcal{T}, g) : \text{true}$;

for any run $r(P)$.

The soundness condition guarantees that the verifiability test returns true only if the goal holds in a run. However, this condition alone is not sufficient: a verifiability test that always returns false is sound but useless. Such kind of possibilities is ruled out with the completeness condition. Completeness implicitly states that the verifiability test cannot fail if all principals execute programs that converge towards the goal. It follows that P is correct as it meets the goal when all principals behave honestly.

Both soundness and completeness conditions can be checked automatically with cryptographic tools as reachability properties. For soundness, we check that there exists no trace in which we reach a state where the verifiability test returns true while the goal does not hold. For completeness, we check that there exists no trace in which we reach a state where the verifiability test returns false assuming all principals being honest. The analysis of three case studies considered later in this paper demonstrates that such mechanisation is possible.

Next, we focus on accountability, more precisely on a test that can be used to identify those principals who are responsible in the case a goal is not reached.

Definition 4 (Accountability Test). *An accountability test* $\text{at}_{\alpha_y}(\mathcal{T}, g, A)$: bool *is an efficient and terminating algorithm such that:*

- $\mathcal{T}$ *is a set of witness traces;*
- g *is a goal in* G;
- α_y *is an indicted principal over the set of principals* A.

The definition of the accountability test is methodologically close to the definition of verifiability. The test should return true if according to the witness traces the indicted principal α_y did not run a goal-convergent program, namely $\pi_{\alpha_i} \notin \Pi^g_{\alpha_y}$. The test should return false otherwise.

Now, we can advance a definition of accountability that is centred around a principal and a protocol's goal.

Definition 5 ((α_y, g)-accountability). *A Protocol P is* (α_y, g)-accountable *if given an indicted principal* $\alpha_y \in A$, *a goal* g, *and the set of its goal-convergent programs* $\Pi^g_{\alpha_y}$, *P meets the following conditions*

1. *P is* g-*verifiable;*

and P admits an accountability test at_{α_y} *that meets the following conditions:*

2. *(soundness)* $\text{at}_{\alpha_y}(\mathcal{T}, g) : \text{false} \implies \pi_{\alpha_y} \in \Pi^g_{\alpha_y}$;
3. *(completeness)* $\pi_{\alpha_y} \in \Pi^g_{\alpha_y} \implies \text{at}_{\alpha_y}(\mathcal{T}, g) : \text{false}$.

for any run $r(P)$.

Condition 1 guarantees that the event that triggers the failure can be identified, namely anyone can be convinced that a run of P failed to ensure the goal. The relation between verifiability and accountability becomes clear here. If a goal is not verifiable, then we cannot account any principal because we cannot state whether the protocol run met the goal or not. Hence, verifiability is a precondition for accountability. Note that condition 1 is goal-centred and independent from the indicted principal α_y.

Conditions 2 and 3 are defined similarly to the corresponding conditions for verifiability: the accountability test returns `true` if it accepts the set of witness traces, and `false` otherwise. Soundness guarantees that the accountability test returns `false` only if the indicted principal runs a goal-convergent program. Completeness states that the accountability test cannot return `true` if the indicted principal runs a goal-convergent program.

Remark. Verifiability is essential to have a meaningfulness definition of accountability. For example, let us assume a protocol P with three principals α_1, α_2, and α_3 of which only α_1 is partially g-accountable (i.e. P is partially (α_1, g)-accountable) according to conditions 2 and 3 only. If α_1 is not guilty (i.e. the accountability test fails), then we cannot say anything else about accountability in P without condition 1 since α_1 is the only culpable principal. In particular, we cannot say whether P failed because either or both α_1 and α_2 misbehaved or due to an external attacker. We cannot even say if the protocol meets the goal. If we can rule out the possibility for an external attacker, thanks to Condition 1, we know that at least either or both α_1 and α_2 misbehaved although P is neither (α_1, g)-accountable nor (α_2, g)-accountable, something that we would miss without Condition 1.

Finally, we propose the definition of *full* **g**-*accountability*. It states that a protocol is fully accountable for a goal if the protocol is accountable for each principal on that goal.

Definition 6 (Full g-accountability). *A Protocol P is fully* **g**-accountable *if* $\forall \alpha \in \mathsf{A}$, P *is* $(\alpha, \mathbf{g})$-*accountable for any run* $r(P)$.

It is easy to see that all three conditions in our definition of accountability can be checked automatically. Condition 1 regards verifiability, and we have already seen that soundness and completeness conditions of g-verifiability can be modelled as reachability properties to be automatically checked by cryptographic tools. Conditions 2 and 3 can also be modelled as reachability properties. In particular, soundness can be checked by showing that there exists no trace in which we reach a state where the accountability test returns `false` when all principals but the indicted are honest, and the verifiability test fails. For completeness, we check that there exists no trace in which we reach a state where the accountability test returns `true` when all principals but the indicted are dishonest.

Table 1 describes the systematic approach that can be used to check verifiability and accountability as reachability properties. This approach is validated

Table 1. Strategies to model verifiability and accountability as reachability properties.

Property	Condition	Principals controlled by the attacker	Strategy
Verifiability	Soundness	All (modulo the goal)	$\mathtt{vt}(\mathcal{T},\mathtt{g}) : \mathtt{true} \rightsquigarrow$ $\mathtt{g\_holds}$
	Completeness	None	$\mathtt{vt}(\mathcal{T},\mathtt{g}) : \mathtt{true}$
Accountability	Soundness	Indicted	$\mathtt{vt}(\mathcal{T},\mathtt{g}) : \mathtt{false} \rightsquigarrow$ $\mathtt{at}_{\alpha_y}(\mathcal{T},\mathtt{g}) : \mathtt{true}$
	Completeness	All but the indicted	$\mathtt{at}_{\alpha_y}(\mathcal{T},\mathtt{g}) : \mathtt{false}$

with two different tools and three different security protocols in the following sections.

4   Case Study I: Secure Exam Protocol

Bella et al. [18] propose a secure exam protocol that does not rely on any trusted party. Hence it can resist to corrupted candidates and authorities. The protocol involves four roles (i.e. candidate, administrator, examiner, and invigilator), and runs in four phases (i.e. preparation, testing, marking, and notification). The most interesting aspect of the protocol regards the outcome of preparation, in which candidate and administrator jointly generate the candidate's pseudonym as a pair of visual cryptography shares using an oblivious transfer scheme. One visual crypto share is held by the candidate, who prints it on a paper sheet together with signatures generated by the administrator. The other visual crypto share is printed by the administrator as a transparency printout and handed to the candidate at testing. Each share alone does not reveal the pseudonym, which the candidate learns only when the two shares are overlapped at testing. Thus, the goal of preparation is to distribute the generation of the two visual cryptography shares that, when overlapped, reveal an intelligible code. We consider this goal to analyse accountability, hence we leave testing, marking, and notification phases and focus only on the outcome of preparation in our analysis.

The idea underlying the preparation phase is that the candidate provides a commitment to an index into an array while the administrator fills the array with a secret permutation of the characters, and only when the two secrets are brought together is the selection of a character determined. Notably, no one learns anything about the code without the knowledge of both shares. The outcome of preparation is two sheets jointly generated by candidate and administrator using a combination of visual cryptography, commitment, and oblivious transfer schemes. The commitment scheme comes with a function $commit(\cdot, \cdot)$ that takes in a random value and a secret, and outputs the commitment. The oblivious transfer schemes consists of (i) the function $obf(\cdot, \cdot)$, which takes a commitment and a set of secrets, and returns a set of obfuscated values; and (ii) the function $deobf(\cdot, \cdot)$, which takes in a set of obfuscated values and a commitment, and returns the corresponding set of secrets.

The authors prove in ProVerif that the protocol meets a set of authentication, privacy, and verifiability properties. They also prove a form of accountability, but their definitions are specific to the protocol in question. Differently, we prove accountability using our general approach that can be applied to other protocols.

As we shall see later, our accountability tests take in the content of the paper and transparency sheets. The paper sheet contains the candidate visual share β, the set of candidate's chosen indexes I, the random commitment value c, and two signatures $sign1$ and $sign2$ both generated by the administrator and encoded as QR codes. The first signature contains the commitment com_A of the administrator on α. The second signature contains the commitment com_C of the candidate chosen indexes I, and the set of obfuscated values Ω due to the oblivious transfer scheme. The transparency printout contains the visual share α, and the random commitment value a on the administrator's commitment com_A. A succinct representation of the contents of the sheets is outlined in Table 2.

Table 2. The content of the paper and transparency sheets

Sheet	Content			Description
Paper (candidate)	β			Visual cryptography share
	c			Random commitment value on com_c
	I			Set of indexes chosen by the candidate
	$sign1$	com_A		Administrator's commitment
	$sign2$	com_C		Candidate's commitment on I
		Ω		Set of obfuscated values
Transparency (administrator)	α			Visual cryptography share
	a			Random commitment value on com_a

4.1 Analysis

Our analysis focuses on the goal of generating two correct visual shares. If so, an intelligible code should appear when the candidate overlaps paper and transparency sheets. We propose two distinct dispute resolution procedures (i.e. accountability tests) — one for the candidate and the other for the administrator — for which we can have formal guarantees of correctness. Our accountability tests can be used with the same sheets generated at preparation of the original protocol. We use ProVerif, an automatic protocol analyser that can prove reachability and equivalence-based properties in the Dolev-Yao model.

Verifiability. First, we demonstrate that the protocol is g-verifiable. Namely, there exists a verifiability test that is sound and complete according to Definition 3 for the goal of generating an intelligible pseudonym. We specify verifiability in ProVerif as a reachability property and use correspondence assertions to prove soundness. The verification scenario consists of checking that, for any execution of the protocol, all traces in which the verifiability test returns `true`, there is another event, earlier in the trace, that signals that the goal holds. In this case, the goal holds if both candidate and administrator print the correct visual shares on the respective sheets. The attacker may control either the administrator or the candidate, but we force two events to be emitted by candidate and administrator processes only when they print the correct visual shares. ProVerif proves that there exists no trace in which the attacker can input the verifiability test with false data so that the test returns `true` without that the goal holds.

The verification scenario to prove completeness consists of checking that, for any execution of the protocol in which the goal holds, the verifiability test returns `true`. In this case, the ProVerif model enforces only honest principals and prevents the attacker to manipulate the input data of the verifiability-tests. In fact, a complete verifiability-test must succeed if its input data is correct. Specifically, the overlapping of the two visual shares should always produce an intelligible code. ProVerif proves that there exists no trace in which the verifiability test returns `false` when its input data is correct. Since the proposed verifiability test is sound and complete, the protocol is g-verifiable.

Algorithm 1. The accountability test for the Candidate

Data:
- $paper = \beta, c, I, sign1, sign2$ where
  - $sign1 = Sign_A\{com_A\}$.
  - $sign2 = Sign_A\{com_C, \Omega\}$.
- $transp = \alpha, a$.

if $sign1 = \bot$ **or** $sign2 = \bot$ **or** $com_c \neq commit(c, I)$ **or** $\beta \neq deobf(\Omega, c)$ **then**
  | **return true**
else
  | **return false**

Accountability. We propose Algorithms 1 and 2 as accountability tests for candidate and administrator respectively. In the following, we show that both algorithms enable the protocol to meet soundness and completeness according Definition 5.

Accountability can be specified as reachability property, but the verification scenario to check the soundness of the accountability test differs from the one we have seen for verifiability. To check soundness, we leave the indicted principal under the control of the attacker (i.e., we force all principals but the indicted one to be honest). Then, if the protocol fails (i.e. the verifiability test returns

---

Algorithm 2. The accountability test for the Administrator

Data:
- $paper = \beta, c, I, sign1, sign2$ where
  - $sign1 = Sign_A\{com_A\}$.
  - $sign2 = Sign_A\{com_C, \Omega\}$.
- $transp = \alpha, a$.

if $sign1 \neq \perp$ **and** $sign2 \neq \perp$ **and** $com_A \neq commit(a, \alpha)$ **then**
| **return true**
else
| **return false**

`false`, we expect that the accountability test returns `true`, namely it blames the indicted principal for all traces and protocol runs. ProVerif proves that Algorithms 1 and 2 are sound since there exists no trace in which the accountability tests return `false` in such scenario.

The verification scenario to prove completeness is complementary to the scenario outlined above. We assume the indicted principal to be honest and leave all the others principals under the control of the attacker. We expect that the accountability test does not blame the indicted principal, hence it returns `false` for all traces and protocol run. ProVerif proves that Algorithms 1 and 2 are complete since there exists no trace in which the accountability test returns `true` in this verification scenario. Thus, we conclude that the secure exam protocol is verifiable and accountable for the goal of correctly generating and distributing the visual cryptography shares.

5 Case Study II: Certificate Transparency

Public Key Infrastructures (PKI) are the source of accountability for a very common use case: a client C – who wants to establish a secure connection to a server S – receives and checks a certificate issued by a certificate authority CA. A certificate essentially binds an identity S with a public key PK_S, along with other information such as the expiration date and a chain of certificates leading to a root CA, which we denote as $certs = sign_{CA}(PK_S, S, info)$. The strongest limitation of PKI is that the client should maintain a list of all trusted CAs (usually hundreds) and if even one of them becomes compromised and misbehaves, then the whole system is compromised. In fact, a dishonest server colluding with a compromised CA can obtain a signed certificate for another server identity and impersonate them, and this behaviour can go undetected since the dishonest server can show the certificate only to the targeted users. Moreover, the PKI standard does not require a CA to show which certificates it has issued.

5.1   Certificate Transparency

To solve the accountability problem of PKIs, Google proposed Certificate Transparency (CT) [19], an extension of standard PKIs that allows the servers to check that the CAs behave properly. It does so by maintaining a *public, append-only, cryptographic log of issued certificates* that anybody can check. When a client C wants to connect to S, she first receives from S their certificate $cert_S$, along with a cryptographic proof that $cert_S$ is included the log L. Conversely, the log can be audited either as a whole in a heavy-weight fashion, or in small parts by piggy backing a chatter protocol on top of the handshake between C and S, as shown with by the "cloud" in the communication diagram of Fig. 1.

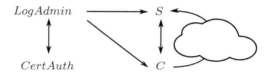

Fig. 1. Certificate Transparency, communication diagram

If a CA misbehaves then their misconduct will appear publicly in the log and will be revealed by auditing. On the other side, a log administrator colluding with a CA could produce two different histories for the client and the server: it could, for example, give S a log where there appears no fake certificate for S, and give C a log where such fake certificate appears, in order to convince her to connect to a rouge server. However, the log signs all histories presented to the various stakeholders, so if the log gives incompatible histories to different entities, their misbehaviour will eventually be detected, by comparing two incompatible histories. All these operations can be implemented efficiently by the use of Merkle trees [20], i.e. they require time and space $O(log(n))$ for n certificates in the log.

It is important to note that CT does not prevent attacks against clients: a CT-enabled client C checks validity and the presence of a certificate in a log, but nothing prevents C from accessing a compromised server S_D if both the validity check and the presence check succeed. CT ensures instead that—as long as the Log Administrators are honest—*eventually* the presence of a fake certificate is revealed to the legitimate owner of a certain domain, who can then take appropriate actions to contain the breach. Furthermore, it claims to support accountability for both the CA and the log administrator, in that if an attack happens there is evidence that they misbehaved: for the CA, this is the presence of a signed certificate without a proper proof of identity given by the legitimate owner, while for the Log Administrator, it is the presence of two incompatible histories, eventually revealed by two different parties exchanging them.

5.2   Analysis

We construct a symbolic model of the Certificate Transparency protocol and show that it satisfies both verifiability and accountability for the Certificate Authorities and the Log Administrators. We model the protocol with AIF-ω [4], which allows to encode stateful protocols by tracking the membership of values in a number of sets, indexed by agent names and other parameters. For example, the logs in our model are represented by a family of sets $log(LogAdmin, Server, Cert, Auth, User)$ of public keys, logged by a $LogAdmin$, issued for a $Server$ by a $CertAuth$, and presented to an $User$, where each camel-case word defines the respective role in the protocol. Therefore we allow an $la \in LogAdmin$ to present two different stories to two different users and treat a log as a database of signed public keys, related to the CAs that produced them and the servers that they represent. We abstract away from the implementation details using Merkle trees and enforce that their properties–efficient querying for the presence of a certificate, and efficient proofs of extension–are maintained in the database.

Verifiability. We show first that the protocol is g-verifiable according to Definition 3 for the goal of producing a valid certificate for a server. The soundness result specifies that, for all execution traces where the verifiability test succeeds, then the protocol has been executed only by an honest and behaving certificate authority and log administrator; in other words, there has not been a trace where a misbehaving CA or LA manage to pass the verifiability test. In this case, the goal holds if there is no scenario where a malicious certificate is produced that does not come with a proof of identity for its server and does not show two incompatible logs (i.e. one with the certificate and one missing it). Algorithms 3 and 4 check these conditions. That is, Algorithm 3 returns **true** if and only if the Certificate Authority lacks a valid proof of identity for the given combination of server and public key, and Algorithm 4 returns **true** iff there is evidence that the Log Administrator produces two logs log_1 and log_2 that are incompatible extensions of one another. It is important to stress that in this model we assume that there is a direct connection between the interested Server and Client comparing the two logs, whereas in reality there is an indirect channel realised by the chatter network, as shown in Fig. 1. Hence in the model, the check of Algorithm 4 is quantified over all possible pairs of logs, and this is not a problem for soundness, but for completeness it requires further justification.

Completeness requires that if a certificate is produced by a dishonest CA and logged only for the client by a dishonest LA, then the client and the server, communicating through the chatter network, will be able to discover the misbehaviour. In this case it is important to stress that this is a reachability property, in that *eventually* the client and server will be able to discover the misbehaviour through the chatter log, but that might be after the client has suffered a man-in-the-middle attack.

Accountability. The accountability test for the Certificate Authority and the Log Administrator coincide with Algorithms 3 and 4 considered singularly. From our

---

Algorithm 3. The accountability test for the Certificate Authority

Data:
- $cert = sign_{CA}(PK, S, info)$
- $poi = proofOfID(PK', S')$

if $poi = \perp$ **or** $PK \neq PK'$ **or** $S \neq S'$ **then**
  | return **true**
else
  | return **false**

Algorithm 4. The accountability test for the Log Administrator

Data:
- log_1
- log_2.

if $log_1 \not\preceq log_2$ **and** $log_2 \not\preceq log_1$ **then**
  | return **false**
else
  | return **true**

---

model, we prove that both algorithms are sound and complete: they do no blame any honest CA/LA, while in any case of a misbehaving CA/LA, there is a proof that they misbehaved.

It is interesting to note that the accountability test amounts to splitting the two checks of the verifiability test, which are aimed at indicting the Certificate Authority and the Log Administrator, respectively. In fact, if a protocol is fully accountable, i.e. if for every principal the accountability test is both sound and complete, we can produce a verifiability test by composing the accountability tests of each principal, therefore obtaining a verifiability test that is also both sound and complete.

6   Case Study III: Bingo Voting

Bingo Voting is a cryptographic voting scheme proposed by Bohli, Müller-Quade and Röhrich in 2007 [21]. It provides individual verifiability based on a trusted random number generator. Each voter receives a receipt that enables the voter to verify that the corresponding vote was counted correctly. But the receipt does not provide any information about how the voter voted to any third party. The original version of Bingo Voting does not include any dispute resolution procedure that enables voters to prove that some manipulation took place and their vote was altered. Küsters et al. [2] demonstrated that the original version also allows dishonest voters to spoil an election by wrongly complaining that the election was manipulated even if this is not the case. Bohli et al. [22] then proposed some improvements to the original scheme that enable dispute resolution procedures during the voting and the tallying phases. In this paper, we consider the improved version of Bingo Voting and focus on the dispute resolution procedure during the voting phase concerning the *cast-as-intended* goal.

The underlying idea of Bingo Voting is that the voting machine encodes the voter's choice in the receipt using random numbers. Each receipt in this election contains each candidate and one random number assigned to it. There are two types of random numbers, *dummy random numbers* generated by the voting authority before the voting phase, and *fresh random numbers* that are generated during the voting phase by the trusted random number generator. The random number used to denote the voter's choice is the fresh random number generated and displayed by the trusted random number generator inside the voting booth. All other random numbers associated to the rest of candidates are dummy random numbers.

At preparation phase, the voting authority generates and publish the set of dummy votes. A dummy vote consists of a pair of Pedersen commitments that hide a dummy random number and the corresponding candidate. The voting authority generates a number of dummy votes equal to the product of the number of candidates and the number of the voters. In addition to the set of dummy votes, the voting machine generates a proof using randomized partial checking [23] to show that each candidate has received the same number of dummy votes. At voting, the voter enters the voting booth and records her choice on a paper ballot that is then fed into the scanner of the voting machine. The scanner prints a random barcode onto one margin of the paper ballot. The barcode is used as alignment information in case of a dispute as the receipt contains an identical barcode. The trusted random number generator generates one fresh random number that is sent to the voting machine and displayed on a screen inside the voting booth so that the voter sees the number. The voting machine generates a receipt such that the fresh random number generated by the trusted random generator is printed next to the candidate chosen by the voter, while unused dummy random numbers are printed next to the other candidates. If the voter thinks that the receipt is correct, she destroys the paper ballot and leaves the voting booth keeping the receipt. The paper ballot needs to be destroyed to prevent vote-buying and coercion.

In the case of a dispute, the voter can put paper ballot and receipt inside privacy sleeves. The privacy sleeves aim at solving a dispute without revealing how a voter voted. There are two types of privacy sleeves. The first type leaves uncovered the barcodes and the candidate names (see Fig. 2). This would allow the voter to prove that the candidates are not placed identically with respect to the barcode on the receipt and the paper ballot. The second type of sleeve uncovers the barcodes and one row of the marking area on the paper ballot and of random numbers on the receipt (see Fig. 3). This would allow the voter to prove a mismatch between her choice and the random numbers that appear on the receipt and on the screen.

The next phase of Bingo Voting is the tallying phase, which we do not cover here since our focus is on the dispute resolution procedure during the voting phase.

Fig. 2. The type of privacy sleeve to check the correctness of the alignment of candidates

Fig. 3. The type of privacy sleeve to check the correctness of the encoding of the voter's choice

6.1 Analysis

We analyse verifiability and accountability of the improved version of Bingo Voting in ProVerif. We assume two candidates are competing for the election and, as we shall see later, prove that the improved version of Bingo Voting meets verifiability but not accountability.

Verifiability. Our analysis strategy to check verifiability of Bingo Voting is similar to the one adopted to check verifiability of the secure exam protocol in Sect. 4. We prove soundness using correspondence assertions and checking that, for any execution of the protocol, all traces in which the test returns `true`, the vote was cast as intended. Since either the voting authority/machine or the candidate can be malicious, we prove the soundness of the verifiability test in each of these scenarios. The verifiability test is as in Algorithm 5. It takes in the *paper* ballot, the *receipt* and the random number displayed in the *screen*, and checks whether the barcodes of paper ballot and receipt match. It also checks that the choice on the paper ballot is associated to the correct random number, which matches with the one displayed in the screen. ProVerif proves that the verifiability test is sound. To prove completeness, we check in ProVerif that when the input data of the test is correct, the test never returns `false`. Since the verifiability test is sound and complete, Bingo Voting allows any one to verify that a vote has been cast as intended.

Accountability. The accountability test for the dispute resolution coincides with the verifiability test. In fact, the failure of the verifiability test (i.e., it returns `false`) is a sufficient condition to blame the Voting Authority since the random generator is trusted by assumption. Hence, the soundness of the accountability test can be trivially checked by proving that if the verifiability test fails, then the accountability test never returns `false` when the indicted principal is the Voting Authority and it is controlled by the attacker. Since the accountability test and the verifiability test coincide, ProVerif trivially proves the soundness of the accountability test. To check completeness, we set the Voting Authority honest and the voter controlled by the attacker. We aim at showing in ProVerif that the accountability test never returns `true`, namely it does not blame the honest Voting Authority. ProVerif fails to prove completeness and shows an attack trace in which two corrupted voters can collaborate to falsely blame an honest Voting Authority. The attack consists of a voter who hands his receipt to the next voter. The latter, on the isolation assumption of the voting booth, swaps the fresh receipt printed by the Voting Machine with the one handed previously by the colluding voter. Then, he puts the fresh paper ballot and the old receipt in the privacy sleeves so that the two barcodes mismatch. The attack is meaningful unless voters are searched before entering the voting booth. We believe this is unlikely to happen as it would decrease the applicability and acceptance of the voting system. Thus, the improved version of Bingo Voting still fails in that of allowing dishonest voters to spoil an election by wrongly complaining that the election was manipulated even if this is not the case.

Algorithm 5. The verifiability test for Bingo Voting

Data:
 - $screen = r$.
 - $paper = choice, barcode\_p$.
 - $receipt = r1, r2, barcode\_r$.

if $(choice = c1$ **and** $r = r1$ **and** $barcode\_p = barcode\_r)$ **or** $(choice = c2$ **and** $r = r2$ **and** $barcode\_p = barcode\_r)$ **then**
 | **return** `true`
else
 | **return** `false`

---

7   Conclusion

Accountability is an essential property for critical systems. Although it has been studied in several security protocols, it has never been defined in a way that fully enables its automated analysis with cryptographic tools. To the best of our knowledge, we advance the first approach that enables the accountability analysis of security protocols automatically. Soundness and completeness conditions are tailored so that verifiability and accountability can be specified as reachability, a property that many cryptographic tools can check automatically nowadays. We validate our approach by applying our definitions to the analysis of three different protocols: a secure exam protocol, Certificate Transparency, and Bingo Voting. We propose the accountability tests that make exam administrators and candidates accountable for the failure of the exam. We show in ProVerif that our accountability tests are sound and complete. We prove in AIF-ω that Certificate Transparency meets its goal of blaming Certificate Authorities and Log administrators if they misbehave. Finally, we find that the improved version of Bingo Voting does not satisfy accountability, although we consider a trusted random generator.

Extending the applicability of automated verification methods to security protocols is a major direction for future work. Manual proofs are complicated and hard to follow as they may involve reasoning about probability and computational complexity, hence prone to human errors. We believe that our mechanised approach will favour the adoption of automated formal verification techniques for the analysis of accountability.

References

1. Cortier, V., Galindo, D., Küsters, R., Müller, J., Truderung, T.: SoK: verifiability notions for e-voting protocols. In: 2016 IEEE Symposium on Security and Privacy (SP), pp. 779–798 (2016)
2. Küsters, R., Truderung, T., Vogt, A.: Accountability: definition and relationship to verifiability. In: Proceedings of the 17th ACM Conference on Computer and Communications Security, CCS 2010, pp. 526–535. ACM, New York (2010)
3. Blanchet, B.: An efficient cryptographic protocol verifier based on prolog rules. In: CSFW, pp. 82–96. IEEE Computer Society (2001)
4. Mödersheim, S., Bruni, A.: AIF-ω: set-based protocol abstraction with countable families. In: Piessens, F., Viganò, L. (eds.) POST 2016. LNCS, vol. 9635, pp. 233–253. Springer, Heidelberg (2016). doi:10.1007/978-3-662-49635-0_12
5. Milner, K., Cremers, C.J.F., Yu, J., Ryan, M.: Automatically detecting the misuse of secrets: Foundations, design principles, and applications. IACR Cryptol. ePrint Arch. 234 (2017)
6. Jagadeesan, R., Jeffrey, A., Pitcher, C., Riely, J.: Towards a theory of accountability and audit. In: Backes, M., Ning, P. (eds.) ESORICS 2009. LNCS, vol. 5789, pp. 152–167. Springer, Heidelberg (2009). doi:10.1007/978-3-642-04444-1_10
7. Bella, G., Paulson, L.C.: Accountability protocols: formalized and verified. ACM Trans. Inf. Syst. Secur. 9, 138–161 (2006)
8. Zhou, J., Gollmann, D.: A fair non-repudiation protocol. In: Proceedings of the 1996 IEEE Conference on Security and Privacy, SP 1996, pp. 55–61. IEEE Computer Society, Washington, DC (1996)
9. Abadi, M., Blanchet, B.: Computer-assisted verification of a protocol for certified email. In: Cousot, R. (ed.) SAS 2003. LNCS, vol. 2694, pp. 316–335. Springer, Heidelberg (2003). doi:10.1007/3-540-44898-5_17

10. Kremer, S., Ryan, M., Smyth, B.: Election verifiability in electronic voting protocols. In: Gritzalis, D., Preneel, B., Theoharidou, M. (eds.) ESORICS 2010. LNCS, vol. 6345, pp. 389–404. Springer, Heidelberg (2010). doi:10.1007/978-3-642-15497-3_24

11. Benaloh, J., Tuinstra, D.: Receipt-free secret-ballot elections (extended abstract). In: Proceedings of the 26th Symposium on Theory of Computing (STOC 1994), pp. 544–553. ACM, New York (1994)

12. Hirt, M., Sako, K.: Efficient receipt-free voting based on homomorphic encryption. In: Preneel, B. (ed.) EUROCRYPT 2000. LNCS, vol. 1807, pp. 539–556. Springer, Heidelberg (2000). doi:10.1007/3-540-45539-6_38

13. Cohen, J., Fischer, M.: A robust and verifiable cryptographically secure election scheme (extended abstract). In: Proceedings of the 26th Annual Symposium on Foundations of Computer Science (FOCS 1985), Portland, Oregon, USA, pp. 372–382. IEEE Computer Society (1985)

14. Benaloh, J.: Verifiable Secret-Ballot Elections. Ph.D. thesis, Yale University (1996)

15. Smyth, B., Ryan, M., Kremer, S., Kourjieh, M.: Towards automatic analysis of election verifiability properties. In: Armando, A., Lowe, G. (eds.) ARSPA-WITS 2010. LNCS, vol. 6186, pp. 146–163. Springer, Heidelberg (2010). doi:10.1007/978-3-642-16074-5_11

16. Dreier, J., Jonker, H., Lafourcade, P.: Defining verifiability in e-auction protocols. In: Proceedings of the 8th ACM Symposium on Information, Computer and Communications Security (ASIACCS 2013), Hangzhou, China, pp. 547–552. ACM (2013)

17. Guts, N., Fournet, C., Zappa Nardelli, F.: Reliable evidence: auditability by typing. In: Backes, M., Ning, P. (eds.) ESORICS 2009. LNCS, vol. 5789, pp. 168–183. Springer, Heidelberg (2009). doi:10.1007/978-3-642-04444-1_11

18. Bella, G., Giustolisi, R., Lenzini, G., Ryan, P.Y.: Trustworthy exams without trusted parties. Comput. Secur. **67**, 291–307 (2017)

19. Laurie, B., Langley, A., Kasper, E.: Certificate transparency. Technical report (2013)

20. Merkle, R.C.: A digital signature based on a conventional encryption function. In: Pomerance, C. (ed.) CRYPTO 1987. LNCS, vol. 293, pp. 369–378. Springer, Heidelberg (1988). doi:10.1007/3-540-48184-2_32

21. Bohli, J.-M., Müller-Quade, J., Röhrich, S.: Bingo voting: secure and coercion-free voting using a trusted random number generator. In: Alkassar, A., Volkamer, M. (eds.) Vote-ID 2007. LNCS, vol. 4896, pp. 111–124. Springer, Heidelberg (2007). doi:10.1007/978-3-540-77493-8_10

22. Bohli, J.M., Henrich, C., Kempka, C., Muller-Quade, J., Rohrich, S.: Enhancing electronic voting machines on the example of bingo voting. IEEE Trans. Inf. Forensics Secur. **4**, 745–750 (2009)

23. Jakobsson, M., Juels, A., Rivest, R.L.: Making mix nets robust for electronic voting by randomized partial checking. In: Proceedings of the 11th USENIX Security Symposium, Berkeley, CA, USA, pp. 339–353. USENIX Association (2002)

Network and System Security

Visualization of Intrusion Detection Alarms Collected from Multiple Networks

Boyeon Song[(⊠)], Sang-Soo Choi, Jangwon Choi, and Jungsuk Song

Korea Institute of Science and Technology Information, 245 Daehak-ro, Yuseong-gu, Daejeon 34141, Korea
{bysong,choiss,jwchoi,song}@kisti.re.kr

Abstract. A Cyber Security Operations Center (CSOC) is a facility where target networks are monitored, analyzed and defended. To detect suspected intrusions, it in general installs an Intrusion Detection System (IDS) at a strategic point within each target network. Security operators in a CSOC should check and analyze security event logs generated by IDSs as fast as they could. However, the amount of security events detected by IDSs of a CSOC is massively increasing owing to ever-increasing cyber threats. It goes beyond the control of security operators using a text-based user interface (TUI) that an IDS typically provides.

Therefore, we propose a novel real-time visualization to effectively display a lot of security event logs collected by IDSs of a CSOC, as a complementary tool to the existing TUI. To the best of our knowledge, it is the first visualization designed for security events of IDSs installed in multiple networks. It is a three-dimensional coordinate system that consists of three parallel plane-squares representing global source networks, target networks, and global destination networks. Security events are displayed between the three planes according to intrusion detection methods, traffic direction, IP addresses and port numbers. We apply it to a public CSOC, and present its beneficial effects.

1 Introduction

A lot of cyber security mechanisms have been devised and developed to counteract the ever increasing cyber threats. An Intrusion Detection System (IDS) is one of fundamental security mechanisms which is in general use in most network security infrastructures. It primarily detects suspicious intrusions or malicious activities by monitoring a network or systems and reports them to an administrator.

Cyber Security Operations Center (CSOC) is a facility where target networks are monitored, accessed, and defended [1]. It compromises security experts who are charged with detecting, analyzing, and preventing cyber attacks within target networks [7,15]. To detect cyber security incidents, it in general installs IDSs at strategic points within target networks. Security operators of a CSOC should quickly discern the security sate of the traffic of target networks by checking

P.Q. Nguyen and J. Zhou (Eds.): ISC 2017, LNCS 10599, pp. 437–454, 2017.
https://doi.org/10.1007/978-3-319-69659-1_24

and analyzing logs of security events (referred to herein as s-events) collected
through IDSs.

However, as cyber threats are rapidly increasing, the amount of s-events
generated by IDSs of a CSOC is massively increasing, and thus it exceeds a
CSOC's manpower supply available. In addition, an IDS typically provides a
text-based user interface (TUI) which displays intrusion detection logs in text
mode. It is not user-friendly to perceive the current sate of network security from
massive s-event logs.

Various mechanisms have been proposed to make effective analysis of large
amounts of security data. One of the mechanisms is information visualization.
It has been increasingly applied as a key method to understand huge volumes of
information at once, by turning them into interactive graphical displays. There
exist many prior art to visualize network security data including network traffic
or IDS alarms, to observe and understand large textual data effectively. However,
to the best of our knowledge, there is no any visualization for security data
collected through multiple networks, while there are many visualizations for
security data of a single network.

Therefore, we design a new visualization suitable for s-events collected from
IDSs installed in multiple networks. The proposed Visualization of Intrusion
Detection Alarm Collection (VisIDAC) consists of three parallel plane-squares
that represent global source networks, target networks, and global destination
networks, respectively. An s-event is represented by a moving object between
two adjacent planes which is shaped, colored and located according to its main
features. It provides a three-dimensional (3-D) comprehensive view of the flow
of s-events in real-time.

We apply VisIDAC to a public CSOC, Science and Technology Cyber
Security Center (S&T-CSC), which takes charge of cyber security defence of
government-supported organizations of science and technology in Korea. It
makes use of an extended version of network-based IDSs, named Threat Management System (TMS), as a core intrusion detection mechanism. TMS consists
of sensors and managers: each sensor is installed in a target network and detects
suspicious outbound and inbound traffic; a manager stores and displays s-events
collected by sensors, so that security operators monitor and analyze them.

The application of VisIDAC to TMS s-events demonstrates its beneficial
effects. It helps to understand more intuitively the overall flow of security events
and grasp their trend, makes it easy to recognize large-scale security events such
as network scanning, port scanning, and DoS/DDoS attacks, and is also effective
to distinguish security event types: which target network they are related to;
whether they are inbound or outbound traffic; what protocol and port number
are mainly used; and whether they are momentary or continuous.

We first review and compare related work in Sect. 2. Next, we introduce
TMS and its s-events, and present our motivation for designing a visualization
of s-events collected by IDSs of a CSOC in Sect. 3. Section 4 proposes a novel
visualization method of s-event collection, and the following section shows its

application to S&T-CSC. Finally, we summarize our work and suggest future work.

2   Related Work

A large number of visualizations of security-related network data have been researched and proposed. Several of them utilize 3-D coordinate systems as a visual structure, as the proposed visualization does. We here review them and compare their features.

The spinning cube of potential doom (referred to herein as SCPD) [4] is a 3-D visual display of network traffic, especially TCP connections, collected through the Bro intrusion detection system [8]. It displays all instances of successful and unsuccessful TCP connections within a 3-D cube using scatter diagram. Bro passively monitors network links over which an intruder's traffic transits, to search for malicious traffic that potentially violates a site's access and usage policies [4,8]. The three axes of the cube represent different components of a TCP connection [4]. The x-axis is the local IP address space, the z-axis is the global IP addresses space, and the y-axis is the port numbers used in connections to locate services and coordinate communication [4]. TCP connections are displayed as single points for each connection. Successful TCP connections are shown as white dots, while incomplete TCP connections are shown as colored dots varying by port number [4].

NetBytes Viewer [13] is a 3-D cube visualization tool designed to show the historical network flow data per port of a single host or subnetwork over a certain time [13]. It visualizes NetFlow data processed using the CERT open source traffic analysis tool suite, SiLK. NetFlow is an industry standard network protocol developed by Cisco for monitoring traffic of a network and collecting IP traffic information. It shows the per port outbound NetFlow volumes for a certain time interval over a specified time period, in order to find anomalous data transmission patterns on suspicious port on an entity or a subnetwork [13]. In its cube display, the z-axis represents port numbers for a single host or subnetwork [13]. The x-axis represents time which is set as a specified time period (e.g. a week), and y-axis represents the magnitude of traffic (in flows, packets, or bytes) seen by the host (or subnet) for a certain time interval (e.g. hourly) [13]. The processed network flow is shown using an orthogonal 3-D impulse graph plot in the cube. Color is used to identify clearly all the data for a specific port.

Cube [12] is a cubic dimensional visualization system to display traffic of a darknet [2,5]. which is a set of unsigned IP addresses of National organization of Information and Communications Technology (NICT) without real systems [3]. In Cube, the left face, called source plane, shows source IP addresses and port numbers of network packets from the Internet, and the right face, called destination plane, shows destination IP addresses and port numbers of network packets toward the darknet. On both the faces, The x-axis represents port numbers and The y-axis represents IP addresses. Each packet is represented by a thin rectangle moving from the source plane to the destination plane. A thin rectangle glides from a point on the source plane to a point on the destination plane taking about several seconds according to its source IP address, source port number, destination IP address, and destination port number. Color is used to distinguish five different packet types: TCP/SYN, TCP/SYN-ACK, TCP/except above, UDP, and ICMP.

P3D [6] is a 3-D coordinate visualization tool to display network packets named P3D flow packet [6]. P3D flow packet is defined as a network connection between two nodes or a set of packets with the same source IP, destination IP, source port and destination port, and is categorized by its connection as various scans such as FIN, ACK, SYN, and Ping scans [6]. It is designed to display these scanning clearly. It consists of two planes based the x, y, and z coordinate systems. One plane represents a range of source IP addresses along the y-axis and a range of destination port numbers along the z-axis, and the other plane represents a range of destination IP addresses and port numbers in the same way. The port numbers range from 0 to 65535, and the IP address range depends on the monitored network. A network connection is denoted by a line in a flow between two planes. Color can be used to distinguish TCP connection types.

Though the existing visualization systems have their own benefits depending on their purposes, they are less effective for monitoring the large amount of IDS data from the multiple networks of different organizations. Thus, we design a new visualization system appropriate for our own target data and visualization goal, which is inspired and influenced by the prior art described above.

Table 1. Comparison between the prior art and VisIDAC

Name	Target data	Target network	Structure	Data shape	Time	Main parameters
SCPD [4]	IDS data	A network	Cube	Dot	Non-real-time	Local IP, global IP, and port
NetBytes Viewer [13]	Network flow	A network	Cube	Impulse	Certain time	Port, time, period and traffic volume
Cube [12]	Darknet packets	A darknet	Two planes	Thin rectangle	Real-time	SRC IP, SRC port, DST IP and DST port
P3D [6]	Network packets	A network	Two planes	Line	Non-real-time	SRC IP, SRC port, DST IP and DST port
VisIDAC	IDS data	Networks	Three planes	Short arrow or straight line	Real-time	TN IP, TN port, SRC IP, SRC port, DST IP and DST port

In Table 1, we compare the above 3-D coordinate visualization systems to VisIDAC, with respect to the following features: target data, target network, structure, data shape, time, and main parameters, where SRC, DST, and TN mean source, destination, and target network, respectively.

3   Motivation and Background

We first introduce an extended version of IDSs, TMS which is made for the usage of a CSOC, and then explain the motives of designing a new visualization system of s-events.

3.1   Threat Management System

TMS monitors target networks, identifies and logs possible malicious attacks, and reports the attempts to administrators [10,11]. TMS consists of *managers* and *sensors*, as follows:

- **Sensor**: It is a type of network-based IDSs, and is installed at a strategic point within the network of a target organization, to monitor traffic to and from all systems in the network. It examines the network traffic for signs of malicious activity, and detects suspected intrusions by comparing them with patterns (also known as signatures) of known attacks. Once malicious behavior is sensed, it transmits the relevant traffic information, i.e. an s-event, to a manager described below.
- **Manager**: It is responsible for management of sensors and s-events. It checks the state of sensors and updates their patterns. It also collects and stores s-events transmitted by sensors, and provides a user interface via which security operators monitor and analyze s-events and get statistics of them.

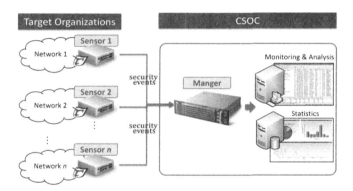

Fig. 1. TMS configuration diagram

Figure 1 shows TMS configuration diagram. Each sensor deployed in the network of an organization detects s-events and sends them to a manager located in a CSOC. Security operators of a CSOC examine s-events of target networks via a user interface providing by managers.

The information of an s-event includes the following elements:

- *Event name*: It is an s-event's name defined as a pattern (e.g. TCP service scanning and UDP flooding).
- *Time*: It is the date and time when the s-event is detected by a sensor.
- *Src IP*: It is the source IP address of the s-event.
- *Src port*: It is the protocol and source port number used (e.g. TCP 6000).
- *Dst IP*: It is the destination IP address of the s-event.

- *Dst port*: It is the protocol and destination port number used.
- *Num*: It is the number of the s-event detected for a second.
- *In/Out*: *In* and *Out* mean inbound and outbound traffic, respectively.
- *Location*: It displays the site of a sensor by which the s-event is detected.

A manager's console screen lists the information of s-events in text mode, as shown in Fig. 2, where confidential information such as IP addresses and location is covered. But the number of s-events which its TUI can display is as limited as the size of the screen, and even they are updated every second to display new s-events.

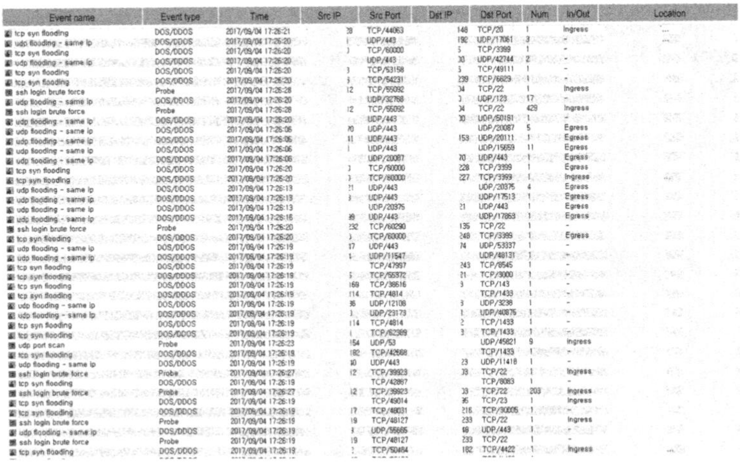

Fig. 2. Screen snapshot of TMS TUI

The volume of s-events collected by sensors of a CSOC is normally a lot, because it monitors more than one network. In case of S&T-CSC that is responsible for cyber defense of more than 50 organizations, the number of s-events detected from its target networks in 2016 is 5,142,182,012; the average number of daily TMS s-events is 15,395,755. That is, security operators of S&T-CSC should be able to examine on average 178 s-events per second, to check whether they are false positives or true positives. Then how many skilled security operators are required! But, it is difficult to increase the number of security operators proportionally to the amount of TMS s-events because of many restrictions including financial constraints and finite skilled manpower.

A variety of mechanisms have been researched and developed to make effective analysis of such large amounts of information. One of the mechanisms is information visualization. S&T-CSC adopts it to quickly discover and identify malicious activities and network behaviors from s-event collection.

4   Visualization of IDS alarms from multiple networks

4.1   Design Goals

The proposed visualization VisIDAC is designed for efficiently displaying alarms of IDSs in real-time, which are installed in more than one target networks.

It has the following three features. First, it classifies s-events with shape, color, and location, for quick grasp of the main properties of s-events. The classification methods are as follows: (a) it sorts s-events according to target networks, (b) it separates inbound s-events and outbound s-events to distinguish them, (c) it groups s-events according to protocols (i.e. TCP, UDP and ICMP) and destination port numbers used, (d) it could segregate s-events by specific source and destination IP addresses, or specific source and destination port numbers, and (e) it distinguishes between a single s-event and multiple s-events.

Next, it shows the overall traffic of s-events in real-time, to be able to understand its scale and current at a glance, and to observe the packet flow of s-events: where they come from and where they are going to; what port numbers are frequently used; what types of s-events are mainly occurred; which monitored networks are mostly targeted; and which source continues generating abnormal traffic.

Lastly, it is for distinguishing large-scale cyber threats noticeably from other individual s-events, such as network scanning, port scanning, and DoS/DDoS attacks. They are popularly exploited by attackers to find vulnerabilities of a system or attack a system. In VisIDAC, such types of s-events can be clearly separated by distinct displays.

The framework of VisIDAC takes the following elements of s-events as its main parameters for effective visibility: *event type, source IP and port*, and *destination IP and port*. It is because the basic core information of an s-event is what, from where, and to where attributes. It separates three network areas: global source networks, target networks, and global destination networks. Between the areas, s-events flow in real-time (more accurately, near real-time in implementation), according to its key properties.

4.2   Structure and Components

VisIDAC consists of three parallel plane-squares. The planes are named source network (referred to as SN), target networks (referred to as TN), and destination network (referred to as DN). S-events are represented by either an arrowhead or a straight line between the three plane-squares. Figure 3a shows the structure of VisIDAC, which is comprised of three plane-squares and two different shaped s-events.

Three Plane-Squares. VisIDAC has three parallel plane-squares, i.e. SN, TN, and DN planes. SN plane represents global source networks, where the horizontal axis represents a range of source IP addresses, and the vertical axis represents a range of source port numbers from 0 to 65535. DN plane represents global

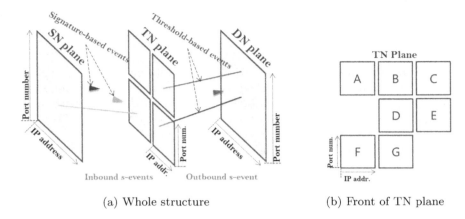

(a) Whole structure   (b) Front of TN plane

Fig. 3. Structure of VisIDAC

destination networks, where the horizontal axis represents a range of destination IP addresses, and the vertical axis represents a range of destination port numbers from 0 to 65535.

TN plane represents target networks, and is divided into square cells, according to the number of target networks. A cell represents a target network, where the horizontal axis represents the IP address space of the target network, and the vertical axis represents the port numbers of the target network. The position of a cell on TN plane is based on a user's selection. The acronym or abbreviation of each target network is shown on each cell transparently to distinguish one from another.

For example, assume that there are 7 target networks. Then TN plane can be divided into 3 by 3 square cells. The 7 of 9 cells are matched with the 7 target networks, and are arranged on TN plane according to a user's choice. The other 2 cells remain empty. Figure 3b shows the example of TN plane. In the figure, TN plane has 7 occupied cells as the number of the target network, and letters A to G on cells are examples of the short names of target networks.

S-Event Display. S-events have two different shapes according to intrusion detection methods, are colored according to s-event groups, and are placed in two different spaces according to traffic direction.

Shape. S-events can be categorized into two major types according to detection methods: *signature-based event* and *threshold-based event*. The former is an s-event type detected by signatures that are specific patterns to identify malware, such as byte sequences in network traffic, or known malicious instruction sequences used by malware. The latter is an s-event type detected when the number of packets including specific patterns is more than a certain threshold, and in most cases it is large-scale, for example, network scanning, port scanning, login brute force attacks, DoS attacks, and DDoS attacks.

VisIDAC displays the two types of s-events in different shapes. A signature-based event is represented by an arrowhead, which moves one plane to the other plane – either from SN plane to TN plane or from TN plane to DN plane – over the s-event appearance duration set by a user (in general several seconds). A threshold-based event is represented by a straight line which connects between two adjacent planes – either from SN plane to TN plane or from TN plane to DN plane – over the s-event appearance duration, as shown in Fig. 3a.

Space. S-events can also be divided into two groups according to traffic direction: inbound s-events and outbound s-events. VisIDAC displays them in two different areas. Inbound s-events are visualized in the space between the right two adjacent planes, while outbound s-events are visualized in the space between the left two adjacent planes. More specifically, when a target network is the destination of an s-event, an arrowhead (resp. a straight line) moves (resp. connects) from a point on SN plane to a point on TN plane; when a target network is the source of an s-event, an arrowhead (resp. a straight line) moves (resp. connects) from a point on TN plane to a point on DN plane.

Color. VisIDAC displays s-events with different colors to distinguish character-istics of s-events. S-events can be grouped in the following ways, and each group can be displayed in a unique color.

First, s-events can be categorized according to protocols and destination port numbers. They are firstly divided into three groups according to protocols, i.e. TCP, UDP, and ICMP, and are secondly subdivided according to port numbers, i.e. the well-known port numbers and other port numbers. Therefore, s-events basically have five groups: TCP & the well-known port numbers, TCP & other port numbers, UDP & the well-known port numbers, UDP & the well-known port numbers, and ICMP. Additionally, an individual protocol and specific port number can be added as an s-event group for independent observation, for exam-ple, TCP 1443 and UDP 53. Table 2a shows the five basic groups and the two additional group types.

Next, VisIDAC can group s-events according to source and destination IP addresses, which has three group types. Type 1 is an s-event group type in which destination IP address or IP address range is specified (e.g. 122.34.155.0/24 → ANY), Type 2 is an s-event group type in which source IP address or IP address range is specified (e.g. ANY → 231.156.89.11), and Type 3 is an s-event group type in which both source and destination IP addresses or IP address ranges are specified (e.g. 122.34.155.11 → 231.156.89.0/24). Table 2b shows the three types of s-event groups divided by source and destination IP addresses.

Also, VisIDAC can separate s-events associated with specific source/destination port numbers from others by color. There are three group types according to source and destination port numbers. Type 1 is an s-event group type in which destination port number is specified (e.g. Any → 12345), Type 2 is an s-event group type in which source port number is specified (e.g. 123 → Any), and Type 3 is an s-event group type in which both source and destina-tion port numbers are specified (e.g. 123 → 12345). It is useful when observing s-events sourced from a specific port number and/or destined for a specific port

Table 2. S-event group types

(a) Groups by protocols and destination port numbers

Group	Protocol	Destination port number
Basic	TCP	The well-known port numbers
		Other port numbers
	UDP	The well-known port numbers
		Other port numbers
	ICMP	N/A
Type 1	TCP	Specific port number
Type 2	UDP	Specific port number

(b) Groups by IP addresses

Group	Source IP address	Destination IP address
Type 1	Any	Specific IP or IP range
Type 2	Specific IP or IP range	Any
Type 3	Specific IP or IP range	Specific IP or IP range

(c) Groups by port numbers

Group	Source port number	Destination port number
Type 1	Any	Specific port number
Type 2	Specific port number	Any
Type 3	Specific port number	Specific port number

number, Table 2c shows the three types of s-event groups divided by source and destination port numbers.

Additionally, s-events can be colored by source countries. It is useful for observing s-events sourced from a specific country.

4.3 Additional Functions

When clicking an s-event appeared on screen, a small window is pop up to show the s-event's detailed information, whose background color is the same as its group color. The window shows the following information of an s-event:

- *Event*: The field is the s-event name, e.g. UDP flooding.
- *Source*: The field is the information of the s-event source IP address, port number, protocol type, and the name of country or organization, e.g. 173.18.254.1 (80) [CN].
- *Destination*: The field is the information of the s-event destination, i.e. IP address, port number, protocol type, and the name of country or organization, e.g. 21.119.22.18 (8080) [KISTI]
- *Time*: The field is the time and date of the s-event detection, e.g. 12:33, 06/07/2017.

- *Packets*: The field is the size of packets of the s-event.
- *The number of detection*: The field is the number of the s-event detected for a second.

Table 3 shows an example of an s-event information window display which gives the detailed information of an s-event, UDP flooding.

Table 3. S-event information window display

Security Event Information	
Event	UDP flooding
Source	173.18.254.1 (80) [CN]
Destination	21.119.22.18 (8080) [KISTI]
Time	12:33, 06/07/2017
Packets	34.04 Kbps
# of detection	35

In VisIDAC, s-events are visualized in near real-time. They are shown on screen for several seconds and soon thereafter disappeared. To have enough time to keep an eye on some s-events, VisIDAC provides a *pause* function, by which all the movements of s-events can stop for a while. It makes it easy to point and click an s-event on screen, and makes it possible to check the details of multiple s-events shown on screen at the same time.

It also has *zoom in, zoom out*, and *360° rotation* functions for users to be able to observe s-events in more detail. There is a *replay* function to search s-events of the past, by setting a specific period of time. It allows users to review the movements of s-events occurred for the period repeatedly.

4.4 Display of Special S-Events

We add noticeable visualization effects to some of large-scale s-event types, i.e. network scanning, port scanning, and DoS/DDoS attacks, to attract extra attention. It is because cyber-attacks is often accompanied by these s-events.

We also gives a distinct mark to s-events that are sourced from a target network and destined for a target network, to pay attention. The visualization methods of the above s-event types are specified below.

Network Scanning. Network scanning is a procedure scanning IP addresses for identifying active hosts on a network, for mainly network security assessment, which returns information about which IP addresses map to live hosts that are active on the Internet. But it can also be employed by attackers to identify potential network vulnerabilities. In most cases of network scanning events (e.g. TCP syn scanning and ICMP scanning), the destination IP address of the s-events is a range of IP addresses. If a host(s) is scanning systems in target networks, it should be carefully observed, because it could be a preparation step for the following attack attempts.

Thus, VisIDAC highlights such an s-event type in a triangular shape; an s-event is shown to connect from a point on SN (resp. TN) plane based on its source IP address and port number to a horizontal line on TN (resp. DN) plane based on its destination port number, as shown in Fig. 4a. It looks like a upward-facing triangle connecting one plane and the other plane, whose base is on the second plane.

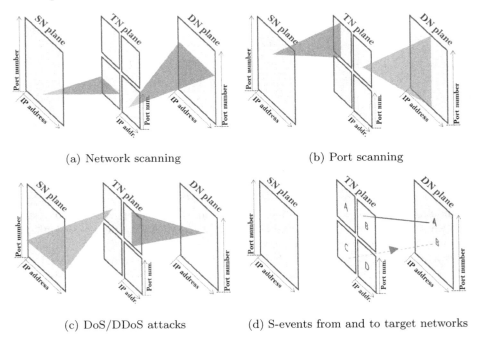

(a) Network scanning   (b) Port scanning

(c) DoS/DDoS attacks   (d) S-events from and to target networks

Fig. 4. Visualization methods of special s-events

Port Scanning. Port scanning is a procedure for probing a system for open ports to identify running services on the system. It can be employed by attackers to look for a weakened access point to break into a system. Port scanning events (e.g. TCP port scanning and UDP port scanning) have a range of destination port numbers in most cases. If a host(s) is scanning ports of a system(s) in a target network, it should be carefully observed, because it may be precedent activities to an attack attempt(s).

Thus, VisIDAC distinguishes such an s-event type in a triangular shape. It is shown to connect from a point on SN (resp. TN) plane based on its source IP address and port number to a vertical line on TN (resp. DN) plane based on its destination IP address, as shown in Fig. 4b. It looks like a front-facing triangle connecting one plane and the other plane, whose base is on the second plane.

DoS/DDoS Attacks. A DoS attack is a cyber-attack that makes a system or network resource unavailable to its intended users by preventing them from accessing information or services. The most common type of DoS attack is accomplished by flooding the targeted system or resource with superfluous requests to overload the system and thus prevent legitimate users of a service from using that service. A DDoS attack is a type of DoS attacks where more than one, often thousands of, unique IP addresses are used to flood a targeted system. When such s-events are detected, it is necessary to examine them thoroughly, because they are explicit attack attempts.

In some of DoS/DDoS s-events (e.g. TCP syn flooding and UDP flooding), their source IP address is a range of IP address, or their source port number is more than one. In such cases, VisIDAC makes them noticeable in a triangular shape. When a range of IP addresses is the source of an s-event, it is shown to connect from a horizontal line on SN (resp. TN) plane based on its source port number to a point on TN (resp. DN) plane based on its destination IP address and port number. It looks like a upward-facing triangle connecting one plane and the other plane, whose base is on the first plane. When an s-event has many source port numbers, it is shown to connect from a vertical line on SN (resp. TN) plane based on its source IP address to a point on TN (resp. DN) plane based on its destination IP address and port number. It looks like a front-facing triangle connecting one plane and the other plane, whose base is on the first plane. In Fig. 4b, the left triangle shows the former s-event and the right triangle shows the latter s-event.

S-Events Occurred Between Target Networks. Some s-events are sourced from a target network and destined for a target network. VisIDAC gives a discernable mark to such s-events, because there is a possibility that a system infected by a malware(s) attempts to attack another system in target networks.

In VisIDAC, they are visualized in the space between TM plane and DN plane. On DN plane, the acronym or abbreviation of the destination target network is written nearby the destination point over the s-event appearance duration to indicate that the s-event's destination is the target network.

Figure 4d shows the visualization method of s-events occurred between target networks. In the figure, there are four target networks named A, B, C and D on TN plane, and there are two examples of s-events occurred from and to target networks; one is a threshold-based event sourced from B and destined for A, and the other is a signature-based event sourced from C and destined for B. The short names of target networks, A and B, are displayed on DN plane to indicate their destination network clearly.

5   Application of VisIDAC to S&T-CSC

VisIDAC is implemented in C++ on CentOS, and developed for practical use in S&T-CSC. The CSOC provides information security services to more than 50 organizations of science and technology, and uses TMS as its core intrusion detection tool for the target networks.

5.1   Basic Setting

In S&T-CSC, the data source of VisIDAC is s-events collected by TMS sensors which are installed in the networks of the target organizations. The information of a TMS s-event consists of *Event name, Time, Src IP, Src port, Dst IP, Dst port, Num, In/Out,* and *Location* (see Sect. 3.1 for details).

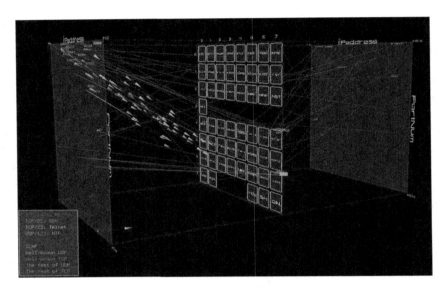

Fig. 5. Screen snapshot of S&T-CSC VisIDAC

The number of cells on its TN plane is matched with the number of the target networks. Figure 5 is a screen snapshot of S&T-CSC VisIDAC, where each cell on TN plane represents each target network of S&T-CSC, and the acronym or abbreviation of each target network is shown on cells to distinguish them.

S&T-CSC VisIDAC basically divides TMS s-events into the five basic s-event groups, TCP & the well-known port numbers, TCP & other port numbers, UDP & the well-known port numbers, UDP & other port numbers, and ICMP (see Sect. 4.2). It also has additional s-event groups for indicating the most often used protocols and destination port numbers.

The top five protocol and destination port numbers of S&T-CSC in 2016 are TCP 22, TCP 80, UDP 123, TCP 23, and UDP 53, whose percentage in the total s-events are 29.7%, 7.1%, 4.6%, 3.9%, and 3.4%, respectively. The sum of their percentages is 49%; it is almost half of the total s-events of 2016. Figure 6a shows the list of the top 10 destination port numbers of the s-events of 2016.

Accordingly, color legends in S&T-CSC VisIDAC are currently configured to distinguish TCP 22, TCP 80, UDP 123, TCP 23, UDP 53, and the five basic s-event groups, as shown in Fig. 6b, where the upper five legends represent the additional s-event groups, and the lower five legends the basic s-event groups.

Rank	Protocol & DST port	Num. of s-events of 2016	Pct	
1	TCP 22	1,525,647,889	29.7%	
2	TCP 80	363,123,762	7.1%	
3	UDP 123	236,052,709	4.6%	49%
4	TCP 23	199,402,511	3.9%	
5	UDP 53	173,587,953	3.4%	
6	UDP 443	147,594,130	2.9%	
7	UDP many	65,057,919	1.3%	
8	UDP 4500	41,430,907	0.8%	
9	UDP 46224	40,861,722	0.8%	
10	UDP 53413	38,920,599	0.8%	
	Total s-events	5,142,182,012	100%	

(a) Top 10 DST ports of 2016 s-events

(b) Color legends

Fig. 6. S-event groups of S&T-CSC VisIDAC

5.2   Overall Effects

The application of VisIDAC to S&T-CSC demonstrates the it provides many useful benefits. First, it allows users to get the information of s-events quicker than TUI can do, by performing further classifications: which target networks they are related to; where they are coming from and where they are going to; whether they are a threshold-based event or a signature-based event; whether they are a single event or multiple events; and whether they are momentary or continuous.

Also, it makes it easier to recognize large-scale events and also distinguish whether they are port scanning, network scanning, or DoS/DDoS attacks by using different noticeable displays.

We here introduce two visualization examples of large-scale s-events. S&T-CSC detected massive Domain Name Server (DNS) amplification attacks [9,14] toward the networks of the target organizations from July 2013 to 2015. It is still one of the top 10 popular s-events detected in S&T-CSC until now. The attack is a popular form of DDoS attacks that relies on the use of publicly accessible open DNS servers to overwhelm a victim system with DNS response traffic, which uses UDP and a port number 53 in general [9,14]. Figure 7a is a screen snapshot of massive DNS amplification attacks which started from Turkey and went toward the network of a target organization. It was colored by red to indicate s-events using UDP 53.

A huge amount of xmas scanning and full xmas scanning events were detected for three months in 2014, which were sourced from several European countries and destined for systems in many target organization networks. Figure 7b is a screen snapshot of these xmas scanning events, and the s-event information window displays the information of a full xmas scanning which was sourced from Denmark and destined for a target organization, including IP addresses, port numbers, protocols, traffic packets, and detection time. The s-event was colored in pink which was assigned for s-events of TCP & other port numbers.

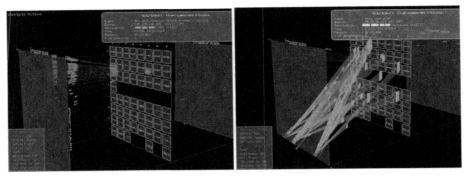

(a) DNS amplification attacks   (b) Xmas scanning

Fig. 7. Screen snapshots of large-scale s-events of S&T-CSC VisIDAC

As shown in the above examples, VisIDAC is very effective in discerning the flow of large-scale events in real-time: where they are from and are going toward. It also makes it much easier to grasp the trend of such s-events than reading logs listed on a TUI.

Next, it is very helpful in observing the overall traffic flow of s-events in real-time and understand their trend: how many s-events are occurring right now; which target networks they are mostly headed for or started from; what sort of s-events are mainly happened; and what port numbers are often destined.

Finally, it makes it possible to find s-events repeated in the same pattern, by remembering its graphical patterns which is much easier than remembering textual patterns. In such a case, security operators can track the related s-events over time.

There is a scalability issue. As the number of target networks increases, the amount of security events is getting larger, while the size of cells on TM plane is getting smaller. Thus, if target networks is too many to display on a screen, it would be better to divide them into few groups to display them separately with different visualization settings.

In conclusion, S&T-CSC is making good use of VisIDAC as a helpful supplementary monitoring interface of TMS.

6   Conclusion and Future Work

We have first discussed a difficulty in monitoring a large number of IDS logs of a CSOC in text mode, which are collected across multiple target networks, The massive volume of the s-events goes beyond the control of security operators.

We have proposed a real-time 3-D visualization of s-event collection, VisIDAC, as a solution for it. It consists of three parallel plane-squares, and each plane represents different control information of the packet of s-events. The left plane represents a range of global source IP addresses along the horizontal axis and a range of source port numbers along the vertical axis, and the right plane represents a range of global destination IP addresses along the horizontal axis and a range of destination port numbers along the vertical axis. The middle plane is divided into cells according to the number of target networks, and each cell on the plane represents a range of IP addresses of a target network along the horizontal axis and a range of port numbers of a target network along the vertical axis. S-events represented by either a moving arrowhead or a straight line are displayed between two adjacent planes, according to intrusion detection methods, traffic direction, IP addresses and port numbers.

We have applied VisIDAC to S&T-CSC, and have presented its useful effects. It provides a 3-D comprehensive view of the overall s-events of target networks in near real-time. It makes it much easier and faster to identify s-events collected from multiple target networks by providing the following features: (a) classification according to target networks, traffic direction, and detection methods, (b) grouping by protocols & destination port numbers, IP addresses, or port numbers, (c) apparent displays of three types of large-scale events, i.e. network scanning, port scanning, and DoS/DDoS attacks, (d) noticeable marks of s-events occurred between target networks, and (e) near real-time visualization of the current s-events.

We will discuss the feedback of security operators using VisIDAC on its usability in near future. We will also provide more beneficial use cases of it, and monitor and track its improvements.

Acknowledgements. This research was supported by Korea Institute of Science and Technology Information (KISTI). Authors would like to thank Koei Suzuki, Daisuke Inoue, and Koji Nakao from National Institute of Information and Communications Technology (NICT) for their help in implementing VisIDAC.

References

1. Bidou, R.: Security Operation Center Concepts & Implementation, August 2005. http://www.iv2-technologies.com/SOCConceptAndImplementation.pdf
2. D. Moore, C. Shannon, G.M.V., Savage, S.: Network telescopes: Technical report. Cooperative Association for Internet Data Analysis (CAIDA), July 2004
3. Inoue, D., Eto, M., Yoshioka, K., Baba, S., Suzuki, K., Nakazato, J., Ohtaka, K., Nakao, K.: nicter: An incident analysis system toward binding network monitoring with malware analysis. In: Information Security Threats Data Collection and Sharing, pp. 58–66, April 2008
4. Lau, S.: The spinning cube of potential doom. Commun. ACM **47**(6), 25–26 (2004). http://doi.acm.org/10.1145/990680.990699
5. Moore, D.: Network telescopes observing small or distant security events. In: 11th USENIX Security Symposium, Invited talk, August 2003
6. Nunnally, T., Chi, P., Abdullah, K., Uluagac, A.S., Copeland, J.A., Beyah, R.: P3D: a parallel 3d coordinate visualization for advanced network scans. In: 2013 IEEE International Conference on Communications (ICC), pp. 2052–2057, June 2013

7. Onwubiko, C.: Cyber security operations centre: Security monitoring for protecting business and supporting cyber defense strategy. In: 2015 International Conference on Cyber Situational Awareness, Data Analytics and Assessment (CyberSA), pp. 1–10, June 2015

8. Paxson, V.: Bro: a system for detecting network intruders in real-time. Comput. Netw. Int. J. Comput. Telecommun. Networking **31**(23–24), 2435–2463 (1999)

9. Rozekrans, T., M.M., de Koning, J.: Defending against DNS reflection amplification attacks. University of Amsterdam, Technical report, February 2013

10. Scarfone, K., Mell, P.: Guide to Intrusion Detection and Prevention Systems (IDPS) - Recommendations of the National Institute of Standards and Technology. National Institute of Standards and Technology, Gaithersburg (2007)

11. Sequeira, D.: Intrusion Prevention Systems - Security's Silver Bullet? GSEC Version 1.4B. SANS Institute (2002)

12. Suzuki, K.: Studies on Network Monitoring Systems to Reveal Suspicious Activities. Ph.D. thesis, Graduate School of Informatics, Kyoto University (2011)

13. Taylor, T., Brooks, S., McHugh, J.: NetBytes Viewer: an entity-based netflow visualization utility for identifying intrusive behavior. In: Goodall, J.R., Conti, G., Ma, K.L. (eds.) VizSEC 2007: Proceedings of the Workshop on Visualization for Computer Security, pp. 101–114. Springer, Heidelberg (2007). doi:10.1007/978-3-540-78243-8_7

14. Vaughn, R., Evron, G.: DNS amplification attacks (preliminary release) (2006). http://packetstormsecurity.com/files/download/44824/DNS-Amplification-Attacks.pdf

15. Zimmerman, C.: Ten Strategies of a World-Class Cybersecurity Operations Center. MITRE Corporation (2014)

Curtain: Keep Your Hosts Away from USB Attacks

Jianming Fu[1,2](✉), Jianwei Huang[2], and Lanxin Zhang[2]

[1] Key Laboratory of Aerospace Information Security and Trusted Computing,
Wuhan University, Wuhan, China
jmfu@whu.edu.cn
[2] School of Computer Science, Wuhan University, Wuhan, China

Abstract. In recent years, many attacks targeting USB were proposed. Besides spreading virus through USB storage, attackers are tending to attack USB stacks because in most cases, any information from devices will be trusted. In this paper, we design a system named Curtain on Windows to defend those attacks by analyzing their IRP flows. Curtain is deployed as a filter driver in USB stack on Windows. It'll sniff all the IRP flows of each USB device and analyze them. It's based on the fact that an attack always happens in a short time and that will be reflected in IRP flows. In short, Curtain provides a solution to defend USB attacks on Windows by inserting a filter driver to USB stacks and catch the behaviors of each device.

Keywords: USB · Device security · Windows driver

1 Introduction

As the Universal Serial Bus (USB) provides the convenience for host computers to easily attach various external devices through the USB ports, we can hardly find one common PC without USB ports. From USB 2.0 to USB 3.1, updated USB ports become more and more powerful for supporting high-speed transmission of almost all common data types. Computer manufactures think highly of USB ports, for example, Apple's latest Macbook only sustains four type-c USB ports.

Due to USB's prevalence, attackers exploit many ways to carry out their attacks [1,3]. In the early stages, USB storage has served as a delivery media for many malicious softwares. For a striking example, the famous "Stuxnet" [4] tried to modify the PLC to change the actions of Industrial production control system in 2010, which caused huge social impact. This kind of attack only uses the storage as a carrier, so antivirus softwares are able to defend from this by detecting the virus [2]. In recent years, a new means called Human Interface Device Attack (HID Attack) has emerged [5]. During the enumeration [26] phase defined in the USB protocol, a single USB device can register itself as a different type device and enable its ability to inject malicious scripts. For an

© Springer International Publishing AG 2017
P.Q. Nguyen and J. Zhou (Eds.): ISC 2017, LNCS 10599, pp. 455–471, 2017.
https://doi.org/10.1007/978-3-319-69659-1_25

instance, RUBBER DUCKY [6,7] penetration tool can declare itself to be a keyboard and inject malicious keyboard input to the host, which is already a mature product. An even more insidious form of USB attack called BadUSB [9,10] has come up at Black Hat in 2014. Without using human interface devices as the HID attack, the BadUSB attack [11] only needs to modify the firmware inside and disguise itself as a standard USB device. For it can perform firmware attack (e.g. adding keyboard emulation to a storage device), USB security faces more severe situation. What's more, security researchers of Bastille Networks raise a new channel-based USB attack called MouseJack [14], which targets on wireless USB devices [8]. Utilizing the vulnerability of unencrypted communication signals between wireless mouse and its receiver, attackers can sniff or even hijack the device so as to control user's host. Another newly raised attack Keyboard Sniffer [15], which targets on wireless keyboards, performs the same trick. These new attacks can bypass the antivirus software's detecting becasue they hide malicious code in the firmware or just sniffer the communication of USB devices. However, existing antivirus softwares just perform static analysis on the files of USB storage, they have no ideas of these new attacking modes.

Therefore, there is a great need for us to consider why existing technologies can't defend from these new attacking modes. First of all, the root cause of the HID attack and the BadUSB attack is a lack of access control for drivers in Windows. During the enumeration phase of USB protocol, malicious USB can make spurious claims defined by its identity, so malicious device is unlimited to request any device drivers. Also, the root cause of the channel-based attack of MouseJack and Keyboard Sniffer is a lack of protection for the communication between the wireless USB devices and the USB interface. Second, it is tempting to conclude that, a technology which can monitor USB device's behaviors is urgently needed. This technology can effectively protect the host from untrusted devices without modifying the communication mechanism of wireless USB devices on the market. Last but not the least, while USB Implementers Forum leaving the authentication of malicious USB devices to users, it is unlikely for users to verify the functionality and the intent of USB devices independently.

In order to make USB secure again, Dave Tian proposed the GoodUSB [13], a host-side defense for Linux against HID attack and BadUSB attacks in 2015. Then he optimized this work and proposed the USBFILTER [12], an access control system, on USENIX in 2016. However, both technologies are designed for Linux system. Although many users are familiar with Linux system, there is no doubt that most normal computer users are using Windows system. Also, GoodUSB needs to modify the kernel of Linux system. If other implementations need to modify the kernel or users have to update the kernel, it might disable the defense function or even cause the disruption of the system. More importantly, both defenses can't protect the host from channel-based USB attacks like MouseJack or Keyboard Sniffer.

Based on the working process of USB authorization and the working process of USB devices, this paper proposed Curtain, a multi-layered USB defending system installed as a filter driver [19] in Windows. Utilizing the programmability and the flexibility of filter driver, Curtain system don't need to modify any upper layer software or lower level device drivers. Based on I/O request packet (IRP) tracking [17], Curtain can monitor, hook, and modify the IRP flow, so as to monitor the activity of USB. What's more, Curtain system can not only successfully protect the host from HID attack or BadUSB, but also can defend channel-based USB attack by analyzing the IRP traffic. Furthermore, users of Curtain can take part into the security process by choosing the expected intention of the USB device.

Our contribution can be summarized as follows:

- **Design and propose a multi-layered USB defense framework and USB attack model.** For no one has proposed a recognized USB working model, it is often obscure for developers to make progress on USB security. At first, we define main working layers of the USB working process on Windows. Then, we summarize the main points of existing USB attacks respectively and precisely abstract these attacks to related USB working layers. By declaring this multi-layered USB working model, developers can fast and clearly find where the vulnerabilities are, then developers are able to produce effective defense towards new attack forms.
- **Propose new effective technologies for the USB defense on Windows.** Our system is the first to apply an IRP tracking and analyzing mechanism for USB on Windows, in order to monitor the USB's package from the enumeration phase till it gets plugged out. This analyzation process can identify the true intention of the USB device, and stop unauthentic USB behaviors before attacks performing out. Also, Curtain realizes an anomalous detection on detecting the abnormal USB behavior based on the concepts of Intrusion Detection System. It is made up of three methods to detect attacks. One of them is based on user's choice. The second one is based on the Isolation Forest algorithm and the last one is based on static rules. The combination of these three methods is much stronger than IDS with static rules only.
- **Demonstrate validity in real-world scenarios and characterize performance.** In the experiment stage, we explore how Curtain can defend against various USB attacks and provide convenience for benign devices. Also, we demonstrate how Curtain causes minimal burden on USB traffic in Windows system. Furthermore, our system is not only able to protect USB storage device and human interface devices, but can also cope with devices like wireless keyboards. As a result, our system is well-suited for protecting any USB workload for the public.

2   Background and Threat Model

In this section, first we will introduce how USB devices work generally. Second, we'll show more details about how USB devices work in Windows. After that, attackers' methods to exploit USB devices will be described and our threat model will be proposed based on this.

2.1   USB Work Flow

In general, when connecting to a host, the USB and the host controller start to negotiate about how to transfer data later. Details about this process is shown in Fig. 1 [9,23].

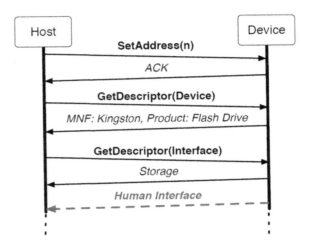

Fig. 1. USB devices enumeration

First, the host will appoint an address for the device and the device will send an ACK message to the host. Then, the host controller will try to get descriptors from the device so that it can load corresponding functional drivers to operate the device. If the device claims itself to be a keyboard, the host controller will load a keyboard driver and hand over control to the keyboard driver. After loading drivers, the enumeration process is done. The functional driver starts to work as a middleware between application and the device.

In the process, the host trusts all the data from the device with no hesitation. Whatever the device claims it to be, the host controller will load the corresponding functional driver for the device. Also, the functional driver will send the data from the device to all the application related no matter what the data is.

2.2   USB Devices' Enumeration in Windows

While in Windows, some differences exist in enumeration. When a USB device connects to the host, the host controller driver starts to work. Then, the descriptors will be sent to the driver. Depending on the content of the descriptor, the host controller driver will assign different functional drivers for the device to work for applications. It's worth mentioning that several functional drivers can be applied for the same device at the same time. They will make up a stack called device driver stack [16,18]. When transmitting data from the device to the host, the functional driver will poll the host controller to receive all the data from device by sending IRP from the top of driver stack [17]. When transmitting data from the host to the device, IRP will be sent to the functional driver at the top of the stack and those drivers will call the next driver until the driver at the bottom of the stack. It will then return the data of URB.

2.3   Existing Attack Methods

Many USB attacking methods are proposed these years. Since USB was invented, many virus were spread by USB disks. Then, many attackers modified the human interface devices (HID) to insert malicious input to the host, which exploits the vulnerability in the enumeration phase defined by USB protocol. This attacking method is called HID attack. In 2014, SRLabs proposed a method named BadUSB in BlackHat [9,10]. They rewrite the firmware of USB devices to disguise them as any device the attackers want. In 2015, Bastille Security Group proposed a channel-based attack to attack wireless mouses and keyboards using the flaw of USB communication [14,15]. They sniff the wireless transmitted data, then edit it or directly replay it to control the I/O of the host in a short time. By using scripts, of course an attack can be done with given conditions.

2.4   Threat Model

USB protocol itself is secure superficially. But why USB devices always under attack these years? In our research, the followings are concluded. For the whole system related to USB, a model can be built like Fig. 2. USB protocol works between Interface Layer and Driver Layer. When a device connects to the host, the host controller collects the device's descriptors stored in the firmware, which contains the type ID of the device. (vulnerabilities between Interface Layer to and Driver Layer) What's worse, vulnerabilities also exist between Application Layer and Driver Layer (data-based attack), and between Physical Device Layer and Interface Layer (channel-based attack). The problem is that in most cases, we can only do access control between Driver Layer and Interface Layer, but we have to defend all attacks shown in Sect. 1 (vulnerabilities excluded). That's why our system is meaningful.

3   System Design

Attribute to the complex architecture of USB working mechanism in Windows kernel [16,18], it is difficult to build an efficient system to intercept the USB's behavior. While the calling process between the driver layer and hardware is twisted, controlling inserted USB devices effectively is challenging. In this section, we introduce the main architecture of Curtain system and how can it protect us from malware USB devices by illustrating every module's function and communication with other modules in detail. The whole system is as described in Fig. 3. In the User Layer, Device Identifier is used for identifying device type,

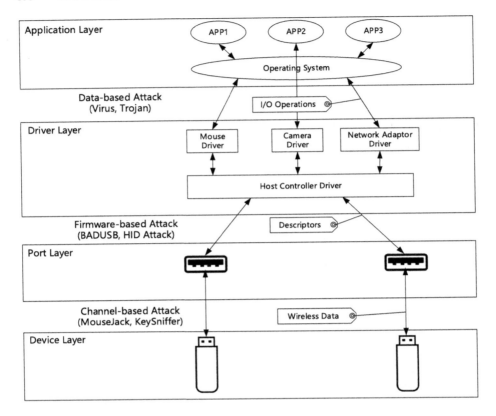

Fig. 2. USB threat model

IRP Analyser is responsible for counting IRP features and sending statistic to Anomaly Detector, which can judge whether a USB device's behavior is malicious. Then Anomaly Detector sends decisions to the IRP Collector & Filter, a filter driver in the Driver Layer, to accomplish the management on USB device's specific behaviors.

3.1 IRP Collector & Filter

As the name implies, one of the main function of this module is collecting IRP from USB Client Driver. In brief, this is a filter driver [19] we built between USB Driver Stack and USB Client Driver. As we illustrated in Sect. 2.2, when a USB device want to carry out an operation, drivers will be called and the message transmitted from USB Client Driver to hardware is IRP. So through the Driver Development Interface (DDI) provided by Windows, this filter driver is actually built in the Client Driver Stack to take part into the transmission of IRP. As a result, this module enables our system to intercept every behavior of USB devices by obtaining all IRPs of USB's behaviors.

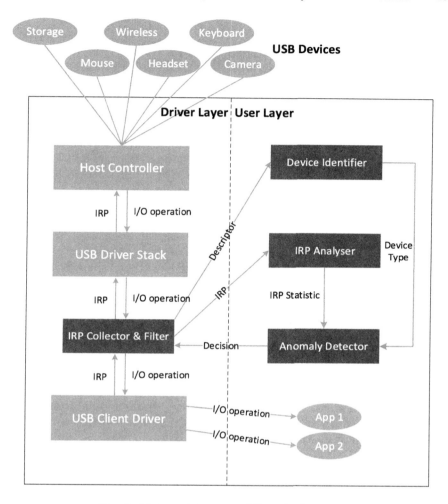

Fig. 3. Main architecture of Curtain System

Also, as a filter driver, this module has the ability to supervise USB devices by dropping specific IRPs and controlling the data transferring speed indirectly. As we discuss in Sect. 2.2, many polling IRPs from upper level drivers often return null if USB devices don't have any operations. However, with the method of dropping non-null IRPs, we can indirectly control the speed of IRP transmission. The specific operation of this module responses to the Decision received from the Anomaly Detector. After dropping specific IRPs from USB Client Driver if IRP Collector & Filter is requested to, it will send IRP flow to the USB Driver Stack to complete the normal IRP transmitting process.

3.2 Device Identifier

When a USB device first connects to a host with Curtain System, new device will enter the device enumeration phase. In this phase, new device will request for drivers. Windows will detect the device and generate specific IRPs, which will be transferred to the IRP Collector & Filter. This module will then generate specific IRPs which can request for USB's descriptor. Then the IRP Collector & Filter will send the descriptor to the Device Identifier. The Device Identifier module will be awakened during the Device Enumeration phase and examine the Device Type [20] in the descriptor. In the meantime, Curtain will let users to name the device and choose the expectative device type, in order to obtain user's acknowledgement of the USB devices. Then, our system can compare these two device types. If user's choice is not consistent with the device's declaration of its type, our system can easily catch this potentially malicious device which tries to disguise itself from its appearance. Our system will warn users and stop its following operations at once. If two choices are the same, the device can be used normally. In the end, the Device Identifier module will send the Device Type to the Anomaly Detector module in order to help our system to use certain type of default basal IRP statistic for supervising the new device.

3.3 IRP Analyser

Receiving IRP flow from the IRP Collector & Filter, IRP Analyser is responsible for checking the content of each IRP and counting the types of IRPs. In a certain period of time, this module will count the proportion of each type's IRP numbers in all received IRPs. For certain type of USB device has specific IRP flow, this statistic can indicate whether the device is doing normal operations. Also, this module will check if an IRP's content contains system sensitive directory. It is because that if a USB device tries to send unknown files to system key locations may achieve attacks, so we must warn the users. In the end, IRP Analyser will send these information to the Anomaly Detector.

3.4 Anomaly Detector

Anomaly Detector is the most important module in Curtain System because it will judge whether a USB device is doing illegal operation and make decisions for the filter driver to control the IRP transmission. Based on the fact that certain type of USB devices share similar IRP flow, we can set default IRP type statistics for each kind of common USB devices in this module in advance. In this module, the Anomaly Detector will first compare the received IRP statistics with the default basal IRP statistics. If there is a huge difference between these two statistics, this module will identify this abnormal operation and catch the potential malware. Otherwise, we use Isolation Forest algorithm [24] to modify the basal IRP statistics in the module with received IRPs statistics in order to generate specific IRP statistics for unique devices. This process will be fully explained in the following. The constantly changing basal IRP statistics will help the judging process more and more accurate. However, if the judging process of Anomaly Detector finds the IRP flow suspectable, the Anomaly Detector will ask IRP Collector & Filter to stop or slow down the IRP transmitting and send warnings to the user, in order to defend user from the potential malware. Through using Isolation Forest algorithm to recalculate the IRP statistic for every USB device under our management respectively, the judging process for each USB device will be more and more accurate.

4 Malicious Objects Detection

As mentioned in Sect. 3.4, the most important module of Curtain is Anomaly Detector. In fact, Anomaly Detector is based on several malicious objects detection algorithm. Of course, to detect an anomaly behavior of devices is not that simple in user mode because in user mode, applications receive data from drivers and process those data. Attackers are tend to be familiar with the process and design specific data so that applications will become one of their assistants. It's difficult to defend such attacks except attackers is unaware of our defense system, which is difficult to achieve. So we turn to kernel mode, we insert a filter driver in driver stack to help us capture information in kernel mode as mentioned in Sect. 3.1. Based on those IRP information, we design three algorithms to detect malicious objects. That's the key why Curtain can defend most of attacks shown above. Those three algorithms are introduced below.

4.1 Unauthorized Access to Important Files Detection

In Sect. 2.2, it has been shown that in Windows systems, USB devices exchange data with host by IRP created by the top driver of driver stack. So when a device is trying to transmit a file to/from an important directory, the action must be completed with a sequence of IRP.

In Curtain, the sequence is detected as follows. First we catch all the IRPs of a device by IRP collector. Then, IRP collector will send all IRP information (IRP type and its properties) to IRP analyzer. When resolving IRP_MJ_CREATE, IRP analyzer will get the path of the file that the USB device is trying to access and send those pre-processed data to Anomaly Detector. Anomaly Detector maintains a blacklist set in which files are not allowed to be accessed by devices except with user's special permission. If the path in IRP is included in blacklist set, the following IRPs related to files will all be cut off by IRP filter. While if not, Curtain keeps spying on them but allowing the following IRPs.

4.2 Abnormal Behaviors Detection

As shown above, there exists many channel-based attacks. When talking about IRP type statistics or properties of IRPs, no difference exists between attacked devices and normal devices because attackers always use normal function of the device to complete an attack. For example, MouseJack and KeyboardSniffer

Table 1. Features to detect abnormal behaviors

No	Feature	Description
1	Number of IRP type	The number of IRP type can reflect what kind of device it is in some way
2	Number of IRP related with file system	The number of IRP related with file system can reflect whether the device is trying to attach file system. It is used to figure out whether the device is performing unauthorized operations
3	Number of IRP related with HID devices	The number of IRP related with HID devices can reflect whether the device
4	average time interval of two adjacent IRP	The speed of opearations is a great feature to judge if those operations are performed by the user or an attacker. That's because there always exist differences between two human-beings and between human-beings and scripts
5	Whether impossible IRP appears	A device type corresponds to a set of IRP types. Any IRP type not included in the set is impossible to appear when the device of that type is woring

enable attackers to control the input of a wireless mouse or keyboard. When we look into IRP flow, there only exist IRP_MJ_READ and no harmful value can be found. But they still can be detected. The reason is that if the attackers send the input value one by one just as the user is coding, the user will find the problem at once as the malicious script is running on the screen. So attackers always send the input value in a fast speed and that's different with normal input process. In Curtain, IRP flow will be divided into many pieces and each piece contains 20 IRPs. Then, we choose 5 features for each piece. They are shown in Table 1. Based on these features of each piece, we use Isolation Forest to detect abonormal behaviors [24]. In the algorithm, those abnomral behaviors should be outliers. So if some piece were judged as a outlier, we think maybe an abonormal behavior is performing. Then we send warning messages to users.

4.3   Fake Device Type Claim

It's obvious that if devices can always claim themselves to be anything they want, hosts will never be able to defend BadUSB attacks. In identifing the fake device, GoodUSB tried to solve the problem with the only trust input, user's choice [13]. Usbfilter is tend to work like a firewall to defend some known attacks [12]. But both of them cannot solve the problem effective and convenient for users. We solve the problem by the steps following. First, we get the descriptors of the new device just as the normal device enumeration does. Then depending on the descriptors, we find the device type that the device claiming itself to be. Meanwhile, we'll ask users for the main device type of the new device (e.g. Mouse, Keyboard, Printer). Finally, we combine user's choice and the result from descriptors. If they match, we call it success and allow the following enumeration steps. But if not, we will ask user about this inconformity. Then users can choose to trust the device or to ban the device. Curtain will kill the device's enumeration steps and deny this device connecting the host.

5   Evaluation

In this section, we will evaluate Curtain. We provide a functionality evaluation of Curtain, where Curtain is tested against a variety of malicious and benign devices. After that, we provide a performance evaluation of Curtain to show that it won't cost too much.

5.1   Functionality Evaluation

The authors of BadUSB have published a proof-of-concept implementation online. The POC is able to rewrite the firmware of some specific devices with malicious scripts. But rather than use such highly specific instance of BadUSB, we use some common penetration tools to launch the BadUSB attack. Besides that, Bastille shared their proof-of-concept implementation of MouseJack and KeySniffer on GitHub. We launch these attacks with the shared code. After that, we compared our results with those of some famous anti-virus softwares.

We prepared two host machines with Windows 10 in VMware, named PC-A and PC-B. They are almost the same but Curtain is installed in PC-A and Kaspersky Anti-Virus is installed in PC-B.

BadUSB Attack. In this part, we launched two attacks. First we tried to claim a U-disk to be a keyboard when Windows trying to get descriptors from our attack device. Later the "keyboard" will input some malicious code into the host (test-1). Second, we tended to claim one more keyboard while the U-disk still works well (test-2).

In test-1, we use Teensy 3 [22] development board as attack device. First, we installed Arduino Development Kit in Kali Linux, which is a tool to rewrite development boards like Teensy. Then, we rewrote the Teensy to be a keyboard exactly but it still looked like a U-disk in appearance. The code inside Teensy will claim itself to be a keyboard and after installation, it will start to input our malicious code immediately. In the test, the code was to download a Trojan generated by Metasploit Kit from the Internet and launch it. Then we plugged the Teensy into PC-A first. Curtain detected that a new device was plugged in and popped up a window, requesting the user to select expected device type. Because the Teensy here was masked to be a U-disk, we chose USB storage. Then it was detected that user's choice was different with the device's claim. So Curtain threw a warning. The attack has been defended. While in PC-B, we performed the same operations but nothing trying to defend the attack happened. The Teensy successfully downloaded the Trojan and we saw PC-B was online in our control side of the Trojan.

In test-2, we still use Teensy 3 development board as attack device. The difference is that we rewrote the Teensy to be a multi-purpose device. It can work as a U-disk and a keyboard at the same time. The function of malicious code was the same in the first test. After preparation, we plugged the Teensy into PC-A. Everything went well. But Curtain detected that two devices were plugged so it popped up two windows, requesting the user to choose expected device type. Of course, in our mind, we only plugged in a U-disk. So we rejected the second device to work. In fact, the attack was defended here. While in PC-B, the malicious code worked well. We also saw PC-B was online in our control side of Metasploit.

Two tests above have shown that Curtain really works when talking about BadUSB attacks. In fact, any attack trying to mask the device to be another device or inject one more device descriptor to send malicious operations will be detected by Curtain.

Table 2. Functionality evaluation result

Test name	Attack	Machine	Installed system	Result
test-1	BadUSB: Fake Device Type Claim(mask to be another device)	PC-A	Curtain	Attack detected. Device claim not corresponding to user's choice.
		PC-B	Kaspersky Anti-Virus	Attack success.
test-2	BadUSB: Fake Device Type Claim(Add malicious device)	PC-A	Curtain	Attack detected. One more device detected.
		PC-B	Kaspersky Anti-Virus	Attack success.
test-3	KeySniffer: Operations Replay	PC-A	Curtain	Attack detected. An outlier of IRP flows detected.
		PC-B	Kaspersky Anti-Virus	Attack success.
test-4	KeySniffer: Operations Injection	PC-A	Curtain	Attack detected. An outlier of IRP flows detected.
		PC-B	Kaspersky Anti-Virus	Attack success

MouseJack and KeySniffer Attacks. In this part, we also launched two attacks. One is to replay I/O operations of the keyboard (test-3) and the other one is to inject some I/O operations of keyboard to attack the target (test-4). The attack device in this part is Crazyradio PA Dongles and we used Logitech K345 keyboard as target device.

In test-3, we performed the test as Bastille introduced in their papers [15]. First, we rewrote the Crazyradio PA Dongles to make sure the scripts shared by Bastille on GitHub can work on it. Then, we plugged the receiver of K345 to PC-A and typed the story of Little Red Riding Hood in Word. Meanwhile, the Crazyradio PA Dongles was sniffing and recorded the data sniffed into test-3.log. After that, we used Crazyradio PA Dongles to replay the operations recorded in test-3.log. The result is that, the replay attack was detected by Curtain while only two words was typed. Then, we performed the same operations in PC-B. The result was that there existed two same story in Word, which means that the replay attack had been successful.

In test-4, first we used Crazyradio PA Dongles to sniff and record the data transferred by K345.. Then, we pressed each button of K345, whose receiver was plugged in my own laptop. After that, we had already known how to map a command string to data transferred to receiver. Then K345's receiver was plugged in PC-A again. We developed a script to automatically transform input into data can be received by the receiver and send them through Crazyradio PA Dongles. With the script, we tried to open CMD and download our Trojan. But Curtain detected our attack while only the first input Win+R was received and resolved. After that, anything we are trying to send to PC-A was rejected. So the attack was unable to continue.

While in PC-B, whatever we tried to input, PC-B would resolve them normally. The result is that we had got the control of the keyboard of PC-B. Then, we downloaded a Trojan generated by Metasploit and ran it. We saw PC-B was online later.

Test-3 and test-4 have shown that those channel-based attacks cannot be defended by traditional anti-virus systems like Kaspersky, but Curtain solved the problem.

As a conclusion, tests shown above have proved that Curtain really works when talking about channel-based attacks and firmware-based attacks. From Table 2, we can conclude that Curtain can detect attacks shown before while traditional anti-virus systems cannot.

5.2 Performance Evaluation

In this part, we use the software named USB Flash Benchmark as our test tool. It's aimed to test the read and write speed of any USB Flash Drive. Our host machine is a PC, with a 3.30GHz Intel(R) Core(TM) i5-4590 CPU and 16 GB of RAM and Windows 10 installed in it. Two virtual machines of Windows 10 named PC-C and PC-D are deployed on the PC, each of them works with 4GB of RAM. The file system type of them is NTFS. The testing USB device is a Kingston DataTraveler Ultimate 3.0 G3 (64 GB). Besides that, Kaspersky Anti-Virus is installed in PC-C and Curtain is installed in PC-D. Then, we plug the Kingston USB Flash Drive to PC-C and PC-D and start USB Flash Benchmark to test the performance of the device on them. The result is shown in Table 3. The write speed of PC-D is slower than that of PC-C by 4.93% and the read speed of PC-D is slower by 4.21%. In fact, we think that such latency is tolerable in most cases.

Table 3. Performance evaluation result

Test name	Machine	Result
Write speed	PC-C	82.79 MB/s
	PC-D	78.71 MB/s
Read speed	PC-C	185.73 MB/s
	PC-D	177.92 MB/s

6   Future Work

Curtain is the first USB defending system for Windows based on IRP analyzing. While Curtain is able to prevent malicious from installing unknown files to system key location, it currently cannot detect the USB storage and find the malicious virus in advance. In future work, we intend to strengthen its detecting ability on USB virus. In order to customize our system for all types of USB devices more precisely, we intend to train Curtain with more USB devices. By refining the classification for USB devices types and functions, we can improve the accuracy of our system and reduce the training cost for diverse USB devices. In short, a more efficient and accurate math model should be defined. Although the USB devices' working process must comply with Windows' USB working mechanism, we may bypass the analyzing of IRP flow of upper level drivers and try to work on analyzing USB's I/O operations. We may apply this idea without modifying original system architecture and improve Curtain's efficiency. A commercial software named USB monitor pro [28] can monitor both IRP and URB flows. So in the future, we may tend to find an algorithm to combine IRP and URB flows to detect malicious behaviors.

7   Discussion

7.1   Automatically Device Type Identification

As our system will ask users to choose the expectable type of the USB devices, is it possible for us to release users from this burden? However, based on the defense method of Curtain, we treat USB devices as untrusted, while we treat users as trusted. As we proposed, users' choice is meaningful to us because we will compare their choice with the device type which the USB device itself declare it to be. Without user's assistance to tell us which kind of USB device should the plugged-in USB device should be, we can only blindly trust the device type inside the descriptor of the USB device. In the case of the BadUSB attack, attackers can modify the firmware of the USB device and disguise it as any type of USB devices, so it is able to request any device drivers to perform its attack. To prevent this, it is essential for us to ask for users' assistance with choosing the expectable type of the USB device they used. Through this, Curtain is able to warn users timely. Further, we are also keen to find a new way to complete our defense goal without users' assistance, because in some cases we cannot treat users as trusted either. It would be much better if we are able to construct our whole defense process on our own. Unfortunately, we are unable to find such way to optimize our defense system up to now. In our further research, we will keep working on this, in order to make our system better.

7.2   Migration to Other OS

It's worth mentioning that Curtain can only work in Windows now. But when talking about adapting Curtain to some other operating systems like Ubuntu or CentOS, what should we do? Of course, the main idea of Curtain can be totally applied to other systems if needed. We are facing attacks shown in Fig. 2 no matter which system we are using. In fact, we can also monitor the traffic of USB devices and analyze them to figure out how to detect abnormal behaviors from them. But in our research, there are still many challenges. First of all, Curtain contains a component named IRP collector, which is based on the Driver Stack of Windows. So when adapting Curtain to other systems, we should know how those systems' device drivers work and find a way to insert a "filter driver". Then, different operating systems implement USB protocol in a different way. We have to find something similar to IRP in those systems so that we can extract features from it. Besides this, Device Identifier, IRP Analyser and Anomaly Detector are easy to be immigrated to other systems.

8   Conclusion

USB attacks are becoming more and more sophisticated. They make the security both of USB devices and communications between USB devices and hosts fragile. What's worse, no practical defensive solution against these USB attacks is well-developed till now. In this paper, we present the design and implementation of Curtain, which will catch all the IRP flows of each device and analyze their behaviors to detect attacks. With this tool, users can possess a more reliable system to protect their valuable data and devices.

Acknowledgement. This work is sponsored by the National Natural Science Foundation of China (61373168).

References

1. Al-Zarouni, M.: The reality of risks from consented use of USB devices. School of Computer and Information Science, Edith Cowan University (2006)

2. OLEA Kiosks Inc: Malware Scrubbing Cyber Security Kiosk. https://www.olea.com/product/california-cyber-security-kiosk/
3. Tetmeyer, A., Saiedian, H.: Security threats and mitigating risk for USB devices. IEEE Technol. Soc. Mag. **29**(4), 44–49 (2010)
4. Falliere, N., Murchu, L., Chien, E.: W32. stuxnet dossier. White paper, Symantec Corp., Security Response. vol. 5, p. 6 (2011)
5. Pavković, N., Perkov, L.: Social Engineering Toolkit-A systematic approach to social engineering. In: the 34th International Convention, pp. 1485–1489 (2011)
6. Hak5. Episode 709: USB Rubber Ducky Part 1. http://www.hak5.org/episodes/episode-709
7. Hak5. USB Rubber Ducky Payloads. https://github.com/hak5darren/USB-Rubber-Ducky/wiki/Payloads
8. MouseJack, KeySniffer and Beyond: Keystroke Sniffing and Injection Vulnerabilities in 2.4GHz Wireless Mice and Keyboards. https://media.defcon.org/DEFCON24/DEFCON24presentations/DEFCON-24-Marc-Newlin-MouseJack-Injecting-Keystrokes-Into-Wireless-Mice-WP-UPDATED.pdf
9. Karsten, N., Sascha, K., Jakob, L.: BadUSB-On accessories that turn evil. In: BlackHat (2014)
10. Karsten, N., Sascha, K., Jakob, L.: BadUSB-On accessories that turn evil. In: PacSec (2014)
11. Caudill, A., Wilson, B.: Phison 2251–03 (2303) Custom Firmware & Existing Firmware Patches (BadUSB). https://github.com/adamcaudill/Psychson/tree/master/firmware/
12. Tian, D., Scaife, N., Bates, A., Butler, K., Traynor, P.: Making USB great again with USBFILTER. In: the 25th USENIX Security Symposium, pp. 415–430 (2016)
13. Tian, D., Bates, A., Butler, K.: Defending against malicious USB firmware with GoodUSB. In: The 31st Annual Computer Security Applications Conference, pp. 261–270 (2015)
14. Bastille: MouseJack. https://www.bastille.net/research/vulnerabilities/mousejack/
15. Bastille: Keysniffer. https://www.bastille.net/research/vulnerabilities/keysniffer-intro/
16. Microsoft Hardware Dev Center: Driver Stacks. https://docs.microsoft.com/en-us/windows-hardware/drivers/gettingstarted/driver-stacks
17. Microsoft Hardware Dev Center: I/O request packets. https://docs.microsoft.com/zh-cn/windows-hardware/drivers/gettingstarted/i-o-request-packets
18. Microsoft Developer Network: USB host-side drivers in Windows. https://msdn.microsoft.com/en-us/library/hh406256(v=vs.85).aspx
19. Microsoft Windows Embedded 8.1 Industry: Usb flter (industry 8.1). https://msdn.microsoft.com/en-us/library/dn449350(v=winembedded.82).aspx
20. Universal Serial Organization: USB Class Codes. http://www.usb.org/developers/defined_class
21. Zaitcev, P.: The usbmon: USB monitoring framework. In: Linux Symposium, pp. 291–296 (2005)
22. PJRC: Teensy 3.2&3.1-New Features. https://www.pjrc.com/teensy/teensy31.html
23. Kamkar, S.: USBdriveby. http://samy.pl/usbdriveby/
24. Liu, F., Ting, K., Zhou, Z.: Isolation forest. In: the 8th IEEE International Conference on Data Mining, pp. 413–422 (2008)

25. Pham, D., Haigamuge, M., Sysed, A., Mendis, P.: Optimizing windows security features to block malware and hack tools on USB storage devices. In: Progress in Electromagnetics Research Symposium, pp. 350–355 (2010)
26. Universal Serial Bus Specification. http://sdphca.ucsd.edu/lab_equip_manuals/usb_20.pdf
27. USB-IF Statement regarding USB security. http://www.usb.org/press/USB-IF_Statement_on_USB_Security_FINAL.pdf
28. USB Monitor Pro. http://www.usb-monitor.com/

Author Index

Printed in the United States
By Bookmasters